ENCYCLOPEDIA OF THE CENTRAL INTELLIGENCE AGENCY

W. THOMAS SMITH, JR.

Facts On File, Inc.

This encyclopedia is dedicated to

CIA Operations Officer Johnny Michael "Mike" Spann,
a former captain of U.S. Marines and
the first American killed in combat
during the war against terrorism,
November 2001.

It is also for
Dad,
the late William Thomas "Bill" Smith,
and for my brother,
the late Michael Robert Smith.

Encyclopedia of the Central Intelligence Agency

Copyright © 2003 by W. Thomas Smith, Jr.

Facts On File, Inc.
132 West 31st Street
New York NY 10001

Library of Congress Cataloging-in-Publication Data
Smith, W. Thomas.
Encyclopedia of the Central Intelligence Agency / by W. Thomas Smith
p. cm.
Includes bibliographical references.
ISBN 0-8160-4666-2 (hc)
1. United States. Central Intelligence Agency—Encyclopedias.   I. Title

UB251.U5 S63   2003
327.1273′003—dc21   2002029951

Facts On File books are available at special discounts when purchased in bulk quantities for businesses, associations, institutions, or sales promotions. Please call our Special Sales Department in New York at (212) 967-8800 or (800) 322-8755.

You can find Facts On File on the World Wide Web at
http://www.factsonfile.com

Text and cover design by Cathy Rincon

Illustrations by Sholto Ainslie

Printed in the United States of America

VB TB 10 9 8 7 6 5 4 3 2 1

This book is printed on acid-free paper.

CONTENTS

ACKNOWLEDGMENTS

There are many to thank for assisting me with this project. I am especially indebted to Alexandra Owens and Brett Harvey of the American Society of Journalists and Authors, James C. Vines of the Vines Agency, Owen Lancer and Gary Goldstein of Facts On File, Gordon Witkin of *U.S. News & World Report,* retired CIA officer Norman Glasser, and the incredibly helpful librarians and library assistants at the South Carolina State Library, the Richland County Public Library, and the Thomas Cooper Library at the University of South Carolina in Columbia.

I would like to thank my immediate family, including Mom (Alba Antointette "Tita" Smith Rowell), Howard Tobias Rowell, Annette Smith Fowler, James David Smith, Michael Paul Fowler, and William Maxwell Fowler, as well as so many in my extended family for their unwavering support on all fronts. I would also like to thank my magazine writing students at USC's College of Journalism and Mass Communications for allowing me to see that there is life beyond the office. So, to Emily Bame, Jane Barwick, James Battle, Lindsey Bonds, Amy Boyd, Crystal Boyles, Ramsey Brantley, Mike Brugh, Justin Capek, Françoise Cerdan, Cheyliece Gamble, Jennifer Gesimondo, Meagan Gudridge, Jason Harvey, Ali Jansen, Katherine Knodell, Brandon Larrabee, Verlanda Mitchell, Julie Scott, Nicole Smallman, Sheila Taylor, Philip "Big Phil" Watson, Sharon White, and Gene Wilson, thanks for the enthusiasm you brought to your work. Teaching you was one of my greatest pleasures during this project. And thanks to all of my newspaper and magazine editors who have been so patient with me since this project began.

Beyond that, there is an army of friends and supporters who deserve special recognition for keeping my spirits from flagging, often unwittingly. Some of those include Gil, Mary Ann, and Edmund Bagnell; Debbie Jones Hart; Daniel Patrick "Danny" Smith; Aida Rogers; Bill McDonald; Jan K. Collins; Jenny Maxwell; Kevin Hyde; Cecile Holmes; Pat McNeely; Emily Cooper; John Temple Ligon; Judy Bistany South; Bonny Millard; Judy Henrichs; Tony Banco; Cindy Mixon; Judith Trotsky; Danelle Germino Haakenson; and Uncle Woody and Aunt Sandy's girls.

Though it would be almost an independent work to recognize everyone, special thanks to all those not named in Columbia, Charleston, Aiken, and Myrtle Beach, South Carolina; Savannah, Georgia; Raleigh, Durham, and Charlotte, North Carolina; Omaha, Nebraska; Chicago; Washington, D.C.; New York; and New Jersey who in some way contributed to the completion of this book. And finally to God—for without Him, this work would not have been possible.

—*W. Thomas Smith, Jr.*
Columbia, S.C.

INTRODUCTION

The Central Intelligence Agency (CIA) is arguably one of the most fascinating, yet least understood, intelligence-gathering and covert-action organizations in the world. The mere mention of "CIA" evokes images of foreign-based spies maneuvering in a shadowy "cloak and dagger" world, or, perhaps, small teams of parachuting commandos operating in some remote region of Latin America, Africa, or Southeast Asia.

In its brief history, the CIA has been all of that. But it is much more. As the federal government's incarnation of the world's second-oldest profession, the CIA employs tens of thousands of workers, with only a fraction serving at the agency's clandestine "tip of the spear." Those numbers, like much of the CIA's inner workings, remain classified. But the Agency's reputation, stemming from its direct involvement in some of history's most important events, has earned those men and women who serve at the tip a place among the pantheon of great American heroes and heroines.

Born of a series of federal organizations that sought to bring all of America's foreign intelligence gathering efforts under one roof, the CIA has existed as the senior member of the U.S. intelligence community for over fifty years. The Agency's responsibilities run the gamut from the collection and analysis of information from a variety of sources to producing finished intelligence, conducting worldwide covert operations, and overseeing the myriad federal agencies tasked with the collection of both foreign and domestic intelligence.

But it has not been without its detractors. John "J." Edgar Hoover, the infamous director of the Federal Bureau of Investigation, fought tooth and nail for FBI control of all foreign intelligence-gathering activities before, during, and after World War II. During the highly publicized congressional investigations into CIA misdeeds during the mid-1970s, Senator Frank Church referred to the Agency as a "rogue elephant on a rampage." In his best-selling expose *Inside the Company: CIA*

Diary, former CIA operative turned Agency backbiter Philip Agee would proclaim to his readers that it is "difficult for people to understand what a huge and sinister organization the CIA is."

CIA critics from all corners, in fact, have attempted to put teeth into such statements by pointing to the disastrous Agency-led invasion of Cuba at the Bay of Pigs in 1961, the unrestricted mail-intercept operation from 1952 to 1973, a series of mind-control drug experiments conducted on unwitting human beings, and numerous allegations of CIA-backed assassinations and assassination attempts. "The CIA should be shut down because its banner has too many Cold War stains," said Lt. General William Odom, a former chief of the National Security Agency, the U.S. government's super-secret eavesdropping and code-cracking entity.

But "shutting down" the largest, most important arm of secret defense in and for the United States would be nothing less than catastrophic for the free world. The CIA, according to an article in *U.S. News & World Report,* is an agency with a multibillion-dollar annual budget, "satellites that can see through clouds, more secret compartments than a Tudor castle, and an army of analysts who can dissect everything from the Ukrainian military to Hindu fundamentalism." Even so, the CIA has been unable to eliminate completely the rash of highly sophisticated terror attacks that—though international in scope—have often directly targeted America and her allies.

Failures will always be held up to the cruel glare of scrutiny, though the successes of the men and women who work for the CIA's directorates, offices, and centers are often unknown. Still, those same men and women have and will continue to put their often-anonymous lives in peril all for the sake of freedom and the great experiment of democracy.

Since the Agency's inception in 1947, countless books have been written in an attempt to shed light on this little-known U.S. government entity. But until now, there has been no single, comprehensive reference work detailing the particulars of the CIA from its pre–World War II beginnings as the Office of the Coordinator of Information to the wartime Office of Strategic Services through the dark years of the Cold War to its current role in America's uncertain war on terrorism.

Here the Agency comes to life through nearly 550 historical, biographical, and general entries followed by an extensive list of CIA-related acronyms, abbreviations, and code names. But the encyclopedia can never be complete.

As the writing of this encyclopedia came to a close and I realized that there was always going to be just one more entry, I concluded that such a book is always a work in progress. The *Encyclopedia of the Central Intelligence Agency* is even more so, as the surface information and the secrets of America's most colorful but shadowy arm grudgingly reveal themselves.

—*W. Thomas Smith, Jr.*
March 2002

A

Abel, Colonel Rudolf Ivonovich (1902–1971)

Colonel Rudolf Ivonovich Abel (a.k.a. Emil R. Golfus, Mark, and Martin Collins) was the infamous Russian spymaster who, having been captured and incarcerated by the United States, was exchanged in 1962 for CIA pilot Francis Gary Powers, a prisoner of the Soviet Union.

Abel was born in 1902 in czarist Russia into a family of great wealth and privilege. In 1903, the Abels moved to England (according to one account, Abel was actually born William Fischer in England). Soon after, the family moved to Scotland. There, young Abel learned to speak both Russian and English, the latter with a Scottish accent. He also learned to speak German, Polish, and Yiddish.

In 1921, Abel's father moved the family back to Russia in order to assist in the communist revolution. There, he was considered a language expert and was soon selected by Soviet intelligence officers to become a language instructor for the Narodnyi Komissariat Vnutrennikh Del, or NKVD, the predecessor intelligence organization to the KOMITET GOSUDARSTVENNOY BEZOPASNOSTI, or KGB.

When World War II erupted, Abel joined the Soviet army as an intelligence officer and saw a great deal of action against the German invaders. Time and again, he displayed remarkable battlefield courage and was several times decorated for his service. In one instance, Abel purportedly impersonated a German officer and was able to slip behind enemy lines and penetrate the Abwehr, the Nazi intelligence organization. During that mission, he was able to glean vital information about the disposition of German forces. This information was forwarded to Russian commanders.

When the war ended, Abel was selected by the KGB for the position of "resident director" of a Soviet spy network that would be established in North America. The network would be tasked with uncovering U.S. military secrets. Abel was the perfect choice. Aside from his language and intelligence skills, he was considered to be an expert with radios and radio transmitters. He had previously studied engineering and was well versed in chemistry and nuclear physics. He was also an accomplished photographer, artist, and jeweler—and he was unknown to the West as a Soviet intelligence officer.

In 1946, Abel moved to East Germany, entered a camp for displaced persons, and applied for immigration to Canada. His COVER was that of a struggling Bohemian artist. False documents provided to him by the KGB identified him as a man of German-Irish descent. Canada bought the ruse and accepted him as a German émigré.

In 1948, Abel slipped across the border into the United States and made contact with members of the American Communist Party. The latter provided him with a new identity and a New York birth certificate as proof of that identity. Abel took as his new name Emil R. Goldfus (the name of a Manhattan-born child who had died 40 years earlier, in infancy).

Abel then began to contact Soviet spies who were already in place. He gave them specific instructions on what information to obtain and how to forward that information to him. He also met with and recruited known Marxist-leaning American citizens, communists, and other political malcontents to work as agents for the Soviet Union. He was careful, however, never to reveal his cover name, Goldfus; that cover was used exclusively to establish Abel's legitimacy as an American citizen. Instead, he was known to his agents by the code-name "Mark."

Initially, Abel lived in substandard hotels in Manhattan. He then rented a small photographer's studio in Brooklyn, where he often stayed overnight. He also established relationships with area artists and was known to loan money and host small parties. But his agents were totally unaware of any aspect of his life as Goldfus.

As Mark, Abel met with his agents in parks, public restrooms, and train and bus stations. His agents were also able to convey messages by way of dead DROPs located in the hollows of trees, beneath broken sidewalk slabs, and in the false bottoms of reconfigured pay telephones.

Abel's agents were responsible for obtaining top-secret U.S. military information on underwater detection devices, missiles, and nuclear weapons. Abel himself was tasked with monitoring United Nations (UN) operations and gleaning as much military information as possible relating to the New York ports system. As Abel gathered his information, he transferred it into microfilm or microdot form and forwarded it to Moscow via Soviet-recruited couriers. He also transmitted and received information directly from Moscow in coded radio messages. The transmissions were conducted on an irregular schedule so as to avoid American radio-monitoring systems.

In time, Abel's spy network expanded so much that it became wholly unmanageable. As a consequence, in 1954, Moscow sent him an assistant, Reino Hayhanen. Hayhanen was to serve as Abel's deputy director (actually a CUT-OUT), in order to handle the enormous amount of information coming in to Abel and alleviate his workload. This would allow Abel to concentrate on relaying messages to Moscow. Unfortunately for Abel, Hayhanen proved to be something of a liability. The new deputy director seemed to scoff at Abel's security measures. His knowledge of CODE breaking, SECRET WRITING, and photography was sorely lacking. Also, he drank too much. Still, he was all Abel had to work with, so Abel helped him get settled and spent time training him.

In 1955, a physically exhausted Abel was ordered to return to the Soviet Union for a six-month leave period. When he returned to New York in 1956, he found that his meticulously constructed spy network had nearly collapsed. Hayhanen had violated countless security measures.

He had failed to retrieve any of the messages left by agents at dead drops. What was worse, he had consistently sent radio transmissions to Moscow from the same location. Abel was furious, but his admonitions had little effect on his deputy. Hayhanen had become a womanizing drunkard who spent much of his Moscow-generated advance money on prostitutes.

The following year, the KGB ordered Hayhanen back to Moscow. Hayhanen feared that he would be disciplined for his poor work in the United States. In an unsuccessful attempt to allay those fears, Moscow promoted him to the rank of major. Hayhanen then told Abel that he was departing for Europe. Instead, he drove to a remote section of New York's Hudson Valley and dug up $5,000 (previously forwarded for espionage purposes) he had buried during Abel's leave.

Hayhanen then sailed for Le Havre, France. Once in Le Havre, he was to travel directly to Moscow. Instead, he made a side trip to Paris, where he drank and frequented the city's bordellos. In time, Hayhanen became convinced that he would be imprisoned or executed, so he made a decision to defect. In early May 1957, he telephoned the U.S. embassy in Paris and subsequently walked into the complex requesting political asylum, promising that he would reveal an intricate Soviet spy network operating in North America. He also promised to identify its director. Hayhanen was returned to the United States and placed in the custody of the FEDERAL BUREAU OF INVESTIGATION (FBI).

Learning of Hayhanen's defection, Moscow immediately ordered Abel out of New York. Abel fled to Florida and remained under ground for several weeks. Soviet spies in New York, believing that Abel's haunts were not under surveillance by the FBI, claimed that the proverbial coast was clear. They were wrong. Abel returned to New York and was arrested on June 21 in Manhattan's Latham Hotel, where he had registered under the alias Martin Collins.

Abel was charged with espionage but denied everything. FBI agents, however, discovered numerous pieces of incriminating evidence in one of his rooms, including microfilm concealed in hollow coins, microdots contained in a hollow shaving brush, hollow pencils, hollow cuff links, ciphering and secret-writing materials, a short-wave transmitter, and photographs of known Soviet spies.

For his testimony against Abel, Hayhanen was granted immunity from prosecution. But the U.S. Justice Department needed corroboration; Roy Rhodes, a U.S. Army master sergeant who was arrested for disclosing American secrets to the Soviets, was their man. Hayhanen recalled having met Rhodes, known only as "Quebec," through Abel. Rhodes, who served as one of Abel's couriers, testified against the Russian spymaster.

The prosecution sought the death penalty for Abel. But his court-appointed attorney, James Donovan, successfully argued that Abel might one day be a valuable holding in a

Colonel Rudolf Abel   (NATIONAL ARCHIVES)

spy swap with the Russians. That he was. On October 25, Abel was found guilty of conspiracy to transmit defense information to the Soviet Union, conspiracy to obtain defense information, and conspiracy to act in the United States as an agent of a foreign government without notification to the U.S. secretary of state.

On November 15, Abel was sentenced to 45 years in prison. He appealed his convictions, claiming that rights guaranteed to him under the Constitution and the laws of the United States had been violated. By a five-to-four decision handed down on March 28, 1960, the Supreme Court upheld the previous ruling.

Abel ultimately became a bargaining chip in one of the most dramatic spy-swapping episodes of the COLD WAR. On the morning of February 10, 1962, he was exchanged for FRANCIS GARY POWERS, a CIA pilot who had been captured by the Russians when his U-2 spyplane was shot down over the Soviet Union in 1960. Abel and Powers were brought by their respective captors to opposite sides of the Glienecker Bridge, which spanned a lake separating West Berlin from the East German city of Potsdam. Negotiators discussed the swap in the center of the bridge, where a white painted line marked the geographical division of East and West. The two spies stared at each other from opposite sides.

Eventually, the negotiators signaled to their respective officers to start the two men across the bridge. Both walked cautiously, each keeping pace with the other. "As I walked toward the line, another man—thin, gaunt, middle-aged—approached from the other side," recalled Abel. "We crossed at the same time."

Abel returned to Russia, where he was given a country cottage, a pension, and numerous other rewards for his service. A heavy smoker, he was also provided with three packs of Lucky Strike cigarettes every day.

What Abel actually did in the last decade of his life remains a subject of conjecture. Some reports suggest that he returned to operational service in the West. Others claim that he worked as a KGB espionage instructor in the Soviet Union. But however he was employed, if he was employed at all, Abel was never fully trusted again. His superiors felt that since he had spent so many years in an American prison, he might have been brainwashed or even converted into a double agent, willing to work for the West.

Abel died on November 16, 1971. He was 68. The Soviets took little notice of his passing, and news of his death did not reach Western news outlets until the following year. As a result, some accounts have incorrectly listed his death as occurring in 1972.

accommodation address

An accommodation address is a prearranged temporary address or location where an intelligence operative (a spy or a CUT-OUT) may receive mail clandestinely from a third party. Of course, the operative would not work or reside at the address and, in most cases, would have no visible connection with anyone who did.

For instance, in Europe—where transient persons traditionally receive mail from small businesses, which charge them small fees—an agent working for the CIA might receive mail from a CIA field officer. By using a COVER name and no permanent address, agents could maintain their anonymity. If they were compromised, their mail could not be traced to them unless they were apprehended or spotted at the time of pickup. The accommodation address itself may be, and often is, serviced by an intermediary.

Administration, Directorate of

See DIRECTORATES, CIA.

Afghanistan, operations in

In 1979, the Southwest Asian country of Afghanistan was invaded and subsequently occupied by ground and air forces of the Soviet Union. For the next 10 years, the Mujahideen—the anticommunist Afghan rebels fighting the Soviets in an attempt to repel them—received military training and equipment from a host of nations, chief among them the United States. Much of America's direct involvement in that country was conducted by officers and agents working for the CIA.

In 1989, the Soviets, unable to conquer the nation, withdrew. That same year, the U.S. embassy in Kabul, Afghanistan's capital, was closed for security reasons as fighting increased among the various Afghan factions. A handful of CIA operatives purportedly remained in the country.

On September 27, 1996, forces of the Taliban—a militant, fundamentalist Islamic sect—captured Kabul, and by 1998 it had firm control of more than 90 percent of Afghanistan. Thirteen years later, in the wake of the

SEPTEMBER 11, 2001, TERRORIST ATTACKS ON THE UNITED STATES, the CIA again found itself operating in force in Afghanistan. Aside from gathering intelligence, CIA operatives were tasked with assisting Northern Alliance forces opposed to the Taliban as well as working closely with American and British special operations forces entering the country.

Unfortunately for the Agency, the first U.S. combat fatality in America's war against terrorism was CIA operations officer JOHNNY MICHAEL SPANN. On November 25, 2001, Spann was interrogating captured Taliban soldiers in the fortress of Kala Jangi, near Mazar-e-Sharif, when the prisoners, who had smuggled weapons into the compound, revolted. In the ensuing battle to regain control of the fortress, Spann was killed. Though the Agency did not release the details of Spann's death, some reports indicated that he was greatly outnumbered in close quarters and died in a violent hand-to-hand struggle.

The CIA continues to operate in Afghanistan.

See also BIN LADEN, OSAMA; TERRORISM, CIA'S INVOLVEMENT IN THE WAR AGAINST.

Agee, Philip Burnett Franklin (1935–   )

A former Latin America–based case officer, Philip Burnett Franklin Agee resigned from the CIA in 1969 and became one of its most outspoken and controversial critics. At that time—before the exposed betrayals of ALDRICH AMES, EDWARD LEE HOWARD, and DAVID H. BARNETT—the CIA boasted that it had never had to cull a traitor from within its ranks. But Agee's postcareer actions became somewhat problematic for the Agency.

Agee was born in Florida on July 19, 1935. He graduated from the University of Notre Dame in June 1956. He had previously been approached by a CIA recruiter, who proposed a career with the Agency. But with dreams of law school, Agee shelved the offer, only to accept it when threatened by the draft in 1957.

For the next 12 years, Agee served as a covert operations officer in places like Quito, Ecuador; Montevideo, Uruguay; and Mexico City. His duties involved everything from bugging phones and picking up drops to recruiting and training agents.

In 1969, Agee resigned from the Agency, citing personal reasons. But his subsequent writings revealed an ideological about-face. "When I joined the CIA I believed in the need for its existence," wrote Agee in his best-selling expose *Inside the Company: CIA Diary.* "After twelve years with the Agency, I finally understood how much suffering it was causing, that millions of people all over the world had been killed or had had their lives destroyed by the CIA and the institutions it supports. I couldn't sit by and do nothing and so began work on this book. Even after recent revelations about the CIA, it is still difficult for people to understand what a huge and sinister organization the CIA is."

The book, published in 1975 and subsequently translated into 28 languages, sparked considerable controversy within the U.S. intelligence community and seriously compromised the covers of many American operatives. It was not so much Agee's criticism of the CIA and its inner workings that damaged the Agency but his listing of the names of hundreds of CIA employees, overseas operatives, and affiliated organizations that were damaging. When the book was released, several exposed operatives, their lives endangered, were forced to withdraw from their posts.

In December 1975, *Counterspy*—a periodical with which Agee reportedly had ties—published the name, title, and home address of the CIA's Athens CHIEF OF STATION (COS), RICHARD WELCH. That same month, masked gunmen shot and killed Welch on his doorstep as he returned home with his wife from a Christmas party. A group calling itself "November 19" later claimed responsibility for the assassination. The CIA blamed Agee, but the former spy denied any responsibility.

Ironically, the same edition of *Counterspy* published the following statement by Agee to potential enemies of the CIA: "The peoples victimized by the CIA and the economic exploitation that CIA enforces can bring pressure on their so-often compromised governments to expel the CIA people. And, in the absence of such expulsion, which will not be uncommon, the people themselves will have to decide what they must do to rid themselves of CIA."

Agee was later accused by U.S. congressman Lawrence McDonald (D-Georgia) of exposing the identity and espionage deeds of Colonel Jerzy Pawlowski, a Polish Olympic fencer who served as an undercover agent for the West. In 1976, the KGB arrested and convicted Pawlowski of spying for the CIA. He was sent to prison for 25 years.

In 1978, Agee published *Dirty Work: The CIA in Western Europe*, which, like his other writings, created great consternation among the intelligence rank and file. The book revealed names, street addresses, telephone numbers, biographical data, and professional activities of nearly 800 employees and agents working for both the CIA and the NATIONAL SECURITY AGENCY (NSA) in Western Europe. The CIA, insiders claimed, would be forced to modify operations after the book's release.

Agee, who at the time was living in Great Britain, was ordered to leave the country. Four other NATO countries deported him, and in 1981 his U.S. passport was revoked. Over the next two decades, Agee spent most of his time in Cuba, living in a house with Cuban aides, granting interviews, and writing several CIA-bashing essays, often covering the same ground he had with *Inside the Company: CIA Diary* and *Dirty Work: The CIA in Western Europe*.

In the late 1980s, Agee wrote and published *On the Run*, a memoir of what he contended had been his hectic life after the CIA. In 1997, the *Los Angeles Times* published an article claiming that a Cuban DEFECTOR to the United States had told its reporters in 1992 that Agee had "repeatedly" accepted from the Cuban intelligence service money that the latter had received from the KGB. It was also stated that he had been working for Cuban intelligence since the early 1970s—allegations he vehemently denied.

On June 23, 2000, Agee held a press conference in Havana, where he announced the launching of an Internet-based travel agency aimed at luring American tourists to Cuba—Cubalinda.com Inter-Active Travel. The website, www.cubalinda.com, urges Americans to visit the island despite a trade embargo prohibiting U.S. citizens from doing business with or spending money in Cuba. "I would like to see people ignore the law," Agee was quoted in a June 2000 wire story for the Associated Press. "The idea is to disdain this law to the point our grandfathers disdained Prohibition."

agent, notional

A "notional agent" is a term used by the CIA and other intelligence agencies to describe an operative who does not exist but is concocted by an intelligence organization to deceive and misdirect the actions of hostile forces.

For instance, during World War II, British intelligence created a notional agent in the person of Royal Marine major William Martin, or "Major Martin," a fictional identity given to a male corpse launched from a Royal Navy submarine off the coast of Spain. The ruse was made to give the impression that Martin had been en route to North Africa when his plane crashed into the sea.

The body was picked up by fishermen on April 30, 1943, near an area on the Spanish coastline known to be frequented by Abwehr operatives (the Abwehr was Nazi Germany's military intelligence agency). Attached to the body were forged documents and personal effects, including theater tickets, cash receipts, letters from a fictional girlfriend, and detailed plans for an Allied invasion of Sardinia that would never be—the Allies were actually planning to invade Sicily.

The Germans bought the deception and were caught completely by surprise when British and American forces began storming the beaches of southern Sicily on July 9.

agent of influence

Also known as FIFTH COLUMNISTS, because of their allegiance to enemies of their own country, "agents of influence" are spies operating in "high" or "influential places."

They are usually in such places because they are unwittingly trusted by their countrymen.

Often the agent of influence is a high-ranking government official, politician, or business leader who, as a recruited agent, is responsible for influencing policy or behavior rather than gathering intelligence.

agent or employee

Anyone who has ever worked for the CIA is quick to say, "There is no such thing as a CIA agent." CIA "officers," "operatives," or "employees?" Yes. Though authors, screenwriters, and journalists often loosely refer to all intelligence field officers as "agents," there is a stark distinction, particularly within the Agency.

CIA *officers* are loyal citizens of the United States, dutifully sworn, employed by the U.S. government, and on the federal payroll. *Agents,* on the other hand, are foreign nationals usually recruited by CIA staff officers to perform clandestine missions in their respective countries. In most cases, agents' missions involve extracting secret information from either their own governments or privately held businesses producing war materials for the same. Once working for the CIA, the foreign nationals—who may or may not have worked previously for their own governments' intelligence services—are now foreign intelligence operatives, classified by the CIA as "agents."

The distinction between officers and agents in the CIA stems from official policy in the OFFICE OF STRATEGIC SERVICES (OSS), the World War II precursor organization to the CIA. In OSS manuals, an "officer" was described as "an individual employed by and responsible to the OSS and assigned under special programs to field activity." An "agent," on the other hand, was "an individual recruited in the field who is employed or directed by an OSS operative or by a field or substation." Agents are sometimes referred to in the CIA as "assets."

Unlike the CIA, the FEDERAL BUREAU OF INVESTIGATION (FBI) draws no distinction between its officers and agents. In fact, FBI officers are referred to as "special agents"—a title created by FBI director J. EDGAR HOOVER to highlight the difference between FBI agents and all other law enforcement agents.

agent provocateur

Agent provocateur is a French term that means simply an "agent" who "provokes." In CIA parlance, an agent provocateur is just that—a person employed to infiltrate an organization for the purposes of inciting it to mischievous actions or rioting. If successful, the agent provocateur's efforts could ultimately subject the organization's members to punishment. In some cases, stirring up trouble is important to create a diversion from another operation.

In the 1950s, agent provocateurs were referred to as TREE SHAKERS. They are the traditional enemies of revolutionaries and organized labor.

Air America

One of the most dramatic images of the last days of the Vietnam War is the famous photograph of a UH-1 helicopter on top of a Saigon building, refugees streaming up a stair toward it. Most Americans are familiar with the picture. However, few are aware that the aircraft and the crew were from one of the CIA's most famous proprietary companies, Air America.

Air America appeared to be an ordinary U.S. commercial air-charter service. In reality, it was an effective COVER for the largest of three airline operations supporting the Agency's policy objectives in Southeast Asia during the Vietnam War and the secret war in Laos. (The Agency also utilized the services of Continental Air Services, a subsidiary of Continental Airlines; and Lao Air Development, a separate privately owned charter company.) Air America was owned and operated by the CIA, which during the war denied its existence. The airline company evolved from the lesser-known Taiwan-registered CIVIL AIR TRANSPORT (CAT), which was formed by Lt. Gen. Claire Lee Chennault in 1946. Chennault, commander of the famous Flying Tigers, had established CAT as a civilian air cargo service operating out of China. In 1949, the service begin to supplement its cargo business by flying covert missions funded by the CIA. Ejected from China in 1950 and facing imminent bankruptcy, CAT was purchased by the Agency, but its new ownership was concealed through complex financial arrangements. In 1959, the air service's name was changed to Air America, and it was placed under the control of a Delaware-based holding company, the Airdale Corporation (later renamed the Pacific Corporation), which was also owned by the CIA.

Like CAT, Air America flew a variety of aircraft and missions in support of American intelligence operations.

A C-47 transport used by Air America   (UNIVERSITY OF TEXAS ARCHIVES)

Its pilots, mostly ex-military aviators, were attracted by high adventure and even higher wages. Their motto was "Anything, Anywhere, Anytime, Professionally."

Operating primarily out of Laos and Thailand, Air America missions included everything from food drops to photo reconnaissance, to the delivery and recovery of covert operatives and special-missions teams across national borders. But the job was fraught with danger.

Ron Zappa, a C-123 transport pilot with Air America, best summed up the hazards associated with working for the Agency's airline when he said, "Not a day went by without one of our aircraft coming back with a hole in its fuselage. In a normal war, the army would not have sent us under such conditions: knowing that anti-aircraft [fire] was in existence, combat aircraft would have accompanied us to attack the installation. In Laos, we had to do it alone."

During the height of the Vietnam War, Air America maintained nearly 167 fixed and rotary-wing aircraft, served by over 300 aviators, mechanics, and freight specialists. The total number of employees on the Air America payroll was 5,600, making it one of the largest air fleets in the world.

In 1972, DIRECTOR OF CENTRAL INTELLIGENCE (DCI) RICHARD M. HELMS ordered the Agency to "divest itself" of the airline at the close of hostilities. In 1974, Air America ceased operations in Laos. In 1975, it assisted in the evacuation of Saigon. In 1976, Air America was dissolved, its assets sold to private businesses. In all, 243 employees of Air America died during the war; 100 of those were killed during the last three years.

See also SOUTHEAST ASIA, CIA OPERATIONS IN.

Air Force intelligence, U.S.

Air Force intelligence is an arm of the U.S. Air Force responsible for collecting, controlling, exploiting, and defending information pertaining to Air Force air and space operations while denying any potential adversary the ability to do the same.

An additional Air Force intelligence responsibility is operation of the NATIONAL RECONNAISSANCE OFFICE (NRO), under the oversight of the CIA. The NRO is responsible for a myriad of aerospace intelligence activities, including, among other tasks, satellite surveillance.

Like its U.S. Army, Navy, and Marine Corps counterparts, the Air Force intelligence service is overseen by the DEFENSE INTELLIGENCE AGENCY (DIA). The Air Force intelligence service also reports to the president, through the NATIONAL SECURITY ADVISOR. Additionally, the service's activities are overseen—and coordinated with the efforts of the other members of the U.S. INTELLIGENCE COMMUNITY—by the CIA's DIRECTOR OF CENTRAL INTELLIGENCE (DCI).

See also ARMY INTELLIGENCE; MARINE CORPS INTELLIGENCE; NAVAL INTELLIGENCE; SATELLITE INTELLIGENCE/SURVEILLANCE OPERATIONS.

AJAX, Operation

AJAX was the code name for the CIA's Iranian operation of 1953 that overthrew the de facto regime of Dr. Mohammad Mossadegh and subsequently restored the shah of Iran, Mohammad Reza Pahlavi, to his throne.

See also ANGLO-IRANIAN OIL COMPANY; IRAN, COUP D'ÉTAT IN; ROOSEVELT, KERMIT "KIM," JR.

Alabama Air National Guard

A key component of the CIA's air arm during Operation ZAPATA (the ill-fated BAY OF PIGS invasion of 1961) was represented by aircraft, pilots, and ground-crew personnel of the Alabama Air National Guard.

In October 1960, six months prior to the invasion, CIA air staff planners realized that the nearly 100 air-crew candidates selected from the ranks of the Cuban exiles were not sufficient. As a consequence, and against White House orders, the Agency approached Major General George Reid "Poppa" Doster, the commander of the Alabama Air National Guard, and requested his assistance.

Doster agreed and assembled a force of 80 pilots and crew members with experience in B-26 bomber and C-54 transport aircraft. Less than two months later, Doster and his airmen joined their Cuban counterparts at Retalhulea, a small airstrip in Guatemala, and began training.

Like the invasion force's ground component, the air element was doomed from the start. In April 1961, the combined ground-sea-air operation was launched and almost immediately began to fall apart. When the invaders became pinned down on the beaches, President John Kennedy refused to authorize American air and naval gunfire support and ordered U.S. warships in the vicinity of the battle to withdraw.

On-station U.S. pilots protested their inability to engage Cuban targets; they knew that the order "not to engage" was a virtual death sentence for the men on the beach. But Kennedy believed that if the United States became directly involved in the shooting, the Soviets might move on Western Europe, thus launching a third world war. In the invasion's final hours, however, six of the Alabama Air National Guard pilots flew combat missions without authorization. Four were shot down and subsequently killed.

Albanian operations

Code named VALUABLE, the Albanian operations were a series of joint CIA/British Secret Service (MI6) paramilitary/covert action projects from 1949 to 1953. The operations were aimed at overthrowing the totalitarian government of Albanian prime minister Enver Hoxha.

It was the first such attempt by the CIA, and it was one that FRANK GARDINER WISNER, then head of the CIA's OFFICE OF POLICY COORDINATION (OPC), described as a "clinical experiment to see whether larger rollback operations would be feasible elsewhere." Unfortunately for the Agency, the operations were a dismal failure.

The seeds for the unrest in Albania were sown during World War II. On April 7, 1939, Italian troops invaded Albania. When the Italians surrendered to the Western allies in September of 1943, the still-undefeated German army moved into and occupied Albania.

The leader of the Albanian underground forces was Enver Hoxha, a former schoolteacher turned communist revolutionary. In resisting the Nazi invaders, Hoxha formed an alliance with Josip Broz Tito, the leader of the Yugoslav partisans. Tito was also a communist. The Nazis were driven out of Albania in 1944. Tito then assisted Hoxha in overthrowing Albania's government, forcing King Zog I (the former Ahmed Bey Zogu) into exile in Egypt. Not long after, Hoxha dispatched troops to help Tito's forces crush Albanian nationalists in Kosovo. By 1946, Hoxha had consolidated power and declared himself president of that Balkan nation.

Great Britain, which feared the swelling Soviet sphere of influence in Eastern Europe, favored a noncommunist government for Albania. The United States was initially less interested; after all, in 1946 most Americans viewed Albania as an obscure state, and few could even locate the country on a map.

In 1947, MI6 began parachuting operatives into the region. The operatives then made contact with a number of Albanian émigrés—called "Pixies"—who were willing to launch a civil war to unseat Hoxha. MI6-supported Albanian insurgents based in Greece and Italy also began launching raids against pro-Hoxha forces. But those raids proved ineffective against Hoxha's regulars. World War II had drained the British government's coffers, and the funds it could provide to support the Albanian resistance movement were wholly insufficient. However, the situation changed in 1948, when Tito severed ties with Soviet premier fellow communist, Josef Stalin. Tito felt that Stalin was trying to manipulate Yugoslav government policy in an attempt to control the destiny of that nation. Rejected by what he perceived to be a lesser communist nation, the Soviet leader expelled Yugoslavia from Cominform, the initial postwar organization of communist states.

Hoxha, despite his ties with Tito, felt a greater sense of loyalty to Stalin. Consequently, Albania severed relations with Yugoslavia, its natural ally, and granted the Soviet Union a foothold in the heart of the Balkans. Making matters worse, Albania began supporting communist insurgents in Greece. There was a growing fear among both the British and the Americans that Italy might be next.

In late 1948, Great Britain's "Russia Committee" appealed directly to Wisner for American assistance. In 1949, Wisner agreed to limited assistance. He offered to fund, train men for, and oversee operations in Albania but stipulated that no American would be directly involved on the ground.

The operations were to be a two-part effort—one a paramilitary entity, the other a clandestine action entity—coordinated in Washington, D.C., by a four-member SPECIAL POLICY COMMITTEE of representatives from the U.S. STATE DEPARTMENT, the CIA, the British Foreign Office, and MI6.

The State Department representative was ROBERT PRATHER JOYCE, an expert on the Balkans and a former member of the OFFICE OF STRATEGIC SERVICES (OSS), the wartime predecessor organization of the CIA. The CIA representative was FRANKLIN ANTHONY LINDSEY, also a former OSS operative. He had fought alongside Tito's partisans during the war and was currently serving as chief of OPC's East European Division. The British Foreign Office representative was George Jellico, a wartime veteran of the elite Special Air Service (SAS). The MI6 representative was HAROLD ADRIAN RUSSELL PHILBY, one of the infamous CAMBRIDGE FIVE, who had been working for the Soviets and would ultimately betray the Albanian operation to the communists. The CIA's man in the man in the Mediterranean was Michael Burke, another former OSS veteran. Burke was responsible for overseeing the operations in the region.

That same year, the CIA and MI6 selected four émigré leaders with whom they would work: Zog, who was living in Egypt; Midhat Frasheri, who was living in Turkey; Abas Ermenji, who was living in Greece; and Said Kryeziu, who was living in Italy. The émigré leaders, whose families harbored long-standing religious and political animosities toward one another, were initially apprehensive about working with each other. However, by July 1949 they had all come to an agreement: Abas Kupi, a Zog supporter, would chair a military junta, with Ermenji and Kryeziu as deputies. Frasheri was placed at the head of the Albanian National Committee, created to promote the supposedly coming "Albanian revolution" around the world. Meanwhile, British commandos were training Albanian freedom fighters and agents at a staging base in Malta. The officers of this paramilitary entity were recruited from among Zog's Royal Guard, which had accompanied him in exile.

Agents recruited for clandestine work were also being trained at bases in Cyprus and West Germany.

In September 1949, the first paramilitary mission was launched. It was a disaster. The Pixies came ashore by boat, immediately met Albanian security forces, and were driven back into the sea. Three of the raiders were killed during the assault. A second mission was attempted in 1950, when a team of Pixie soldiers was sent from Malta overland across Greece into Albania. Its members were arrested by Greek authorities before they reached the border (but were eventually released).

Several more attempts were made to infiltrate Albania. Some were parachuted into the country by C-47 transport planes flown by CIA pilots out of Bari, an Italian air base. Others were transported to the coast by submarine. In most cases, the infiltrators were shot on sight. Some were captured and condemned to death. Others were tortured to death by Hoxha's secret police.

By 1952, it was evident that the operations were being compromised by a MOLE, and the project was abandoned. It was later revealed that Philby had been passing to the Soviets insider information about the operations, thus ensuring the failure of the project at every turn.

Several hundred Albanian émigrés are estimated to have been killed during the Albanian operation. Hoxha remained in power until his death in 1985.

ALERT, Operation

Operation ALERT was a COLD WAR exercise wherein American citizens living or working in "nuclear target cities" were required upon alarm to take cover for 15 minutes. Instituted by the U.S. Civil Defense Agency, the exercise was designed to test the readiness of the American people to seek safety in the event of a nuclear attack on the United States.

The operation, which began in 1954, consisted of a series of civil defense drills in which ordinary citizens in target areas sought cover in fallout shelters when air raid sirens were sounded. Simultaneously, federal civil defense officials tested their own readiness and communications systems, and key government officials, including senior CIA and other U.S. intelligence community officials, conducted practice evacuations of Washington, D.C.

On June 15, 1955, an ALERT drill was conducted in which 55 American cities participated. President Dwight Eisenhower himself evacuated the White House for a tent city outside of the capital. For days, newspapers around the country published reports of the fictitious attacks.

The mock reports included numbers of bombs dropped, cities hit, and casualties. Millions of Americans participated in the exercise. But in New York City, some 28 antinuclear activists from the Catholic Worker Movement, the Fellowship of Reconciliation, and the War Resisters League remained above ground in New York's City Hall Park. The protestors, who viewed the drills as a ludicrous assertion of the survivability of nuclear war, were arrested and charged with violating the State Defense Emergency Act of 1951, which mandated participation in drills. However, none

were given prison terms, because the state of New York did not want further publicity in the matter. Operation ALERT was abandoned in 1962.

all-source intelligence

"All-source intelligence" is a CIA term for intelligence gathered from all sources, including HUMINT (human intelligence)—the CIA's primary intelligence resource), COMINT (communications intelligence), IMINT (imagery intelligence—formerly PHOTINT, or photographic intelligence), ELINT (electronic intelligence), MASINT (measurement and signature intelligence—collected from special technical sensors, by which a missile's target can be determined by its trajectory), TELINT (telemetry intelligence—a form of MASINT), RADINT (intelligence gathered from radars, also a form of MASINT), SIGINT (signals intelligence—essentially an amalgamation of both COMINT and ELINT), TECHINT (technical intelligence—essentially an amalgamation of IMINT and SIGINT), and OSINT (OPEN-SOURCE INTELLIGENCE—gleaned from foreign television and radio broadcasts, as well as articles and photographs published in foreign newspapers, magazines, and trade journals).

According to the U.S. DEPARTMENT OF DEFENSE (DoD), the five primary intelligence disciplines in all-source intelligence are HUMINT, IMINT, MASINT, SIGINT, and OSINT.

Amazon Natural Drug Company

One of the least known of the CIA's proprietary FRONT companies, the Amazon Natural Drug Company was established in 1966 as a supporting enterprise for Project MKSEARCH, the ascendant project of MKULTRA, the Agency's infamous MIND-CONTROL DRUG TESTING program.

Located near Iquitos, Peru, on the Amazon River, the Amazon Natural Drug Company operated as a bottom-tier drug-collection company, in which Agency-employed botanists, anthropologists, and Peruvian tribesmen led by CIA officer JOSEPH CALDWELL KING, gathered all manner of roots, barks, mushrooms, and native vegetation in order to extract toxic and hallucinogenic compounds for Agency experimentation.

King, a former U.S. Army officer and FEDERAL BUREAU OF INVESTIGATION (FBI) agent who became the CIA's chief of clandestine operations in the Western Hemisphere, had directed the ZAPATA (BAY OF PIGS) operation during its initial planning stages and was eased out of the Agency soon after it failed. As head of the Amazon Natural Drug Company, King supervised the CIA's "drug gatherers"—often with a glass of scotch in hand—from the deck of a houseboat on the Amazon River. At least two other CIA field officers worked out of offices in Iquitos. The company's extracts were forwarded to CIA laboratories in the United States.

The Amazon Natural Drug Company ceased operations when the Agency shut down MKSEARCH in 1972.

Ames, Aldrich Hazen (Ricky) (1941–)

With the exception of Benedict Arnold, there has never been a more notorious turncoat in the history of American espionage than CIA counterspy Aldrich Hazen "Ricky" Ames. As one of the Agency's top COUNTERINTELLIGENCE officers, Ames was tasked with uncovering potential spies who had infiltrated the Western intelligence community. Instead, he became a spy himself for the Soviet Union, betraying over 100 American intelligence operations and compromising the covers of countless officers, agents, and Russian-based DOUBLE AGENTS, several of whom were arrested and executed by the Soviets. A 31-year veteran of the Agency, Ames was arrested by the FEDERAL BUREAU OF INVESTIGATION (FBI) in 1994.

Born on June 26, 1941, to Carleton Cecil Ames, a hard-drinking college professor, and Rachel Aldrich Ames, a high school English teacher, Ames spent the first decade of his life climbing trees, skinny-dipping in a local creek, attending Cub Scout meetings, and developing a passion for poetry in the backwater farming community of River Falls, Wisconsin. In 1951, his father suddenly and unexpectedly accepted a job with the CIA, uprooted the family, and moved to McLean, Virginia. How the elder Ames came to be recruited by the Agency is not known, but his language skills and knowledge of Asian history were certainly factors. From 1957 to 1959, the younger Ames found summer work as a CIA records analyst, marking classified documents for filing. In 1959, Ames entered the University of Chicago with dreams of pursuing a career in theater arts. In the summer of 1960, he returned to Virginia and again obtained employment at the Agency, this time as a painter. He returned to Chicago in the fall but failed to complete his sophomore year. For the next two years he worked at a Chicago theater as an assistant technical director.

In February 1962, Ames returned home and with the help of his father landed a full-time job as a clerk typist within the Agency's DIRECTORATE of Plans (Operations). For the next five years, he worked at the Agency, while attending nearby George Washington University.

In 1967, Ames's father retired from the Agency. That same year, Ames graduated from GWU with a history degree and was accepted into the CIA's CAREER TRAINEE program. He completed training in October 1968.

In October 1969, Ames was assigned to Ankara, Turkey, where he was made responsible for recruiting new agents. Unfortunately, it was a marginal tour of duty, and Ames earned less than stellar proficiency marks. It is widely held that in Turkey his cynicism toward the Agency began to develop.

According to an abstract of the 1994 Ames investigation by the CIA, "Ames's first overseas posting took place between 1969 and 1972. It was not a successful tour, and the last Performance Appraisal Report (PAR) of his tour stated, in effect, that Ames was unsuited for field work and should spend the remainder of his career at Headquarters. The PAR noted that Ames preferred 'assignments that do not involve face-to-face situations with relatively unknown personalities who must be manipulated.' Such a comment was devastating for an operations officer, and Ames was discouraged enough to consider leaving the Agency." In 1972, Ames was reassigned to CIA headquarters in LANGLEY, VIRGINIA, specifically the Directorate of Plans' Soviet–East European Division, where in 1973 he attended Russian-language school. From 1973 to 1974, he was tasked with recruiting American-based Soviet officials.

Like his father, Ames had a drinking problem. In the early 1960s, he had at least two alcohol-related run-ins with local law enforcement. By the early 1970s, the problem was beginning to surface at Agency functions. At a CIA Christmas party in 1973, he became so unmanageably intoxicated that he had to be helped home by members of the Agency's Office of Security. At a Christmas party the following year, he again got drunk and was discovered in a compromising position with a female officer. Both incidents were recorded in his employee security file.

In 1976, however, Ames received "proficient" and "strong performer" ratings as a headquarters officer supporting CIA operations in the field. The evaluation, however, also made note of his procrastination and a lack of attention to detail. That same year, he was transferred to New York and given charge of two Soviet agents for the CIA. He was also responsible for recruiting new agents among citizens of Eastern bloc countries who were in New York as members of missions to the United Nations.

Ames received substantially higher evaluations during his tenure in New York. He was considered "interested," "articulate," and "capable," with his efforts "invariably exceeding work standards." But his chronic procrastination, overdue reports, and occasional security violations were also noted.

Ames's most unsettling operational slips included one in which he left a briefcase containing classified documents on a subway train, and another wherein he left top-secret materials unsecured in his office. In both cases, he received only verbal reprimands. It was also in New York that his personal life began to unravel. His marriage to his first wife, Nancy, began to show signs of strain when in 1981, after turning down several overseas assignments, he

Aldrich Ames   (AP PHOTO/DENIS PAQUIN)

accepted a posting to Mexico City. Nancy Ames remained in New York.

In Mexico, Ames was tasked with monitoring Cuban and Soviet espionage activity in Central America, as well as recruiting new agents to the CIA. One of those recruits was an attractive social butterfly and Colombia's cultural attaché to Mexico, Maria del Rosario Casas Dupuy. Against Agency policy, Ames became intimately involved with his new recruit.

In 1983, Ames was placed in charge of the Agency's regional counterintelligence branch, where he came in contact with a number of KGB operatives. Whether or not they recruited him or he initially volunteered information is not known. What is known is that two years after he moved to counterintelligence, the lure of quick money became too strong.

For Ames, 1985 was a red-letter year. He divorced Nancy, married Rosario, and began selling secrets to the KGB, quickly becoming the highest-paid spy for the Soviet Union in the history of espionage. His misdeeds began on April 16 while assigned to the CIA's Soviet/East European Division. He met with the KGB at the Soviet

embassy in Washington; shortly thereafter, he received $50,000 from the same source. That summer, he met with a Washington-based Soviet diplomat and passed information regarding anti-Soviet operations as well as information about CIA and FBI assets. Then, in December, he met with a KGB agent in Bogotá, Colombia.

In July 1986, Ames was transferred to Rome. He took his new bride, who was now assisting him in his betrayal of American intelligence, and for three years the couple engaged in their treasonous trade. In 1985 and 1986, both the CIA and the FBI, when a number of their Soviet assets were exposed and subsequently arrested by the KGB, began looking inward. Shortly after the two returned to the United States in 1989, the CIA began to take a hard look at Ames, whose Agency salary could ill support the $540,000 home (for which he had paid cash) in upstate Virginia and other high-end purchases he had begun to make.

In 1991, Ames was transferred to the CIA's Counternarcotics Center, the FBI was notified of his newfound wealth, and both the FBI and the CIA began putting two and two together. An investigation was launched, overwhelming evidence was compiled, and on February 21, 1994, he was arrested by the FBI. Soon after, Rosario was also arrested.

In the ensuing trial, it was determined that Ames had met with and sold secrets to the Soviets about Western operatives and Russian assets who were working for the Americans and the British, providing the names of every agent operating in the USSR. All total, the KGB had paid Ames $2.7 million for information that resulted in the compromising of at least 100 intelligence operations and the execution of at least 10 agents working for the West.

On April 28, Ames pled guilty to charges of conspiracy to commit espionage and tax evasion. He avoided the death penalty by agreeing to cooperate fully and was subsequently sentenced to life in prison without the possibility of parole. Rosario was sentenced to five years.

In a 2000 CNN interview, CIA officer RICHARD L. HAVER, who led the Agency's damage-assessment team in the Ames case, described Ames's spying for the Soviets as "catastrophic" for the Agency's HUMINT (human intelligence) operations. According to Haver, "In the spy game, when you're penetrated, when someone is working for the other side inside your security world, they then own you."

Ames himself has never expressed remorse for the deaths of those resulting from his betrayals, and he has at times discredited the importance of the Western intelligence community. In a CNN interview for its televised documentary *Cold War,* Ames said, "The reasons that I did what I did in 1985 were personal, banal, and amounted really to a kind of greed and folly." He added, "I trafficked with the devil. This I hadn't factored in."

analyst

In the CIA, an analyst is a professional intelligence officer, usually with a science or engineering background, responsible for evaluating intelligence gathered from clandestine or open sources. Working within the Agency's DIRECTORATE of Intelligence, analysts assess information about key foreign countries, regional conflicts, terrorism, weapons development and proliferation, information warfare, and narcotics trafficking. This analyzed information, or FINISHED INTELLIGENCE, is then presented to intelligence consumers either through reports called NATIONAL INTELLIGENCE ESTIMATES (NIEs) or briefings.

Analysts also produce the CURRENT INTELLIGENCE BULLETIN, which is delivered daily to the president of the United States.

Angleton, James Jesus (1917–1987)

The legendary "master spy hunter"—so christened because of his reputation as a spy catcher during World War II—James Jesus Angleton was a former operative in the OFFICE OF STRATEGIC SERVICES (OSS) who has since been credited as the unofficial founder and developer of the CIA's COUNTERINTELLIGENCE (CI) arm during the first two decades of the COLD WAR. But his abrupt retirement from the Agency in 1974 is mired in controversy.

Born in Boise, Idaho, on December 9, 1917, to James Hugh Angleton, a former cavalry officer and National Cash Register Company businessman who himself would become an OSS colonel, and Mexican-born Carmen Mercedes Moreno, young Angleton was destined to be the stuff of spy novels. Angleton, a tall, thin, chain-smoking fly fisherman and lover of poetry, graduated from Yale in 1941. Like many of his CIA compatriots, including RICHARD MERVIN BISSELL; WILLIAM PUTNAM BUNDY; WILLIAM SLOAN COFFIN, JR.; WILLIAM F. BUCKLEY, JR.; and future U.S. president GEORGE BUSH, Angleton became a member of Yale's secret SKULL & BONES SOCIETY. He attended Harvard Law School and was inducted into the U.S. Army on March 19, 1941.

In August, as Allied forces were mopping up in Sicily, Angleton was recruited into the OSS through the efforts of his father and NORMAN PEARSON, his former English professor at Yale. Pearson, head of the OSS's London-based counterintelligence (X-2) division, assigned Angleton to the OSS Rome desk after the fall of Italy in 1944. As a 27-year-old OSS lieutenant, he was the youngest member of X-2. But, as a man of considerable intellectual gifts, he was made responsible for CI activities from Spain to Germany to the Mediterranean. He quickly assumed the reigns of the OSS's Special Counterintelligence UNIT Z,

and he was the only American X-2 operative who was allowed access to Britain's ULTRA code-breaking system.

In August 1945, World War II ended. Angleton was promoted to captain. He also received the Legion of Merit for "successfully capturing over a thousand enemy intelligence agents."

When President Harry Truman disbanded the OSS in October, the office's operational arm was redesignated the STRATEGIC SERVICES UNIT (SSU) and moved to the War Department. OSS research and analysis units were transferred to the STATE DEPARTMENT. Angleton was still in Italy as the senior American intelligence officer with SSU in 1946 (when Truman signed a presidential directive establishing the CENTRAL INTELLIGENCE GROUP and folding SSU into the same) and 1947 (when the NATIONAL SECURITY ACT established the CIA). He is considered a key player in the postwar efforts that prevented Italy from going communist. Also during those years Angleton developed close contacts with the Jewish underground, and he helped create solid collaboration between the CIA and the MOSSAD, Israel's counterpart organization to the CIA.

In the summer of 1947 Angleton returned to the United States, and within a few months he was reassigned as a senior aide to the director of the CIA's OFFICE OF SPECIAL OPERATIONS (OSO). At OSO, he oversaw espionage and counterespionage activities, particularly those regarding the discovery of MOLES who he believed were passing America's most closely guarded nuclear secrets to the Soviets.

In 1954, DIRECTOR OF CENTRAL INTELLIGENCE (DCI) ALLEN WELSH DULLES named Angleton chief of counterintelligence, under the Directorate of Plans (Operations). He would serve in that capacity for 19 years.

Despite his sterling CI efforts and loyalty to the United States, Angleton's keen focus on counterintelligence began to evolve into an unhealthy paranoia. He doubted almost everything, and he suspected almost everyone. He accurately believed that the KGB was charting a course to support worldwide communist domination. But he inaccurately believed that the division between China and the USSR and the break between the latter and Yugoslavia were merely plots hatched between the three nations to lure the United States into dropping its guard. Worse, he recklessly suggested that British prime minister Harold Wilson may have worked with the Soviets.

Angleton's overall suspicions were further stoked in 1963 when HAROLD ADRIAN RUSSELL "KIM" PHILBY, a treasonous MI6 officer turned KGB general, defected to the Soviet Union after having supplied the Russians with Western secrets for nearly 30 years. Philby, a member of the infamous CAMBRIDGE FIVE, had been lunching and drinking with Angleton every week for months when the former was stationed in Washington. Angleton had considered him a close friend.

Additionally, Anatoli Golitsyn, a KGB defector who knew of Philby's betrayal of the West, convinced Angleton that spies had penetrated the CIA, stolen secrets, and disseminated KGB misinformation. Angleton began to look inward. He believed—his critics have said, to a fault—that moles had permeated every aspect of the Western spy network, and he set out to cleanse the American intelligence community.

Though officially he reported directly to the deputy director of plans, during the 1950s and 1960s Angleton was granted unofficial carte blanche powers to circumvent the chain of command. He was allowed to bug the residences and office telephones of high-ranking government officials and foreign dignitaries as he saw fit. Directors Allen Welsh Dulles and RICHARD MCGARRAH HELMS looked the other way. Not so with DCI WILLIAM EGAN COLBY, who was not fond of Angleton and his unrestrained activities.

Despite his brilliance as an intelligence-gathering "fundamentalist" and a "spook" of the old school, by the early 1970s, Angleton's obsessions and implausible theories were perceived as serious liabilities. There were even whispers that he had become the victim of a Soviet plot, that he himself had been a Soviet spy, though no such allegation has ever been proven.

In 1974, Colby purportedly leaked word that Angleton had been involved in the opening of domestic mail by the CIA. On December 17, Colby called Angleton into his office, relieved him as CI chief, offered him a choice between consultancy or retirement, and allowed him a few days to think it over. An embittered Angleton resigned.

"As if the external wounds were not enough, Langley had long engaged in its own bloodletting," wrote author Ted Gup in his *The Book of Honor.* "The self destructive hunt for Soviet moles inside the CIA, led by the brilliant but obsessed James Angleton, was finally brought to an end with his forced retirement in December 1974—but not before the careers of honorable officers had been ruined and vast resources squandered chasing phantoms."

Angleton died in 1987. He was 70.

Anglo-Iranian Oil Company (AIOC)

The Anglo-Iranian Oil Company (AIOC) was a British-owned corporation that became a bone of contention between the United Kingdom and Iran in 1950 and ultimately led to Operation AJAX—the CIA-sponsored COUP D'ÉTAT IN IRAN in 1953.

The AIOC, initially doing business as the Anglo-Persian Oil Company, had been operational for a half century, granted oil rights on over 1.5 million square miles of Iranian territory. The British government purchased 51 percent of the company in 1913 to provide fuel for Royal Navy warships operating in the Persian Gulf and elsewhere.

The problem stemmed from 1950 legislation by the Majlis, the Iranian parliament, rejecting a Soviet-proposed oil agreement for northern Iran and declaring that all such agreements would be subject to review. In 1950, British oil operations were up for renegotiation. Under a previous arrangement, which was not slated for renewal until 1993, the British—through the AIOC—had complete autonomy in pumping, refining, and shipping oil from southern Iran throughout the world. AIOC was critical to Iran's financial well-being. In addition to paying the salaries of company employees, AIOC paid rent for individual housing, as well as taxes. The payouts amounted to over half of Iran's budget. But the company was making 10 times as much as it was paying Iran, and it was paying more in taxes to Great Britain.

In 1950, the AIOC agreement was reviewed. The British offered minor concessions. Then they arranged for AIOC supporters in the Majlis to create a commission and issue a parliamentary report stating that nationalization of AIOC would not be in Iran's best interest.

On March 3, 1951, Iranian prime minister Ali Razmara appeared before the Majlis and read a poorly translated version of the report. He was shouted down by other ministers, who accused him of being in league with the British. Four days later, Razmara was shot to death while praying in a mosque.

On March 15, Dr. Mohammad Mossadegh, a procommunist hard-liner and one of the most rabid nationalists in the Majlis, introduced a bill that would nationalize the AIOC.

On April 19, the Majlis elected him prime minister, and on May 2, Iran took control of the AIOC.

On August 19, 1953, Mossadegh was ousted during a coup organized and financed by the CIA, and AIOC was returned to its stockholders. The following year, the Anglo-Iranian Oil Company was renamed British Petroleum—known to most American motorists as "BP."

ARGON

ARGON was the code name for a satellite-intelligence mapping project that was operational from May 1962 until August 1964. Utilizing the existing framework of CORONA (a satellite/high-altitude-aircraft photo reconnaissance project operational from 1959 to 1972), 12 satellite missions were conducted under ARGON. Seven of those missions were successful.

ARGON was the predecessor satellite project to LANYARD.

See also SATELLITE INTELLIGENCE/SURVEILLANCE OPERATIONS.

Armed Forces Security Agency (AFSA)

The Armed Forces Security Agency (AFSA) was the predecessor organization to the NATIONAL SECURITY AGENCY (NSA), a senior member of the U.S. INTELLIGENCE COMMUNITY. Established on May 20, 1949, under the direct command of the JOINT CHIEFS OF STAFF (JCS), the AFSA was responsible for directing the COMINT (communications intelligence) and ELINT (electronic intelligence) activities of the organic SIGINT (signals intelligence) units within each of the U.S. armed forces.

The AFSA was the first substantive attempt on the part of the U.S. DEPARTMENT OF DEFENSE to eliminate a duplication of cryptologic activities by centralizing those efforts. The AFSA, however, lacking legal authority to provide "central direction," was ineffective.

On December 29, 1952, the NSA was created and superseded the AFSA.

l'Armée Clandestine

L'Armée Clandestine ("the Secret Army") was a special military force composed of Laotian tribesmen and managed by the CIA during the secret war in Laos (1962–72). Established in 1962, l'Armée Clandestine was organized, recruited, and trained by the Far East Division of the Agency's Clandestine Service.

The army, which grew to some 30,000 Laotian fighters and 17,000 Thai mercenaries, was responsible for combatting Pathet Lao and North Vietnamese soldiers who were attempting to overthrow the government of Laos.

When the Paris Peace Accords of 1973 ended America's involvement in Southeast Asia, l'Armée Clandestine was disbanded. Soon thereafter, the force's commanding general, Vang Pao, left Laos and settled in the United States.

See also SOUTHEAST ASIA, CIA OPERATIONS IN.

Army intelligence, U.S.

Army intelligence is a branch of the U.S. Army responsible for collecting, controlling, exploiting, and defending information pertaining to Army ground and air operations while denying any potential adversary the ability to do the same.

Like its Air Force, Navy, and Marine Corps counterparts, the Army Intelligence Service is overseen by the DEFENSE INTELLIGENCE AGENCY (DIA). Army intelligence also reports to the president, through the NATIONAL SECURITY ADVISOR. Additionally, the service's activities are overseen—and coordinated with the efforts of the other members of the U.S. INTELLIGENCE COMMUNITY—by the CIA's DIRECTOR OF CENTRAL INTELLIGENCE (DCI).

See also AIR FORCE INTELLIGENCE; MARINE CORPS INTELLIGENCE; NAVY INTELLIGENCE.

assassination plots

Though the CIA has been implicated in numerous assassination plots around the world, no successful assassination connected with the CIA has ever been substantiated.

During the CHURCH COMMITTEE (officially, the Select Committee to Study Governmental Operations with respect to Intelligence Activities) hearings of the mid-1970s, it was determined that the CIA had plotted to assassinate foreign leaders. In at least two instances, the Agency had moved beyond the planning phase. In his book *A Season of Inquiry,* Church Committee investigator Loch K. Johnson wrote, "The details we pieced together during the summer (1975) documented an unhappy truth; the government of the United States did plot, in peacetime, the death of foreign leaders."

According to the Church Committee's findings, attempts to assassinate both Cuban leader FIDEL CASTRO and Congolese leader Patrice Emery Lumumba had moved into the operational phase. But the Agency was not successful in either case. Castro was too elusive and too heavily guarded; Lumumba was killed by Congolese rivals before the CIA could get to him.

Other foreign leaders who were on the CIA's assassination list but were actually killed during non-Agency-sponsored coups d'état or by local dissidents include Iraqi general Abdul Karim Kassem, General Rafael Trujillo of the Dominican Republic, Ngo Dinh Diem of South Vietnam, and General René Schneider of Chile.

DIRECTORS OF CENTRAL INTELLIGENCE (DCI) RICHARD MCGARRAH HELMS and WILLIAM EGAN COLBY, expressly forbade, in writing, assassinations as a means of achieving operational objectives. Helms issued such a directive in 1972, Colby in 1973.

In 1976, President Gerald Ford issued EXECUTIVE ORDER (EO) 11905, which forbade government-sponsored assassinations. A portion of Ford's EO reads: "No employee of the United States Government shall engage in, or conspire to engage in, political assassination."

In 1978, President Jimmy Carter issued Executive Order 12036, revoking EO 11905 but continuing the ban on government-sponsored assassinations. A portion of Carter's EO reads: "No person employed by or acting on behalf of the United States government shall engage in, or conspire to engage in, assassination."

In 1981, President Ronald Reagan issued Executive Order 12333, which, like EOs 11905 and 12036, prohibited assassinations but did not define the term "assassination."

In the 1990s, a debate emerged within the U.S. INTELLIGENCE COMMUNITY as to whether government-sponsored assassinations should be banned in all circumstances. In the wake of the SEPTEMBER 11, 2001, TERRORIST ATTACKS ON THE UNITED STATES, the prohibition of assassination was publicly criticized, forcing the federal government to rethink its policy.

On September 17, following President George W. Bush's remark that terrorist Osama bin Laden was "wanted dead or alive," White House spokesman Ari Fleischer said that EO 12333 "remains in effect." Fleischer declined to interpret the text, stating, "I'm going to just repeat my words and others will figure out the exact implications of them, but it does not inhibit the nation's ability to act in self-defense."

See also CHILE, OPERATIONS IN; CONGO, OPERATIONS IN THE; EXECUTIVE ACTION.

assassins

The word "assassin" is derived from an 11th-century Persian military cult known as the Hashashin, or Hashishan. This group—born of a Shi'ite Muslim sect known as the Ismalites—comprised devoutly religious, though cruel, professional killers who often ingested hashish (either smoking or drinking it in a mixed brew) before participating in their grisly trade—thus their name. Eventually, the title evolved into the English "assassin."

In the modern world, an assassin is a professional killer or a killer for hire.

Many intelligence organizations around the world have at times maintained assassination teams. The CIA has never maintained such, preferring to subcontract its WET WORK.

See also ASSASSINATION PLOTS; EXECUTIVE ACTION.

Association of Former Intelligence Officers (AFIO)

The Association of Former Intelligence Officers (AFIO) is a nonprofit, nonpolitical association composed of both former intelligence professionals and supporters of the U.S. INTELLIGENCE COMMUNITY. Founded in 1975 by retired Agency operations officer DAVID ATLEE PHILLIPS, the AFIO seeks to build a strong public constituency through education.

See also CENTRAL INTELLIGENCE RETIREES ASSOCIATION.

A-12 Blackbird aircraft

The A-12 Blackbird was the CIA's single-seat predecessor aircraft to the twin-seat SR-71 BLACKBIRD, a high-altitude strategic reconnaissance aircraft.

Unlike the SR-71, A-12s were flown by CIA pilots.

See also BLACKSHIELD, OPERATION; OXCART.

awards, medals, and decorations

Like American military forces and police departments, the CIA presents awards, medals, and decorations to employees who distinguish themselves in a manner reflecting credit upon the Agency.

Officially, the awards include

1. Distinguished Intelligence Cross—awarded for a voluntary act or acts of heroism involving acceptance of existing dangers and conspicuous fortitude and exemplary courage.
2. Distinguished Intelligence Medal—awarded for outstanding services or for achievement of a distinctly exceptional nature in a duty or responsibility.
3. Intelligence Star—awarded for a voluntary act or acts of courage performed under hazardous conditions, or for outstanding achievements or services rendered with distinction under conditions of grave risk.
4. Intelligence Medal of Merit—awarded for the performance of specially meritorious service or for acts of achievements conspicuously above normal duties.
5. Career Intelligence Medal—awarded for a cumulative record of service that reflects exceptional achievement.
6. Intelligence Commendation Medal—awarded for specially commendable service or for an act or achievement significantly above normal duties that results in an important contribution to the mission of the Agency.
7. Exceptional Service Medallion—awarded for injury or death resulting from service in an area of hazard.
8. Gold Retirement Medallion—awarded for a career of 35 years or more with the Agency.
9. Silver Retirement Medallion—awarded for a career of 25 years or more with the Agency.
10. Bronze Retirement Medallion—awarded for a career of at least 15 but less than 25 years with the Agency.

As much as the awards are treasured, decorations awarded to covert operatives in the CIA are sometimes referred to as "jock-strap medals." Such officers' decorations are retained by the Agency until recipients retire. In some cases, if security warrants, the officer may never receive it. CIA employees often make light of these facts by saying that such medals can only be worn concealed on jock straps.

AZORIAN

AZORIAN was the code name for the preparatory phase of a joint CIA/U.S. Navy mission that successfully recovered a portion of a sunken Soviet Golf II Class submarine in 1974.

Prior to its initiation, the CIA approached billionaire industrialist Howard Hughes and requested his assistance in the recovery operation. Hughes agreed, and Project AZORIAN was officially launched. Hughes's Summa Corporation designed and built a $350 million salvage vessel, the *GLOMAR EXPLORER,* specifically for the mission.

On November 4, 1972, *Glomar Explorer* set sail, and AZORIAN was renamed Project JENNIFER.

B

Bagley, Tennent Harrington (1925–)

CIA operations officer Tennent Harrington Bagley was one of the first conspiracy theorists to come forward in the aftermath of the assassination of President John F. Kennedy.

Ironically, Bagley was born in Annapolis, Maryland (home of the U.S. Naval Academy), on November 11, 1925–Veterans Day, and exactly 150 years and one day after the birth of the U.S. Marine Corps (an organization in which Harrington would serve with distinction during World War II). His father was Admiral David Worth Bagley, and his mother, Mary Louise Harrington Bagley, was a niece of Fleet Admiral William D. Leahy. Both of Harrington's brothers also attained the rank of admiral. Bagley joined the Marines in 1943 and was honorably discharged at the rank of first lieutenant in 1946. The following year, he attended the University of Southern California. He then studied political science at the University of Geneva (Switzerland), earning a bachelor's degree in 1948 and a Ph.D. in 1951.

After completing his studies, Bagley joined the CIA. He held a number of posts in the Agency, including service as a political officer at the U.S. embassies in Vienna, Austria (1951–52) and Bern, Switzerland (1958–61). He also held the posts of deputy chief of the Soviet Bloc Division in the Agency's CLANDESTINE SERVICE. While serving in that capacity, he became one of the original conspiracy theorists in the investigation of the assassination of Kennedy. On November 23, 1963, the day after the assassination, Bagley sent to his superiors a memo that read, "Putting it baldly, was [Lee Harvey] Oswald, wittingly or unwittingly, part of a plot to murder President Kennedy in Dallas?" Bagley later became CHIEF OF STATION (COS) in Brussels, Belgium.

In 1990, Bagley coauthored a book, *The KGB: Masters of the Soviet Union*, with Peter Deriabin, a former KGB officer who had defected to Vienna, Austria, in 1954.

bang and burn

"Bang and burn" is a CIA term for demolition and sabotage operations. For instance, during the CUBAN MISSILE CRISIS of 1962, WILLIAM KING HARVEY, the director of a CIA covert action program known as TASK FORCE W, sent several teams into Cuba that attacked farming and industrial complexes and, in one instance, destroyed a factory. Those missions were known as "bang and burn" operations.

Bank of Credit and Commerce International (BCCI)

The Bank of Credit and Commerce International (BCCI) was a FRONT for a multinational, multibillion-dollar money-laundering operation that allegedly supported international terrorism, arms trafficking, illegal sales of nuclear technologies, prostitution, income tax evasion, drug smuggling, illegal immigration, illicit purchases of banks and real estate, and a myriad of other disreputable financial schemes.

The CIA had a somewhat conflicting and controversial relationship with the BCCI. In a 1992 report to the U.S. Senate's Foreign Relations Committee, Senators John Kerry (D-Massachusetts) and Hank Brown (R-Colorado) stated that by early 1985, the Agency "knew more about BCCI's goals and intentions concerning the U.S. banking system than anyone else in government, and provided that information to the U.S. Treasury and the Office of the Comptroller of the Currency, neither of whom had the responsibility for regulating the First American Bank that BCCI had taken over." The report added that the CIA had not provided the information gathered to its proper users, the U.S. Justice Department and the Federal Reserve. According to the senators, the CIA had been aware of the fact that BCCI was a "fundamentally corrupt criminal enterprise." However, they claimed, the Agency used both BCCI and its secretly held U.S. subsidiary First American for a variety of covert operations.

BCCI originated in Pakistan but was a global institution by the 1970s. The CIA's relationship with BCCI lasted from 1979 through 1991. In 1991, Congress began pressuring the Agency to reveal its involvement with the bank. The following year, a number of documents related to the CIA's involvement with BCCI were released to the congressional intelligence committees, but questions regarding the depth to which the CIA was involved in any BCCI operations remain unanswered.

Barker Terry, Bernard Leon (1917–)

Bernard Leon Barker Terry, also known by his childhood nickname "Macho," was one of the five burglars arrested for breaking into the WATERGATE complex in the summer of 1972. He was also a CIA operative who was directly involved in the ill-fated invasion of Cuba at the BAY OF PIGS in 1961.

Barker was born in Havana, Cuba, on March 17, 1917, to Bernard L. Barker, a descendant of Russian immigrants to the United States, and Alicia Terry, a hot-tempered Irish-Cuban woman and a member of the old Cuban aristocracy. Raised in a strict Catholic household, young Barker learned to speak both English and Spanish at a very young age, and he developed a lifelong passion for fishing. In 1933, still a teenager, he joined a revolutionary group opposed to Cuban president Gerardo Machado Morales. Barker's father was warned by the police that his son's association with the group was dangerous. Consequently, Barker was sent to Long Island, New York, in

order to finish high school. When he turned 18 he applied for and received American citizenship. He then worked briefly in a Baltimore, Maryland, steel mill, before returning to Cuba.

When the Japanese attacked Pearl Harbor on December 7, 1941, Barker was a 24-year-old engineering student at the University of Havana. The following day, he walked into the American embassy in Havana and offered his services to the United States, thus becoming the first Cuban-American to volunteer for the American armed forces.

Barker was soon shipped to Tampa, Florida, for basic training. From there, he was transferred to Houston, Texas, where he became an aviation cadet. After earning his wings and a second lieutenant's commission, he was assigned aerial reconnaissance missions over the Gulf of Mexico. He then trained as a bombardier and in October 1943 was shipped to England, where he became a bombardier with the famous Eighth Air Force.

On the morning of February 2, 1944, Barker's B-17 Flying Fortress was mortally hit by antiaircraft fire over the Ruhr Valley in Germany's industrial heartland. Barker managed to bail out, but moments after his parachute opened an enemy fighter nosed toward him in what Barker felt were to be the last seconds of his life. Instead of shooting him, however, the German fighter pilot roared past the young bombardier and saluted. Barker returned the salute.

Picked up by the Germans, Barker was sent to a prisoner of war camp, where he spent the remainder of the war. Discharged with the rank of captain, he returned to Cuba and joined the National Police as an assistant to the chief. Soon, Barker was recruited by and joined the FEDERAL BUREAU OF INVESTIGATION (FBI). He then left the bureau to join the newly established CIA.

In 1959, a guerrilla army under Marxist leader FIDEL ALEJANDRO CASTRO RUZ toppled the pro-American Cuban regime of President Fulgencio Batista y Zaldívar. Barker, who was in Cuba with his family, was soon ordered to Miami, Florida, where he began working with the influx of Cuban exiles.

At some point in 1960, Barker was introduced to his new boss, Eduardo Hamilton, the code name for EVERETTE HOWARD HUNT, the CIA's infamous DIRTY TRICKS expert. Barker was then directed to help organize and recruit men for a CIA-trained and equipped paramilitary force composed of Cuban exiles. The force would ultimately become known as the 2506 BRIGADE, the ill-fated brigade destined to invade Cuba at the BAY OF PIGS.

The Bay of Pigs invasion was arguably the worst operational disaster in the CIA's history. In April 1961, over 1,500 exiled Cuban freedom fighters hit the beaches along Cuba's southwestern coastline in an attempt to rally Cubans on the island, defeat the Cuban army, and overthrow Castro. Instead the invasion was crushed by Castro in three days. Though it was both a strategic and moral victory for the Cuban president, the outcome of the invasion had less to do with Castro's combat talents than with the Agency's inability to assess properly the willingness of the Cuban people to rise up against Castro and U.S. president John Kennedy's refusal to provide previously promised air and naval gunfire support for the émigrés on the ground.

Back in Miami, Barker felt betrayed by the U.S. government but remained loyal to the CIA. He worked for the CIA in Miami for the next 10 years. There he was purportedly connected in some manner to projects against the Castro regime.

In 1971, on the anniversary of the Bay of Pigs Invasion, Barker was contacted by Hunt. "I came home and found a message in the door of the house," said Barker in an interview years later. "The message was from E. Howard Hunt and said, 'If you are the same Barker I once knew, meet me at . . . ,' signed Eduardo.

"We met and talked about the old times and remembered mutual friends. Hunt told me he was working in Washington now, at the White House, and needed my help for a big and important project.

"Without asking the nature of the project I told him he could count on me. I was very excited thinking that the fight against Castro was continuing. I had been waiting a long time for this moment, being reactivated to start the fight again in Cuba."

But the fight wasn't against Castro. It was against those opposed to the administration of President Richard Nixon. Hunt was establishing a special White House unit tasked with stopping leaks to the press from Washington, D.C., insiders, many of whom were suspected of undermining American policy in Vietnam. The unit was to become known as the PLUMBERS. Barker agreed to work with Hunt and was directed by the latter to recruit "plumbers" from among the CIA's former assets in Miami.

On the night of June 17, 1972, Barker and four other plumbers—Eugenio Martinez, Virgilio Gonzalez, Frank Sturgis, and JAMES WALTER MCCORD, JR.—broke into Washington's Watergate complex with the objective of obtaining information from the Democratic Party's national headquarters office there. The five men were discovered and arrested.

The burglary proved to be one of the greatest political malefactions in U.S. history. The scandal, which involved the highest levels of government in a number of illegal activities, forced Nixon to resign from the presidency in 1974 in order to avoid impeachment proceedings. It also resulted in the exposure of CIA activities to public scrutiny to a degree that the Agency had never before experienced.

Of his involvement in the Watergate scandal, Barker would later say, "The word burglar doesn't bother me any-more, now I wear it as a badge of honor. I don't regret what I did, I was aware of the risks involved, after all they are just part of the life of an intelligence agent."

Barnes, Charles Tracy (ca. 1912–1972)

Often compared to a character in an F. Scott Fitzgerald novel, Charles Tracy Barnes was regarded as a polished prince with a rough edge—traits that would serve him well as a World War II commando and later as a senior planning officer with the CIA.

Born (circa 1912) to Courtlandt Barnes, a wealthy financier, and Katherine, a society woman who taught young Barnes to play tennis and cards, he became something of a risk taker and rebellious child. His difficult behavior soon forced his parents to send him to Groton, an elite college preparatory school near Boston, where he became a star quarterback. After Groton, he attended Yale University, where he earned a bachelor's degree. He later graduated from the Harvard University School of Law.

When World War II erupted in Europe, Barnes was living in New York City practicing law at the Wall Street firm of Carter Ledyard. Barnes was a respected attorney who spent his leisure time reading, roller skating, and attending grand parties thrown by members of New York society. But he was bored with his life.

On December 8, 1941, the Monday morning after the Japanese attack on Pearl Harbor, Barnes skipped breakfast and rushed down to the local U.S. Army recruiting office. Well connected and with a graduate degree, he could have easily managed an officer's commission. Instead, he enlisted as a private, preferring to serve in the ranks.

Barnes's first station after basic training was the Army Air Corps intelligence school in Harrisburg, Pennsylvania. He was a bright student, but his independent spirit clashed with military discipline. In one instance in 1942, he flatly refused to obey the orders of a second lieutenant who commanded him to stand up straight in formation. Barnes, who at six feet one inch towered above the officer, looked down and said, "I won't."

Not long after, Barnes reluctantly accepted a commission and a position as an aide to the U.S. air attaché in London. In London, he witnessed at first hand the horrors of the Nazi air campaign against the British Isles, and he chafed at not being in the thick of the fight. He briefly pondered joining the British merchant marine. He also considered becoming a waist-gunner on an Army Air Corps bomber. Instead, his athletic ability and cognitive skills led to his recruitment by the OFFICE OF STRATEGIC SERVICES (OSS), the wartime precursor to the CIA.

With the OSS, Barnes trained to become a member of one of the famous JEDBURGHS, three-man commando teams tasked with slipping behind enemy lines, gathering intelligence, running sabotage missions, and coordinating the efforts of the local resistance forces. On August 5, 1944, he made the first of his many parachute jumps behind German lines in France.

Near the end of the war, Barnes operated out of the OSS station in Bern, Switzerland. There he worked closely, and developed a long-standing friendship, with ALLEN WELSH DULLES, the future DIRECTOR OF CENTRAL INTELLIGENCE (DCI). Dulles would later refer to Barnes as the "bravest man" he had ever known.

By war's end, Barnes had received a Silver Star and a French Croix de Guerre for actions with the OSS. He returned to the United States, moving to Providence, Rhode Island, where he practiced law and served as president of the state's Urban League.

When the Korean War broke out in 1950, Barnes relocated to Washington, D.C., where he briefly served as legal counsel to the Undersecretary of the Army. Not long after, he was recruited into the CIA.

With the Agency, Barnes initially served in the DIRECTORATE of Plans (Operations) as deputy director of the Psychological Strategy Board (PSB). In 1952, he was made head of the Agency's newly established Psychological and Paramilitary Warfare Staff. In 1954, he was made officer in charge of Operation PBSUCCESS, which led to the COUP D'ÉTAT IN GUATEMALA. For the next four years, he served as CIA CHIEF OF STATION (COS) in both Frankfurt, Germany (1954–56), and London (1957–59).

From 1960 to 1961, Barnes served as the assistant to Deputy Director of Plans (DDP) RICHARD MERVIN BISSELL. In this capacity, he was a key player in the planning and conduct of Operation ZAPATA, the ill-fated invasion of Cuba at the BAY OF PIGS in 1961. Bissell was fired after the Bay of Pigs and was made chief of the Agency's DOMESTIC OPERATIONS DIVISION (DOD). The DOD was responsible for setting up proprietary companies, FRONTS, and COVERS for the CIA's operations within the United States.

In 1968, Barnes retired from the CIA and returned to Yale, accepting a position in community relations. He left Yale in 1970.

Barnes died on February 19, 1972. He was 60.

Barnett, David H. (1933–1993)

David H. Barnett was the first CIA field officer (active or former) to be convicted of espionage activities against the United States.

From the 1960s until 1970, Barnett was employed by the CIA, working in both the United States and Asia (he was stationed in Indonesia from 1967 until 1970). He then entered private business. But within six years, he had amassed debts of over $100,000 and faced imminent financial ruin.

To rectify his problems, Barnett chose to sell classified information to the Russians. In 1976, he approached Indonesia-based Soviet intelligence officers and offered to sell them the names of CIA assets.

Over the next three years, Barnett revealed to the KGB the identities of some 30 American officers or foreign agents working for the CIA. Additionally, he handed over a great deal of classified information gathered by the CIA on Soviet SA-2 surface-to-air missiles and the Soviet Whiskey diesel-powered submarines. The Soviets paid him a total of $92,000 for information received between 1976 and 1977.

In April 1980, American intelligence operatives spotted Barnett meeting with KGB officers in Vienna, Austria. When he returned to the United States that same year, he was immediately arrested by the FEDERAL BUREAU OF INVESTIGATION (FBI).

On October 24, Barnett was indicted on charges of espionage. He subsequently pled guilty and was sentenced to 18 years in prison. He died on November 19, 1993.

Baynes, Virginia Jean (unknown)

Virginia Jean Baynes was a CIA office secretary convicted of espionage in 1992.

Having been employed by the Agency since 1987, Baynes began her illegal activities in 1990 after meeting JOSEPH GARFIELD BROWN, an American civilian who worked as a martial-arts instructor in Manila, the Philippines. Baynes had been assigned to the U.S. embassy in Manila, where she held a top-secret clearance. While off duty, she attended karate classes taught by Brown at the embassy annex.

According to Baynes's testimony, she developed a "friendship" with Brown, who in the summer of 1990 asked her to smuggle CIA documents from her office and deliver them to him. The requested documents contained secret information pertaining to assassinations planned by a local terrorist group that were to be carried out in the Philippines. She complied.

In April 1991, the FEDERAL BUREAU OF INVESTIGATION (FBI) launched an investigation after an internal CIA probe determined that Baynes had passed two or three documents to Brown. As part of the investigation, the FBI conducted a "sting" operation whereby Brown unwittingly provided an undercover FBI agent illegally obtained CIA documents on Iraqi terrorist activities during the PERSIAN GULF WAR. Brown also provided the agent with information pertaining to the assassination plans of a Philippine insurgent group.

Baynes was soon arrested, and on May 22, 1992, she pled guilty to espionage. She was subsequently sentenced to a 41-month term of imprisonment. Brown was also arrested and convicted. He was sentenced to five years, to be followed by three years' probation.

Bay of Pigs (Bahía de los Cochinos) invasion

On April 19, 1961, on the southwestern shoreline of a Cuban inlet known as the Bay of Pigs, JOSE PEREZ "PEPE" SAN ROMAIN, the commander of a CIA-trained force of Cuban expatriates, made his last frantic radio transmission to the Americans he was counting on for combat support during the U.S.-sponsored invasion of Cuba. "I have nothing left to fight with," he shouted as communist tanks moved against his position. "Am taking to the woods. I can't wait for you." The Americans never came. The invasion was crushed.

Launched on April 17, 1961, the Bay of Pigs invasion—code-named OPERATION ZAPATA—may well be the worst operational disaster in CIA history. It was hoped that the invasion, financed and directed by the CIA, would result in a popular uprising against the communists and the ultimate overthrow of FIDEL CASTRO. But it was not to be.

Initiated from a CIA staging area at Puerto Cabezas (a seaport on Nicaragua's Caribbean coast), the preliminary phase of the operation began with a number of ineffective air raids by "Free Cuba" pilots flying eight vintage B-26 bombers against communist air bases on April 15. Castro's air force consisted of six B-26s, four T-33 trainers redesigned as fighters, and a handful of British Sea Fury fighters.

The Free Cuba pilots had been recruited by the CIA and trained by members of the ALABAMA AIR NATIONAL GUARD, who had also been recruited by the Agency. Alabama guardsmen actually flew some of the sorties themselves, but without authorization. Four of them were shot down and killed.

Two days after the first bombing run against Castro's airfields, San Romain and his 1,543 Cuban freedom fighters, known as BRIGADE 2506, or the "Brigada Asalto," began hitting the beaches. The men disembarked from a number of transport vessels, landing craft, and small aluminum and fiberglass boats at several points along the Cuban coastline. The principal landing site was the Bay of Pigs. (The majority of the Bay of Pigs invasion force landed at Playa Girón, a short stretch along the bay's shoreline. Consequently, Cuba refers to the invasion as the Battle of Girón.) The primary transports included five 2,400-ton chartered vessels—the *Houston*, the *Rio Escondido*, the *Caribe*, the *Atlantico*, and the *Lake Charles*—as well as two CIA-owned infantry landing craft, the *Blagar* and the *Barbara J.* Additionally, 177 Free Cuba paratroopers landed north of the beachhead.

It was an ambitious venture, and it depended on the element of surprise to defeat Castro's numerically superior force of 32,000. But the invasion was doomed from the start, at both the strategic and tactical levels. The strategic problems included a miscalculation of the Cuban people's willingness to rise up against Castro once hostilities commenced. The CIA's DIRECTORATE of Plans (Operations) was so concerned with operational secrecy that it failed to consult the Directorate of Intelligence for such an assessment. CIA officials also believed incorrectly that the operation could be conducted without the communists' knowledge of U.S. support. At the tactical level, early beach reconnaissance data was misinterpreted by the planners. In the event, the invading force was overwhelmed, its only escape options to cross 80 miles of impenetrable swampland toward the mountains or to retreat into the sea. Instead of destroying Castro's air force, bombing raids served only to alert Castro's commanders of an imminent amphibious or airborne assault. Castro's planes soon began freely strafing the disembarked invading force as well as the transports and boats, sinking a number of the latter. Making matters worse, shallow water covered coral reefs along the Bay of Pigs, forcing substantial numbers of the landing troops to disembark at great distances from the beach.

Hours into the invasion, the *Rio Escondido* was hit. She sank when the aviation fuel she was carrying ignited in a tremendous ball of fire. The *Houston* was also hit and forced to run aground to avoid sinking.

Even when the invaders became pinned down on the beaches, President John Kennedy refused to grant authorization for American air and naval gunfire support, and U.S. warships in the vicinity of the battle were ordered to withdraw. On-station U.S. pilots protested against their inability to engage Cuban targets. They knew that the order "not to engage" was a virtual death sentence for the men on the beach. But Kennedy believed that if the United States became directly involved in the shooting, the Soviets might move on Western Europe, thus launching a third world war.

As a result, 114 members of the invading force were killed, nearly 1,200 were taken prisoner, and America's credibility on the world stage was severely tarnished. Despite their victory, Castro's forces reportedly suffered even greater losses—some 1,650 killed and 2,000 wounded.

Ted Gup, author of *The Book of Honor: Covert Lives and Classified Deaths at the CIA,* described the failure at the Bay of Pigs during an interview for C-Span's *Booknotes* on August 27, 2000. "The plan was continually cut back and curtailed to preserve presidential deniability and prevent the U.S. from being linked," Gup said. "This was absurd. Even as the operation was ongoing, the U.S. hand was all over it. But we condemned ourselves to failure."

Almost immediately after the mission was aborted, the Kennedy administration began bargaining with Castro for the release of those captured during the attack. After months of negotiations, Castro agreed to the release in exchange for $53 million worth of food and medicine.

In October 1962, the world was again brought to the brink of war during the CUBAN MISSILE CRISIS. Two

The Bay of Pigs, 1961

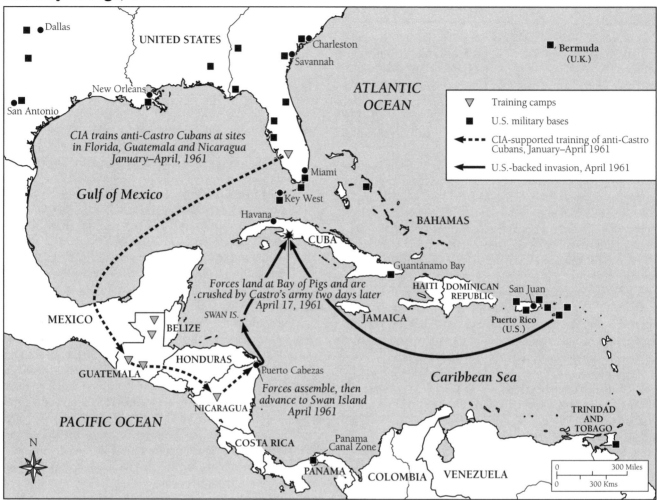

Dallas

UNITED STATES

Charleston
Savannah

Bermuda
(U.K.)

New Orleans

San Antonio

*CIA trains anti-Castro Cubans at sites
in Florida, Guatemala and Nicaragua
January–April, 1961*

ATLANTIC
OCEAN

▽ Training camps

■ U.S. military bases

◀--- CIA-supported training of anti-Castro
Cubans, January–April 1961

◀— U.S.-backed invasion, April 1961

Gulf of Mexico

Miami

Key West

Havana

CUBA

BAHAMAS

Guantánamo Bay

*Forces land at Bay of Pigs and are
.crushed by Castro's army two days later
April 17, 1961*

SWAN IS.

MEXICO

BELIZE

HAITI DOMINICAN
REPUBLIC

San Juan

Puerto Rico
(U.S.)

JAMAICA

HONDURAS

Puerto Cabezas

GUATEMALA

Caribbean Sea

*Forces assemble, then
advance to Swan Island
April 1961*

NICARAGUA

PACIFIC OCEAN

TRINIDAD
AND
TOBAGO

N

COSTA RICA

Panama
Canal Zone

PANAMA COLOMBIA VENEZUELA

0   300 Miles

0   300 Kms

months later, Castro began releasing the surviving Bay of Pigs prisoners to the United States.

Conceived in May 1960 during the presidency of Dwight Eisenhower, the invasion of Cuba had been first proposed to President Kennedy within weeks of his assuming office, by DIRECTOR OF CENTRAL INTELLIGENCE (DCI) ALLEN WELSH DULLES. Kennedy was initially cool to the idea. But as proof that such an invasion was doable, Dulles pointed to the Agency's successful 1954 COUP D'ÉTAT IN GUATEMALA, which had resulted in the installation of a pro-American regime.

Castro, a Soviet-supported communist revolutionary, had been a thorn in America's side since overthrowing Cuban dictator Fulgencio Batista in 1958. Eisenhower had severed diplomatic ties with Cuba before leaving office in January 1961. The CIA had since held that a brigade of Cuban exiles trained by the U.S. military under Agency supervision and backed by American air and naval power would rid the Western Hemisphere of a developing Soviet base of operations.

Some of the initial training for Operation ZAPATA took place in Florida, Mississippi, Louisiana, and Panama. But the majority of the training took place in Guatemala, in mountains near the town of Retalhulea and at a CIA base known as Camp Trax.

As the Cuban émigrés began honing their skills for the operation, Radio Swan—a powerful radio station located on one of the Swan Islands off Honduras—began broadcasting anti-Castro messages. The Radio Swan project was supervised by DAVID ATLEE PHILLIPS, an experienced Agency operative who—despite the failure of ZAPATA—was destined to become the head of the CIA's Western Hemisphere Division.

Three days after the collapse of the operation, Kennedy established the TAYLOR COMMISSION, an executive-level body that was to ascertain the reasons for the failure of ZAPATA. Chaired by former Army chief of staff General Maxwell Taylor, the commission compiled a 53-page classified report, which was submitted to Kennedy on June 13, 1961. Declassified in 1977, the report criticized the operation's conception, development, and implementation. Blame was also leveled at the U.S. DEPARTMENT OF STATE, the JOINT CHIEFS OF STAFF (JCS), the Kennedy administration, and the CIA.

Concurrent with the Taylor Commission, the CIA established its own Bay of Pigs investigative entity, headed by the CIA INSPECTOR GENERAL (IG), LYMAN B. KIRKPATRICK, JR., under the direction of Dulles. After a five-month examination, the 170-page Kirkpatrick Report was issued to selected intelligence executives. Though it remains classified, insiders believe that much of the report was unjustly critical of Dulles and the Agency.

Three senior CIA officials were dismissed as a result of the Bay of Pigs. In November, Kennedy replaced Dulles with JOHN ALEX MCCONE. Within the next few months, GENERAL CHARLES P. CABELL, the DEPUTY DIRECTOR OF CENTRAL INTELLIGENCE (DDCI), and RICHARD MERVIN BISSELL, the deputy director of plans (operations), were also fired.

Years later, General David Shoup, who as Marine Corps commandant had advised the CIA during the planning stages, would say, "I don't think any military man would ever think that this force could overthrow Castro without support. They could never expect anything but annihilation."

See also LYNCH, GRAYSTON; ROBERTSON, WILLIAM.

Beerli, Colonel Stanley W. (unknown)

Air Force colonel Stanley W. Beerli was the organizer/commander of air operations during OPERATION ZAPATA—the 1961 invasion of Cuba at the BAY OF PIGS. Having previously overseen the U-2 spy plane program for the CIA's Deputy Director of Plans (Operations) RICHARD MERVIN BISSELL, JR., Beerli was brought on board in the planning phase of ZAPATA to organize the air-support arm of the invasion force.

Beerli chose the World War II–era B-26 bomber. His reasoning was that countless B-26s had been sold as surplus to countries around the world; FIDEL CASTRO's air force maintained six of them. Beerli believed that if the "Free Cuba" pilots flew B-26s during the invasion, it could be argued if necessary that they were defectors flying former Cuban air force aircraft.

The operation began on April 15, with a number of ineffective strikes by eight of Beerli's vintage bombers against communist air bases. Unfortunately for Beerli and the other commanders, the strikes were soon canceled, and the mission ultimately failed.

Berg, Morris (Moe) (1902–1972)

Part professional baseball player, part spy, Morris "Moe" Berg was one of the most colorful covert operatives to parachute behind enemy lines for the OFFICE OF STRATEGIC SERVICES (OSS), the World War II precursor to the CIA. He has the distinction of being the only major league ballplayer whose baseball card is on display at the CIA's headquarters in LANGLEY, VIRGINIA.

Born in New York City on March 2, 1902, to Russian Jewish immigrants, young Berg seemed an unlikely future spy. In 1906, the family moved across the Hudson River to Newark, New Jersey, where Berg developed a passion for baseball. The first organized play for the young Jewish boy was on a Methodist church team, where he assumed the pseudonym "Runt Wolfe." He lettered in baseball at Newark's Barringer High School. At Princeton University, where he majored in foreign languages, he played shortstop on the varsity team.

In 1923, Berg graduated from Princeton with honors and embarked on a 16-year professional baseball career—first with the Brooklyn Dodgers, later with the New York Robins, the Chicago White Sox, the Cleveland Indians, the Washington Senators, and the Boston Red Sox. Professionally, he was a marginal player, spending most of his game days "schmoozing and reading in dugouts and bullpens." His father saw the game as a waste of time. Between seasons, he studied at Columbia Law School and the Sorbonne, in Paris.

In 1928, Berg was admitted to the New York State bar and entered private practice in the law firm of Satterlee and Canfield. But that didn't stop his baseball career, nor did it slow his progress toward becoming a spy.

Interestingly, his first espionage project, in 1934, took place while traveling with the American all-star baseball team. During a tour of Japan, Berg, who spoke Japanese, took home movies of the Japanese skyline. When no one was looking, he lowered his camera to film Tokyo Harbor, anchored Japanese warships, and various military installations along the Japanese coastline. His films proved invaluable to the U.S. government. When General James H. Doolittle began preparing for his famous raid on Tokyo, he closely studied Berg's films, basing much of his planning on them.

Berg spent the remaining two years of his baseball career as a coach for the Red Sox. He abandoned baseball altogether on January 14, 1942, the date of his father's death.

Recognizing the value of Berg's language skills, Nelson Rockefeller, the coordinator of the U.S. Office of Inter-American Affairs, offered him a position. After a brief fact-finding tour of South and Central America, Berg left Inter-American Affairs to accept a job with the OSS, becoming a field officer in 1943. That same year, he parachuted into Yugoslavia, reporting back to OSS officials arguments for Allied support for Josip Broz Tito and his partisans, who were fighting the Nazis in the Balkans.

Berg later flew secretly into German-occupied Norway, met with Free Norwegian guerrillas, and gathered vital information about a German heavy-water plant that had been constructed for Nazi atomic-power experiments. His information led to the Allied bombing, and total destruction, of the plant.

Berg's most fascinating mission was carried out in December 1944. He was dispatched under COVER to neutral Zurich, Switzerland, to attend a lecture of Werner Heisenberg, one of Germany's leading scientists, who was working on the atomic bomb project. He had orders to assassinate Heisenberg if the scientist presented any evidence that Germany was close to developing the bomb. Fortunately for Heisenberg, Berg didn't know enough physics or German to be sure whether or not he should kill him. So he did not.

After the war, while traveling with several other officers through Soviet-occupied Czechoslovakia, Berg was confronted by Soviet soldiers who demanded to see his credentials. Americans were not authorized to be in the area. Berg immediately produced a letter with a red star emblazoned on it; the Soviets let him pass. He had shown them a copy of the Texaco Oil Company letterhead.

In 1946, Berg was offered the American Medal of Merit, the highest award presented to an American civilian for service during time of war. But for reasons that have never been determined, he refused to accept the award.

Berg served briefly as a scientific adviser for the North Atlantic Treaty Organization (NATO), and it is widely held that he accepted classified assignments for the American intelligence community during the 1950s and 1960s, though, no proof of that has ever been established.

A lifelong bachelor, Berg spent the last 25 years of his life jumping from one job to the next. He lived for 17 years with his brother, Sam, and eight with his sister, Ethel.

Berg died of an abdominal aneurysm on May 29, 1972, in Belleville, New Jersey. His body was cremated, and his sister took his ashes to Israel for burial. The actual site of his burial remains a mystery.

Berlin blockade and airlift

The Berlin blockade and subsequent airlift was the first serious confrontation between the Western allies and the Soviet Union during the COLD WAR.

In 1948, the Soviet Union attempted to limit the ability of U.S., British, and French occupation forces to travel to their respective sectors in the German capital of Berlin, which was within Soviet-occupied East Germany. The Soviets blockaded the city by land, thus forcing the Western powers to enter by air.

Seeds for the crisis had been planted during the famous Crimea Conference (Yalta) in February 1945. With World War II nearing its conclusion, the Allied leaders—specifically, American president Franklin Roosevelt, British prime minister Winston Churchill, and Soviet pre-

mier Joseph Stalin—began making preparations for the future of Germany. Among the arrangements made between the "Big Three" was that Berlin would be divided into occupational zones. However, there was no stipulation concerning access to those zones. Making matters worse, the long-strained relationship between the Soviet Union and the West began deteriorating rapidly after the war.

In July 1945, the Potsdam Conference, between new American president Harry Truman, Churchill, and Stalin, was held. During the conference, it was decided that Germany would be administered as a single economic entity under an Allied Control Council. The council would be headed by U.S. Army general Lucius Clay, West Germany's new military governor and the commander of American occupation forces in that country.

In March 1946, less than a year after the close of hostilities, Churchill traveled to Fulton, Missouri, where he made his famous "IRON CURTAIN" speech. In it he asserted that a dangerous communist line had been drawn across the middle of Europe: "From Stettin in the Baltic to Trieste in the Adriatic, an iron curtain has descended across the [European] Continent." The prime minister's statements were considered provocative by the Soviets, and many historians have since argued that his speech officially launched the cold war. That same year, Stalin issued his own terse warning, proclaiming that World War II had been unavoidable, an inevitable consequence of "capitalist imperialism"—implying that such a war might recur.

Beyond the rhetoric, a developing trend among U.S. foreign policy makers to contain communist expansion throughout the world was perceived by the Soviets as overtly hostile. The Soviets also became unnerved by the rebuilding of Germany under the Marshall Plan, as well as by a growing desire on the part of the Western powers to establishing a separate capital in West Germany.

In late 1947, discussions between the Soviets and the West completely broke down over charges that the Western powers were violating a number of the Potsdam agreements. The following year, a Soviet-sponsored coup d'état in Czechoslovakia brought that country under communist domination. Almost immediately, Clay cabled the following message to the Army intelligence chief, Lt. Gen. Stephen J. Chamberlin: "For many months, based on logical analysis, I have felt and held that war was unlikely for at least ten years. Within the last few weeks, I have felt a subtle change in Soviet attitude which I cannot define but which now gives me a feeling that it may come with dramatic suddenness. I cannot support this change in my own thinking with any data or outward evidence in relationships other than to describe it as a feeling of a new tenseness in every Soviet individual with whom we have official relations. I am

Transport airplanes taking part in the Berlin airlift (NATIONAL ARCHIVES)

unable to submit any official report in the absence of supporting data but my feeling is real. You may advise the Chief of Staff of this for whatever it may be worth if you feel it advisable." The CIA was immediately directed to analyze the developing situation in Europe and report to the president.

On March 16, the Agency delivered to President Truman a NATIONAL INTELLIGENCE ESTIMATE (NIE) stating that war with the Soviets "was not probable within the next sixty days." By the end of the month, the CIA's estimate was even less reassuring. While Clay's cable and the CIA estimate were under consideration, the occupying forces of the United States, Great Britain, and France began to consolidate their respective zones in West Germany. This was the first step toward the reestablishment of a single, independent German state. As part of that process, and to promote economic recovery, the Western powers also attempted to reform the existing monetary system with a new West German currency. The proposed

currency, over which the Soviets would have no control, would be legal tender in the western sectors of Berlin. The city of Berlin, divided between East and West, was located approximately 100 miles inside East Germany. Berlin was essentially an island, surrounded by Russian soldiers.

The idea of a unified Germany alarmed the Soviets. Unification meant strength. After all, the USSR had been invaded by the Germans, twice.

On March 20, the Soviets withdrew from the Allied Control Council. On March 31, they declared that Western military passenger trains bound for Berlin would not be allowed to enter the city unless all passengers submitted to physical searches.

The Soviets also established their own new currency in East Berlin, as a response to the West's monetary reforms; the Soviet currency was released just 24 hours before the new West German mark was to begin circulation. Less than three months later, on June 24, the Soviets closed the doors on West Berlin, cutting off all highway and rail routes into the western zones.

The blockade effectively placed West Berlin's 2.5 million civilians at the mercy of the Soviets, unless the Western powers could circumvent the blockade. Reeling from the aftermath of a world war, the Berliners were totally dependent on reserve stores of food and medicine and airlifted supplies. Clay later wrote, "It was one of the most ruthless efforts in modern times to use mass starvation for political coercion."

Several options to counter the blockade were considered. One of the more provocative ideas was proposed by FRANK GARDINER WISNER, a former operative with the OFFICE OF STRATEGIC SERVICES (the wartime precursor to the CIA), who had become chief of the CIA's OFFICE OF POLICY COORDINATION (OPC).

Wisner, along with several top-ranking U.S. Army officers, believed that Berlin could be taken by force. After all, the Soviets had yet to develop the atomic bomb. The idea was to send in a self-contained task force, complete with engineers, artillery, armor, and a small force of infantry. The force would jump off from one of the Western-occupied zones and fight its way toward the capital city.

The proposal was shelved in favor of something less confrontational—the Berlin airlift. Under the command of the U.S. Air Force's brash, cigar-chewing General Curtis LeMay, C-54 transport planes began supplying Berlin on July 1. Code-named Operation VITTLES (unofficially, "LeMay's Feed and Coal Company"), Western pilots flew nearly 300,000 transport sorties into West Berlin, delivering an average of 5,000 tons of life necessities every day, for the next 321 days. The effort, which gained wide public support around the world, was an enormous success.

On May 12, 1949, the Soviets conceded and reopened the land routes. That same month, East and West Germany were established as separate republics.

Berlin Tunnel

Code-named OPERATION GOLD, the Berlin Tunnel (1953–56) was a CIA-MI6 underground communications-monitoring facility extending from just inside West Berlin to a point deep in the communist eastern sector. Constructed by CIA employees, the tunnel stretched across the East-West border to a point directly below Soviet and East German telephone cables. The cables, also underground, were then tapped by MI6 (British Secret Service) personnel.

The tunnel's entrance (in the western sector) was concealed by an above-ground U.S. radar station. A narrow equipment-moving rail line ran the length of the tunnel. Amplifying equipment used to monitor the phone transmissions was located in a steel-reinforced exclusion area, or communications chamber, at the eastern end.

Construction began on the 1,476-foot subterranean station in 1953. The project was completed, and the tunnel became operational, in 1955. For nearly a year, MI6 personnel inside the tunnel were able to monitor communications between Soviet military headquarters in East Berlin and Moscow.

Considered one of the West's most ambitious intelligence operations of the COLD WAR, the tunnel enabled the British and the Americans to gather intelligence pertaining to Soviet army units, and it would conceivably have provided warning if the Soviets had planned an invasion of the West.

The tunnel was compromised and immediately vacated when it was discovered by East German telephone repairmen in 1956. It was later discovered that George Blake, a DOUBLE AGENT working for both MI6 and the KOMITET GOSUDARSTVENNOY BEZOPASNOSTI, or KGB (the Soviet state security and intelligence service), had revealed the operation to his Soviet employers. Interestingly, the KGB—unaware that the CIA had the capability to decipher the coded messages intercepted by MI6—did not inform the GLAVNOYE RAZVEDYVATELNOYE UPRAVLENIYE, or GRU (the Soviet military intelligence service). In April 1956, the Soviets invited journalists to inspect the facility.

The Berlin Tunnel was the brainchild of WILLIAM KING HARVEY, the CIA's Berlin CHIEF OF STATION (COS).

Berlin Wall Monument

Located along a path leading from the south parking lot to the southwest entrance of the original CIA headquarters building at the George Bush Center for Intelligence is the CIA's Berlin Wall Monument.

The monument incorporates three concrete panels from the original Berlin Wall, with interpretive plaques that describe the historical significance of the monument, and antitank obstacles that had been positioned near the original wall. The markings on the wall include cartoon-like graffiti and spray-painted statements: "And the wind cries," "MNP," "Endlich Frei," "Tear down the wall," "Democracy," and "Freedom."

In the summer of 1961, the Berlin Wall was erected by the Soviet-backed East Germans to prevent East Germans from immigrating to the West. The wall split the city of Berlin into two parts—communist East Berlin and noncommunist West Berlin. The city itself was located deep in the heart of communist East Germany, but West Germany and her allies controlled West Berlin. The Berlin Wall was brought down in November 1989, foreshadowing the collapse of the Soviet Union two years later.

The CIA's Berlin Wall Monument was dedicated on December 18, 1992. A smaller portion of the wall is on display in the CIA EXHIBIT CENTER.

BfV

See BUNDESAMT FÜR VERFASSUNGSSCHUTZ.

bin Laden, Osama (1957–)

America's most wanted man and the CIA's greatest nemesis at the turn of the 21st century, Osama bin Laden (aka Osama bin Muhammad bin Laden, Shaykh Osama bin Laden, the prince, the emir, Abu Abdallah, Mujahid Shaykh, Hajj, the director) was the chief perpetrator of the SEPTEMBER 11, 2001, TERRORIST ATTACKS ON THE UNITED STATES.

Bin Laden was born in 1957 in Saudi Arabia to billionaire Yemeni construction magnate Mohammed bin Oud bin Laden and one of his four wives, a Syrian woman named Al-Khalifa bin Laden. Young bin Laden was raised, one of 52 children, among the conflicting trappings of Western capitalism, Saudi nationalism, and Islamic piety. When his father died (circa 1970), bin Laden inherited approximately $300 million. When he was 17 years old, bin Laden married a related Syrian woman. He traveled widely and earned a degree in public administration from King Abdul-Aziz University in Jeddah, Saudi Arabia.

Bin Laden left Saudi Arabia several times beginning in 1979 to participate in the fighting against the Soviets, who had invaded Afghanistan. In Afghanistan, he used his own wealth to raise money for the Mujahideen forces fighting the Soviets. He eventually became affiliated with Egyptian Islamic extremist groups, such as Egyptian Islamic *Jihad* (Arabic for "holy war" or "struggle").

In 1986, bin Laden began constructing a series of camps inside Afghanistan and organizing and funding independent rebel forces, leading them in attacks against the Soviet army. The Afghan rebels fighting the Soviets were also financially supported by the United States, which was itself engaged in a proxy war with the communist invaders. It was during that period that bin Laden allegedly received security and special-operations training from the CIA (an allegation that both the Agency and bin Laden's supporters have denied).

While in Afghanistan, bin Laden founded the Maktab al Khidimat (MAK)—an organization that recruited "freedom fighters" from around the world and imported weapons and equipment for the Afghan resistance. He also founded and became the principal source of direction and funding for al-Qaeda (Arabic for "the base")—a worldwide network of terrorist cells whose primary tactic was suicide bombings of civilian and military targets.

After the Soviet pullout in 1989, bin Laden's faction turned its focus to opposing the United States and its allies in the Middle East. Like many Arabs, bin Laden hated Israel and wanted nothing less than the collapse of that nation. He also hated Israel's allies, chief among them the United States. Also, he believed that Western culture in general was corrupting Islamic society.

As the Soviet Union collapsed from within, bin Laden returned to Saudi Arabia to work in one of his family's construction enterprises. His anti-Americanism, however, intensified during the buildup phase of the PERSIAN GULF WAR in 1990, when American military forces were stationed in Saudi Arabia. He believed that the presence of U.S. troops was nothing less than a desecration, as Saudi Arabia was the birthplace of the prophet Mohammed and the home of two of Islam's holiest shrines.

In 1994, bin Laden was stripped of his Saudi citizenship and expelled from the country because of his vocal opposition to the Saudi government. He then moved to Khartoum, Sudan, where his family had business operations. Two years later, U.S. pressure led the Sudanese government to expel him from that country. He returned to Afghanistan, where he began to ply his grisly trade in earnest.

According to American intelligence sources, bin Laden was involved in numerous attacks on Western targets prior to the attacks of September 11—the 1992 bombing of a Yemeni hotel where American servicemen were lodging, killing two Australians; the 1993 World Trade Center bombing, which killed six people and wounded more than 1,000; a 1995 car-bomb detonation in Riyadh, Saudi Arabia; a 1993 attack on American troops in Somalia in which 18 American soldiers were killed; a 1995 truck-bomb detonation in Dhahran, Saudi Arabia, in which 19 American soldiers were killed; the 1995 assassination attempt on Egyptian president Hosni Mubarak; the 1998 embassy bombings in Kenya and Tanzania, which killed 224 people and wounded nearly 5,000; and the 2000 attack on the guided-missile destroyer USS *Cole* in Aden, the port of Yemen, killing 17 American sailors and wounding 40 others.

But the U.S. government was not sitting on its hands. In 1998, American air and naval forces launched a cruise-missile attack against bin Laden's training camps in Afghanistan. It was believed that the Saudi-born terrorist leader would be in one of the camps and thus would be killed. Western intelligence miscalculated, and he survived.

The following year, the CIA—now under the leadership of DIRECTOR OF CENTRAL INTELLIGENCE (DCI) GEORGE JOHN TENET—allegedly trained and equipped approximately 60 Pakistani commandos who were to enter Afghanistan and either capture or kill bin Laden. The operation had been arranged by then-Pakistani prime minister Nawaz Sharif and his chief of intelligence. In turn, the administration of President Bill Clinton promised to lift sanctions against Pakistan and provide that country with economic assistance. Unfortunately, Sharif was removed from power in a military coup d'état, and the operation was aborted.

On February 7, 2001, Tenet expressed grave concern over bin Laden's increasing capabilities. "Osama bin Laden and his global network of lieutenants and associates remain the most immediate and serious threat," Tenet stated before the Senate Select Committee on Intelligence (SSCI). "Since 1998, bin Laden has declared all US citizens legitimate targets of attack. As shown by the bombing of our Embassies in Africa in 1998 and his Millennium plots last year, he is capable of planning multiple attacks with little or no warning. His organization is continuing to place emphasis on developing surrogates to carry out attacks in an effort to avoid detection, blame, and retaliation. As a result it is often difficult to attribute terrorist incidents to his group, Al Qaeda."

In August, the CIA received information from a number of sources suggesting that bin Laden was "increasingly determined" to strike on American soil. Unfortunately, that intelligence was not specific enough to prevent the attacks of September 11. Additionally, it was determined by early 2002 that both the CIA and the FEDERAL BUREAU OF INVESTIGATION (FBI—the Agency's domestic counterpart) had failed to share related information that might have produced more precise FINISHED INTELLIGENCE. The CIA, the FBI, and the NATIONAL SECURITY AGENCY (NSA—the U.S. INTELLIGENCE COMMUNITY member primarily responsible for electronic intelligence) were also blamed for failing to develop a single, cooperative counterterrorism plan and a single definition of terrorism. By the time of the attacks, George W. Bush had become president and bin Laden and his chief lieutenants were still in Afghanistan, protected by that country's ruling Taliban (Arabic for "the students") Party—a hard-line Islamic militia sect sympathetic to al-Qaeda. The Taliban was also engaged in a civil war with the Northern Alliance, a marginally equipped group of Afghan freedom fighters opposed to the Taliban's iron-fisted rule.

In the aftermath of September 11, American and British warships steamed toward South Asia, and special-forces commandos reportedly began preliminary scouting in and around Afghanistan. Bin Laden denied any involvement in the attacks, but he issued the following statement: "We hope that these brothers [the suicide hijackers] will be the first martyrs in the battle of Islam in this era against the new Jewish and Christian crusader campaign that is led by the Chief Crusader Bush under the banner of the cross."

On October 7, the United States and the United Kingdom launched a massive retaliatory air and naval assault against the forces of the Taliban and al-Qaeda. The CIA, which was on the ground in the region almost immediately after the attacks of September 11, began coordinating the efforts of the Northern Alliance with the military forces of America and her allies.

Hours after the attack began, bin Laden—still denying involvement in the September 11 attacks—stated, "There is America, hit by God in one of its softest spots. Its greatest buildings were destroyed, thank God for that. There is America, full of fear from its north to its south, from its west to its east. Thank God for that."

Meanwhile, a small number of cases of deadly anthrax contamination began to appear in a variety of locations within the United States, particularly along the eastern seaboard. By year's end, some 18 cases would be confirmed—11 would be of the dangerous inhalation form of anthrax, seven would be the less serious skin form. Five people would ultimately die. On October 25, a trace amount of anthrax was found in the mail room at CIA headquarters in LANGLEY, VIRGINIA. The mail room was closed, and some CIA employees were treated with antibiotics. Some members of the U.S. INTELLIGENCE COMMUNITY suggested that the anthrax attack might well have been the work of a domestic terrorist. Others believed it might have been the work of bin Laden and al-Qaeda, though there was no substantive evidence to suggest that.

The day following the discovery of anthrax in the Langley mail room, Bush signed into law the Anti-Terrorism Act (also known as the USA Patriot Act of 2001, or

Osama bin Laden   (GETTY IMAGES)

Public Law 107-56). The act is a sweeping set of guide-lines granting unfettered power to all agencies involved in combating terrorism.

As of March 2003, Osama bin Laden was still at large.

biographic leverage

"Biographic leverage" is a CIA euphemism for blackmail. It is essentially the leverage acquired from some piece of negative information about the past or personal life of an individual that gives Agency operatives the upper hand when persuading that person to do something he or she may not be inclined to do.

For example, a CIA field officer might be able to use biographic leverage as a means of coercing foreign nationals to disclose information about their governments that they are reluctant to disclose. If a field officer, for instance, knows that a foreign national has been having an adulterous affair without the knowledge of the latter's spouse, that information may provide biographic lever-age.

Birch, John (1918–1945)

Missionary, Army officer, and OFFICE OF STRATEGIC SER-VICES (OSS) operative, John Birch is best known as the eponym of the John Birch Society, an ultra-right-wing advocacy organization.

Birch was born the son of American Baptist missionar-ies in Landour, India, on May 28, 1918, and seemed des-tined to a life of foreign evangelical work. That life would be cut short at age 26.

In 1920, the Birch family returned to the United States and settled in Macon, Georgia, a quiet, mid-sized south-ern town that had been home to generations of Birches. John Birch, the oldest of seven children, expressed a desire to become a missionary when he was only 11 years old. He chose China as his mission field; his parents had served there. But his pastor cautioned him about the dan-ger to Western Christian missionaries preaching the gospel in China. "More will be killed," the pastor report-edly told him. But Birch was not dissuaded. "I know the big enemy is communism," he replied. "But the Lord has called me. My life is in his hands, and I am not turning back."

As a young man, Birch attended Mercer University, graduating magna cum laude. He also won a Rhodes scholarship. But instead of attending Oxford University, in England, he elected to attend a seminary in Fort Worth, Texas.

In 1939, Birch journeyed to China as a missionary, though much of that country was occupied by the Japan-ese, who had invaded three years prior. Birch found China war ravaged, plagued by famine, disease, and

Japanese bombs. He was initially frustrated at his inability to ease the suffering; while his fellow missionaries fed the hungry and tended to the sick and wounded, he attended Chinese language school. But in less than a year his stud-ies were complete.

Birch took to his work enthusiastically. He became a traveling preacher, covering thousands of miles on foot, bicycle, and sampan, often eluding Japanese patrols and venturing far behind Japanese lines. At times he was stricken with malaria, but he continued to work in some of the most remote areas of China.

When the U.S. STATE DEPARTMENT ordered all mission-aries out of China, Birch refused to leave. But after the Japanese attacked Pearl Harbor on December 7, 1941, Birch decided to join the war effort. Dying his hair black and dressing in the garb of the local working population, he began working behind enemy lines as an unofficial intelligence operative.

Birch gained notoriety on April 19, 1942, when a Chinese innkeeper directed him to the nearby Chienteng River and a cabin-boat where it was believed a group of Americans was hiding. In the boat, he found Colonel James H. Doolittle and several of his airmen who, follow-ing their famous bombing raid on Tokyo, had crash-landed in China. With his solid grasp of geography and ability to communicate in Chinese, Birch assisted in the escape of Doolittle and his raiders to areas in China free of Japanese occupation.

When Doolittle arrived in Chungking, he met with General Claire Chennault, commander of the famed Fly-ing Tigers, and told him about Birch's mastery of the lan-guage, understanding of local cultures, and navigational skills in the back country. Doolittle added that Birch had expressed a desire for an Army commission, but as a chaplain. Chennault had a chaplain, but he needed an intelligence officer, and Birch met the requirements.

On July 4, 1942, Chennault awarded Birch a commis-sion as a first lieutenant. That same day, the Army Air Corps 14th Air Force was created, with Chennault as commanding officer. Birch was made head of the 14th's intelligence department, a post he would hold for nearly three years.

In May 1945, Birch, then a 26-year-old captain, was transferred from Chennault's intelligence department to WILLIAM J. "WILD BILL" DONOVAN and the OSS, the World War II predecessor organization to the CIA. On August 14, the defeated Japanese accepted unconditional surren-der. During that period Birch wrote of his longing to "live slowly, to relax with my family before a glowing fire-place . . . to enjoy a good book . . . to reach the sunset of my life sound in body and mind, flanked by strong sons and grandsons." That dream would never be realized.

On August 25, Birch was leading an 11-man OSS team on a mission to accept the surrender of a remote Japanese base in an area of northern China. The area was also actively patrolled by both Nationalist and Communist forces. Separated from the main body, Birch and an aide were several times stopped and accosted by Communist soldiers, who often threatened to kill the two if they did not turn over their weapons and equipment.

When Birch and the aide attempted to pass a roadblock, they were again detained and forcefully questioned by Communist soldiers. Birch requested a meeting with the soldiers' commanding officer; instead, the soldiers tried to disarm Birch. When he resisted, a scuffle ensued wherein Birch and his aide were both shot in the legs. Birch's hands were then bound behind his back at the ankles, and he was forced to kneel for execution. The soldiers shot him in the back of the head and disfigured his body with their bayonets. Birch's wounded aide was left for dead. Fortunately, he survived to tell of Birch's tragic death.

In an attempt to keep the incident from escalating into a new regional conflict, the circumstances surrounding Birch's death were covered up. His family was told that he was killed by crossfire from a clash between Chinese Nationalist and Communist forces. Years later, the truth was disclosed by U.S. congressman William Knowland (R-California).

In December 1958, the founders of a right-wing political-education group named their organization after Birch, declaring Captain John Birch the first casualty of the COLD WAR—hence, the John Birch Society.

Bissell, Richard Mervin, Jr. (1909–1994)

The CIA's deputy director of Plans (operations) from 1959 to 1962, Richard Mervin Bissell, Jr., is unfortunately best known for his involvement in the ill-fated BAY OF PIGS INVASION in 1961. But as the "father" of the U-2 spy-plane program, he was also one of the most influential and effective deputies in the Agency's history.

Bissell was born in Hartford, Connecticut, on September 18, 1909, to Richard Mervin Bissell, Sr., an insurance executive, and Marie Truesdale, whom Bissell would later call "a refuge from the cruel world." As a child, Bissell was timid and prone to temper tantrums. But he had impeccable manners, as well as an uncanny mechanical acumen and sense of detail. Trains were a passion, as were reading and mathematics. Bissell grew up among the well-heeled set. He spent the first nine years of his life living in a house his father had purchased from author Mark Twain, and he later attended Groton, an elite college-preparatory school near Boston, Massachusetts.

In the late 1920s, he entered Yale University. Like so many of his future CIA compatriots, including JAMES JESUS ANGLETON, WILLIAM SLOAN COFFIN, JR., WILLIAM F. BUCKLEY, JR., WILLIAM PUTNAM BUNDY, and future U.S. president GEORGE H. W. BUSH, Bissell became a member of

the school's secret SKULL & BONES SOCIETY. He graduated from Yale in 1932.

From 1932 to 1933, Bissell studied at the London School of Economics. He returned to Yale in 1935 as a professor of economics and taught there for six years. In 1939, he earned his Ph.D. in economics from Yale with a dissertation entitled, "The Theory of Capital under Static and Dynamic Conditions."

When war broke out in 1941, Bissell followed Yale colleague and White House diplomat W. Averell Harriman into government service and for several years and in different organizations was one of Harriman's chief lieutenants. During the war, Bissell served as an economist for the Combined Shipping Adjustment Board. At the close of hostilities, he spent a brief time teaching at the Massachusetts Institute of Technology. He left MIT to become a consultant for U.S. Steel, followed by a term as the executive secretary of the President's Commission on Foreign Aid. Then he went on to work in West Germany as an administrator for the Marshall Plan, the ambitious postwar German infrastructure-rebuilding program. Bissell also worked for the Washington, D.C.–based Edward E. Ford Foundation.

Despite his lack of experience in the field of intelligence, Bissell was recruited into the CIA as an aide to DIRECTOR OF CENTRAL INTELLIGENCE (DCI) ALLEN WELSH DULLES in 1952. But it wasn't his experience Dulles was interested in. Instead, the DCI was impressed with his reported organizational skills and his ability to follow a project through to completion.

In 1954, he was made special assistant for planning and coordination. That same year, he was a member of the CIA's organizational staff for the Agency-backed COUP D'ÉTAT IN GUATEMALA—a "textbook operation" that looked good in the personal files of everyone involved.

When Dulles promoted Bissell to deputy director of plans for operations in 1958, he told him flatly, "The only thing I want you to plan is how to get more intelligence about Russia." That's exactly what he did.

Bissell was directly responsible for overseeing the building and operational success of the CIA's famous U-2 spy plane, as well as the development of sophisticated satellite cameras. He also proclaimed that there would be no communist government in Latin America as long as he was the head of Plans. Unfortunately, Cuban leader FIDEL CASTRO would confound that statement.

Not long after the election of President John Kennedy in 1960, Bissell was ordered to begin counterrevolutionary operations against the Cuban communists under Castro. This also led to Bissell's involvement in the ASSASSINATION PLOTS against Congolese prime minister Patrice Emery Lumumba, General Rafael Trujillo of the Dominican Republic, and Iraqi general Abdul Karim Kassem—all of which would be exposed in future congressional hearings.

But his ultimate fall from grace came when, like his boss Allen Dulles, he was forced to resign from the Agency for his involvement in the disastrous OPERATION ZAPATA—the Bay of Pigs invasion (the Agency-sponsored invasion of Cuba aimed at overthrowing the Castro regime). In his memoirs, Bissell recalls his dismissal: "I was called into the president's office, where Kennedy explained that I could not continue as deputy director of Plans," wrote Bissell. "Then he used a phrase that I have always remembered. He said, 'If this were a parliamentary government, I would have to resign and you, a civil servant, would stay on. But being the system of government that it is, a presidential government, you will have to resign.'" As something of a consolation prize for his spy plane and satellite work, Bissell was offered the deputy directorship of the CIA's Science and Technology DIRECTORATE. But he rejected the offer, viewing it only as a demotion from Plans.

When Bissell left the Agency in 1962; he reentered the private sector, joining the Institute for Defense Analyses (IDA) and serving as its president until 1964. He then took an executive position with United Aircraft Corporation (later United Technologies), from which he retired in 1974.

When U.S. senator Frank Church launched his 1975 probe into CIA misdeeds, Bissell had returned to his primary trade as an economist and a business consultant. However, he was called to testify during the CHURCH COMMITTEE hearings (officially, the Select Committee to Study Governmental Operations with Respect to Intelligence Activities).

Bissell, a recipient of the National Security Medal, died in his sleep on February 7, 1994. He was 84.

See also CONGO, OPERATIONS IN THE; SATELLITE INTELLIGENCE/SURVEILLANCE OPERATIONS.

black

"Black" is a term frequently used by CIA employees, and those of other intelligence agencies, to indicate a reliance on false or illegal concealment rather than on true COVER.

black-bag operation

Black-bag operations, sometimes referred to as a "black-bag jobs," are missions individual CIA field officers and covert operatives from other intelligence organizations are sometimes tasked with but are looked upon with distaste by the general public. A black-bag operation might be anything illegal or "under the table," from burglary to bribery, kidnapping, and assassination.

Though an unpopular method of conducting covert work, many intelligence officers would argue that a black-bag operation is sometimes a necessary evil.

The term "black-bag operation" is derived from the fact that lock-picking tools and other surreptitious-entry devices were once carried in black leather cases.

See also BLACK OPERATION.

Blackbird aircraft

See A-12 BLACKBIRD AIRCRAFT; BLACKSHIELD, OPERATION; SR-71 (A-12) BLACKBIRD AIRCRAFT; OXCART, OPERATION.

black boxes

In CIA parlance, "black box" refers to any form of equipment used in gathering intelligence. For instance, spy satellites, telephone taps, room wires, and BUGs are all considered black boxes.

black operation

In CIA parlance, a "black operation" is a clandestine mission, with negative particulars, not attributable to the organization carrying it out.

See also BLACK-BAG OPERATION.

black propaganda

More commonly referred to as "disinformation," black propaganda is a method used by CIA officers to disseminate or spread inaccurate or misleading information without revealing the source of the deception. Black propaganda is often used to reduce the morale of enemy troops or disrupt enemy operations or routine work.

For instance, during the Korean War, the CIA created convincing forgeries of Chinese military documents and command orders. Agents managed to slip them into the Chinese command network, where they confused the Chinese soldiers. Another example of a successful black-propaganda operation occurred during the 1954 COUP D'ÉTAT IN GUATEMALA. The CIA, employing a textbook disinformation technique, broadcast a series of radio announcements that greatly exaggerated the numerical strength of the rebel force moving against the Guatemalan government army. Also, in at least one instance CIA officers staged a mock rebel takeover of the radio station by firing weapons inside the studio, while acting radio announcers began screaming on the air as if they were actually under attack. This panicked many of Guatemala's military commanders, many of whom defected or fled the country.

It doesn't always work. When the CIA employed similar black-propaganda methods during the BAY OF PIGS INVASION in 1961, many of Cuban leader FIDEL CASTRO's chief lieutenants remembered Guatemala and refused to bite.

See also GRAY PROPAGANDA; WHITE PROPAGANDA.

BLACKSHIELD, Operation

BLACKSHIELD was the code name for high-altitude air reconnaissance operations conducted by CIA pilots flying A-12 BLACKBIRDs out of Kadena Air Base, Okinawa, from May 1967 to June 1968. In what was considered to be the highlight of the A-12 aircraft's history, BLACKSHIELD pilots flew numerous sorties over Vietnam and North Korea.

The A-12s were replaced by SR-71 BLACKBIRDs, flown by Air Force pilots. But photographic intelligence (PHOTINT) gleaned from SR-71 missions continued to be forwarded to the Agency.

black trainees

"Black trainees" are foreigners brought to the United States and trained at CIA facilities without their knowing that they are actually in the United States.

Black trainees are figuratively blindfolded so that in the event they are captured or apprehended during a future operation on foreign soil, they cannot be forced into admitting that they were trained in any sovereign territory or protectorate of the United States. Keeping foreign trainees "in the dark" serves a fourfold purpose. First, the foreigners' inability to connect their training with North America protects American citizens from repercussions by the foreigner's captors. Second, it reduces the possibility that the CIA or any other U.S. government entity might be connected with the operation being conducted by the foreigner. Third, the foreigner, if he or she ever switches allegiance, can never betray the location of the training site to potential enemies of the United States. Lastly, like all clandestine or paramilitary training, the less the trainee knows of his or her whereabouts, the more authoritative can be the control held by the training instructors.

See also CAREER TRAINEE.

blow back

"Blow back" is a CIA term that describes the end result of false information or propaganda deliberately planted in a foreign country that is picked up by its media and then reprinted as fact in the actual country of origin.

For example, during the CHURCH COMMITTEE hearings of 1975 (officially, the Select Committee to Study Governmental Operations with Respect to Intelligence Activities), WILLIAM E. COLBY testified that material the CIA disseminated in foreign countries was often "blown back" into the United States and published as truth in American newspapers.

Reporters and editors can usually avoid "blown-back" material by reporting their own facts rather than repeating what has been previously reported in another country.

BND

See BUNDESNACHRICHTENDIENST.

Bond, James

James Bond was the famous fictional British intelligence officer created by real-life British intelligence officer and novelist IAN LANCASTER FLEMING.

See also MOVIES, TELEVISION, AND POPULAR CULTURE, CIA IN.

bonesmen

"Bonesmen" are former members of Yale University's secret SKULL & BONES SOCIETY. Many of the early members of the CIA were "bonesmen," including JAMES JESUS ANGLETON, RICHARD MERVIN BISSELL, WILLIAM PUTNAM BUNDY, WILLIAM SLOAN COFFIN, JR., WILLIAM F. BUCKLEY, JR., and U.S. president GEORGE HERBERT WALKER BUSH.

book message

A book message is an official, usually nonsensitive, dispatch forwarded from CIA headquarters in LANGLEY, VIRGINIA, to every Agency station and installation in the world. Most book messages address administrative matters, like new appointments or policy changes.

Book of Honor

Located in the lobby of the main headquarters building in LANGLEY, VIRGINIA, the CIA's Book of Honor contains over 40 names of those killed while serving the United States through the Agency.

Unlike most CIA operatives killed in the line of duty, whose names cannot be listed for reasons of national security, the revealed names are calligraphically inscribed in the book on handmade paper next to a gold star. The deceased whose names cannot be inscribed in the book are honored with blank spaces next to gold stars. Nearly 80 stars are in the book, each symbolizing a lost CIA operative.

Designed by Harold Vogel, the Book of Honor is bound in black leather with a gold embossed CIA seal on the cover. The book is displayed, open, in a glass case on a marble shelf below the same number of stars on the CIA MEMORIAL WALL.

The Book of Honor was begun in 1974.

books and Bibles

During the COLD WAR, the CIA published and smuggled behind the IRON CURTAIN countless miniature books containing the works of such writers as Alexander Solzhenitsyn,

Václav Havel, and George Orwell. Miniature Bibles were also published and smuggled to Eastern Bloc countries by agents who then covertly distributed them to Christian dissidents living under communist rule.

In communist countries throughout most of the Cold War, such books and Bibles were forbidden.

Boren-McCurdy initiative

At the early days of the post–COLD WAR world, two federal lawmakers proposed a restructuring of the U.S. intelligence community to eliminate the CIA director's responsibilities for it.

The initiative was launched by U.S. senator David Boren, the chairman of the Senate Select Committee on Intelligence, and U.S. representative Dave McCurdy, the chairman of the House Permanent Select Committee on Intelligence in 1992. The initiative consisted of two separate bills (one proposed by Boren, the other by McCurdy), which differed slightly but were similar in overall content. The bills were to serve as an intelligence counterpart to the Goldwater-Nichols DEPARTMENT OF DEFENSE (DoD) Reorganization Act of 1986 (the Goldwater-Nichols Act integrated armed service capabilities, strengthened DoD joint elements, and broadened the executive and advisory powers of the chairman of the JOINT CHIEFS OF STAFF).

Both the Boren and McCurdy bills would have called for the creation of a DIRECTOR OF NATIONAL INTELLIGENCE. The DNI would have had the authority to program and reprogram intelligence funds and direct their expenditure throughout the U.S. Intelligence Community. The DNI would also have been responsible for tasking intelligence organizations and temporarily transferring personnel from one agency to another as new requirements dictated.

A DNI was first proposed in the SCHLESINGER REPORT of 1971, and then in the TURNER PROPOSAL of 1985). It was later proposed by Senator Dianne Feinstein (D-California) in June 2002, and lastly by a congressional panel (tasked with investigating possible intelligence shortcomings leading to the SEPTEMBER 11, 2001, TERRORIST ATTACKS ON THE UNITED STATES) in December 2002.

The initiative also would have created two deputy directors of National Intelligence positions. One DDNI would have been responsible for intelligence analysis and estimates, the other for U.S. intelligence community affairs. Under the initiative, the existing DIRECTOR OF CENTRAL INTELLIGENCE (DCI) would have had responsibilities only for the CIA. Accordingly, the DCI, would have been subordinate to the DNI.

A National Imagery Agency would have been established within the DoD. This agency would be responsible for collecting, exploiting, and analyzing imagery (the National Imagery and Mapping Agency was in fact established on October 1, 1996, as a DoD entity).

The Boren-McCurdy initiative was never passed, though particulars survived to be included in future legislation.

Boyce, Christopher John (the Falcon)

Christopher John Boyce (aka the "Falcon," because of his lifelong passion for training birds of prey) was convicted of espionage in 1977. He, together with accomplice ANDREW DAULTON LEE, sold top-secret CIA satellite documents to the KOMITET GOSUDARSTVENNOY BEZOPASNOSTI (or KGB, the chief Soviet intelligence and counterintelligence entity) in Mexico City.

Boyce was sentenced to a 40-year term of imprisonment. He escaped in January 1980 and—after committing a string of bank robberies across Montana, Idaho, and Washington State—was recaptured and sentenced to an additional 90 years in prison.

See also FALCON AND SNOWMAN.

Brigade 2506

Brigade 2506 was the CIA-sponsored, anti-CASTRO landing force that invaded Cuba during OPERATION ZAPATA— the BAY OF PIGS INVASION in April 1961.

Composed of 1,400 Cuban émigrés under the command of JOSE PEREZ "PEPE" SAN ROMAIN, the brigade was organized into six small battalions, a heavy weapons force, a commando team, and 500 reinforcement soldiers.

The numerical strength of each battalion was between 167 and 185 men, less than the standard 200-man infantry company in the U.S. Army or Marines.

The soldiers of the First Battalion were trained as paratroopers. The Fourth Battalion soldiers were trained as tankers (the battalion was equipped with five M41A2 tanks and several trucks mounted with 50-caliber machine guns). The remaining four battalions were trained as naval infantry (marines). The commando team (168 men) was trained to create a diversion at another point on the Cuban coastline.

The name "2506" was adopted by the brigade's soldiers to honor their comrade recruit Carlos Rodriguez Santana, who was killed in a training accident. Rodriguez fell to his death from a cliff during mountain-warfare training near the town of Retalhulea in Guatemala. At the beginning of the training cycle, each of the anti-Castro freedom fighters was assigned a number in the 2,000 series. Rodriguez was number 2,506.

Brigade 2506 was also known as "La Brigada Asalto" or simply "La Brigada."

Brown, Joseph Garfield (unknown)

Joseph Garfield Brown was a former enlisted member of the U.S. Air Force who was imprisoned in 1993 for illegally obtaining and selling secret CIA documents. Brown, who served in the Air Force from 1966 to 1968, lived in the Philippines, working as a martial arts instructor for the Department of Tourism.

Brown's activities began in 1990 after meeting VIRGINIA JEAN BAYNES, a CIA secretary who was working at the U.S. embassy in Manila. Brown was teaching karate classes at the embassy annex, and Baynes was one of his students.

According to Baynes, she developed a "friendship" with Brown, who in the summer of 1990 asked her to smuggle CIA documents from her office and deliver them to him. The requested documents contained secret information pertaining to assassinations that had been planned by a local terrorist group and were to be carried out in the Philippines. She complied.

In April 1991, the FEDERAL BUREAU OF INVESTIGATION (FBI) launched an investigation after an internal CIA inquiry determined that Baynes had passed two or three documents to Brown. As part of the investigation, the FBI conducted a sting operation wherein Brown unwittingly provided an undercover FBI agent with illegally obtained CIA documents on Iraqi terrorist activities during the PERSIAN GULF WAR. Brown also provided the agent with information pertaining to the assassination plans of a Philippine insurgent group.

Brown was then lured to the United States by FBI officials who promised him a job teaching self-defense tactics to FBI agents. On December 27, 1992, he was arrested at Dulles International Airport in Washington, D.C. He was subsequently indicted on three counts of espionage.

Brown pled guilty to a charge of conspiring to commit espionage in April 1993, when it was revealed that he had delivered CIA materials to an official of the Philippine government. He was convicted and sentenced to a prison term of 5.9 years. Baynes was also arrested and convicted; she served a 41-month prison term.

Bruce-Lovett Report

The Bruce-Lovett Report was a study conducted in the mid-1950s that apparently criticized the CIA for "being too heavily involved in Third World intrigues" while "neglecting the collection of hard intelligence on the Soviet Union." It also allegedly criticized the close relationship between former DIRECTOR OF CENTRAL INTELLIGENCE (DCI) ALLEN WELSH DULLES and his brother, Secretary of State John Foster Dulles, arguing that the two by virtue of their lofty positions could unduly influence American foreign policy. The report, having not been located by either the Agency's Center for the Study of Intelligence or by private researchers, is presumably still classified.

The report was initiated in 1956 by James Killian, chairman of the PRESIDENT'S BOARD OF CONSULTANTS ON FOREIGN INTELLIGENCE ACTIVITIES (PBCFIA) and president of the Massachusetts Institute of Technology. Killian directed PBCFIA members David Bruce, a well-known diplomat, and former secretary of defense Robert Lovett, who would in 1962 serve on President John Kennedy's Executive Council during the CUBAN MISSILE CRISIS, to prepare a report on the CIA's covert-action programs for President Dwight Eisenhower. Despite its elusiveness, the report was referred to in author Peter Grose's biography of DCI Dulles, *Gentleman Spy*. According to Grose, Bruce and Lovett prepared such a report.

The CIA's History staff has since attempted to obtain a copy from several sources, but to no avail. Grose later stated that he had not actually seen the report but had used notes made from it by Professor ARTHUR MEIER SCHLESINGER, JR., an author/historian and former intelligence analyst with the OFFICE OF STRATEGIC SERVICES (OSS), the World War II predecessor organization to the CIA. Schlesinger stated that he had once seen the report but that it had been acquired by the John F. Kennedy Presidential Library in Boston, Massachusetts. Interestingly, the library has no record of the report.

See also EXCOMM.

brush contact

In CIA parlance, a brush contact is a brief encounter between two field operatives (usually a case officer and an agent) wherein secret material is passed from one to the other.

A brush contact is also known as a "brush pass."

Buckley, William (1928–1985)

A CIA CHIEF OF STATION in Beirut, Lebanon, during President Ronald Reagan's administration, William Buckley (not to be mistaken with famed author WILLIAM F. BUCKLEY, JR., also a onetime CIA officer) was captured by Lebanese-based Hezbollah (Party of God) terrorists with links to the Iranian regime of the Ayatollah Ruhollah Moussavi Khomeini. The terrorists who snatched Buckley were a group of Shiite Muslims calling themselves Islamic Jihad (Islamic Holy War or Islamic Holy Struggle).

Buckley was born in Bedford, Massachusetts, on May 30, 1928. He was a former U.S. Army Special Forces officer who won a Silver Star for gallantry during the Vietnam War. He later transferred from the Green Berets to the CIA.

With the Agency, Buckley worked in numerous countries around the world, including Angola, Saudi Arabia, and Afghanistan, where he was directly involved in the CIA's efforts to launder guns and money to the Mujahideen rebels fighting the Soviets.

In 1983, he and fellow CIA officer Leslie Aspin (also trained as a Special Forces soldier) were sent to the Middle East with the task of leading an Agency-sponsored kidnapping squad. The squad was tasked with snatching Lebanese terrorists. Instead, Buckley was himself captured, on March 16, 1984.

Buckley was one of several Americans who had been kidnapped in Beirut in recent months, but his "station chief" status—as well as his alleged links to the kidnaping squad—impelled his captors to torture him unmercifully. Reportedly, their primary method was to force an inflatable tube down his throat. Air was then pumped in, expanding the tube to a point of unbearable pain. Eventually, Buckley's lungs were irreparably damaged, and he developed pneumonia. On June 3, 1985, the CIA station chief died of strangulation. Hezbollah sent a videotape of his torture and murder to CIA headquarters. Before his death, Buckley had been forced to confess to "crimes" against the Islamic people and to sign a 400-page document that outlined in great detail the White House's plot to kidnap Lebanese terrorists.

During the 444 days Buckley was held in captivity, DIRECTOR OF CENTRAL INTELLIGENCE (DCI) WILLIAM CASEY worked tirelessly for his release, convinced that Iran exercised control over the Shiite group that held Buckley. Both the CIA and the White House were contacted by intermediaries who claimed to represent the Iranian authorities. The intermediaries presented a plan wherein Buckley and other American hostages might be released in return for the sale of weapons and weapons-related materials to Iran.

The initial approach was allegedly made by the Israeli government, which was working through Israeli and Iranian weapons dealers (during the Iran-Iraq War, the Israelis had reportedly established a secret relationship with Iran, because it believed that a victorious Iraq would be a more dangerous enemy). The weapons dealers believed they could free Buckley, but he had already been tortured to death.

Buckley was a lifelong bachelor who aside from his CIA work owned an antiques shop, collected fine art and miniature soldiers, avidly read history and politics, and was the principal artisan of the panorama at the Lexington Battlefield Tourist Center in Massachusetts. He was the recipient of countless decorations, including the Intelligence Star, the Exceptional Service Medallion, and the Distinguished Intelligence Cross.

During a public memorial service for Buckley three years after his death, DCI WILLIAM WEBSTER said, "Bill's success in collecting information in situations of incredible danger was exceptional, even remarkable." Buckley is buried in Arlington National Cemetery. At the time of his death, he was 57.

See also IRAN-CONTRA.

Buckley, William F., Jr. (1925–)

Best-selling author, famed political pundit, and the recipient of over 35 honorary degrees, William Frank Buckley, Jr., is best known for founding the conservative opinion magazine *National Review* and hosting *Firing Line,* the longest-running television debate program in the United States. But Buckley (not to be confused with CIA CHIEF OF STATION WILLIAM BUCKLEY, who was captured and murdered by Lebanese Shiites in the mid-1980s) was also a CIA officer who served in Mexico during the early 1950s.

Buckley was born in New York City on November 24, 1925, the sixth of 10 children to Catholic oil baron William Frank Buckley, Sr., and Aloise Steiner Buckley. Soon thereafter, the Buckley family moved to Sharon, Connecticut, where, raised by Mexican housekeepers, young Buckley spoke his first words in Spanish. At six years old he attended his first school—in Paris, where he learned French. At age seven, he learned English at a day school in London. In 1943, he attended the University of Mexico, and in 1944, he joined the U.S. Army as a second lieutenant.

At the end of World War II, Buckley enrolled in Yale University. Like many of his future CIA compatriots, including future U.S. president GEORGE HERBERT WALKER BUSH and JAMES JESUS ANGLETON, RICHARD BISSELL, WILLIAM PUTNAM BUNDY, and WILLIAM SLOAN COFFIN, JR., Buckley became a member of Yale's secret SKULL & BONES SOCIETY. He also distinguished himself as a skilled debater and became chairman of the *Yale Daily News.* Buckley graduated from Yale with honors in 1950. The following year, he penned *God and Man at Yale,* a scathing accusation that the institution had turned away from its founding premise that God exists. According to Buckley, Yale had evolved into a secular bastion of atheism. Many of Buckley's former professors were unsettled, as much of Buckley's work stemmed from their lectures. However, the book effectively launched his career.

In May 1951, he was recruited into the CIA. Buckley would later recall, "I did training in Washington as a secret agent and was sent to Mexico City." In Mexico City, he served as a field officer of the Agency's recently established OFFICE OF POLICY COORDINATION (OPC) under the direct supervision of E. HOWARD HUNT, a station chief destined to become one of the key players in the infamous WATERGATE SCANDAL. The OPC, the CIA's covert-action wing, was responsible for everything from propaganda to economic warfare and from sabotage to assisting underground resistance forces. Buckley, however,

William F. Buckley, Jr., ca. 1967 (LIBRARY OF CONGRESS)

spent the majority of his time at OPC editing and translating *The Road from Yenan,* an anticommunist book by Eudocio Ravines, a former Marxist from Chile.

In 1952, Buckley left the Agency for a career in journalism. Two years later, he met and became close friends with Whitaker Chambers, a journalist and former member of the American Communist Party who had worked as an agent for Soviet intelligence during World War II. Chambers, who had made an ideological about-face in the late 1930s and had become an outspoken anticommunist, was best known for his 1948 revelation that Alger Hiss, a respected U.S. State Department official, had also been a spy for the Soviets. In the last years of Chamber's life, he wrote Buckley a voluminous series of letters, which the latter published in book form as *Odyssey of a Friend 1954–1961.*

In 1955, Buckley founded *National Review,* one of the most widely circulated political opinion journals in the United States and required reading for every staff member in President Ronald Reagan's administration. For 10 years, he served as the magazine's editor in chief. His

friend Chambers became a senior editor with the magazine, serving in that capacity until his death in 1961. Buckley also began a syndicated column, "On the Right," in 1962. Today, it appears three times a week in over 300 newspapers worldwide.

In 1965, Buckley ran unsuccessfully for mayor of New York. The following year, he launched *Firing Line*—a television interview program featuring world political and intellectual leaders, with Buckley as host. By 1971, the show was carried nationally on the Public Broadcasting System. Buckley's interviewees have included U.S. presidents Nixon, Ford, Carter, Reagan, and Bush; British prime ministers Harold Wilson, Margaret Thatcher, and Edward Heath; and comedian Groucho Marx and best-selling author James Michener.

In the late 1970s, Buckley produced a series of successful spy novels featuring a fictionalized CIA agent, Blackford Oakes. In addition to *God and Man at Yale, Odyssey of a Friend,* and the Blackford Oakes series, Buckley authored a number of books on communicating, history, and political thought. In 2000, Buckley published *Let Us Talk of Many Things,* a collection of his speeches, as well as a CIA-based novel entitled *Spytime: The Undoing of James Jesus Angleton.*

In November 1991, Buckley was awarded the Presidential Medal of Freedom. He has received many other awards.

In a 1999 interview for *Salon* magazine, Buckley said, "For 50 years, I never talked about what I did in the CIA because I had pledged not to. But I just picked up a book (*Who Paid the Piper* by France Stonor Saunders) in England that describes what I did do." That book convinced Buckley that he no longer needed to keep the knowledge of his CIA tenure a secret. But, despite his unwavering patriotism, he also revealed many of the inner workings of the unseen world of espionage in his Blackford Oakes novels.

bug

A bug is a small, hidden audio device used by CIA officers and other intelligence operatives to eavesdrop on and record closed door conversations. Bugs, often referred to as "wires" or "listening devices," are often placed in hotel rooms, telephone receivers, vehicles, and other places where the intended target might talk more freely with friends, lovers, or close associates, thus unwittingly disclosing vital information.

Some of the more clever methods of employing bugs or listening devices have been concealing them in book spines and ballpoint pens. During the 1950s, a Soviet-planted bug was discovered behind a wooden carving of the U.S. seal at the American embassy in Moscow. The seal was on the wall directly behind the desk of U.S. ambassador GEORGE FROST KENNAN, the man considered to be the architect of the CIA's covert-action arm. In 1964, some 40 eavesdropping devices were discovered and pried out of the walls of the same American embassy in Moscow. In 1985, construction was halted on a new American embassy in Moscow after it was determined that bugs had been planted throughout the building.

CIA operatives in foreign countries are also wary of being bugged themselves. Consequently, they often employ Agency counterintelligence specialists known as EXTERMINATORS to locate and remove the devices.

Bunche, Ralph Johnson (1903–1971)

Dr. Ralph Johnson Bunche, a political science professor and United Nations diplomat, was, as an African American, the first person of color to receive the Nobel Peace Prize. He also served in both the OFFICE OF THE COORDINATOR OF INFORMATION (COI) and the OFFICE OF STRATEGIC SERVICES (OSS), predecessor organizations to the CIA.

Bunche was born on August 7, 1903, in Detroit, Michigan, to Fred Bunche, a barber, and Olive Johnson, an amateur pianist and poet. Young Bunche was raised in an integrated section of the city by several adult members of a large extended family including his parents, aunts and uncles, and his maternal grandmother, Lucy Taylor Johnson, a former slave. When Bunche was 11 years old, the family moved to Albuquerque, New Mexico, where he found himself one of two black students in a class of 36. He was an excellent student, and he soon developed a deep love for geography.

In October 1916, Bunche's father left Albuquerque, never to return. His mother died the following year, and his favorite uncle committed suicide. Bunche's grandmother then moved the family to a predominately white neighborhood in Los Angeles, California.

Bunche graduated from high school as the class valedictorian. He then attended the University of California at Los Angeles (UCLA) on an athletic scholarship, supporting himself as a part-time janitor. In 1927, he graduated summa cum laude with a bachelor's degree in international relations and, again, as class valedictorian. In 1928, Bunche earned a master's degree in political science from Harvard University. He then began teaching at Howard University in Washington, D.C. At Howard, he established the school's first political science department. He also continued his formal education, at Harvard.

In 1932, Bunche secured a Rosenwald Fellowship, which enabled him to travel to Africa and conduct research on the impact of race and segregation in the lives of black South Africans. During his research he also attended Northwestern University, the London School of Economics, and the University of Cape Town.

In 1934, he earned a Ph.D. from Harvard. Three years later, Bunche collaborated with Gunnar Myrdal, a Swedish sociologist who was researching race relations in America. With Bunche's assistance, Myrdal wrote *An American Dilemma: The Negro Problem in Modern Democracy*. Myrdal's book proved to be one of the period's definitive works on American race relations.

On September 10, 1941, Bunche left Howard to accept a position as an analyst with the COI, the predecessor organization to the OSS, which in turn was the World War II precursor to the CIA. When Bunche joined the COI, there were only 40 employees there. After the Japanese attacked Pearl Harbor in December, the COI's ranks swelled to over 600.

On June 13, 1942, President Franklin Roosevelt redesignated the COI as the OSS, and Bunche was selected to head the Africa section of its Technical and Research Division. In that capacity, he played a key role in developing intelligence that would be used in the American invasion of North Africa.

On January 4, 1944, Bunche left the OSS to accept an appointment to the Near East and African section of the U.S. DEPARTMENT OF STATE. Initially, some members of the State Department resisted his being brought into what was then considered "an exclusive white man's club." It was a resistance that reportedly impelled Secretary of State Cordell Hull to say, "I don't care whether his skin is white, blue, black, green, or pink. . . . The only thing I care about is having the best possible man for the job. . . . I want him hired." In July, Bunche was assigned to the State Department's International Security Organization section. There he worked on matters related to "trusteeship," involving postwar planning for "dependent territories." Bunche joined the United Nations Secretariat as head of the Trusteeship Division in December 1946.

On December 11, 1950, Bunche was awarded the Nobel Prize for Peace. He received the award for his successful mediation of a series of armistice agreements signed by the fledgling nation of Israel (which had been established two years earlier) and its four Arab neighbors—Egypt, Jordan, Lebanon, and Syria. During the award ceremony at Oslo University in Norway, Bunche said, "In the dynamic world society which is the objective of the United Nations, all peoples must have equality and equal rights."

During the 1960s, Bunche was discredited by black activists like Malcolm X and Stokely Carmichael, who believed that he was more concerned with solving international problems than in tackling the problems of American racism. Nothing could have been further from the truth. Many black leaders advocated separatist policies. Bunche disagreed. He believed that full integration of the races was the only way in which marginalized African Americans would ever achieve economic and social parity. As demands for equal rights for African Americans were met with hostile resistance by white Americans, riots erupted in many major cities across the United

States. These events greatly agitated Bunche. However, he continued to dismiss the concept of black separatism.

In 1965, Bunche joined a number of black leaders, including Martin Luther King, Jr., in the famous Selma-to-Montgomery voting rights march in Alabama. "I am a Negro, I am also an American," Bunche later stated. "This is my country. I own a share in it, I have a vested interest in it. My ancestors helped create it, to build it, to make it strong and great, and rich. All of this belongs to me as much as [it] belongs to any American with a white skin. What is mine I intend to have and to hold, to fight, if necessary, to uphold it. I will not give up my legacy in this society willingly. I will not run away from it by pursuing an escapist fantasy of an all-black road to an all-black society—the illusion of a black heaven."

Bunche died in 1971 in New York City. He was 68.

Bundesamt für Verfassungsschutz (BfV)

Established as a West German entity in 1950, the Bundesamt für Verfassungsschutz (Federal Office for the Protection of the Constitution) is Germany's current COUNTER-INTELLIGENCE agency. Though its officers have no police authority, many of the BfV's functions parallel those of America's FEDERAL BUREAU OF INVESTIGATION (FBI). Some of its functions also parallel those of the CIA.

Bundesnachrichtendienst (BND)

Established in 1956, the Bundesnachrichtendienst (Federal Information Service) was West Germany's foreign intelligence service. Unlike the CIA, it was responsible for both foreign and domestic intelligence. The BND was the descendent of the GEHLEN ORGANIZATION which was developed and overseen by the CIA beginning in 1949.

The current German BND functions in much the same manner as it did under the West German government. The BND's counterpart American organization is the CIA.

Bundy, William Putnam (1917–2000)

One of the initial targets of Senator Joseph McCarthy's communist witch-hunt, William Putnam Bundy was an early CIA ANALYST who would later be referred to as the man whose name was "on more pieces of paper dealing with Vietnam" than any other Vietnam analyst during the Kennedy-Johnson years. Yet he was the man "about whom the least was known."

Born in Washington, D.C., on September 24, 1917, to Harvey Hollister Bundy, a prominent attorney who served as secretary of both state and war, and Katherine Lawrence Putnam, a respected member of New England society, young Bundy grew up in world of wealth, privi-

lege, and constant intellectual stimulation. His family's unofficial motto was, "Don't talk while I'm interrupting." Not surprisingly, Bundy was destined to make his mark on the world stage. He spent most of his boyhood in Boston, Massachusetts; he attended nearby Groton, an elite college-preparatory school, where he graduated top of his class.

Bundy attended Yale University, where he studied history, played hockey, was president of the Yale Political Union, and worked for the *Yale Daily News*. Like many of his future CIA compatriots, including JAMES JESUS ANGLE-TON, RICHARD BISSELL, WILLIAM SLOAN COFFIN, JR., WILLIAM F. BUCKLEY, JR., and future U.S. president GEORGE HERBERT WALKER BUSH, Bundy became a member of Yale's secret SKULL & BONES SOCIETY. He graduated from Yale in 1939. The following year, he earned a master's degree in history from Harvard. He then briefly attended the Harvard Law School.

When World War II erupted, Bundy was commissioned a second lieutenant in the U.S. Army. He served as a Signal Corps officer, rising to the rank of major. In the Army, he was stationed at London's Bletchley Park, where he was responsible for decoding intelligence intercepts. He would later describe his wartime service in London as the most rewarding of his career. He was subsequently awarded the Legion of Merit and the Order of the British Empire. After the war, Bundy returned to Harvard, earning a law degree in 1947. For the next three years, he practiced law at the Washington, D.C., firm of Covington and Burling.

Bundy briefly considered rejoining the Army when the Korean War broke out in 1950. Instead, in 1951, he joined the CIA. With the Agency, he became an intelligence analyst and prepared NATIONAL INTELLIGENCE ESTIMATES (NIE). He soon was made chief of staff of the NIE.

In 1953, Bundy was appointed to the post of assistant to the DEPUTY DIRECTOR OF INTELLIGENCE. That same year, Senator Joseph McCarthy, the infamous anticommunist inquisitor, targeted Bundy for having contributed $400 to the defense fund of Alger Hiss, a former aide to President Franklin Roosevelt who was being tried as a spy for the Soviet Union. Bundy, who had disclosed his support of Hiss during a previous background check, argued that he simply wanted Hiss to receive a fair trial. McCarthy, believing Bundy was a communist sympathizer, attempted to investigate him, as a first step toward investigating the entire Agency. Bundy was vigorously defended by DIRECTOR OF CENTRAL INTELLIGENCE (DCI) ALLEN WELSH DULLES. McCarthy backed off, and the matter was dismissed.

In 1960, Bundy left the CIA to serve on President Dwight Eisenhower's Commission on National Goals. In 1961, President John Kennedy appointed him deputy to the assistant secretary of defense for international security affairs; he became assistant secretary in 1963. The following year, President Lyndon Johnson appointed him to the post of assistant secretary of state for Far Eastern affairs. Throughout those years, Bundy was intimately involved in a number of critical national matters, including the ill-fated invasion of Cuba at the BAY OF PIGS in 1961, the CUBAN MISSILE CRISIS in 1962, and the developing situation in SOUTHEAST ASIA.

In 1964, Bundy was the focus of an article in the *New York Times* that described him as a political "tiger." The article went on to say that unlike his more famous brother McGeorge Bundy (a Republican who served as national security advisor to both Presidents Kennedy and Johnson), Bundy was a Democrat, and he did not like being mistaken for anything else. Once when a newspaper referred to him as a Republican, Bundy demanded and received a published correction.

During the Vietnam War, Bundy served the Johnson administration as one of the president's chief policy makers and supporters of the war effort. In 1970, he retired from government service, accepting a position at the Massachusetts Institute of Technology Center for International Studies. There he became a continual target of the antiwar movement. In one instance, protesters attempted to place a bomb in his office. Not long after, he became an editor of *Foreign Affairs* magazine, where he served until 1983. But at *Foreign Affairs,* he again came under harsh criticism, this time by the magazine's advisory council, which claimed that "his [Bundy's] role in planning and executing illegal and criminal war policies in Indo-China should disqualify him from holding an editorial position of this kind." But council chairman David Rockefeller stood by Bundy, and he continued as editor.

At some point soon after, Bundy began to realize that America's involvement in the Vietnam War had been doomed from the start. "I was never able to convince myself that there was a cost-free alternative course, as from 1961, or that any of the different strategies since proposed, especially those involving stronger military action, would have made sense," he wrote in a publication celebrating his 50th Yale University reunion, in 1989. "In a nutshell, my present feeling is that it was a tragedy waiting to happen, but one made much worse by countless errors along the way, in many of which I had a part."

New York Times journalist Seymour Hersh would later describe Bundy as a man who learned from his mistakes. "He changed an awful lot," said Hersh. "He began to see the other side of the Vietnam War more."

In the 1990s Bundy penned *A Tangled Web: The Making of Foreign Policy in the Nixon Presidency.* The book, a critical analysis of American foreign policy during the Nixon era, including the latter years of the Vietnam War, was published in 1998.

Bundy died of heart disease at his Princeton, New Jersey, home on October 6, 2000. He was 83.

Bush, George Herbert Walker (1924–)

The 41st president of the United States, George Herbert Walker Bush was also the 11th DIRECTOR OF CENTRAL INTELLIGENCE (12th, counting MAJOR GENERAL WILLIAM J. "WILD BILL" DONOVAN's directorship).

Bush was born in Milton, Massachusetts, on June 12, 1924, to Prescott Sheldon Bush, an investment banker and U.S. senator, and Dorothy Walker, an amateur athlete whose father had established the famous Walker Cup Golf tournament. Like his parents, the younger Bush was a keen competitor with a passion for sports. He attended both Greenwich Country Day School in Connecticut and Philips Academy in Andover, Massachusetts, where, despite a quiet, unassuming manner, he excelled in nearly all sports, edited the school newspaper, and became president of the senior class. He was a natural leader, and, despite what the critics of his presidency would say, he was a "tough guy"—but in his own urbane manner.

Media consultant Roger Ailes would later describe Bush as unlike John Wayne. "He's more like Gary Cooper in *High Noon.* He's very gentle. He would much rather talk than fight. But he's capable of taking care of himself." He could take care of himself, indeed. In June 1943, Bush, barely 19 years old, earned ensign's bars and the gold wings of a naval aviator. Surviving a crash during a training mishap five months later, he shipped out with a Navy torpedo bomber squadron and flew combat missions against the Japanese over Wake Island, Guam, and Saipan.

Bush was shot down by antiaircraft fire twice. But his most heroic exploit took place on September 2, 1944, while dive-bombing a Japanese radio center on Chichi Jima. His plane was severely hit. His wings were on fire, smoke was filling the cockpit, and his tail gunner was dead. But he continued diving on the target, unloaded his ordnance on the enemy position, and then struggled to regain altitude, pointing his crippled aircraft's nose out to sea. When he was far enough out, he ordered his radioman to bail out. The radioman jumped and was killed when his parachute failed to open. Bush then jumped himself and slammed into the aircraft's tail as he was swept from the cockpit, splitting his head open and ripping his own parachute. Three hours later, the injured aviator was pulled from the Pacific by the crew of an American submarine, the *Finback.* Bush spent the next three months aboard the *Finback* as the sub continued to attack Japanese ships. After 58 combat missions, three crashes, three air medals, one Distinguished Flying Cross, and a brief combat tour on a submarine, the pilot who was for a time the youngest aviator in the Navy was honorably discharged.

After the war, Bush enrolled in an accelerated two-and-a-half-year program at Yale, where he lettered in baseball and soccer. Like many of his CIA compatriots, including JAMES JESUS ANGLETON, RICHARD BISSELL, WILLIAM PUTNAM BUNDY, WILLIAM SLOAN COFFIN, JR., and WILLIAM F. BUCKLEY, JR., Bush became a member of Yale's secret SKULL & BONES SOCIETY. He graduated with honors and a bachelor's degree in economics in 1948.

After considering several career tracks, including farming, he entered the oil business as a floor sweeper and warehouse manager with an Odessa, Texas, company, International Derrick and Equipment. He eventually moved up to sales, worked briefly for Pacific Pumps, and in 1950 cofounded the Bush-Overby Oil Development Company. Four years, one merger, and several reorganizations later, he found himself as the president and later board chairman of Zapata Off-Shore, a multinational offshore drilling platform construction company.

In the early 1950s, Bush also became involved in Republican Party politics, campaigning for future president Dwight Eisenhower and eventually earning the chairmanship of the Harris County Republican Party in Houston. From 1967 to 1971, Bush served in the U.S. Congress. He was appointed U.S. ambassador to the United Nations in 1971. From 1973 to 1974, he served as chairman of the Republican National Committee. From 1974 to 1975, he became chief U.S. liaison in China.

In 1976, President Gerald Ford appointed Bush director of central intelligence. Ford's first choice, attorney Edward Bennett Williams, had declined the post, and Bush accepted it only because his father had advised him never to reject an offer from the president of the United States. Bush felt that the CIA was a "political graveyard" and would kill any dreams he had of the White House.

Bush's nomination came under fire from Democratic opponents—chief among them Senator Frank Church, who believed that Bush's strong Republican connections linked him, at least collaterally, to the WATERGATE SCANDAL.

Nevertheless, Bush was confirmed. As DCI, Bush was the first professional politician to head the Agency. In the wake of Watergate and the CHURCH COMMITTEE congressional investigations of CIA ASSASSINATION PLOTS in the developing world, Bush was careful to avoid any appearance of partisanship, refusing to accept invitations to Republican Party functions during his 51-week tenure.

Bush was a "strictly business" DCI who wasted no time cleaning house. He fired many top Agency administrators, lobbied for increased funding for reconnaissance satellites, advocated a program of intelligence sharing with the nation's strongest allies, and created a non-Agency organization, known as Team B, that independently evaluated Soviet military capabilities and served as a check and balance for the Agency's own assessment of the same.

Despite his initial disinclination to accept the DCI appointment, Bush was reluctant to give up the post when Jimmy Carter became president in 1976. Bush requested that he be retained as DCI. Carter instead appointed ADMIRAL STANSFIELD TURNER as Bush's successor. Bush resigned quietly and moved back to Texas.

In 1980, he reemerged as a presidential contender, campaigning unsuccessfully for the Republican nomination. It was during one of his nomination speeches that he expressed his desire for a strong CIA. "We are up against a tough adversary [the Soviet Union]," Bush said. "We have to have the best intelligence service money can buy."

Down but not out after losing the nomination, he was chosen as Ronald Reagan's running mate. In January 1981, he became the 43rd vice president of the United States. After two terms as vice president, he was elected president in 1988.

From the beginning of his presidency, Bush directed a great deal of energy toward foreign policy. In December 1989, he ordered an invasion of Panama aimed at arresting and toppling the regime of [General Manuel Antonio Noriega, who was heavily involved in the trafficking of] drugs from Latin America to the United States. The following year, before the Soviet Union collapsed, Bush signed a mutual nonaggression pact with President Mikhail Gorbachev.

On August 2, 1990, Iraqi president Saddam Hussein invaded Kuwait, an oil-rich but defenseless Persian Gulf nation bordering Iraq. On January 15, 1991, after one of the most remarkable mobilizations and deployments in military history, Bush launched OPERATION DESERT STORM, a counterinvasion into Kuwait with the objective of expelling the Iraqi army.

Led by the United States, a 700,000-man, 28-nation coalition force routed the Iraqis in less than six weeks and virtually destroyed Saddam Hussein's army during its retreat to Baghdad. The PERSIAN GULF WAR was the highlight of Bush's presidency, but his popularity was short-lived. Bush's reversal of a "no new taxes" pledge and a developing economic recession began to plague him in the public opinion polls. He lost his bid for reelection to former Arkansas governor Bill Clinton in 1992.

In the final weeks of his administration, Bush dispatched a contingent of U.S. Marines and Army Rangers to Somalia in order to help feed starving civilians during a period of civil unrest. The mission, which ultimately led to the deaths of 18 soldiers, was to lead to an unmanageable situation for the Clinton administration.

Though his tenure at the CIA lasted less than a year, Bush found his Agency directorship one of the most rewarding periods of his professional life. On April 26, 1999, President Clinton and the Agency honored Bush by renaming the CIA's headquarters compound in LANGLEY, VIRGINIA, the GEORGE BUSH CENTER FOR INTELLIGENCE.

George H. W. Bush is sworn in as the director of the CIA, with his wife, Barbara Bush, and President Gerald Ford on either side   (NATIONAL ARCHIVES)

During the dedication ceremony, Bush expressed his devotion to the Agency. "I left here some 22 years ago after a limited tenure, and my stay here had a major impact on me," Bush said. "The CIA became part of my heartbeat back then, and it's never gone away. In my opinion, of the many agencies comprising the Executive Branch, the men and women of CIA—many of whom I'm privileged to say are here—exemplified the best about public service. Here service to country comes first. You're ever vigilant, always looking out for the nation's best interests, but rarely getting the credit that you deserve. You never sit at the head table; never get singled out. You are there out of love of country."

Bush's oldest son, former Texas governor George W. Bush, became the 43rd president of the United States in 2001.

C

Cabell, General Charles Pearre (1903–1971)

A distinguished U.S. Army Air Corps and U.S. Air Force officer, Charles Pearre Cabell was the longest-serving DEPUTY DIRECTOR OF CENTRAL INTELLIGENCE (DDCI) in CIA history. Unfortunately, he is best known as the DDCI who—along with DIRECTOR OF CENTRAL INTELLIGENCE (DCI) ALLEN WELSH DULLES and other top Agency officials—was forced out of the CIA after the disastrous invasion of Cuba at the BAY OF PIGS in 1961.

Cabell was born in Dallas, Texas, on October 11, 1903. He graduated from the U.S. Military Academy at West Point in 1925 and was commissioned a second lieutenant of field artillery. For the next five years, he served with the 12th Field Artillery at Fort Sam Houston, Texas.

In 1930, Cabell was assigned to the Army Air Corps flight school at Brooks Field, Texas. He earned his wings in 1931. From then until the beginning of World War II, he held a variety of posts, including a stint as an observer with the Royal Air Force. During the early years of the war, he held a number of planning and advisory positions and attended staff officer courses.

In October 1943, Cabell was assigned to the famous Eighth Air Force in the European Theater of Operations, and on December 1 he assumed command of the Eighth's 45th Combat Bombardment Wing. In April 1944, Cabell, then a brigadier general, was made director of plans for

the U.S. Strategic Air Force in Europe. Three months later, he was posted to Caserta, Italy, where he was made director of operations and intelligence for the Mediterranean Allied Air Forces. He was reassigned to Air Force Headquarters in May 1945. There for the remainder of the war he served as chief of the Strategy and Policy Division in the Office of the Assistant Chief of Air Staff for Plans. For his actions during the war, Cabell was awarded a number of decorations, including the Bronze Star, the Legion of Merit, the Distinguished Service Medal, and the Distinguished Flying Cross.

In December 1945, he was assigned to the Military Staff Committee of the United Nations. In August 1947, Cabell returned to Air Force Headquarters as special assistant to the assistant chief of Air Staff for plans, and, for the next two months he served as acting deputy to the director of the Joint Staff. In November, Cabell, then a major general, became chief of the Air Intelligence Requirements Division in the Office of the Director of Intelligence. In May 1948, he was appointed director of intelligence for the U.S. Air Force. In 1951, he was named director of the Joint Staff, in the Office of the JOINT CHIEFS OF STAFF.

President Dwight Eisenhower appointed Cabell to the post of deputy director of central intelligence on April 23, 1953. He served in that capacity until 1962, when he was directed to resign from the CIA in the aftermath of the ill-fated Bay of Pigs invasion. He left the Agency on January 31.

Cabell collapsed and died after a physical examination at Fort Myer, Virginia, on May 25, 1971. He was 67.

See also AIR FORCE INTELLIGENCE.

Cambridge Five

"Cambridge Five" was the nickname given to a network of five of the most notorious DOUBLE AGENTs to ever betray the West. So named because each of the spies was educated at Cambridge University in the 1930s, the five were HAROLD ADRIAN RUSSELL "KIM" PHILBY, Donald Maclean, Guy Burgess, Anthony Blunt, and John Cairncross. The Cambridge Five betrayals, particularly those committed by Philby, proved catastrophic to many operations conducted by both the CIA and MI6.

The Cambridge Five were also known as the "Ring of Five" and, to the Soviets, the "Magnificent Five."

cameras, miniature

One of the most important tools used in the collection of intelligence has been the miniature camera. Operatives from the CIA and its predecessor and related agencies have depended on such devices in order to surreptitiously to photograph documents, persons, objects, and such physical sites as bridges, airstrips, manufacturing facilities, and military installations.

The most famous of the miniature photographic devices is the Minox camera. Developed in Latvia in the late 1930s, the Minox is a tiny camera developed for commercial use. But its small size and durable construction made it one of the most effective intelligence-collection tools of World War II and later the COLD WAR—the nonshooting conflict between the United States and the Soviet Union that lasted from 1945 until 1991.

Other miniatures followed the creation of the Minox camera, including cameras developed to look like ordinary cigarette lighters, matchboxes, and wristwatches.

During the cold war, personal spy cameras developed for use by the CIA were concealed in a number of ways. Cameras were mounted behind vehicle license plates, men's neckties, and trenchcoat waist belts. Others were concealed within cigarette packs, books, umbrellas, hats, and briefcases.

Microdot cameras, ultratiny cameras that use easily concealable microdot film, were used extensively by the intelligence agencies of Eastern bloc countries during the cold war. Microdot film, in fact, was so small that it could be hidden in hollowed-out coins and secret chambers in finger rings.

Miniature cameras, including the Minox and the microdot, are still in use today by spies from intelligence organizations throughout the world.

Canadian Security Intelligence Service (CSIS)

The CSIS, or Canadian Security Intelligence Service, is Canada's counterpart to the CIA. The CSIS, however, is unique in that it serves as the Canadian government's principal adviser on matters of security. The service was established by an act of the Canadian Parliament in 1984 that disbanded the Royal Canadian Mounted Police Security Service.

In the weeks immediately following the SEPTEMBER 11, 2001, TERRORIST ATTACKS ON THE UNITED STATES, the CSIS provided the CIA credible threat intelligence gleaned from intercepted cell-phone conversations between members of al-Qaeda, the worldwide terrorist network headed by OSAMA BIN LADEN.

Canine Corps, CIA

Established during the PERSIAN GULF WAR, in January 1991, the CIA's Canine Corps is responsible for training, maintaining, and employing dogs for security purposes. The Canine Corps falls under the DIRECTORATE of Administration's Center for CIA Security.

Cannistraro, Vincent M. (Vince) (unknown)

A former NATIONAL SECURITY ADVISOR on terrorism for President Ronald Reagan who would go on to head the CIA's Counterterrorist Task Force under President George H. W. Bush, Vincent M. "Vince" Cannistraro is today an international security consultant for news organizations and private companies.

From 1984 to 1987, Cannistraro served as director of the NATIONAL SECURITY COUNCIL (the NSC is the highest-ranking executive council responsible for advising the president of the United States on the integration of domestic, foreign, and military policies that affect national security). He went on to serve as chief of operations for the CIA's COUNTERTERRORIST CENTER. In that capacity, he directed the CIA's investigation into the bombing of Pan Am flight 103 in 1988.

In the wake of the SEPTEMBER 11, 2001, TERRORIST ATTACKS ON THE UNITED STATES, Cannistraro has addressed both the U.S. Congress and the American public on the particulars of global terrorism.

Career Trainee (CT)

Career trainees, often referred to as CTs, are CIA "recruits" undergoing the Agency's rigorous two-year Career Trainee Program. Drawn from a cross section of America, career trainees are all college-educated men and women who have demonstrated an aptitude for mastering foreign languages and an ability to make critical decisions rapidly.

The brainchild of former DIRECTOR OF CENTRAL INTELLIGENCE (DCI) WALTER BEDELL SMITH, the Career Trainee Program is the gateway for inductees into the CIA. As the CIA's "boot camp," the Career Training Program begins with a rigorous one-year formal training program at Camp Peary, Virginia, the Agency's primary training center. After completion of the initial program, inductees begin an equally difficult year of on-the-job training.

Currently, American taxpayers pay an average of $150,000 per recruit for the first year in the Career Trainee Program.

See also BLACK TRAINEES.

Carlucci, Frank Charles, III (1930–)

Frank Charles Carlucci III, a DEPUTY DIRECTOR OF CENTRAL INTELLIGENCE (DDCI), a NATIONAL SECURITY ADVISOR, and a secretary of defense, in his early years of government service had a colorful career as a CIA operations officer in Africa.

Carlucci was born in Scranton, Pennsylvania, on October 18, 1930, to Frank Charles Carlucci, Jr., and Roxanne Bacon. As a boy, he was recognized as a tough, natural leader who in time became known for his prowess on the wrestling mat. Carlucci graduated from Princeton University in 1952. Upon graduation, he was commissioned an officer in the U.S. Naval Reserve. He was discharged at the rank of lieutenant (junior grade) in 1954. He began graduate studies at the Harvard University School of Business in 1956. That same year, he became a foreign service officer with the U.S. STATE DEPARTMENT.

Carlucci's first posting was to Johannesburg, South Africa, in 1957. There he served as vice consul and economic officer for nearly three years. In 1960, Carlucci was sent to the Congo (modern Zaire), where he served as second secretary and political officer in Kinshasa (formerly Léopoldville).

Located in central Africa, northeast of Angola, the Congo had been a Belgian colony for over a half-century. When the country gained its independence on June 30, 1960, hostile factions began grappling for political control, chief among them the Congo National Movement, under the charismatic, though somewhat unpredictable, Patrice Emery Lumumba.

No place in the country was safe that first year; in one instance, Carlucci was nearly killed. Seeing his daughter being threatened with a bayonet, he dashed to her rescue but was himself stabbed and arrested. He later directed an evacuation of Europeans and Americans from that country.

In early 1961, Lumumba was arrested and executed by rival forces. (Years later, unfounded rumors that Carlucci had had a hand in Lumumba's death surfaced. Carlucci has adamantly denied them, pointing out that "young junior officers are not in the habit of deciding on assassination attempts.")

In 1962, Carlucci was promoted to officer in charge of Congolese Political Affairs. He left the Congo in 1964 to accept the post of consul general in Zanzibar. In 1965, he was made counselor for political affairs in Rio de Janeiro, Brazil, a post he held for the next four years.

When Richard Nixon entered the White House in 1969, Carlucci returned to the United States, where he served in a variety of domestic-policy posts. Initially, he worked as assistant director of operations for the White House Office of Economic Opportunity (OEO). In that capacity, he served under future wartime secretaries of

Defense Secretary Frank Carlucci   (AP PHOTO/IRA SCHWARZ)

defense Richard B. "Dick" Cheney (also a future vice president) and Donald H. Rumsfeld.

In 1970, Carlucci became director of the OEO. He then served in three positions with future secretary of defense Caspar W. Weinberger: first as associate director of the Office of Management and Budget (OMB), in 1971; then as deputy director of the OMB, in 1972; and finally as undersecretary of the Department of Health, Education, and Welfare, a post he would hold from 1972 to 1974. In 1975, he returned to foreign service when President Gerald Ford appointed him U.S. ambassador to Portugal, a position he held for the next three years, including reappointment by Ford's successor, President Jimmy Carter.

In 1978, Carter appointed Carlucci to the post of DEPUTY DIRECTOR OF CENTRAL INTELLIGENCE (DDCI). He served in that capacity from February 10, 1978, until February 5, 1981. It was during his tenure as DDCI that Carlucci, serving under DIRECTOR OF CENTRAL INTELLIGENCE (DCI) STANSFIELD TURNER, was allegedly involved in gutting the Agency's covert-action capabilities (i.e., spies and special operatives on the ground)—an allegation that became a hot topic in the weeks following the SEPTEMBER 11, 2001, TERRORIST ATTACKS ON THE UNITED STATES.

Some media-hired defense analysts argued that had the CIA retained its covert-action capabilities, America might have been forewarned of a terrorist plan to strike. Defenders of the Turner-Carlucci years have argued that it was overwrought congressional scrutiny following the CHURCH and PIKE COMMITTEE hearings that eradicated the Agency's ability to conduct covert operations.

When Ronald Reagan entered the White House in 1981, he appointed Weinberger secretary of defense and Carlucci as deputy secretary. In 1982, Carlucci left the Department of Defense for the private sector, where he served as president and then chairman and chief executive officer of Sears World Trade, Inc.

In 1986, during the IRAN-CONTRA SCANDAL (an illegal U.S. government transaction wherein weapons were secretly sold to Iran in exchange for hostages, with proceeds from those sales funneled to American-supported contra rebels, who were attempting to overthrow the Nicaraguan government), Carlucci was asked to return to Washington. There he replaced Admiral John M. Poindexter as National Security Advisor. Carlucci appointed U.S. Army general Colin Powell (future chairman of the JOINT CHIEFS OF STAFF and a future secretary of state) as his deputy. In 1987, Weinberger resigned. Carlucci became secretary of defense, a post he would hold until 1989, and Powell became NATIONAL SECURITY ADVISOR.

Carlucci returned to private business in 1989, accepting a vice chairmanship with the Washington, D.C.–based Carlyle Group, a merchant bank founded in 1987 as a private global investment firm. In 1993, he was named chairman.

Carlucci has earned three honorary doctorates. His government service awards include, among others, the State Department's Superior Service Award, the Superior Honor Award, the Defense Department's Distinguished Civilian Award, the Distinguished Intelligence Medal, the National Intelligence Distinguished Service Medal, the Presidential Citizens Award, the Woodrow Wilson Award, the James Forrestal Memorial Award, and the George C. Marshall Award.

See also CONGO, OPERATIONS IN THE.

Carver, George A., Jr. (ca. 1930–   )

A retired CIA officer, George A. Carver, Jr., is best known as a witness for the plaintiff in the libel suit brought by General William C. Westmoreland against CBS in 1984.

Born (around 1930) in Shanghai, China, where his father was chairman of the English Department at the University of Shanghai, Carver spent most of his boyhood in the Far East. He graduated from Yale University.

Carver joined the CIA in 1962 and returned to Asia as an officer in the Agency's Far East Division. In this capacity, he served as special assistant to the director for Vietnamese affairs from 1966 to 1973. He was a realist, and unlike many of his peers he was somewhat pessimistic about America's involvement in Vietnam. His prepared assessments suggested that the war was "unwinnable," was being "clumsily prosecuted," and that the bombing of North Vietnam was having little, if any, effect on the Communists' ability to wage war.

However, Carver's pessimism diminished over time. In 1967, a dispute arose between the CIA and U.S. Army intelligence personnel over enemy strength figures to be used in a NATIONAL INTELLIGENCE ESTIMATE (NIE). Carver sided with the Army, which was of the opinion that local Vietcong self-defense units did not represent a significant element of the enemy's overall strength.

Near the end of the war, Carver served as NATIONAL SECURITY COUNCIL aide to President Richard Nixon. He also chaired the White House Special Action Group's (WSAG) Indochina Subcommittee on Strategic Intelligence. He retired from the Agency in 1979.

In 1984, Carver testified as a witness for General William Childs Westmoreland, the plaintiff in a libel case against CBS, several CBS employees, and former CIA officer Samuel Adams. Westmoreland, who commanded American and allied forces in Vietnam from 1964 and 1968, had sued the defendants after CBS aired a television documentary, *The Uncounted Enemy: A Vietnam Deception,* that suggested that Westmoreland had deliberately lied about North Vietnamese troop strength between 1966 and

1968. The case was settled out of court in 1985, with both sides claiming victory.

In retirement, Carver founded C&S Associates, a consulting firm. He also held a senior fellowship at Georgetown University's Center for Strategic and International Studies.

See also SOUTHEAST ASIA, OPERATIONS IN.

case officer

A case officer is a CIA employee in a foreign country who is responsible for managing and directing agents (assets) in the field. Case officers are sometimes referred to as "operations officers."

Casey, William Joseph (1913–1987)

Author, attorney, entrepreneur, and intelligence chief, William Joseph "Bill" Casey was one of the CIA's most brilliant—albeit autocratic—directors, and he was responsible for one of the most aggressive expansions in Agency history. But he wasn't without his detractors.

Casey was born in the Elmhurst neighborhood of Queens, New York, on March 13, 1913, to William J. Casey and Blanche La Vigne. He attended Fordham University, where he graduated with a B.S. degree in 1934. He studied briefly at the Catholic University of America, and in 1937 he earned his law degree from St. Johns University. Casey then took a job with the Washington, D.C.–based Research Institute of America, where he was tasked with—and exhibited an uncanny talent for—absorbing and then rewriting complicated federal regulations into public guidebooks for conducting business with the U.S. government.

When America entered World War II in late 1941, Casey briefly went to work for the Bureau of Economic Warfare. He then obtained a commission as a lieutenant (junior grade) in the U.S. Navy and was posted to the Navy's Office of Procurement.

WILLIAM J. "WILD BILL" DONOVAN recruited Casey into the OFFICE OF STRATEGIC SERVICES (OSS), the wartime predecessor organization to the CIA, after the two met and became fast friends at a cocktail party. Casey had no experience in espionage, and his eyesight was too poor for field work. But his energy and natural cognitive abilities so impressed Donovan that he made him chief of intelligence in London (officially, the OSS Secretariat for the European Theater of Operations).

Casey, a spy-novel enthusiast, was a quick study in the mysterious world of espionage, and he relished his new role in the OSS. He worked tirelessly throughout the war, creating solid personal alliances with British intelligence officers, mastering the art of intelligence analysis, and organizing and supervising complex clandestine opera-

tions in Europe. Years later, he would tell British prime minister Margaret Thatcher that he had learned everything he knew about foreign intelligence work from his British counterparts during the war. When the war ended, Casey briefly headed American intelligence in Europe, working with several former Nazis, including REINHARD GEHLEN, a former Nazi intelligence officer who had become head of the West German intelligence service.

Back in the States, Casey amassed a small fortune as a tax attorney and an investor. He taught tax law at New York University from 1948 to 1962. He authored numerous "how to" books and articles on business and entrepreneurism, including *The Lawyers' Desk Book* (1965), *Tax Sheltered Investments* (1952), *The Estate Planning Book* (1956), *Forms of Business Agreements* (1966), and *The Accounting Desk Book* (1967). Casey is credited with coining the term "tax shelter." In addition to his business publications, Casey wrote histories of both the American Revolution and his service in the OSS. In 1966, he ran an unsuccessful campaign for a seat in the U.S. Congress.

Throughout the 1970s, Casey held a myriad of public posts, including chairman of the Securities and Exchange Commission (1971–73), undersecretary of state for economic affairs (1973–74), and president of the U.S. Export-Import Bank (1974–75). In 1976, he became a member of the FOREIGN INTELLIGENCE ADVISORY BOARD.

A conservative Republican with close ties to both the Nixon and Ford presidencies, Casey served as Ronald Reagan's national campaign manager during the future president's race for the White House in 1980. When Reagan assumed office in 1981, he appointed Casey DIRECTOR OF CENTRAL INTELLIGENCE (DCI), granting him cabinet-level status and broad powers to revitalize the CIA (no other DCI would be granted cabinet-level status, thus keeping them out of the White House policy-making loop, until President Bill Clinton appointed DR. JOHN M. DEUTCH as DCI in 1995).

In *Presidents' Secret Wars,* John Prados writes, "There has never been a closer team of President and DCI than Ronald Reagan and William J. Casey. No director of Central Intelligence ever spent as much time with a president as did Casey in the first year of the administration." CIA projects and assets had been drastically reduced under President Jimmy Carter, and Reagan was determined to restore the Agency's waning credibility and effectiveness.

Casey approached his new job with the same zeal with which he had tackled his OSS duties during the 1940s. Throughout the Reagan years, Casey increased the number of CIA employees by more than 2,500, creating new jobs and rehiring most of the 820 officers who had been dismissed during the Carter administration. He approved construction of a million-square-foot addition to the Agency's headquarters complex in LANGLEY, VIRGINIA.

William Casey meeting with President Ronald Reagan (RONALD REAGAN LIBRARY)

Also, he stepped up the number of covert operations in regional hotspots around the world.

With the escalation of global terrorism, there was strong public support for Casey's expansion efforts. Congress, historically leery of the CIA, approved substantial budget increases during the 1980s. In 1986, Casey established a Counterterrorism Center (CTC) under the DIRECTORATE of Operations. In an attempt to support the Reagan doctrine of opposing communist-supported wars of liberation in the developing world, Casey began focusing on the defeat of communist armies and insurgents from Afghanistan to Angola to Central America.

Despite his creditable revitalization of the CIA, Casey's career and life ended with a number of unanswered questions in a controversy known as IRAN-CONTRA. The affair, wherein American weapons were illegally sold to Iran in exchange for hostages, with profits being used to support Nicaraguan rebels (contras), once again exposed the Agency to harsh criticism. It threatened to topple the Reagan presidency. Marine Corps lieutenant colonel Oliver North, an obscure NATIONAL SECURITY COUNCIL (NSC) staffer who had directed the arms sales to Iran, testified before a congressional inquiry that Casey had master-

minded the entire project. But just before Casey was to testify, in December 1986, he was stricken with brain cancer. He died the following May in Glen Cove, New York, taking his secrets to the grave. He was 73.

Iran-contra notwithstanding, the Center for Security Policy, a Washington, D.C.–based national-security think tank, recognized Casey's achievements by posthumously presenting him its *Freedom Flame* award in 1996. That same year, the center created the William J. Casey Institute, to stimulate debate with respect to the intersection of international economics, trade, finance, energy, and technology developments with traditional U.S. national security policy. The center also created the Casey Medal of Honor.

Castelli, Leo (1907–1999)

Leo Castelli is considered in many circles to be the most important influence in the world of American art during the second half of the 20th century. Few know that he was also an intelligence operative who worked with the OFFICE OF STRATEGIC SERVICES (OSS), the World War II predecessor organization to the CIA.

Castelli was born in Trieste, Italy, on September 4, 1907, the son of Ernest Krauss, a banker from Hungary, and Bianca Castelli, daughter of the prominent Castellis of Trieste. At that time, Trieste was part of the Austro-Hungarian Empire. When Trieste was annexed by Italy in 1919, Castelli changed his name from Krauss to Krauss-Castelli. He eventually dropped the Krauss and became known simply as Castelli.

Though a marginal math student, young Castelli was noticeably bright. He learned to read and write fluently in Italian, English, French, German, and Greek. He also developed a passion for art history. In 1924, he earned a law degree from the University of Milan. He then returned to Trieste, where he accepted a position at an insurance company. In 1932, he was transferred to Bucharest, Romania. In 1937, he moved to Paris, where he briefly worked for a bank. In Paris, Castelli befriended several contemporary surrealist artists, including Salvador Dali and Max Ernst. Such contacts enabled Castelli to cofound (with architect/designer René Drouin) an art gallery on the Place Vendôme, the Galerie René Drouin, in 1939.

However, when World War II erupted in Europe, Castelli, who was Jewish, left for the United States. He settled in New York City in 1941. From 1942 to 1943, he attended Columbia University, taking graduate art courses. Castelli was soon drafted into the U.S. Army, where his language skills attracted the attention of the OSS. He was transferred from the Army to the OSS and dispatched to Bucharest. Following his service, Castelli was granted U.S. citizenship. He then returned to New York, where his father-in-law arranged a job for him with a sweater-manufacturing company. Castelli purchased and sold art during his free time. By 1951, he was involved in the establishment of the famed New York School.

Throughout the 1950s and 1960s, Castelli discovered and promoted such emerging artists as Jasper Johns, Robert Rauschenberg, Frank Stella, Cy Twombly, Andy Warhol, Roy Lichtenstein, Claes Oldenburg, and James Rosenquist. He also established one of the most respected galleries for pop art in New York, the Leo Castelli Gallery. "While he did not single-handedly transform the American art world, Leo Castelli did more than any other individual to see to it that American art was appreciated both here and abroad," wrote Tom DiEgidio in an article for Salon.com. "It seems perhaps improbable that this should have been accomplished by a suave, reticent European ladies' man who often downplayed his own importance. But perhaps it was a job that could only be pulled off by a literary, mercantile, polyglot, Jewish, Italian, Austro-Hungarian, banking, lawyering, art-dealing veteran of the OSS."

Castelli's career awards include the Chevalier de l'Ordre Nationale de la Légion d'Honneur (France); the New York City Mayor's Award of Honor for Arts and Culture; the Manhattan Cultural Awards Prize; the Bowery Savings Bank Distinguished New Yorker Award; the Butler Medal, from the Butler Institute of American Art; the Adam Elsheimer Preis Award, from the City of Frankfurt, Germany; the Academy Award, from the American Academy; and the Medal of Honor for Citizenship, from the City of Arles, France. He also received honorary doctorate degrees from the New York City School of Visual Arts and Brenau University in Georgia.

Castelli died in New York City on August 21, 1999. He was just shy of 92.

Castro Ruz, Fidel Alejandro (1926–)

A thorn in America's southern flank since becoming the leader of Cuba in 1959, Fidel Alejandro Castro Ruz evolved into one of the most colorful and charismatic political leaders of the second half of the 20th century and the beginning of the next. His distinctive beard, army fatigues, and perpetual cigar are recognizable by schoolchildren throughout the world. But the survivability and political acumen of this communist revolutionary has baffled his opponents for decades, not the least of whom has been the CIA.

Born near Biran, Cuba, on August 13, 1926, to Angel Castro Argiz, a Jesuit-educated Spanish immigrant and sugar cane farmer, and Angel's housekeeper, Lina Ruz González, young Castro was one of seven children growing up in a strict Roman Catholic household. As a boy, he attended a Catholic boarding school near his home in Cuba's eastern backcountry, where he quickly developed a reputation as an outstanding athlete and a lover of history. He attended Belén High School in Havana. In 1945, he entered the University of Havana's School of Law.

When he was a college student, Castro's insurrectionist spirit began to manifest itself in overt attacks on his political opponents. At the University of Havana, he organized a number of violence-prone political groups, and in 1947 he participated in a failed effort to overthrow General Rafael Trujillo, the president of the Dominican Republic. In 1948, he was directly involved in a series of urban riots in Bogotá, Colombia.

But it was after graduating from law school in 1950 that Castro began to make a name for himself among Central America's revolutionary factions. Castro joined the "Ortodoxos," a radical Cuban Peoples Party, and he became a practicing attorney. He also became a candidate for a seat in Cuba's House of Representatives, campaigning for the election of June 1952. But the election was not to be.

In March, General Fulgencio Batista y Zaldívar, a former Cuban president, toppled the government of President Carlos Prios Socarras, and scrapped the June election. Castro attempted to remove Batista through litigation, and when his efforts failed, he organized a rebel army. On July 26, 1953, he led 160 followers in an attack on the Moncada Military Barracks, in the town of Santiago. He was counting on a people's uprising to aid in the ousting of Batista. Instead, the attack failed. Most of the men were killed, and their 27-year-old commander was arrested.

After a brilliant legal defense, he proclaimed, "Condemn me. It does not matter. History will absolve me." Castro, however, evaded the death penalty when the local Roman Catholic bishop interceded on his behalf. Sentenced to a prison term of 15 years, he was granted amnesty in 1955.

Castro then went to Mexico to begin planning his next campaign. It was there that he met the infamous Argentinian revolutionary ERNESTO "CHE" GUEVARA. Castro also spent a brief period in the United States raising funds for his cause. Declaring those killed in the Moncada Barracks attack to be martyrs, he organized the "July 26 Movement," an organization of Cuban exiles with the goal of overthrowing Batista.

On December 2, 1956, Castro and some 80 armed men landed on a stretch of Cuban coastline not far from his birthplace and almost immediately clashed with Batista's forces. The Castro forces were defeated. Only a handful survived, including Castro, his brother Raúl, and Guevara, all of whom escaped into the Sierra Maestra. Over the next three years, Castro waged a successful guerrilla war against Batista's 30,000-man army with less than 1,000 of his own fighters, at peak strength.

His army demoralized and political support crumbling, Batista fled Cuba on January 1, 1959. Two days later, Manuel Urritia was installed as president, and Castro was named commander in chief of the armed forces.

Soon after the Batista ouster, the U.S. government officially recognized the new Cuban government. But relations between the two nations quickly began to deteriorate. In February, Castro declared himself prime minister. He had initially proclaimed that he was opposed to communism; during an April visit to the United States, he laid wreaths at the memorials of Jefferson and Lincoln. In addition, as a gesture of positive relations and in support of mutual prosperity, American-based businesses in Cuba advanced some $1.5 million in future taxes to the Cuban coffers.

But word soon began to spread that Castro's inner circle was executing hundreds of former Batista officials whom they accused of war crimes. The trials were conducted in a circuslike atmosphere, with defendants being herded before the members of a revolutionary tribunal who shouted accusations and then sentenced most to death. Firing squads were averaging close to 30 executions per week. Both the American and Mexican press were having a field day, the U.S. Congress issued sharp condemnations, and tens of thousands of Cubans began fleeing to Miami, Florida.

In July, Castro forced Urritia to resign. This move essentially granted Castro power for life. He had the support of the Catholic Church and the unwavering loyalty of the Cuban armed forces. He also turned to the local communist party for support and assistance in organizing the labor unions.

In his book *Fidel Castro,* Robert E. Quirk contends that despite Castro's initial inclination toward a Western-style democracy, he began to believe that the only true path to reform was communism. "If Fidel Castro would not allow a Western-style democracy, with representative institutions freely chosen by the people, or an economic system characterized by private enterprise, competition, and profit incentives, there seemed to be no alternative but Marxism," wrote Quirk. "It had become clear too that the communists, no democrats themselves, were perfectly willing to see Fidel Castro continue as Maximum Leader for the rest of his life. They praised him unconscionably. They never criticized or complained, and if the United States refused to aid the Cubans, the Soviets could provide both economic and military assistance. Before the end of 1959 Castro was willing to believe that the road map to Cuba's New Jerusalem might be found in the covers of *Das Kapital.*"

Like Guatemala under Jacobo Arbenz Guzmán, and Iran under Dr. Mohammad Mossadegh, Castro began instituting a number of sweeping economic reforms that rattled foreign investors. Chief among the reforms was the expropriation of private American land holdings and an oil agreement with the Soviet Union.

Meanwhile, the CIA began implementing plans for either an assassination of Castro or a Cuban counterrevolution based on the Guatemalan model. The United States also launched a trade embargo against Cuba.

On January 3, 1961, the United States severed diplomatic relations with Cuba. Four months later, over 1,500 Cuban exiles began hitting the beaches along Cuba's southwestern coastline in a CIA-sponsored operation known as OPERATION ZAPATA, or the BAYS OF PIGS INVASION. Doomed from the start, the invasion was crushed by Castro in three days. Though it was both a strategic and moral victory for the Cuban president, the outcome had less to do with Castro's combat talents than with the CIA's inability to assess the willingness of the Cuban people to rise up against Castro and President John Kennedy's failure to provide previously promised air and naval gunfire support for the émigrés on the ground.

In November, in the wake of the failed invasion, Kennedy gave the CIA authorization to begin a covert-action project, code-named OPERATION MONGOOSE, aimed at removing Castro from power. The project included sabotage, paramilitary operations, psychological warfare, direct U.S. military intervention, and even the assassination of Castro himself.

Castro began acquiring weapons from the Soviet Union, and in October 1962 American U-2 spy planes photographed Soviet ballistic missiles capable of delivering nuclear warheads positioned on launching sites in Cuba. The weapons, which threatened most of the southeastern United States, forced Kennedy to consider an immediate invasion of Cuba. Instead, the president opted for a naval blockade of the island nation and threatened war if the Soviets attempted to deliver additional offensive weapons.

After 13 days of intense back-and-forth negotiations during which the two superpowers came dangerously close to a nuclear confrontation, Soviet premier Nikita Khrushchev blinked. He ordered Soviets ships loaded with missiles and bound for Cuba to return to the USSR. He also agreed to remove previously stationed missiles and halt work on existing missile sites in Cuba, if Kennedy would promise never to invade Cuba and also to remove U.S. ballistic missiles stationed in Turkey. Kennedy agreed. Castro felt betrayed, but the CUBAN MISSILE CRISIS was over. Operation MONGOOSE was also terminated, though assassination planning continued for another three years.

According to findings revealed during the Senate CHURCH COMMITTEE hearings in 1975, the CIA was involved in no less than eight government-authorized plots to assassinate Castro from 1960 to 1965. Apparently, however, none of the plots moved far enough beyond the planning stages to make an actual attempt to kill the Cuban president. The alleged plots to kill Castro included lacing a box of his favorite cigars with botulism so potent that it would kill him as soon as he put one in his mouth, and injecting him with botulism from a hypodermic needle concealed in a ballpoint pen. The cigars were given to one of the CIA's Cuban agents, who claimed he could get them to Castro. The pen was presented to another, who requested something "more sophisticated." Neither attempt materialized.

A CIA-Mafia plot was also hatched; it progressed beyond the planning stages, but with no results. Unlike the KGB, the CIA had no internal corps of trained assassins. Consequently, the Agency's WET WORK had to be subcontracted. For the task of killing Castro, the CIA's deputy director of plans (operations) RICHARD M. BISSELL, JR., decided to commission the Mafia. Bissell asked Sheffield Edwards, the CIA's security director, to approach Johnny Roselli about the job. Roselli, who had once been one of Al Capone's chief lieutenants, called upon fellow Mafiosos Salvatore "Sam" Giancana and Santos Trafficante. Giancana was on the FBIs 10-most-wanted list.

Trafficante was the head of La Cosa Nostra's Cuban interests.

Bissell proposed a guns-blazing, gangland-style assassination. The CIA was willing to pay $150,000 for the job; Bissell believed that if gangsters handled the project, there would be little chance of its being traced back to the Agency. After all, the Mafia's lucrative prostitution and gambling works in Havana had been quashed after Castro seized power from Batista. Therefore, Bissell surmised, the motivation to kill him must be there. Indeed, it was. The Mafia counterproposed a "poison pill" hit. The Agency agreed. Pills were allegedly sent to Cuba, but Castro never ingested any.

Additionally, the Agency considered planting explosive devices inside unusual-looking sea shells and then placing them along the seafloor near one of Castro's favorite diving spots. If, during one of his treasure seeking jaunts, Castro were to pick up one of the shells, the device would detonate and either kill or cripple him. Another plan was to infect Castro's diving suit with a fungus and his scuba breathing tubes with a particularly virulent strain of tuberculosis. Outrageous schemes aimed at discrediting Castro—thus "assassinating" his character—were also considered, including spraying his broadcast studio or impregnating his cigars with a hallucinogen, like LSD, just before he was to give a speech, dusting his shoes with potent thallium salts to make his beard fall out, or initiating rumors that Castro was the anti-Christ.

In February 1963, the Kennedy administration announced that American citizens would be prohibited from traveling to, and making financial transactions with, Cuba. Castro then began taking measures to strengthen his own political base. Organizing his government into a one-party dictatorship, he effectively eradicated all internal opposition to his power. This forced a swell of Cuban immigration to the United States.

In 1976, Castro established a Cuban National Assembly, of which he proclaimed himself president. He dropped the title of "premier" but retained his positions as secretary general of the Communist Party and commander in chief of the armed forces. Cuban troops began assisting other communist causes throughout Latin America and the world, including Angola (1975–89), Ethiopia (1978), and Nicaragua (1979). In 1980, Castro released a flood of some 125,000 immigrants—including mental patients and jailed criminals—to the United States, during the infamous "Mariel boatlift."

The 1991 collapse of the Soviet Union isolated Castro both politically and economically. As a result Castro began to warm up to the idea of greater economic freedom, allowing some free market restraints to be loosened in Cuba. After his daughter sought asylum in the United States in 1993, he lifted restrictions on Cubans wanting to leave the island.

Fidel Castro   (NATIONAL ARCHIVE)

Speaking before a group of Canadian and American religious leaders in 1996, Castro said, "We have also lived through a huge moral fast for over 35 years, a moral fast imposed by those trying to destroy our Revolution, those who have tried to starve us to death and hinder any kind of progress in our country."

For 50 years, Castro's resiliency has baffled his opponents. No targeted foreign leader in the history of American central intelligence has been as fortunate in evading death, the toppling of his or her government, or simply the assassination of his or her character as has Fidel Castro. Today, in his 70s and with his Soviet power base gone, Castro, once called the "guerrilla prince" of the Western Hemisphere, is not nearly as threatening to American interests in the region as he was during the height of the cold war. He remains committed to Cuba and to his Marxist-Leninist ideology. To many Latin Americans, he is a symbol of revolutionary triumph.

See also ASSASSINATION PLOTS.

Central Imagery Office (CIO)

The Central Imagery Office (CIO), a joint activity between the U.S. INTELLIGENCE COMMUNITY and the DEPARTMENT OF DEFENSE (DoD), is designated as a combat support agency under the DoD. Established in 1992 by the DIRECTOR OF CENTRAL INTELLIGENCE (DCI) and the secretary of defense, the CIO is responsible for ensuring responsive imagery support to the intelligence community and other key departments and agencies of the federal government. The CIO is also responsible for ensuring that timely imagery support is made available to American military commanders in the field.

In order to accomplish its mission, the CIO develops techniques, recommends courses of action, and implements policy that pertains to the tasking, collection, processing, exploitation, and dissemination of imagery (all products of reconnaissance that provide a likeness of any natural or manmade feature or related objective or activity). The CIO also tasks the national imagery-collection assets of the Intelligence Community and DoD, in accordance with intelligence requirements established by the DCI during periods of peace, and by the secretary of defense in wartime.

As a member of the U.S. Intelligence Community, the CIO is ultimately overseen by the DCI.

Central Intelligence Agency (CIA)

Though the American intelligence community traces its lineage back to the American Revolution, no centrally controlled federal intelligence organization existed until the beginning of World War II. No permanent intelligence agency appeared until two years after the close of hostilities.

When the Japanese attacked Pearl Harbor in late 1941, the only centrally controlled U.S. intelligence entity was WILLIAM J. "WILD BILL" DONOVAN's marginally staffed OFFICE OF THE COORDINATOR OF INFORMATION (COI), which had been established only four months prior. Previous intelligence and counterintelligence efforts had fallen under the respective domains of the Departments of Navy and War and the FEDERAL BUREAU OF INVESTIGATION (FBI). But those efforts had suffered from poor coordination, duplication of services, and sometimes rabid organizational rivalries.

On June 13, 1942, President Franklin Roosevelt redesignated the COI as the OFFICE OF STRATEGIC SERVICES (OSS). The latter, which quickly morphed into one of history's most famous intelligence/counterintelligence organizations, is often referred to as the direct predecessor of the Central Intelligence Agency. However, the OSS was dissolved in October 1945, its services transferred to other government entities; a CENTRAL INTELLIGENCE GROUP (CIG) was established in January 1946. On September 18, 1947, the NATIONAL SECURITY ACT reorganized America's defenses and established a Central

Intelligence Agency (CIA) under a new NATIONAL SECURITY COUNCIL (NSC).

Today, the CIA is an enormous federal bureaucracy, employing an estimated 12,000–14,000 field officers, analysts, administrators, scientists, and technicians. As one of the world's most highly regarded, though sometimes controversial, agencies, the CIA is also the single cabinet-level agency responsible for the tasks of engaging in, coordinating, developing, and disseminating global intelligence and COUNTERINTELLIGENCE, as well as participating in covert special operations and even diplomatic missions outside of the United States.

Uncompromising performance of these tasks on the part of the CIA ensures that "the intelligence consumer—whether Washington policymaker or battlefield commander—receives the best intelligence possible." Headquartered at the GEORGE BUSH CENTER FOR INTELLIGENCE in LANGLEY, VIRGINIA, the CIA advises the NSC and other executive-branch agencies concerning all foreign intelligence matters. It also coordinates U.S. intelligence activities, and, as an independent source of intelligence analysis, provides support to other agencies.

The CIA is the "hub" of an expansive intelligence network referred to as the U.S. INTELLIGENCE COMMUNITY, which includes the Agency itself, the Federal Bureau of Investigation, the NATIONAL SECURITY AGENCY, the NATIONAL RECONNAISSANCE OFFICE, the NATIONAL IMAGERY AND MAPPING AGENCY, the DEPARTMENT OF THE TREASURY, the DEPARTMENT OF ENERGY, the DEPARTMENT OF STATE, the DEFENSE INTELLIGENCE AGENCY, ARMY INTELLIGENCE, NAVAL INTELLIGENCE, MARINE CORPS INTELLIGENCE, and AIR FORCE INTELLIGENCE.

In recent years, the Agency has tailored its traditional intelligence services for policy makers, key agencies, and major military commands. For instance, a number of multidisciplinary centers within the Agency have been created to address high-priority issues. These centers include special staffs for nonproliferation, counterterrorism, counterintelligence, international organized crime, narcotics trafficking, environment, and arms control.

For most of its existence, the CIA has comprised four primary DIRECTORATES: the Directorate of Administration, the Directorate of Intelligence, the Directorate of Operations (until 1973, the Directorate of Plans), and the Directorate of Science and Technology. However, on June 4, 2001, the Directorate of Administration was "abolished" and its functions centralized in five entities—Information Technology, Finance, Security, Global Support, and Human Resources—under the CIA's Executive Board. The heads of each entity are on a par with the leaders of the Agency's three primary directorates.

Though it is the first permanent American intelligence organization, the CIA is directly descended from four predecessor organizations, including the COI, which existed from 1941 to 1942; the OSS, which existed from 1942 to 1945; the STRATEGIC SERVICES UNIT (SSU) and collateral offices under the Departments of State and War, which existed from 1945 to 1946; and the CIG, which existed from 1946 to 1947.

Some of the CIA's current foreign parallel organizations include MI6 (United Kingdom), SVR (Russia), MOSSAD (Israel), DGSE (France), and CSIS (Canada).

Central Intelligence Group (CIG)

The Central Intelligence Group (CIG) was the short-lived interim intelligence organization that bridged the gap between the abolition of the OFFICE OF STRATEGIC SERVICES (OSS) in 1945 and the creation of the modern CIA in 1947. America's first postwar intelligence group and the direct predecessor of the CIA, the CIG was established under the NATIONAL INTELLIGENCE AUTHORITY (NIA) by presidential directive on January 22, 1946.

The directive issued to the secretaries of state, war, and navy by President Harry Truman created the NIA and the CIG and outlined the general responsibilities of both entities. Truman's directive ordered the three secretaries to assign "from time to time" personnel and facilities from their respective departments to a "Central Intelligence Group" under an appointed DIRECTOR OF CENTRAL INTELLIGENCE (DCI) in order to assist the NIA. The CIG was responsible for planning and coordinating foreign intelligence activities.

In the spring of 1946, the NIA began dismantling the STRATEGIC SERVICES UNIT (SSU, the descendant organization of the OSS's operational arm). Some of the SSU's components were assigned to the CIG. Others were assigned to the War Department. The SSU was officially abolished on October 19, 1946.

As necessary as the CIG was during the early days of the COLD WAR, Truman was reluctant to establish such a group. After all, the consensus was that peacetime espionage activities were unfair, hence "un-American."

In his book *For the President's Eyes Only,* author Christopher Andrew describes Truman's formal celebration of the CIG as a "notably eccentric White House lunch." That it was. The attending guests received black cloaks, matching hats, and toy daggers. Truman then called Admiral William Leahy forward and pressed a large black moustache above his upper lip. The president then somewhat condescendingly proclaimed ADMIRAL SIDNEY WILLIAM SOUERS as the "Director of Centralized Snooping." Souers was in fact the CIG's first DCI.

Both the CIG and the NIA were abolished by the National Security Act of 1947, which created the CIA. In its 13-month existence, the CIG was headed by two DCIs:

first Souers, then Air Force lieutenant general HOYT SAN-FORD VANDENBERG.

See also NATIONAL SECURITY ACT OF 1947.

Central Intelligence Retirees Association (CIRA)

The Central Intelligence Retirees Association (CIRA) is an exclusive, nationwide organization of retired Agency employees. Founded in 1979, CIRA is an apolitical association that exists only as a social entity for its 3,200 members. CIRA maintains 14 chapters, coast to coast.

See also ASSOCIATION OF FORMER INTELLIGENCE OFFICERS.

CHAOS, Operation

Operation CHAOS was a CIA program of domestic spying on American citizens; it lasted for approximately 15 years. Initiated in 1959 under the administration of President Dwight Eisenhower, Operation CHAOS was a successful project in terms of information gathered. But the operation came under tremendous scrutiny as a perceived violation of an American citizen's right to privacy.

CHAOS escalated in 1965, when President Lyndon Johnson instructed DIRECTOR OF CENTRAL INTELLIGENCE (DCI) JOHN MCCONE to provide an independent analysis of the developing ideological movement against the Vietnam War. Johnson had previously relied on information provided by the FEDERAL BUREAU OF INVESTIGATION (FBI). But growing distrust between the president and FBI director J. EDGAR HOOVER impelled the former to order a second opinion of the situation by the CIA.

During CHAOS, the Agency compiled extensive individual profiles on tens of thousands of people and organizations, including files on more than 7,000 U.S. citizens and over 1,000 domestic groups.

CHAOS was revealed and abandoned as a result of the Senate CHURCH COMMITTEE investigations of 1975.

chief of outpost (COO)

A chief of outpost (COO) is a CIA officer in charge of one of the Agency's field offices in a foreign country. A field office is subordinate to a CIA station; thus the COO answers to the CHIEF OF STATION (COS) in his or her chain of command.

chief of station (COS)

A chief of station (COS) is a CIA officer in charge of one of the Agency's stations, usually in the capital city of a foreign country. To provide a natural cover and to ensure diplomatic immunity if arrested, a COS usually falls under the umbrella of an embassy's staff.

See also CHIEF OF OUTPOST.

Child, Julia McWilliams (1912–   )

Julia McWilliams Child is a best known as the culinary "queen mother" who turned American cookery on its head with her best-selling classic *Mastering the Art of French Cooking.* But few know that she was also an employee of the OFFICE OF STRATEGIC SERVICES (OSS), the World War II precursor organization to the CIA.

Born Julia McWilliams in Pasadena, California, on August 15, 1912, to John McWilliams and Julia Carolyn Weston McWilliams, the future Julia Child was recognized early on as a natural leader with a mischievous bent. As a young woman, she grew to a statuesque six feet two inches, a height that made her stand out from her peers. She had few dates, even fewer romantic relationships, but she was a fun-loving person with many friends. She graduated from Smith College in 1934. She then worked in the advertising department of W. & J. Sloane, a New York–based furniture store.

When World War II erupted, McWilliams (Child) joined the OSS. She wanted to be a spy but was instead made an office manager. Still, she had what she considered to be the adventure of sailing on troopships, sleeping on army cots, and wearing military fatigues. She was stationed first in Washington, D.C. She was then reassigned to Ceylon (modern Sri Lanka), where she met future husband, Paul Child, an OSS mapmaker. The couple was eventually transferred to China.

It was during her time in the OSS that Child developed an interest in the culinary arts. "Army food was terrible," she said during a 1997 interview for *Grand Times* magazine. "We were hungry, so we were interested in eating."

When the war ended, Child's husband was assigned to the U.S. Information Service office at the American embassy in Paris. There, Child, at 37, began her cooking career, at the famous Cordon Bleu. She took to cooking with a passion, and for the next 10 years she explored the kitchens and food markets of Europe—experimenting, learning, documenting, and eventually opening L'Ecole des Trois Gourmandes, a cooking school, with chefs Simone Beck and Louisette Bertholle. In 1961, Child's classic work, *Mastering the Art of French Cooking,* was published.

In early 1963, *The French Chef,* Child's first televised cooking program, aired. Some 200 episodes later, she decided to tackle contemporary American cuisine with a series of successful programs including *Julia Child and Company, Julia Child and More Company, Dinner at Julia's,*

Baking with Julia, Master Chefs, and *Julia and Jacques Cooking at Home,* with chef Jacques Pepin.

Child has published a number of cookbooks and cooking-related books. Her awards include a Peabody, an Emmy, the Ordre de Mérite Agricole (France), Ordre National de Mérite (France), the Ralph Lowell Award, the Corporation for Public Broadcasting Award, and the TV Cooking Show Award from the James Beard Foundation, among others.

Her classic programs still appear on the Food Network.

Chile, operations in

The decade between 1963 and 1973 was a period of tremendous activity for the CIA in Chile. According to the CHURCH COMMITTEE's findings in 1975, the Agency was involved in almost every major election during that time and at least one assassination.

The CIA's operations in Chile began in 1962, when the Agency received executive authorization to carry out covert-action projects in support of the pro-American Chilean Radical Party and Christian Democratic Party. The CIA projects, which were primarily antisocialist propaganda programs, were designed to assist the parties to attract larger followings, improve their organizational structures, and support American interests in the region. A secondary purpose of the CIA projects was to support efforts to split the Socialist Party in Chile.

In 1963, the 5412 GROUP, a special CIA covert-action branch, began funding propaganda efforts aimed at influencing selected Chilean radio stations and newspapers. As the Chilean national elections of 1964 drew close, those efforts were stepped up in an attempt to prevent Dr. Salvador Allende Gossens, a Marxist candidate for the presidency, from gaining power. Fortunately for the Agency, public opinion was swayed, and on September 4, 1964, Allende lost the election to Eduardo Frei, a pro-American Christian Democrat. In all, the 303 COMMITTEE (formerly the 5412 Group) approved over 3 million dollars to keep Allende from gaining the presidency.

With Frei in power, on February 5, 1965, the 303 Committee approved a new propaganda campaign aimed at supporting pro-American candidates for congressional elections in March. The campaign, considered a success, was terminated in June.

Throughout 1965 and 1966, the Agency continued its propaganda through the mass media in Chile. Those efforts helped shift public opinion against anti-American parties and candidates. In 1967, the CIA began promoting "anticommunist themes," specifically against the growing Soviet presence in the region. In 1968, an Agency-backed "propaganda workshop" was established to coordinate the work of agents, officers, and the local press.

The CIA's efforts in Chile continued with some success until 1969. But the socialists were steadily gaining ground. Allende emerged as the leading candidate for president in the upcoming 1970 election campaign, and several American-owned companies in Chile—including the International Telephone & Telegraph Corporation, Anaconda Copper, and Kennecott Copper—feared that they might be nationalized if he won.

In March, the 40 COMMITTEE, the successor to the 303 Committee, approved a second propaganda campaign aimed at preventing Allende from gaining the office. The committee directed officers in the field to conduct "spoiling operations" to thwart his campaign.

But unlike in 1964, the CIA lost. Allende won and became the first Marxist leader to achieve power through democratically held elections. However, Allende (with 36.3 percent of the vote) had not won an overwhelming majority of the votes; his conservative opponent Jorge Allesandri had received 34.9 percent. The Chilean constitution required that both houses of its congress choose between them. Allende being in the lead, it was assumed that he would be selected by the Chilean congress.

On September 15, President Richard Nixon summoned NATIONAL SECURITY ADVISOR Henry Kissinger, Attorney General John Mitchell, and DIRECTOR OF CENTRAL INTELLIGENCE (DCI) RICHARD MCGARRAH HELMS to a closed-door meeting in the Oval Office. Nixon began issuing orders and Helms took notes. "One in ten chance perhaps, but save Chile," Helms wrote, " . . . worth spending . . . not concerned risks involved . . . no involvement of Embassy . . . $10,000,000 available, more if necessary . . . full time job—best men we have . . . game plan . . . make the economy scream . . . 48 hours for plan of action."

The game plan, code-named PROJECT FUBELT, was divided into two options, or "tracks." Track I was an undetermined covert-action option wherein the CIA would find some way to persuade the Chilean congress not to vote Allende into office. Under Track I, the CIA suggested a plan in which the Congress would elect Allesandri, who would immediately resign. At that point, a second election would be held between Allende and Frei; this suggested plan was known as the "Rube Goldberg gambit." The Track II option was a military coup d'état, which the Agency hoped to avoid. In his book *For the President's Eyes Only,* Christopher Andrew states that Nixon "gave instructions that Track II, unlike Track I, was to be kept secret from State, Defense, and the Embassy in Santiago. Even the 40 Committee was not told. Probably only four officials in Chile and five at Langley knew of it."

Frei's high regard for the Chilean constitution compelled him to reject the Track II offer. The CIA's only other option was Track II, the military coup.

From October 5 through 20, CIA officers and agents orchestrated numerous contacts with key Chilean military and national police (Carabinero) officers to persuade them to carry out a coup. During that period, the U.S. embassy's military attaché was placed under operational control of the CIA station in Santiago. The attaché relayed similar messages to his own Chilean military contacts.

Chilean army general Roberto Viaux, who had led a minor insurrection in 1969, was viewed as a prime candidate to lead a coup. But against the advice of the CIA, Viaux and a group of pro-American Chilean military officers attempted to abduct General René Schneider, the Chilean army's commander in chief. Schneider was a staunch supporter of the Chilean constitution and an obstacle to any coup attempt. Schneider's car was ambushed on the morning of October 22; he drew his weapon and was gunned down. Schneider's death had an adverse reaction on the Chilean proponents of a coup; soldiers and civilians alike were shocked. Viaux was arrested, and the coup was effectively crushed before it could be launched. On October 24, the Chilean congress elected Allende.

For the next three years, the CIA continued to support propaganda efforts against Allende, spending upward of $6.5 million in support of opposition parties and candidates.

On September 11, 1973, Allende was killed and his government overthrown in a military coup led by General Augusto Pinochet. The Pinochet forces were not supported by the CIA. However, the CIA was aware of a plot, and there were "intelligence collection relationships" between the Agency and many of the coup planners. Chile's new government was a military junta that consisted of Pinochet, air force general Gustavo Leigh, navy admiral José Merino, and national police chief general Cesar Mendoza.

On the day following the coup, a decree was released to the public proclaiming the junta as Chile's "supreme power" and Pinochet as president. A verbal agreement was made between the four senior officers to rotate the office of president. Pinochet, however, quickly established a presidential advisory committee, staffing it with army officers loyal to himself. The committee abolished the concept of a rotating presidency, and Pinochet's power was consolidated.

In the ensuing months, CIA field officers working in concert with Pinochet's security forces became aware of a growing campaign of human-rights abuses against Pinochet's political enemies in the country. It was an awkward arrangement, wherein CIA operatives, whose primary purpose was to assist Pinochet's government in gathering intelligence on external targets, found that the Chilean forces were not concerned with combatting subversion and terrorism from abroad. Instead, Pinochet was attempting to eradicate internal opponents of his government, through persecution and physical torture. The U.S. intelligence community realized that the CIA's relationship with Pinochet might result in a public perception that the Agency somehow sanctioned the abuses. But in order to maintain an intelligence foothold in Chile, the CIA had to continue its relationship with Pinochet on the surface. The Agency, however, did suspend funding for covert action in Chile.

In January 1974, CIA officers and agents were ordered to report on human-rights violations by the Pinochet government. By June, all CIA covert-action plans for Chile had been officially terminated. Officers and agents, however, continued gathering intelligence in Chile.

Much of the CIA's involvement in Chile came to light during the Senate Church Committee hearings in 1975 (the committee was tasked with investigating previous illegal activities on the part of the CIA). Addressing the committee, U.S. SENATOR FRANK CHURCH stated, "The only plausible explanation for our intervention in Chile is the persistence of the myth that Communism is a single, hydra-headed serpent, and that it remains our duty to cut off each ugly head, wherever and however it may appear."

Chin, Larry Wu-Tai (ca. 1923–1986)

Larry Wu-Tai Chin was a retired CIA employee who in 1986 was convicted of espionage for the People's Republic of China.

A native of Beijing, China, Chin was recruited by communist intelligence operatives while attending college during the early 1940s. He became a naturalized citizen of the United States and worked with the U.S. Army's Liaison Office in China in 1943.

In 1952, he joined the CIA, serving with the Agency until 1981. During that time, Chin—who served in the CIA's FOREIGN BROADCAST INFORMATION SERVICE—provided the Chinese government with an untold amount of classified materials, receiving as much as a million dollars for his services. Among his actions, he purportedly removed secret documents from his office, photographed them, and presented the photographs to Chinese couriers at meetings in Toronto, Hong Kong, and London between 1976 and 1982. He also met with Asian-based Chinese intelligence officers as late as March 1985.

On November 22, 1985, Chin was arrested. He was subsequently indicted on 17 counts of espionage-related and income-tax violations. He admitted that he had provided the Chinese with information over a period of

11 years, but only for the purpose of reconciliation between the two nations.

On February 8, 1986, Chin was convicted on all counts. Sentencing was scheduled for March 17. The 63-year-old Chin, however, skirted formal punishment by committing suicide in his cell on February 21.

Church Committee

In the wake of the WATERGATE SCANDAL, allegations about CIA plots—some true, some false—began emerging in congressional circles and in the proverbial court of public opinion. As a result, on January 27, 1975 (the so-called YEAR OF INTELLIGENCE), the Senate established a 14-member fact-finding panel chaired by U.S. senator Frank Church (D-Idaho), to conduct investigations and hold hearings in an attempt to shed light on alleged abuses of power by the CIA and its domestic counterpart, the FEDERAL BUREAU OF INVESTIGATION (FBI).

Officially titled the "Select Committee to Study Governmental Operations with Respect to Intelligence Activities," the Church Committee conducted numerous interviews and held 60 days of open hearings into CIA activities worldwide, including possible Agency-sponsored ASSASSINATION PLOTS against foreign leaders, foreign coups d'état, unauthorized spying on American citizens, and a lack of governmental oversight. The committee accumulated over 110,000 pages of documentation, including 8,000 pages of sworn testimony. At its peak, the Church Commission had 155 staff members investigating the Agency.

Soon after the Senate launched its Church Committee investigations, the U.S. House of Representatives also began holding similar hearings, with a 10-member investigative panel chaired by Congressman Otis Pike (D-New York) and known as the PIKE COMMITTEE. Like the Church Committee, The Pike Committee subpoenaed current and former CIA employees to testify as to their knowledge of or participation in illegal activities sanctioned by the CIA.

Neither committee was able to establish proof that a successful CIA-sponsored assassination of any foreign leader had ever been committed, though it was revealed that aborted attempts had probably been made.

At the conclusion of the hearings, on April 26, 1976, the Church Committee issued a final report. The report, a six-volume treatise, made some 100 recommendations, including the curbing or complete elimination of illegal wiretaps, clandestine opening of mail, break-ins, surveillance, harassment of political dissidents, plots to assassinate political leaders, and campaigns to smear civil rights activists.

Church, who during the hearings referred to the CIA as a "rogue elephant on a rampage," appended the follow-

ing note to the committee's report: "Certainly we do not need a regiment of cloak-and-dagger men, earning their campaign ribbons—and, indeed, their promotions—by planning new exploits throughout the world. Theirs is a self-generating enterprise." He added, "I must lay the blame, in large measure, to the fantasy that it lay within our power to control other countries through the covert manipulation of their affairs. It formed part of a greater illusion that entrapped and enthralled our Presidents—the illusion of American omnipotence."

Both houses of Congress assumed responsibility for negligence in overseeing the previous activities of the CIA. As a direct result of the Church and Pike Committees, President Gerald Ford relieved WILLIAM COLBY of his position as DIRECTOR OF CENTRAL INTELLIGENCE (DCI). Ford believed that Colby had been too forthcoming with the FAMILY JEWELS, an Agency-generated list of its own misdeeds.

Colby was replaced with future U.S. president GEORGE BUSH—a nomination frowned upon by Church, who believed that Bush had connections with many members of the CIA's old guard. Ford also issued EXECUTIVE ORDER 11905, which clarified the authority and responsibilities of American intelligence departments and agencies—basically, who would do what. The order also restricted the means by which such agencies and departments could collect intelligence and conduct clandestine operations. In addition, the order established oversight measures to ensure compliance.

Despite the Church Commission's expressed intention to weed out the bad seeds and revive the Agency, Ford's opinion of the commission—specifically its chairman, Frank Church—was not wholly favorable. Indeed, the president held the senator in a certain amount of contempt; he later wrote in his memoirs, "The Church probe was sensational and irresponsible—Church made no secret of his presidential ambitions—and it was having a devastating impact on morale at the CIA." The following year, newly elected president Jimmy Carter replaced DCI Bush with ADMIRAL STANSFIELD TURNER and embarked on a campaign of Agency housecleaning. Turner dismissed some 820 CIA officers during his tenure.

Both the Church and Pike Committees were formed as a result of an inconclusive investigation of unauthorized CIA activities by the ROCKEFELLER COMMISSION in January 1975. The latter had been established by President Ford and chaired by Vice President Nelson Rockefeller. Congress, however, felt that the commission's findings had been "whitewashed"—thus, the establishment of their own investigative bodies.

A public outcry arose in the wake of the SEPTEMBER 11, 2001, TERRORIST ATTACKS ON THE UNITED STATES, with many leveling blame at the Church Committee for its eradication of the CIA's ability to gather intelligence from human sources (HUMINT).

CIA Act of 1949

The Central Intelligence Agency Act of 1949 provides for special administrative authorities and responsibilities for the Agency and the DIRECTOR OF CENTRAL INTELLIGENCE.

Section 1 (Definitions) of the Act defines terms used throughout the act.

Section 2 (Seal of Office) directs the DCI to create a seal of office for the CIA, to be approved by the president.

Section 3 (Procurement Authorities) lists four subsections that authorize the CIA to exercise its powers contained in the various sections and subsections of the Armed Services Procurement Act of 1947. It states that the term "Agency head" shall mean the director, deputy director, or the executive of the Agency. It also grants the "Agency head" the authority to make determinations and decisions with respect to purchases and contracts, stipulating that the "Agency head" may delegate that authority to any other officer(s) or officials of the Agency.

Section 4 (Education and Training) provides in two subsections for the training of CIA employees outside of the Agency.

Section 5 (Travel, Allowances, and Related Expenses) outlines in 18 subsections the Agency's authorization for travel and transport pay, physical examinations, and hospitalization for officers and their dependents as prescribed in the Foreign Service Act of 1946.

Section 6 (General Authorities) authorizes the CIA, in the performance of its functions, to transfer and receive monies from other government agencies, provide armed couriers for the transporting of confidential materials, and improve and maintain premises.

Section 7 further implements a section of the NATIONAL SECURITY ACT OF 1947 that outlines the responsibilities of the DCI in protecting against unauthorized disclosure of intelligence sources and methods, exempting the Agency from specific provisos in the acts of 28 August 1935 and 30 June 1945.

Section 8 provides rules for the director, attorney general, and the commissioner of immigration in determining and allowing for the entry into the United States of illegal aliens when in the interest of national security or essential to the national intelligence mission.

Section 9 authorizes the director to establish and fix compensation for not more than three positions in the professional and scientific field within the Agency.

Section 10 (Appropriations) allows for the expenditure of monies made available to the Agency for the purposes necessary to carry out its functions. This section also stipulates that such monies may be expended "without regard to the provisions of law and regulations relating to the expenditure of Government funds."

Section 11 (Separability of Provisions) stipulates that if any of the act's provisions are held invalid, the other provisions shall not be affected.

Section 12 (Short Title) states that the act may be cited as the "Central Intelligence Agency Act of 1949."

The act was signed into law on June 20, 1949.

CIA Information Act of 1984

The CIA Information Act of 1984 exempts the Agency from the ordinary search and review requirements found in the FREEDOM OF INFORMATION ACT (FOIA) with respect to operational materials and other sensitive files. For operational or security considerations, many CIA documents can be withheld from the public. The CIA Information Act of 1984 was signed into law by President Ronald Reagan on October 15, 1984.

cipher

A cipher is a form of secret writing based on the use of symbols representing single digits or letters of the alphabet. Unlike CODEs or CRYPTONYMs, which represent entire words, phrases, or sentences, ciphers systematically substitute numbers and letters for those of an open, or plaintext, message.

CI Project

The CI Project was the unofficial name for HT-LINGUAL, the CIA's MAIL INTERCEPT project, which existed from 1952 to 1973.

Civil Air Transport (CAT)

The predecessor air cargo service to AIR AMERICA, Civil Air Transport (CAT) was the brainchild of Army Air Corps general Claire Lee Chennault, commander of the famed Flying Tigers.

Chennault, along with Whiting Willauer, a businessman with financial and legal connections in Washington and New York, founded the airline in China as a private venture in 1946. For the next three years, CAT pilots flew countless relief missions in Asia, as well as a number of covert operations sorties, primarily in support of the Nationalist Chinese under Jiang Jieshi (Chiang Kai-shek). But in 1949, faced with imminent bankruptcy, the threat of a communist takeover in China, and the desire of the Nationalists to control the airline, Chennault appealed for government funding under a plan that would "militarize" the airline if the need arose.

The plan was tentatively approved on October 10, and the airline began supplementing its transport business by flying covert missions for the CIA. In January 1950, CAT was ordered out of China by the Communists, and the company moved to Taiwan (Formosa). In March, the CIA's OFFICE OF POLICY COORDINATION purchased CAT under an agreement that placed the airline under a COVER holding company, Airdale Corporation. Under absolute CIA control, CAT continued operating over the next decade; CAT pilots flew missions over Korea, Indochina (Vietnam), Indonesia, Tibet, and Nepal. In 1959, the CIA changed the name of its expanding proprietary air arm from CAT to Air America.

clandestine mentality

"Clandestine mentality" is an unofficial term by which CIA operatives, and those of other intelligence agencies, describe the overreactive, paranoid behavior of some spymasters who have become a bit too suspicious of others. The term is often used to describe the mind-set of the CIA's famous chief of COUNTERINTELLIGENCE JAMES JESUS ANGLETON. Many other phrases and monikers have been used to describe clandestine mentality, including CONSPIRATORIAL NEUROSIS, dream-world spookology, and SICK THINK.

Clandestine Service (CS)

The CIA's Clandestine Service (CS) was the forerunner to the Agency's current DIRECTORATE of Operations. It was responsible for conducting intelligence-gathering operations, covert action, and other espionage-related activities in the field.

The CS was established in January of 1951, when then DIRECTOR OF CENTRAL INTELLIGENCE (DCI) WALTER BEDELL SMITH brought the Agency's two clandestine arms—the OFFICE OF SPECIAL OPERATIONS, or OSO (the secret intelligence arm), and the OFFICE OF POLICY COORDINATION, or OPC (the covert-action arm)—under the newly created post of deputy director for plans (DDP).

A cargo plane of the Civil Air Transport (CAT) (UNIVERSITY OF TEXAS ARCHIVES)

The new DDP was future DCI ALLEN WELSH DULLES. The following year, the CS's two offices merged to form the Directorate of Plans.

In 1973, the Directorate of Plans was renamed the Directorate of Operations. However, "Clandestine Service" and "Plans Directorate" are still used synonymously with "Directorate of Operations."

Clark Study

The Clark Study was an evaluation conducted by the Clark Committee (officially the Task Force on Intelligence Activities), under the chairmanship of U.S. Army general Mark W. Clark, from 1954 to 1955. The study evaluated the organization and administration of the CIA and its related agencies, then issued classified and unclassified reports.

In 1955, the classified report was completed and forwarded directly to President Dwight Eisenhower (according to available information, that report remains classified). The unclassified version was sent to Congress. The unclassified report was a 76-page document that briefly described the evolution and coordination of the existing American intelligence agencies. Describing the relationship between those agencies, the report initiated the official use of the term "U.S. INTELLIGENCE COMMUNITY." The report also contained nine recommendations, beginning with the CIA's internal organization. It recommended that the DIRECTOR OF CENTRAL INTELLIGENCE (DCI) focus on issues of intelligence facing all members of the intelligence community. The administration of the Agency should be left to an executive officer.

Executive and congressional oversight of intelligence activities was also recommended, as was systematic five-year reevaluation of all personnel within the intelligence community, in order to ensure that "the passage of time has not altered the trustworthiness of any employee, and to make certain that none has succumbed to some weakness of intoxicants or sexual perversion."

The committee also recommended that the Agency replace the U.S. State Department in the acquisition of foreign publications and the collection of scientific intelligence. It further recommended that a NATIONAL INTELLIGENCE SURVEY be published (the survey was the forerunner publication to the CIA's current *WORLD FACTBOOK*).

A portion of the report reads: "The National Intelligence Survey is an invaluable publication which provides the essential elements of basic intelligence on all areas of the world. There will always be a continuing requirement for keeping the Survey up-to-date."

Additional recommendations included the need to build a new CIA complex, improve foreign language training, and raise the salary of the DCI.

The Clark Committee was the key element of the second Hoover Commission, an executive panel chaired by former U.S. president Herbert Hoover.

classification of materials

Materials handled by the CIA and other members of the U.S. INTELLIGENCE COMMUNITY are classified as either confidential, secret, top secret (TS), or special compartmented information (SCI). Such materials are considered to be classified information and are defined as materials owned by, produced by, produced for, or which fall under the control of the U.S. government. Such materials are within one or more of the following categories: intelligence sources/methods, cryptology, military plans, systems' vulnerabilities or capabilities, installations, and projects or plans related to the national security of the United States.

Levels of classification are:

- Confidential   Information of which the unauthorized disclosure could cause damage to national security.
- Secret   Information of which the unauthorized disclosure could reasonably result in "serious" damage to national security.
- Top Secret (TS)   Information of which the unauthorized disclosure could reasonably result in "exceptionally grave" damage to national security.
- Special Compartmented Information (SCI)   The most sensitive secrets of the U.S. government.

Access to classified information at any level is on a "need to know" basis and may be further restricted from foreign nationals, contractors, or consultants.

Classified Information Procedures Act (CIPA)

In 1982, the Classified Information Procedures Act (CIPA) established statutory procedures for the handling of classified information in federal criminal proceedings. The purpose of the CIPA was, and is, to protect classified "sources and methods" from being publicly disclosed, as such disclosure could degrade national security.

Clifford and Cline proposals

During U.S. Senate hearings by the Committee on Government Operations in 1976, former secretary of defense Clark Clifford (who had served Presidents Harry Truman and Lyndon Johnson and had been directly involved in the legislation surrounding the establishment of the CIA in 1947) proposed the creation of a DIRECTOR GENERAL OF INTELLIGENCE (DGI)—who would serve as the president's chief adviser on all matters of intelligence and as a principal point of contact with the congressional intelligence committees. Under Clifford's proposal, the post of DIRECTOR OF CENTRAL INTELLIGENCE (DCI) would continue, but the DCI's duties would be restricted to day-to-day CIA operations.

That same year, former DEPUTY DIRECTOR OF CENTRAL INTELLIGENCE (DDCI) Ray Cline also recommended a number of sweeping changes to the CIA. Cline proposed that the DCI be granted broad supervisory powers over the entire U.S. intelligence community and that the CIA be divided into two entities—one for analysis, one for clandestine services. Cline also recommended that the DCI be granted cabinet-level status. The latter recommendation ultimately found support in the administrations of Presidents Ronald Reagan and Bill Clinton.

cloak and dagger

"Cloak and dagger" is the romantic term used to describe the activities of a spy in the field who operates in a covert manner. The term is derived from the stereotypical spy in Western history in a cloak and carrying a dagger. CIA officers often use the term "cloak and dagger" to refer to deep-cover activities.

Cockroach Alley

Cockroach Alley was the nickname of the CIA's first office complex in Washington, D.C., during the late 1940s. The complex consisted of four buildings, which, according to many who worked there, "shuddered in the slightest breeze," were infested with cockroaches, smelled, had rotting wood floors, walls with peeling paint, and a cafeteria as "gloomy as a prison camp."

Cockroach Alley is a far cry from today's sterling headquarters complex—the GEORGE BUSH CENTER FOR INTELLIGENCE—in LANGLEY, VIRGINIA.

code

A code is a secret system of symbols that represent words, terms, phrases, or sentences. Unlike CIPHERs (which represents only numbers or letters of the alphabet), codes may be any form of symbol or signal, representing an idea or conveying an entire message. However, most codes can be encrypted or put into cipher form as an added measure of security.

Codes are based on the transposition or substitution of the symbols or characters. Transposition is simply the distortion of word patterns. Substitution is the replacement of symbols, characters, or word patterns with other symbols, characters, or word patterns. Substitution keys (tables) are often contained in code books possessed by both the sender and the recipient. Substitution is generally used to secure the most sensitive messages. Additionally, code books are often disguised as other types of books (novels, dictionaries, religious texts, etc.).

Codes may be combined with "ciphony" (sound messaging, as in the transmission of Morse code or other sound signals). Codes may also be transmitted visually. Flags, colored smoke, light signals, and physical markings are all forms of visually transmitted codes.

Coffin, William Sloan, Jr. (1924–   )

A career clergyman and a onetime antiwar and anti–civil rights activist, William Sloan Coffin, Jr., was also a CIA case officer during the early years of the COLD WAR. But he considered his work in the Agency futile.

Born in New York City on June 1, 1924, to William Sloane Coffin, Sr., and Catherine Butterfield, young Coffin was born into wealth and privilege. When he was nine years old, his family left New York for Carmel, California. As a teenager, he studied music in both Paris and at Phillips Academy in Andover, Massachusetts. In 1942, he entered Yale University's Music School.

The following year, with World War II in full swing, Coffin joined the U.S. Army. He was fluent in French, a skill that garnered him a position in Army intelligence as a liaison officer attached to the Free French forces. He later learned Russian and held a similar post with the Soviet army. In 1947, he was discharged with the rank of captain.

That same year, he returned to Yale. There, like many of his future CIA compatriots, including future U.S. president GEORGE BUSH, JAMES JESUS ANGLETON, RICHARD MERVIN BISSELL, WILLIAM PUTNAM BUNDY, and WILLIAM F. BUCKLEY, JR., Coffin became a member of the university's secret SKULL & BONES SOCIETY. In 1949, he graduated with a B.A. degree in government. During his senior year, he had been recruited by the CIA. But, with dreams of a career in the ministry, he instead chose to enter New York's Union Theological Seminary.

When the Korean War erupted in 1950, Coffin put the ministry on hold and entered the CIA. He would later contend that his decision to join the CIA was based on his wartime experiences with anti-Stalinist Russians who were repatriated to the USSR at the close of World War II. Aware that they would face execution and torture in their native land, some of the Russians committed suicide. Coffin was deeply moved, and he felt that by serving with the Agency he could help eradicate communism.

Coffin's first post was in the Eastern European Division of the OFFICE OF POLICY COORDINATION (OPC), the covert-action arm of the CIA. With the OPC, he served as a case officer in Germany. There he recruited and trained anti-Soviet Russian agents and infiltrated them into the Soviet Union on intelligence-gathering missions. Unfortunately, all were captured, having been betrayed by HAROLD ADRIAN "KIM" PHILBY, a British DOUBLE AGENT loyal to the Soviets. Coffin would later refer to his efforts as a "spectacular failure."

In 1953, Coffin left the Agency and entered the Yale University Divinity School. In 1956, he earned a bachelor of divinity degree. For the next several years, he held chaplaincies at Phillips Academy (his alma mater); Williams College in Williamstown, Massachusetts; and Yale.

During his tenure at Yale, Coffin served as a Peace Corps adviser and director. He also became involved in the civil rights and antiwar movements of the 1960s. In 1968, he was convicted of conspiracy to aid and abet disobedience to the Selective Service Act when he encouraged young men to burn their draft cards. His conviction was overturned. In 1976, he left his post at Yale and soon became the senior pastor at New York City's Riverside Church.

In 1979, Coffin was one of four American clergymen permitted by the Iranian government to spend Christmas with the American hostages in Tehran. During an address on February 7, 1981, at San Francisco's Trinity Institute, he stated, "The world is too dangerous for anything but truth and too small for anything but love." It was a comment destined to become one of the great American quotes.

Coffin has written and published extensively. Among his works are *Once to Every Man* (an autobiography published in 1977) and two debates on civil disobedience, published in 1967 and 1972. In 1985, he published *Living the Truth in a World of Illusions,* a collection of his personal reflections on religious ideology.

Colby, William Egan (1920–1996)

A former OSS commando during World War II who later headed up the controversial PHOENIX Program in SOUTHEAST ASIA, William Egan Colby is best known as the DIRECTOR OF CENTRAL INTELLIGENCE who "too" willingly turned over the CIA's FAMILY JEWELS to the CHURCH COMMITTEE in 1975.

Colby was born January 4, 1920, in St. Paul, Minnesota, to Elbridge Colby, a career Army officer and devout Roman Catholic, and Margaret Mary Egan Colby, a doting mother. Growing up in a military family, young Colby was widely traveled by the time he graduated from high school at age 16. Like his father, he decided to pursue a military career. He was too young to be accepted at West Point, so he enrolled in Princeton University. When he turned 17, he applied to West Point but was rejected because of nearsightedness. Undaunted, he remained at Princeton, joined the Army Reserve Officer Training

Corps (ROTC), and attained the rank of cadet captain. In 1940, he graduated from Princeton.

In August 1941, four months before the Japanese attacked Pearl Harbor, Colby was commissioned a second lieutenant in the U.S. Army. Eager for combat duty, he volunteered for airborne training, and in the fall of 1942 he was sent to jump school at Fort Benning, Georgia. A broken ankle during his second jump put his dreams on hold, but only temporarily. In March 1943, he was briefly posted as a staff officer in the 462nd Parachute Artillery Battalion. But when presented with an opportunity to join the OFFICE OF STRATEGIC SERVICES (OSS), Colby immediately accepted.

The OSS, the World War II precursor to the CIA, was only two years old in 1943. But its growing reputation as a clandestine force of educated, physically fit young men seeking high adventure was a tremendous lure for soldiers like Colby. Soon, Colby was at England's Milton Hall, undergoing a rigorous program of weapons instruction and special operations training led by British commandos and intelligence officers from the SPECIAL OPERATIONS EXECUTIVE (SOE). Once his training was completed, Colby was given command of one of the famous JEDBURGH teams and assigned a number of tasks involving parachuting into Nazi-occupied France; training, arming, and leading resistance fighters; blowing up bridges and communications centers; ambushing enemy patrols; gathering intelligence; and generally doing whatever needed to be done to disrupt German military operations. He returned to London, where he was given command of an OSS operational group that was sent to Nazi-held Norway. There he led the group on numerous special-operations missions. By war's end, he had won many decorations, including the Silver Star, the Croix de Guerre (France), and the St. Olaf's Medal (Norway).

Colby returned to school in 1946, earning a law degree from Columbia University in 1947. He practiced law in New York from 1947 to 1949, and he served with the National Labor Relations Board in Washington, D.C., from 1949 to 1950.

Colby joined the CIA in 1950. His first post was in Stockholm, Sweden, where he was tasked with overseeing STAY-BEHIND NETS, networks of clandestine operatives who would remain in Scandinavia in the event of a Soviet attack on the West. Colby then served as the Agency's CHIEF OF STATION (COS) in Rome from 1953 to 1958, and as the COS in Saigon from 1959 to 1962. In Saigon, he directed Operation PHOENIX, a controversial special project wherein Vietcong leaders were identified by intelligence officers and subsequently targeted by U.S. forces.

In 1963, he was promoted to the head of the Agency's Far Eastern Division. He held that post until 1967. The following year, he was granted leave from the CIA to accept a position as director of civil operations and rural development support with the Agency for International Development in Saigon (South Vietnam). He served in this capacity until 1971; his rank was equivalent to that of a full ambassador. He returned to the CIA in 1972. From March 2, 1973, until August 24, he served as deputy director for operations (concurrently serving as executive secretary of the CIA's Management Committee).

On September 4, Colby was appointed director of central intelligence by President Richard Nixon. Unfortunately for Colby, much of his tenure was spent putting out the proverbial fires of scrutiny. While he was serving as DCI, the CIA supported opponents of Chilean president Salvador Allende, a Marxist who was later killed during an attempted coup d'état.

But Colby is perhaps best remembered for his disclosure of the "family jewels"—a list of over 300 "questionable" CIA activities compiled by the Agency and publicly exposed during the U.S. Senate's Church Committee hearings in 1975. Colby was also directed to turn over classified meterial to the U.S. House of Representative's PIKE COMMITTEE. When he hedged on that order, the committee threatened to charge him with contempt of Congress. In late 1975, President Gerald Ford asked Colby for his resignation, purportedly for failure to obey a presidential order to destroy the Agency's stockpile of poisons. Colby stepped down on January 30, 1976.

His awards for military and civilian government service include the Silver Star, the Bronze Star, St. Olaf's Medal (Norway), the Croix de Guerre (France), the State Department's Distinguished Honor Award, the Distinguished Intelligence Medal, the National Security Medal, the Intelligence Medal of Merit, and the Career Intelligence Medal.

Among his published works are *Honorable Men: My Life in the CIA* (1978) and *Lost Victory* (1989).

In retirement, Colby practiced law first at the Washington, D.C.–based firm of Reid & Priest and then the Los Angeles firm of Donovan, Leisure, Newton & Irvine. He also worked as a business consultant and a lecturer. In 1994, the former DCI signed with Activision, an entertainment and video-game publisher, to develop spy thriller video games.

On April 27, 1996, Colby disappeared while canoeing on the Potomac River. For nine days, law enforcement officers combed the shoreline, as speculation of foul play began to surface across the country. Eventually, his body was discovered in a tributary. An autopsy suggested that he had suffered a heart attack or a stroke before falling into the river and drowning.

Colby is considered to have been one of the last true "gentleman spies," respected by friend and foe alike—a fact evident at his funeral, where one of the mourners was MAJOR GENERAL OLEG DANILOVICH KALUGIN, former head

CIA director William Colby before the House Intelligence Committee, August 1975   (LIBRARY OF CONGRESS)

of the KGB's First Chief Directorate, the counterpart agency to the CIA.

Colby was buried in Arlington National Cemetery. He was 76.

See also CHILE, OPERATIONS IN.

cold war

The "cold war" (as opposed to a hot war) is the term generally used to describe the long-term, but nonshooting, conflict or state of tension between the United States and Soviet Union that lasted from the close of World War II in 1945 until the collapse of the Soviet Union in 1991. Characterized by ideological competition in the Third World, global political-military alliances, limited wars fought by proxies, and a nuclear arms race, the cold war was a matter of great concern and strategic focus for the CIA. Though historians have debated its genesis, most agree that the cold war arose from disputes between the West-

ern democracies and the Soviet Union, particularly the latter's takeover of Eastern European states, after World War II.

In March 1946, less than a year after the close of hostilities, British prime minister Winston Churchill traveled to Fulton, Missouri, where he made his famous IRON CURTAIN speech. In the speech, he asserted that a dangerous communist line had been drawn across the middle of Europe. "From Stettin in the Baltic to Trieste in the Adriatic, an iron curtain has descended across the [European] Continent," said Churchill. The prime minister's statements were considered provocative by the Soviets, and many historians have since argued that his speech officially launched the cold war.

That same year, Soviet premier Josef Stalin proclaimed that World War II had been unavoidable and an inevitable consequence of "capitalist imperialism," implying that such a war might reccur.

U.S. president Harry Truman issued his own terse statement in an address before a joint session of Congress on March 12, 1947. Requesting military and economic aid for Greece and Turkey in their struggle against communist insurgents, he said, "I believe that it must be the policy of the United States to support free peoples who are resisting attempted subjugation by armed minorities or by outside pressures." Truman's statement was, of course, a thinly veiled reference to communist expansion around the world and to the U.S. goal of containing it.

As to who actually coined the phrase "cold war," no one knows for sure. Some historians have credited financier and longtime presidential adviser Bernard Baruch with having first used the term during a speech in 1947. Others have credited Walter Lippmann, an American newspaper columnist who actually brought the term into wide use in a series of essays entitled *The Cold War.*

In recent years, the West's contentious relationships with both China and the Russian Federation have been said to have spawned new, developing cold wars.

COMINT (communications intelligence)

COMINT is an acronym for "communications intelligence." In most cases, COMINT is gathered via CODE-breaking and the technical interception of foreign communications.

Occasionally, COMINT is gleaned by CIA officers and agents through the surreptitious entry of communications facilities. In that case, COMINT would overlap HUMINT, or human intelligence.

See also ALL-SOURCE INTELLIGENCE; INTELLIGENCE CYCLE.

Command Organization Chart, CIA
See appendices.

COMMO
COMMO is a CIA term for the Agency's Office of Communications. Operating under the umbrella of the DIRECTORATE of Administration, COMMO is responsible for providing communications between CIA headquarters and the Agency's overseas stations and outposts. Though some calls, messages, and dispatches are placed over landlines, the majority of the CIA's communications traffic travels via satellite.

Community Management Staff (CMS)
The Community Management Staff is the coordinating element of the U.S. INTELLIGENCE COMMUNITY and, as such, is the right arm of the DIRECTOR OF CENTRAL INTELLIGENCE (DCI). Established in 1992, the CMS is tasked with developing, maintaining, coordinating, and executing all of the DCI's intelligence community responsibilities as they relate to intelligence resource and collections management, assessments of intelligence programs, and evaluations of intelligence policies.

As the descendant entity of the Intelligence Community Staff (ICS), the CMS is headed by an executive director for intelligence community affairs, who reports directly to the DCI.

company, the
"The company" is an affectionate euphemism often used by CIA employees when referring to the Central Intelligence Agency.

Other terms include "the Agency," "Langley" (which is the Virginia location of CIA headquarters), or simply "CIA" (without "the"). For instance, a former CIA officer might say, "I spent 20 years with the Company," "I spent 20 years with the Agency," "I spent 20 years with Langley," or "I spent 20 years with CIA."

Euphemisms like "the Company" reflect the CIA employees' constant elusiveness even at the most superficial level when it comes to intelligence work. CIA employees sometimes skirt the "Company" connection altogether, by saying simply that they work for the federal government or the State Department.

For some, like excommunicated CIA officer PHILIP BURNETT FRANKLIN AGEE, the euphemism "the Company" reflects a CIA big-business mind-set. In a 1975 interview for *Playboy* magazine, Agee stated, "The Big Business mentality pervades everything. Agents, for instance, are called assets. The man in charge of the

United Kingdom desk is said to have the 'U.K. account.'"

Congo, operations in the
One of the CIA's earliest African crisis projects was that of stabilizing the developing unrest in the former Belgian Congo (Congo Belge) in 1960. Located in Central Africa, northeast of Angola, the Congo had been a Belgian colony, ruled by the latter for over a half-century. When the country gained its independence on June 30, 1960, hostile factions began grappling for political control, chief among them the Congo National Movement, under the direction of its charismatic, though somewhat unpredictable, leader Patrice Emery Lumumba.

The year before the Congo had gained its independence, Lumumba had boldly proclaimed, "The divorce between Belgium and the Congo is definitive. . . . I am launching a decisive plan of action for the liberation of the Congo. It is better to die than to put up with the regime of servitude any longer. We must win our independence."

Minerally rich, politically fragmented, and bordered by nine other nations, the Congo was ripe for an insertion of power from either the United States or the Soviet Union. At that time, the United States was extracting 75 percent of its cobalt, 50 percent of its tantalum, as well as measurable percentages of zinc, manganese, bauxite, iron, and gold from the Congo, all of which were critical in developing the American aerospace industry.

On July 2, a number of Congolese tribes began openly clashing with one another. Several days later, Congolese troops mutinied against their Belgian officers (Belgium had continued managing the country's military and business affairs even after June 30). The Belgian government appealed to Lumumba to allow it to send in regular Belgian troops. Lumumba, who had just become the Congo's prime minister, refused. But with the lives of European citizens at stake and Belgian businesses threatened, Belgian soldiers moved in unilaterally.

On July 11, the situation deteriorated further when the Congolese province of Katanga declared its own independence. That same month, the United Nations (UN) requested that Belgium withdraw its forces and ordered in UN peacekeeping troops.

Meanwhile, Lumumba traveled to Washington, met with U.S. officials, and appealed for economic assistance for his struggling nation. The prime minister was not impressive during his visit. Lumumba alienated American leaders with wordy diatribes, failure to look anyone in the eye, and alleged demand that a white prostitute be sent to his presidential guest quarters at the Blair House. His worst mistake was threatening to invite Soviet troops into the Congo in order to cast out the Belgians.

CIA deputy director of plans (operations) RICHARD MERVIN BISSELL, JR. referred to Lumumba as a "mad dog." During a July 21 meeting of the NATIONAL SECURITY COUNCIL, DIRECTOR OF CENTRAL INTELLIGENCE (DCI) ALLEN WELSH DULLES said that Lumumba had been "bought by the communists." By August, large numbers of Soviet supplies and support personnel were being airlifted into the Congo, and the CIA was ordered into action.

On August 25, a meeting was convened of President Dwight Eisenhower's SPECIAL GROUP, or 5412 GROUP—a covert plans-oversight body consisting of the director of central intelligence, the NATIONAL SECURITY ADVISOR, and the deputy secretaries of state and defense. In the meeting, national security advisor Gordon Gray stated that the president "had expressed extremely strong feelings on the necessity for very straightforward action in this situation." The following day, Dulles wired a message to LAWRENCE DEVLIN, the CIA CHIEF OF STATION (COS) in the Congo capital, Léopoldville (modern Kinshasa): "In high quarters here it is the clear-cut conclusion that if [Lumumba] continues to hold high office, the inevitable result will at best be chaos and at worst pave the way to communist takeover of the Congo with disastrous consequences for the prestige of the U.N. and for the interests of the free world generally. Consequently, we conclude that his removal must be an urgent and prime objective and that under existing conditions this should be a high priority of our covert action." As ambiguous as the message was—some historians have argued that it was an assassination order—it was in fact an "executive" order to rid the Congo of Lumumba.

Bissell ordered DR. SIDNEY GOTTLIEB of the CIA's TECHNICAL SERVICES STAFF (TSS) to select a poison to be used against an "unspecified African leader." The poison was to be an extract, indigenous to Central Africa, that could be injected into Lumumba's food or toothpaste by a CIA-hired executioner. In September, Gottlieb traveled to the Congo with a package consisting of gloves, gauze masks, hypodermic needles, and a vial containing a toxic virus. He met with Devlin, who seemed compliant, though somewhat reluctant to oversee the operation. Impatient, Bissell began recruiting others who would be more willing to carry out the task.

In November, Lumumba gave both the CIA and his Congolese rivals the slip. But his good fortune was short-lived. Having lost a governmental power struggle to Joseph Kasavubu, the Congolese president, and to Joseph Désiré Mobutu, the chief of staff of the Congolese armed forces, Lumumba had been placed under house arrest. He escaped on November 27 and fled to the safety of UN troops in Léopoldville. Unfortunately for the prime minister, he was captured by Mobutu's troops on December 2 and imprisoned. On January 17, 1961, he was executed

by a firing squad, and his remains were destroyed in an acid bath.

In 1971, the Congo was renamed Zaire, in an attempt by Mobutu, now the ruler, to strengthen the nation's African identity after the postcolonial turmoil of the 1960s. Mobutu also changed his own name to Mobutu Sese Seko Kuku Ngbendu wa za Banga ("Mobutu, the all-powerful warrior who, because of his endurance and inflexible will to win, will go from conquest to conquest leaving fire in his wake"). However, Mobutu was overthrown in 1997, and the country's name was restored to the Democratic Republic of the Congo.

See also ASSASSINATION PLOTS.

conspiratorial neurosis

Conspiratorial neurosis is synonymous with CLANDESTINE MENTALITY.

See also DREAM-WORLD SPOOKOLOGY; SICK THINK.

Coordinator of Information, Office of the (COI)

The Office of the Coordinator of Information (COI) was the predecessor organization to the OFFICE OF STRATEGIC SERVICES, or OSS (the wartime precursor to the CIA), and as such was the original predecessor organization to the CIA. Established on July 11, 1941, by order of President Franklin Roosevelt, the COI was given executive authority to "collect and analyze all information and data, which may bear upon national security; to correlate such information and data, to make such information and data available to the President and to such departments and officials of the government as the President may determine; and to carry out, when requested by the President, such supplementary activities as may facilitate the securing of information important to national security not now available to the government." The order designated WILLIAM J. "WILD BILL" DONOVAN as the "Coordinator of Information."

According to historian Thomas F. Troy, the COI was "a novel attempt in American history to organize research, intelligence, propaganda, subversion, and commando operations as a unified and essential feature of modern warfare; a 'Fourth Arm' of the military services." Donovan viewed it as a means of organizing the American government's intelligence resources. According to Donovan, "We have, scattered throughout the various departments of our government, documents and memoranda concerning military and naval and air and economic potentials of the Axis which, if gathered together and studied in detail by carefully selected trained minds, with a knowledge both of the related languages and technique, would yield valuable and often decisive results."

The COI grew rapidly during its 11-month existence. Initially, there was only Donovan and a handful of men. By September, there were 40 employees working for the office. But after the Japanese attacked Pearl Harbor in December, the COI's ranks swelled to over 600.

On June 13, 1942, President Roosevelt redesignated the COI the Office of Strategic Services.

Coordinator of National Intelligence (CNI)

The Coordinator of National Intelligence (CNI) was a position proposed by future DIRECTOR OF CENTRAL INTELLIGENCE (DCI) JAMES RODNEY SCHLESINGER in his SCHLESINGER REPORT to President Richard Nixon in 1971. Had the idea been adopted, the CNI would have acted as an executive-level overseer of the U.S. intelligence community, thus allowing the DCI to focus his attention on fiscal and intelligence-production issues.

The CNI, Schlesinger believed, would provide more direct presidential representation in all intelligence issues.

See also DIRECTOR OF NATIONAL INTELLIGENCE.

core beliefs and values, mission statement, and vision; CIA

Like all expansive organizations, the CIA has set official standards of excellence to which all of its employees must adhere. Those standards include a set of core beliefs and values, a mission statement, and a vision.

Core beliefs and values

What the CIA stands for

- Intelligence that adds substantial value to the management of crises, the conduct of war, and the development of policy.
- Objectivity in the substance of intelligence, a deep commitment to the customer in its form and timing.

How the CIA conducts itself

- Personal and organizational integrity.
- Teamwork throughout the Agency and the U.S. INTELLIGENCE COMMUNITY.
- Total participation of an excellent and diverse workforce.
- Innovation and risk-taking to get the job done.
- Adaptation to both a changing world environment and evolving customer needs.
- Accountability for our actions.
- Continuous improvement in all that we do.

Mission statement

We support the President, the NATIONAL SECURITY COUNCIL, and all who make and execute U.S. national security policy by:

- Providing accurate, comprehensive, and timely foreign intelligence related to national security.
- Conducting counterintelligence activities, special activities, and other functions related to foreign intelligence and national security as directed by the President.

Vision

To be the keystone of a U.S. Intelligence Community that is preeminent in the world, known for both the high quality of our work and the excellence of our people.

CORONA

CORONA was the code name for the satellite/high altitude-aircraft photo-reconnaissance project operated by the U.S. NATIONAL RECONNAISSANCE OFFICE (NRO) from 1959 to 1972. Though managed and staffed by the NRO (one of the 13 members of the U.S. intelligence community), the CORONA project also employed personnel from both the CIA and the U.S. DEPARTMENT OF DEFENSE.

On October 14, 1957, the Soviet Union launched Sputnik, the first satellite to orbit the earth. As a result, U.S. president Dwight Eisenhower endorsed CORONA in February 1958; the first test launch was attempted on February 28, 1959.

On May 1, 1960, a U-2 high altitude/surveillance aircraft piloted by FRANCIS GARY POWERS was shot down over the Soviet Union. Three months later, CORONA began producing the first images ever made from a satellite. It was, according to ADMIRAL WILLIAM O. STUDEMAN, future acting DIRECTOR OF CENTRAL INTELLIGENCE (DCI), "an era when facts were scarce and fears were rampant."

In the early days, CORONA's imaging resolution was eight meters, or 25 feet. But over time it improved to two meters, or 6.25 feet. Each satellite produced images that on average covered an area approximately 10 miles by 120 miles.

The last CORONA satellite was launched on May 25, 1972, and the last images of the CORONA series were taken on May 31.

In February 1995, CORONA was declassified, and 800,000 CORONA images (2.1 million feet of film in 39,000 cans) were transferred to the National Archives and Records Administration.

In a speech presented to fellow CIA employees in 1995, Admiral Studeman stated, "The most important contribution of the CORONA system to national security came from the intelligence it provided. CORONA looked through the IRON CURTAIN and helped to lay the groundwork for disarmament agreements and the collapse of the

Berlin Wall. With satellites, we could verify reductions in missiles without on-site inspections. Satellite imagery gave the United States the confidence to enter into negotiations and to sign arms control treaties with the Soviet Union. Successor programs continued to monitor ICBM sites, and verify strategic arms agreements and the Nuclear Nonproliferation Treaty."

See also ARGON, LANYARD; SATELLITE INTELLIGENCE/ SURVEILLANCE OPERATIONS.

counterespionage (CE)

Counterespionage (CE) is the act of conducting COUN- TERINTELLIGENCE operations that involve the penetration of an opposing intelligence service.

counterinsurgency

Counterinsurgency is the comprehensive (military, para- military, political, economic, civic, and psychological) action taken by a government to combat subversive resis- tance or guerrilla activities (insurgency) within its own borders or an area of military operations. For example, during the war in SOUTHEAST ASIA, the CIA—in concert with American military forces—conducted counterinsur- gency operations against communist guerrillas in the region.

Agency field officers and the U.S. troops conducting such operations were considered counterinsurgent forces.

counterintelligence (CI)

Counterintelligence (CI) is a broader term than COUNTER- ESPIONAGE (CE). CI is the total action taken by an intelli- gence agency by which information is gathered and activ- ities are conducted to protect that agency against espionage, theft of materials, sabotage, assassinations, or other intelligence activities conducted by, or on behalf of, hostile foreign governments or other "threatening" for- eign organizations (terrorist groups, rogue military units, etc.).

One of the CIA's most important offices is the Counter- intelligence Center, within the DIRECTORATE of Opera- tions.

countersurveillance

Countersurveillance is the total action taken to detect and frustrate hostile surveillance. For instance, the CIA's EXTERMINATORs engage in countersurveillance when they seek out and remove wires and BUGGING devices (devices used to eavesdrop on closed-door conversations).

Counterterrorist Center (CTC)

Established in 1986 by DIRECTOR OF CENTRAL INTELLI- GENCE (DCI) WILLIAM CASEY, the CIA's Counterterrorist Center (CTC) was formed as an arm of the Agency's DIRECTORATE of Operations to conduct offensive action against global terrorism.

The CTC's genesis lay earlier in the mid-1980s. At that time, the COLD WAR between the United States and the Soviet Union was nearing its end. But a number of high- profile terrorist attacks had convinced U.S. policy makers that more needed to be done to combat the new, increas- ingly dangerous, and less predictable threat of terrorism. As a result, a task force chaired by Vice President (and former DCI) GEORGE HERBERT WALKER BUSH was created to address the threat. The task force concluded that though U.S. government agencies did collect information on terrorists and terrorist activities, little was being done that was effective in disrupting those activities. Thus, the CTC was established.

Testifying before a House Judiciary subcommittee on April 6, 1995, acting DIRECTOR OF CENTRAL INTELLI- GENCE (DCI) WILLIAM O. STUDEMAN stated, "CTC has been responsible for anticipating and preempting terror- ist operations and for penetrating, disrupting, and destroying terrorist groups that target the interests of the United States and its allies." He added, "Counterterrorist work by necessity must be done out of the glare of pub- licity if we are to protect those who would provide us with vital information and to protect methods critical to us if we are to continue to keep Americans out of harm's way."

The CTC is composed of hundreds of operations offi- cers, analysts, and other technical experts. Most CTC staffers are CIA employees, but a considerable number are detached from the FEDERAL BUREAU OF INVESTIGATION (FBI), the U.S. DEPARTMENT OF STATE, the U.S. DEPART- MENT OF DEFENSE (DoD), and other members of the U.S. INTELLIGENCE COMMUNITY.

In the wake of the SEPTEMBER 2001 TERRORIST ATTACKS ON THE UNITED STATES, the CIA dramatically increased its numbers of CTC professionals; their num- bers are classified.

courier

A courier is a person who picks up, carries, and delivers secret materials or messages for an intelligence agency like the CIA. The courier may pass the materials or mes- sages to the CIA from a third party, or vice versa.

Couriers are not always aware that they are delivering materials or messages. For instance, a businessman trav- eling overseas may be delivering a gift from his company to another party. He may not be aware that concealed within the gift are secret CODEs, film strips, etc. CUT-OUTs and GO-BETWEENs often act as couriers.

cousins

An unofficial term used by American and British intelligence officers when referring to one another. The term "cousins" stems from both North America's deeply rooted British heritage and the historically close coordination between the two national intelligence communities.

Israeli officers also make reference to "cousins," but the term is not quite as affectionate. To an officer in the MOSSAD, a "cousin" is an Arab, usually a Palestinian. The Mossad refers to Arabs as "cousins" because Israelis and Arabs have a common ancestry, both being descended from the Judeo-Christian-Islamic patriarch Abraham.

cover

"Cover" is a term used by CIA officers and members of other intelligence services to describe a given, pre-arranged story that conceals either the name and background of an operative, or the title and raison d'être of a clandestine organization. For instance, during the war in SOUTHEAST ASIA, the CIA's operational air arm was provided a cover identity, AIR AMERICA, and a cover mission, civilian air transport, in order to conceal the Agency's primary purpose—that of gathering intelligence as well as transporting covert operatives and ammunition across national borders. Covers are also known as FRONTs.

See also LEGEND.

Covert Mission Protocols

The CIA's Covert Mission Protocols were seven clandestine operations particulars spelled out in NATIONAL SECURITY COUNCIL (NSC) Resolution 10/2 during the early years of the Agency. The CMPs included covert political actions, covert psychological warfare, covert paramilitary operations or guerrilla warfare, covert sabotage, economic warfare, evasion-and-escape plans for downed pilots, and STAY-BEHIND NETS in the event of enemy takeover.

NSC Resolution 10/2, which became effective on June 19, 1948, also provided for the establishment of the OFFICE OF POLICY COORDINATION (OPC), the CIA's then-covert operations arm.

Cowboys, the

"The Cowboys" were a group of five CIA officers who planned and directed the 1953 COUP D'ÉTAT IN IRAN from a SAFE HOUSE in Tehran.

See also ROOSEVELT, KERMIT.

cowboys vs. scholars

The CIA is a mixed bag of intelligence-gathering talents. In his book *The Very Best Men*, Evan Thomas describes what CIA officer DESMOND FITZGERALD believed was the perfect clandestine operative—a cross between a cowboy and a scholar. "He [Fitzgerald] wanted his spies to be at once intellectual and macho," writes Thomas. "His idea of perfection, said one of his case officers, was a Harvard Ph.D. who could handle himself in a barfight."

British intelligence officer WILLIAM "INTREPID" STEPHENSON adopted a similar policy in recruiting agents for MI6 during World War II. Like Fitzgerald, he believed that "the best agents" were those who "in peacetime make good bankers, physicians, or creative artists."

cryptanalysis

Cryptanalysis is the term used to describe the analyst's art of "breaking" CODEs or CIPHERs into legible text.

cryptography

Cryptography is the term used to describe the enciphering or coding of legible text into a form that will be unintelligible to an unauthorized person who might gain access to it.

cryptonym

A cryptonym is a code name. For example, AJAX was a cryptonym for the CIA's covert operation aimed at restoring the shah of Iran to power in 1953. ZAPATA was a cryptonym for the CIA's invasion of Cuba at the BAY OF PIGS.

CSIS

See CANADIAN SECURITY INTELLIGENCE SERVICE.

Cuba, operations in

See BAY OF PIGS INVASION; CASTRO, FIDEL ALEJANDRO RUZ; CUBAN MISSILE CRISIS; ZAPATA, OPERATION.

Cuban missile crisis

No incident in history has brought the world closer to the brink of all-out nuclear war than the Cuban missile crisis of 1962. For 13 days, the United States and the Soviet Union faced off in a dangerous confrontation over Soviet nuclear missile installations in Cuba. It ended in a concession on the part of the Soviets, a victory for the Americans, and a fortunate conclusion for the entire world.

On October 16, 1962, President John F. Kennedy called two emergency meetings with his top advisers in the Oval Office to discuss a startling revelation. On the previous night, the CIA had produced detailed aerial photographs of Soviet missile installations being constructed on the island of Cuba. The missiles, once operational, would be able to destroy much of the continental United States within minutes after being launched.

U.S. secretary of defense Robert McNamara presented Kennedy with three possible courses of action. The first was "the political course of action." This option would involve openly approaching Cuban leader FIDEL CASTRO, Soviet premier Nikita Khrushchev, and America's key allies to arrange negotiations aimed at resolving the crisis diplomatically. This option was considered unlikely to succeed. The second option was "a course of action that would involve a declaration of open surveillance" coupled with a "blockade against offensive weapons entering Cuba." The third option was "direct military action against Cuba." This option would have been initiated by a massive conventional air attack against the Soviet missile sites in Cuba.

For most of the day, discussions centered on the third option and the dangerous probability of a Soviet retaliation—which included the possibility of a nuclear exchange. "I don't know quite what kind of a world we'll live in after we've struck Cuba," McNamara told Kennedy. "And we've started it. How do we stop at that point?" In the end, the president opted for a naval blockade around,

Picture from a spy satellite showing a missile launch site in Cuba   (JOHN F. KENNEDY LIBRARY)

or "quarantine" of, Cuba to prevent Soviet freighters carrying missile equipment from entering Cuban waters.

On October 22, 1962, President Kennedy announced the establishment of the blockade, and just under 200 warships were dispatched to the Caribbean. U.S. naval commanders received instructions to halt, board, and search all cargo vessels bound for Cuba. Meanwhile, Soviet cargo ships proceeded toward Cuba. As American warships closed with the freighters, tensions heightened. Both sides were aware that their actions might initiate World War III. The situation degraded further on October 27, when the Soviets shot down a U-2 spyplane photographing missile positions on the island. The pilot, Major Rudolph Anderson, was killed. Almost immediately, the U.S. DEFENSE DEPARTMENT proposed an attack against Cuba. President Kennedy shelved the proposal.

Like the Americans, the Soviets were desperately seeking ways in which war might be averted. Throughout the crisis, the United States and the Soviet Union exchanged communiqués through both back-channel proxies and official letters. Khrushchev initially declared to Kennedy that the missiles were for deterrent purposes and that the Soviet Union had only peaceful intentions. The Soviet leader later offered a proposal wherein the missile installations would be dismantled if Kennedy guaranteed that neither the United States, its allies, nor proxy forces would ever invade Cuba. On October 27, the day the U-2 was shot down, Kennedy received another missive from Khrushchev, this time proposing to dismantle the missiles if the United States dismantled its own missile installations in Turkey.

In the end, the Kennedy administration accepted a modified version of the proposals, including a commitment not to invade Cuba and a demand that the Soviets also remove several light bombers from Cuba. Months later, the American missiles in Turkey were dismantled.

"In those nerve-wracking days, when it seemed that a military conflict was about to break out, both sides had enough courage and wisdom to begin intensive diplomatic discussions and make mutual concessions,"

recalled Soviet Air Defense Forces colonel Alexander Orlov. "After the Cuban missile crisis, the tensions of the global secret 'air war,' in which the U-2 had played a central role, began to abate. Incursions into Soviet airspace by reconnaissance aircraft became less necessary with the emergence of U.S. satellites, although U.S. reconnaissance flights along the USSR's borders continued—and occasionally violated Soviet airspace."

In Russian history and political science textbooks, the Cuban missile crisis is known as the "Caribbean crisis." The actual crux of the confrontation between the United States and the USSR took place at sea; therefore, the Caribbean is the Soviets' primary point of reference. Cuban texts, on the other hand, refer to the event as the "Crisis of October."

See also EXCOMM; McCONE, JOHN A.

Current Intelligence Bulletin (CIB)

The *Current Intelligence Bulletin (CIB)* is a CIA 24-*hour* intelligence publication delivered daily to the president of the United States. Created by analysts in the Agency's DIRECTORATE of Operations, the CIB has been issued each day since February 21, 1951, providing critical FINISHED INTELLIGENCE for the president. Prior to that date, the bulletin was known simply as the *PRESIDENT'S DAILY BRIEF,* the *President's Daily Intelligence Publication,* or the *Daily Summary.*

cut-out

A cut-out is a clandestine operative who acts as a liaison or contact person between spies in the field and a handler, or controller, who supervises the activities of field officers and agents. Cut-outs also act as COURIERs and intermediaries between members of intelligence organizations and networks of spies. This increases security for all parties involved, as actual contact between spies is prevented.

Cut-outs often make bottom-tier decisions. They also instruct spies as to their responsibilities during given missions. Cut-outs are sometimes referred to as GO-BETWEENs.

D

dead drop

See DROP.

Deep Throat

Deep Throat is the unofficial code name for *Washington Post* reporter Bob Woodward's anonymous deep background source who during the investigation surrounding the infamous WATERGATE SCANDAL provided Woodward solid information no other journalist was able to garner.

The Watergate scandal, which lasted from 1972 to 1974, was the greatest political misdeed in U.S. history. The scandal involved the highest levels of government in a number of illegal activities designed to help President Richard Nixon win reelection in the 1972 presidential campaign. It forced Nixon to resign from the presidency in order to avoid impeachment proceedings in 1974. It also resulted in exposure of CIA activities to the light of public scrutiny to a degree that the Agency had never before experienced.

The events began to unfold on the night of June 17, 1972, when five men—Eugenio Martinez, Virgilio Gonzalez, Frank Sturgis, BERNARD BARKER, and JAMES WALTER MCCORD, JR. (under the direction of former CIA operations officer HOWARD HUNT)—broke into the Washington, D.C., Watergate apartment complex with the

objective of obtaining information from the Democratic Party's national headquarters office there. Barker had once allegedly been recruited by the Agency while a Cuban policeman. McCord was also a former CIA officer.

Woodward, who broke the story, initially referred to his source as "my friend." But the source's insistence on deep anonymity, including no direct quotations, spurred the *Post*'s managing editor, Howard Simons, to coin the nickname "Deep Throat," after a famous pornographic film of the same title and era.

There has been a great deal of speculation as to who might have been Deep Throat, but the only persons believed to have known his or her true identity were Woodward, reporter Carl Bernstein (Woodward's partner), and former *Washington Post* executive editor Ben Bradlee. It has been suggested in a number of circles that Deep Throat was none other than Hunt, one of the Watergate break-in leaders; however, there has never been enough hard evidence to prove it.

defector

A defector is a person who, for political or personal reasons, rejects his or her country of origin and requests temporary or permanent asylum in another country. Often defectors to free Western nations are viewed by the CIA as rich sources of human intelligence (HUMINT).

Agency officers, however, are always cautious with defectors, who might be "plants" sent out by hostile intelligence services to lure the West into a misinformation trap.

Defense, U.S. Department of (DoD)

The U.S. Department of Defense is a cabinet-level organization composed of the three U.S. military departments, 14 defense agencies, nine unified combatant commands, and seven field activity groups. DoD's three military departments are: the Departments of the Army, Navy, and Air Force. The four traditional armed forces (each of which maintains a separate intelligence organization, all of which are members of the U.S. INTELLIGENCE COMMUNITY) are subordinate to their individual departments. The Marine Corps is in the Department of the Navy.

DoD's 14 defense agencies are the:

- Ballistic Missile Defense Organization
- Defense Advanced Research Projects Agency
- Defense Commissary Agency
- Defense Contract Audit Agency
- Defense Finance and Accounting Service
- Defense Information Systems Agency
- The DEFENSE INTELLIGENCE AGENCY (a member of the U.S. intelligence community)
- Defense Legal Services Agency
- Defense Logistics Agency
- Defense Security Cooperation Agency
- Defense Security Service
- Defense Threat Reduction Agency
- The NATIONAL IMAGERY AND MAPPING AGENCY (a member of the U.S. intelligence community)
- NATIONAL SECURITY AGENCY (a member of the U.S. intelligence community).

DoD's nine unified combatant commands are the:

- U.S. European Command
- U.S. Pacific Command
- U.S. Joint Forces Command
- U.S. Southern Command
- U.S. Central Command
- U.S. Space Command
- U.S. Special Operations Command
- U.S. Transportation Command
- U.S. Strategic Command.

DoD's seven field activities are the:

- American Forces Information Services
- Defense Prisoner of War/Missing Personnel Office
- Defense Human Resources Activity
- DoD Education Activity
- TRICARE Management Activity

- Office of Economic Adjustment
- Washington Headquarters Services.

Each of the three military departments under DoD is responsible for recruiting, training and equipping its respective forces. Operational control of those forces, however, is assigned to one of the unified combatant commands.

The above-mentioned DoD organizations that are members of the U.S. intelligence community fall under the coordinating jurisdiction of the DIRECTOR OF CENTRAL INTELLIGENCE (DCI).

Defense Intelligence Agency (DIA)

As the senior military intelligence component of the U.S. INTELLIGENCE COMMUNITY, the Defense Intelligence Agency is a combat-support arm providing ALL-SOURCE INTELLIGENCE to the American armed forces, defense policy makers, and other members of the U.S. intelligence community.

The brainchild of President John Kennedy and his secretary of defense, Robert McNamara, the DIA was established in 1961 as a military intelligence authority that would provide independent information while circumventing the "turf" problems arising from interservice rivalries. Today, the DIA effectively reduces the role of the individual services in the realm of strategic intelligence. However, the armed forces each continue to maintain organic intelligence branches for tactical intelligence, technical intelligence, and COUNTERINTELLIGENCE.

Ultimately overseen by the DIRECTOR OF CENTRAL INTELLIGENCE (DCI) and with a direct line to the president through the NATIONAL SECURITY ADVISOR, the DIA is tasked with coordinating and providing intelligence support for operational forces at home and abroad. The agency's responsibilities include targeting, and assessing battle damage assessment on, enemy forces; monitoring weapons proliferation; warning of impending crises and "hot spots"; providing support to U.S. forces participating in peacekeeping operations; maintaining databases on foreign military forces, to include equipment, activities, and numerical strength; and providing support to the United Nations and allies of the United States. In addition to the support of operational forces, the DIA provides intelligence to DEPARTMENT OF DEFENSE (DoD) policy makers, and members of the JOINT CHIEFS OF STAFF (JCS). The DIA is headed by a military director of three-star rank (either a lieutenant general or a vice admiral) and is staffed by military and civilian personnel in offices scattered throughout Washington, D.C.

The headquarters of the agency is located at the Defense Intelligence Analysis Center at Bolling Air Force

Base in Washington, D.C. A few DIA employees are based at the Armed Forces Medical Intelligence Center in Maryland and at the Missile and Space Intelligence Center in Alabama. DIA's military attachés are also assigned to U.S. embassies around the world and as liaison officers to each unified military command.

The DIA's Russian counterpart, or parallel, organization is the GLAVNOYE RAZVEDYVATELNOYE UPRAVLENIYE, or GRU (Main [Chief] Intelligence Administration).

See also AIR FORCE INTELLIGENCE; ARMY INTELLIGENCE; MARINE CORPS INTELLIGENCE; NAVAL INTELLIGENCE.

deputy director(s) of central intelligence

The deputy director of central intelligence (DDCI) is second in command to the DIRECTOR OF CENTRAL INTELLIGENCE (DCI). In the absence of the DCI, the DDCI assumes the director's responsibilities.

In the early days, DDCIs were appointed by the DCI. But in April 1953, Congress recognized the importance of the position by amending the NATIONAL SECURITY ACT OF 1947 to provide for the appointment of the DDCI by the president, with the advice and consent of the Senate. This amendment also stipulated that commissioned officers of the armed forces, whether active or retired, could not occupy the DCI and DDCI positions simultaneously. Since 1946, 21 appointees have held the post of DDCI—six serving as acting directors, and four ultimately assuming the reins of DCI.

(For a complete list of deputy directors see Appendix III.)

deputy directors and other senior positions in the CIA (other than the deputy director of central intelligence)

DEPUTY DIRECTOR OF CENTRAL INTELLIGENCE FOR COMMUNITY MANAGEMENT (DDCI/CM)

The deputy director of central intelligence for community management is a senior CIA position established in 1997. Nominated by the president and confirmed by the Senate, the DDCI/CM carries out the responsibilities of the DIRECTOR OF CENTRAL INTELLIGENCE (DCI) in the realm of planning and developing the intelligence budget, managing requirements and collection, as well as overseeing analysis, production, and acquisition. The DDCI/CM is assisted by the assistant DCI (ADCI) for administration, the ADCI for collection, the ADCI for analysis and production, and a senior acquisition executive. An executive director for intelligence community affairs reports to both the DDCI/CM and the DCI, and directs the COMMUNITY MANAGEMENT STAFF.

EXECUTIVE DIRECTOR (EXDIR)

The executive director (EXDIR) is the CIA's chief operating officer. Appointed by the DCI, the EXDIR manages the Agency on a day-to-day basis, creating and implementing policies and programs that affect the corporate interests of the CIA and those of the Agency's employees. With input from the primary deputy directors (the heads of the DIRECTORATES), the EXDIR is responsible for directing such Agency functions as budget and resource issues, strategic planning issues, and senior personnel assignments, as well as other matters that affect Agency operations. Whenever the DCI or the DDCI is acting as the representative of the U.S. INTELLIGENCE COMMUNITY, the EXDIR represents the Agency.

DIRECTOR OF CENTRAL INTELLIGENCE FOR MILITARY SUPPORT (ADCI/MS)

The position of associate director of central intelligence for military support was established in 1995. As the DCI's chief adviser and senior representative on military issues, the ADCI/MS coordinates the efforts of the U.S. intelligence community in order to provide senior military commanders with timely finished intelligence. Additionally, the ADCI/MS supports members of the DEPARTMENT OF DEFENSE (DoD) responsible for overseeing military intelligence training and the acquisition of intelligence systems and technology for their respective services. The ADCI/MS, a general or admiral, coordinates the policies and plans of the U.S. intelligence community as they relate to American military forces.

CHAIRMAN OF THE NATIONAL INTELLIGENCE COUNCIL

The chairman of the NATIONAL INTELLIGENCE COUNCIL (together with his or her vice chairman, director for evaluations, and other council members) serves the DCI as leader of the U.S. intelligence community by producing NATIONAL INTELLIGENCE ESTIMATEs.

DEPUTY DIRECTOR FOR ADMINISTRATION (DDA)

The deputy director for administration (DDA) was the senior manager of the CIA's DIRECTORATE of Administration. The office of the DDA was abolished on June 4, 2001.

DEPUTY DIRECTOR FOR INTELLIGENCE (DDI)

The deputy director for intelligence (DDI) is the senior manager of the CIA's Directorate of Intelligence.

DEPUTY DIRECTOR FOR OPERATIONS (DDO)

The deputy director for operations (DDO) is the senior manager of the CIA's Directorate of Operations.

DEPUTY DIRECTOR FOR SCIENCE AND TECHNOLOGY (DDS&T)

The deputy director for science and technology (DDS&T) is the senior manager of the CIA's Directorate of Science and Technology.

GENERAL COUNSEL (GC)

The general counsel (GC) is the senior legal adviser to the DCI and is responsible for the conduct of all the Agency's legal affairs. Nominated by the president and confirmed by the Senate, the GC is responsible for providing a legal interpretation of any statute, regulation, directive, or EXECUTIVE ORDER relevant to the DCI.

INSPECTOR GENERAL, OFFICE OF THE (OIG)

The Office of the Inspector General (OIG) is an Agency entity responsible for promoting "efficiency, effectiveness, and accountability" in the administration of all CIA activities. The inspector general is nominated by the president and confirmed by the Senate. The activities of the OIG are independent of those of any other office or Directorate within the Agency. The OIG conducts inspections, investigations, and audits at CIA headquarters and in the field, as well as overseeing the Agency's grievance-handling system. Additionally, the OIG provides a semiannual report to the DCI, which the latter is required to forward to the various intelligence committees of the Congress within 30 days. The OIG reports directly to the DCI and is otherwise subordinate only to the DDCI.

DESERT SHIELD, Operation

Operation DESERT SHIELD was the U.S. code name for the deployment and mobilization phase of the PERSIAN GULF WAR, the American-led invasion that liberated Kuwait from Iraq.

See also DESERT STORM, OPERATION.

DESERT STORM, Operation

Operation DESERT STORM was the U.S. code name for the combat operational phase of the PERSIAN GULF WAR, the American-led invasion that liberated Kuwait from Iraq.

See also DESERT SHIELD, OPERATION.

De Silva, Peer (1917–   )

Peer De Silva was chief of security for America's atomic bomb project during World War II. He went on to hold a variety of posts throughout the world as a CIA CHIEF OF STATION (COS) and an expert on counterinsurgency operations.

De Silva was born on June 26, 1917, in San Francisco, California. In 1936, he enlisted in the U.S. Army but soon won an appointment to the U.S. Military Academy at West Point, New York. He graduated from West Point and was commissioned a second lieutenant a few months before America's entry into World War II in 1941. His first posting was to Army intelligence; he attended the Army's Advanced COUNTERINTELLIGENCE Corps School, graduating in 1942.

De Silva was then assigned to the security detail for the Manhattan Project, the first atomic weapons development program. Serving in both San Francisco and Los Alamos, California, he was responsible for security for the atomic weapons development sites and for the physical protection of J. Robert Oppenheimer, the project director. When the bomb to be used against Nagasaki, Japan, was transported to the island of Tinian in 1945, De Silva provided an escort. By war's end, he was a lieutenant colonel.

De Silva joined the postwar STRATEGIC SERVICES UNIT (SSU), the operational remnant of the recently disbanded OFFICE OF STRATEGIC SERVICES (OSS). (The OSS was the World War II precursor to the CIA; when the office was dissolved in late 1945, espionage and counterespionage activities were rolled into the U.S. War Department and renamed the SSU.) In the SSU, De Silva and others began studying the Soviet Union. De Silva himself studied the Russian language at Columbia University (1946–47) and attended a special U.S. Army school (1947–48) taught by Russian émigrés in Germany. From 1948 through 1949, De Silva served as a diplomatic courier between the U.S. embassies in Moscow and Helsinki, Finland.

In December 1949, De Silva was transferred from the Army to the new CIA, where he served as deputy chief of the CIA base in Pullach, West Germany. In that capacity, he worked directly with the famous GEHLEN ORGANIZATION, a group of former Nazi intelligence operatives headed by German lieutenant general REINHARD GEHLEN that conducted post–World War II espionage operations for the West against the Soviets and their Eastern European satellite countries.

In 1951, De Silva was reassigned to Washington, D.C., and soon became operations chief of the Soviet Russia division of the OFFICE OF SPECIAL OPERATIONS (OSO). Two years later, he resigned completely from the Army in order to remain with the Agency in a civilian status. In 1955, he was named deputy COS in Vienna, Austria; in 1956, he became COS. Following Vienna, he held three major COS posts: stations in Seoul, Korea (1959–62), Hong Kong (1962–63), and Saigon, South Vietnam (1963–65).

In Saigon, De Silva was seriously injured when a car bomb set by the Vietcong exploded outside the U.S. embassy. De Silva, who lost an eye in the attack, was ordered to return to Washington. There he was named special assistant for Vietnam affairs to DIRECTOR OF CENTRAL

INTELLIGENCE (DCI) WILLIAM FRANCIS RABORN, JR. In 1966, De Silva was "loaned" by the CIA as a counterinsurgency adviser to the American ambassador to Thailand, Graham Martin.

De Silva briefly returned to the United States in 1968. From 1971 through 1972, he served as COS in Canberra, Australia. The following year, he retired from the Agency.

Detachment 101

Detachment 101 was the first paramilitary unit operated by the OFFICE OF STRATEGIC SERVICES (OSS), the World War II predecessor organization to the CIA. Established in 1942, the detachment, under the command of then Major CARL FREDERICH EIFLER, was responsible for conducting sabotage and resistance operations behind Japanese lines in Burma.

The detachment was the brainchild of intelligence guru MILLARD PRESTON GOODFELLOW, a former Brooklyn newspaper publisher and Boy's Club executive. Goodfellow, who served in the Secret Intelligence Branch of the OFFICE OF THE COORDINATOR OF INFORMATION or COI (the precursor to the OSS), first proposed the concept of an American irregular-warfare unit to be employed against the Japanese in the rugged backcountry of Burma. However, the idea was flatly rejected by General Joseph "Vinegar Joe" Stilwell, commander of U.S. forces in the China-Burma-India theater. Stilwell was of the opinion that regular forces were far superior to small teams of irregulars. Eventually, Stilwell conceded, and Detachment 101 was established in May 1942 under the newly created OSS. Soon thereafter, the detachment, led by Eifler, was shipped to the Far East.

About to launch an offensive against the Japanese, Stilwell ordered Eifler into action, to conduct sabotage and resistance operations against the enemy. Stilwell told Eifler, "The next thing I want to hear out of you are some loud booms from behind the Jap lines." Soon, the men of Detachment 101 were proving themselves along a 600-mile front, gathering vital intelligence, coordinating air strikes, destroying bridges and railroads, cutting communications lines, and training and equipping Kachin tribesmen to fight the Japanese.

Eifler himself was injured in a plane crash during an aerial reconnaissance mission in 1943. He was subsequently discharged at the rank of colonel, and command of Detachment 101 was passed to Lt. Col. WILLIAM R. PEERS.

In time, Detachment 101 grew to a force of more than 10,000 guerrillas, most of them Kachin tribesmen. When Allied troops invaded Burma in 1944, Detachment 101 teams advanced far ahead of the regular forces, disseminating misinformation, rescuing downed Allied aviators, destroying isolated enemy units, and gathering intelligence.

In all, Detachment 101 chalked up an estimated 5,447 enemy killed and another 10,000 wounded or reported missing. The detachment also destroyed over 50 bridges and nearly 300 military vehicles, while suffering the loss of 184 Kachin tribesmen and 18 Americans.

Detachment 101 was disbanded on July 12, 1945.

Deuel, Wallace Ranking (1905–1974)

A former correspondent and editorial writer for the *Chicago Daily News*, Wallace Ranking Deuel served with the CIA's first two predecessor organizations, the OFFICE OF THE COORDINATOR OF INFORMATION (COI) and the OFFICE OF STRATEGIC SERVICES (OSS). He later served as a senior employee of the CIA.

Deuel was born in Chicago, Illinois, on June 14, 1905. He graduated from the University of Illinois in 1926 and for the next three years taught political science and international law at the American University in Beirut, Lebanon. In 1929, he returned to his hometown, where he joined the *Chicago Daily News* as an editorial writer, editorial assistant, and foreign correspondent. The latter position took him to Rome and Berlin.

In Germany, Deuel wrote a scathing profile of Adolf Hitler, *People under Hitler.* The book earned him the distinction, according to Columbia University Press, of being one of the 15 American authors Hitler would execute first if the Germans defeated the United States.

In 1941, Deuel joined the COI. When COI functions were transferred to the OSS in June 1942, he became a special assistant to OSS director WILLIAM J. "WILD BILL" DONOVAN. Not cut out for clandestine work, Deuel took on myriad nonfield responsibilities. At one point, he worked with Walt Disney on a cartoon propaganda project.

After the war, Deuel wrote the initial draft of what would become the official history of the OSS, *Records of the Office of Strategic Services.* He then accepted a position as diplomatic correspondent with the *St. Louis Post-Dispatch.*

In January 1954, having been laid off by the *Post*, Deuel joined the CIA. There, he held a variety of posts, including chief of staff of current intelligence publications, deputy chief and then chief of foreign intelligence requirements, and as a staffer with the Agency's Office of the Inspector General. He also served as a CIA representative to the White House during the administration of President John Kennedy.

Tragically, Deuel's son, Mike—also a CIA officer—was killed in a helicopter crash during the "secret war" in Laos in 1965. Three years later, on August 1, 1968, Deuel retired from the CIA.

Deuel died on May 10, 1974. He was 69.

Deutch, John Mark (1938–)

Dr. John Mark Deutch, one of U.S. defense secretary Robert S. McNamara's Pentagon "whiz kids" during the Vietnam War years, would be known in some congressional circles during the 1990s as the worst DIRECTOR OF CENTRAL INTELLIGENCE (DCI) in CIA history.

Born in Brussels on July 27, 1938, to Michael Joseph Deutch and Rachel Felicia Fisher, young Deutch arrived in America in 1940. He became a naturalized U.S. citizen in 1946. In 1961, he earned a bachelor's degree from Amherst College, in Massachusetts. That same year, he also earned a bachelor's degree in chemical engineering from the Massachusetts Institute of Technology. He soon became systems analyst in the Office of the Secretary of Defense. In 1965, he earned a Ph.D. in physical chemistry from MIT. From 1967 to 1970, he served as an assistant professor at Princeton University, in New Jersey. He then became a member of the faculty at MIT, eventually rising to full professor, dean of science, and provost. Deutch also earned honorary doctorates from Amherst (1978) and the University of Massachusetts at Lowell (1986). Additionally, he won a Sloan Fellowship (1969 to 1971) and a Guggenheim Fellowship (1974). In 1993, he was named undersecretary for acquisition and technology at the U.S. DEPARTMENT OF DEFENSE. From 1994 to 1995, he served as deputy secretary of defense.

On May 10, 1995, President Bill Clinton appointed Deutch as director of central intelligence, a post he would hold until December 15, 1996. His position was elevated to cabinet status. (The office of DCI had been first elevated to the cabinet level during the tenure of DCI WILLIAM JOSEPH CASEY, beginning in 1981. Casey's successors, however, had not been made cabinet members, keeping them out of the White House policy-making loop, until Deutch's appointment.)

During his tenure, Deutch implemented a number of reforms, including assigning more women to top Agency posts and establishing an open-door policy for junior employees who wanted access to the director—a move that created consternation among senior CIA officers. He also tailored a greater number of the CIA's intelligence products to military and law enforcement agencies and proposed a new NATIONAL IMAGERY AND MAPPING AGENCY.

But things began to sour for both Deutch and the Agency days after he stepped down as DCI. A CIA security officer turned up at his Maryland home in order to conduct a routine security inspection of Deutch's Agency-supplied Macintosh computers. The security officer discovered numerous files containing classified information, many of them secret, top secret, or "Special Access." Many of the documents were stored as unencrypted Microsoft Word files. Further investigation revealed some 17,000 pages of data, including budgeting information from the NATIONAL RECONNAISSANCE OFFICE (NRO), the U.S. INTELLIGENCE

John Mark Deutch   (NATIONAL ARCHIVES)

COMMUNITY agency that handles spy satellites; highly sensitive details of covert operations; a message to the Oval Office; and a lengthy journal of Deutch's activities for several years. It was a shocking revelation.

A report issued by the CIA inspector general's office found that Deutch had knowingly violated Agency and U.S. government regulations requiring that his government-owned computers be used solely for government-related work. The computers were connected to the Internet via America Online; Deutch's user name was a recognizable variation of his actual name. Worse, it was revealed that a member of the Deutch family had used one of the computers to access pornographic and other "high risk" websites where hackers would have been able to plant devices that could have monitored Deutch's online activities and possibly gained access to, or stolen, sensitive CIA files. Deutch had also employed as a housekeeper a resident alien whom he had provided a code to his home alarm/security system. The housekeeper thus had unmonitored access to his residence. The Agency had offered to place a 24-hour security officer at Deutch's home during his tenure as DCI, but he had refused, citing privacy concerns.

Deutch initially denied any wrongdoing. He then arranged to retain the computers by arguing that they contained personal data. Attempting, though unable, to delete the personal files from the computers' hard drives, he contacted the Agency's technical support personnel for assistance.

Concluding that Deutch had mishandled national security information on personal computers at his residences in Maryland and Massachusetts, Deutch's successor, DCI GEORGE JOHN TENET, was forced to act. On August 20, 1999, Tenet suspended Deutch's security clearance at the CIA. His clearance at the DEFENSE INTELLIGENCE AGENCY (DIA) was also suspended.

Reluctantly, Deutch agreed to testify before a closed-door hearing of the Senate Select Committee on Intelligence on February 22, 2000. He later told reporters, "The director of Central Intelligence is not above the rules," adding that he regretted his errors.

"While serving as Director of Central Intelligence I erred in using CIA-issued computers that were not configured for classified work to compose classified documents and memoranda," Deutch said in a 1999 interview for the *Washington Post*. "While it was absolutely necessary for me to work at home and while on travel, in hindsight it is clear that I should have insisted that I be provided the means of accomplishing this work in a manner fully consistent with all the security rules."

Falling on his sword was not enough for congressional committee members like John Millis, staff director of the House Permanent Select Committee on Intelligence. According to Millis, Deutch was the "first, second, and third-worst" DCI in Agency history. In addition to Deutch's mishandling of national security information, it was discovered that he had made the decision to replace a number of human field operatives with high-tech spy equipment—a revelation that garnered him little sympathy in the wake of the SEPTEMBER 11, 2001, TERRORIST ATTACKS ON THE UNITED STATES.

Devlin, Lawrence Raymond (1922–   )

CIA officer Lawrence Raymond Devlin was a key player in the Agency's attempted assassination of Congolese leader Patrice Emery Lumumba in 1960. But it wasn't a position he relished.

Devlin was born in New Hampshire on June 18, 1922. From 1942 to 1946, he served in the U.S. Army, rising to the rank of major. In 1947, he earned a bachelor's degree from San Diego State University; in 1949, he earned a master's from Harvard University. From 1950 to 1953, he worked as an editor. In 1953, he became a political affairs analyst for the U.S. Department of the Army.

In 1957, Devlin joined the CIA, where he accepted a post as a political officer in the U.S. embassy in Brussels, Belgium. He was reassigned in 1960 to the Congo (today Zaire). He served as the CIA's CHIEF OF STATION (COS) in Léopoldville (today Kinshasa) until 1963.

The Congo, which had gained its independence from Belgium on June 30, 1960, was in a state of tremendous unrest when Devlin arrived. Hostile factions were grappling for control of the West African nation, chief among them the Congo National Movement, under the charismatic, though somewhat unpredictable, Patrice Emery Lumumba.

On August 18, Devlin cabled CIA headquarters the following message: "Embassy and station believe Congo experiencing classic Communist effort takeover government . . . whether or not Lumumba actually commie or just playing commie game to assist his solidifying power. Anti-West forces rapidly increasing power Congo and there may be little time left in which take action to avoid another Cuba." The decision was made by the CIA to assassinate Lumumba. In September, DR. SIDNEY GOTTLIEB, the Agency's chief science adviser, traveled to the Congo with a package consisting of protective rubber gloves, gauze masks, hypodermic needles, and a vial containing a toxic virus. There Gottlieb met with Devlin, who was willing, though somewhat reluctant, to oversee the operation.

Assassination seemed a nasty business to Devlin, though he had no qualms about tough fieldwork. That same year he had wrestled to the ground a gunman who was attempting to assassinate Joseph Mobutu, the chief of staff of the Congolese armed forces.

In 1963, Devlin returned to the United States, serving at CIA headquarters in LANGLEY, VIRGINIA. He returned to the Congo in 1965 and was reportedly instrumental in the establishment of Congolese president Joseph Mobutu's administration.

With the fighting in Southeast Asia heating up, Devlin was assigned to Vientiane, Laos, in 1968. He oversaw the CIA's paramilitary operations in that country. He served in that capacity until 1970 and then returned to Langley, becoming chief of the Agency's Africa Division.

Devlin retired from the Agency in 1974. The following year, he was called to testify before the U.S. Senate's CHURCH COMMITTEE (the Select Committee to Study Governmental Operations with respect to Intelligence Activities) regarding his involvement in the attempt to assassinate Lumumba. Devlin testified before the committee using the pseudonym "Victor Hedgman." "If I had had Hitler in my sights in 1941 and I'd pulled the trigger, maybe 20 or 30 million people would be alive today," said Devlin. "But I just never felt it was justified with Lumumba. I was hoping the Congolese would settle it amongst themselves, one way or another."

In retirement, Devlin returned to the Congo, obtaining an audience with President Mobutu. "Poor Lumumba," Devlin would say in an interview for *New African* magazine. "He was no communist. He was just a poor jerk who thought, 'I can use these people.' I'd seen that happen in

Eastern Europe. It didn't work very well for them, and it didn't work for him."

See also ASSASSINATION PLOTS; CONGO, OPERATIONS IN THE; SOUTHEAST ASIA, OPERATIONS IN.

Direction Générale de la Sécurité Extérieure (DGSE)

Established in 1981, the Direction Générale de la Sécurité Extérieure (DGSE) is France's "external" or foreign intelligence service. The DGSE's American counterpart, or parallel, agency is the CIA.

directive, CIA

A CIA directive is an official statement issued in order to amend or add to existing policy regulations. A CIA directive is often referred to as a DIRECTOR OF CENTRAL INTELLIGENCE directive, or simply a DCID.

directorates, CIA

There are currently three primary directorates within the CIA: the Directorate of Intelligence, the Directorate of Operations (formerly Plans), and the Directorate of Science and Technology. Five independent departments also exist that were once under the now-defunct Directorate of Administration: the offices of Information Technology, Finance, Security, Global Support, and Human Resources.

THREE EXISTING CIA DIRECTORATES

Directorate of Intelligence (DI)

Formerly known as the Office of Research and Reports (ORR), the Directorate of Intelligence (DI) is the analytical arm of the CIA, responsible for evaluating intelligence gathered from both clandestine and open sources. Information about key foreign countries, regional conflicts, terrorism, weapons proliferation, and narcotics trafficking is then provided to intelligence consumers through reports called "intelligence estimates." Recipients of these intelligence estimates include, but are not limited to, the president, the vice president, the cabinet, the National Security Council, congressional committees, and such federal law enforcement agencies as the Federal Bureau of Investigation (FBI), the U.S. Customs Service, and the Drug Enforcement Administration (DEA)—each on an individual need-to-know basis. The DI also supports diplomatic negotiations and military operations.

Overseen by the deputy director for intelligence (DDI), the DI comprises 12 internal components:

- Collection Requirements and Evaluation Staff
- DCI Crime and Narcotics Center

- Office of Asian Pacific and Latin American Analysis
- Council of Intelligence Occupation
- DCI Environmental Center
- Office of Near Eastern, South Asian, and African Analysis
- Office of Policy Support
- DCI Nonproliferation Center
- Office of Russian and European Analysis
- Office of Support Services
- Office of Advanced Analytic Tools (this office also falls under the umbrella of DS&T)
- Office of Transnational Issues.

Directorate of Operations (DO)

The Directorate of Operations (DO) is the most fascinating to the general public, yet least understood branch, of the CIA. The DO is the glamorous cloak-and-dagger arm of the Agency, responsible for both the clandestine collection of foreign intelligence and covert paramilitary operations. This directorate was, until 1973, referred to as the Directorate of Plans. Prior to that, it was simply referred to as the CLANDESTINE SERVICE. Some of the Operations Directorate's more colorful, albeit unofficial, monikers include the "Department of Spies," the ELITE DIRECTORATE, the "Untouchables," and the DEPARTMENT OF DIRTY TRICKS (a name also used to describe the CIA's Office of Policy Coordination).

Overseen by the DEPUTY DIRECTOR OF OPERATIONS (DDO), the DO is composed of four components:

- Counterintelligence Center
- DCI Counterterrorist Center
- National HUMINT Requirements Tasking Center
- Clandestine Information Technology Office (this office also falls under the umbrella of DS&T).

Directorate of Science and Technology (DS&T)

When an officer in the field employs a hidden device used to monitor communications or a satellite records troop movements somewhere in the Middle East, the odds are that some or all of the technical components required were developed by the CIA's Directorate of Science and Technology (DS&T). Established in 1962 as the Directorate of Research and renamed the following year the Directorate of Science and Technology, DS&T is the Agency's ever-evolving life-support system. The details of the work conducted by the DS&T are closely guarded secrets. The directorate employs numerous scientific researchers who constantly develop new technologies to improve the intelligence-gathering process, making that process faster, more adaptive, and more effective. The DS&T also applies new technologies to the processing and analysis of information.

Overseen by the deputy director for science and technology (DDS&T), the DS&T comprises eight components:

- Office of Advanced Analytical Tools (this office also falls under the umbrella of DI)
- Office of Development and Engineering
- Investment Program Office
- Office of Technical Collection
- Office of Technical Service
- Clandestine Information Technology Office (this office also falls under the umbrella of DO)
- Open Source Collection
- NIMA Systems and Technology Directorate.

TWO OBSOLETE CIA DIRECTORATES

Directorate of Administration (DA)

The Directorate of Administration (DA) was, until 2001, the largest branch of the CIA, and it was responsible for running the day-to-day operations of the Agency. Everything from employee pay to training to medical services fell under the DA. One of its key functions was to provide security for the Agency's employees, facilities, and information.

Overseen by the deputy director of administration (DDA), the DA had 15 components:

- Agency Technology Services
- Business Process Transformation Program Office
- Center for CIA Security
- Center for Support Coordination
- CIA Recruitment Center
- DCI Center for Security Evaluation
- Human Resource Management
- Printing and Photography Group
- Office of Communications
- Office of Finance and Logistics
- Office of Facilities Management
- Office of Information Management
- Office of Medical Services
- Office of Training and Education
- Business Enterprises.

On June 4, 2001, the Directorate of Administration was abolished and its functions distributed to five entities—Information Technology, Finance, Security, Global Support, and Human Resources—under the CIA's Executive Board. The heads of each entity are on a par with the leaders of the Agency's three primary directorates.

Directorate of Plans (DP)

The Directorate of Operations was, until 1973, referred to as the Directorate of Plans. This directorate was overseen by the deputy director of plans. The DP was the descendant of the CIA's CLANDESTINE SERVICE (CS). The latter entity comprised the Office of Policy Coordination of OPC (the CIA's covert-action arm) and the Office of Special Operations (the CIA's secret intelligence arm).

director general of intelligence (DGI)

Though never established, the post of a "Director General of Intelligence" (DGI) was proposed by former secretary of defense Clark Clifford during 1976 U.S. Senate hearings by the Committee on Government Operations. The DGI would serve as the president's chief adviser on all matters of intelligence and as a principal point of contact for congressional intelligence committees.

The post of DIRECTOR OF CENTRAL INTELLIGENCE (DCI) would continue, but the DCI's duties would be restricted to day-to-day CIA operations.

See also CLIFFORD AND CLINE PROPOSALS.

director of central intelligence (DCI)

The director of central intelligence (DCI) may best be described as the chief executive officer of the CIA. But the DCI's authority extends well beyond the Agency's inner sanctum. The DCI also serves as the coordinating head of all other U.S. INTELLIGENCE COMMUNITY organizations (though the DCI has no direct authority over them) and is the primary adviser to the president on matters relating to foreign intelligence.

The DCI has four primary responsibilities: to serve as the senior intelligence officer of the federal government; to establish requirements and priorities for the efforts of the U.S. intelligence community; to develop and justify the NATIONAL FOREIGN INTELLIGENCE PROGRAM (NFIP); and, like all other Agency officers, to protect sources and methods.

The DCI also serves as chairman of the NATIONAL SECURITY COUNCIL's senior interagency group when it meets to consider intelligence matters. This committee addresses issues requiring interagency attention, deals with interdepartmental matters, and monitors the execution of approved intelligence policies and decisions. Collateral responsibilities of the DCI can be inferred, including planning, evaluation, and coordination.

The position of DCI was created as part of President Harry Truman's directive establishing the NATIONAL INTELLIGENCE AUTHORITY (NIA) and the CENTRAL INTELLIGENCE GROUP (CIG) on January 22, 1946. The office of DCI was elevated to a cabinet-level position under President Ronald Reagan for the tenure of DCI WILLIAM JOSEPH CASEY, beginning in 1981. However, Casey's successors were not made cabinet members (keeping them out of the White House policy-making loop) until President Bill Clinton appointed DR. JOHN DEUTCH as DCI in 1995.

Since 1946, 18 presidential appointees have held the post of DCI. This figure does not include MAJOR GENERAL WILLIAM J. DONOVAN, director of the OFFICE OF STRATEGIC SERVICES (OSS), who is considered to be America's first director of Central Intelligence.

(See Appendix III for a listing of directors of the Central Intelligence Agency.)

director of foreign intelligence (DFI)

In 1975, the MURPHY COMMISSION (officially the Commission on the Organization of the Government for the Conduct of Foreign Policy, under former deputy secretary of state Robert D. Murphy) recommended, among other matters, that the title of DIRECTOR OF CENTRAL INTELLIGENCE be changed to "Director of Foreign Intelligence" (DFI). The recommendation was not adopted.

director of national intelligence (DNI)

The director of national intelligence, had that proposed post been established, would have had the responsibilities for the U.S. intelligence community currently held by the DIRECTOR OF CENTRAL INTELLIGENCE (DCI). The position of DNI has been proposed five times: by future DCI JAMES RODNEY SCHLESINGER in 1971 (whose proposal specified "coordinator of national intelligence"), by DCI STANSFIELD TURNER in 1985, and finally in the BOREN-MCCURDY INITIATIVE of 1992, in June 2002 by U.S. senator Dianne Feinstein (D-California), and in December 2002 by a congressional panel tasked with investigating possible intelligence shortcomings leading to the SEPTEMBER 11, 2001, TERRORIST ATTACKS ON THE UNITED STATES.

See also SCHLESINGER REPORT.

Dirty Tricks, Department of

The "Department of Dirty Tricks" is the unofficial title sometimes used to describe both the CIA's former OFFICE OF POLICY COORDINATION (or OPC, the Agency's first-ever covert-action arm) and the Agency's current DIRECTORATE of Operations (formerly the DIRECTORATE of Plans).

disinformation

Disinformation is synonymous with BLACK PROPAGANDA.

Domestic Operations Division (DOD)

The Domestic Operations Division (DOD) was a supersecret branch of the CIA responsible for establishing proprietary companies, FRONTS, and COVERS for the Agency's operations within the United States. Authorized by President Lyndon Johnson and overseen by DIRECTOR OF CENTRAL INTELLIGENCE (DCI) JOHN MCCONE, the DOD was officially created in 1964 to "exercise centralized responsibility for the direction, support, and coordination of clandestine operational activities within the United States." By the 1970s, the DOD had been phased out of existence.

Donovan, William Joseph (Wild Bill)
(1883–1959)

Major General William Joseph "Wild Bill" Donovan will forever be regarded as "the father of American central intelligence." A native New Yorker of humble origins, Donovan was a second-generation Irish American Catholic. He served as a U.S. Army colonel during World War I, earning the Congressional Medal of Honor. After the war, he became a successful Wall Street lawyer, unsuccessfully campaigned for governor of New York, and was briefly considered for the posts of either U.S. attorney general or secretary of war. Donovan founded the OFFICE OF STRATEGIC SERVICES (OSS) during World War II and was one of the foremost proponents of a postwar central intelligence service. Nevertheless, his initial plan was scrapped, and he declined any role in the CIA.

Born on January 1, 1883, in a working-class neighborhood of Buffalo, New York, Donovan attended Christian Brother's School, where he developed passions for literature, especially poetry, and athletics. As a young man, he briefly attended New York's Niagara University before transferring to Columbia College (now Columbia University). Working his way through college, he also found time for athletics. At Columbia, he rowed on the second varsity crew and earned the starting quarterback position on the varsity football team. Many sources contend that it was Donovan's fellow athletes who bestowed on him his lifelong nom de guerre "Wild Bill." Others claim he earned the title years later in the Army. He graduated from Columbia with a B.A. degree in 1905; in 1907, he received his law degree and entered private practice.

In 1912, Donovan was one of the first to enlist in the newly formed Troop One, First New York Cavalry, New York National Guard. Enlisting as a private trooper, he was elected captain of the unit in less than five months. When Pancho Villa's raids into Texas and New Mexico forced the U.S. Army's hand in 1916, Donovan's horsemen were federalized. Troop One saw no combat action. But the unit, under the leadership of the former Columbia quarterback, trained relentlessly, often pushing beyond the limits of other units. The demands Donovan placed on his troopers earned him a reputation as a merciless drillmaster that remained with him for the rest of his life.

When America entered World War I, Donovan was offered a colonel's commission and an administrative post. He opted instead for a field command in the grade of major and a posting to the crack 69th New York—the descendant of the American Civil War's famed "Fighting Irish" Brigade. In France, he distinguished himself time and again, and was eventually promoted to colonel. At the Battle of l'Ourq, he won the Distinguished Service Cross. During the Meuse-Argonne offensive, Donovan—severely wounded and refusing evacuation—directed the 165th Infantry Regiment (the old 69th New York) in a fierce attack against the Germans. The Germans counterattacked but were driven back. For this action, Donovan received the Congressional Medal of Honor.

Between the world wars, Donovan held several public posts. In 1922, he was appointed U.S. district attorney for western New York, where he was charged with enforcing Prohibition laws. From 1924 to 1929, he served as assistant attorney general, initially in charge of the U.S. Justice Department's Criminal Division before moving "upstairs" to the Anti-Trust Division. In the latter capacity he argued and won six cases before the U.S. Supreme Court. Twice he made unsuccessful bids for elected office on Republican Party tickets in New York State—for lieutenant governor in 1922 and for governor in 1932. President Herbert Hoover briefly considered Donovan for the post of U.S. attorney general in 1929. When he changed his mind, he offered Donovan the governor-generalship of the Philippines as something of a consolation prize. Donovan refused it.

In *Donovan and the CIA*, Thomas Troy quotes a journalist as remarking, "[Donovan is] ready and fit now, whether he should be called upon to die, to box Jack Dempsey, or to be President." Troy also quotes President Franklin Roosevelt, one of Donovan's law school classmates: "If Bill Donovan had been a Democrat, he'd be in my place today."

In the 1930s, Donovan reentered private practice and established one of the most powerful law firms in Manhattan's financial district. But in 1935, his focus again began to shift beyond America's shores. President Roosevelt, whose New Deal policies had been publicly challenged by the former colonel, understood the value of creating alliances with former opponents. In 1935, Roosevelt sent Donovan abroad on a series of fact-finding missions to places like Germany, Italy, Ethiopia, Yugoslavia, and Czechoslovakia. It was even rumored, in 1939, that Donovan was to be named secretary of war. But his career path was taking another, more covert, turn. One of his fact-finding missions included a trip in 1940 to London, where Donovan met with officials from M16, M15, and the newly formed SPECIAL OPERATIONS EXECUTIVE (SOE). British intelligence officers, taking an immediate liking to Donovan, often referred to him as "our man." From the British Donovan gleaned great insight

into the world of organized intelligence and special operations. In July 1941, FDR named Donovan to the OFFICE OF COORDINATOR OF INFORMATION (COI), the forerunner of the OSS.

Following the Japanese attack on Pearl Harbor, Donovan began the task of organizing, staffing, and directing what would become, in June 1942, the OSS. Donovan was directly involved in all aspects of the OSS, including actual participation in field operations. In March 1943, he was made a brigadier general in the Army. In November 1944, he was promoted to major general. Despite the fact that the OSS demonstrated remarkable proficiency in both special covert operations and intelligence gathering, not everyone understood or appreciated the organization's modus operandi. Prior to the end of World War II, Donovan proposed a postwar "centralized intelligence service." His plan would have combined clandestine warfare and intelligence-gathering operations under one roof. But the general public, fearful of an "American Gestapo," was wary. President Harry Truman also rejected Donovan's idea, telling the general that he was opposed to any form of "international spying" on the part of the United States. "It's un-American," Truman said.

In October 1945, the OSS was abolished. Its primary operations moved to the War Department; research and analysis units were transferred to the State Department. On January 22, 1946, Truman issued a directive establishing the NATIONAL INTELLIGENCE AUTHORITY (NIA) and the CENTRAL INTELLIGENCE GROUP (CIG). That same month, Donovan was awarded the Distinguished Service Medal and left the Army. He returned to his private law practice.

The following year, the CIA was created by the NATIONAL SECURITY ACT OF 1947. The new agency, a variation of Donovan's plan, combined intelligence operations under a single DIRECTOR OF CENTRAL INTELLIGENCE (DCI), and it was to recruit heavily from Donovan's wartime operatives. Donovan offered advice, particularly in the realm of developing covert-action programs to counter communist expansion around the world, but he refused any role in the new CIA.

From 1953 to 1954, Donovan served as ambassador to Thailand. During that period, he was involved in increasing the number of Thailand-based American military advisers.

As an end-of-service award, President Dwight Eisenhower presented him the National Security Medal, making Donovan the first and only American to win his country's top four military and civilian honors.

Donovan died in Washington, D.C., on February 8, 1959. He was buried in Arlington National Cemetery.

Today, a statue of Donovan stands in the main lobby of the CIA's headquarters in LANGLEY, VIRGINIA. The inscription on the marble base reads:

William "Wild Bill" Donovan   (NATIONAL ARCHIVE)

MAJOR GENERAL
WILLIAM J. DONOVAN
DIRECTOR
OFFICE OF STRATEGIC SERVICES
THE FORERUNNER OF THE
CENTRAL INTELLIGENCE AGENCY

See also GESTAPO FEAR, THE GREAT.

Donovan proposal

The Donovan proposal, also known as "The Basis for a Permanent U.S. Foreign Intelligence Service," was embodied in a series of documents by Major General WILLIAM J. "WILD BILL" DONOVAN outlining a plan for a third branch of the armed services—a "Strategic Service." The plan, drafted during the waning days of World War II, proposed a permanent, centrally controlled intelligence service that would exist on an equal footing with the Army, Navy, and Air Force. It would conduct intelligence-gathering and analytical operations during peace as well as war. Donovan's service would also maintain a covert-action arm.

Donovan drew on his own experiences with both the OFFICE OF THE COORDINATOR OF INFORMATION (COI)

and the OFFICE OF STRATEGIC SERVICES (OSS), the two predecessor organizations of the CIA. Donovan was also heavily influenced by the British, with whom he worked so closely during World War II.

During a wartime trip to Washington, D.C., William Cavendish-Bentinck, then head of the British Joint Intelligence Committee, advised Donovan to keep intelligence operations and covert-action projects under one roof. In Phillip Knightly's acclaimed book *The Second Oldest Profession,* Cavendish-Bentinck recalled a conversation he had with Donovan: "I remember saying to Bill Donovan 'Don't have two organizations; one for skullduggery, tripping people up, cutting throats, and any other nasty business like our SOE [SPECIAL OPERATIONS EXECUTIVE]; and another like our SIS [Secret Intelligence Service] for intelligence. Because they'd be quarreling the whole time and trying to get the better of one another instead of getting the better of the enemy. Have one control organization.' I didn't know that I was acting as a midwife for that monster, the CIA."

Though rejected in its initial form, the idea of establishing such an agency was never quashed. The modern CIA was created under the NATIONAL SECURITY ACT OF 1947.

Doole, George Arntzen, Jr. (1909–1985)

George Arntzen Doole, Jr., was a pre–World War II Army Air Corps pilot who was later credited with founding AIR AMERICA, the largest of the CIA's proprietary airlines.

Doole was born in Quincy, Illinois, on August 12, 1909. He graduated from the University of Illinois in 1931. He then entered the U.S. Army Air Corps flight school as an aviation cadet. Upon earning his pilots wings, he was commissioned a second lieutenant and began flying with active units in Hawaii, France, and Panama.

In 1934, Doole left the Air Corps for a job as an apprentice pilot and flight mechanic with Pan American (Pan Am) World Airways. Five years later, he was granted temporary leave from Pan Am in order to pursue an MBA at Harvard University Business School. Upon graduation, he briefly returned to Pan Am.

When the United States entered World War II, Doole rejoined the Army Air Corps. After the war, he returned to Pan Am, serving as the airline's regional director for Asia and the Middle East.

In 1951, Doole, by then a colonel in the Air Force Reserve, was called to active duty. The Korean War was in its second year, but Doole was sent to the Middle East as chief of estimates for Air Force intelligence. There, he served under GENERAL CHARLES PEARRE CABELL, the future DEPUTY DIRECTOR OF CENTRAL INTELLIGENCE (DCI), who would be ousted after the ill-fated BAY OF PIGS

INVASION of 1961, and an officer whom Doole had known during his Air Corps service in the 1930s.

In April 1953, Cabell was appointed DIRECTOR OF CENTRAL INTELLIGENCE (DCI). Three months later, he recruited Doole into the CIA to oversee the Agency's troubled CIVIL AIR TRANSPORT (CAT) service. CAT was the CIA's covert-mission air service, operating out of Taiwan (Formosa). CAT had been purchased by the Agency from Lt. Gen. Claire Chennault in 1950, but ownership had been concealed through a number of complex financial arrangements. In 1959, the air service's name was changed to Air America and placed under the control of a Delaware-based holding company, the Airdale Corporation (later renamed the Pacific Corporation); also owned by the CIA. Doole, who was instrumental in the company's evolution, was made the company's president as a COVER.

Like CAT, Air America flew a variety of aircraft and missions in support of American intelligence operations. During the war in Southeast Asia, Air America operated primarily out of Laos and Thailand; the airline's missions including everything from food drops to photo reconnaissance, to the delivery and recovery of covert operatives and special-operations teams across national borders. Air America pilots, mostly ex-military aviators, were attracted by the lure of high adventure and even higher wages. The Agency's airlines were profitable during the Doole years; Air America developed into one of the largest air fleets in the world.

Doole retired from the CIA in 1971. The following year, DCI RICHARD M. HELMS ordered the Agency to divest itself of the largest of its air proprietaries, Air America, when the war in Vietnam was ended. For the next several years, Doole was involved in Arntzen Enterprises, a family holding company with several aircraft-related subsidiary businesses.

Doole died on March 9, 1985. He was 75.

Doolittle Report

The Doolittle Report was, in effect, a mission statement, based on a presidentially commissioned study that addressed the "rules of the game" in American espionage during the COLD WAR. Issued on September 30, 1954, the Doolittle Report was the product of a committee appointed by President Dwight Eisenhower and chaired by Lt. Gen. James H. Doolittle, the famous U.S. Army Air Corps commander.

Following a three-month study, Doolittle submitted directly to Eisenhower a 69-page classified report containing 42 recommendations. It began with a summary of contemporary American cold war attitudes following the Korean War. A portion of that summary reads: "It is now clear that we are facing an implacable enemy whose avowed objective is world domination by whatever means and at whatever cost. There are no rules in such a game. Hitherto, acceptable norms of human conduct do not apply. If the United States is to survive, long-standing American concepts of fair play must be reconsidered. We must develop effective espionage and counterespionage services and must learn to subvert, sabotage, and destroy our enemies by more clever, more sophisticated, and more effective methods than those used against us."

The report went on to make several recommendations as to how American espionage capabilities might be improved through better organization, training, and strategic intelligence-gathering efforts.

The Doolittle Report was declassified in 1976.

double agent

A double agent is a clandestine operative who works for two opposing espionage organizations but who is loyal to one of the organizations and betrays the other. For example, former CIA COUNTERINTELLIGENCE officer ALDRICH HAZEN "RICKY" AMES spied for the Soviet Union during the same period he was employed by the Agency. He was paid by both, but he was loyal only to the Soviets. Thus, he was a double agent. A double agent is also known as a "counterspy."

Douglas, Kingman (1896–1971)

Kingman Douglas is considered to be the first DEPUTY DIRECTOR OF CENTRAL INTELLIGENCE (DDCI), though his position was officially "acting DDCI."

Douglas was born in Oak Park, Illinois, on April 16, 1896. He attended Yale University, earning a bachelor's degree in 1918. He then began a career as an investment banker.

During World War II, Douglas served as an intelligence officer with the U.S. Army Air Corps—first as an intelligence liaison officer with the British Air Ministry in the European theater of operations, then as an Allied Intelligence Group officer in the Pacific theater. When the war ended, he joined the CENTRAL INTELLIGENCE GROUP (CIG), the short-lived interim intelligence organization that bridged the gap between the abolition of the OFFICE OF STRATEGIC SERVICES (OSS) and the creation of the CIA.

In March 1946, Douglas was appointed as both assistant director and acting deputy director of central intelligence under DIRECTOR OF CENTRAL INTELLIGENCE (DCI) SIDNEY WILLIAM SOUERS. In July, he transferred from the CIG's front office to the OFFICE OF SPECIAL OPERATIONS. In September, he resigned from the CIG. He joined the CIA on January 4, 1951, as assistant director for current intelligence. He served in that capacity until his resignation from the Agency on July 11, 1952.

Douglas died on October 8, 1971. He was 75.

Downey, John Thomas (Jack) (1930–)

John Thomas "Jack" Downey was a CIA covert-operations officer who in 1952, during a clandestine operation in China, was captured by the communists and sentenced to life in prison for espionage. He was released after 21 years.

Born in 1930, Downey was raised in New Britain, Connecticut. He attended the Choate School and later Yale University, where he earned a bachelor's degree in 1951. After graduation, he joined the CIA and was soon posted to the OFFICE OF POLICY COORDINATION (OPC), then the Agency's covert-action arm.

Downey spent his first three months with the CIA training at Fort Benning, Georgia. He was then assigned to the OPC's Far East Division at the U.S. Naval Air Station, Atsugi, Japan.

Downey was an active participant in OPERATION TROPIC, a series of Agency-supported insurgency operations conducted by "third force" teams (anticommunists who were not allied with the Nationalist Chinese on Taiwan) against communist forces on the Chinese mainland). During one such mission, on November 29, 1952, a CIVIL AIR TRANSPORT (CAT) aircraft with Downey on board was shot down by communist ground forces. The pilot and copilot were killed in the crash. Downey and fellow CIA officer RICHARD GEORGE FECTEAU were taken prisoner. Initially, the U.S. government denied that Downey and Fecteau were CIA officers; the official story was that the two men were civilian employees of the U.S. Army who had been on a "routine flight" from Seoul, Korea, to Japan.

Fecteau was sentenced to 20 years in prison and was released in December 1971, after serving 19 years. Downey, who was sentenced to life, was released in March 1973 after President Richard Nixon admitted publicly that both men were in fact CIA officers.

In a 1998 ceremony honoring Downey and Fecteau with Director's Medals, DIRECTOR OF CENTRAL INTELLIGENCE (DCI) GEORGE TENET referred to the two men as "true legends." Tenet added, "You demonstrated heroism of a whole other magnitude during those dark decades of captivity. Your story, simply put, is one of the most remarkable in the fifty-year history of the CENTRAL INTELLIGENCE AGENCY."

Downey currently serves as a Superior Court judge in Connecticut.

Dragon Lady aircraft

See POWERS, FRANCIS GARY; U-2 (DRAGON LADY); U-2 INCIDENT.

dream-world spookology

"Dream-world spookology" is synonymous with CLANDESTINE MENTALITY.

See also CONSPIRATORIAL NEUROSIS; SICK THINK.

drop

In most instances, a drop is simply a predetermined secret location where officers and agents leave messages and other items for undetected collection by other parties. Such a location is also referred to as a "dead drop," as opposed to a "live drop," where operatives actually meet face to face in order to deliver messages and items.

drycleaning

In CIA parlance, the term "drycleaning" refers to the methods used by a pursued subject to elude pursuers. For instance, during a surveillance on foot, the pursued subject might dash down an alley, suddenly change his route, or dart into an elevator or subway.

Dulles, Allen Welsh (1898–1969)

One of the best known of the senior CIA chiefs, DIRECTOR OF CENTRAL INTELLIGENCE (DCI) Allen Welsh Dulles was the first civilian director of the CIA, and he presided over one of the most dramatic periods in the Agency's history.

Dulles was born on April 7, 1898, in Watertown, New York, to Allen Macy Dulles, a Presbyterian pastor, and Edith Foster, daughter of former secretary of state John W. Foster. As a boy, Dulles attended school in both Auburn, New York, and at the École Alsatienne in Paris, France. In 1910, he enrolled at Princeton, earning a bachelor's degree in 1914 and a master's in 1916. Soon after graduation, he was recruited by the U.S. STATE DEPARTMENT and began a lifelong career in foreign service.

Following a brief course in espionage taught by WILLIAM STEPHENSON, the famous British intelligence officer known as INTREPID, Dulles was posted to Vienna, Austria. Arriving on July 7, 1916, he was tasked with collecting political information on Germany and the Austro-Hungarian Empire.

When America entered World War I on April 7, 1917, all U.S. intelligence and diplomatic operations in Vienna were relocated to Bern, Switzerland. Arriving in Bern on April 23, Dulles was made chief of intelligence. The war ended on November 11, 1918. During the Paris Peace Conference in 1919, he served in the U.S. State Department's intelligence unit. He remained with the department but transferred to the American legation in Berlin.

In May 1920, Dulles was assigned to gather military and economic intelligence on oil-related activities in Southwest Asia. In 1922, he became chief of the State Department's Near Eastern Affairs Division. In 1925, he served as an American delegate to the Geneva Arms Traffic Conference.

In 1926, Dulles earned a law degree from George Washington University. He then joined New York–based Sullivan & Cromwell, an international law firm where his older brother, John Foster Dulles, was a senior partner (the elder Dulles was destined to become secretary of state under President Dwight Eisenhower). The following year, Dulles returned to Europe, this time as a legal adviser to the American delegation attending the Three Powers Naval Conference. He also served as legal adviser to the Geneva Disarmament Conferences of both 1932 and 1933.

Dulles campaigned unsuccessfully for the Republican nomination to a New York congressional seat in 1938. Two years later, he was active in the presidential campaign of Wendell Wilkie.

In 1941, Dulles was ordered to Bolivia to help "neutralize" German influence on Bolivian airlines. The following year, he joined the OFFICE OF THE COORDINATOR OF INFORMATION (COI), the precursor to the OFFICE OF STRATEGIC SERVICES (OSS), the World War II predecessor organization to the CIA. Soon, he was made chief of the OSS's New York office, which coordinated much of the North American training and intelligence-gathering effort between the OSS and the British Secret Service in North America.

In November 1942, Dulles returned to Switzerland, this time to establish an OSS secret intelligence station in Bern. He remained in Bern for the remainder of the war. When the Nazis surrendered in the spring of 1945, he was made CHIEF OF STATION (COS) in Wiesbaden, West Germany. In November, he returned to his law practice in New York.

The following year, Dulles was named president of the Council on Foreign Relations. He also became an adviser to GENERAL HOYT S. VANDENBERG and REAR ADMIRAL ROSCOE H. HILLENKOETTER during their terms as DCI. During that period, Dulles assisted in drafting the NATIONAL SECURITY ACT OF 1947. The act, which became effective on September 18, reorganized America's national defense system and established a permanent CENTRAL INTELLIGENCE AGENCY under a new NATIONAL SECURITY COUNCIL (NSC).

In 1948, Dulles again entered politics, this time as an adviser to presidential candidate Thomas Dewey. That same year, Dulles, future DEPUTY DIRECTOR OF CENTRAL INTELLIGENCE (DDCI) William Jackson, and Matthias Correa, a former assistant to Secretary of Defense James V. Forrestal, embarked on a study that resulted in a scathing critique of the newly established CIA.

In August 1951, Dulles became DDCI. On February 26, 1953, President Dwight Eisenhower appointed him DCI. As DCI, Dulles became known as "the great white CASE OFFICER"—a nickname that suggested his personal involvement in the particulars of covert operations. Indeed, it was covert operations, not intelligence gathering, that best characterized the Agency's efforts under his tenure. During the Dulles years, the CIA was involved in such ventures as the IRAN COUP D'ÉTAT, the GUATEMALA COUP D'ÉTAT, and the U-2 reconnaissance aircraft program. But the most memorable event of Dulles's term was the ill-fated invasion of Cuba (code named ZAPATA) at the BAY OF PIGS in 1961.

The invasion, considered to be the worst operational disaster in CIA history, forced President John Kennedy to ask for Dulles's resignation. On November 29, 1961, Dulles left the Agency. Despite being forced into retirement, he was heartily praised by Kennedy during ceremonies dedicating the CIA's new LANGLEY headquarters building on November 28, 1961. "I know of no man who brings a greater sense of personal commitment to his work, who has less pride in office than he [Dulles] has," said Kennedy. "Your successes are unheralded—your

Allen Welsh Dulles (NATIONAL ARCHIVE)

failures trumpeted. I sometimes have that feeling myself. But I am sure you realize how important your work is, how essential it is, and how in the long sweep of history, how significant your efforts will be judged."

In addition to his intelligence career, Dulles was also an accomplished author. His works include *Germany's Underground* (1947), *The Craft of Intelligence* (1963), and *Secret Surrender* (1966).

On January 28, 1969, Dulles died at his home of an acute case of influenza. He was 71.

See also DULLES-JACKSON-CORREA REPORT; KOLBE, FRITZ.

Dulles-Jackson-Correa Report (Dulles Report)

Submitted to the NATIONAL SECURITY COUNCIL (NSC) in January 1949, the Dulles-Jackson-Correa Report (or Dulles Report) was the result of a year-long study that addressed problems in the CIA's execution of both its intelligence and its operational missions. Conducted by future DIRECTOR OF CENTRAL INTELLIGENCE (DCI) ALLEN WELSH DULLES, future DEPUTY DIRECTOR OF CENTRAL INTELLIGENCE (DDCI) William Jackson, and Matthias Correa, a former assistant to Secretary of Defense James V. Forrestal, the report was highly critical of the CIA, attacking it on countless fronts, including its alleged "failure to take charge of the production of coordinated national estimates."

The Dulles Report consisted of 193 pages containing 56 recommendations. "It [the report] was quite a devastating critique of CIA," said J. Kenneth McDonald, former chief historian of the CIA, during a 1994 lecture to the Center for the Study of Intelligence. "The criticisms were principally that the Central Intelligence Agency and the DCI were not carrying out the coordinating functions like they were supposed to do." McDonald contends that the Dulles Report suggested that the CIA was "an organization that was adrift." He added that the report was also a "vote of no-confidence" for REAR ADMIRAL ROSCOE HENRY HILLENKOETTER, then the director of central intelligence.

Among the particulars addressed by the report was an argument that the CIA's trend toward intelligence-gathering activities should be reversed in favor of its previously mandated role as a coordinator of intelligence. Other items addressed the CIA's internal security issues, including the high turnover rate of employees, an excessive number of military personnel, inadequacies in the realm of scientific intelligence, and an overall lack of coordination between the CIA and the FEDERAL BUREAU OF INVESTIGATION (FBI). Recommendations included elevating the FBI to membership in the Intelligence Advisory Committee (IAC) and a reorganization of the CIA to avoid duplication of effort.

The Dulles Report was partially declassified in 1976.

E

Eberstadt Study (Eberstadt Report)

The Eberstadt Study, of January 1949 concluded that the CIA should be the "logical arbiter" of differences of opinion regarding intelligence matters between the American armed forces and the DEPARTMENT OF STATE. The report was produced by the HOOVER COMMISSION's Committee on National Security Organization (best known as the Eberstadt Committee) under the leadership of New York investment banker Ferdinand Eberstadt, a staunch proponent of a strong centralized intelligence capability. Hearings began in June 1948. On January 13, 1949, the committee's 121-page unclassified report was submitted to Congress.

According to the report, the "National Security Organization, established by the NATIONAL SECURITY ACT OF 1947," was "soundly constructed, but not yet working well." The report cited fundamental shortcomings in the national intelligence effort and the newly established CIA. Among those shortcomings was an "adversarial relationship and lack of coordination" between the CIA, the U.S. State Department, and the armed forces. The report suggested that such a relationship resulted in an unnecessary duplication of effort and departmental intelligence estimates that "have often been subjective and biased."

Much of the blame was heaped on the State Department and the military for failing to consult the CIA and acquaint it with, pertinent information. The report recommended "that positive efforts be made to foster relations of mutual confidence between the CIA and the several departments and agencies that it serves." Establishment within the CIA of a top-echelon evaluation board of "competent and experienced personnel who would have no administrative responsibilities and whose duties would be confined solely to intelligence evaluation" was recommended, as was a civilian director of central intelligence with a long term in office. The report also stressed that the CIA "must be the central organization of the national intelligence system."

Regarding special operations, the report suggested that all covert operations be integrated into one CIA office overseen by the NATIONAL SECURITY COUNCIL (NSC). During time of war, those clandestine operations would be the direct responsibility of the JOINT CHIEFS OF STAFF (JCS).

CIA budget, organizational, and strategic intelligence-collection matters were also addressed in the report. Briefly considered and rejected by the committee was the idea of placing the COUNTERINTELLIGENCE responsibilities of the FEDERAL BUREAU OF INVESTIGATION (FBI) under CIA control.

edible paper

Edible paper is simply water-soluble, digestible paper used in writing secret messages. In an emergency, a spy carrying a message written on edible paper would swallow the paper to avoid its being compromised.

See also SECRET WRITING.

Eifler, Colonel Carl Frederich (1906–)

Colonel Carl Frederich Eifler was the commander of the famed DETACHMENT 101, the first of the OFFICE OF STRATEGIC SERVICES (OSS) paramilitary units during World War II.

Eifler was born the son of Carl Frederich Eifler, Sr., and Pauline Engelbert Eifler in Los Angeles, California, on June 27, 1906. When he was 16 years old, Eifler enlisted in the U.S. Army; he served for one year. As a young man, he joined the Los Angeles Police Department. He then served as a chief inspector with the U.S. Border Patrol along the Mexican border.

When the Japanese attacked Pearl Harbor in 1941, Eifler was living in Honolulu serving as deputy director of the U.S. Customs Bureau and as a U.S. Army Reserve captain. He was immediately called to active duty with the Hawaii-based 25th Infantry Regiment. But Eifler was not an ordinary army officer. He was a skilled pilot, an accomplished rifleman, a former professional boxer and martial arts expert, and a good friend of General Joseph "Vinegar Joe" Stillwell, commander of U.S. forces in the China-Burma-India Theater.

Recognizing Eifler's "unique qualities," WILLIAM J. "WILD BILL" DONOVAN, head of the OFFICE OF THE COORDINATOR OF INFORMATION (the first predecessor organization to the CIA), arranged for his transfer to COI. There, Eifler was promoted to major and tasked with developing, training, and commanding the office's first special-operations unit. The unit, known as Detachment 101, was established in May 1942 under the newly created OSS, the wartime precursor to the CIA.

The detachment was soon shipped to India. In India, Eifler and his 25 officers and men sat idle for several weeks. Despite Eifler's relationship with Stillwell, the general was not yet convinced of the value of special, paramilitary forces. Stillwell's opinion changed, however, when ordered to lead an American offensive against the Japanese in the rugged Burmese countryside. Stillwell directed Eifler to conduct sabotage and resistance operations against the enemy in Burma: "The next thing I want to hear out of you are some loud booms from behind the Jap lines." Soon, Eifler's men were proving themselves—gathering vital intelligence, coordinating air strikes against the enemy, destroying bridges, cutting communications lines, and training and equipping native Kachin tribesmen to fight the Japanese.

Unfortunately for Eifler, he was injured in a plane crash during an aerial reconnaissance mission in 1943.

He was subsequently discharged at the rank of colonel, and command of Detachment 101 was passed to LT. COL. WILLIAM R. PEERS.

After the war, Eifler briefly returned to work as a U.S. Customs inspector. He then became a Protestant clergyman and a psychologist. In 1954, he accepted a position as business manager at Jackson College in Honolulu, Hawaii. Two years later, he earned a bachelor of divinity degree from that institution. In 1959, he began working as an instructor and graduate research assistant at the Illinois Institute of Technology (IIT) in Chicago. In 1962, he earned a Ph.D. from IIT. He returned in 1964 to California, where he worked as a psychologist for the Monterey County Mental Health Services in Salinas. He retired in 1973.

Eifler's military and civilian awards include the U.S. Army's Combat Infantryman's Badge, the Legion of Merit with two oak-leaf clusters, the Bronze Star, the Air Medal, and the Purple Heart. He has also been named to Military Intelligence Corps Hall of Fame. He is a recipient of the Albert Gallatin Award from the U.S. Department of the Treasury, the General William J. Donovan Award, and the Knowlton Award for Military Intelligence. The Eifler Sports Plaza and Museum in Fort Huachuca, Arizona, is named in his honor.

ELINT (electronic intelligence)

ELINT is the acronym for "electronic intelligence." This form of intelligence is usually gathered by monitoring, collecting information, and analyzing technical data and electronic signals emitted from radar, jamming devices, and airborne missiles and aircraft.

See also ALL-SOURCE INTELLIGENCE; INTELLIGENCE CYCLE.

Elite Directorate

Elite Directorate is a nickname of the CIA's DIRECTORATE of Operations (DO), the "spy side" of the house.

The term was coined by Herbert E. Hetu, the Agency's public affairs officer during the tenure of DIRECTOR OF CENTRAL INTELLIGENCE (DCI) STANSFIELD TURNER. Turner himself referred to Agency employees working in the DO as the "untouchables."

Ellsberg, Daniel (1931–)

A U.S. defense consultant turned antiwar activist, Daniel Ellsberg is best known for leaking the 47-volume secret study of America's involvement in Vietnam, the *PENTAGON PAPERS,* to the *New York Times* in 1971.

Ellsberg was born in Chicago in 1931. He attended both Harvard and Cambridge Universities, eventually receiving a master's degree in economics from Harvard.

In 1954, Ellsberg entered the U.S. Marine Corps, rising to the rank of first lieutenant. When his two-year term of service was completed in 1956, he requested an extension in order to ship out with his battalion, which was deploying to the Middle East and the developing crisis in the Suez.

After leaving the Marines, Ellsberg returned to Harvard, where he earned a Ph.D. in 1962. He then joined the RAND Corporation, an academic "think tank" specializing in research and analysis projects for decision makers in the corporate world and the federal government. By 1967, he was a senior research associate at the Massachusetts Institute of Technology (MIT) Center for International Studies. That same year, Secretary of Defense Robert McNamara commissioned Ellsberg and 34 other researchers to compile a history of American/Vietnamese relations from 1945 through 1968. Ellsberg was responsible for researching the escalation period during President John Kennedy's administration in 1961. The project took 18 months.

Initially, Ellsberg supported American military intervention in the Vietnam War. But as the war escalated and he got deeper into his research, Ellsberg grew disillusioned with U.S. policy and became a staunch opponent of any American involvement in SOUTHEAST ASIA. "I think now to a large extent it was an American president's war," he would write years later. "No American president, Republican or Democrat, wanted to be the president who lost the war or who lost Saigon." He added, "To call a conflict in which one army is financed and equipped entirely by foreigners a 'civil war' simply screens a more painful reality: That the war is, after all, a foreign aggression. Our aggression."

In mid-1969, Ellsberg and several of his associates wrote President Richard Nixon a letter expressing their opposition to the war. Ellsberg's protests became more public when in 1970 he participated in an antiwar rally at Georgetown University.

In 1971, Ellsberg released to the media the completed *Pentagon Papers*—a 47-volume history of the war, some 3,000 pages of classified analysis and another 4,000 pages of appended documents, much of it top secret and top secret–sensitive. The *Pentagon Papers* first appeared on the front page of the *New York Times* on June 13. The story was then picked up by a number of other newspapers, including the *Washington Post* and the *Boston Globe*. The U.S. government obtained an injunction that temporarily prevented the publication of further stories. But the U.S. Supreme Court ruled in favor of the media, and the stories continued to be published.

Ellsberg, who contended that he was willing to risk a prison sentence to end the war, was indicted on several counts, including converting government property to personal use (via a copy machine), possessing government documents, conspiracy, theft, and espionage. The first trial was declared a mistrial in 1972 after Ellsberg's attorneys successfully argued that the papers were in the public domain and therefore did not constitute a threat to national security. The following year, just as Ellsberg was preparing for a second trial, the judge dismissed all charges when it was revealed by the WATERGATE prosecutors that the Nixon White House had directed former CIA dirty-tricks master EVERETTE HOWARD HUNT to burglarize the offices of Dr. Lewis J. Fielding—Ellsberg's psychoanalyst—in an attempt to uncover personal information that might prove damaging to Ellsberg's reputation. It would later be discovered that the CIA had supplied Hunt with a wig, a camera, a speech-altering device, and false identification papers for the operation.

Citing government misconduct, the judge declared that Ellsberg and the American public had been "victims of a conspiracy to deprive us of our civil liberties." Ellsberg regarded the judge's ruling as "the defrocking of the Wizard of Oz."

Since the end of the Vietnam War, Ellsberg has been an outspoken opponent of the nuclear arms race and nuclear proliferation. To that end, he has lectured all over the country, and he has been arrested on nearly 70 occasions in acts of civil disobedience.

From 1992 to 1995, he served as a lobbyist for the Washington, D.C.–based Physicians for Social Responsibility, a group with antinuclear goals. On January 10, 1999, Ellsberg was interviewed by CNN reporter Bruce Kennedy for CNN's *Perspectives* series *Cold War*. Asked about the White House's alleged willingness to "neutralize" him, Ellsberg claimed to believe that CIA operatives had once been assigned the task of physically harming him. A portion of that interview reads: "Charles Colson, who was the counsel to the president, called Jeb Magruder, who was running the Committee to Reelect the President (CREEP), to arrange for counter-demonstrators to disrupt physically a demonstration, a rally at which I would be speaking on May 3 [1972]. Magruder turned to Gordon Liddy and Howard Hunt, who arranged for 12 Cuban Americans, all of whom had worked for the CIA or were still on the CIA payroll, to be flown up from Miami for this purpose. They have testified that they were shown my photo, told that this was their target and that I was to be beaten up. Eventually the special prosecutor, Watergate prosecutor, who was investigating this action told me that their orders were 'to incapacitate Daniel Ellsberg totally.' I asked him, "What does that mean? To kill me?' And he simply repeated the orders. But you have to realize that these guys never used the word 'kill.' He believed the intent was to kill me. My own judgment, looking at several other things, including over 1,000 pages of Watergate special task force documents, [is] that the intention was not to kill me but simply to shut me up physically at that particular moment. That is, to put me in the hospital."

emblem, CIA

See SEAL OF OFFICE, CIA.

Enduring Freedom

Enduring Freedom is the code name for the series of military actions and intelligence-gathering operations conducted by the American-led coalition of nations against terrorist leader OSAMA BIN LADEN in Afghanistan. The operations, initially known as INFINITE JUSTICE (the original code name was dropped as it was deemed insensitive to the Islamic faith), were launched in the aftermath of the SEPTEMBER 11, 2001, TERRORIST ATTACKS ON THE UNITED STATES.

See also TERRORISM, CIA'S INVOLVEMENT IN THE WAR AGAINST.

Energy, U.S. Department of (DOE)

The U.S. Department of Energy (DOE) is one of three non–Defense Department components of the U.S. INTELLIGENCE COMMUNITY. Aside from its primary responsibilities of providing national leadership in the related domains of energy, science, technology, the economy, the environment, and national security, the DOE maintains a foreign intelligence program that provides intelligence analyses of foreign countries bent on acquiring sensitive DOE information, as well as technical and analytical expertise to the other members of the intelligence community. The DOE is the successor of the Atomic Energy Commission (AEC). In July 1947, the AEC was authorized a seat on the Intelligence Advisory Board.

When the NATIONAL SECURITY ACT OF 1947 was passed, the AEC's role in foreign intelligence was affirmed by NATIONAL SECURITY COUNCIL (NSC) Intelligence Directive Number 1 on December 12. Nearly three decades later, the Energy Reorganization Act of 1974 transferred the AEC's intelligence responsibilities to the U.S. Energy Research and Development Administration. With the passing of the Department of Energy Organization Act in 1977, those responsibilities were transferred to the DOE.

The department's foreign intelligence program is a component of the U.S. intelligence community. Its missions are to provide the department and other U.S. government policy and decision makers with timely, accurate, high-impact foreign intelligence analyses; to detect and defeat foreign intelligence services bent on acquiring sensitive information on the Department's programs, facilities, technology, and personnel; to provide technical and analytical support to the DIRECTOR OF CENTRAL INTELLIGENCE (DCI); and to make the department's technical and analytical expertise available to other members of the community.

On December 4, 1981, President Ronald Reagan issued EXECUTIVE ORDER 12333, clarifying the ambigui-ties of previously issued orders and outlining the goals of the intelligence community. The order directed the DOE to provide "expert technical, analytical and research capability to the Intelligence Community; to formulate intelligence collection and analysis requirements where the expert capability of the Department can contribute; to produce and disseminate foreign intelligence necessary for the Secretary of Energy's responsibilities; and to participate with the Department of State in overtly collecting information with respect to foreign energy matters."

The DOE's intelligence responsibilities include issues of global nuclear proliferation, nuclear weapons technology, fossil-fuel and nuclear energy, and science and technology. The DOE's responsibilities related to nuclear energy and weapons proliferation were expanded with the passing of the Nuclear Non-Proliferation Act of 1978.

The DOE is headed by the secretary of energy. But like its fellow intelligence community members, the department's intelligence efforts are coordinated by the DIRECTOR OF CENTRAL INTELLIGENCE (DCI). The department also reports directly to the president, through the NATIONAL SECURITY ADVISOR.

espionage, economic

Economic espionage is the open-source and clandestine acquisition of a nation's sensitive financial, trade, technological, or economic policy information by government intelligence agencies, such as the CIA. This form of espionage is also employed to clandestinely influence economic policy decisions of foreign governments in order to inflict loss on the economy of that foreign government's nation.

The term "economic espionage" is often, though incorrectly, used interchangeably with the term "INDUSTRIAL ESPIONAGE." The latter is normally conducted by competing businesses, not by governments.

espionage, industrial

Industrial espionage is the open-source and clandestine acquisition of a business's proprietary or secret information by another business or a nongovernment entity. Unlike ECONOMIC ESPIONAGE, which involves opposing governments, industrial espionage is normally conducted by competing firms.

At the international level, industrial espionage is most commonly used against businesses involved in the development of war materials (ground, sea, air, or space). Industrial espionage may be practiced as a means of increasing one's share of a highly competitive international market, thus protecting the spying country's own industrial power.

Spies employed by businesses use the same procedures and equipment as those in economic espionage. The only exception is that, in the event of exposure, they rarely face death or imprisonment for criminal activity. In most cases, they only lose their jobs. Not surprisingly, the term "industrial espionage" is often, though incorrectly, used interchangeably with the term "economic espionage."

EXCOM

EXCOM is the acronym for the CIA's Executive Committee, which comprises the DEPUTY DIRECTORS and is chaired by an executive director.

EXCOMM

EXCOMM was the acronym for the Executive Committee of the NATIONAL SECURITY COUNCIL (NSC) during the CUBAN MISSILE CRISIS in 1962.

President John Kennedy created EXCOMM as a short-term think tank to help him find ways of coping with the Soviet missiles in Cuba without going to war. Referred to unofficially as a "bunch of men Kennedy wanted to see when he first heard about the missiles," EXCOMM was in fact a hand-picked group of 19 senior military, diplomatic, and political advisers, some of whom had no previous connection with the NSC. The committee managed the crisis in a number of ways, including providing intelligence briefings to the president, editing the president's letters, and discussing the best courses of action to be taken.

Created on October 16 (the first day of the crisis) and officially constituted on October 22, EXCOMM comprised Vice President Lyndon Johnson, Secretary of State Dean Rusk, Secretary of Defense Robert McNamara, General Maxwell Taylor (chairman of the JOINT CHIEFS OF STAFF), NATIONAL SECURITY ADVISOR McGeorge Bundy, Secretary of the Treasury Douglas Dillon, Attorney General Robert Kennedy, Undersecretary of State George Ball, Deputy Secretary of Defense Roswell Gilpatric, Ambassador at Large Llewellyn Thompson, and DIRECTOR OF CENTRAL INTELLIGENCE (DCI) JOHN MCCONE. All of these were official members.

Unofficial members of EXCOMM included Alexis Johnson, deputy undersecretary of state; Paul Nitze, assistant secretary of defense; Dean Acheson, former secretary of state; Adlai Stevenson, United Nations ambassador; Donald Wilson, deputy director of the U.S. Information Agency; Edwin Martin, assistant secretary of state for inter-American affairs; Charles Bohlen, former U.S. ambassador to the Soviet Union; and personal presidential advisers John McCloy and Robert Lovett.

executive action

"Executive action" is a euphemism for assassination. The term came to light during the congressional hearings (CHURCH and PIKE COMMITTEES) of the mid-1970s in a number of CIA documents describing projects aimed at overthrowing or, if necessary, assassinating foreign leaders. According to the Church Committee's findings, no executive action ever actually occurred, though there were ASSASSINATION PLOTS during certain periods in the CIA's history, in particular the 1960s, when a number of attempts were made against the life of Cuban leader Fidel Castro.

In the wake of the SEPTEMBER 2001 TERRORIST ATTACKS ON THE UNITED STATES, the justifiability of executive action has been revisited.

executive orders, primary (EO)

The primary executive orders (presidentially mandated) affecting the conduct and organization of the CIA and other members of the U.S. INTELLIGENCE COMMUNITY are Executive Orders 9621, 11828, 11905, 12036, 12333, 12958, and 12968.

EXECUTIVE ORDER 9621

Signed by President Harry Truman on September 20, 1945, EO 9621 officially terminated the OFFICE OF STRATEGIC SERVICES (OSS) and transferred its operational functions to the War Department. OSS research and analysis units were transferred to the State Department and designated the INTERIM RESEARCH AND INTELLIGENCE SERVICE.

The order is broken down into six "paragraphs," which address: (1) the transfer and consolidation of OSS research and analysis functions to the Department of State, (2) the pending abolition of the Interim Research and Intelligence Service, (3) the transfer of all other OSS functions to the Department of War, and the abolition of the OSS, (4) The authority of the director of the Bureau of the Budget in this matter, (5) prior presidential orders in conflict with the order, which were to be amended, and (6) the effective date of the order (October 1, 1945).

EXECUTIVE ORDER 11828

Signed by President Gerald Ford on January 4, 1975, EO 11828 created the "Commission on CIA Activities within the United States," also known as the ROCKEFELLER COMMISSION.

The order's summary paragraph reads: "The CENTRAL INTELLIGENCE AGENCY as created by the NATIONAL SECURITY ACT OF 1947 fulfills intelligence functions vital to the security of our nation, and many of its activities must necessarily be carried out in secrecy. Such activities are nevertheless subject to statutory limitations. I have determined that in order to insure scrupulous compliance with these statutory limitations, while fully recognizing the statutory missions of the Agency, it is advisable to establish a commission on CIA activities within the United States."

The order is broken down into six "sections," which address: (1) establishment of the commission, (2) functions of the commission, (3) cooperation by and with executive departments and agencies, (4) compensation, personnel, and finance, (5) administrative services, and (6) report and termination.

EXECUTIVE ORDER 11905

Signed by President Gerald Ford on February 18, 1976, EO 11905 established policies to improve the quality of American intelligence as it related to national security. Drafted in the wake of the 1975 congressional inquiries (Church and Pike Committees) into alleged CIA misdeeds, EO 11905 clarified the authority and responsibilities of the various members of the intelligence community. It also established oversight guidelines to ensure that intelligence agencies complied with the law.

Section 1 of the order addressed the purpose of the order. Section 2 of the order addressed definitions. Section 3 (control and direction of intelligence organizations) is broken down into four subsections for (3-a) the National Security Council, (3-b) the Committee on Foreign Intelligence, (3-c) the Operations Advisory Group, and (3-d) the Director of Central Intelligence. Section 4 (responsibilities and duties of the U.S. intelligence community) has seven subsections: (4-a) the senior official of each organization of the community, (4-b) the Central Intelligence Agency, (4-c) the Department of State, (4-d) the Department of the Treasury, (4-e) the Department of Defense, (4-f) the Energy Research and Development Administration, and (4-g) the Federal Bureau of Investigation.

Section 5 (restrictions on intelligence activities) is broken down into eight subsections, which address (5-a) definitions, (5-b) restrictions on collection, (5-c) dissemination and storage, (5-d) restrictions on experimentation, (5-e) assistance to law enforcement authorities, (5-f) assignment of personnel, (5-g) prohibition of assassination, and (5-h) implementation. Section 6 addresses oversight of intelligence organizations. Section 7 discusses secrecy protection. Section 8 provides enabling data.

EXECUTIVE ORDER 12036

Signed by President Jimmy Carter on January 24, 1978, EO 12036 reshaped the American intelligence structure and provided explicit guidance on organization and control of all foreign intelligence activities by the United States.

EO 12036 is most often referred to as the order that effectively banned assassinations by, or sponsored by, the Agency. This prohibition is found in Section 2 (2.305), "Prohibition on Assassination," which reads: "No person employed by or acting on behalf of the United States

government shall engage in, or conspire to engage in, assassination."

The order also addresses a number of other topics, including physical searches, mail surveillance, and participation in "special activities."

Section 1 (goals, direction, duties, and responsibilities with respect to the national intelligence effort) is broken down into 15 "subsections": (1.1) the NATIONAL SECURITY COUNCIL, (1.2) the NSC Policy Review Committee, (1.3) the NSC Special Coordination Committee, (1.4) the National Foreign Intelligence Board, (1.5) the National Intelligence Tasking Center, (1.6) the DIRECTOR OF CENTRAL INTELLIGENCE, (1.7) senior officials of the intelligence community, (1.8) the CENTRAL INTELLIGENCE AGENCY, (1.9) the DEPARTMENT OF STATE, (1.10) the Department of the Treasury, (1.11) the DEPARTMENT OF DEFENSE, (1.12) intelligence components utilized by the secretary of defense, (1.13) the DEPARTMENT OF ENERGY, (1.14) the FEDERAL BUREAU OF INVESTIGATION, and (1.15) the Drug Enforcement Administration.

Section 2 (restrictions on intelligence activities) of the order has 21 "subsections," which address (2.1) adherence to law, (2.2) restrictions on certain collection techniques, (2.201) general provisions, (2.202) electronic surveillance, (2.203) television cameras and other monitoring, (2.204) physical searches, (2.205) mail surveillance, (2.206) physical surveillance, (2.207) undisclosed participation in domestic organizations, (2.208) collection of non–publicly available information, (2.3) additional restrictions and limitations, (2.301) tax information, (2.302) restrictions on experimentation, (2.303) restrictions on contracting, (2.304) restrictions on personnel assigned to other agencies, (2.305) prohibitions on assassination, (2.306) restrictions on special activities, (2.307) restrictions on indirect participation in prohibited activities, (2.308) restrictions on assistance to law enforcement authorities, (2.309) permissible assistance to law enforcement authorities, and (2.310) permissible dissemination and storage of information.

Section 3 (oversight of intelligence organizations) is broken down into four "subsections" for (3.1) the INTELLIGENCE OVERSIGHT BOARD, (3.2) inspectors general and general counsel, (3.3) the attorney general, and (3.4) congressional intelligence committees.

Section 4 (general provisions) has two "subsections" which address (4.1) implementation and (4.2) definitions.

EO 12306 superseded Executive Orders 11905, 11985, and 11994, all of which addressed "United States Foreign Intelligence Activities."

EXECUTIVE ORDER 12333

Signed by President Ronald Reagan on December 4, 1981, EO 12333 clarified the ambiguities of previous orders and set clear goals for the American intelligence community in accordance with law and with due regard for the rights of Americans.

The order designates the Director of Central Intelligence as "the primary intelligence adviser" to the president and National Security Council on all foreign intelligence activities. In this capacity, the DCI is responsible for implementing special or covert actions activities, serving as a liaison to the nation's foreign intelligence and counterintelligence components, and protecting the community's sources, methods, and analytical procedures. The order also grants the DCI "full responsibility for the production and dissemination of national foreign intelligence." This responsibility also includes the authority to task non-CIA intelligence organizations. Like previous orders, EO 12333 prohibits assassinations.

A portion of the order's summary reads: "Timely and accurate information about the activities, capabilities, plans, and intentions of foreign powers, organizations, and persons, and their agents, is essential to the national security of the United States. All reasonable and lawful means must be used to ensure that the United States will receive the best intelligence available. For that purpose, by virtue of the authority vested in me by the Constitution and statutes of the United States of America, including the NATIONAL SECURITY ACT OF 1947, as amended, and as President of the United States of America, in order to provide for the effective conduct of United States intelligence activities and the protection of constitutional rights, it is hereby ordered."

Part 1 (goals, direction, duties, and responsibilities with respect to the national intelligence effort) is broken down into 14 "sections," which address: (1.1) goals, (1.2) the National Security Council, (1.3) national foreign intelligence advisory groups, (1.4) the intelligence community, (1.5) DIRECTOR OF CENTRAL INTELLIGENCE, (1.6) duties and responsibilities of the heads of executive branch departments and agencies, (1.7) senior officials of the intelligence community, (1.8) the Central Intelligence Agency, (1.9) the Department of State, (1.10) the Department of the Treasury, (1.11) the Department of Defense, (1.12) intelligence components utilized by the secretary of defense, (1.13) the Department of Energy, and (1.14) the Federal Bureau of Investigation.

Part 2 (conduct of intelligence activities) of the order is broken down into 12 "sections": (2.1) need, (2.2) purpose, (2.3) collection of information, (2.4) collection techniques, (2.5) attorney general approval, (2.6) assistance to law enforcement authorities, (2.7) contracting, (2.8) consistency with other laws, (2.9) undisclosed participation in organizations within the United States, (2.10) human experimentation, (2.11) prohibition on assassination, and (2.12) indirect participation.

Part 3 (general provisions) has six "sections," which address: (3.1) congressional oversight, (3.2) implementa-

tion, (3.3) procedures, (3.4) definitions, (3.5) purpose and effect, and (3.6) revocation.

EXECUTIVE ORDER 12958

Signed by President Bill Clinton on April 17, 1995, EO 12958 outlines a system for classifying, declassifying, and safeguarding information deemed vital to the national security interests of the United States. This EO was designed to prevent "overclassification" of CIA documents, by upgrading standards for federal classifiers. Officially, the Agency contends that EO 12958 serves the public by promoting "openness" by encouraging declassification of intelligence records and other documents, especially those which may be of "permanent historical value."

A portion of the order's summary reads: "Our democratic principles require that the American people be informed of the activities of their Government. Also, our Nation's progress depends on the free flow of information. Nevertheless, throughout our history, the national interest has required that certain information be maintained in confidence in order to protect our citizens, our democratic institutions, and our participation within the community of nations. Protecting information critical to our nation's security remains a priority. In recent years, however, dramatic changes have altered, although not eliminated, the national security threats that we confront. These changes provide a greater opportunity to emphasize our commitment to open Government."

Part 1 (original classification) is broken down into nine "sections," which address: (1.1) definitions within the order, (1.2) classification standards, (1.3) CLASSIFICATION levels, (1.4) classification authority, (1.5) classification categories, (1.6) duration of classifications, (1.7) identification and markings on the face of classified documents, (1.8) classification prohibitions and limitations, and (1.9) classification challenges.

Part 2 (derivative classification) has three "sections": (2.1) definitions within the order, (2.2) use of derivative classifications, and (2.3) classification guides.

Part 3 (declassification and downgrading) has eight "sections" on (3.1) definitions within the order, (3.2) authority for declassification, (3.3) transferred information, (3.4) automatic declassification, (3.5) systematic declassification review, (3.6) mandatory declassification review, (3.7) processing requests and reviews, and (3.8) a declassification database.

Part 4 (safeguarding) is broken down into four "sections," which address: (4.1) definitions within the order, (4.2) general restrictions on access, (4.3) distribution controls, and (4.4) special-access programs.

Part 5 (implementation and review) is broken down into seven "sections," on (5.1) definitions within the order, (5.2) program direction, (5.3) information security oversight office, (5.4) interagency security classification appeals panel, (5.5) information security policy advisory council, (5.6) general responsibilities, (5.7) sanctions.

Part 6 (general provisions) has two "sections": (6.1) general provisions, and (6.2) the effective date (October 1995).

The order revoked EO 12356, which on April 2, 1982, had prescribed a uniform system for classifying, declassifying, and safeguarding national security information.

EXECUTIVE ORDER 12968

Signed by President Bill Clinton on August 2, 1995, EO 12968 established the current personnel security program for federal employees having access to classified information. This EO was designed to bring previous personnel security (or reliability) programs under a single, uniform system for improved management.

A portion of the order's summary reads: "The national interest requires that certain information be maintained in confidence through a system of classification in order to protect our citizens, our democratic institutions, and our participation within the community of nations. The unauthorized disclosure of information classified in the national interest can cause irreparable damage to the national security and loss of human life.

"Security policies designed to protect classified information must ensure consistent, cost effective, and efficient protection of our Nation's classified information, while providing fair and equitable treatment to those Americans upon whom we rely to guard our national security.

"This order establishes a uniform Federal personnel security program for employees who will be considered for initial or continued access to classified information."

Part 1 (definitions, access to classified information, financial disclosure, and other items) of the order is broken down into five "sections," which address: (1.1) definitions within the order, (1.2) access to classified information, (1.3) financial disclosure, (1.4) use of automated financial record data bases, and (1.5) employee education and assistance.

Part 2 (access eligibility policy and procedure) has six "sections": (2.1) eligibility determinations, (2.2) level of access approval, (2.3) temporary access to higher levels, (2.4) reciprocal acceptance of access eligibility determinations, (2.5) specific access requirement, and (2.6) access by non-U.S. citizens.

Part 3 (access eligibility standards) is broken down into four "sections" on (3.1) standards, (3.2) basis for eligibility approval, (3.3) special circumstances, and (3.4) reinvestigation requirements. Part 4 (investigations for foreign governments) addresses authority. Part 5 (review of access determinations) is broken down into two "sections" on (5.1) determinations of need for access and (5.2) review proceedings for denials or revocations of eligibility for access.

Part 6 (implementation) has four "sections," which address: (6.1) agency implementing responsibilities, (6.2) employee responsibilities, (6.3) security policy board responsibilities and implementation, and (6.4) sanctions. Part 7 (general provisions) is broken down into two "sections": (7.1) the CLASSIFIED INFORMATION PROCEDURES ACT, and (7.2) general information.

No prior executive orders were revoked by EO 12968.

executive oversight of intelligence

Executive (presidential) oversight of Intelligence is managed through the NATIONAL SECURITY COUNCIL (NSC), the PRESIDENT'S FOREIGN INTELLIGENCE ADVISORY BOARD (PFIAB), the PRESIDENT'S INTELLIGENCE OVERSIGHT BOARD (IOB), and the DIRECTOR OF CENTRAL INTELLIGENCE (DCI).

exfiltration

Exfiltration is the term used to describe the surreptitious extraction of operatives in the field (as opposed to INFILTRATION, the insertion of operatives).

Exhibit Center, CIA

The CIA Exhibit Center is a permanent intelligence history museum located at CIA headquarters in LANGLEY, VIRGINIA. Unlike any other museum in the country, the Exhibit Center contains a fascinating collection of artifacts and declassified photographs that tell the story of American intelligence from the colonial era to the present day, with special emphasis on certain periods in U.S. intelligence history.

Memorabilia from the OFFICE OF STRATEGIC SERVICES (OSS), the World War II predecessor organization of the CIA, is on display, as are Agency-related items from the COLD WAR. All items displayed in the Exhibit Center are authentic (no reproductions are permitted), and all have, of course, been declassified. Some of the more interesting pieces housed in the center include the personal effects of MAJOR GENERAL WILLIAM J. "WILD BILL" DONOVAN, the director of the OSS; an ENIGMA cipher machine used by the Nazis during World War II; the first flag to fly over the CIA compound; as well as some dead-DROP SPIKES, several spy cameras, an AIR AMERICA cap, some CIA-produced leaflets, a model of the U-2 spy plane flown by FRANCIS GARY POWERS, and a 300-pound chunk of the BERLIN WALL.

Like the CIA LIBRARY, the CIA Exhibit Center is not open to the general public.

exterminator

In CIA parlance, an "exterminator" is a COUNTERINTELLIGENCE operative who specializes in locating and removing planted listening devices, known as BUGs.

F

Factbook, World

One of several CIA publications available to the general public (and one of the Agency's two primary publications), the *World Factbook* is a comprehensive single-volume reference guide of facts, maps, and statistics on nearly 300 countries. It is produced annually by the Agency's DIRECTORATE of Intelligence. Created as an update yearbook to the encyclopedic *National Intelligence Survey* (NIS), the *World Factbook* was first published in a classified edition in 1962. The first unclassified version of the *World Factbook* was released in 1971.

Born of the 1954 HOOVER COMMISSION—an executive-branch organization chaired by former president Herbert Hoover tasked with finding ways to reduce the size and increase the efficiency of the postwar federal bureaucracy—the NIS was first issued to members of Congress in 1955. According to the commission report, "The *National Intelligence Survey* is an invaluable publication which provides the essential elements of basic intelligence on all areas of the world. There will always be a continuing requirement for keeping the Survey up-to-date"—thus the *World Factbook*.

In 1973, the NIS program was terminated, but annual publication of the *World Factbook* continued. The *Factbook* was first made available to the general public through the U.S. Government Printing Office in 1975. Today, the CIA publishes the *Factbook* in both print and Internet versions. Though it is a CIA publication, content information for the book is provided by the National Science Foundation; the Departments of STATE, DEFENSE, Commerce, Labor, Interior, Transportation; and other public and private sources, as well as the Agency. The *World Factbook* is currently one of the most widely used reference texts in the English-speaking world.

Factbook on Intelligence

One of several CIA publications available to the general public (and one of the Agency's two primary publications), the *Factbook on Intelligence* is an unclassified, 36-page overview of the Agency's organization, history, and mission.

The *Factbook on Intelligence* covers the genesis of the CIA; the original headquarters building cornerstone ceremony; key events in the CIA's history; an overview of American intelligence until World War II; directors and DEPUTY DIRECTORS OF CENTRAL INTELLIGENCE; diagram of DIRECTOR OF CENTRAL INTELLIGENCE (DCI) responsibilities; the DCI and his principal deputies; vision, mission, and values of the Central Intelligence Agency; the INTELLIGENCE CYCLE; the U.S. INTELLIGENCE COMMUNITY; EXECUTIVE OVERSIGHT of intelligence; LEGISLATIVE OVERSIGHT of intelligence; the CIA headquarters buildings; the Memorial Stars; the OFFICE OF STRATEGIC SERVICES Memorial; The MEMORIAL GARDEN; CIA LIBRARY; the Center for the Study of Intelligence; the Office of Equal Employment Opportunity; CIA AWARDS AND MEDALS; the CIA SEAL, frequently asked questions; how to obtain publications and maps available to the public; and public affairs and employment information.

Falcon and Snowman

In 1975—the so-called YEAR OF INTELLIGENCE, when the CIA underwent congressional investigations into alleged illegal activities—two young Americans were also engaging in their own misdeeds—selling U.S. defense-technology secrets to Soviet agents south of the border.

CHRISTOPHER JOHN BOYCE (aka the "Falcon," because of his lifelong passion for training birds of prey) was the brains behind the sellout. He was employed as a cipher clerk with TRW, an aerospace defense contractor and repository of U.S. intelligence community materials based in Redondo Beach, California. Boyce, an aimless 22-year-old who dropped out of college in 1973, had landed the job at TRW through the efforts of his father, a former special agent with the FEDERAL BUREAU OF INVESTIGATION (FBI).

Boyce's accomplice, ANDREW DAULTON LEE (the "Snowman," so-named because of his involvement in cocaine trafficking), was a small-time drug dealer and Boyce's childhood friend.

While at TRW, Boyce stole documents from a security exclusion area (known as the "black vault") that contained vital CIA materials related to spy satellites. Boyce presented the documents to Lee and instructed him to deliver them to KGB agents based in Mexico City.

The treason began in April 1975. Boyce gave Lee a slip of 12-inch paper tape used in TRW's cryptographic machines. On the tape were top-secret messages from Rhyolite, one of the CIA's satellites. Lee flew to Mexico City, walked up to the main gate of the Soviet embassy, and matter-of-factly informed the guard that he could provide information that would be of great interest to the USSR. He was immediately shown inside, where, over vodka and caviar, he met the KGB's Mexico station chief, Boris Alexei Grishin. The Soviets reviewed the tape, and Grishin gave Lee $250 for a flight back to Los Angeles. He also promised a great deal of money to the young Californian if he could in fact deliver on his promise. Upon his return, Lee relayed Grishin's message to Boyce. Almost immediately, Boyce began making copies of satellite materials and giving them to Lee for delivery to the Russians.

Thereafter, each time Lee embarked on one of his courier missions to Mexico City, he returned with thousands of dollars in cash. Boyce, who did not want to disclose his identity to the Soviets, told Lee to tell Grishin that he was a disgruntled black man who hated the United States.

Over time, Grishin offered to pay the two Americans $10,000 for every shipment of ciphers that were scheduled for installation in the Rhyolite satellite. Boyce agreed, and Lee delivered. But things began to unravel in 1976. Boyce began to suspect that Lee was sandbagging on the payments. In fact, Lee was sharing only $3,000 out of every $10,000 he received from the Soviets.

Breaking cover, Boyce flew to Mexico City and met with Grishin personally. He described his duties at TRW in detail. Grishin then offered to finance Boyce's college education, provided that he choose a major that would be suited to future employment with the CIA. Boyce accepted the offer. He also agreed to deliver a final shipment of top-secret documents to the Soviets, for $75,000. The shipment, which was never delivered, was to have been a thick file of photographed documents detailing the development of a network of covert satellites (code-named PYRAMIDER) that could be manipulated with miniature receiver/transmitters by American spies in China and the Soviet-bloc countries.

Before the delivery could be made, Lee appeared unexpectedly at the Soviet embassy. He needed advance money to supply his drug addiction. A Mexican police officer, suspecting that Lee was a terrorist, arrested him. During a physical search, the Mexican authorities discovered suspicious-looking filmstrips of photographed documents; the FBI was contacted. Lee implicated Boyce, and the latter was arrested in Los Angeles.

On June 20, 1977, Lee and Boyce were convicted of espionage. Boyce was sentenced to 40 years in prison. Lee was given a life term.

On January 21, 1980, Boyce scaled a 10-foot security fence at a maximum security federal prison facility at Lompoc, California, and escaped. He became involved in a string of bank robberies across Montana, Idaho, and Washington State. He was eventually recaptured and convicted of bank robbery, conspiracy, and firearms violations charges. Boyce returned to prison to serve out his term for espionage; when that term is completed, he will be required to serve an additional 90 years for the convictions after his escape.

false flag recruit

"False flag recruits" is a term sometimes used by CIA officers to describe recruited agents who believe they are working for one country when in fact they are working for another.

"family jewels"

Also known as "the skeletons," the "family jewels" was a list of over 300 "questionable" CIA activities compiled by the Agency and publicly exposed during Senate hearings in the 1970s. The list was conceived on May 9, 1973, in an in-house directive issued after it was learned that Agency facilities and perhaps agents had been used in illegal activities surrounding WATERGATE.

Two weeks prior, Judge Matthew Byrne, presiding over the trial of DANIEL ELLSBERG for leaking the PENTAGON PAPERS, had learned that former CIA officer E. HOWARD HUNT had burglarized Ellsberg's psychiatrist's office. Hunt had already been convicted in the Watergate break-in. As a result, newly appointed DIRECTOR OF CENTRAL INTELLIGENCE (DCI) JAMES R. SCHLESINGER—a virtual outsider when it came to the CIA's clandestine affairs—decided to find out what else he might not be aware of.

The directive, drafted by Schlesinger and DEPUTY DIRECTOR of operations (DDO) WILLIAM COLBY, "asked" current and former CIA employees to report (to the DCI) any illegal CIA activities of which they were aware. A portion of the directive reads: "All the senior operating officials of this Agency are to report to me [Schlesinger] immediately on any activities now going on, or that have gone on in the past, which might be construed to be outside of the legislative charter of this Agency." Thus was assembled of the "family jewels," a 693-page compendium of some 300 possible CIA transgressions including domestic spying, MIND-CONTROL DRUG TESTING, MAIL INTERCEPTIONS, and foreign ASSASSINATION PLOTS.

When Colby succeeded Schlesinger as DCI, public and political pressure forced him to release the list to the ROCKEFELLER COMMISSION, a presidentially appointed eight-member panel tasked with investigating the CIA in early 1975. When U.S. senator FRANK CHURCH requested the list for his own CHURCH COMMITTEE probe of the CIA, President Gerald Ford was reluctant to turn it over. Ford felt that exposing the "family jewels" might put U.S. national security interests at risk. He eventually conceded, but ultimately he replaced Colby with future-president GEORGE BUSH. Ford believed Colby had been too willing to turn over the list.

"Family jewels" is a euphemism for testicles. The list was so named because Agency insiders believed that if the list were ever made public, the CIA would be effectively emasculated.

Farm, the

CAMP PEARY, Virginia, the CIA's top-secret "boot camp" for fledgling spies, is often referred to by Agency insiders as "the Farm," CAMP SWAMPY, or ISOLATION.

See also CAREER TRAINEES.

Fecteau, Richard George (1927–   )

Richard George Fecteau was a CIA covert operations officer who in 1952, during a clandestine operation in China, was captured by the communists and sentenced to life in prison for espionage. He was released after 19 years.

Born in 1927, Fecteau spent much of his early life in Lynn, Massachusetts. He attended Boston University. In 1952, he joined the CIA and after five months was assigned to the Far East.

Fecteau was an active participant in OPERATION TROPIC, a series of Agency-supported insurgency operations conducted by "third force" teams (anticommunists who were not allied with the Nationalist Chinese on Taiwan) against communist forces on the Chinese mainland.

During one such mission, on November 29, 1952, a CIVIL AIR TRANSPORT (CAT) aircraft on which Fecteau was a passenger was shot down by communist ground forces. The pilot and copilot were killed in the crash. Fecteau and fellow CIA officer JOHN THOMAS "JACK" DOWNEY were taken prisoner. Initially, the U.S. government denied that Fecteau and Downey were CIA officers, insisting that the two men were civilian employees of the U.S. Army on a "routine flight" from Seoul, Korea, to Japan.

Fecteau, who was sentenced to 20 years in prison, was released in December 1971. Downey, who was sentenced to life, was released in March 1973, after President Richard Nixon admitted publicly that both men were in fact CIA officers.

In a 1998 ceremony honoring Fecteau and Downey with Director's Medals, DIRECTOR OF CENTRAL INTELLIGENCE (DCI) GEORGE TENET referred to the two men as "true legends." Tenet added, "You demonstrated heroism of a whole other magnitude during those dark decades of captivity. Your story, simply put, is one of the most remarkable in the fifty-year history of the CENTRAL INTELLIGENCE AGENCY."

Federal Bureau of Investigation (FBI)

In terms of COUNTERINTELLIGENCE activities, the Federal Bureau of Investigation (FBI) is often considered to be the CIA's domestic counterpart. But it is much more. Established in 1924, the modern FBI is the U.S. national police force and internal counterintelligence service. The federal government's largest investigative agency, it is largely responsible for conducting investigations whenever and wherever there is a federal interest. The exceptions are instances in which another federal agency, such as the CIA, has been specifically assigned that responsibility by executive mandate. The FBI is a branch of the Department of Justice, and its primary mission revolves around investigations of criminal activities; it reports its findings to the attorney general of the United States and to the U.S. Attorney's offices in federal judicial districts across the nation.

Headquartered in Washington, D.C., the FBI maintains field offices in major cities throughout the United States and in Puerto Rico. Additionally, the bureau has special agents posted as liaison officers in several cities overseas in order to facilitate the exchange of information with foreign countries on matters relating to international criminal activity.

The bureau's senior officer is its director. Until 1968, the director was appointed by the attorney general. Today, the director is appointed by the president, with the advice and consent of the Senate.

The FBI traces its lineage back to 1908, when Attorney General Charles J. Bonaparte created a Bureau of Investigation (BI) within the Justice Department. The bureau, then as now, was tasked with investigating federal criminal cases. In 1924, Attorney General Harlan Fiske Stone ordered the reorganization of the BI and appointed JOHN EDGAR HOOVER as its director. The bureau was then transformed from an obscure agency into a nationally respected federal police force. Granted virtual carte blanche, Director Hoover set about creating a centrally managed fingerprint database, an investigations laboratory, and a federal police academy.

A congressional mandate in 1934 renamed the entity the "Federal Bureau of Investigation." The new name implied independent agency status, although the FBI remained a quasi branch of the Justice Department. In 1939, President Franklin Roosevelt expanded the powers of the FBI by directing it to investigate espionage, sabotage, and subversion on all fronts; all domestic intelligence gleaned by the various military agencies was to be turned over to the FBI. Hoover took that directive as a mandate to expand his investigations and COUNTERINTELLIGENCE efforts. In 1940, Hoover began working closely with SIR WILLIAM STEPHENSON, the Canadian-born head of the Anglo-American intelligence effort in New York (Stephenson is often referred to by his wartime code name, INTREPID). However, Hoover didn't completely trust Stephenson; at one point, Hoover purportedly complained to Roosevelt that he was directing a British hit squad assassinating Nazi collaborators on U.S. soil. But there was no hard evidence, and the complaint was dismissed by the president. The British in turn criticized the FBI's "heavy-handed" police tactics, which they argued clashed with pure espionage operations. Non-FBI American intelligence officers like WILLIAM J. "WILD BILL" DONOVAN, head of the OFFICE OF STRATEGIC SERVICES (OSS), tended to agree. The bureau, it seemed, was more interested in crushing spy rings and making arrests than it was in letting the spy game run its course and lead to bigger fish.

Throughout the war, Hoover fought hard for jurisdictional control of all American intelligence activities. He won in the struggle against Donovan's OSS for jurisdiction of Latin America. But he lost in his bid for control of all postwar global intelligence operations, retaining only the FBI's domestic counterintelligence responsibilities (all foreign intelligence operations would eventually fall under the jurisdiction of the CIA). When the war ended, Hoover's focus turned toward ridding the North American continent of all vestiges of communism; the FBI kept files on anyone he deemed suspect.

Hoover adamantly opposed the creation of the CIA in 1947 and once even directed his men not to communicate or associate in any manner with Agency officers. When the CIA began assuming control of all espionage activities in Latin America, FBI officers were ordered to destroy their files rather than turn them over to the Agency. It was a "scorched earth" policy, according to EVERETT HOWARD HUNT, who, as the CHIEF OF STATION (COS) in Mexico City, had to sift through the remains. For several decades, unofficial competition existed between the FBI and the CIA, as it had with the CIA's predecessor organizations like the OSS. However, the death of Hoover in 1972 and subsequent changes in the American intelligence infrastructure (after the congressional hearings of the mid-1970s that investigated previous CIA and FBI misdeeds) eradicated much of the intra-Agency rivalry and control problem.

Over the next few decades, the FBI evolved into one of the most effective and critical components of the U.S. INTELLIGENCE COMMUNITY. In the wake of the SEPTEMBER 11, 2001, TERRORIST ATTACKS ON THE UNITED STATES, wartime reorganization and mobilization plans were developed for the FBI. Much of the Bureau's resources and jobs in the Washington, D.C., area were shifted to field offices around the nation. Numbers of special agents were increased, and improving technology and countering terrorism became priority missions.

Prior to September 11, the FBI had approximately 1,000 special agents assigned to counterterrorism. Today, that number is more than 2,100. In summer 2002, FBI director Robert S. Mueller III acknowledged the fact that the United States had treated its domestic intelligence/law enforcement as separate from foreign intelligence but added that the FBI and the CIA were currently coordinating efforts far better than before: "We had a CIA that looked overseas and an FBI that looked within the United States," he said. "That division worked in the past. It doesn't work in countering terrorism, which floods across borders."

In November, media reports indicated that President George W. Bush and some of his top NATIONAL SECURITY ADVISORS were discussing the possibility of creating a new, separate domestic intelligence agency that would assume responsibility for counterterrorist spying within U.S. borders. The FBI, which currently handles all domestic intelligence, would relinquish those duties to the new agency and focus its attention on law enforcement. If established, the new agency would be the true domestic parallel organization to the CIA. Bush later dismissed the reports saying that there are no plans to create a separate domestic intelligence agency. Domestic intelligence gathering and analysis will continue to fall under the jurisdiction of the FBI.

The FBI is represented on the United States Intelligence Board, a panel created by the NATIONAL SECURITY COUNCIL. The bureau is also a member of the intelligence community, which is ultimately overseen by the DIRECTOR OF CENTRAL INTELLIGENCE.

field information report (FIR)

A field information report is a CIA report generated by an officer or an agent operating in the field. FIR's are submitted to the nearest CIA station, from where they are forwarded to CIA headquarters in LANGLEY, VIRGINIA. A FIR is the most basic CIA report.

fifth columnist

A fifth columnist is a subversive who acts out of secret sympathy for an enemy of his or her own country. The term was coined in 1936, during the Spanish Civil War. It was said then that the Spanish rebels had four columns of troops marching on the city of Madrid—and an additional "fifth column" of sympathizers within the city itself, ready to take up arms at a moment's notice.

A fifth columnist may also be an AGENT OF INFLUENCE—a spy operating in "high" or influential places where he or she is able to influence a government's or other organization's policy or behavior.

Fifty CIA Trailblazers

On September 18, 1997, the CIA marked its 50th anniversary by naming "50 trailblazers" whose accomplishments throughout the first 50 years of the Agency's history best exemplified the Agency's strict standards of excellence. The 50 were selected from among 300 nominations representing the DIRECTORATES of Operations, Intelligence, Science and Technology, and Administration.

Congratulating the select group during the Agency's 50th anniversary celebration, DIRECTOR OF CENTRAL INTELLIGENCE (DCI) GEORGE TENET made the following remarks: "Secrecy is a necessary part of the intelligence profession. Your achievements probably will never be known in their fullness by the American people. I am convinced, however, that the American people would be enormously proud if they knew of your service, and I hope you will accept this award as an expression of thanks from a grateful nation."

The 50 CIA trailblazers include:

1. Robert C. Ames, who served the CIA from 1960 to 1983
2. Joseph A. Baclawski, who served the CIA from 1972 to 1991
3. Matthew Baird, who served the CIA from 1953 to 1965
4. RICHARD MERVIN BISSELL, JR., who served the CIA from 1954 to 1962
5. David H. Blee, who served the CIA from 1972 to 1985
6. Paul A. Borel, who served the CIA from 1947 to 1972
7. Patricia L. Brannen, who served the CIA from 1952 to 1964, and then from 1977 to 1994
8. Archie R. Burks, who served the CIA from 1956 to 1984
9. Joseph B. Castillo, Jr., who has served the CIA from 1971 to the present
10. David E. Coffey, who served the CIA from 1968 to 1995
11. John E. Craven, who has served the CIA from 1968 to the present
12. James H. Critchfield, who served the CIA from 1948 to 1974
13. Benedetto Defelice, who served the CIA from 1953 to 1987
14. Leslie C. Dirks, who served the CIA from 1961 to 1982
15. William F. Donnelly, who served the CIA from 1954 to 1990
16. Janet V. Dorigan, who has served the CIA from 1989 to the present
17. Carl E. Duckett, who served the CIA from 1964 to 1977
18. ALLEN WELSH DULLES, who served the CIA from 1951 to 1961
19. Agnes D. Greene, who served the CIA from 1947 to 1972
20. Howard P. Hart, who served the CIA from 1966 to 1990
21. Earl M. Harter, who served the CIA from 1950 to 1972
22. RICHARD MCGARRAH HELMS, who served the CIA from 1947 to 1973
23. R. Evans Hineman, who served the CIA from 1964 to 1989
24. LAWRENCE R. HOUSTON, who served the CIA from 1947 to 1973
25. Paul L. Howe, who served the CIA from 1956 to 1987

26. SHERMAN KENT, who served the CIA from 1950 to 1967

27. LYMAN B. KIRKPATRICK, JR., who served the CIA from 1947 to 1965

28. George G. Kisevalter, who served the CIA from 1952 to 1970

29. Lloyd Lauderdale, who served the CIA from 1963 to 1969

30. Richard Lehman, who served the CIA from 1949 to 1982

31. Henry S. Lowenhaupt, who served the CIA from 1947 to 1990

32. Arthur C. Lundahl, who served the CIA from 1953 to 1974

33. Harold N. McClelland, who served the CIA from 1951 to 1965

34. John N. McMahon, who served the CIA from 1951 to 1986

35. Antonio J. Mendez, who served the CIA from 1965 to 1990

36. CORD MEYER, JR., who served the CIA from 1951 to 1977

37. Eloise R. Page, who served the CIA from 1947 to 1987

38. John Parangosky, who served the CIA from 1948 to 1974

39. Walter L. Pforzheimer, who served the CIA from 1947 to 1974

40. Carol A. Roehl, who served the CIA from 1967 to 1996

41. Linus F. Ruffing, who served the CIA from 1962 to 1976

42. Howard Stoertz, Jr., who served the CIA from 1949 to 1980

43. John R. Tietjen, who served the CIA from 1947 to 1975

44. Omego J. C. Ware, Jr., who served the CIA from 1955 to 1982

45. John S. Warner, who served the CIA from 1947 to 1976

46. Albert D. Wheelon, who served the CIA from 1962 to 1966

47. Lawrence K. White, who served the CIA from 1947 to 1972

48. FRANK G. WISNER, who served the CIA from 1948 to 1962.

For security reasons, the names of two additional "trailblazers" were not disclosed.

5412 Group

The 5412 Group, named after National Security Council Directive 5412 reaffirming the CIA's responsibility for covert actions abroad, was a senior-level interdepartmental organization tasked with overseeing the CIA's high-risk covert operations during the 1950s and early 1960s. The 5412 Group traced it lineage to the early OPERATIONS COORDINATING BOARD (OCB), which was later renamed the 5412 Group, and was often referred to simply as the SPECIAL GROUP. During the administration of President John Kennedy, the 5412 Group was known as the 303 COMMITTEE—after a room number in the executive office complex in Washington, D.C. The group was later known, respectively, as the 40 COMMITTEE and then the OPERATIONS ADVISORY GROUP.

Members of the 5412 Group included representatives from the U.S. DEPARTMENT OF STATE, the U.S. DEPARTMENT OF DEFENSE, the JOINT CHIEFS OF STAFF (JCS), the Oval Office, and the CIA.

finished intelligence

Finished intelligence is the result of analysis of data or raw information within the "ALL-SOURCE analysis and production" step of the INTELLIGENCE CYCLE. Finished intelligence is delivered to intelligence consumers.

firefly

A "firefly" was a simple gasoline-based explosive device, similar to a Molotov cocktail, that was used extensively by commandos of the OFFICE OF STRATEGIC SERVICES (OSS), the CIA's predecessor organization during World War II.

A firefly, though crude, is simple and quick to make. Thus it is still considered a part of the CIA unconventional-weaponry arsenal.

Fitzgerald, Desmond (Dizzy Fits)
(ca. 1910–1967)

Desmond "Dizzy Fits" Fitzgerald was considered one of the CIA's "golden boys." He was once described by a fellow CIA officer as a man with "the silken grace and easy manners of a courtier and the imagination and dash of a Renaissance soldier of fortune." Had Fitzgerald lived beyond his 57 years, he might well have risen to the Agency's top post.

Fitzgerald was born in New York City (ca. 1910). As a boy he attended St. Mark's School in Southboro, Massachusetts. He had a keen interest in a myriad of subjects, made many friends, and developed the prototypical personality of an eastern establishment elitist. But he never shirked work or difficult tasks. In 1932, he earned an undergraduate degree from Harvard University. He then enrolled in the Harvard Law School, earning his degree in 1935. For the next six years, he practiced law in New York City.

When the United States entered World War II in 1941, Fitzgerald was a 31-year-old attorney with a wife and a child. But his sense of patriotism and adventure proved irresistable. Fitzgerald enlisted in the army as a private, initially believing that rank was insignificant and that all that really mattered was the opportunity to fight for one's country. However, that belief was short-lived; he found his fellow enlisted soldiers somewhat less than intellectually gifted. "I think what angers me about the local dopes is that they are so utterly uncurious," he wrote in a 1942 letter to his wife. He soon managed a transfer to Officer Candidate School, where he performed well, even boasting that he was "potentially hot stuff as a combat officer."

During the war, Fitzgerald served as a liaison officer attached to the Chinese army operating in the China-Burma-India theater. By 1945, he had risen to the rank of major. He had also earned a Bronze Star and several foreign decorations. Unfortunately, he returned home to find that his wife had been having an extramarital affair with film director John Huston and that she wanted a divorce.

When the Korean War erupted in 1950, Fitzgerald was recruited into the CIA by FRANK GARDINER WISNER, the head of the Agency's covert-action arm, the OFFICE OF POLICY COORDINATION (OPC). In 1951, Fitzgerald was appointed deputy chief to the OPC's Far East Division, and he soon became chief of the Far East Division's China Command. He then served as the DIRECTORATE of Plans (Operations) chief of political and paramilitary warfare. It was during that time that he warned fellow officers against any CIA participation in the 1958 INDONESIAN rebellion. Nevertheless, the Agency supported the rebellion, and it failed. That same year, Fitzgerald was posted to the head of the Far East Division.

In 1963, Fitzgerald was assigned to the head of the Special Affairs Staff, a covert unit tasked with removing Cuban leader FIDEL CASTRO from power. The unit was part of an overall Castro-elimination project known as OPERATION MONGOOSE. The following year, Fitzgerald was named chief of the CIA's Western Hemisphere Division.

In 1966, Fitzgerald became DEPUTY DIRECTOR of Plans (DDP). As DDP, he was responsible for gathering the intelligence presented to President Lyndon Johnson that accurately predicted the June 1967 Six Day War between the Israelis and the Arabs. His star was clearly rising.

Fitzgerald was highly respected by his colleagues. Former DIRECTOR OF CENTRAL INTELLIGENCE (DCI) ALLEN WELSH DULLES once referred to him as an officer of "imagination and sense of daring, backed by his credentials as a fellow Wall Street lawyer and his impeccable social connections, coupled with his ability to get things done."

On July 23, 1967, Fitzgerald, 57, suffered a heart attack and died while playing tennis. He was posthumously presented the National Security Medal.

fix

"Fix" is a COLD WAR term for a person who is to be blackmailed or compromised so that he or she may be manipulated by Agency operatives. In such a scenario, the compromised person is said to have been "fixed."

flaps and seals

Also known as the "kettle and stick" method, "flaps and seals" is an Agency tradecraft term for the secret opening, examining, closing, and resealing of envelopes and packages without the knowledge of the recipient.

During the 1950s, the CIA began instructing field officers in the art of opening mail undetected. In fact, a flaps-and-seals course was taught by the Agency's OFFICE OF TECHNICAL SERVICES (OTS) as part of HT-LINGUAL, the COVER name for a CIA mail-intercept project that lasted for 20 years. Officers attending the course learned to open envelopes by softening the glue with steam from a tea kettle, then easing the flap open with a narrow implement.

Field officers often carried a flaps-and-seals briefcase containing tools used in the surreptitious opening of mail. Those tools include an electric heat table with a temperature gauge, blotting paper, sticks, brushes, gloves, as well as containers of water, glue, and other chemicals. The three most common techniques used in flaps-and-seals work were steam opening, dry opening, and wet opening. Steaming was usually the most effective. In the 1960s, the OTS developed a special letter steamer designed to open 100 letters simultaneously. Unfortunately, the glue often hardened on the letter flap before the contents could be removed. Thus, the new steamer was scrapped.

The steaming open of flapped envelopes is one of the oldest methods of gathering intelligence. British intelligence operatives actually perfected the technique prior to World War II and began teaching special agents of the FEDERAL BUREAU OF INVESTIGATION (FBI) how to get into the mail of Axis diplomats. The British technique is referred to as "chamfering."

Other methods of surreptitiously removing letters included tightly rolling a letter inside an envelope using a special set of pincers, and then extracting it from the unsealed gap at the top corner of the envelope. The letter would then be replaced by simply reversing the technique. Known as the ROLL-OUT method, this could be done with all manner of long, thin instruments, including a split chopstick or a pair of knitting needles.

The term "flaps and seals" is derived from the original opening-and-resealing procedure used to open surreptitiously letters and dispatches inside either a flapped envelope or folded and fastened with a wax seal.

Fleming, Ian Lancaster (ca. 1908–1964)

No person in either the United States or the United Kingdom better epitomizes the resourcefulness and derring-do of a foreign intelligence operative than the fictional character JAMES BOND, created by real-life British intelligence officer Ian Lancaster Fleming. Bond is the stuff of legends. Fleming, though a bit more tame than Bond, was the genuine article. An officer in Royal Navy intelligence, Fleming was also instrumental in the establishment of America's OFFICE OF STRATEGIC SERVICES (OSS), the World War II precursor to the CIA.

Fleming was born in Oxfordshire, England, around 1908, the son of Valentine Fleming (a British army officer, landowner, and member of Parliament) and Evelyn St. Croix Rose. The Flemings were of Great Britain's privileged class, the family having obtained much of its wealth from Scottish banker Robert Fleming, young Fleming's grandfather. In 1914, Great Britain entered World War I. Three years later, Valentine Fleming was killed on the western front. Growing up in the shadow of his father's sacrifice, Fleming seemed destined for an army career. But after formal schooling at Eton (1921–26) and the British Military Academy at Sandhurst (1926–27), he decided that army life was not for him. He dropped out of Sandhurst before earning his commission and began working as a journalist. Prior to World War II, he worked for the *London Times,* served in Moscow as a wire correspondent for Reuters, and was for a brief period a London-based stockbroker.

In 1939, Fleming joined British naval intelligence and was assigned by Sir Winston Churchill (then First Lord of the Admiralty) as aide to Rear Admiral Sir John H. Godfrey, the head of Great Britain's Naval Intelligence Division (NID). That same year, Fleming became directly involved in the war effort, developing and carrying out a myriad of clandestine methods used to confuse and harass the Germans.

In 1940, he slipped into France, where he assisted Allied forces in their escape after the disastrous amphibious landing at Dieppe. Reflecting the flair that his future readers would find in the character James Bond, Fleming successfully eluded the Nazis—but never turned down a dinner invitation from the locals.

Touring the United States with Godfrey in the spring of 1941, Fleming met a number of American intelligence chiefs, including WILLIAM J. "WILD BILL" DONOVAN, future director of the OSS, and JOHN EDGAR HOOVER, the director of the FEDERAL BUREAU OF INVESTIGATION (FBI). It was also during that period that Godfrey met with President Franklin Roosevelt and described what he perceived to be "inadequacies" in the American intelligence system. Godfrey noted to the president, however, that there were some "useful strengths" in American intelligence and that Donovan was the man to build on those strengths. Upon his return to Britain, Godfrey left Fleming behind, as a liaison and intelligence adviser to Donovan.

On July 11, 1941, Roosevelt ordered the establishment of an OFFICE OF THE COORDINATOR OF INFORMATION (COI) with Donovan as the actual "coordinator." Fleming, still in town, advised Donovan during the early stages, writing a lengthy report on intelligence operations to aid in the development of an American wartime espionage organization. In the summer of 1942, Fleming assisted Donovan in the organization of the OSS. For his work with the OSS, Donovan presented Fleming with an engraved pistol. The engraving read, "For Special Services."

Soon after the establishment of the OSS, Fleming was ordered to Camp X, WILLIAM STEPHENSON's commando training center in Canada on Lake Ontario. There, under the code name "17F," he observed U.S. and British special-operations exercises, and he personally participated in underwater demolition training. As the war progressed, Fleming became more involved in special operations. At one point he commanded a special commando group tasked with dangerous missions deep behind German lines. Occasionally, Fleming led his men in the field. But more often than not, he was ordered to direct operations from behind his desk in London.

In 1945, Fleming was ordered to Jamaica for a naval conference. He fell in love with the country, and when the war was over he purchased a tract of land there and began construction of his paradise home. In January of 1946, he moved to Jamaica. In March, however, he returned to England to accept a part-time newspaper position. For the next six years he alternated between his Jamaican home and his house in England.

In 1951, Fleming, then 43 years old, married his pregnant lover, Lady Anne Rothermore, a previously married woman with whom he had been having an affair. That same year, he penned the first draft of his first novel, *Casino Royale.*

Fleming wrote 12 James Bond novels between 1952 and 1964: *Casino Royale* (1953), *Live and Let Die* (1954), *Moonraker* (1955), *Diamonds Are Forever* (1956), *From Russia with Love* (1957), *Doctor No* (1958), *Goldfinger* (1959), *For Your Eyes Only* (1960), *Thunderball* (1961), *The Spy Who Loved Me* (1962), *On Her Majesty's Secret Service* (1963), and *You Only Live Twice* (1964). Bond novels published after his death include *The Man with the Golden Gun* (1965), *Octopussy, The Living Daylights,* and *The Property of a Lady* (1966).

Many James Bond movies have been produced since 1962.

Fleming died in 1964. He was 56.

See also MOVIES AND POPULAR CULTURE, CIA IN.

flutter

In CIA parlance, a flutter is a polygraph or lie-detector test. All potential CIA hires are fluttered as part of their pre-employment screening. Regular polygraph testing is also administered throughout an employee's career.

Ford, John (1895–1973)

John Ford was an Academy Award–winning film director whose moviemaking career spanned nearly a half-century. He was also chief of the World War II film documentaries branch of the OFFICE OF STRATEGIC SERVICES (OSS), the wartime predecessor organization of the CIA.

Born Sean Aloysius O'Feeney (O'Fearna), or John Martin Fenney, in Cape Elizabeth, Maine (February 1, 1895), young Ford was the 10th of 11 children of Irish immigrants. When he was 12 years old, Ford contracted diphtheria, but he was otherwise considered a healthy, strapping boy and a natural athlete. During his teenage years, he played football and was nicknamed "Bull" by his teammates. As a young man, he reportedly attended classes at the University of Maine—a claim, though often disputed, that he made throughout his life.

In 1914—at the behest of his older brother Francis, an actor and Broadway director—Ford moved to Hollywood. Assuming his brother's stage surname and first name, Jack, he began his career as a stuntman and prop assistant. He also garnered bit roles in several silent movies, including D. W. Griffith's controversial film *Birth of a Nation,* where he donned the hood of a Ku Klux Klansman. By 1917, he was writing and directing his own films. In 1924, after changing his first name to "John," he began making his mark as one of Hollywood's most promising young writer/directors. Over the next 18 years, he produced a variety of highly touted films, many of them Westerns, including: *The Iron Horse* (1924), *Three Bad Men* (1926), *Four Sons* (1928), *Judge Priest* (1934), *The Lost Patrol* (1934), *Steamboat 'round the Bend* (1935), *Drums along the Mohawk* (1939), *Young Mr. Lincoln* (1939), *Stagecoach* (1939), *The Grapes of Wrath* (1940), and *How Green Was My Valley* (1941).

In 1942, Ford was commissioned a commander in the Naval Reserve and placed under the direct command of WILLIAM J. "WILD BILL" DONOVAN, the director of the OSS, who in turn made him chief of the intelligence organization's Field Photographic Branch. With nearly 200 officers and men (cameramen, sound men, and special effects and laboratory technicians), Ford made a number of wartime documentaries of military action, often in a combat environment. He was wounded filming the Battle of Midway, but he was never disheartened. In addition to his work at Midway, he flew with General James H. Doolittle and his raiders over Tokyo; he marched with guerrillas in Burma; and his cameras were rolling at Normandy on June 6, 1944. His wartime awards included a Legion of Merit, a Purple Heart, and an Academy Award for best documentary.

When the war ended in 1945, Ford began supervising an eight-hour documentary on the Nuremberg war crimes trials. But the project was abandoned, and he returned to Hollywood.

Ford, who became known as an unmatched director of the great American westerns (many of which starred actor John Wayne), went on to direct such films as *They Were Expendable* (1945), *My Darling Clementine* (1946), *Fort Apache* (1948), *She Wore a Yellow Ribbon* (1949), *Rio Grande* (1950), *The Quiet Man* (1952), *The Searchers* (1956), *Mogambo* (1953), *The Last Hurrah* (1958), *The Horse Soldiers* (1959), *The Man Who Shot Liberty Valance* (1962), one of three segments of *How the West Was Won* (1963), *Seven Women* (1966), and documentaries on the conflicts in Korea and Vietnam.

In all, Ford won four Academy Awards and the American Film Institute's first-ever Lifetime Achievement Award. President Richard Nixon promoted him to the Naval Reserve rank of rear admiral.

John Ford died in Palm Desert, California, on August 31, 1973. He was 78.

Foreign Broadcast Information (Intelligence) Service (FBIS)

The Foreign Broadcast Information Service (FBIS)—sometimes referred to as the Foreign Broadcast Intelligence Service—is the CIA's broadcast journalism arm.

FBIS is directly descended from the Princeton Listening Center, an independent radio project initiated in 1939 by Hadley Cantril, a Princeton University psychologist and public opinion researcher. Cantril and several of his colleagues had intended to study Nazi propaganda broadcasts on the radio. But in 1941, the Federal Communications Commission (FCC) assumed control of the project, as it was deemed a wellspring of vital open-source intelligence. As a unit of the FCC, the project became known as the Foreign Broadcast Monitoring Service. Not long after, the FCC combined forces with the British Broadcasting Company (BBC), and the two services shared information and divided their areas of responsibility. The BBC focused on stations broadcasting from Europe, the FCC on the rest of the world. The joint FCC-BBC effort became a vital source of daily intelligence; Axis broadcasts were translated into written transcripts and forwarded to intelligence analysts for study.

On December 30, 1945, the American entity, then known as FBIS, was transferred to the Department of War, and later to the CENTRAL INTELLIGENCE GROUP (CIG). When the CIA was officially established in 1947, the FBIS was placed under permanent Agency control. However, a close liaison between the FBIS and the BBC continued. Today, FBIS activities extend far beyond broadcast listening. All manner of open-source intelligence, from foreign-published scientific journals to foreign television news programs, is gathered by FBIS.

foreign intelligence services

The following foreign intelligence services are their respective nations' counterpart or parallel agencies to the CIA:

- Australia—Australian Security Intelligence Organization, or ASIO (M09)
- Belgium—Veiligheid van de Staat, or SV (federal intelligence and security agency)
- Canada—Canadian Security Intelligence Service, or CSIS
- China—Guojia Anquan Bu, or Guoanbu (Ministry of State Security)
- Cuba—Direccion General de Intelligencia, or DGI (Directorate General of Intelligence)
- France—Direction Générale de la Sécurité Extérieure, or DGSE
- Germany—Bundesnachrichtendienst, or BND (Federal Intelligence Service)
- India—Cabinet Secretariat Research and Analysis Wing, or RAW
- Iran—Savama (Information and Security Service of the Nation)
- Iraq—Al Mukharbarat (Department of General Intelligence)
- Israel—Mossad Merkazi Le-modiin U-letafkidim Meyuhadim, or Mossad (Central Institute for Intelligence and Security)
- Italy—Servizio per le Informazioni e la Sicurezza Democratica (Intelligence and Democratic Security Service)
- Japan—Naikaku Chosashitsu Betsushitsu, or Naicho (Cabinet Research Office)
- Jordan—General Intelligence Department, or GID
- Libya—Mukharbarat (Central Security Bureau)
- The Netherlands—Binnenlandse Veiligheidsdienst, or BVD (national intelligence and security agency)
- New Zealand—Security Intelligence Service, or SIS
- Nigeria—National Intelligence Agency, or NIA
- North Korea—Cabinet General Intelligence Bureau

- Norway—Kontrollutvalget for overvakings og sikkerhetstjenesten (Control Committee for the Intelligence and Security Services)
- Pakistan—Directorate for Inter-Service Intelligence, or ISI
- Russia—Sluzhba Vneshney Razvedki Rossii, or SVR (Foreign Intelligence Service)
- Serbia—Sluzba Informaitvna u Dokumenti, or SID (Information and Documentation Service)
- Slovenia—Slovenska Obvešèevalno Varnostna Agencija (Slovenian Intelligence and Security Agency)
- South Africa—South African Secret Service, or SASS
- South Korea—Agency for National Security Planning, or NSP
- Spain—Centro Superior de Informacion de la Defensa, or CESID (Higher Defense Intelligence Center)
- Ukraine—Sluzhba Bespeky Ukrayiny, or SBU (Security Service of Ukraine or SSU)
- United Kingdom—Secret Intelligence Service or SIS (MI6).

Foreign Intelligence Surveillance Act (FISA)

The Foreign Intelligence Surveillance Act (FISA) requires that a court order be obtained before any electronic surveillance operations be conducted within the United States.

Enacted in 1978, the FISA is divided into "four" subchapters.

Subchapter I (electronic surveillance) of the act is broken down into eleven "sections," which address: (1.1) definitions; (1.2) electronic surveillance authorization without court order, certification by attorney general, reports to congressional committees, transmittal under seal, duties and compensation of communication common carrier, applications, and jurisdiction of court; (1.3) designation of judges; (1.4) applications for court orders; (1.5) issuance of order; (1.6) use of information; (1.7) report to administrative office of the United States Supreme Court and to Congress; (1.8) report of attorney general to congressional committees, limitation on authority or responsibility of information gathering activities of congressional committees, and report of congressional committees to Congress; (1.9) criminal sanctions; (1.10) civil liability; and (1.11) authorization during time of war.

Subchapter II (physical searches) has nine "sections": (2.1) definitions, (2.2) authorization of physical searches for foreign intelligence purposes, (2.3) application for order, (2.4) issuance of order, (2.5) use of information, (2.6) congressional oversight, (2.7) penalties, (2.8) civil liability, and (2.9) authorization during time of war.

Subchapter III (pen registers and trap and trace devices for foreign intelligence purposes) is broken down into six "sections," which address: (3.1) definitions, (3.2) pen registers and trap and trace devices for foreign intelligence and international terrorism investigations, (3.3) authorization during emergencies, (3.4) authorization during time of war, (3.5) use of information, and (3.6) congressional oversight.

Subchapter IV (access to certain business records for foreign intelligence purposes) has three "sections": (4.1) definitions, (4.2) access to certain business records for foreign intelligence and international terrorism investigations, and (4.3) congressional oversight.

40, Operation

Operation 40 was the code name for a CIA-sponsored counterintelligence group composed of Cuban exiles. The group was organized during the planning phases of the ill-fated invasion of Cuba at the BAY OF PIGS in 1961 and continued to operate unofficially for nearly a decade after the invasion.

The group was disbanded in 1970 after allegations surfaced that a cargo plane flying in support of Operation 40 that had crashed in California had been transporting a large cache of cocaine and heroin.

40 Committee

The 40 Committee was a senior-level interdepartmental organization tasked with overseeing the CIA's high-risk covert operations during the 1970s. The 40 Committee traced its lineage to the early OPERATIONS COORDINATING BOARD (OPB). The OPB was later renamed the SPECIAL GROUP; it was also known as the 5412 GROUP. During the administration of John Kennedy, the Special (5412) Group was known as the 303 COMMITTEE—after a room number in the executive office complex in Washington, D.C. During the administration of President Richard Nixon, the 303 Committee became known as the 40 Committee. After the CHURCH COMMITTEE hearings of 1975 and the subsequent establishment of the INTELLIGENCE OVERSIGHT BOARD (IOB), the 40 Committee was renamed the OPERATIONS ADVISORY GROUP.

Members of the 40 Committee included representatives from the U.S. DEPARTMENT OF STATE, the U.S. DEPARTMENT OF DEFENSE, the JOINT CHIEFS OF STAFF, the Oval Office, and the CIA.

founding fathers of American intelligence

According to the CIA, the three founding fathers of American intelligence were American Revolutionary leaders George Washington, John Jay, and Benjamin Franklin.

- George Washington is considered to be the founding father of the acquisition of foreign intelligence. A spymaster in his own right, Washington directed numerous agent networks throughout his military career. He provided guidance on intelligence tradecraft to his operatives, and he used their gathered intelligence effectively in planning and conducting military operations.
- John Jay, who ultimately became chief justice of the United States, is considered to be the founding father of American counterintelligence. Though best known for his political and judicial efforts, Jay was also the first national-level American counterintelligence chief.
- Benjamin Franklin is considered to be the founding father of American covert action. During the American Revolution, Franklin engaged in an effective series of propaganda and disinformation operations. He also directed paramilitary operations against British property targets in the colonies.

In 1997, the CIA opened the doors of its Liaison Conference Center, which consists of three meeting rooms for hosting foreign visitors. The three rooms are named, respectively, for the three founding fathers of American intelligence.

four mission areas

The Four Mission Areas are those primary areas of focus that the CIA has deemed to be vital to both the U.S. INTELLIGENCE COMMUNITY and consumers of FINISHED INTELLIGENCE.

In 1995, DIRECTOR OF CENTRAL INTELLIGENCE (DCI) JOHN M. DEUTCH initiated a mission-based intelligence budget for fiscal year 1997. In it Deutch specified "four mission areas" for U.S. intelligence, including:

- Support to military operations (SMO)
- Support to policy
- Support to law enforcement
- COUNTERINTELLIGENCE (CI).

The four mission areas were based on President Bill Clinton's Presidential Directive 35 (March 2, 1995), which specified operational requirements for American intelligence, dividing them into the same four categories.

Freedman, Lawrence N. (Larry) (1941–1992)

Lawrence N. Freedman was a former Army Special Forces commando who was killed in 1992 while working for the CIA in Somalia.

Born to devout Jewish parents in Philadelphia, Pennsylvania, on April 13, 1941, Freedman was known as a "tough kid" and a natural athlete who excelled in diving and gymnastics. At 13 he attempted to rob a service station with a bow and arrow—less for the money than for the adrenaline rush. He attended Kansas State University (KSU) in the late 1950s. At KSU, he quickly developed a reputation as a motorcycle-riding lady's man and a leader of his peers. Antics like climbing buildings by their balcony railings earned him a moniker he would proudly carry with him for the rest of his life—"Super Jew."

A colorful character indeed, in 1965 Freedman enlisted in the U.S. Army and volunteered for Special Forces training. After earning his green beret, he was shipped to Vietnam, where time and again he distinguished himself under fire. When the war ended, he remained in service but chafed in inactivity. In 1978, he joined the Army's newly formed counterterrorist group Operational Detachment D (better known as Delta Force). There, he honed his proficiency in hand-to-hand combat, marksmanship, and battlefield medicine.

In 1980, while serving with Delta Force, Freedman was directly involved in the ill-fated attempt to rescue the 81 Americans held hostage by Iranian terrorists in Tehran. He left Delta Force in October 1982. After that, according to Ted Gup, author of *The Book of Honor,* Freedman's military record became somewhat "murky," and it remains so. "Only weeks after leaving Delta, Pentagon records note he was an 'infantry man (special project),'" wrote Gup. "A year later, he became a 'special projects team member.' None of those operations have come to light." From 1984 to 1986, Freedman trained Army fledgling commandos. But by 1986, Freedman, who had attained the rank of sergeant major, was ready to get back into the fight. He briefly considered working as a mercenary for the MOSSAD, Israel's secret intelligence service. Instead, he applied to the U.S. Drug Enforcement Administration (DEA). He was in perfect physical condition, running and lifting weights every day. But he was nearly 50 years old, and the DEA wasn't interested.

Freedman then joined the CIA. He had worked with Agency officers on previous joint operations between the CIA and the Army, and he saw it as a way to get back into fieldwork.

On December 23, 1992, while operating with the CIA in Somalia, Freedman's luck ran out. He was killed when a jeep he was driving hit a land mine. On December 31, he was posthumously awarded the CIA's Intelligence Star for exceptional service by DIRECTOR OF CENTRAL INTELLIGENCE (DCI) ROBERT M. GATES. The citation reads in part, "For superior performance under hazardous combat conditions with the Central Intelligence Agency."

Since Freedman's death, contributions have been made in his honor to a Special Warfare museum at Fort Bragg, North Carolina. The museum has been appropriately named the "Lawrence 'Super Jew' Freedman Memorial Theater."

Freedom of Information Act, CIA's exclusion from

Signed by President Ronald Reagan on October 15, 1984, the CENTRAL INTELLIGENCE AGENCY INFORMATION ACT OF 1984 specifically exempted the CIA from the search and review requirements under the U.S. Freedom of Information Act (FOIA). The act exempted the Agency only with respect to operational files and other sensitive materials that for security reasons cannot be released.

French Room

"The French Room" is the unofficial name of the headquarters conference room of the DIRECTOR OF CENTRAL INTELLIGENCE (DCI). The origin of the name is unknown.

front

In spy parlance, a "front" is a legitimate operation created by an intelligence organization as a COVER for its operatives. For instance, during the CIA's wartime OPERATIONS IN SOUTHEAST ASIA, the Agency's proprietary airline company, AIR AMERICA, served as a front for clandestine air operations.

On the surface, the company appeared to be an American-based Southeast Asian air cargo service that transported only rice and livestock. In reality, the service also transported guns, ammunition, and special-operations troops over national borders.

FUBELT, Project

Project FUBELT refers to operations conducted during the early 1970s aimed at undermining the government of President Salvador Allende Gossens of Chile and at promoting a coup d'état in that country.

See also CHILE, OPERATIONS IN.

G

Gade, John Allyne (1875–1955)

A career U.S. naval officer, John Allyne Gade was one of the earliest proponents of a "central intelligence" organization.

Gade was born in Cambridge, Massachusetts, on February 10, 1875. As a boy, he attended schools in Norway, Germany, and France. In 1896, he graduated from Harvard University, and for the next 15 years he practiced architecture in New York City.

Gade joined the Navy during World War I, serving as a reserve captain and a naval attaché with the U.S. legation in Copenhagen, Denmark, from 1917 to 1919. (During that period, his brother, Horace Upton Gade, served as a naval attaché in Norway.) In Copenhagen, Gade worked closely with foreign intelligence services, gleaning a great deal of insight into espionage and counterintelligence work.

In 1919, Gade served as a U.S. STATE DEPARTMENT representative in the Baltic region. He soon returned to New York, working briefly in the Wall Street banking firm of White, Weld. But he continued to show a keen interest in intelligence activities. In 1929, he presented to both the U.S. Army's and the Navy's intelligence services a "critical analysis" of what he perceived to be the "foreign information service" of the United States. The analysis compared and contrasted U.S. intelligence capabilities with those of other nations, concluding that "we were amateurs where

they were past masters." He added that "some sort of central intelligence agency" would be beneficial to national security.

Gade's concept of a centrally controlled intelligence agency was not unlike that of WILLIAM J. "WILD BILL" DONOVAN. Donovan—the future director of the OFFICE OF STRATEGIC SERVICES (OSS), the World War II precursor organization to the CIA—would draft during the waning days of World War II a plan proposing a permanent, centrally controlled intelligence service that would exist on an equal footing with the traditional military services. Unfortunately for both Gade and Donovan, the plans were scrapped.

Gade returned to the Navy in 1938, retiring two years later. He was the recipient of numerous awards and decorations, including the Navy Cross. His memoirs of his service as a naval attaché, *All My Born Days*, were published in 1942.

Gade died on August 16, 1955. He was 80.

See also ARMY INTELLIGENCE; DONOVAN PROPOSAL; NAVAL INTELLIGENCE.

Gates, Robert Michael (1943–)

Dr. Robert Michael Gates is, thus far, the only career officer in the history of the CIA to rise from the entry-level ranks to become the DIRECTOR OF CENTRAL INTELLIGENCE (DCI). It almost didn't happen.

Born in Wichita, Kansas, on September 25, 1943, young Gates was the proverbial all-American boy. As a Boy Scout in the 1950s, he earned numerous badges and leadership awards, including a God and Country Award in 1957 and Eagle Scout rank in 1958. Decades later, he would say, "Earning my Eagle gave me the confidence, for the first time in my life, that I could achieve whatever I set out to do." That he did.

In the early 1960s, Gates attended the College of William and Mary. In addition to his studies, he worked part-time as a school-bus driver and a dormitory manager. He also worked with the college-level Boy Scouts organization. In 1965, he earned a B.A. degree from William and Mary, and in 1966 he graduated from Indiana University with a master's degree in history.

Gates' first professional employment was as an ANALYST with the CIA, which he joined almost immediately after finishing his studies at IU. In 1974, he earned a Ph.D. in Russian and Soviet history from Georgetown University, and he was soon thereafter posted to the staff of the NATIONAL SECURITY COUNCIL (NSC). He served in this capacity until 1980. For the next two years, he held several administrative positions, including as national intelligence officer for the Soviet Union.

In 1982, Gates was appointed DEPUTY DIRECTOR FOR INTELLIGENCE (DDI). In September of the following year, he was assigned the additional post of chairman of the NATIONAL INTELLIGENCE COUNCIL (NIC), the entity responsible for producing NATIONAL INTELLIGENCE ESTIMATES (NIE).

During the early 1980s, Gates was a key player in securing CIA and U.S. DEPARTMENT OF DEFENSE funding for a 10-university consortium project aimed at strengthening Soviet and Russian studies nationwide. The project was led by Harvard University. In 1986, Gates developed a collaborative research project involving the CIA and Harvard's John F. Kennedy School of Government to develop case studies on the role of intelligence in American government decision making.

On April 18, 1986, President Ronald Reagan appointed Gates DEPUTY DIRECTOR OF CENTRAL INTELLIGENCE (DDCI), a post he would hold until March 20, 1989. During his tenure as DDCI, he also held the post of acting director (December 18, 1986–May 26, 1987) during the terminal illness of DCI WILLIAM JOSEPH CASEY.

In February 1987, Gates was Reagan's nominee as Casey's successor. But the appointment was not to be. Gates's knowledge of the IRAN-CONTRA affair prompted Congress to delve deeper into his CIA background before confirmation. (The Iran-contra affair was a secret U.S. government project in which American weapons were illegally sold to Iran in exchange for hostages, with the profits from those sales being secretly used to fund contra rebels fighting in Nicaragua.) Congress was also chafing at the fact that the White House had failed to inform it of Gates's knowledge of Iran-contra. Though confident of eventual confirmation, Gates chose to spare the U.S. intelligence community, which would have, no doubt, been embarrassed by the political scrutiny of such a debate. He consequently withdrew his nomination. Gates was, in fact, close to many key players in the Iran-contra affair and could have easily been privy to many activities that would have implicated him. However, the evidence developed by the independent counsel for Iran-contra matters in 1991 did not warrant an indictment of Gates.

Gates served as assistant to the president and deputy NATIONAL SECURITY ADVISOR at the White House from January 20, 1989, until November 6, 1991. President GEORGE HERBERT WALKER BUSH appointed him to the post of DCI; he was confirmed, and he served in that capacity from November 6, 1991, until January 20, 1993. He was the first DCI to come up through the ranks of the Agency, the first former analyst to attain the post, and the only person nominated by two U.S. presidents to direct the CIA.

Gates assumed the directorship during a watershed period in the history of American foreign policy. The Soviet Union collapsed in 1991, and with it came the end of the Cold War. With its primary foe thus eliminated, the CIA found itself redefining its role. This, combined with a public and congressional demand to downsize the American military and the U.S. intelligence community, created an unexpected challenge for the new DCI.

Gates was quick to assess future intelligence needs and priorities. He identified available resources, initiated organizational changes, and recommended new budgetary and legislative proposals. He also established a number of new Agency-overseen task forces. He replaced the Office of Soviet Analysis with an Office of Slavic and Eurasian Analysis. Additionally, he created a sense of greater openness with Congress and the American public by allowing more liberal media accessibility and declassification standards for historical research.

Following his retirement in 1993, Gates entered the private sector and the lecture circuit. He is currently the dean of the George Bush School of Government and Public Service at Texas A&M University. He is a member of various boards of trustees and directors for several large American corporations. He serves in an advisory capacity to several major international firms. Additionally, he serves as a member of the National Executive Board of the Boy Scouts of America and as president of the National Eagle Scout Association.

Gates is the recipient of the Intelligence Medal of Merit, the Arthur S. Fleming Award, the National Security Medal, the Presidential Citizens Medal, the National Intelligence Distinguished Service Medal (three awards), and the Distinguished Intelligence Medal (three awards).

Gates authored *From the Shadows: The Ultimate Insider's Story of Five Presidents and How They Won the Cold War*, a 1996 memoir of his service in the U.S. intelligence community.

Gehlen, Reinhard (1902–1979)

A former Nazi intelligence officer who was destined to become the head of West Germany's Foreign Intelligence Service, Reinhard Gehlen was considered a vital CIA asset during the early years of the COLD WAR.

Born in Erfurt, Germany, on April 1, 1902, young Gehlen was the son and grandson of career army officers. As such, he grew up among the trappings of traditional Prussian militarism and during a world war that would bring Germany to its knees. Gehlen was too young to fight when World War I erupted in 1914, but he would later serve as a junior officer during a time of frenzied German nationalism. In 1920, he enlisted in the army. His star rose over the next two decades, which also saw the rise to power of Adolf Hitler and the revitalization of the German army, which had been decimated after World War I.

On December 1, 1921, after completing infantry and artillery schools and an officer candidate course, Gehlen was commissioned a second lieutenant. In 1933, having served in the artillery and completed cavalry school, he was selected to attend the Armed Forces Academy. Two years later, he graduated with honors. For the next four years, he held a number of operational posts, two of which enabled him to participate in the planning of both the annexation of Czechoslovakia and the invasion of Poland.

On May 29, 1942, three days before his 40th birthday, Gehlen was promoted to lieutenant colonel and made chief of military intelligence for Fremde Heere Ost, or FHO (Foreign Armies East). The FHO was the German army fighting on the Russian front. Gehlen's unit, the Eastern Front Intelligence Service, operated as an independent entity, gathering information on the enemy's regular and partisan forces.

Understanding the Soviet officer corps was of particular importance to Gehlen and his organization. FHO intelligence compiled detailed dossiers on not only Soviet senior officers but junior officers who seemed destined to lead the Russian military in the future. Gehlen also created files on Soviet political leaders. He painstakingly categorized and broke Soviet codes and ciphers. Additionally, he created an encyclopedic file on Soviet espionage and special operations methods.

Throughout the war, Gehlen developed a vast network of agents and spies. He often recruited Russian nationals who had extensive connections to Germany. These spies slipped behind Soviet lines at every point along the front, gathering vital intelligence that aided the Nazis during their retreat from Russia.

Despite Gehlen's stellar work, he was personally disliked by Hitler, who felt that the intelligence chief was far too pessimistic. Actually, Gehlen was a realist. He warned Hitler as early as 1942 that the Soviets would never surrender and that the individual Russian soldier would "fight to the death." By early 1945, Gehlen, then a major general, was convinced of both the insanity of Hitler and the impending defeat of Germany.

Less than a year earlier, a number of like-minded officers had conspired and attempted to assassinate Hitler in an ill-fated bomb plot/coup d'état attempt known as the Black Orchestra. In the aftermath, Hitler ordered the execution of some 5,000 military and political leaders suspected of being involved. Additionally, Hitler had previously purged his general officer corps, firing many of Germany's best military minds, including Gehlen's boss, Admiral Wilhelm Canaris.

Just before committing suicide in April 1945, Hitler dismissed Gehlen, proclaiming the German spymaster as an "unreliable defeatist." Gehlen was unmoved by the firing. In fact, the month before he was relieved of command, he had begun implementing personal plans to survive the war. Placing all of their files on microfilm, Gehlen and his FHO men struck out for the Austrian Alps, where they buried their intelligence records in 50 large metal containers. He planned, once in American hands, to use the documents as a bargaining chip in order to gain immunity from war crimes prosecution.

On May 28, Gehlen and his men surrendered to advancing American troops. After interrogation by officers of the U.S. Army's Counterintelligence Corps, he was transported first to a prisoner of war camp at Wiesbaden, then to a former Nazi concentration camp at Oberusal. It was determined that Gehlen was an inconsequential prisoner.

The Soviets knew better. Not long after his surrender, the Americans and the Soviets began separate, concerted efforts to track down all German intelligence officers. The Soviets desperately wanted Gehlen. Instead, the Americans brought him before U.S. Army general Edwin L. Sibert, chief of military intelligence in Germany. Gehlen warned Sibert that the Soviets would attempt to occupy much of Eastern Europe, turn Germany into a Communist state, and risk a third world war to achieve those aims.

Gehlen drafted a 129-page report outlining what he believed were Soviet plans of global conquest. He also surrendered his prized bargaining chip, the steel containers.

Wholly convinced, Sibert issued an order on the authority of his superior, GENERAL WALTER BEDELL SMITH (a future DIRECTOR OF CENTRAL INTELLIGENCE)—Gehlen was to establish a new intelligence group, created from the remnants of FHO Intelligence, and begin espionage operations for the West. Known simply as the GEHLEN ORGANIZATION, the group included some 350 former Nazi intelligence operatives, many of whom had been members of the infamous SS, or Schutzstaffel (Protection Team), Hitler's most fanatical police/military force. The new FHO intelligence was officially, though secretly, part of the Army's Counterintelligence Corps (CIC).

The Gehlen Organization's first headquarters was in the Spessart Mountains of central Germany. When its personnel swelled to 3,000, the headquarters was relocated to a sprawling 25-acre compound near Munich. The organization also assumed a cover name—the South German Industrial Development Organization.

In 1947, the CIA was established from the disbanded OFFICE OF STRATEGIC SERVICES (OSS). In 1949, the year that the Federal Republic of Germany (West Germany) was officially established, FRANK GARDINER WISNER, chief of the CIA's OFFICE OF POLICY COORDINATION, recruited Gehlen and directed him to carry out espionage against the Soviets in several regions of Eastern Europe.

Gehlen proved to be a master of employing his own AGENTS OF INFLUENCE in East Germany. He warned the Americans about the impending blockade of Berlin, but his warning was ignored.

His other successes included identifying the existence of Smersh, the KGB's infamous assassination arm. He assisted in the development of the BERLIN TUNNEL enabling the CIA and MI6 to tap into Soviet communications lines. He secured for the CIA a copy of Nikita Khrushchev's secret speech to the 20th Communist Party Congress denouncing Joseph Stalin. He also obtained information in advance of the Six Day War in the Middle East in 1967. However, he failed to warn the West that the Berlin Wall would be built.

In April of 1956, the Gehlen Organization was absorbed into the new Bundesnachrichtendienst or BND (West Germany's Foreign Intelligence Service). Gehlen was named chief of the BND. He served in that capacity until his retirement in 1968.

Gehlen died in 1979.

See also BERLIN BLOCKADE AND AIRLIFT.

Gehlen Organization

The Gehlen Organization was a group of former Nazi intelligence operatives tasked with conducting post–World War II espionage operations for the West against the Soviets and their Eastern European satellite countries. Recruited from the ranks of German prisoners by the U.S. Army's Counterintelligence Corps in 1946, the Gehlen Organization was transferred to the CIA in 1949. The

chief of the Gehlen Organization was LT. GEN. REINHARD GEHLEN, former head of Nazi Germany's "Foreign Armies East," or Eastern Front Intelligence Service.

In 1956, the Gehlen Organization evolved into the BUNDESNACHRICHTENDIENST, or BND, West Germany's Foreign Intelligence Service.

George Bush Center for Intelligence

The official designation of the CIA's headquarters compound in LANGLEY, VIRGINIA, is the George Bush Center for Intelligence. Named for former president GEORGE HERBERT WALKER BUSH, who served as DIRECTOR OF CENTRAL INTELLIGENCE (DCI) from January 30, 1976, to January 20, 1977, the center was dedicated on April 26, 1999. President Bill Clinton forwarded the following letter to Bush on the date of the commemoration (the letter was read aloud by DCI GEORGE J. TENET to the Bush family as well as Agency employees in attendance at the dedication ceremonies): "I want to join the men and women of the Intelligence Community—and all Americans—in saluting you, as our nation designates the Central Intelligence Agency complex as the George Bush Center for Intelligence.

"When you assumed your duties as Director of Central Intelligence in January 1976, the nation had just endured one of the most tumultuous periods in its history. Many Americans had lost faith in government. Many asked whether the CIA should continue to exist.

"As Director, you accomplished a great deal. You restored morale and discipline to the Agency while publicly emphasizing the value of intelligence to the nation's security. You also restored America's trust in the CIA and the rest of the Intelligence Community.

"Of course, we honor you today for more than your tenure as Director; in your lifetime of service to America, you served not only as the head of the Intelligence Community but also, as President, as the nation's chief intelligence consumer. As President, you stood for American leadership around the world—leadership for freedom and democracy, peace and prosperity.

"As you know, in my time as President, I have turned to you more than once for your wise counsel, and I have benefitted greatly from it. And I have been well served by the talented and dedicated men and women who make up the Intelligence Community that you did so much to preserve and strengthen.

"On behalf of all Americans, I want to thank you for your patriotism and leadership, and I want to convey to you my warmest congratulations on receiving this fitting tribute."

The new headquarters designation was signed into law by Clinton on October 20, 1998, as part of the Intelligence Authorization Act for fiscal year 1999.

Gestapo

Gestapo was the acronym for Nazi Germany's feared Geheime Staatspolizei (Secret State Police). The Gestapo existed from 1933 to 1945. At the end of World War II, Americans feared that a Gestapo-like organization might be created from the remnants of the OFFICE OF STRATEGIC SERVICES (OSS), the CIA's first predecessor organization.

See GESTAPO FEAR, THE GREAT.

Gestapo Fear, the Great

"The Great Gestapo Fear" evokes the general public's wariness of a postwar Central Intelligence Agency, which many believed would become a de facto American GESTAPO organization.

The fear began in late 1944, when MAJOR GENERAL WILLIAM J. "WILD BILL" DONOVAN began lobbying for a strong centralized intelligence agency that would replace the wartime OFFICE OF STRATEGIC SERVICES (OSS). Donovan, who had directed the OSS since its inception in 1941, believed that if it instituted a centrally controlled system of intelligence gathering and COUNTERINTELLIGENCE, the United States would be better able to avoid any future surprise attacks like the Japanese strike on Pearl Harbor. Unfortunately for Donovan, there were a number of opponents to such an agency. Chief among them were the heads of the various military services and J. EDGAR HOOVER, the director of the FEDERAL BUREAU OF INVESTIGATION (FBI).

Like many American generals and admirals, Hoover believed that a postwar OSS would encroach on the jurisdictional intelligence responsibilities of other government entities, specifically the FBI. Hoover raised the specter of an American secret police, by leaking to *Chicago Tribune* reporter Walter Trohan a copy of a memo from Donovan to President Franklin Roosevelt outlining Donovan's plans. The *Tribune* subsequently published an article that read in part: "New Deal plans to spy on world and home folks; and Super Gestapo Agency is under consideration." Thus the Great Gestapo Fear.

See also DONOVAN PROPOSAL.

Glavnoye Razvedyvatelnoye Upravleniye (GRU)

The GRU, or Glavnoye Razvedyvatelnoye Upravleniye (the Chief Intelligence Directorate, i.e., of the General Staff), is the Russian Federation's military intelligence corps.

The GRU was also the military intelligence branch of the former Soviet Union. When the USSR dissolved in the early 1990s, the GRU existed for a brief time as the principal intelligence body of the Main Command of the Commonwealth of Independent States Armed Forces. However, when the new Russian Ministry of Defense was created in the spring of 1992, the GRU became Russia's military intelligence arm.

See also KGB.

Global Trends 2015 (GT-2015)

Global Trends 2015, or *GT-2015*, is a nontraditional intelligence assessment of the world situation as it is projected to evolve from the beginning of the 21st century to the year 2015.

The CIA and the NATIONAL INTELLIGENCE COUNCIL (NIC), in close collaboration with a variety of U.S. government specialists as well as experts outside the government, developed the plan to identify major "drivers" and "trends" that will, according to their assessment, shape the world of 2015.

As of this writing, *GT-2015* is being used to make future projections and identify troubling uncertainties of strategic importance to the United States. This assessment will ideally enable intelligence planners to address potential problems before they become unmanageable. The assessment also encourages dialogue from global experts outside the U.S. INTELLIGENCE COMMUNITY.

There are seven key areas of focus addressed by *GT-2015*:

1. Demographics
2. Natural resources and environment
3. Science and technology
4. The global economy and globalization
5. National and international governance
6. Future conflict
7. The role of the United States.

In an open letter to the public (December 13, 2000), DIRECTOR OF CENTRAL INTELLIGENCE (DCI) GEORGE TENET wrote, "From the beginning of the ambitious project in the fall of 1999, we intended to make GT-2015 an unclassified assessment to be shared with the public. Experts from academia, think-tanks, and the corporate world have made major contributions, and their reactions, along with those of other specialists who will see our work for the first time, will strengthen our continuing analysis of the issues covered in GT-2015. Grappling with the future is necessarily a work in progress that I believe should constantly seek new insights while testing and revising old judgements."

Conducted by the NIC under CIA direction, *GT-2015* was 15-month study initiated by Tenet in 1999.

Glomar Explorer

The *Glomar Explorer* was a salvage ship constructed for the CIA in the early 1970s by billionaire industrialist Howard Hughes. The vessel was used in the 1974 recovery of a portion of a sunken Soviet submarine some 1,700

Glomar Explorer   (AP/WIDE WORLD PHOTOS)

miles northwest of Hawaii. The ship was dispatched to the site on what was ostensibly an undersea mining expedition. In reality, the vessel had been designed to raise the sub from the seafloor.

Glomar Explorer is enormous. It stretches the length of three football fields and weighs more than 50,000 tons. In the 1970s, its decks were crammed with all manner of technical devices used to locate and salvage items thousands of feet below the surface. Its weather decks were equipped with pivoting cranes; its main deck was fitted with a 209-foot derrick that could send a giant claw nearly 17,000 feet below the sea surface and lift at one time up to 800 tons. Special refrigerated storage could handle up to 100 bodies. Additionally, *Glomar Explorer's* officers carried religious texts for American and Russian burial services.

Glomar Explorer was only marginally successful. The vessel recovered the bodies of six Soviet sailors and approximately 10 percent of the Soviet submarine.

When the CIA ended Project JENNIFER, the recovery operation, the U.S. Navy retained ownership of the *Glomar Explorer.* The vessel was then leased as a commercial salvage vessel. *Glomar Explorer* was converted into an ultra-deepwater drillship and became the first ship to conduct deep-sea mining for minerals.

In November 1998, *Glomar Explorer* set a world water-depth record after it drilled in 7,718 feet of water in the Gulf of Mexico. Today, the ship continues operating as an ultra-deepwater drillship. She is leased from the U.S. Navy to GlobalSantaFe, a multinational drilling corporation.

go-between

In CIA parlance, a "go-between" is a spy who operates as a COURIER/liaison between two parties. A go-between is also known as a CUT-OUT.

GOLD, Operation

Operation GOLD was the code name for the BERLIN TUNNEL, a joint CIA–British Secret Service underground communications-monitoring facility extending from just inside West Berlin to a point deep in the communist eastern sector.

Goldberg, Arthur Joseph (1908–1990)

Writer and lawyer Arthur Joseph Goldberg held the posts of secretary of labor, Supreme Court justice, and U.S. ambassador to the United Nations (UN). He also served in the OFFICE OF STRATEGIC SERVICES (OSS), the World War II precursor organization to the CIA.

Goldberg was born on August 8, 1908, in Chicago to Russian Jewish immigrants Joseph Goldberg and Rebecca Perlstein. As a boy, Goldberg helped his parents, who earned the family's income by selling vegetables from a pushcart. When he was older, he attended Chicago's public schools and simultaneously worked as a delivery boy for a local shoe factory. He later worked on a construction crew while attending first Crane Junior College of the City College of Chicago, then De Paul University. He eventually transferred to Northwestern University, where he earned a B.S. degree in 1929. Following his undergraduate work, Goldberg was admitted to the Illinois bar and worked as an associate lawyer in a Chicago firm. That income enabled him to earn a law degree, graduating first in his class, from Northwestern in 1930.

When America entered World War II in 1941, Goldberg was developing something of a reputation as a pro-labor attorney, particularly after representing the Newspaper Guild in a strike in 1938. Goldberg, however, put his practice on hold and joined the U.S. Army, where he won an officer's commission and was detached to the OSS. He served as chief of the OSS's European Labor Division from 1942 to 1944. By war's end he had risen to the rank of major.

Goldberg returned to the practice of law in Chicago, simultaneously teaching at the John Marshall Law School and the Chicago School of Industrial Relations. In 1948, he became general counsel to the Congress of Industrial Organizations (CIO) and the United Steelworkers. With Goldberg's assistance, the CIO merged with American Federation of Labor (AFL) to form the AFL-CIO.

In December 1960, U.S. president-elect John Kennedy named Goldberg secretary of labor. Goldberg served in that capacity until 1962, when he was named to the U.S. Supreme Court. In 1965, President Lyndon Johnson persuaded Goldberg to relinquish his seat on the Supreme Court and accept the position of ambassador to the United Nations (UN). He held that post until 1968, then returned to his law practice.

In 1970, Goldberg made an unsuccessful bid for governor of New York. He then moved to Washington, D.C., and resumed teaching and practicing law. His final post was that of U.S. ambassador-at-large for President Jimmy Carter. In retirement, Goldberg spent much of his time at his vacation home in the Virgin Islands.

Goldberg was a prolific writer. He authored, among other works, *AFL-CIO: Labor United* (1956), *The Defenses of Freedom: The Public Papers of Arthur J. Goldberg* (1966),

and *Equal Justice: The Warren Era of the Supreme Court* (1971). His awards included the Outstanding Labor Personality of the Year for 1961, by the New York Newspaper Guild; and the Herbert H. Lehman Medal, from the Jewish Theology Seminary. He was also the recipient of numerous honorary degrees.

On January 19, 1990, Goldberg died of coronary artery disease at 82 in Washington, D.C. He was buried in Arlington National Cemetery.

Goodfellow, Millard Preston (1892–1973)

Millard Preston Goodfellow, a former Brooklyn newspaper publisher and Boy's Club executive who served in the Secret Intelligence Branch of the OFFICE OF THE COORDINATOR OF INFORMATION or COI (the pre–World War II predecessor of the CIA), first proposed the concept of an American irregular warfare unit to be employed against the Japanese operating in Burma. The unit would become a reality known as DETACHMENT 101.

Goodfellow was born May 22, 1892, in Brooklyn, New York. He attended the New York University School of Journalism and then landed a job as a reporter for the *Brooklyn Eagle*. He later served on the staffs of both the *Brooklyn Times* and the *New York Evening Mail*.

When America entered World War I, Goodfellow joined the U.S. Army, becoming a second lieutenant in the Signal Corps. He later served as freelance correspondent for the *New York Times* on the Mexican border. He returned to the *Brooklyn Eagle,* eventually becoming its publisher.

When World War II erupted in Europe, Goodfellow returned to the Army, where he received a major's commission and an assignment to Army intelligence. In that capacity, he served as liaison between the Army and the Office of the Coordinator of Information. The COI was the predecessor organization to the OFFICE OF STRATEGIC SERVICES or OSS (the wartime precursor to the CIA), and as such was the earliest predecessor organization of the CIA.

In January 1942, Goodfellow was tasked with organizing the COI's special-operations branch. In that capacity, he suggested to Coordinator of Information WILLIAM J. "WILD BILL" DONOVAN that a unit comprising irregular or special-warfare forces would be effective against the Japanese who were operating in the rugged backcountry of Burma. However, the idea was flatly rejected by General Joseph "Vinegar Joe" Stilwell, commander of U.S. forces in the China-Burma-India theater. Stilwell was of the opinion that regular forces were far superior to small teams of irregulars. Eventually, Stilwell conceded, and Detachment 101 was established in May.

In June, the COI was redesignated the OSS, and Goodfellow was made deputy director of Operations. While serving in the OSS, he befriended exiled Korean leader Syngman Rhee. The U.S. STATE DEPARTMENT had dismissed Rhee as having no legitimacy as a Korean head of state. But through the sponsorship of Goodfellow, Ree's standing was eventually elevated in the eyes of the U.S. government.

When World War II ended, Goodfellow was dispatched to Korea, where he served as political adviser to the American occupation forces. At that time Korea was under a joint occupation pact between the United States and the Soviet Union. When the two nations failed to reach an agreement as to how Korea should be governed, Goodfellow proposed the establishment of a separate government for South Korea.

Goodfellow returned to the private sector to serve as publisher of the *Pocatello Tribune* in Idaho and later as president of the Overseas Reconstruction, Inc., a multinational corporation based in Washington, D.C.

Goodfellow died on September 5, 1973. He was 81.

Gottlieb, Dr. Sidney (1919–1999)

Dr. Sidney Gottlieb (aka Joseph Scheider) was the controversial chief science adviser and head of the CIA's TECHNICAL SERVICES STAFF (TSS), which detractors have referred to as a "house of horrors."

Gottlieb, a native New Yorker, was born Joseph Scheider in 1919. He stuttered and had a club foot, but he overcame the emotional effects of his physical challenges, mastering his schoolwork and becoming an accomplished folk dancer.

In 1951, Gottlieb earned a Ph.D. in chemistry from the California Institute of Technology and joined the CIA. At the CIA, he worked feverishly, climbing his way up through the ranks of the TSS and ultimately becoming chief of the Agency's Chemical Division.

As a cover for his work, Gottlieb lived on a 15-acre farm outside of Washington, D.C. There he, his wife, and four children grew and sold Christmas trees and raised goats. Each morning, Gottlieb milked his own goats before driving to his laboratory at CIA headquarters.

A self-proclaimed "Dr. Strangelove," Gottlieb was best known in intelligence circles as the man who prepared and delivered deadly poisons to Agency-commissioned assassins during the 1950s and 1960s. He was also responsible for much of the CIA's mind-controlling drug experimentation during Operations MKULTRA and MKSEARCH.

In 1973, Gottlieb's deadly trade was exposed with the revelation of the Agency's FAMILY JEWELS—a lengthy compendium of some 300 possible CIA legal transgressions, including domestic spying, mind-controlling drug experiments, mail interception, and foreign ASSASSINATION PLOTS. As a consequence, Gottlieb was ordered to destroy his records. Soon after, he retired from the CIA

and traveled to India, where he briefly volunteered at a hospital for lepers.

Gottlieb died on March 7, 1999. He was 80.

See also MIND-CONTROL DRUG TESTING and OLSON, FRANK E.

gray man

"Gray man" is an espionage term describing the "perfect" covert operator. Former DIRECTOR OF CENTRAL INTELLIGENCE (DCI) WILLIAM EGAN COLBY may have expressed it best when he said that a gray man was a person "so inconspicuous that he could never catch the waiter's eye in a restaurant."

Colby, probably because of his statement, was also widely regarded as "the gray man." As he aged, his nickname evolved into "the old gray man."

gray propaganda

In CIA parlance, gray propaganda is information in broadcast or published statements of which the source is either unattributed or confusing—unlike BLACK PROPAGANDA, where the source is simply not known.

See also WHITE PROPAGANDA.

Groat, Douglas Fred (1947–)

Douglas Fred Groat was a former CIA ANALYST who, when caught selling secrets to two unnamed foreign governments, attempted to extort money from the Agency to keep him from continuing his illegal activities.

Groat was employed by the CIA as a technical officer in the Agency's DIRECTORATE of Science and Technology from 1980 to 1996. However, by early 1993, the Agency began to suspect that he was a security risk and consequently placed him on a three-year paid administrative leave. For the next three years, he had no access to classified information.

During his 16 years with the Agency, Groat, an expert in CRYPTOGRAPHY, was involved in a number of clandestine operations aimed at breaking the secret CODEs and communication systems employed by foreign governments. It was also during that time that he revealed classified information to two undisclosed foreign governments. The information revealed pertained to CIA operations against the communications systems of those governments. Oddly, Groat never received any money for his misdeeds. Instead he purportedly betrayed his country because he felt slighted by the CIA (he had not received assignments he felt he deserved).

Groat was arrested by the FBI on April 3, 1998, and was charged with four counts of espionage and one count of attempted extortion. The latter charge was leveled against him after he boldly demanded between $500,000 and $1 million from the CIA in return for his not disclosing any additional secrets.

The day after Groat's arrest, DIRECTOR OF CENTRAL INTELLIGENCE (DCI) GEORGE TENET made the following statement: "Yesterday he [Groat] was arrested on charges of espionage and attempted extortion based on information alleging that he disclosed information concerning the targeting and compromise of the cryptographic systems of two foreign governments to those governments and that he threatened to reveal intelligence activities and methods unless the CIA agreed to pay him more than half a million dollars for his silence." Tenet added that the U.S. government would not be "intimidated by threats of blackmail."

On July 27, 1998, Groat accept a plea bargain, pleading guilty to the single extortion charge. As part of the agreement, federal prosecutors agreed to drop the four counts of espionage, which could have easily placed him behind bars for the remainder of his life. On September 25, he was sentenced to five years in prison for attempted extortion.

GRU
See GLAVNOYE RAZVEDYVATELNOYE UPRAVLENIYE.

Guatemala, coup d'état in
In its efforts to contain the global spread of communism during the first decade of the COLD WAR, the CIA had a number of initial successes, including one of the Agency's best-known operations—the 1954 coup d'état in Guatemala.

Less than a year after the Agency's ousting of Iranian prime minister Mohamed Mossadegh, who had threatened to nationalize the British-owned ANGLO-IRANIAN OIL COMPANY, a similar upheaval was threatening American business interests in the third-largest country in Central

Some of the troops of the Guatemalan "liberation army"   (NATIONAL ARCHIVES)

America, Guatemala. Its strategic location below America's southern flank was of great concern to Washington.

In March 1951, Socialist-Democrat Jacobo Arbenz Guzmán, a former revolutionary who had the support of both the Guatemalan army and the Communist Party, was elected to the presidency on a popular platform of land reform. When he assumed office, 70 percent of Guatemala's arable lands were owned by less than 2.5 percent of the planter class, most of whom were not even resident in the country. Almost immediately, Arbenz Guzmán began to institute a number of social and economic reforms, including a strengthening of the unions and a redistribution of land to some 100,000 peasants whose incomes averaged less than eight dollars per month. Unfortunately for American business interests in Guatemala, Arbenz Guzmán's reforms included the 1953 expropriation of private property including over 400,000 acres of banana plantation lands owned by the U.S.-based UNITED FRUIT Company, effectively the largest landowner in the country. Arbenz Guzmán also demanded that United Fruit and other such companies pay more taxes. Arbenz Guzmán initially offered to purchase United Fruit—its expansive banana lands, railroads, and telephone lines—for a paltry $600,000 in long-term nonnegotiable bonds. The offer was essentially what the company had declared was the taxable land value. United Fruit then made an unsuccessful counteroffer of $16 million.

President Dwight Eisenhower, who inherited the developing Guatemalan problem from Harry Truman, described Arbenz Guzmán's offer as "woefully inadequate," adding that the government confiscation of United Fruit land was a "discriminatory and unfair seizure."

United Fruit had close ties to the CIA. GENERAL WALTER BEDELL SMITH, a former United Fruit executive who was later named to the company's board of directors, was a former DIRECTOR OF CENTRAL INTELLIGENCE (DCI). The Dulles brothers, Secretary of State John Foster Dulles and DCI ALLEN WELSH DULLES, had provided legal services for United Fruit through their association with the New York–based law firm of Sullivan & Cromwell. Eisenhower was more concerned, however, with containing communism in Central America than he was with supporting a multinational banana corporation.

The year after the United Fruit expropriation, the CIA learned that Arbenz Guzmán had purchased some 2,000 tons of armaments—mostly rail guns, antitank weapons, and small arms—from Czechoslovakia. Eisenhower soon authorized the CIA to begin operations aimed at the ultimate overthrow of Arbenz Guzmán. Code-named PBSUCCESS, the efforts to oust the Guatemalan president began with a series of covert arrangements with several Guatemalan military officers, offers of money deposited in Swiss bank accounts to persuade Arbenz Guzmán to resign, and signed security treaties with Honduras and Nicaragua. The CIA also began flying planes over Guatemala dropping anti-Arbenz Guzmán leaflets, as well as broadcasting messages over Guatemalan airwaves from locales in Honduras, Nicaragua, and the Dominican Republic. The psychological-warfare campaign against Arbenz Guzmán was headed up by CIA operatives EVERETTE HOWARD HUNT, destined for infamy as one of the White House "PLUMBERS" in the WATERGATE SCANDAL; and DAVID ATLEE PHILIPS, who would eventually direct all CIA activities in the Western Hemisphere.

On May 24, 1954, the U.S. Navy began a blockade against Guatemala. On June 15, Eisenhower gave the attack a green light. "I want you all to be damn good and sure you succeed," he told DCI Dulles. "When you commit the flag, you commit it to win." On June 18, a CIA-sponsored army of some 150 Guatemalan expatriates, Hondurans, Nicaraguans, and American mercenaries led by rebel colonel Carlos Castillo Armas crossed the Honduran border into Guatemala and began marching on Guatemala City. Though trained and equipped by the CIA, Armas's meager force was no match for the 6,000-man Guatemalan army and air force. But the size of the force had been greatly exaggerated by CIA-sponsored radio announcements directed by Hunt and Phillips, which Guatemalan government troops believed to be legitimate broadcasts. This misperception panicked many of Arbenz Guzmán's military commanders. Less than two weeks before the ground attack was launched, the commanding general of the Guatemalan air force, unsettled by the anti–Arbenz Guzmán broadcasts, had defected to Nicaragua and urged his pilots to do the same. This action forced the Guatemalan president to ground his entire air force, the most effective arm of the Guatemalan military.

CIA pilots flying vintage P-47 and P-51 fighters at once achieved air superiority and began bombing and strafing military installations. By June 25, most of the soldiers in the demoralized Guatemalan army were refusing to fight. Two days later, Arbenz Guzmán resigned and fled to Mexico.

Armas was installed as president by the United States. Land-reform policies were rescinded. The CIA began basking in the light of its first successful Latin American coup. The CIA's enthusiasm for such operations would, in seven years, lead the Agency into the fiasco known as the BAY OF PIGS INVASION.

See also IRAN, COUP D'ÉTAT IN.

Guevara, Ernesto (Che) (1928–1967)

Ernesto "Che" Guevara was Cuban leader FIDEL CASTRO's second in command during both the Cuban Revolution (1956–59) and the CIA-supported BAY OF PIGS INVASION in 1961.

Born Ernesto Guevara de la Serna on June 14, 1928, in Rosario, Argentina, Guevara was the eldest of five children in a middle-class family of Spanish-Irish descent with Marxist leanings. Though he suffered from asthma as a boy, he was a superb athlete and a scholar. After graduating from high school with honors in 1947, he entered medical school at the University of Buenos Aires. His dreams of becoming a physician stemmed from a desire to find a cure for cancer; his grandmother had died from the disease, and his mother would later be diagnosed with it. Guevara's studies, however, were briefly interrupted in 1952 when he and a friend, Alberto Granados, embarked on a 3,000-mile motorcycle jaunt across South America through Chile, Peru, Ecuador, Colombia, and Venezuela. The two men earned money along the way by working as truck drivers, dishwashers, porters, and even doctors.

In 1953, Guevara completed medical training. He then went to GUATEMALA, where Socialist-Democrat Jacobo Arbenz Guzmán had recently been elected president on a platform of radical land reform that threatened U.S. interests in the region.

The subsequent overthrow of Arbenz Guzmán's regime by CIA-backed rebels in 1954 led Guevara to believe that the United States would always oppose Marxist governments in Latin America. This belief compelled him to become more deeply involved in the growing concept of fostering revolutions to bring about global socialism.

After the coup, Guevara left Guatemala for Mexico. There, he met future Cuban president Fidel Castro and his brother, Raúl. Both were political exiles who were making preparations to overthrow the Cuban government of Fulgencio Batista. Guevara joined the Castros, and in November 1956 the three men led a force of revolutionaries in a landing on the Cuban coast near the province of Oriente. Almost immediately, the force was discovered by Batista's army and was nearly annihilated. Guevara himself was wounded, but he escaped into the Sierra Maestra mountains along with his commander, Castro.

By the time Castro's forces had overthrown Batista's government in 1959, Guevara had become one of the Cuban leader's most trusted aides. Once Castro's power was firmly established, Guevara was authorized to conduct public "war crimes" trials, resulting in the hanging and firing-squad executions of some 600 civilian and military officials from the Batista regime. Under Castro's "Revolutionary Code of Justice," Guevara ordered the arrests, trials, and executions of anyone deemed suspect. He also assisted Castro's brother in the reorganization of the national army. This included purging the officer corps of suspected dissidents.

Soon, Guevara developed an international reputation as a staunch anti-American revolutionary. In Havana, he was posted chief of the Industrial Department of the National Institute of Agrarian Reform, president of the National Bank of Cuba, and minister of industry. He also wrote several widely read books that reflected his political ideology.

In the spring of 1965, Guevara disappeared from public life. Though his whereabouts were kept secret for two years, American intelligence operatives discovered that he had spent much of his time outside of Cuba, serving with and helping to train revolutionary armies in both Africa and South America.

On October 8, 1967, while leading a guerrilla force near Santa Cruz, Bolivia, Guevara was ambushed and captured by American-trained Bolivian rangers. The following day, he was executed in Vallegrande, Bolivia.

H

Hale, Nathan (1755–1776)

Everyone passing through the main entrance of the CIA's headquarters building in LANGLEY, VIRGINIA, is at once taken aback by an imposing statue of Nathan Hale, the revolutionary hero who allegedly proclaimed before his execution in 1776 that he regretted having only one life to lose for his country. Hale, widely regarded as the father of American espionage, was the first American in history executed for spying.

Born in Coventry, Connecticut, on June 6, 1755, to Richard Hale, a farmer and devout Puritan, and Elizabeth Strong Hale, young Hale was considered something of a child prodigy. He was recognized by his contemporaries as a natural athlete; he was both intellectually gifted and strikingly handsome. At only 14 years he entered Yale, thus beginning a tradition of American spies who attended Ivy League institutions. He graduated with honors in 1770 and for two years served as a schoolmaster, first at East Haddam, then in New London. But his academic career was short-lived.

In 1774, Hale joined the seventh Connecticut Militia and was soon elected to first sergeant. On April 19, 1775, British troops clashed for the first time with American militia at Lexington Green, thus heralding the beginning of the American Revolution. On July 6, 1775, three days after General George Washington assumed command of the Continental Army in Cambridge, Massachusetts, Hale was awarded a lieutenant's commission. Six months later, the army was reorganized, and Hale was commissioned captain in the new 19th Connecticut Regiment.

In the spring of 1776, the Continentals marched on Manhattan in an attempt to prevent the British from capturing all of New York. Many sources contend that Hale, soon after arriving in New York, participated in the seizing of a British provision ship under the guns of a man-of-war. However, that story has more legendary elements than factual ones.

In early September 1776, Washington ordered the forming of four companies of rangers under the command of Lt. Col. Thomas Knowlton. Hale was given command of one of the companies and was tasked with reconnoitering areas forward of the American positions. It was a great opportunity for Hale, but it was bittersweet.

The Continental Army's situation in New York was, at best, tenuous. Facing an approaching winter, increasing desertion, and a numerically superior British army, Washington became keenly aware that he would not be able to defend all of Manhattan. Expressing his dilemma to his officers, he also explained the need to determine at what point along his lines the British would attack. Good intelligence was critical.

Nathan Hale, about to be hanged by the British for spying   (LIBRARY OF CONGRESS)

Hale then offered to penetrate British lines dressed as a civilian and report to Washington the disposition of British troops. Washington accepted the offer. But Hale was an unlikely spy. He had no training in the art of espionage. His physical appearance—tall, handsome, and with a facial burn from a gunpowder explosion—would cause him to stand out from real civilians. Also, his cousin Samuel Hale, who could easily identify him, was a loyalist serving under British general Sir William Howe in New York. It was a dangerous venture. But Hale's sense of patriotism far outweighed the risks.

Prior to embarking on his mission, Hale purportedly told a fellow officer, Captain William Hull, "I am not influenced by the expectation of promotion or pecuniary award; I wish to be useful, and every kind of service necessary to the public good becomes honorable by being necessary. If the exigencies of my country demand a peculiar service, its claims to perform that service are imperious."

Though the date is uncertain, at some point in mid-September Hale secretly crossed Long Island Sound from Norwalk, Connecticut, spending several days behind enemy lines. His COVER was that of an out-of-work schoolteacher. During his mission, the British invaded Manhattan, thus negating his efforts. He then crossed into British-held New York City and continued gathering intelligence. On September 20, fires were set and rioting broke out within the city; all suspicious-looking characters were arrested on the spot. The following night, a British ranger company confronted Hale in what is today midtown Manhattan. He was questioned, searched, and found to be carrying intelligence information that would be useful to the Americans. He was then arrested and brought before General Howe, to whom he denied nothing, freely disclosing his identity and mission.

The following morning, Sunday, September 22, 1776, Hale was marched north nearly six miles to a gallows next to a public house known as Dove Tavern. There, bound by the hands and feet and standing before a detachment of British soldiers, Hale uttered his last words, "I only regret that I have but one life to lose for my country." The remark was similar to one in Joseph Addison's renowned play *Cato,* but it would be immortalized by the 21-year-old former schoolmaster. Hale was then hanged, and though he had earned the admiration of his executioners, his body was ordered left on display. After several days, his body was cut down and buried in an unmarked grave.

On October 1, 1985, the Connecticut General Assembly officially proclaimed Nathan Hale as Connecticut's state hero.

The CIA's statue of Hale, by artist Bela Lyon Pratt, is a duplicate of an original at Yale University.

Hall, Virginia (1906–1982)

The only American civilian woman to win the Distinguished Service Cross, Virginia Hall (aka Maria Monin, Germaine, Diane, Camille, Nicolas, and the Limping Lady) was a covert operative for both the OFFICE OF STRATEGIC SERVICES (OSS) and its descendant agency, the CIA.

Hall was born on April 9, 1906 in Baltimore, Maryland. As a child, she was regarded as having a passion for knowledge and for the world around her. In the early 1920s, Hall studied foreign languages (French, Italian, and German) at Radcliffe and Barnard Colleges, completing her studies in Paris and Vienna. In 1929, she returned to the United States and enrolled in George Washington University, where she studied French and economics. In the early 1930s, she served as a clerk at the U.S. embassy in Warsaw, Poland.

Hall had dreams of a career in foreign service, but her dreams would not be realized before some serious obstacles were overcome. During a hunting trip near Izmir, Turkey, an accident took place that would change her life: she accidentally fired her shotgun into her left foot. By the time she was able to receive medical treatment gangrene had set in, and her leg below the knee had to be amputated. She was fitted with an artificial leg. Later, when she applied to take the Foreign Service board exams, she was rejected because of her physical handicap. In May 1939, she left her position at the U.S. embassy and made her way to France.

When World War II erupted in Europe, Hall, who was in Paris, joined the French Ambulance Service as a private second class. In June 1940, France fell to the Germans, and she fled to England. There she took a job as a code clerk for the military attaché in the American embassy.

Not long after, Hall joined the SPECIAL OPERATIONS EXECUTIVE (SOE), the newly formed British clandestine-warfare organization. With the SOE, she learned every-thing about the special operations trade, from weaponry to communications to resistance activities. Her training completed, Hall was sent to Vichy, France, in August 1941. There, under the COVER of being a reporter for the *New York Post,* she was to establish a spy network for the Allies. That she did. She also aided escaping Allied prisoners of war and downed air crews, as well as working closely with the French Underground. She, in fact, was so successful in her espionage efforts that the Nazis launched a focused manhunt for her.

By 1942, the Germans were hot on Hall's trail. But just before they were to arrest her, she slipped away, escaping over the Pyrenees Mountains into Spain. What made the event even more dramatic was that she made her escape on foot despite her physical handicap, and in the dead of winter.

In Spain, Hall was briefly incarcerated by the local authorities, released at the urging of the American consul, and resumed her work. She spent a few months in Madrid, operating as a spy under the cover of a reporter for the *Chicago Times.* She then was ordered back to England in order to receive training as a wireless operator. Upon her return to England, she was awarded the "Member of the Order of the British Empire" by King George VI. Soon after, she transferred to the OSS.

In November 1943, Hall journeyed back to Nazi-occupied France and resumed her work. By day, she appeared to be a harmless milkmaid. At night, she transmitted radio dispatches to London from haylofts all over the French countryside. When the Germans discovered that she had returned to France, they again began to track her. The GESTAPO, Germany's notorious Secret State Police, circulated a wanted poster that stated, "the woman with the limp is one of the most valuable Allied agents in France and we must find and destroy her." Fortunately, Hall was constantly disguised and had taught herself to walk without a limp; she eluded the enemy at every turn.

Hall was a vital asset to the Americans and the British. Aside from her invaluable intelligence-gathering missions, she helped coordinate air drops in support of the Normandy invasion in June 1944. Additionally, she trained and led French resistance forces in numerous sabotage operations and raids against the occupying Germans.

When the war ended, Hall returned to the United States and was awarded the Distinguished Service Cross—the only American civilian women to receive it. She left intelligence work in 1945 but returned in 1951, when she joined the fledgling CIA. Her first Agency post was with the OFFICE OF POLICY COORDINATION, the CIA's early covert-action arm, where she became an intelligence ANALYST on French paramilitary affairs.

In 1952, Hall became one of the first female operations officers in the new office of the DEPUTY DIRECTOR of plans (operations). She prepared political-action projects, interviewed exiles, and planned resistance and sabotage networks to be used against Soviet forces in the event of a third world war. Over the next 14 years, she was given several overseas assignments. But in 1966, at the mandatory retirement age of 60, she closed the book on her espionage career.

In retirement she spent time gardening and taking care of her French poodles. After a period of declining health, Hall died in 1982 at age 76 at the Shady Grove Adventist Hospital in Rockville, Maryland. She was buried in Pikesville, Maryland.

Halloween Massacre

"Halloween Massacre" was the name given to the day, October 31, 1977, when DIRECTOR OF CENTRAL INTELLIGENCE (DCI) STANSFIELD TURNER issued some 820 pink slips to CIA employees.

Turner, a former admiral and President Jimmy Carter's newly appointed DCI, conducted the mass firing as a method of "cleaning house" after the 1975–76 congressional investigations of Agency misdeeds. It forced 147 career officers into early retirement, sacked an additional 17, and eliminated nearly all of the OSS veterans and CIA charter officers.

Turner's action severely damaged Agency morale. Opponents of the mass firing—like THEODORE SHACKLEY, a former deputy to the director of the Agency's CLANDESTINE SERVICE—argued that the reduction in force could have been accomplished through "peer review and attrition." As it was, the firings were "insensitive" and wholly demoralizing to the Agency.

The Halloween Massacre was the second such wave of firings at the CIA in less than five years. In early 1973, DCI JAMES SCHLESINGER, an unpopular appointee of President Richard Nixon, fired or retired nearly 1,400 CIA employees. Officially, Schlesinger's actions were the result of downsizing after the Vietnam War. But Agency insiders felt that Schlesinger was hauling out what he perceived to be deadwood left over from the earliest days of the Agency. Unlike Turner's "Halloween Massacre," Schlesinger's firings were conducted over a period of four months, and senior career officers were not disproportionately targeted.

handler

In the CIA, a handler is a field officer (in most instances, a case officer) who is tasked with controlling, or "handling," one or more of the Agency's assets or agents. Handlers are responsible for recruiting and paying agents, as well as directing their activities during operations.

Hanssen, Robert Philip (1944–)

FBI COUNTERINTELLIGENCE officer Robert Philip Hanssen (aka "B," Ramon Garcia, Jim Baker, and G. Robertson) was the first high-profile DOUBLE AGENT of the 21st century arrested for conducting espionage activities against the United States. His activities proved to have been catastrophic for the CIA.

Hanssen was born in Chicago on April 18, 1944, the only child of Howard Hanssen, a Chicago police lieutenant, and his wife Vivian. In 1966, Hanssen earned an A.B. degree in chemistry from Knox College in Illinois. He then studied dentistry at Northwestern University from 1966 to 1968. In 1971, he received an MBA degree in accounting and information systems from Northwestern. During his college years, he studied the Russian language.

Hanssen briefly considered a career as a dentist but dropped out of dental school in 1971 and began working as a junior accountant at a Chicago-based accounting firm. The following year, he joined the Chicago Police Department as an investigator in the Financial Section of the Inspection Services Division.

Hanssen was a model officer, but he wanted more. On January 12, 1976, he joined the FEDERAL BUREAU OF INVESTIGATION (FBI), a primary member of the U.S. INTELLIGENCE COMMUNITY and the CIA's domestic intelligence counterpart. He was initially posted in Indiana and in New York City. In 1981, he was transferred to FBI headquarters in Washington, D.C. There, he was tasked with tracking white-collar criminals and monitoring foreign diplomats assigned to the United States. From 1983 to 1985 he served in the bureau's highly sensitive Soviet analytical unit. In that capacity he had access to classified information relating to the foreign intelligence and counterintelligence activities of various U.S. intelligence community agencies, including the CIA.

In 1985, Hanssen transferred to New York City in order to head an FBI foreign counterintelligence squad in the Manhattan Bureau. Other agents there were either requesting transfers from the city or leaving the FBI altogether because they found it nearly impossible to support their families adequately in New York on an FBI salary. Hanssen nonetheless moved his wife and six children from a comfortable four-bedroom home in a Washington-area suburb to a cramped dwelling north of Manhattan.

Though his motives have yet to be fully determined, within nine days of joining the Manhattan Bureau, Hanssen decided to become a double agent. In 1986, he sent the following note to his KGB handlers: "As far as the funds are concerned, I have little need or utility for more than the 100,000. It merely provides a difficulty since I can not spend it, store it or invest it easily without triping [sic] 'drug money' warning bells. Perhaps some diamonds as security to my children and some good will so that when the time comes, you will accept by [sic] senior services as a guest lecturer. Eventually, I would appreciate an escape plan. Nothing lasts forever."

According to U.S. Justice Department allegations, the Russians paid Hanssen more than $600,000 in cash and diamonds and set up an escrow account for him in a Moscow bank worth at least $800,000. For his part, he allegedly passed to the Russians some 6,000 pages of documents that revealed the identities of double agents (most of whom were working for the CIA), disclosed how the United States was intercepting Soviet satellite transmissions, and provided outlines of how the nation might retaliate against nuclear attack. He also allegedly tipped off the KGB to the FBI's secret investigation of Felix Bloch, a foreign service officer suspected of spying for Moscow in 1989 (Bloch was never arrested).

Hanssen, who dressed in black so often that colleagues called him "Dr. Death," was considered to be an unflappable agent and something of a loner. "His reputation was of a quiet, professional man," said Jim Kallstrom, former director of the FBI's New York office, in an interview for CNN. "He kept to himself, thought of himself as a deep thinker."

On February 18, 2001, Hanssen was arrested by the FBI after making a DEAD DROP in a park in northern Virginia. Cutting a deal with his prosecutors, he pled guilty on July 6 to 15 counts of espionage and conspiracy charges in exchange for a promise that federal prosecutors would not seek the death penalty. On May 10, 2002, he was sentenced to life in prison without parole.

In a letter released by the FBI, Hanssen claimed that he derived his treasonous inspiration from the published memoirs of British-born double agent HAROLD ADRIAN RUSSELL "KIM" PHILBY, one of the infamous CAMBRIDGE SPIES. "I decided on this course when I was fourteen years old," Hanssen wrote. "I had read Philby's book [*My Silent War*]. Now that is insane, eh?"

hard rice

"Hard rice" was a slang or jargon term used by employees of the CIA's famous proprietary airline, AIR AMERICA, to describe shipments of small arms ammunition. The term was derived from the fact that much of what Air America transported over SOUTHEAST ASIA in the 1960s and early 1970s was in fact "rice." But the rice loads on Air America transport planes were often mixed with ammunition destined for points in Laos and Vietnam.

hard target

"Hard target" is a CIA term used to describe a hostile nation that covert operatives find difficult to penetrate, much less operate in or obtain information from. During the PERSIAN GULF WAR, Iraq was considered to be a hard target.

See also SOFT TARGET.

Harvey, William King (1915–1976)

A former FBI special agent who was unable to conform to what he considered to be Director J. EDGAR HOOVER's "petty rules," William King Harvey became a pistol-wielding CIA COUNTERINTELLIGENCE officer with a photographic memory whom U.S. president John Kennedy once reportedly labeled "America's JAMES BOND."

Harvey was born in Danville, Indiana, on September 13, 1915. In 1937, Harvey earned a law degree from the University of Indiana. For the next three years, he practiced law in Maysville, Kentucky.

In 1940, Harvey joined the FEDERAL BUREAU OF INVESTIGATION (FBI). After briefly serving in the Pittsburgh, Pennsylvania, field office, he was assigned a counterespionage post in Washington, D.C. In 1947, J. Edgar Hoover reassigned Harvey to a lesser post in Indianapolis, Indiana, for violating minor bureau rules. Not long after, Harvey resigned from the FBI and joined the CIA, which was then actively seeking officers with espionage experience. He was hired and assigned to a counterintelligence post in Washington. There, he befriended and ultimately "unmasked" one of the infamous CAMBRIDGE SPIES, HAROLD ADRIAN RUSSELL "KIM" PHILBY, as MI6 officer who sold Western secrets to the Russians.

In December 1952, Harvey became the Agency's CHIEF OF STATION (COS) in Berlin, where he earned a reputation as the "father of the BERLIN TUNNEL." Discovering that the Soviets had several telephone and telegraph cables buried beneath a highway just inside Berlin's eastern sector, Harvey convinced his Agency superiors and officials of the British Secret Service (MI6) that a tunnel could intercept those lines and tap into highly classified Soviet/East German communications. The CIA began construction on the tunnel in 1953. The project was completed, and the subterranean station became operational, in 1955. Code-named OPERATION GOLD, Harvey's line-tapping project was considered one of the West's most ambitious intelligence operations of the COLD WAR. The tunnel enabled the British and the Americans to gather intelligence pertaining to Soviet army units, and it would conceivably have provided a warning if the Soviets had planned an invasion of the West.

The tunnel's entrance (in the western sector) was concealed by an above-ground U.S. radar station. A narrow equipment-moving rail line ran the length of the tunnel. Amplifying equipment used to monitor the phone transmissions was located in a steel reinforced exclusion area, or communications chamber, at the eastern end. For nearly a year, MI6 personnel inside the tunnel were able to monitor communications between Soviet military headquarters in East Berlin and Moscow. The tunnel was compromised and immediately vacated when it was discovered by East German telephone repairmen in 1956. For the Berlin Tunnel operation, Harvey was awarded the CIA's Distinguished Service Medal.

Harvey had a natural gift for espionage work, but he was a paradox. With a drinking problem—exacerbated by the fact that martini lunches were not only the norm but in vogue—he was known for throwing free-pouring afternoon cocktail parties at his Berlin residence. He was also known for carrying a pearl-handled revolver (sometimes two pistols), even when patronizing local restaurants and beer halls. Fellow officers viewed it as nonsensical badge of rank. Harvey felt he was simply being prepared for any scenario in a city that was considered a cold war trip wire—and prepared he was. He is known to have stored rifles and thermite grenades in his office.

Harvey loved the CIA, but he loathed the elitism that permeated its ranks in the 1950s and 1960s. He preferred the cowboy mentality of the barroom brawler to the scholarly virtues of the Ivy League set. In fact, he so resented the Ivy Leaguers that he reputedly rarely let pass an opportunity to derail their careers.

Physically, Harvey was not an impressive man. In his book *The Very Best Men*, Evan Thomas describes Harvey as "short, fat, and hideous looking; he had bulging eyes, attributed to a thyroid condition, and a froglike voice." According to Thomas, Harvey's officers and agents referred to him as "the Pear." Harvey sometimes referred to himself as "God."

In 1959, Harvey left Berlin and returned to the United States, where he was placed in charge of an Agency communications-intercept unit known as Staff D. In 1961, he was placed in charge of the CIA's EXECUTIVE ACTION program, wherein the Agency was developing means and methods of eliminating certain foreign leaders.

In November, he was placed in charge of TASK FORCE W, the sabotage/paramilitary arm of OPERATION MONGOOSE (the CIA's all-encompassing covert-action effort to eliminate Cuban leader FIDEL CASTRO). During the CUBAN MISSILE CRISIS of 1962, Harvey sent more than one intelligence team into Cuba without the knowledge of either President John Kennedy's Executive Committee (EXCOM) or DIRECTOR OF CENTRAL INTELLIGENCE (DCI) JOHN MCCONE. One of the teams was captured by the Cubans (October 25). Another team destroyed a Cuban industrial complex (November 8). Harvey's actions elicited strong criticism of the Agency from Attorney General Robert Kennedy, who wanted to terminate Task Force W. Instead, Harvey was transferred to Rome as COS.

While in Rome his drinking increased, his output decreased, and he suffered a heart attack. He was recalled from Rome and reassigned a lesser task of reporting on security at CIA facilities around the world.

Harvey retired from the Agency for medical reasons in 1969 and accepted an editor's position with the Bobbs-Merrill publishing house in Indianapolis.

In 1975, he was called to testify about his involvement in Operation MONGOOSE during the congressional CHURCH COMMITTEE hearings into CIA misdeeds.

Harvey died of complications from heart disease on June 9, 1976. He was 60.

See also COWBOYS VS. SCHOLARS.

Hasenfus, Eugene (1941–)

Eugene Hasenfus was a pilot for one of the CIA's cover airlines, Southern Air Transport. Over Nicaragua his C-123 cargo plane was shot down by Sandinistas (Nicaraguan government troops) on October 5, 1986. Hasenfus's aircraft was transporting military weapons to the contra rebels, who were fighting the Sandinistas. Hasenfus was the lone survivor in the crash, which claimed the lives of two other crew members. He was captured by the Sandinistas and jailed for 73 days.

The significance of Hasenfus and the crash stems from the fact that up until that point, President Ronald Reagan had claimed that the U.S. government was not illegally arming the contra rebels. The Reagan administration denied any knowledge of Hasenfus's cargo or activities.

The Hasenfus crash incident, among other revelations related to the arming of the contra rebels, eventually led to the congressional investigations of the government's involvement in the IRAN-CONTRA SCANDAL.

Haver, Richard Leonhardt (1945–)

A former executive director of the CIA's COMMUNITY MANAGEMENT STAFF, Richard Leonhardt Haver headed up the Agency's damage-assessment teams in the cases of ALDRICH AMES, JONATHON POLLARD, and the WALKER FAMILY SPY RING.

Haver was born on January 30, 1945, in Syracuse, New York, to Richard Marriott Haver and Bertha Elizabeth Leonhardt. Haver earned a bachelor's degree from Johns Hopkins University in 1967. He joined the U.S. Navy in 1969, serving through the end of America's involvement in Vietnam in 1973.

Following his active naval service, Haver accepted a post as a civilian analyst with the Naval Intelligence Support Center in Suitland, Maryland. He served in that capacity until 1976. He was then named technical director of the Naval Ocean Surveillance Information Center, also in Suitland, where he served until 1978. From 1978 until 1981 he served as technical director of the Navy

Field Operations Intelligence Office at Fort Meade, Maryland. He then transferred to the Washington, D.C., Office of NAVAL INTELLIGENCE (ONI), where he served as special assistant until 1983. He was then appointed deputy director to the Chief of Naval Operations.

In 1989, Haver was named assistant for intelligence in the Office of the Secretary of Defense in Washington. In 1992, he was named executive director of intelligence community affairs for the CIA.

After heading up the Agency's damage-assessment team in the spy case of Aldrich Ames, Haver was named to the post of national intelligence officer for special activities. He served in that capacity from 1996 until 1998.

In 1999, Haver joined TRW Systems & Information Technology Group, where he currently serves as a senior-level executive in the firm's Intelligence Business Development branch. He is also a private consultant and lecturer.

Haver's awards include the Department of the Navy's Distinguished Civilian Award, the Department of Defense Distinguished Civilian Award, the Presidential Meritorious Executive Award, the Presidential Distinguished Executive Award, and the National Intelligence Distinguished Service Medal.

Hawkins, Jack (unknown)

A dashing, highly decorated Marine Corps officer whose striking face could have easily graced a Marine recruiting poster, Colonel Jack Hawkins (aka John Haskins) was the CIA's chief paramilitary specialist on the Cuban Task Force, the planning entity for the BAY OF PIGS INVASION.

A graduate of the U.S. Naval Academy at Annapolis, Maryland, Hawkins epitomized the tough, cool-headed leadership qualities associated with Marine officers. During World War II, he saw action in the Philippines at Bataan and Corregidor, was captured by the Japanese, escaped from his prisoner of war camp, linked up with U.S. Army–led guerrilla forces, and led raiding parties in attacks against the enemy. He later rejoined regular Marine infantry forces and fought in the Okinawa campaign, earning a reputation as one of the Corps's wartime "supermen." For his service, he was awarded the Distinguished Service Cross and a Bronze Star. He was fluent in Spanish, and his postwar career led him to a brief posting in Venezuela, where he served as a naval attaché.

When hostilities in Korea broke out, Hawkins again saw combat, this time as the commanding officer of the famed First Battalion, First Marine Regiment. For his actions with the First Marines, he won a Silver Star. For the next several years, he held several posts within the Corps, and his career progressed in a direction that could only have been the envy of his peers.

Unfortunately for Hawkins, his career took a detour when the planned invasion of Cuba at the Bay of Pigs expanded from an infiltration plan to an amphibious landing. Detailed from the Marine Corps to the CIA in October 1960, Hawkins, who had recently been promoted to colonel, set about creating a blueprint for an amphibious assault by Cuban exiles somewhere along the Cuban coastline. His plan called for absolute air supremacy over the operational area. It was not to be.

Code-named OPERATION ZAPATA, the Bay of Pigs invasion was launched on April 15, 1961, but within three days it evolved into what would be known as the CIA's greatest operational disaster. The "Free Cuba" landing force encountered Marxist leader FIDEL CASTRO's forces almost immediately upon landing and were pinned down on the beaches. Making matters worse, U.S. president John Kennedy, fearing an escalating conflict that might pit the United States against the Soviet Union, refused to authorize American air and naval gunfire support. U.S. warships in the vicinity of the battle were subsequently ordered to withdraw.

Hawkins retired from the Marine Corps in 1965. In a 1996 interview with author Peter Kornbluh, the former Marine stated that the failure of the operation had not been the fault of the Agency or its military planners. "We wanted to use enough aircraft to do what had to be done," said Hawkins. "[The DEPARTMENT OF STATE] opposed that from the very first they ever heard about it and never stopped opposing it. They opposed the use of American pilots. They opposed the use of American bases. It was really State that convinced the President to cut down the airstrikes. That was Mr. [Dean] Rusk, the Secretary of State. So the Department of State crippled and destroyed this operation. That is my considered judgement that I thought at the time and for years after, and they were never blamed for anything."

Hayden, Sterling (1916–1986)

Nicknamed "the most beautiful man in the movies" and "the beautiful blond Viking god," Sterling Hayden is best known as one of Hollywood's all-time leading tough-guy actors. He was also a real-life "tough guy" with the OFFICE OF STRATEGIC SERVICES (OSS), the World War II precursor to the CIA.

Hayden was born Sterling Relyea Walter to George Walter and Frances Simonson on March 26, 1916, in Montclair, New Jersey. His father died when he was nine years old, and he received his surname from his stepfather, James Hayden. As a boy, Hayden was known as an ultra-extrovert who thrived on adventure. When he was 16 years old, the lure of the sea compelled him to drop out of school. By the time he was 20, he was first mate on the schooner *Yankee*. But he soon grew restless and decided to try his hand at acting. He went to New York, took a screen test, and in 1940 signed a contract with Paramount Pictures. But by 1941, the escalating war in Europe was tempting Hayden to make yet another career move, this time as a British army commando. Unfortunately, he broke his ankle during parachute training in Scotland and was medically discharged.

Hayden returned to the United States seeking a Navy lieutenant's commission and an assignment to a patrol torpedo (PT) boat squadron. But he had only a 10th-grade education, and his request was denied. He was, however, offered an ensign's commission. Instead, he enlisted in the Marine Corps as a private. In 1942, Hayden attended boot camp at Parris Island, South Carolina. There he was known as "Recruit John Hamilton" (he had legally changed his name to avoid any celebrity status). After boot camp, Hayden was shipped to Officer Candidate School (OCS) at Quantico, Virginia. At OCS, he was one of three men selected from a class of nearly 300 for the OSS.

The OSS was only two years old in 1943. But its growing reputation as a clandestine force of educated, physically fit young men seeking high adventure was a tremendous lure for thrill seekers like Hayden. Hayden also knew the OSS's director, WILLIAM J. "WILD BILL" DONOVAN. While sailing in the 1930s, he had collected information for Donovan.

Hayden's first OSS posting was to Cairo, Egypt. There, he was tasked with both gathering intelligence and reviewing reports from operatives in the region. He then traveled to the Balkans, where Marshal Josip Broz Tito gave him command of some 400 Yugoslav partisans.

Eventually, Hayden's sailing experience and Marine training led to an assignment with the OSS Maritime Unit in Monopoli, Italy. There he was placed in command of a small flotilla of schooners, ketches, and brigs that ran supplies through the German blockade in the Adriatic Sea to Yugoslavia.

In November 1944 Hayden briefly returned to the United States, where he met with a number of Washington chiefs, including President Franklin Roosevelt. In early 1945, he returned to Europe as an OSS officer attached to the U.S. First Army. When the war ended, Hayden, now a captain, was awarded a Silver Star, a Yugoslav decoration, and an honorable discharge.

Hayden's friendship with the Yugoslav partisans led him to consider briefly joining the Communist Party—a relationship that he would later confess apologetically to the House Un-American Activities Committee (a now-defunct congressional committee established to investigate disloyalty and potentially subversive organizations).

Hayden returned to Hollywood after the war and played a number of lead and character roles. His postwar films were: *Manhandled* (1949), *The Asphalt Jungle*

(1950), *The Star* (1952), *Flat Top* (1952), *So Big* (1953), *Prince Valiant* (1954), *Johnny Guitar* (1954), *Battle Taxi* (1955), *The Last Command* (1955), *The Killing* (1956), *The Iron Sheriff* (1957), *Zero Hour* (1957), *Dr. Strangelove* (1964), *Hard Contract* (1969), *Loving* (1970), *The Godfather* (1972, playing the memorable role of a corrupt police chief who is shot to death by Al Pacino in a restaurant), *The Long Goodbye* (1973), *1900* (1977), *King of the Gypsies* (1978), *9 to 5* (1980), and *Venom* (1982). In 1966 Hayden wrote an autobiography, entitled *Wanderer*.

Hayden died in Sausalito, California, on May 23, 1986. He was 70.

heavy mob

"Heavy mob" is an unofficial CIA term for CIA officers who because of their imposing size and muscularity are often tasked with duties wherein physical strength might be needed. An example of a heavy-mob responsibility would be escorting a DEFECTOR through a train station or an airport terminal where operatives from his or her own country's intelligence services might interfere. Heavy-mob officers also serve as bodyguards for the DIRECTOR OF CENTRAL INTELLIGENCE (DCI) and other high-ranking CIA officers.

The FEDERAL BUREAU OF INVESTIGATION (FBI) has a similar group of agents, whom the bureau refers to as the "heavy squad."

Helms, Richard McGarrah (1913–2002)

A recipient of the National Security Medal and one of the CIA's most devoted DIRECTORS OF CENTRAL INTELLIGENCE (DCI), Richard McGarrah Helms was one of the original "cold warriors" and the first CIA career officer to head the Agency.

Born May 30, 1913, to Herman H. Helms and Marion McGarrah in an upper-class neighborhood in St. David's, Pennsylvania, young Helms attended prep schools in Germany and Switzerland, becoming fluent in both German and French. In 1935, he graduated from Williams College in Williamstown, Massachusetts, and became a correspondent for United Press International (UPI) in Berlin. At UPI, he covered the 1936 Olympic games, and later managed to land a lengthy interview with Adolf Hitler. Two years later, he returned to the United States and became an advertising manager for the *Indianapolis Times*. He was there when the Japanese attacked Pearl Harbor on December 7, 1941.

In 1942, Helms joined the U.S. Navy and served in a fund-raising capacity for the Navy Relief Society in New York. Not long after, he attended a two-month officers'-training course at Harvard University. He was subsequently awarded a lieutenant's commission and assigned to anti-submarine operations in the Navy's Eastern Sea Frontier command.

Helms's previous experience in Germany led him in August 1943 to transfer to the OFFICE OF STRATEGIC SERVICES (OSS), the World War II precursor of the CIA. Following training, he went to work for another future DCI, ALLEN WELSH DULLES, in the OSS's Secret Intelligence branch. For the remainder of the war, he ran espionage operations against the Nazis from posts in Great Britain, France, Luxembourg, as well as Washington, D.C. Germany surrendered in the spring of 1945.

When President Harry Truman disbanded the OSS in October 1946, the Office's operational arm was redesignated the STRATEGIC SERVICES UNIT (SSU) and moved to the War Department. OSS research and analysis units were brought under an INTERIM RESEARCH AND INTELLIGENCE SERVICE and transferred to the STATE DEPARTMENT. Helms remained with the SSU and became CHIEF OF STATION (COS) in Berlin. When the SSU was rolled into the new CENTRAL INTELLIGENCE GROUP (CIG), Helms's Secret Intelligence branch was renamed the OFFICE OF SPECIAL OPERATIONS (OSO). Helms himself was dis-

charged from the Navy at the rank of lieutenant commander, becoming a civilian employee with CIG. He continued with the organization when it was reestablished as the CIA in 1947.

In the early days of the COLD WAR, Helms was directly involved in West German espionage operations, particularly those involving the intricate spy network created by REINHARD GEHLEN, a former Nazi intelligence officer who was destined to become the head of West Germany's Foreign Intelligence Service.

In 1951, Helms returned to Washington and assumed the post of deputy assistant director for operations and began succeeding one superior after another. First, he succeeded LYMAN KIRKPATRICK as the assistant director for operations in July 1952. Kirkpatrick was forced to leave office after being stricken with polio. During that same period, the OSO merged with the OFFICE OF POLICY COORDINATION to form the new DIRECTORATE OF PLANS (OPERATIONS). At Plans, Helms became second in command to both FRANK GARDINER WISNER, the first DEPUTY DIRECTOR of plans (DDP), and later RICHARD MERVIN BISSELL, JR., the DDP who in February 1962 was forced to resign from the CIA after the ill-fated invasion of Cuba at

Richard Helms meeting with President Lyndon B. Johnson   (NATIONAL ARCHIVES)

the BAY OF PIGS in 1961. Helms then became DDP, and served in this capacity for the next four years.

In 1965, DCI JOHN A. MCCONE purportedly recommended that Helms be appointed his successor. President Lyndon Johnson instead chose Vice Admiral WILLIAM F. RABORN, JR., to be the next DCI, with Helms as deputy DCI. Raborn, however, stepped down after only a few months in office, and, on June 30, 1966, Helms became CIA director.

Helms's tenure was not an easy one. He had replaced Raborn because Johnson had lost confidence in the admiral. For the next seven years, Helms presided over an agency that was losing face in the public eye. It was during the height of the Vietnam War. Revelations were beginning to emerge in the American press that suggested that the CIA had been involved in a number of illegal and/or immoral activities at home and abroad. Making matters worse, in 1972, the public learned that the Agency may have had a hand, either directly or indirectly, in the burglary of the Democratic National Headquarters at the Watergate Hotel.

It was also during this time that Helms initiated covert OPERATIONS IN CHILE in an attempt to overthrow the regime of Socialist president Salvador Allende Gossens (Allende would be killed and his government ousted seven months after Helms stepped down as DCI). "We're not in the Boy Scouts," Helms was fond of saying. "If we'd wanted to be in the Boy Scouts, we'd have joined the Boy Scouts."

Helms loved the CIA, and he did everything he could to protect the Agency. When President Richard Nixon attempted to divert the FBI's investigation of the WATERGATE SCANDAL away from the White House by deepening the CIA's implication in the matter, Helms resisted. This action was viewed as disloyalty by the president. On February 2, 1973, Nixon relieved Helms as DCI, replacing him with JAMES R. SCHLESINGER.

Helms then accepted a position as ambassador to Iran, a post he would hold until 1976. But during routine confirmation hearings before the Senate Foreign Relations Committee, he swore under oath that the CIA had not been involved in a plot to overthrow Chilean president Allende. It was a lie that would come back to haunt him. He was found guilty of perjury, and, on November 4, 1977, he was given a two-year suspended sentence and fined $2,000. Presiding Judge Barrington D. Parker concluded by leveling harsh words at Helms. "You [Helms] stand before this court in disgrace and shame," he said.

Many CIA insiders viewed Helms's conviction and subsequent punishment as unjust. After all, they believed, it was sheer loyalty to the Agency that compelled him to commit perjury. Helms himself remained unrepentant. "I found myself in a position of conflict," he said. "I had sworn my oath to protect certain secrets. I didn't want to

lie. I didn't want to mislead the Senate. I was simply trying to find my way through a very difficult situation in which I found myself."

In October 1983, President Ronald Reagan attempted to polish Helms tarnished reputation by awarding him the National Security Medal. His other awards included the Career Service Award by the National Civil Service League and the Distinguished Intelligence Medal.

In retirement, Helms worked both as president of the Safeer Company, a publishing house, and as a private consultant.

Helms died on October 22, 2002, at age 89.

Hersh story, the

Seymour Hersh was the investigative reporter for the *New York Times* who broke the story on illegal CIA operations against the antiwar movement during the administration of Richard Nixon.

On December 18, 1974, the day after COUNTERINTELLIGENCE chief JAMES JESUS ANGLETON was relieved of his duties by DIRECTOR OF CENTRAL INTELLIGENCE (DCI) WILLIAM EGAN COLBY, Hersh informed the latter of his intention to write what he believed was the "biggest story" of his career. Colby would later recall that his telephone conversation with Hersh had the effect of "ruining not only the Christmas season for me, but nearly all of the next year as well." In a meeting two days later, Hersh told Colby that he had uncovered information about numerous illegal operations conducted by the CIA against dissidents opposed to America's involvement in Vietnam.

On December 22, the lead story in the *Times* was a piece by Hersh that began, "The Central Intelligence Agency, directly violating its charter, conducted a massive illegal domestic intelligence operation during the Nixon administration against the anti-war movement and other dissident groups in the United States, according to well-placed Government sources."

Hersh's exposé created a public outcry against what was perceived as an unrestrained CIA. As a result, three investigative groups—the presidentially appointed ROCKEFELLER COMMISSION and the congressionally appointed CHURCH and PIKE COMMITTEES—would be formed over the next several months. These groups would ultimately uncover Agency misdeeds including ASSASSINATION PLOTS against foreign leaders, foreign coups d'état, unauthorized spying on American citizens, and a lack of governmental oversight.

Hillenkoetter, Rear Admiral Roscoe Henry (1897–1982)

Rear Admiral Roscoe Henry Hillenkoetter was the first "official" director of the post–World War II Central

Intelligence Agency (not counting the OFFICE OF STRATE-GIC SERVICES director WILLIAM J. "WILD BILL" DONOVAN, who is unofficially considered to have been the first DIRECTOR OF CENTRAL INTELLIGENCE). Hillenkoetter, known in some circles as "the amiable Dutchman," had a stellar wartime Navy career. But his tenure as director was considered to be less than effective.

Hillenkoetter was born in St. Louis, Missouri, on May 8, 1897. He graduated from the U.S. Naval Academy at Annapolis in 1919. Following his commissioning, he held a variety of shore and sea-duty posts, including a teaching assignment at Annapolis and service aboard a submarine.

In 1933, Hillenkoetter was assigned to the Office of NAVAL INTELLIGENCE (ONI). That assignment led him to a posting to the U.S. embassy in Paris, where he served as an assistant naval attaché.

Much of Hillenkoetter's service throughout the 1930s was spent as a diplomatic courier and naval observer. He was able to travel widely and witness firsthand the war-conducive conditions developing across Europe. He also spent time aboard the battleship USS *Maryland*. During the Spanish Civil War, he served in Paris, Madrid, and Lisbon. In 1940, he moved up to become naval attaché in Paris.

When France fell to the Germans in June, Hillenkoetter recorded and reported on the events. He then moved with the Free French government to Vichy in unoccupied France, where for over a year he worked with the French resistance forces. He also traveled across the Mediterranean, observing and reporting on German operations in North Africa.

In November 1941, Hillenkoetter returned to sea duty as executive officer of the battleship USS *West Virginia*. When the Japanese attacked Pearl Harbor on December 7, the ship took several bomb and torpedo hits and sank. Hillenkoetter was slightly wounded.

In September 1942, Hillenkoetter was made officer in charge (OIC) of intelligence under the Pacific theater commander, Admiral Chester W. Nimitz. Hillenkoetter held this post until March 1943. He then briefly commanded the destroyer tender USS *Dixie*. In 1944, he was assigned to the Bureau of Naval Personnel.

Following the Japanese surrender in 1945, Hillenkoetter took command of the battleship USS *Missouri* for a Mediterranean cruise. In 1946, he returned to his prewar post in Paris. On November 29, 1946, he was promoted to the rank of rear admiral.

On May 1, President Harry Truman appointed Hillenkoetter to the post of DIRECTOR OF CENTRAL INTELLIGENCE (DCI), succeeding Air Force GENERAL HOYT SANFORD VANDENBERG. Hillenkoetter maintained something of a low profile while his predecessor continued a previously initiated campaign for a permanent "central intelligence agency."

The NATIONAL SECURITY ACT, which reorganized America's defenses and established a permanent CENTRAL INTELLIGENCE AGENCY under a new NATIONAL SECURITY COUNCIL (NSC), was passed on September 18, 1947. As the CIA's first "official" DCI, Hillenkoetter was regarded as a likeable boss and an efficient overseer of records but only a marginally effective intelligence director. He presided over a fledgling CIA in an unsure world; unfortunately for the admiral, the Agency failed to provide Washington policy makers with enough solid intelligence to prepare them for the strategic events that were taking place around the world.

When the North Koreans attacked the South in June 1950, Truman's administration was, in effect, "blindsided." Hillenkoetter's career with the Agency was over; he remained DCI only until October 7, 1950. "Admiral Hillenkoetter was an experienced officer who inspired a great deal of loyalty who worked for him and he was a man of considerable intelligence and perception," said J. Kenneth McDonald, former chief historian of the CIA, during a 1994 lecture before the Center for the Study of Intelligence. "But if you compare and contrast him with his predecessor [General Vandenberg] and his successor [GENERAL WALTER BEDELL SMITH], you can begin to see why Hillenkoetter was an unsuccessful director of Central Intelligence."

McDonald argues that Hillenkoetter did not have the enormous reputation that Vandenberg and Smith had. Additionally, Hillenkoetter lacked the "instinct and experience" for "bureaucratic infighting" so common among the Washington power brokers. "He [Hillenkoetter] had no real taste for the kind of cut and thrust that's necessary in Washington," said McDonald.

Following his term as DCI, Hillenkoetter returned to naval service, commanding the Pacific Fleet's Cruiser Division One from October 1950 until August 1951. He was promoted to vice admiral on April 9, 1956, and made inspector general of the Navy in August. He retired from the Navy on May 1, 1957. Following his retirement, Hillenkoetter held several senior executive positions in the private sector.

Hillenkoetter died on June 18, 1982, six weeks shy of his 85th birthday.

Homeland Security, Department of (DHS)

The Department of Homeland Security (DHS) is a cabinet-level agency that was created in the wake of the SEPTEMBER 2001 TERRORIST ATTACKS ON THE UNITED STATES.

Initially established as the Office of Homeland Security by President George W. Bush in October 2001, the DHS became a congressionally mandated department in November 2002 with the passage of the HOMELAND SECURITY ACT. The DHS absorbed 22 federal agencies—or subdepartments thereof—including the U.S. Coast Guard, the Secret

Service, and the Border Patrol. As such, the act became the most sweeping reorganization of the federal government since the passage of the NATIONAL SECURITY ACT OF 1947.

The DHS is primarily responsible for implementing and overseeing a unified federal plan to combat domestic terrorism. The DHS is not an official member of the U.S. INTELLIGENCE COMMUNITY (IC) nor does it oversee any of the IC's member agencies. However, the department is responsible for coordinating and analyzing intelligence and other information from the IC as that intelligence and information relate to homeland defense. The DHS also identifies and assesses existing and future threats to the homeland, maps those threats against current vulnerabilities, issues warnings, and takes preventive and protective actions to defend the North American continent. A key partner with the DHS's intelligence and threat analysis branch is the FBI's Office of Intelligence. Subtasks of the DHS include the coordination of any number of antiterror activities conducted by federal, state, and local law enforcement agencies.

The DHS is headed by a director for Homeland Security, a post which is sometimes referred to in intelligence circles as a domestic version of the NATIONAL SECURITY ADVISOR. The DHS is a primary consumer of FINISHED INTELLIGENCE produced by the CIA.

Homeland Security Act

The Homeland Security Act is the law that reorganized the homeland defense structure of the United States and created the DEPARTMENT OF HOMELAND DEFENSE (DHS), one of the primary consumers of FINISHED INTELLIGENCE produced by the CIA.

The act, approved by Congress in November 2002, is considered the most sweeping reorganization of the federal government since the passage of the NATIONAL SECURITY ACT OF 1947.

honey trap

A honey trap is an often-used espionage technique wherein a person is deliberately targeted for sexual entrapment. If the targeted individual takes the bait and enters into a compromising situation, he or she can be blackmailed by the intelligence team that set the trap. In some cases, an agent posing as a prostitute or interested party can gather additional information before the target is aware of having been honey-trapped. Honey traps are also known as "honey pots."

Hoover, John Edgar (J.) (1895–1972)

No other law enforcement or intelligence chief in the history of the United States has had more influence on a single government agency than the late John "J." Edgar

Hoover, the famous—sometimes infamous—director of the FEDERAL BUREAU OF INVESTIGATION (FBI). No single federal agency felt its very existence challenged by Hoover more than did the CIA. For nearly a half-century Hoover directed the FBI, developing it into the monolithic national police and internal counterintelligence force that exists today. But despite his stellar career, his personal life was the subject of much scrutiny. His detractors accused him of everything from racial and religious intolerance to homosexuality, but his efficiency made it impossible for any American president to fire him—a fact exemplified in a comment made by President Lyndon Johnson to the president-elect Richard Nixon in late 1968. "Dick, you will come to depend on Edgar," Johnson said. "He is a pillar of strength in a city of weak men."

For most of his life, Hoover battled anarchists, gangsters, Nazis, and communists. He also waged a silent war against his two greatest competitors, the OFFICE OF STRATEGIC SERVICES (OSS) and the OSS's descendant organization, the CIA.

Born in Washington, D.C., on January 1, 1895, to Dickerson Naylor Hoover, an official with the U.S. Coast and Geodetic Survey, and Annie Scheitlin, a staunch though principled disciplinarian, young Hoover would have been a perfect psychiatric case study. He worshiped his mother, was emotionally estranged from his chronically depressed father, and was something of an outcast in school. He had no girlfriends. He was a poor athlete. But he did excel in academics; he was a sharp-witted debater; he joined a military drill team; and he ultimately became valedictorian of his class.

After graduation, Hoover worked his way through George Washington University (GWU) by taking a job as a clerk and messenger boy at the Library of Congress. In 1916, he earned an LL.B., and in 1917 an LL.M. While at GWU, Hoover became a member of the Kappa Alpha fraternity, then likened to a college auxiliary of the Ku Klux Klan. His mother was named KA's honorary "housemother," and Hoover remained active in the order all his life. A number of his colleagues at the FBI were also KAs.

Upon graduation from GWU, Hoover skirted the draft and joined the U.S. Department of Justice. There, he quickly developed a reputation as a dapper go-getter with an acute attention for detail.

In 1919, Hoover was appointed special assistant to the U.S. attorney general and placed at the head of the newly established General Intelligence Division (GID). With World War I over, the focus shifted from foreign threats to home-grown radical political groups, individuals suspected of subversive activities, and organized crime. The GID was established to gather intelligence on all of these.

In 1924, Hoover was named director of the Justice Department's Bureau of Investigation (BI). Only 29 years old, he began in his new position an almost feverish quest to transform the bureau from an obscure agency into a nationally respected federal police force. Despite his autocratic style, he was granted virtual carte blanche to create a centrally managed fingerprint database, an investigations laboratory, and a federal police academy. In the late 1920s and 1930s his reputation began to soar as he waged an unofficial war against organized crime and his officers arrested a number of high-profile mobsters and bootleggers.

A congressional mandate in 1934 renamed the Bureau of Investigation the "Federal Bureau of Investigation." The new name implied independent-agency status, although the FBI remained a quasi branch of the Justice Department.

In 1939, President Franklin Roosevelt expanded Hoover's responsibilities by directing the FBI to investigate espionage, sabotage, and subversion on all fronts; all domestic intelligence gleaned by the various military agencies was to be turned over to the FBI. Hoover took that directive as a passkey to expansion of his investigations and counterintelligence efforts. The FBI began investigating anyone it chose, from the obscure to the influential.

In 1940, Hoover began working closely with SIR WILLIAM STEPHENSON, the Canadian-born head of the Anglo-American intelligence effort in New York (Stephenson is often referred to by his wartime code name, INTREPID). Hoover, however, didn't completely trust Stephenson. At one point, Hoover reportedly alleged to Roosevelt that the Canadian operative was directing a British hit squad that was assassinating Nazi collaborators on U.S. soil. But there was no hard evidence, and the complaint was dismissed by the president.

The British in turn criticized Hoover's "heavy-handed" police tactics, which, they argued, clashed with pure espionage operations. Non-FBI American intelligence officers like WILLIAM J. "WILD BILL, DONOVAN, head of the OSS, tended to agree. Hoover, they felt, was more interested in crushing spy rings, making arrests, and garnering headlines than he was in letting a spy game run its course and lead to bigger fish. Hoover, however, was one of the first intelligence chiefs to suspect Britain's infamous CAMBRIDGE SPIES of treason.

Throughout World War II, Hoover fought hard for control of all American intelligence activities. He won in the struggle against Donovan's OSS for jurisdiction over Latin America. But he lost in his bid for control of all postwar global intelligence operations, retaining only the FBI's domestic counterintelligence responsibilities (all foreign intelligence operations would eventually fall under the CIA). When the war ended, Hoover's focus turned to ridding the North American continent of all vestiges of communism; the FBI kept files on anyone he deemed suspect.

Hoover adamantly opposed the creation of the CIA in 1947; he once even directed his men not to communicate or associate in any manner with Agency officers. When the CIA began assuming control of all espionage activities in Latin America, Hoover ordered his men to destroy their files rather than turn them over to the Agency. It was a "scorched earth" policy, according to E. HOWARD HUNT, who, as the CIA's CHIEF OF STATION (COS) in Mexico City, had to sift through such remains. Hoover considered the CIA to be his primary rival, often referring to the Agency as PH.D. INTELLIGENCE—a derogatory term he coined in reference to the number of Ivy League graduates serving in the CIA.

In the early 1950s, Hoover ruled the bureau with an iron fist, distrusting even his own agents who had dissimilar political or social ideologies. But his power was on the wane. In 1956, the FBI director initiated COINTELPRO, a Bureau's "COUNTERINTELLIGENCE" program directed at everyone from black militants and civil rights activists to antiwar protestors and white supremacists. Hoover's COINTELPRO agents engaged in a myriad of suboperations ranging from illegal wiretapping to leaking rumors to the press about personal lives, to secretly writing and mailing letters harassing and blackmailing anyone deemed by Hoover to be "un-American."

One of the primary targets of COINTELPRO was civil rights leader Martin Luther King, Jr., a man Hoover detested. In November 1964, in an attempt to force King to commit suicide, the FBI secretly taped one of his extramarital rendezvous and mailed the tape with a anonymously written letter to King's Atlanta office. A portion of the letter reads: "King, there is only one thing left for you to do. You know what it is. You have just 34 days in which to do it (This exact number has been selected for a specific reason). It has a definite practical significance. You are done. There is but one way out for you. You better take it before your filthy, abnormal fraudulent self is bared to the nation." King rejected the blackmail attempt. In March 1971, COINTELPRO was exposed and consequently abandoned. Hoover retired that same year.

On May 2, 1972, Hoover died at home of undiagnosed heart disease. He was 77.

Hoover Commissions

The Hoover Commissions, two independent, executive-level review boards chaired by former U.S. president Herbert Hoover, directly impacted American intelligence agencies, including the CIA.

FIRST HOOVER COMMISSION

The first Hoover Commission was a 12-person panel that conducted a comprehensive review of the federal bureaucracy, including American intelligence agencies. At the heart of the commission's work was the EBERSTADT STUDY, conducted by the commission's Eberstadt Committee. That report, presented to Congress in January 1949, concluded that the CIA was the "logical arbiter" of differences of opinion regarding intelligence matters between each of the American armed forces and the U.S. DEPARTMENT OF STATE. According to the report, the "National Security Organization, established by the NATIONAL SECURITY ACT OF 1947," was "soundly constructed, but not yet working well."

The report cited fundamental shortcomings in the national intelligence effort and the newly established CIA. Among them was an "adversarial relationship and lack of coordination" between the CIA, the U.S. State Department, and the armed forces. The report suggested that such a relationship resulted in an unnecessary duplication of effort and intelligence estimates that "have often been subjective and biased."

Much of the blame was heaped on the State Department and the military for failing to consult and acquaint the CIA with pertinent information. The report recommended "that positive efforts be made to foster relations of mutual confidence between the CIA and the several departments and agencies that it serves."

The establishment within the CIA of a top-echelon evaluation board composed of "competent and experienced personnel who would have no administrative responsibilities and whose duties would be confined solely to intelligence evaluation" was recommended, as was a civilian DIRECTOR OF CENTRAL INTELLIGENCE with a long term in office. The report also stressed that the CIA "must be the central organization of the national intelligence system."

Regarding special operations, the report suggested that all covert operations be integrated into one CIA office, overseen by the NATIONAL SECURITY COUNCIL (NSC). Additionally, during time of war, clandestine operations should be the direct responsibility of the JOINT CHIEFS OF STAFF (JCS). CIA budget, organizational, and strategic intelligence collection matters were also addressed in the report.

Briefly considered and rejected by the committee was the idea of placing the COUNTERINTELLIGENCE responsibilities of the FEDERAL BUREAU OF INVESTIGATION (FBI) under CIA control.

SECOND HOOVER COMMISSION

The second Hoover Commission was an executive panel that in 1954 created the CLARK Committee (officially the Task Force on Intelligence Activities) under the chairmanship of U.S. Army general Mark W. Clark. The com-

mittee itself was established for the purposes of evaluating the organization and administration of the CIA and its related agencies; it issued classified and unclassified reports of its findings.

In 1955, the classified report was completed and forwarded directly to President Dwight Eisenhower. The unclassified version was sent to Congress.

The unclassified report was a 76-page document that briefly described the evolution of and coordination between the existing American intelligence agencies. In describing the relationship between those agencies, the report initiated the official use of the term "U.S. INTELLIGENCE COMMUNITY."

The report also contained a number of recommendations, beginning with the CIA's internal organization. It recommended that the DIRECTOR OF CENTRAL INTELLIGENCE (DCI) focus his attention on issues of intelligence facing all members of the intelligence community. Executive and congressional oversight of intelligence activities was also recommended, as was a systematic five-year reevaluation of all personnel within the intelligence community. The committee, additionally, recommended that the Agency replace the U.S. STATE DEPARTMENT in the acquisition of foreign publications and the collection of scientific intelligence. It also recommended that a NATIONAL INTELLIGENCE SURVEY be published (the survey was the forerunner publication to the CIA's current WORLD FACTBOOK ON INTELLIGENCE).

A portion of the report reads, "The National Intelligence Survey is an invaluable publication which provides the essential elements of basic intelligence on all areas of the world. There will always be a continuing requirement for keeping the Survey up-to-date."

Additional recommendations included the need to build a new CIA complex, improve foreign-language training, and raise the salary of the DCI.

House Permanent Select Committee on Intelligence (HPSCI)

The House Permanent Select Committee on Intelligence (HPSCI) is one of two congressional bodies tasked with overseeing, and sometimes investigating, the actions of the U.S. INTELLIGENCE COMMUNITY. Established on July 14, 1977, the HPSCI was created as a result of the congressional hearings held in the mid-1970s that investigated alleged misdeeds on the part of the CIA and the FEDERAL BUREAU OF INVESTIGATION (FBI).

The HPSCI's Senate counterpart is the SENATE SELECT COMMITTEE ON INTELLIGENCE (SSCI).

See also CHURCH COMMITTEE; PIKE COMMITTEE; ROCKEFELLER COMMISSION.

Houston, Lawrence Reid (1913–1995)

Lawrence Reid Houston is best known as the principal draftsman of the NATIONAL SECURITY ACT OF 1947, which created the CIA.

In 1935, Houston graduated from Harvard University. He earned an LL.B. from Virginia Law in 1939. In 1944, Houston joined the OFFICE OF STRATEGIC SERVICES (OSS), the wartime precursor organization to the CIA. He served in its Secret Intelligence Branch in the Middle East.

When the OSS was disbanded after the war, Houston served as general counsel in the CENTRAL INTELLIGENCE GROUP (CIG)—the short-lived interim intelligence organization between the OSS and the creation of the modern CIA. It was with the CIG in 1946 that Houston's most important work was done. That year, Houston and his staff drafted the legislation that became known as the National Security Act of 1947. On September 18, the act passed. It reorganized America's defense and established a CENTRAL INTELLIGENCE AGENCY (CIA) under a new NATIONAL SECURITY COUNCIL (NSC).

Houston continued with the CIA as its first general counsel, and he remained in that capacity until his retirement in 1973. As such, he was a key adviser to nine DIRECTORS OF CENTRAL INTELLIGENCE. He is the recipient of the Intelligence Medal of Merit, the Distinguished Intelligence Medal, and the Civil Service League Award.

Howard, Edward Lee (1951–)

Edward Lee Howard (aka "Robert") was the first CIA officer to betray the West and then successfully escape to Moscow.

Born in Albuquerque, New Mexico, on October 27, 1951, to Kenneth Howard, a career Air Force sergeant, and Mary Jaramillo, a Hispanic-American, young Howard never established any real roots. As a boy he lived in a half-dozen states and three countries. By the time he was 11 years old, he spoke fluent German. In 1972, he earned a bachelor's degree with honors in international business and economics at the University of Texas. He then joined the Peace Corps, for which he worked for several years in South America. In 1974, Howard returned to the United States, working first as a Peace Corps recruiter in Dallas, Texas. Then he enrolled in the American University in Washington, D.C., where he earned an MBA in 1976. That same year, he married Mary Cedarleaf, a fellow Peace Corps volunteer, and joined the Agency for International Development (AID). Howard viewed AID as a stepping-stone to a career in foreign service. In 1979, he left AID and worked briefly in the private sector.

In 1981, Howard joined the CIA and—despite an admission that he had previously used illegal drugs—was trained for special duty with the Agency's Soviet/East European Division. Following training, he was briefed on espionage operations in Moscow, including the names and profiles of Moscow-area agents working for the Agency.

Just before being posted to the Soviet capital, Agency officials discovered that Howard had a drinking problem. He was ordered to take a polygraph test. He failed the polygraph test, which indicated that he also may have been involved in petty theft, and in June 1983 was forced to resign from the CIA.

Howard became embittered. He returned to New Mexico and took a job as an economic analyst with the New Mexico State Hospital. There he was arrested and convicted on a minor firearms charge. Paroled, Howard and his wife began making trips to Europe. There he contacted and met with Soviet agents, divulging whatever knowledge he had about his aborted Moscow assignment. The information he disclosed to the Soviets included the names of Russian agents working in Moscow for the United States. For several months Howard sold secrets to the Soviets, who paid him hundreds of thousands of dollars in cash.

On August 1, 1985, a senior KGB official, Vitaly Sergeyevich Yurchenko, defected to the West. Yurchenko revealed that Howard was one of two former CIA employees who sold secrets to the KGB (RONALD W. PELTON was DOUBLE AGENT number two). According to Yurchenko, an agent, code-named "Robert," had met with Soviet officials in Austria in the fall of 1984; Robert had disclosed Western secrets and had consequently been paid large sums. Yurchenko claimed he did not know Robert personally, but he did know that the agent had been trained for a CIA assignment in Moscow but been suddenly removed before being posted.

Yurchenko's information coincided with recent Agency setbacks in Moscow. The Moscow CHIEF OF STATION (COS) had been reporting that many of the CIA's operations were being mysteriously "blown." In one incident, a CIA officer working under diplomatic cover had been suddenly deported from the Soviet Union for espionage. Weeks later, one of the officer's assets had been arrested and executed for treason. A number of other assets, their covers blown, had been rounded up by the KGB.

The CIA had long known that Howard was a security risk. But it wasn't until Yurchenko's revelation that Agency officials notified the FEDERAL BUREAU OF INVESTIGATION (FBI). On August 7, 1985, the CIA contacted the FBI and informed them that "Robert" was in fact Howard. The bureau immediately launched an investigation into Howard's misdeeds and began round-the-clock surveillance of his home and office in Albuquerque.

Nonetheless, Howard, who was trained in surveillance operations as well as escape-and-evasion tactics, managed to elude the FBI and flee the country on September 21, 1985.

Howard was able to make his escape by slipping past an inexperienced FBI agent. With his wife driving a getaway car, Howard deployed a JIB (a makeshift man-sized dummy) to represent his figure and then leaped from the passenger side into a grove of trees.

On August 7, 1986, exactly one year to the day after the FBI was notified of Howard's treachery, the Soviet news agency TASS announced that Howard had been granted political asylum in the Soviet Union.

HT-LINGUAL

HT-LINGUAL was the code name given to the CIA's domestic MAIL-INTERCEPT project that existed from 1952 to 1973.

See also FLAPS AND SEALS.

Hughes-Ryan Amendment

The Hughes Ryan Amendment was the first congressional response to the disclosure of CIA support to noncommunist forces in Angola and the revelation of the CIA's FAMILY JEWELS—an intra-Agency compilation of some 300 possible CIA transgressions including domestic spying, MIND-CONTROL DRUG TESTING, MAIL INTERCEPTION, and foreign ASSASSINATION PLOTS. Though short-lived, the amendment ultimately became the launching pad for substantive congressional oversight of federal intelligence activities. Enacted in December 1974, the Hughes-Ryan Amendment revised the Foreign Assistance Act of 1961 (the Foreign Assistance Act of 1961, signed by President John Kennedy, provided for assistance to less-developed foreign countries).

The amendment restricted CIA covert actions abroad and prohibited the use of appropriated funds for such activities unless and until the president determined that such activities were important to national security. Additionally, the president—through the DIRECTOR OF CENTRAL INTELLIGENCE (DCI)—was to make his knowledge of such activities available to the appropriate congressional committees (initially six committees, then eight), which at that time included the armed services committees, foreign relations committees, and appropriations committees in each house of Congress. Routine intelligence-gathering operations were excepted.

The amendment gave teeth to a Congress that had previously been left out of the intelligence loop. But CIA officials were unnerved. "That [the amendment] effectively kills covert action," said DCI RICHARD MCGARRAH HELMS. "One cannot simply assume that literally scores of Congressmen and Senators and their staffs are all going to keep the secrets." In 1975, Congress in fact terminated funding for a covert program—the secret military support of the UNITA (União Nacional Para a Independência Total de Angola) faction in Angola's civil war.

Five years and several congressional hearings later, the Hughes Ryan Amendment began to lose some of its steam. First, the passing of the INTELLIGENCE OVERSIGHT ACT OF 1980 reduced its committee-notification requirements to two congressional committees instead of eight. Two years later, the INTELLIGENCE IDENTITIES PROTECTION ACT OF 1982 was passed, making it a crime to reveal the identity of intelligence operatives. Finally, the CIA INFORMATION ACT OF 1984 was passed. This act exempted certain Agency operational files from being disclosed under the FREEDOM OF INFORMATION ACT.

The Senate sponsor of the Hughes-Ryan Amendment was Senator Harold Hughes (D-Iowa), best known as a key figure in the establishment of the National Institute on Alcohol Abuse and Alcoholism. The House of Representatives sponsor of the bill was Congressman Leo J. Ryan (D-California), later best known as the congressman who was assassinated in Guyana in the infamous Jonestown mass suicide of 1978.

HUMINT (human intelligence)

A CIA acronym for human intelligence or human-source intelligence, HUMINT is simply intelligence collected by officers, agents, or informers.

In the wake of the SEPTEMBER 2001 TERRORIST ATTACKS ON THE UNITED STATES, the American public leveled blame on the CIA and other members of the U.S. INTELLIGENCE COMMUNITY for what was perceived to be a lack of HUMINT that might have prevented the attacks.

See also ALL-SOURCE INTELLIGENCE; INTELLIGENCE CYCLE; INTELLIGENCE DISCIPLINES, FIVE PRIMARY.

Hunt, Everette Howard (1918–)

Best known for his involvement in the infamous burglary of the WATERGATE complex in 1972, Everette Howard Hunt (aka Eduardo Hamilton, Robert Dietrich, John Baxter, Gordon Davis, and David St. John) was one of the CIA's most colorful DIRTY TRICKS experts.

Born on October 9, 1918, to Everette Howard Hunt, Sr., and Ethel Jean Totterdale, the junior Hunt was raised in the Lake Erie shoreline town of Hamburg, New York. In 1940, he graduated from Brown University and joined the U.S. Naval Reserve.

In 1941, Hunt saw service aboard an American destroyer, but the following year he was medically discharged after a shipboard injury rendered him unable to

Everette Howard Hunt   (NATIONAL ARCHIVES)

perform his duties. He then worked as a screenwriter/editor for a series of World War II documentary films produced from 1942 to 1943. In 1943, he was a war correspondent for *Life* magazine.

That same year, Hunt joined the OFFICE OF STRATEGIC SERVICES (OSS), the wartime precursor organization to the CIA. Thus began a storied espionage career. When the OSS was disbanded by President Harry Truman in October 1945, Hunt went to Mexico to write. He opted out of any posting to the CENTRAL INTELLIGENCE GROUP (CIG), which was established three months later. But by 1949 he had become frustrated with what he perceived to be the West's failure to respond effectively to Soviet aggression and expansion. He then joined the CIA, serving in the Agency's covert-action arm, the OFFICE OF POLICY COORDINATION (OPC).

From 1950 to 1952, Hunt served as OPC's CHIEF OF STATION (COS) in Mexico City. When OPC merged with the OFFICE OF SPECIAL OPERATIONS in August, Hunt became deputy COS.

In 1953, Hunt was reassigned as a Washington, D.C.–based COUNTERINTELLIGENCE officer in the Agency's Southeast Europe Division. His primary responsibility was that of "looking for turncoats" who might betray the CIA's operations in ALBANIA. But when

the CIA received authorization to begin operations against Guatemala in 1954, Hunt was transferred to the Western Hemisphere Division. There he was responsible for planning the political/propaganda particulars for the COUP D'ÉTAT IN GUATEMALA. He completed his duties before the operation was launched and was transferred to the Agency's North Asia Command in Tokyo, Japan, where he was made chief of covert operations.

In 1956, Hunt returned to Latin America, becoming COS in Montevideo, Uruguay. In March 1960 he was named chief political action officer for the project to overthrow FIDEL CASTRO in Cuba. But he was ultimately reassigned for refusing to obey orders. His next assignment was to the DOMESTIC OPERATIONS DIVISION.

In 1964, Hunt offered to spy on Republican senator Barry Goldwater, who was campaigning for president against the Democratic incumbent, Lyndon Johnson. Hunt believed that if he were to obtain copies of Goldwater's speeches before they were delivered, he could keep Johnson in the White House, and, therefore gain influence with the president for the CIA. Hunt's offer was a harbinger of things to come.

In 1970, Hunt retired from the CIA and for a brief period found employment with Robert R. Mullen & Company, a Washington, D.C.–based public relations firm with close ties to the Agency. Not long after, he became an unofficial member of the Nixon White House staff. Initially, he was hired as a freelance propaganda consultant. In this role, he was tasked with researching the Kennedy administration's expansion of American involvement in the Vietnam War. This led to work with the White House Special Investigative Unit. The unit, known as the "PLUMBERS," was organized to find and fix "secret information leaks" originating from the highest levels of government.

In 1971, DANIEL ELLSBERG, the government-commissioned defense ANALYST who leaked the *PENTAGON PAPERS* to the press, was becoming a major thorn in the side of President Richard Nixon. Publicly stating that he was willing to risk a prison sentence to end the war, Ellsberg had presented to the *New York Times* and other newspapers a 47-volume top-secret history of the Vietnam War that he had participated in researching and writing for U.S. defense secretary Robert McNamara. Several indictments were leveled against Ellsberg, including converting government property to personal use (via a copy machine), possessing government documents, conspiracy, theft, and espionage.

The Nixon administration wanted him badly, and it pulled all the stops. In September, the White House directed Hunt to burglarize the offices of Dr. Lewis J. Fielding, Ellsberg's psychoanalyst, in an attempt to uncover personal information that might prove damaging to Ellsberg's reputation. The CIA purportedly supplied Hunt with a wig, a camera, a speech-altering device, and false identification papers for the operation.

But Hunt's infamy stems from his involvement in the Watergate scandal. In 1972, Hunt organized the break-in of the Democratic National Headquarters in the Watergate building, a complex of shops, offices, and condominiums near the White House. He was implicated in the affair when his phone number was found in an address book belonging to one of the burglars.

Hunt was indicted and eventually pled guilty to charges of wiretapping, burglary, and conspiracy. He served 33 months in prison and was released in 1977.

In 1981, Hunt filed and won $650,000 in a libel suit against the Liberty Lobby, a right-wing political action group. The award was for an article that appeared in *The Spotlight*, the Liberty Lobby's newspaper, which suggested that Hunt had been involved in the assassination of President John Kennedy. A second trial in 1985 overturned the original ruling when the article's best-selling author, Mark Lane successfully defended its publication.

Hunt has written under at least four pseudonyms, including Robert Dietrich, John Baxter, Gordon Davis, and David St. John. Many of his books are spy novels featuring a fictitious CIA officer, "Peter Ward."

Hunt currently resides in Florida.

Huston plan

The Huston Plan was a Nixon White House proposal for increasing domestic intelligence gathering by members of the U.S. intelligence community, particularly the FEDERAL BUREAU OF INVESTIGATION (FBI) and the CIA. In a sense, it was the result of President Richard Nixon's desire to create a "super-secret" presidential intelligence agency.

Named for White House attorney Tom Huston, who drafted and presented the proposal in 1969, the Huston plan consisted of a number of covert-action possibilities that Nixon briefly considered employing. They included a resumption of covert MAIL INTERCEPTIONS, increased electronic surveillance (wiretapping), break-ins, and an increase in the number of college-campus informants.

On June 23, 1970, Nixon approved the Huston plan. However, when FBI director J. EDGAR HOOVER and Attorney General John Mitchell objected to the plan, Nixon had second thoughts. He rescinded his approval within days.

I

illegal

An "illegal" is a CIA officer who is operating in a hostile country without the protection of diplomatic immunity. In most cases, an illegal has little or no contact with his or her embassy. Instead, the activities of the illegal are controlled directly from Agency headquarters. An illegal is sometimes referred to as an OUTSIDE MAN.

See also LEGAL.

IMINT (imagery intelligence and geospatial information)

Formerly known as PHOTINT (for PHOTOGRAPHIC INTELLIGENCE), the CIA acronym IMINT represents imagery intelligence and geospatial information.

See also ALL-SOURCE INTELLIGENCE; INTELLIGENCE CYCLE; INTELLIGENCE DISCIPLINES, FIVE PRIMARY.

Indonesia, operations in

In the late 1950s, CIA covert-operations expert FRANK GARDINER WISNER argued that it was "time we held Sukarno's feet to the fire." Wisner was referring to Indonesia's president Sukarno, an Asian leader whose anti-Western sentiment and growing sympathy toward world communism was considered a threat by many within the U.S. intelligence community.

The Agency began by conducting a number of propaganda operations against the Sukarno regime. In the best known of those operations, a pornographic film was produced that featured someone resembling Sukarno. The film and a number of still photographs were distributed throughout Indonesia. But the apparent uninterest among the Indonesian population, as well as Sukarno's willingness to increase Communist Party representation within his government, led the CIA to adopt a more substantial covert-action approach. In 1958, the CIA sponsored an ill-fated rebellion within the officer corps of the Indonesian army in an attempt to overthrow Sukarno.

Though it had no human source (HUMINT) assets in the region, the CIA provided assistance to the rebelling officers in the form of infantry weapons, paramilitary advisers, and B-26 bombers flown by pilots of the CIVIL AIR TRANSPORT (CAT), one of the CIA's better-known proprietary airlines.

The Indonesian operations took on another dimension when on May 18, CAT pilot ALLEN LAWRENCE POPE was shot down by Indonesian troops and captured. Pope had been flying a bombing mission against Sukarno's forces and had accidentally attacked a church during services, killing most of the congregation. Following a brief trial, Pope was sentenced to death. The U.S. government successfully appealed for his release, and he returned to the United States in July 1962.

infiltration

Infiltration is a term used to describe the surreptitious insertion of operatives into the field (as opposed to EXFIL-TRATION, the extraction of operatives).

Inman, Bobby Ray (1931–   )

NAVAL INTELLIGENCE chief, director of the NATIONAL SECURITY AGENCY (NSA), and DEPUTY DIRECTOR OF CEN-TRAL INTELLIGENCE (DDCI), Admiral Bobby Ray Inman was President Bill Clinton's first choice to succeed Les Aspin as secretary of defense. Media scrutiny forced Inman to withdrew his name from consideration.

Inman was born in Rhonesboro, Texas, to Herman H. and Mertie Hinson on April 4, 1931. In 1950, Inman earned a bachelor's degree from the University of Texas. Two years later, he was commissioned an ensign in the U.S. Navy.

As a naval officer, he held a variety of staff posts. One of his early assignments was that of assistant naval attaché in Stockholm, Sweden, from 1965 to 1967. He then attended the National War College. Following grad-uation in 1972, he became executive assistant and senior aide to the vice chief of naval operations, from 1972 to 1973. He then was named assistant chief of staff for intel-ligence on the staff of the commander in chief of the U.S. Pacific Fleet, serving in that capacity until 1974. He served as director of the Naval Intelligence Command in Washington from 1974 to 1976.

Inman's career then began to take a focused path into the highest levels of the U.S. intelligence community. From 1976 to 1977, he served as vice director of the DEFENSE INTELLIGENCE AGENCY (DIA). He then trans-ferred to the National Security Agency, where he served as director until 1981.

On February 12, 1981, Inman was appointed to the post of DDCI by President Ronald Reagan. Inman served in that capacity until June 10, 1982.

In 1983, Inman left the Navy for the private sector. He became chairman of the board, president, and chief exec-utive officer (CEO) of the Austin, Texas–based Microelec-tronics and Computer Technologies Corporation. In 1986, he was named board chairman and CEO of West-mark Systems, also of Austin. In 1990, he became a lec-turer and private investor.

A 1984 article in *Omni* magazine stated, "Because he is unusually quick witted, rapier tongued, and in the spy business, people have always suspected Inman of being something more than he appeared." But two of the big three weekly newsmagazines offered glowing accolades.

Newsweek magazine referred to Inman as "a superstar in the intelligence community." *U.S. News & World Report* would later proclaim him "the former whiz kid of U.S. intelligence."

In 1994, Inman was picked by Clinton to succeed Les Aspin as secretary of defense. However, charges by mem-bers of the media that Inman was "manipulative and deceptive," a "tax cheat," and a "failure as a business executive" forced him to withdraw from consideration. Inman referred to the attacks as "media McCarthyism." The statement he made at the time led many to question his stability, but a background check by the FEDERAL BUREAU OF INVESTIGATION (FBI) proved him to be "clean as a whistle." Inman returned to the private sector.

His decorations include the Defense Distinguished Service Medal, the Navy Distinguished Service Medal, the Legion of Merit, the Defense Superior Service Medal, the Meritorious Service Medal, the National Security Medal, and the Joint Services Commendation Medal.

inside man

In CIA parlance, an "inside man" is a CASE OFFICER who works in an American embassy. Unlike an OUTSIDE MAN, who operates on foreign soil as a private citizen with no overt connection to the American government, an inside man has what is considered a charmed situation. They operate with U.S. STATE DEPARTMENT cover, thus allowing them ease of movement, and in some cases diplomatic immunity. An inside man is sometimes referred to as a "LEGAL."

Intelligence Community, U.S.

The U.S. Intelligence Community is a network of execu-tive-branch agencies and organizations that conduct oper-ations that contribute to the total American national intelligence effort. The DIRECTOR OF CENTRAL INTELLI-GENCE (DCI), the director of the CIA, also coordinates the community, of which the CIA is but one component.

The U.S. Intelligence Community, as defined by the fiscal year 1996 Intelligence Authorization Act, comprises the CIA, the CENTRAL IMAGERY OFFICE (Department of Defense), the FEDERAL BUREAU OF INVESTIGATION (FBI), the NATIONAL SECURITY AGENCY (NSA), the NATIONAL RECONNAISSANCE OFFICE (NRO), the NATIONAL IMAGERY AND MAPPING AGENCY (NIMA), the OFFICE OF INTELLI-GENCE SUPPORT (Department of the Treasury), the DEPARTMENT OF ENERGY (DOE), the BUREAU OF INTEL-LIGENCE AND RESEARCH (Department of State), the DRUG ENFORCEMENT ADMINISTRATION (DEA), the DEFENSE INTELLIGENCE AGENCY (DIA), ARMY INTELLI-GENCE (Department of the Army), NAVAL INTELLIGENCE (Department of the Navy), MARINE CORPS INTELLIGENCE

(Department of the Navy), and AIR FORCE INTELLIGENCE (Department of the Air Force). Members of the Intelligence Community advise the DCI through their respective directors and through representatives who sit on committees that deal with intelligence matters of common concern. Chief among these groups are the NATIONAL FOREIGN INTELLIGENCE BOARD and the Intelligence Community Executive Committee. The DCI chairs both.

In November 2001, the Intelligence Community was faced with a major restructuring—the SCOWCROFT PROPOSAL, a comprehensive recommendation to bring three major defense intelligence agencies under the direct control of the DCI. The proposal, based on the findings of a panel headed by retired lieutenant general Brent Scowcroft (the chairman of the PRESIDENT'S FOREIGN INTELLIGENCE ADVISORY BOARD and a former national security advisor), suggests that the NRO, NSA, and NIMA be transferred to the CIA. If the proposal is accepted, it will constitute one of the largest overhauls of the Intelligence Community.

See also INTELLIGENCE COORDINATION ACT OF 1996.

intelligence cycle

The intelligence cycle is the series of steps by which raw information is converted into FINISHED INTELLIGENCE and made available to policy makers and other intelligence consumers for use in decision making.

There are five steps in the cycle:

1. Planning and direction. This step comprises the determination of intelligence requirements, preparation of a plan for collection, issuance of orders and requests to information-collection agencies, and continuous checks on the productivity of collection agencies. The step is also considered to be "the beginning and the end of the cycle." It is the beginning because it involves drawing up specific collection requirements; it is the end because finished intelligence, which supports policy decisions, generates new requirements.

2. Collection. This step entails the acquisition of information and the provision of this information to processing or production elements. Information is collected from numerous OPEN SOURCEs of intelligence (or OSINT), including newspapers, magazines, books, the Internet, and foreign television and radio broadcasts. Information is also collected from the various traditional intelligence disciplines, such as HUMINT (human intelligence), COMINT (communications intelligence), IMINT (imagery intelligence, formerly PHOTINT for photographic intelligence), ELINT (electronic intelligence), MASINT (measurement and signature intelligence), TELINT (telemetry intelligence), RADINT (intelligence gathered from radars), SIGINT (signals intelligence), and TECHINT (technical intelligence).

3. Processing. In this step collected information is converted through decryption, translation, and data reduction into a form suitable to the production of intelligence.

4. ALL-SOURCE analysis and production. In this step information is converted into finished intelligence through the integration, analysis, evaluation, and interpretation of all-source data and the preparation of intelligence products in support of known or anticipated consumer requirements.

5. Dissemination. In the final step in the cycle, finished intelligence is conveyed to consumers in a suitable form. Each day, finished intelligence is hand-delivered to the president and his key national security advisers. Certain policy makers also receive finished intelligence. They may make on the basis of the information decisions that lead to the need for more information. Thus the intelligence cycle continues.

The North Atlantic Treaty Organization (NATO) also maintains an intelligence cycle. Though encompassing only four steps, the NATO intelligence cycle differs very little from that of the CIA and the U.S. INTELLIGENCE COMMUNITY. The four steps in the NATO intelligence cycle are direction, collection, processing, and dissemination.

Intelligence, Directorate of

See DIRECTORATES, CIA.

intelligence disciplines, five primary

According to the U.S. DEPARTMENT OF DEFENSE (DoD), the five primary intelligence disciplines are HUMINT (human intelligence), IMINT (imagery intelligence), MASINT (measurement and signature intelligence), SIGINT (signals intelligence), and OSINT (open-source intelligence).

See also ALL-SOURCE INTELLIGENCE; INTELLIGENCE CYCLE.

intelligence estimates

Intelligence estimates are CIA-issued reports (based on FINISHED INTELLIGENCE) delivered to intelligence consumers. At the national level, intelligence estimates are called NATIONAL INTELLIGENCE ESTIMATES (NIEs) and SPECIAL NATIONAL INTELLIGENCE ESTIMATES (SNIEs).

Intelligence Identities Protection Act of 1982

The Intelligence Identities Protection Act of 1982 imposes criminal penalties on persons found guilty of revealing the names of covert intelligence operatives.

Signed into law by President Ronald Reagan on June 23, 1982, the act was a direct result of the assassination of CIA officer RICHARD WELCH. In December 1975, Welch, the CIA's Athens CHIEF OF STATION, was gunned down on his doorstep after his name, title, and home address were published in an issue of *Counterspy* magazine. His death—and the revelation that former Agency operative PHILIP BURNETT FRANKLIN AGEE may have released the information to the magazine—prompted Congress to pass the bill.

During the signing ceremony, Reagan read the following comments: "Today I speak again of those heros, the men and women who are locked in a dangerous, sometimes deadly conflict with the forces of totalitarianism, the men and women whose best accomplishments, whose greatest deeds can never be known to their countrymen, but only to a few of their superiors and ultimately only to history. These men and women, these heroes of a grim twilight struggle are those of you who serve here in the CENTRAL INTELLIGENCE AGENCY.

"Whether you work in Langley or a faraway nation, whether your tasks are in operations or analysis sections, it is upon your intellect and integrity, your wit and intuition that the fate of freedom rests for millions of your countrymen and for many millions more all around the globe. You are the trip-wire across which the forces of repression and tyranny must stumble in their quest for global domination. You, the men and women of the CIA, are the eyes and ears of the free world.

"Like those who are part of any silent service, your sacrifices are sometimes unappreciated; your work is sometimes misunderstood. Because you're professionals, you understand and accept this. But because you're human and because you deal daily in the dangers that confront this nation, you must sometimes question whether some of your countrymen appreciate the value of your accomplishments, the sacrifices you make, the dangers you confront, the importance of the warnings that you issue."

intelligence information report (IIR)

An intelligence information report, or IIR, is a raw report that conveys the views of a source (usually HUMINT, or human-source intelligence). It is not yet FINISHED INTELLIGENCE; it must be evaluated by ANALYSTs for its veracity.

Intelligence Organization Act of 1992

The Intelligence Organization Act of 1992 is widely regarding as one of the most far-reaching intelligence bills passed since the NATIONAL SECURITY ACT OF 1947.

The five most important elements of the act include:

- Recognition of the DIRECTOR OF CENTRAL INTELLIGENCE (DCI) as the statutory adviser of the NATIONAL SECURITY COUNCIL (NSC).
- Establishment of the NATIONAL INTELLIGENCE COUNCIL (NIC) as the highest authority for developing and publishing intelligence analysis.
- Assignment to the DCI of the responsibility of establishing priorities for U.S. government intelligence gathering and for coordination of all HUMINT collection.
- Grant to the DCI of authority to approve the budgets of the various intelligence agencies.
- Definition of the composition of the U.S. INTELLIGENCE COMMUNITY.

Intelligence Oversight Act of 1980

The Intelligence Oversight Act of 1980 revised the HUGHES-RYAN AMENDMENT to require notice of covert actions only to the two intelligence committees—the SENATE SELECT COMMITTEE ON INTELLIGENCE (SSCI) and the HOUSE PERMANENT SELECT COMMITTEE ON INTELLIGENCE (HPSCI)—as opposed to the previously required eight congressional committees.

The Intelligence Oversight Act of 1980 also required the heads of intelligence agencies to keep the two oversight committees "fully and currently informed" of their activities, including "any significant anticipated intelligence activity."

interception

Interception is the term used by CIA employees to describe the act of disrupting, stopping, or cutting off from the intended destination either a messenger or a message. For instance, if a clandestine operative were to meet and apprehend a secret-message-carrying COURIER traveling to a specific destination, that courier would be said to have been "intercepted." In the same manner, an electronically forwarded message picked up by communications officers before it has been received (or as it is received) by its intended recipient is considered to be an intercepted message.

Interim Research and Intelligence Service

The Interim Research and Intelligence Service was an entity of the U.S. DEPARTMENT OF STATE created to coordinate and oversee the research and analysis functions of the OFFICE OF STRATEGIC SERVICES (OSS), the World War II precursor to the CIA, when the OSS was disbanded in October 1945. In January 1946, the Interim Research and Intelligence Service was placed under the newly created CENTRAL INTELLIGENCE GROUP (CIG), the direct predecessor organization to the CIA. The Interim Research and Intelligence Service is the predecessor entity of the Agency's DIRECTORATE OF SCIENCE AND TECHNOLOGY.

interrogation

Interrogation is the term used by CIA employees to describe the act of extracting secret information from a captive. The methods used to interrogate may range from coercion to persuasion to deception.

Intrepid

Intrepid was the code name given to Canadian-born spymaster WILLIAM STEPHENSON by British prime minister Winston Churchill during the early days of World War II.

Stephenson, who directed British intelligence operations in the Western Hemisphere during the war, is credited with coordinating the exchange of intelligence between Great Britain and the United States. Intrepid's influence also helped shape American intelligence and special operations capabilities, particularly his work with the OFFICE OF STRATEGIC SERVICES (OSS), the wartime predecessor organization to the CIA.

Iran, coup d'état in

In 1953, the CIA launched an operation in Iran that overthrew the de facto regime of Dr. Mohammad Mossadegh and restored the shah of Iran, Mohammad Reza Pahlavi, to his throne.

The operation, code-named AJAX, was initiated after the shah, a pro-Western leader, was forced out of office in 1951 by the supporters of Mossadegh, a procommunist hard-liner who—as the shah's prime minister—had ordered the nationalization of all foreign oil companies, including the huge British-owned ANGLO-IRANIAN OIL COMPANY (AIOC) on May 2.

Mossadegh contended that the AIOC was bleeding Iran dry of its oil. The British were incensed. The AIOC was a lucrative business venture, and, as the company was responsible for fueling the warships of the Royal Navy, it was of great strategic importance.

Mossadegh, a nervous man prone to fits of crying, had the backing of the Majlis (Iran's parliament), the Tudeh (Iran's communist party), and the poor. The shah, the last ruler in the Pahlavi dynasty, had the backing of Iranian

business leaders and the growing Iranian middle class. But Mossadegh's increasing power base had forced Pahlavi into a self-imposed seclusion in his Tehran palace.

Pahlavi was still the shah, but in title only. He wanted assistance from the British and the Americans. But he did not completely trust the latter. After all, *Time* magazine had named Mossadegh "Man of the Year" in 1952.

The initial planning for AJAX was begun in 1952 by MI6, Great Britain's Secret Intelligence Service, when it was realized that the shah's power was being seriously eroded by Mossadegh. However, the United States, in the lame-duck administration of President Harry Truman, was hesitant to get in involved, though Truman did agree to a naval blockade of Iran. The White House feared that the Americans and the British would be labeled aggressors by the United Nations if they involved themselves in Iran's internal affairs.

On June 27 of the previous year, Truman had issued a NATIONAL SECURITY COUNCIL (NSC) directive recognizing "the rights of sovereign states to control their natural resources and the importance we attach to international contractual relationships." Meanwhile, Mossadegh threatened to dissolve Iran's National Assembly, thus eliminating free elections. He ordered a referendum in which voters casting ballots in favor of dissolving the National Assembly would vote in one booth, while those opposed would vote in another. The voting booths were watched by Mossadegh's supporters. Under those circumstances, it was not surprising to anyone when Mossadegh carried the day with 99 percent of the vote. Mossadegh then opened trade negotiations with Moscow.

When President Dwight Eisenhower moved into the White House in January 1953, U.S.-Iran policy made a 180-degree turn. Eisenhower, fearing that Moscow was either gaining an unwavering ally or a puppet, decided it was time to act. Authorizing a plan that had been previously approved by the U.S. STATE DEPARTMENT, the president gave the CIA the green light on Operation AJAX.

In late July 1953, KERMIT "KIM" ROOSEVELT, President Theodore Roosevelt's grandson and the CIA's chief of the Plans (Operations) DIRECTORATE's Near East and Africa Division, met with the shah and assured him that if he were to attempt to dismiss Mossadegh, he would have the backing of both Eisenhower and British prime minister Winston Churchill. The fearful shah wanted no part of it. Nevertheless, Roosevelt began preparations for a coup d'état with a group of four other Agency operatives, known as the "COWBOYS," in the basement of a SAFE HOUSE in Tehran. The officers hired street thugs and a number of circus performers, including a group of heavily muscled acrobats known as the Zur Khaneh (House of Strength) Giants, paying them cash from a million-dollar Agency expense account, to assist the coup by inciting a mass uprising.

The next step was to convince the shah that AJAX was doable. That task was assigned to U.S. Army colonel H. Norman Schwarzkopf, a former New Jersey police officer and father of the now-famous Persian Gulf War general. Schwarzkopf had trained Iran's secret SAVAK police force and had once commanded the shah's Imperial Iranian Gendarmerie, instilling in his men an unwavering pride of service and a hatred for all things communist. It was a factor that would ultimately ensure the coup's success.

Schwarzkopf met with the shah and proposed that he replace Mossadegh with General Fazollah Zahedi by official decree. Schwarzkopf reminded the shah of the support of the Americans and the British. But it was not enough.

Tudeh officials, learning of the meeting, accused the shah in newspaper articles of conspiring with "brainless agents of international reaction." Mossadegh threatened a second referendum, this time to arrest and depose the shah.

Fearing for his life, the shah fled Tehran for his summer palace on the Caspian Sea. There, after a third attempt to convince him, the shah agreed and signed the decrees. On August 14, 1953, the decrees were delivered to Mossadegh. Characteristically, the prime minister arrested the "messenger," Colonel Nematollah Nassiry, and threw him in jail.

The following morning, Mossadegh began radio broadcasts denouncing the shah, accusing him of initiating a foreign-sponsored coup. Meanwhile, hidden in Roosevelt's safe house, General Zahedi began issuing his own radio statements, denouncing Mossadegh and declaring himself the rightful prime minister. Mossadegh's soldiers began searching for Zahedi. Panicked, the shah fled to Baghdad with his queen, one aide, and no luggage. From there he flew to Rome, where he met with DIRECTOR OF CENTRAL INTELLIGENCE (DCI) ALLEN WELSH DULLES. In Tehran, pro-Mossadegh factions led by the Tudeh Party took to the streets en masse. For two days they looted, destroyed statues, and shouted "Death to Americans" and "Down with the shah."

Secretary of State John Foster Dulles then ordered Loy Henderson, the ambassador to Iran, to assist Roosevelt. It was a decisive move. On August 18, Henderson demanded an immediate audience with Mossadegh. Mossadegh agreed, and at his meeting with Henderson began castigating the U.S. government, specifically the CIA, for "persuading" the shah to sign the decrees. Henderson turned the tables. He demanded that all riotous behavior cease or he would order Americans out of Iran. Mossadegh, fearing a public-relations catastrophe, conceded.

In a move that proved fatal to the Iranian communists, Mossadegh ordered the police to quell the rioting and clear the streets. The police, who had been trained by Schwarzkopf, unleashed their pent-up anger toward the communists and attacked the rioters with tear gas, clubs, and rifle butts.

On August 19, Roosevelt's own demonstrators began parading down the city's streets. Led by some 200 biceps-flexing, handspringing Zur Khaneh acrobats, the demonstrators marched toward Mossadegh's house shouting "Long live the shah." Agents passed out money, pictures of the shah, and small paper Iranian flags to spectators along the way, and soon the ranks of the demonstrators swelled. At least two pro-Mossadegh newspaper offices were sacked and burned, radio stations were seized, and isolated clashes took place between pro-shah and pro-Mossadegh forces. By the end of the day, at least 300 people had been killed. Zahedi was driven in a tank from his home to the studios of Tehran Radio, where he broadcast the coup's success to the nation. Mossadegh, clad only in his pajamas and a coat, jumped over his garden wall and tried to flee the city. He was later arrested.

The shah learned of the news while lunching at Rome's Excelsior Hotel. He reportedly said to his wife, "I always knew the people loved me."

Roosevelt was an instant hero. Eisenhower ordered him to Washington for a personal debriefing. The shah at a private dinner presented Roosevelt with a gold cigarette case and made a toast: "I owe my throne to God, my people, my army, and you." Churchill, who invited Roosevelt to his London bedside, where he was recovering

After being forced to flee to Rome, Mohammad Reza Shah Pahlavi, shah of Iran, authorized a new government for his country (HULTON ARCHIVE)

from a stroke, exclaimed, "Young man, if I had been but a few years younger, I would have loved nothing better than to have served under your command in this great venture."

Despite the fact that the CIA had no more than a handful of operatives in Iran, the operation went off without a hitch. Twenty-five years later, on February 14, 1979, the shah was again forced to flee Iran, when power was seized by an Islamic clergyman, the Ayatollah Ruhollah Moussavi Khomeini. The exiled shah died in Cairo, Egypt, on July 27, 1980.

Iran-contra, CIA involvement in

The 1985–87 Iran-contra scandal was the worst blemish on the Soviet-toppling administration of President Ronald Reagan. It was also a setback for the CIA, which at that time was attempting to regroup itself after the public and congressional scrutiny of the mid-1970s. Seeds for the scandal were sown in the early 1980s, when members of the pro-Iranian terrorist group Hezbollah (Arabic for "Party of God") began jailing and torturing American citizens snatched from the streets of Beirut, Lebanon.

One of the most notorious "snatchings" was that of WILLIAM BUCKLEY (not to be mistaken for famed author WILLIAM F. BUCKLEY, JR., a onetime CIA officer), the CIA's CHIEF OF STATION in Beirut. On March 16, 1984, Buckley was captured by terrorists with links to the Iranian regime of the Ayatollah Ruhollah Moussavi Khomeini. The terrorists who snatched Buckley were a group of Shiite Moslems calling themselves Islamic Jihad (Islamic Holy War, or Islamic Holy Struggle).

Convinced that Iran exercised control over the group that held Buckley, the CIA and the White House took seriously contacts by intermediaries who claimed to represent the Iranian authorities. The intermediaries presented a plan wherein Buckley and other American hostages might be released in return for the sale of weapons and weapons-related materials to Iran. The initial approach was allegedly made by the Israeli government, which was working through Israeli and Iranian weapons dealers. (During the Iran-Iraq War, the Israelis reportedly established a secret relationship with Iran, believing that a victorious Iraq would be a more dangerous enemy. The weapons dealers believed they could free Buckley, but in fact the station chief had already been tortured to death. In the meantime, other Americans were being picked up and detained at undisclosed locations.

Believing a deal could be cut for the release of Buckley and other hostages, the Reagan administration devised a covert plan wherein arms would be secretly sold to Iran in exchange for hostages; proceeds from those sales would be illegally funneled to American-supported contra rebels who were attempting to overthrow the Sandanista regime in Nicaragua. At that time, Iran was running des-

perately short of military hardware in its war with Iraq. It had the money to purchase weapons, but the U.S. Congress had banned the sale of American weaponry to countries, like Iran, that sponsored terrorism. Nonetheless, Reagan was allegedly advised that a deal could be made, and authorization was soon granted at a level never fully disclosed. In August 1985, the first consignment of arms to Iran was shipped via middlemen, and some hostages were soon released.

The deal violated the American policy of refusing to negotiate with terrorists. It also violated legislation that forbade government agencies, including the CIA and the DEPARTMENT OF DEFENSE, from providing military aid to the contra rebels. The White House initially skirted the law by going through the NATIONAL SECURITY COUNCIL (NSC), which was not covered by the policies or legislation in question. The NSC was tasked with overseeing the contra-funding operation. The NSC did so, under the leadership of Robert McFarlane and Admiral John Poindexter, raising private and foreign money, in addition to the Iranian weapons-sale proceeds, for the rebels. The operation was directed by Marine Corps Lieutenant Colonel Oliver North, an NSC staff officer. Despite the American trade and arms embargo, McFarlane and North also became involved in the plan to ship weapons to Iran.

In late 1986 the deal was made public in the Lebanese press, and the Reagan administration was forced to disclose the operations. Poindexter resigned. North was fired. Congressional investigative committees were established, and Lawrence E. Walsh was named as special prosecutor in the investigation.

It was alleged that Reagan, Vice President GEORGE HERBERT WALKER BUSH, a former DIRECTOR OF CENTRAL INTELLIGENCE (DCI), and DCI WILLIAM J. CASEY were directly involved in either the affair or its coverup. But the extent of that involvement was never made clear.

Several criminal convictions resulted from Iran-contra, including those of McFarlane, North, Poindexter, former secretary of defense Caspar Weinberger, and a number of U.S. STATE DEPARTMENT and CIA officials. Most of these men were pardoned. Casey died in May 1987.

See also HASENFUS, EUGENE.

Iron Curtain

The Iron Curtain was a figurative wall constructed that separated East from West during the cold war. For most of the CIA's history, the Agency operated behind the Iron Curtain, and many CIA operatives there were apprehended and imprisoned or executed.

The term was coined in March 1946 by British prime minister Winston Churchill. In a speech to Westminster College in Fulton, Missouri, Churchill asserted that a dangerous communist line had been drawn across the middle of Europe. In the prime minister's words, "From Stettin in the Baltic to Trieste in the Adriatic, an iron curtain has descended across the [European] Continent." Churchill's statements were considered provocative by the Soviets, and many historians have since argued that his speech officially launched the COLD WAR.

isolation

Isolation is a term often used to describe the CIA's top-secret "boot camp" for fledgling spies at CAMP PEARY, Virginia. The training center is also known to Agency insiders as THE FARM or Camp Swampy.

See also CAREER TRAINEES.

Italian operations

In its first-ever series of covert operations, the CIA orchestrated a clandestine political campaign project aimed at defeating the Communist Party candidates in the Italian national elections of 1948. The operation was successful and kept the incumbent Christian Democrats in power.

In the years immediately following World War II, the Communist Party began to gain strength in much of Eastern and Central Europe. Much of this strength was concentrated in Italy, where the largest Communist Party outside the Soviet Union (approximately 2 million members) existed.

In the elections scheduled for the spring of 1948, the Partito Communista Italiano, or PCI (Italian Communist Party) opposed the incumbent Democrazia Cristiana, or DC (Christian Democrat) Party. This concerned U.S. president Harry Truman, who turned to his foreign-policy experts for assistance.

In December 1947, the NATIONAL SECURITY COUNCIL (NSC) authorized a series of "psychological warfare" operations as a means of influencing the outcome of the elections. Initially the operations were to be directed by the U.S. DEPARTMENT OF STATE, but fears of a possible foreign-policy embarrassment led to the operations' being reassigned to the CIA.

At that time, the director of the CIA's OFFICE OF SPECIAL OPERATIONS (OSO) was JAMES JESUS ANGLETON, the Agency's future controversial COUNTERINTELLIGENCE guru. As director of the OSO, Angleton was in charge of covert operations. For the Italian problem he created the SPECIAL PROCEDURES GROUP (SPG), the Agency's first covert-action arm. The SPG launched a staggeringly expensive propaganda war against the PCI. All manner of DISINFORMATION—in the form of leaflets, posters, form-letter mailings, and propagandistic newspaper stories and radio broadcasts—was disseminated throughout the Italian Peninsula. Additionally, some $75 million was fun-

neled—by recruited agents carrying bags of money—into the coffers of the anticommunist politicians. Most of the money went was received by the DC.

As a result, on April 18, 1948, the communists lost the election, and the CIA saw the successful conclusion of its first covert operation. This served to embolden the leadership of the Agency, which would turn to covert action several times during the 1950s and 1960s.

IVY BELLS, Operation

An offshoot of the CIA's PROJECT JENNIFER, IVY BELLS was the code name for a joint NATIONAL SECURITY AGENCY–U.S. Navy operation, overseen by the CIA, wherein Soviet dispatches were intercepted from a Soviet communications cable on the bottom of the Sea of Okhotsk. Initiated in the late 1970s during the tenure of DIRECTOR OF CENTRAL INTELLIGENCE (DCI) ADMIRAL STANSFIELD TURNER, IVY BELLS was an ambitious and highly successful intelligence-gathering project. It was betrayed to the Soviets by an NSA employee in 1981.

On the Okhotsk seafloor, between the Soviet navy's base at Petropavlovsk and its Pacific Fleet headquarters at Vladivostok, specially equipped U.S. Navy submarines installed and maintained large eavesdropping devices, or listening "pods," over a vital Soviet communications line for a period of nearly two years. The pods, designed to tap electronically into the cable without actually connecting to it, were able to intercept communications traffic between key Soviet naval and military units and Moscow. The pods were fashioned to break free of the line and remain on the bottom of the sea, undamaged and undetected if the Soviets ever raised the cable for maintenance purposes. Each pod was a 20-foot-long cylindrical apparatus. It was watertight and able to withstand the tremendous pressure of the ocean at great depths. Inside the pod were tapes that could record information for up to six weeks at a stretch. In order to retrieve the recordings (which was done twice each year), Navy divers using mini-subs and robots had to locate the pod and switch tapes; the old ones were returned to an American submarine.

The missions were dangerous by anyone's standards. In order to reach the Sea of Okhotsk, the submarines had to ease through narrow, shallow channels that snaked through the Soviet-controlled Kuril Islands. If the Americans were discovered, the channels could easily be blocked, rendering escape impossible. Additionally, the divers tasked with retrieving and replacing the tapes had to brave great depths and dangerously cold temperatures. But to the U.S. INTELLIGENCE COMMUNITY, the rewards were worth the risk. Once retrieved, the tapes were delivered to the NSA, where they were decoded and analyzed. By the time the tapes reached Washington, the information was, of course, no longer "real time." Still, vital information was gleaned from the recordings about Soviet ballistic missile tests, naval maneuvers, and other military exercises near the Kamchatka Peninsula.

In 1981, the NSA and the CIA realized that the operation had been compromised when American satellites photographed a small flotilla of Soviet warships at the exact position of the pod's connection to the cable. For four years, the CIA was mystified as to how the IVY BELLS operation could have been compromised. But in 1985, the Agency discovered that the project had been betrayed to the Soviets by RONALD W. PELTON, a bottom-tier staffer at the NSA who had begun selling secrets to the Soviets to avoid bankruptcy. Pelton had resigned from the NSA in 1980.

A few years later, Vitaly Sergeyevich Yurchenko, a former KGB security officer at the Soviet embassy in Washington, defected to the United States and began to provide information to the CIA. Yurchenko's information uncovered the treasonous activities of former CIA officer EDWARD LEE HOWARD. He also disclosed the activities of a "walk-in" from the NSA who had telephoned the Soviet embassy and said, "I have some information to discuss with you, and to give to you." Yurchenko referred to the walk-in as "Mister Long."

The CIA passed the information to the FEDERAL BUREAU OF INVESTIGATION (FBI). The latter researched its archived recordings of wire-tapped calls made to the Soviet embassy and found the tape. The recording was then played to a handful of NSA employees, who recognized Pelton's voice. A voice analysis later confirmed it.

On November 25, 1985, the FBI arrested Pelton in Annapolis, Maryland, where he was working as a sailboat salesman. DCI WILLIAM JOSEPH CASEY wanted Pelton tried without revealing any of the particulars surrounding the IVY BELLS project. Casey believed, despite the fact that Pelton had sold secrets to the USSR, the Soviets could have "missed something" that might be brought to light in a trial. Keeping the lid on what was revealed was crucial.

On June 5, 1986, Pelton was found guilty on two counts of espionage, one count of conspiracy, and one count of disclosing classified communications intelligence. He was subsequently sentenced to three consecutive life terms plus 10 years.

One of the discovered IVY BELLS pods was placed on public display in Moscow.

J

Jackson, Charles Douglas (1902–1964)

Charles Douglas Jackson was president of a CIA FRONT organization known as the Free Europe Committee that managed the Agency's two largest proprietary radio broadcast entities, RADIO FREE EUROPE (RFE) and RADIO LIBERTY (RL).

Jackson was born in New York City on March 16, 1902, to Carl David Jackson, a marble importer, and Eda F. Strauss. Like most of his life, Jackson's beginnings were unusual. He was initially schooled in Switzerland, but his family returned to the United States, where he attended the Hill School in Pottstown, Pennsylvania. As a young man, he attended Princeton University in New Jersey, where he majored in French and literature, and rowed on the Princeton crew. In 1924, he graduated with a B.A. degree and a desire to teach French. His father's death that same year led him to assume the leadership of the family business. Unfortunately, the business failed after the stock market crashed in 1929.

In 1931, Jackson accepted a position with *Time,* Inc., and by 1940 was vice president of that company. He then left *Time* to establish the Council for Democracy, a propaganda organization opposed to isolationism. In 1941, America entered World War II. The following year, he was appointed special assistant to the American ambassador in Turkey.

Jackson left the embassy in 1943 to become deputy chief of psychological warfare for the U.S. Army Air Corps. In 1944, he joined General Dwight Eisenhower's staff and became directly involved in the organization of psychological warfare operations in support of the Normandy invasion.

Jackson returned to *Time* after the war. But in 1951, he was appointed president of the Free Europe Committee, a CIA front organization that operated RFE and RL.

In 1953, Eisenhower (now president) named Jackson as his psychological warfare special assistant for COLD WAR planning. In March, Jackson assisted the White House in a foreign-policy response to a propagandistic peace proposal by the Soviets after the death of Premier Joseph Stalin. Jackson became a target of Senator Joseph McCarthy's controversial campaign to uncover closet communists after Jackson recommended to Eisenhower that he "take a strong stand" against McCarthy and his inquisitors.

Jackson left government service in 1954 and returned to *Time.* In 1960, he became the publisher of *Life* magazine.

Jackson died in New York on September 18, 1964. He was 62.

Jackson, William Harding (1901–1971)

William Harding Jackson is best known as one of three intelligence specialists who issued the 1949 DULLES-

JACKSON-CORREA REPORT, which was highly critical of the CIA. He also became DEPUTY DIRECTOR OF CENTRAL INTELLIGENCE (DDCI).

Jackson was born in Nashville, Tennessee, on March 25, 1901. In 1920, he graduated from St. Mark's School in Southborough, Tennessee. He earned a bachelor's degree from Princeton University in 1924. In 1928, he graduated from Harvard Law School. After Harvard, he worked as a lawyer in New York, first with the firm of Cadwalader, Wickersham, and Taft, then, in 1930, with Carter, Ledyard, and Milburn. He became a partner with the latter firm in 1934.

When World War II erupted, Jackson joined the U.S. Army, where he was commissioned a captain and posted to the Army Air Corps Intelligence School in 1942. Jackson served for a brief period with the OFFICE OF STRATEGIC SERVICES (OSS), the wartime predecessor organization to the CIA. In early 1944, Jackson served on the U.S. Military Headquarters intelligence staff in London. By war's end, he was a colonel and the assistant deputy to General Omar Bradley.

Back in New York, Jackson returned to the practice of law. But in 1947, he accepted a partnership with J. H. Whitney and Company, an investment banking firm. Soon thereafter, Jackson became a member of the Council on Foreign Relations (at that time directed by a future DIRECTOR OF CENTRAL INTELLIGENCE, ALLEN WELSH DULLES).

In 1948, Jackson, Dulles, and Matthias Correa (a former assistant to Secretary of Defense James V. Forrestal) were tasked with conducting a study that would address problems within the U.S. intelligence community, particularly the CIA, in its execution of both its intelligence and operational missions. Submitted to the NATIONAL SECURITY COUNCIL (NSC) in January of 1949, the Dulles-Jackson-Correa Report (or Dulles Report) proved to be highly critical of the CIA, attacking the Agency on countless fronts, including its alleged "failure to take charge of the production of coordinated national estimates."

On August 18, 1950, Jackson was appointed to the post of DDCI and was sworn in the following October. He served in that capacity until August 1951. One of the most important problems Jackson attempted to address as DDCI was bringing the OFFICE OF POLICY COORDINATION or OPC (the Agency's covert-action arm) and the OFFICE OF SPECIAL OPERATIONS or OSO (the Agency's secret intelligence-gathering arm) under one senior CIA officer. This officer was the DEPUTY DIRECTOR for Plans (operations), or DDP. It was believed that by bringing the OPC and the OSO under the DDP, the rivalry between the two offices would be eliminated. The rivalry continued, however, until 1952, when the OPC and the OSO merged to form the CIA CLANDESTINE SERVICE, the forerunner to the Agency's current DIRECTORATE of Operations. Jackson left

the Agency in 1951 and returned to the private sector, but he served as a contract special assistant and senior consultant to the DCI until February 1956.

In 1955, Jackson served as special assistant to the secretary of state. In 1956, he became special assistant to President Dwight Eisenhower.

Jackson died on September 28, 1971. He was 70.

JEDBURGH, Operation

Operation JEDBURGH was a joint effort between the American OFFICE OF STRATEGIC SERVICES (OSS, the wartime precursor to the CIA), the British SPECIAL OPERATIONS EXECUTIVE (SOE), and Free French units during World War II.

The operation consisted of recruiting, training, equipping, and inserting—usually by parachute—three-man teams of specially trained covert operatives into Nazi-occupied France, where they would coordinate Resistance activities supporting the Allied effort. Each team comprised two officers and one enlisted radio operator, ideally, one man from each of the three participating Allied nations. The JEDBURGH teams would link up with French Resistance units. They would then lead resistance forces (usually 30–50 fighters) in harassing commando raids against the Germans—creating diversions, disrupting communications, destroying key installations, and gathering intelligence to be used by the Allied armies.

The "Jedburghs" were equipped with all types of small arms, as well as bazookas, heavy machine guns, and jeeps. Because their insertions had to be clandestine, parachute drops were made at a low altitude, thus reducing the time in the air during which parachutists would be most vulnerable to ground fire. Jumps were made from 500 to 600 feet, as opposed to the more common 1,200-foot jumps made by regular airborne units. Additionally, the Jedburghs were not equipped with emergency reserve parachutes, as they would have been useless at such low altitudes.

Nearly 300 Jedburgh operatives were inserted into France over the course of the war. They included 83 Americans, 93 British, 103 French, and a handful of men from the Netherlands, Belgium, and Canada. The Jedburghs carried out over 100 operations in Europe between the Normandy landings and VE Day. With the surrender of Germany, some of the Jedburghs were transferred to Burma, where they saw action against the Japanese.

One of the best known of the American-led Jedburghs was the team led by future DIRECTOR OF CENTRAL INTELLIGENCE (DCI) WILLIAM EGAN COLBY. It was code-named "Bruce"; Colby, then a major, was code-named "Berkshire." He commanded two Free French commandos, Jacques Favel ("Galway") and Louis Giry ("Piastre").

Legend has it that the "Jedburgh" was taken from the Scottish village of Jedburgh and that there, along the Jed River, much of the training was conducted by British commandos and intelligence operatives from the SOE and OSS. The truth is somewhat less romantic. The code name was randomly picked from an English schoolbook. In addition to the Jedburgh training in Scotland, training was held in England at Milton Hall in Peterborough and Tatton Park in Manchester.

JENNIFER, Project

JENNIFER was the code name for a successful CIA–U.S. Navy mission aimed at recovering a portion of a sunken Soviet Golf II–class submarine in 1974.

On April 11, 1968, the Soviet submarine, K129, surfaced some 1,700 miles (some sources say 750 miles) northwest of the Hawaiian Islands. She was on a routine patrol in international waters, and the crew was attempting to recharge her batteries when several explosions inexplicably ripped through her hull. Within minutes the dead submarine went to the bottom of the sea, entombing 70 men, along with their sensitive coding and decoding devices, targeting materials, three SS-N-5 missiles armed with nuclear warheads, and several torpedoes. Almost immediately, the Soviet navy began searching for the wreck, but without success. The U.S. Navy, on the other hand, knew exactly where she was and considered it to be "an unprecedented opportunity."

The CIA's DEPUTY DIRECTOR for Science and Technology (DDS&T), Carl Duckett, proposed a recovery operation. DIRECTOR OF CENTRAL INTELLIGENCE (DCI) RICHARD MCGARRAH HELMS, initially cool to the idea, was eventually persuaded to gave the project a green light. The White House was contacted, and the wheels were set in motion.

The CIA then approached billionaire industrialist Howard Hughes and asked for his assistance. Hughes agreed, and Project AZORIAN, the preparatory phase of the recovery, was begun. Hughes's Summa Corporation built a $350 million salvage vessel, the GLOMAR EXPLORER, for the recovery operation.

On November 4, 1972, Glomar Explorer set sail, and Project AZORIAN was renamed Project JENNIFER. The ship was dispatched to the Soviet wreck site on what was ostensibly an undersea mining expedition. In reality, the vessel was designed to raise the sub from the seafloor.

Glomar Explorer (today in reserve) is enormous. She stretches the length of three football fields, and her decks were then crammed with all manner of technical devices for locating and salvaging items thousands of feet below the surface. Her weather decks were equipped with pivoting cranes; her main deck was fitted with a 209-foot derrick that could send a giant claw nearly 17,000 feet below the sea surface and lift, at one time, up to 800 tons. Spe-

cial refrigerated storage could handle up to 100 bodies. Additionally, Glomar Explorer's officers carried religious texts for American and Russian burial services.

Over a period of two years, the Glomar Explorer recovered a portion of the sub's hull, as well as some of her internal equipment. But the results of the operation remain classified. Some reports have suggested that only the bow portion was recovered. It purportedly contained the bodies of 70 Soviet sailors. Another report suggests that the conning tower (the prize most highly sought by the CIA) was salvaged, along with at least one intact submarine-launched ballistic missile (SLBM). The most plausible report is that a small portion of the sub (roughly 10 percent) was salvaged and the bodies of six Soviet seamen recovered. In any case, the bodies were then buried at sea with full military honors. The CIA wanted to send the Glomar Explorer back out the following summer, but word of JENNIFER began leaking to the press.

When the CIA closed the book on Project JENNIFER, Hughes employed the Glomar Explorer as a commercial salvage vessel. Glomar Explorer then became the first ship to conduct deep-sea mining for minerals.

jib

A jib is an inflatable man-sized dummy first employed by the CIA during the early 1980s. It is designed to replace an operative escaping from the inside of a moving vehicle. As the escapee rolls from the passenger side of the vehicle, the jib is deployed. Thus, the jib serves as a decoy for pursuers.

On September 21, 1985, EDWARD LEE HOWARD, a turncoat former CIA officer, employed a jib in his successful escape from the United States. Howard, who was under surveillance by agents from the FEDERAL BUREAU OF INVESTIGATION (FBI) managed to elude them, slipping past an inexperienced agent. Then, as his wife drove a getaway car, Howard deployed a jib to represent his figure while he leaped from the passenger side into a grove of trees. He eventually made his way out of the country.

JMWAVE

JMWAVE, also known as WAVE station, was the code name for the CIA's Miami station from which operations against Fidel Castro's Cuba were launched during the early 1960s.

See also ZENITH TECHNICAL ENTERPRISES.

Johnny Walker Red

"Johnny Walker Red," named after a popular blend of Scotch whiskey, was the U.S. Navy's unofficial moniker for former Navy chief warrant officer JOHN ANTHONY WALKER, JR., the ringleader of the notorious WALKER FAMILY SPY RING. The name is derived from the fact that Walker sold U.S. INTELLIGENCE COMMUNITY secrets to the Soviets for nearly two decades. Thus, he was in league with the "Reds," the communists.

Joint Chiefs of Staff (JCS)

The Joint Chiefs of Staff (JCS) is a five-member body consisting of the heads of each of the U.S. armed forces: the chief of staff of the Army, the chief of staff of the Air Force, the chief of naval operations, the commandant of the Marine Corps, and a presidentially appointed chairman chosen from one of the services. Originally, the JCS served collectively as principal military adviser to the president, the secretary of defense, and the NATIONAL SECURITY COUNCIL (NSC). During World War II, the OFFICE OF STRATEGIC SERVICES (or OSS, the wartime predecessor organization to the CIA) was under direct jurisdictional control of the JCS.

Born of the old U.S. Joint Board, the JCS was established in 1942. The Joint Board had existed since 1903 to deal with administrative matters of interservice concern. With the urgent need to develop and execute joint military operations during World War II, the JCS was created on the model of the effective British Chiefs of Staff. Then, as today, the American JCS prepares strategic plans and reviews high-level material, issues of personnel, and logistical requirements of the military. The JCS also formulates policies for joint operations and joint training exercises. As such, the JCS is a primary consumer of CIA-generated FINISHED INTELLIGENCE.

Joyce, Robert Prather (1902–1984)

A World War II intelligence chief who later served as an officer of the U.S. DEPARTMENT OF STATE, Robert Prather Joyce was once credited as being "more CIA than the CIA." Yet he never served a day in the Agency.

Born on October 17, 1902, in Los Angeles, Joyce was recognized early on as a young man of great intellectual gifts and a knack for diplomacy. In 1926, he graduated from Yale University, and for the next year he studied at the Free School of Political Science in Paris. In 1928, he entered the U.S. Foreign Service, and over the next decade he traveled from Asia to Latin America to Eastern Europe.

During the early years of World War II, Joyce served as the first secretary of the U.S. embassy in Havana, Cuba. In 1943, he joined the OFFICE OF STRATEGIC SERVICES (OSS), the wartime precursor to the CIA, as a civilian employee. He was initially assigned to Cairo, then to Bari, Italy, on the Adriatic coast. In Italy, he was placed in charge of the SECRET INTELLIGENCE Branch for the Balkans.

In 1944, OSS director WILLIAM J. "WILD BILL" DONOVAN made Joyce his political officer at the Allied Forces Mediterranean headquarters in Caserta, Italy. In 1945, Joyce was assigned the post of OSS CHIEF OF STATION (COS) in Bern, Switzerland. In 1947, he returned to the Foreign Service and was stationed in Trieste, Italy. The following year, he was transferred to Washington, D.C., where he served on the State Department's Policy Planning Staff.

When the CIA began planning operations aimed at overthrowing the communist government of ALBANIA in 1949, Joyce was assigned to a joint British/American SPECIAL POLICY COMMITTEE as a State Department representative. The committee was responsible for coordinating the paramilitary/clandestine action effort, code-named VALUABLE, against the Albanian communists.

In 1952, Joyce was reassigned to the American embassy in Paris, where he was the State Department counselor. From 1956 to 1957 he served at the American embassy in Rio de Janeiro, Brazil. In 1957, he became special assistant to the director of the Bureau of Intelligence and Research, a component of the State Department; in 1958, he was made its acting director. He returned to Italy the following year to become U.S. consul general in Genoa. He retired from the State Department in 1962.

Joyce died on February 8, 1984. He was 81.

K

Kalugin, Major General Oleg Danilovich (1934–)

Major General Oleg Danilovich Kalugin was a senior officer in the First Chief Directorate of the KOMITET GOSUDARSTVENNOY BEZOPASNOSTI (KGB, Committee for State Security), the Soviet counterpart of the CIA. Today, however, he is a staunch ally, public supporter, and friend of the Agency.

Kalugin was born (1934) in Leningrad (now St. Petersburg), one of the largest cities in the Union of Soviet Socialist Republics (USSR). His father was an officer in the Narodnyi Komissariat Vnutrennikh Del, or NKVD (People's Commissariat for Internal Affairs), one of the several predecessor organizations to the KGB. As a young man, Kalugin attended Leningrad State University.

While in school, he was recruited by the KGB for foreign intelligence work and was posted to the infamous First Chief Directorate, the direct counterpart agency of the CIA. Kalugin was initially posted to the United States, where he conducted Soviet espionage operations under the COVER of a journalist. He also attended New York's Columbia University as a Fulbright scholar in 1958. He also worked as a correspondent for Radio Moscow at the United Nations, conducting espionage and broadcast propaganda operations.

From 1965 to 1970, Kalugin served as deputy resident and acting chief of the KGB residency at the Soviet embassy in Washington, D.C. Rising quickly through the ranks of the First Chief Directorate, he became the youngest general officer in the history of the KGB. He eventually became the KGB's chief of worldwide foreign counterintelligence, with the rank of major general.

Kalugin served at the heart of some of the Soviets' most critical spy operations in North America, including the infamous WALKER FAMILY SPY RING. But he gradually became disillusioned with what he felt was a failed Soviet system. During a 1979 visit to a guard post on the border that separated Czechoslovakia from Austria, Kalugin stared across the IRON CURTAIN with other KGB officials. He later recalled, "Not far from Bratislava, we disembarked and inspected the barbed wire barrier separating Czechoslovakia from Austria, 150 yards away. On the other side of the river, Austrian families picnicked along the riverbank. Children flew kites as parents unpacked food hampers and made campfires. It was a picture of idyllic contentment and peace. Silently, we stood on our side of the barbed wire, surrounded by watchtowers and dour Czech border guards with carbines. The contrast between the two scenes could not have been sharper, and I sensed that everyone in the Soviet delegation was thinking the same thing: They are the ones who are free and we are the ones in a prison camp."

Kalugin was known by his peers as an aggressive officer and a Soviet patriot. But his mounting personal misgivings over what he perceived to be a failed ideology as well as the unchecked lawlessness, arbitrary rule, and an old-boy system within Soviet intelligence unsettled him, as they did much of the KGB leadership. As a result, Kalugin was demoted and ordered back to Leningrad, where he served as first deputy chief of internal security from 1980 to 1987. In that capacity, he began to realize that the KGB's internal functions had little to do with Soviet state security. Instead, he viewed the KGB as an entity whose primary responsibilities had evolved into nothing more than maintaining the power of corrupt Communist Party officials.

When the Soviet system began to collapse, Kalugin realized it was time to cut ties. He retired from the KGB in 1990 and became an outspoken critic of the communist system. His harsh criticism of the KGB earned him both praise and rejection. Soviet president Mikhail Gorbachev signed in 1990 an official decree that stripped Kalugin of his rank, all his awards and decorations, and his pension. Kalugin countered by running a successful campaign for a seat on the Supreme Soviet (the equivalent of Parliament). In the Supreme Soviet, he continued his attacks on the KGB and its abuses of power.

On August 21, 1991, the KGB attempted to overthrow the Soviet government. KGB Spetnaz units were ordered to storm the Russian parliament building and seize a number of key Soviet leaders. Several senior commanders refused to obey the KGB's orders. The operation failed, and the instigators were arrested.

Kalugin then became an adviser to KGB chairman Vadim Bakatin, a reformist officer who succeeded in dissolving the old state security apparatus but was unable to reform it quickly enough. On August 21, Gorbachev signed a decree that abolished the KGB effective October 24. The KGB dissolved, but its First Chief Directorate was immediately reestablished as the Centralnaya Sluzhbza Razvedki (CSR), the Central Intelligence Service.

Kalugin returned to the United States, where he currently teaches and lectures. He appears on news programs and documentaries throughout the United States and the world. He is also chairman of Intercon International, an international information service that provides business-related information for companies operating in the former Soviet Union. Kalugin writes regularly for Intercon's *Daily Report on Russia and the Former Soviet Republics,* as well as for a number of American magazines and newspapers. He has also contributed to a number of books about COLD WAR intelligence and espionage, in some cases writing their forewords.

In 1994, Kalugin published his memoirs, *The First Chief Directorate: My 32 Years in Intelligence and Espionage against the West.* Two years later, he collaborated with former DIRECTOR OF CENTRAL INTELLIGENCE (DCI) WILLIAM E. COLBY and Activision, an entertainment and video game publisher, to develop *Spycraft,* a spy thriller video game.

In a 1999 interview for CNN, Kalugin expressed a mixed opinion of the CIA as it compared with the KGB. "Initially, the CIA did not look too great in the eyes of the KGB," he said. "It was a fairly young organization. It was no match for the old experienced imperial service which represented both the Soviet Union and Imperial Russia. At the same time, the people in the KGB admired American prowess and the technology and the ability to spend money we did not have. Let me tell you, at one time the KGB had one very strong advantage over the CIA. We recruited our agents worldwide on ideological grounds. People who spied for us did not do it for money. They had a goal, world communism. They wanted to help the Soviet Union. However, things started to change as the Soviet system began to degenerate. Ideology lost its appeal, and at this point the CIA made a major breakthrough in becoming a powerful adversary which managed ultimately to help, and I emphasize to help, defeat the Soviet system."

On September 29, 2001, days after the TERRORIST ATTACKS ON THE UNITED STATES, as the United States began to prosecute its WAR ON TERRORISM, Kalugin issued the following statement: "I'm not an admirer of Russian President [Vladimir] Putin, but he was right when he compared the crimes committed by the Moslem extremists with those of the Nazis. It is precisely for this reason that the civilized world should treat these savages as Nazis. The plague of the 21st Century must be stamped out before it plunges the human race into an abyss."

Kampiles, William (1955–)

A lower-echelon CIA employee, William Kampiles was imprisoned in 1978 for stealing and selling a classified technical manual to the KGB.

Kampiles was employed by the CIA from March to November 1977 but resigned after being told that he was not qualified to serve as a field officer. Disgruntled, he stole a top-secret technical manual on a sensitive surveillance system and left for Athens, Greece. There, he met a Soviet intelligence officer who purchased the manual for $3,000. Kampiles's treachery was revealed when he mentioned frequent meetings with the Soviets in Athens in a letter to a CIA employee.

When Kampiles returned to the United States, he was arrested by special agents from the FEDERAL BUREAU OF INVESTIGATION (FBI). He confessed to his crime but claimed that his intention was to become a DOUBLE AGENT for the CIA. He was convicted of espionage, and, on December 22, 1978, he was sentenced to 40 years in prison.

Kaplan, Gabriel Louis (1901–1968)

Gabriel Louis Kaplan was a CIA officer who was instrumental in helping establish free elections in the Philippines during the post–World War II era.

Kaplan was born on September 14, 1901, in New York City. He attended Swarthmore College, Columbia University, and New York University, earning a law degree from the latter in 1925. He then practiced law and became involved in Republican Party politics in New York.

When America entered World War II, Kaplan joined the U.S. Army Air Corps. He served as a personnel officer from 1942 through 1946, eventually attaining the rank of lieutenant colonel.

In 1952, DESMOND "DIZZY FITS" FITZGERALD, a CIA officer who knew Kaplan through New York politics, recruited him into the Agency. Kaplan was dispatched to the Philippines, where he was tasked with assisting GENERAL EDWARD GEARY LANSDALE, the CHIEF OF STATION (COS) for the OFFICE OF POLICY COORDINATION's (OPC) station in Manila. The OPC was the Agency's early covert-action arm. Lansdale himself was assisting the government of the Philippines in its efforts against the communist Huk (Hukbalahap) guerrilla forces, which were trying to topple the legitimate government. One of Kaplan's primary responsibilities was ensuring that the elections in the Philippines were free and just.

Operating within more than one FRONT organization, Kaplan was able to assist in the founding of both NAMFREL (the National Movement for Free Elections) and "The Magsaysay for President Movement," which helped establish Philippine defense minister Ramon Magsaysay as a legitimate national candidate. In 1953, Magsaysay was elected president, and for the next five years Kaplan worked toward building a sound community infrastructure in the Philippines.

In 1958, Kaplan returned to the United States and retired from the Agency. He then founded the Community Development Counseling (CDC) service in Arlington, Virginia. The CDC provided business and other consulting services to Third World nations throughout the Far East and Latin America.

Kaplan died on September 17, 1968, three days after his 67th birthday.

Karamessines, Thomas H. (1916–1978)

Thomas H. Karamessines was head of the CIA's CLANDESTINE SERVICE during the Agency's unsuccessful series of CHILEAN OPERATIONS in the late 1960s and early 1970s.

Karamessines was born to Greek immigrant parents in 1916. He graduated from Columbia University and from the Columbia University School of Law. He then briefly served on the staff of Thomas E. Dewey, New York's famous "racket-busting" district attorney.

Following America's entry into World War II, Karamessines enlisted in the U.S. Army. There his mastery of Greek language and history caught the interest of WILLIAM J. "WILD BILL" DONOVAN, head of the OFFICE OF STRATEGIC SERVICES, the wartime predecessor organization to the CIA. Karamessines was recruited into X-2, the OSS's counterespionage branch. He was dispatched to Greece, where he rose to the rank of major.

When the NATIONAL SECURITY ACT OF 1947 established the CIA as a permanent foreign intelligence entity, Karamessines joined the Agency's Clandestine Service (CS). With the CS, he served as both a CASE OFFICER and a CHIEF OF STATION (COS). As COS, he served in a number of major European capitals including Athens, Vienna, and Rome.

Karamessines became CS chief of operations under its chief (and future DIRECTOR OF CENTRAL INTELLIGENCE) RICHARD MCGARRAH HELMS in 1962. Four years later, he succeeded DESMOND "DIZZY FITS" FITZGERALD as DEPUTY DIRECTOR of plans (operations). Karamessines was head of the CS in the late 1960s and early 1970s when it was directly involved in the CIA's unsuccessful attempts to oust the Marxist government of Chilean president Salvador Allende Gossens. Karamessines retired from the CIA in 1973.

On September 4, 1978, Karamessines died of a heart attack at his vacation home in Grand Lake, Quebec. He was 61.

Kennan, George Frost (1904–   )

Diplomat and Pulitzer Prize winner George Frost Kennan never served a day in the CIA or in any of the Agency's predecessor organizations. But he is considered to be the true architect of the CIA's covert-action arm.

Kennan was born in Milwaukee, Wisconsin, on February 16, 1904, the son of Kossuth Kent Kennan, a tough-minded lawyer of Scotch-Irish ancestry, and Florence James. As a boy, Kennan attended St. John's Military Academy in Delafield, Wisconsin. There he excelled in history, literature, and English. He was elected by his peers to the rank of cadet lieutenant and senior class poet. Kennan would later describe his boyhood personality as "oddball, not eccentric, not ridiculed or disliked, just imperfectly visible to the naked eye." As a young man, he attended Princeton University, earning an A.B. degree in 1925. The following year, he entered the U.S. Foreign Service.

Kennan initially served as vice consul in Geneva and the German cities of Hamburg and Berlin. From 1928 through 1929, he served in the countries of Estonia,

Latvia, and Lithuania. In 1930, he earned a diploma in oriental languages from the Berlin Seminary.

In 1933, the United States officially recognized the Union of Soviet Socialist Republics (USSR), and President Franklin Roosevelt dispatched America's first ambassador to the Soviet Union, William C. Bullitt. Bullitt chose Kennan to be a member of his new embassy staff. In this capacity, Kennan was able to develop strong opinions as to the global implications of Stalinism, including its executions and bloody purges, death threats against dissidents, and concentration camps. He also developed an uncanny ability to discern the difference between the Soviet Union's official hostility toward the West and its unofficial cordial diplomacy.

In 1937, Ambassador Bullitt was replaced by Joseph E. Davies, a respected Democrat whose primary task was to develop good will between the two nations in order to lay the groundwork for a possible future alliance. Kennan, who had seen the dark side of Stalinism, refused to remain in Moscow under Davies. He returned to the United States and served on the Russian desk at the STATE DEPARTMENT. Not long after, he was dispatched to Prague, Czechoslovakia. From there he witnessed the Nazi annexation of the Sudetenland.

When Germany invaded Poland in the fall of 1939, Kennan transferred from Prague to the American embassy in Berlin. When the United States entered the war in December 1941, Kennan and his fellow embassy staffers were detained and prohibited from leaving Germany until May 1942. Kennan's next post was as chargé d'affaires of the U.S. mission to Portugal.

In 1944, Keenan returned to Moscow, where he served as minister-counselor until 1946. He then returned to the United States and joined the faculty of the National War College. In 1947, he was named chairman of the State Department's Policy Planning Committee.

In July, the quarterly journal *Foreign Affairs* ran an article entitled "The Sources of Soviet Conduct." The article, published under the pseudonym "X," became the basis for American policy toward the Soviet Union. The article offered a model of "containing" the Soviets, a model that would remain U.S. policy throughout the cold war. The article stated, "The main element of any United States policy toward the Soviet Union must be that of a long-term, patient but firm and vigilant containment of Russian expansive tendencies." The author was later revealed to be Kennan.

In June 1948 Kennan drafted a national security directive that ultimately provided for the establishment of the CIA's OFFICE OF POLICY COORDINATION (OPC), the CIA's covert-action arm.

In 1950, Kennan temporarily left government service in order to conduct research at Princeton University's Institute for Advanced Studies. In May 1952, he was named ambassador to the Soviet Union. However, critical comments about Soviet treatment of Western diplomats led the Soviets to declare him persona non grata in October. In 1953, he returned to Princeton. From 1957 to 1958, he taught at Oxford University. While at Oxford, his book *Russia Leaves the War* earned him the Pulitzer Prize for history.

In 1961, President John F. Kennedy appointed Kennan ambassador to Yugoslavia. He served in that capacity until 1963. He then held a variety of academic posts, including a professorship at Princeton (1964–66), a university fellowship in history and Slavic civilizations at Harvard (1966–70), and a fellowship at Oxford's All Souls College (1969). He also served as president of the National Institute of Arts and Letters (1965–68) and of the American Academy of Arts and Letters (1967–71).

Aside from numerous honorary doctoral degrees, Kennan was awarded the Pour le Mérite for Arts and Sciences (Germany), the Woodrow Wilson International Center Scholars Award from the Smithsonian Institution, the Albert Einstein Peace Prize, the Grenville Clark Prize, the German Book Trade Peace Prize, the Union Medal from Union Theological Seminary, the Gold Medal in History

George Frost Kennan   (HULTON ARCHIVE)

from the American Academy and Institute of Arts and Letters, the James Madison Award from Princeton University, the Literary Lion Award from the New York Public Library, the Creative Art Award from Brandeis University, the FDR Freedom from the Fear Award—Franklin D. Roosevelt Foundation, the Physicians Award for Social Responsibility, the Toynbee Prize, the British Award from Encyclopedia Britannica, the Presidential Medal of Freedom, New Jersey's Woodrow Wilson Public Service Award, the Distinguished Service Award, two Pulitzers, two National Book Awards, a Bancroft Prize, a Francis Parkman Prize, and an Ambassador Book Award.

Kennan's many published works included *American Diplomacy 1900–1950* (1951), *Realities of American Foreign Policy* (1954), *Das Amerikanisch Russische Verhaltnis* (1954), *Russia Leaves the War,* volume 1 of *Soviet-American Relations 1917–20* (1956) and *Decision to Intervene,* volume 2 (1958), *Russia, the Atom, and the West* (1958), *Russia and the West under Lenin and Stalin* (1961), *On Dealing with the Communist World* (1964), *Memoirs 1925–1950* (1967), *From Prague after Munich* (1968), *Democracy and the Student Left* (1968), *The Marquis de Custine and His Russia in 1839* (1971), *Memoirs 1950–1963* (1972), *The Cloud of Danger: Current Realities of American Foreign Policy* (1977), *The Decline of Bismarck's European Order: Franco-Russian Relations, 1875–1890* (1979), *The Nuclear Delusion: Soviet-American Relations in the Atomic Age* (1982), *The State Department Policy Planning Staff Papers* (1983), *The Decision to Intervene* (1984), *The Fateful Alliance: France, Russia and the Coming of the First World War* (1984), *Soviet-American Relations 1917–1920* (1984), *Sketches from a Life* (1989), *Around the Cragged Hill* (1993), and *At a Century's Ending* (1996).

Kennedy assassination, CIA's alleged involvement in the

Among the many conspiracy theories surrounding the assassination of President John Kennedy on November 22, 1963, is that CIA operatives were either directly or indirectly involved. No proof of such a thing has ever emerged. "Believe me, if the CIA had anything to do with the murder of our president I would have discovered it in the early seventies and I would have revealed it," former DIRECTOR OF CENTRAL INTELLIGENCE (DCI) WILLIAM EGAN COLBY said years after his retirement. "I revealed a lot of other things."

Nearly three decades after the assassination, a (Kennedy) Assassination Review Board (ARB) was established under the John F. Kennedy Assassination Records Collection Act of 1992. The ARB, which began its work in 1994, was tasked with overseeing the processing of some 14,000 CIA documents and the transference of some 100,000 CIA documents related to the Kennedy assassination to the National Archives and Records Administration and the JFK Collection. The project was originally slated for completion in 1997. But President Bill Clinton extended the ARB's deadline through September 1998. On September 30, the ARB reported that the CIA had properly performed all of its responsibilities. Under a post-ARB agreement, the CIA continued transferring Kennedy assassination records to the National Archives.

Kent, Sherman (1903–1986)

If there was ever a cigar-chomping "diamond-in-the-rough aristocrat" who literally brought intelligence to the CIA, it was Sherman Kent.

Kent was born in Chicago on December 1, 1903, to William Kent and Elizabeth Thacher. He attended Yale University, earning a Ph.B. (bachelor of philosophy) in 1926, a Ph.D. in 1933, and an affectionate nickname—"Buffalo Bill, the cultured cowboy"—from his classmates. Kent then taught history at Yale until the outbreak of World War II.

In 1941, Kent left academia to join the war effort, specifically the OFFICE OF THE COORDINATOR OF INFORMATION (COI), America's prewar intelligence agency. In 1942, the COI was reorganized into the OFFICE OF STRATEGIC SERVICES (OSS), the wartime precursor organization to the CIA. Assigned to the OSS's Research and Analysis Branch, Kent was quickly made head of the branch's Africa Section.

In 1943, Kent became head of the Europe Africa Division and remained in that capacity until the end of the war in 1945. That same year, the OSS was disbanded, and the Research and Analysis Branch was transferred to the U.S. DEPARTMENT OF STATE. The branch was then renamed the INTERIM RESEARCH AND INTELLIGENCE SERVICE, and Kent was appointed director. It was also during that time that he became a member of the National War College's resident civilian faculty.

In 1947, Kent returned to Yale and served as a full professor of history. The following year, he published *Strategic Intelligence for American World Policy,* a highly touted work that addressed "the intelligence cycle and it's role in the formulation of foreign policy."

Kent wrote a number of books—in addition to his *Strategic Intelligence for American World Policy*—including *Electoral Procedure under Louis Philippe* (1937), *Writing History* (1942), *A Boy and a Pig, but Mostly Horses* (a children's book of 1974), and *The French Election of 1827* (1975).

In 1950, Kent became deputy director of the National Board of Estimates in Washington, D.C. Two years later he became director, serving in that capacity until 1967. He was the recipient of the President's Award for Distinguished Federal Service, as well as the National Civil Service League Award.

Kent died on March 11, 1986. He was 82.

On May 4, 2000, the CIA held dedication ceremonies for its new Sherman Kent School of Analysis, a headquarters institution for Agency analysts.

KGB

See KOMITET GOSUDARSTVENNOY BEZOPASNOSTI.

King, Joseph Caldwell (J.C.) (1900–1975)

Joseph Caldwell "J.C." King was a former FBI agent who became the CIA's first chief of clandestine operations in the Western Hemisphere.

King, a native New Yorker, was born on October 5, 1900. He graduated from the U.S. Military Academy at West Point in 1923 and was subsequently commissioned a second lieutenant of infantry. In 1924, he resigned from active duty in order to study diplomacy at l'École Libre des Sciences Politiques in Paris.

For the next five years, King was employed by a myriad of companies in a number of countries. From 1925 to 1926, he managed the King and San Bernabe Mines in Durango, Mexico. From 1926 to 1927, he traveled across Europe and Asia. He returned to the United States in 1927 and accepted a vice president's position with the New Jersey–based King Chemical Company. In 1930, he joined pharmaceutical giant Johnson and Johnson. This job took him back to Latin America.

When World War II broke out, King returned to active duty and was posted to Argentina as a military attaché. It was in Argentina that he became an intelligence operative, working for the FEDERAL BUREAU OF INVESTIGATION (FBI).

In 1947, King joined the newly established CIA and was appointed chief of the Agency's Western Hemisphere Division. There he proved a natural middleman. He had an excellent working knowledge of Latin American operations. He recruited into the division many of the former FBI agents with whom he had worked. He also had excellent connections with Latin American security and police officials, as well as business leaders. But he had neither the stomach for paramilitary operations nor the planning and leadership skills for complex operations.

When the initial planning was begun for the ill-fated invasion of Cuba at the BAY OF PIGS, King was deliberately left out of the loop. He maintained his position, on paper, as chief of the Western Hemisphere Division until 1964, when he was eased out of the Agency.

In 1966, the Agency again retained the services of King when they hired him to serve as head of the AMAZON NATURAL DRUG COMPANY, a private enterprise operated by the CIA. The Amazon Natural Drug Company collected plant extracts along the Amazon River and forwarded them to CIA drug-testing laboratories in the United States. The extracts were then used for experimental purposes in the CIA's MIND-CONTROL DRUG TESTING and research programs. King supervised his plant gatherers, often with a glass of scotch in hand, from the deck of a houseboat that served as his mobile office.

King died in 1975. He was 75.

Kirkpatrick, Lyman Bickford, Jr. (1916–1995)

Lyman Bickford Kirkpatrick, Jr., is widely regarded as the CIA officer who—had it not been for a polio attack in 1952—might have become DIRECTOR OF CENTRAL INTELLIGENCE (DCI) after ALLEN WELSH DULLES was forced into retirement in 1961.

Kirkpatrick was born in Rochester, New York, on July 15, 1916, to Lyman Bickford Kirkpatrick, Sr., and Lyde Paull. In 1938, he graduated from Princeton University in New Jersey.

Kirkpatrick wrote and edited for the Bureau of National Affairs and the U.S. News Publishing Corporation. He also served on the editorial staffs of *U.S. News* and the *World Report* (which would eventually merge to become *U.S. News & World Report*).

In 1942, WILLIAM J. "WILD BILL" DONOVAN recruited Kirkpatrick into the OFFICE OF THE COORDINATOR OF INFORMATION (COI), the first of the predecessor organizations to the CIA. That same year, the COI was reorganized into the OFFICE OF STRATEGIC SERVICES (OSS), the World War II precursor to the CIA. Kirkpatrick was transferred to Europe as an OSS operative. He served in the OSS until the end of the war, attaining the rank of major.

When the CIA was established in 1947, Kirkpatrick offered his services. He was hired and assigned duties as a division chief (1947–50), assistant director for special operations (1950–53), inspector general (1953–61), and executive director (1961–65). Unfortunately, Kirkpatrick was stricken with polio while serving with the OFFICE OF SPECIAL OPERATIONS (OSO) in 1952. He survived the disease and continued his work with the Agency, but he was partially paralyzed for the remainder of his life.

Following operation ZAPATA, the ill-fated Cuban invasion at the BAY OF PIGS in 1961, he wrote a harsh critique of the operation known as the KIRKPATRICK REPORT; though well known in the U.S. intelligence community, it was suppressed within the CIA. In a 1972 article for the *Naval War College Review*, Kirkpatrick expressed his opinions publicly. He contended that the ZAPATA planners within the CIA's Directorate of Plans (Operations) had failed to consult adequately with the Agency's Cuban analysts before the commencement of the invasion. He also criticized ZAPATA's overall lack of internal security and the failure to keep President John Kennedy informed. In Kirkpatrick's opinion, the Agency, not the White House, was primarily responsible for the failure at the Bay of Pigs.

Following his retirement from the Agency in 1965, Kirkpatrick taught political science at Brown University, the Naval War College, and the Defense Intelligence College.

Among his published works were *The Real CIA* (1967), *American Security Policy* (1968), *Captains without Eyes: Major Intelligence Failures in World War II* (1969), and *The U.S. Intelligence Community* (1973). Kirkpatrick was also a contributor to the *Britannica Year Book* (1948–60), as well as to political science and military journals.

Aside from winning the Legion of Merit, the Croix de Guerre (France and Belgium), and a Bronze Star with five battle stars, Kirkpatrick was the recipient of the Distinguished Intelligence Medal, the National Civil Service League award, and the President's Award for Distinguished Federal Civilian Service.

Kirkpatrick died of pneumonia in Middleburg, Virginia, on February 27, 1995. He was 78.

Kirkpatrick report

The Kirkpatrick report was the result of an examination of the CIA's shortcomings during Operation ZAPATA, the invasion of Cuba at the BAY OF PIGS in 1961. The study was headed by the CIA INSPECTOR GENERAL (IG), LYMAN B. KIRKPATRICK, JR., under the direction of DIRECTOR OF CENTRAL INTELLIGENCE (DCI) ALLEN WELSH DULLES. It was conducted concurrently with an investigation of ZAPATA by the presidentially appointed TAYLOR COMMISSION.

For the failure of ZAPATA, the Taylor Commission heaped blame upon the CIA, the U.S. DEPARTMENT OF STATE, the JOINT CHIEFS OF STAFF (JCS), and the administration of President John Kennedy. The Kirkpatrick report focused on the CIA.

After a five-month examination, the 170-page Kirkpatrick report was issued to select intelligence insiders. Though it remains classified, insiders believe that much of the report was unjustly critical of the CIA and Dulles, who was relieved as DCI by Kennedy in November 1961.

In a 1972 article for the *Naval War College Review*, Kirkpatrick expressed his opinions publicly. Kirkpatrick contended that the ZAPATA planners within the DIRECTORATE of Plans (Operations) had failed to consult adequately the Agency's Cuban analysts before the commencement of the invasion. He also criticized ZAPATA's overall lack of internal security and the failure to keep Kennedy informed. In Kirkpatrick's opinion, the Agency, not the White House, was primarily responsible for the failure at the Bay of Pigs.

KMSOURDOUGH, Operation

KMSOURDOUGH was the cryptonym for a CIA MAIL-INTERCEPT operation based in San Francisco, California, from September 1969 to October 1971.

See also FLAPS AND SEALS and HTLINGUAL.

Knoche, Enno Henry (1925–)

Henry Enno Knoche was the special liaison between the CIA and the 1975 executive and congressional committees investigating alleged misdeeds on the part of the Agency. He would go on to serve as DEPUTY DIRECTOR OF CENTRAL INTELLIGENCE (DDCI) and acting DIRECTOR OF CENTRAL INTELLIGENCE (DCI).

Knoche was born on January 14, 1925, in Charleston, West Virginia. He attended Washington and Jefferson College, earning an A.B. degree in 1947. He served as a naval officer in both World War II and the Korean War.

In 1953, Knoche, who spoke fluent Chinese, joined the CIA as an intelligence analyst specializing in Far Eastern political and military affairs. Knoche held a variety of posts with the Agency and elsewhere in the U.S. intelligence community. From 1962 to 1967, he served as chief of the National Photographic Interpretation Center. In 1969, he was named deputy director for planning and budgeting. He also chaired the CIA's in-house committee in charge of computerization, which enabled the Agency to place a great deal of emphasis on spy satellites and SIGINT (signals intelligence). Knoche then became director of the FOREIGN BROADCAST INFORMATION SERVICE, or FBIS (1972–73), director of the Office of Strategic Research (1973–75), and associate deputy director of central intelligence for the Intelligence Community (August 1975–July 1976).

In 1975, the YEAR OF INTELLIGENCE, Knoche was assigned the task of special liaison between DCI WILLIAM E. COLBY and the presidentially appointed ROCKEFELLER COMMISSION (officially, the President's Commission on CIA Activities within the United States). The Rockefeller Commission was tasked with investigating alleged illegal domestic activities on the part of the CIA. The alleged misdeeds included ASSASSINATION PLOTS against foreign political leaders.

Knoche also served as liaison between Colby and the Senate's CHURCH COMMITTEE and the House of Representative's PIKE COMMITTEE (congressional bodies established to investigate alleged misdeeds on the part of the Agency). Knoche was critical of Colby's policy of surrendering classified material to the two committees. He purportedly lamented to a group of friends, "There is no COUNTERINTELLIGENCE any more."

On April 22, 1976, President Gerald Ford appointed Knoche DDCI, a post he would hold from July 7, 1976, to August 1, 1977.

In *George Bush: The Unauthorized Biography*, Webster G. Tarpley and Anton Chaitkin write, "Knoche was to function as [DCI GEORGE HERBERT WALKER BUSH's] 'Indian guide' through the secrets of Langley; he knew 'where the bodies were buried.'"

From January 20 to March 9, 1977 (the interim between Bush and STANSFIELD TURNER), Knoche served as acting DCI.

knuckle dragger

A "knuckle dragger" is an affectionate, once derogatory, CIA term for military and paramilitary forces attached to the Agency for covert and special operations. The term suggests that the "paras" were so much like apes that their knuckles would drag the ground when they walked. In the early days of the Agency, such insults might have been met with a fist to the mouth. Today, the level of technical acumen required of special forces or special purpose soldiers is so high that no one could possibly consider them "apes." Thus, the term "knuckle dragger" is considered humorous by all parties.

Koecher, Karl F. (1934–)

Considered to be the first agent to penetrate the CIA, Karl F. Koecher was arrested in 1984 after passing on to Czech intelligence operatives highly classified materials, including names of CIA officers and agents. Koecher, who had been operating as an ILLEGAL for Czech intelligence for nearly 20 years, had been employed by the CIA from 1973 to 1975.

In 1962, Koecher was trained for work as a foreign agent by the Czech intelligence service. Three years later, he and his wife staged a phony defection to the United States. To further develop his COVER, he began making public statements against communism to New York's academic community.

In 1971, the Koechers became naturalized citizens of the United States. Two years later, Koecher became a translator with the CIA. During that time, he was observed making frequent contact with known KGB operatives in the United States. According to the FEDERAL BUREAU OF INVESTIGATION (FBI), from February 1973 to August 1983 Koecher passed highly classified materials and disclosed the names of CIA personnel to Czech intelligence officers. Koecher's wife allegedly operated as a paid COURIER.

On November 27, 1984, the Koechers were arrested as they prepared to board a plane for Switzerland. The case, however, never went to trial. Instead, the Koechers were taken to Berlin, where they were released on February 11, 1985. Koecher was exchanged for Soviet dissident Anatoly Shcharansky.

Kolbe, Fritz (unknown)

Fritz Kolbe was a Berlin-based Nazi Foreign Office official who served the Allies as a spy for the American OFFICE OF STRATEGIC SERVICES (OSS), the World War II precursor organization to the CIA. Code-named "George Wood," Kolbe contacted SECRET INTELLIGENCE station chief ALLEN WELSH DULLES (the future DIRECTOR OF CENTRAL INTELLIGENCE, who was then based in Bern, Switzerland) and offered his services as a DOUBLE AGENT for the Allies.

Kolbe proved to be a highly valuable asset. His information enabled Allied intelligence forces to stay a step ahead of Axis foreign policy and military matters. The intelligence also enabled British forces to capture a key Nazi spy who was operating within the household of the British ambassador to Turkey.

Komitet Gosudarstvennoy Bezopasnosti (KGB)

The most familiar of all the Russian intelligence organizations, the Komitet Gosudarstvennoy Bezopasnosti (KGB, or Committee for State Security), was the chief Soviet intelligence and counterintelligence entity during the COLD WAR. It was the largest espionage organization in world history. It was established in 1954, and before it was disbanded with the collapse of the Soviet Union in 1991, the KGB's reputation as a ruthless secret police force achieved almost mythic proportions. In his book *Secret Agencies: U.S. Intelligence in a Hostile World,* Loch Johnson describes the KGB as "fearsome in [its] aggressive capabilities," exampled by countless instances of murder, torture, and threats of both. Fearsome it was; as the organization's presence was felt it every level of Soviet society and in practically every region of the world that experienced political unrest.

Like the CIA, the KGB was tasked with maintaining a vast network of spies and information analysts. Unlike the CIA, the KGB's jurisdiction was both domestic and foreign. The committee maintained internal political-enforcement officers, security forces, assassination squads, and border troops, equipped with tanks, armored vehicles, aircraft, ships and boats, and specially trained combat units.

The KGB was vast in size (estimated at over 750,000 personnel at peak strength in the late 1980s), and its responsibilities extended far beyond those of its counterpart organizations in the West. The KGB was tasked with all of the primary functions of the CIA, but it also carried out the duties required in the United States of the NATIONAL SECURITY AGENCY (NSA), the Secret Service, and the Marshals Service, as well as many functions of the FEDERAL BUREAU OF INVESTIGATION (FBI), the Customs Service, the Parks Service, COUNTERINTELLIGENCE and security units of the armed forces; the U.S. Bureau of Alcohol, Tobacco, and Firearms (ATF); the U.S. Drug Enforcement Agency (DEA), and the state police agencies of all 50 states.

As a committee with ministerial status, the KGB operated on the basis of a statute, or *polozhenie,* approved by the Soviet Council of Ministers (the equivalent of the U.S. cabinet). The *polozhenie* set forth the KGB's authority and responsibilities, but it was never published. Over time, however, the functions of the KGB were revealed by defectors to the West, Soviet DOUBLE AGENTs, and field officers working for the CIA and Britain's MI6. Information on KGB projects and capabilities were also revealed through official Soviet publications, which either gleaned information through their own sources or secretly released it as a means of instilling in others a respect for the committee's power.

Generally speaking, KGB tasks lay in four broad areas:

1. Addressing the problem of foreign spies and agents
2. Exposing and investigating the political and economic crimes of Soviet citizens
3. Protecting Soviet borders
4. Protecting Soviet secrets.

Officially, the KGB was directed by a chairman, one or two first-deputy chairmen, and five to six deputy chairmen. The chairman of the KGB, the equivalent of the CIA's DIRECTOR OF CENTRAL INTELLIGENCE (DCI), was selected by the Politburo (the Political Bureau of the Communist Party Central Committee, the premier policymaking body of the Soviet Union) and formally appointed by the Supreme Soviet (the Soviet legislative assembly).

Key decisions of the KGB were made by the Collegium, a panel consisting of the KGB chairman, first deputy and deputy chairmen, select chiefs of directorates, and selected chairmen from individual republic KGB organizations.

The KGB was organized into five chief directorates, several unnumbered directorates, and various departments, including:

- The First Chief Directorate (Foreign Intelligence). This directorate was the committee's primary espionage arm. As such, it was the directorate most often intended when outsiders refer to the KGB. This directorate was tasked with collecting and analyzing all political, scientific, and technology-related foreign intelligence; foreign counterintelligence; recruiting and training covert operatives and foreign agents; disseminating foreign propaganda and disinformation; and providing support for international terrorism. Simply put, all international clandestine activities—with the exception of the military intelligence gathered by the GLAVNOYE RAZVEDYVATELNOYE UPRAVLENIYE, or GRU—were under the umbrella of the First Chief Directorate. This directorate also maintained an elite Spetznaz (Voiska Spetzialnogo Noznochenia, or special-mission troops) commando unit, comparable to U.S. Navy Sea-Air-Land (SEAL) Teams or Great Britain's Special Air Service (SAS).
- The Second Chief Directorate (COUNTERINTELLI-GENCE). This directorate was responsible for all domestic counterintelligence and internal security, including hunting for foreign spies and domestic

traitors, as well as working with the other agencies to defeat organized crime and drug trafficking.
- The Third Chief Directorate (Military Counterintelligence). This directorate was responsible for ensuring the loyalty and security of all armed forces personnel in the armed forces, as well as providing physical security for nuclear weapons.
- The Fourth Directorate (Transportation). This directorate was responsible for all transportation security matters.
- The Fifth Chief Directorate (Ideological). This directorate, also known as the "Directorate to Defend the Constitution" and as "Directorate Z," was responsible for monitoring and repressing Soviet dissidents, and eliminating threats of sedition. Special operational departments within this directorate specifically addressed religious dissent, ethnic minorities, the artistic community, and the intelligentsia, as well as the censorship of any literature that failed to toe the party line. Many of its tasks overlapped the responsibilities of the Second Chief Directorate.
- The Sixth Directorate (Economic Security). This directorate was responsible for enforcing financial and trade laws, as well as guarding against economic espionage.
- The Seventh Directorate (Surveillance). This directorate provided to other chief directorates and directorates personnel for physical surveillance purposes. Much of this work was centered around Moscow and Leningrad, where tourists, diplomats, foreign students, and members of the Soviet intelligentsia were concentrated. It also maintained an antiterrorist team.
- The Eighth Chief Directorate (Communications). This directorate was responsible for intercepting, monitoring, and analyzing foreign communications; designing CODEs and safeguards to secure Soviet communications; and running the telephone system used by the highest levels of the Soviet government. Some of these tasks overlapped the responsibilities of the 16th Directorate. The Eighth Directorate also maintained a subdirectorate (the Communications Troops Directorate) of 16,000 communications soldiers. It was considered the counterpart of America's NATIONAL SECURITY AGENCY (NSA).
- The Ninth Directorate (Guards). This directorate was responsible for guarding high-ranking party officials, government leaders, and foreign dignitaries. It also provided uniformed security details for Lenin's Tomb, the Kremlin, and other key state posts.
- The 10th Directorate (Archives). This directorate was responsible for maintaining KGB archives.
- The 12th Directorate (Electronic Surveillance). This directorate was responsible for developing, placing,

maintaining, and monitoring electronic eavesdropping and telephone bugging devices within the Soviet Union.

- The 15th Directorate (Bunkers). This directorate was responsible for providing security at government installations and administering Soviet underground command and control facilities, as well as nuclear-weapons storage sites.
- The 16th Directorate (Communications Security). This directorate was responsible for providing Soviet communications security. Its tasks often overlapped the responsibilities of the Eighth Chief Directorate.

Several other directorates and departments (some lasting only briefly) existed under the KGB umbrella, including the Information Analysis Directorate (which reported directly to top KGB officials) and the Border Guards Chief Directorate (nearly 250,000 troops, with an array of boats and aircraft, organized into nine frontier districts).

The KGB traces its lineage back to the Cheka (or Vse Cheka), a Russian acronym for Vse-Rossiyskaya Chrezvychaynaya Komissiya po Borbe s Kontrrevolutsiay i Sabotazhem—the All-Russian Extraordinary Commission for Combating Counterrevolution and Sabotage. The Cheka was created on December 20, 1917, during the early period of the Bolshevik (predecessor of the Russian Communist Party) government. Earlier that year, Marxist revolutionary leader Vladimir Ilyich Lenin had ordered the elimination of the Okhrana, the czarist intelligence and security service. Under Lenin's supervision, most Okhrana officers were arrested and executed without trial. Some were recruited into the fledgling Cheka.

Not long after, Leon Trotsky, Lenin's fellow Bolshevik and occasional political rival, formed a military intelligence service known as the GLAVNOYE RAZVEDYVATELNOYE UPRAVLENIYE (GRU), the Chief Intelligence Administration. The Cheka, which viewed the GRU as a rival, demanded and won the right to screen all potential GRU officers and agents. The Cheka was also allowed to place its own officers in the GRU. Trotsky and the Soviet generals objected to the arrangement but were overruled by the party leadership.

In 1918, the Narodnyi Komissariat Vnutrennikh Del (NKVD, the People's Commissariat for Internal Affairs) was established. This agency was responsible for providing police officers and detectives, border troops, prison guards, and firefighters. On February 8, 1922, the Cheka was incorporated into the NKVD, which itself was reorganized and renamed the Gosudarstvennoy Politicheskoye Upravleniye (GPU), the State Political Administration.

When the Union of Soviet Socialist Republics (USSR) was officially formed in 1923, the GPU was removed from the NKVD, organized as an independent directorate, and renamed the Obedinennoye Gosudarstvennoye Politich-eskoye Upravleniye (OGPU), the Unified State Political Administration.

In 1934, the OGPU was returned to NKVD control and renamed the Glavnoye Upravleniye Gosudarstvennoy Bezopasnosti (GUGB), the Chief Directorate of State Security. In early February 1941, the GUGB was removed from the NKVD and given people's-commissariat status, thus creating the Narodnyi Komitet Gosudarstvennoy Bezopasnosti (NKGB), the People's Committee for State Security. This organization was responsible for conducting foreign intelligence gathering and domestic counter-intelligence, seeking out and eliminating sedition, and protecting top party and government officials.

In an odd transitional period that clearly demonstrates the former Soviet government's internal instability, the NKGB's people's-commissariat status was removed in June 1941. The organization was again named the GUGB and placed under the direction of the NKVD. The justification for this was that the German army had attacked, and the very existence of the Soviet government was threatened. By returning the NKGB (GUGB) to the NKVD, the party and the government gained tighter control over internal security.

In the spring of 1943, when the war's tide turned in favor of the Soviets, the GUGB was once again removed from NKVD control and renamed the NKGB. In 1946, the Soviet government underwent a major structural reorganization. All people's commissariats were elevated to ministry status. Consequently, the NKGB became the Ministerstvo Gosudarstvennoy Bezopasnosti (MGB), the Ministry of State Security, while the NKVD became the Ministerstvo Vnutrennikh Del (MVD), Ministry of Internal Affairs.

On March 6, 1953, the day after the death of Soviet premier Joseph Vissarionovich Stalin, the MGB and MVD were combined as the MVD. On March 13, 1954, the organization was again split into two bodies. The MVD retained its original "NKVD" internal security responsibilities. The MGB lost its ministerial status but was designated a "state committee attached to the Council of Ministers" and renamed the KGB. Despite its subordination to the council, the KGB was granted far more autonomy than most other state entities and, to a large degree, was able to operate independently of the council.

Twenty-five years later, on July 5, 1978, the KGB was renamed the "KGB of the Union of Soviet Socialist Republics" and accorded ministerial status.

On August 21, 1991, the KGB attempted to overthrow the Soviet government. KGB Spetnaz units were ordered to storm the Russian parliament building and seize a number of key Soviet leaders. Several senior commanders refused to obey the order, the operation failed, and the instigators were arrested. As a result, on October 24, Soviet president Mikhail Gorbachev signed a decree that abolished the KGB.

The activities of the First Chief Directorate were immediately reestablished as the Tsentralnaya Sluzhbza Razvedkyi (TsSR), the Central Intelligence Service. The Eighth Chief Directorate and 16th Directorate were folded into the Federalnaya Agenstvo Pravitelstennoy Svayazi i Informatsii (FAPSI), the Federal Agency for Government Communications and Information (the equivalent of the NSA). The Ninth Directorate was folded into the new Federalnaya Sluzhba Okhrani (FSO)—the Federal Protective Service—and the Prezidentskaya Sluzhba Bezopasnosti (PSB). The PSB, the Presidential Security Service, is the equivalent of the U.S. Secret Service.

After falling under two short-lived government entities, Second, Third, and Fifth Chief Directorates and the Seventh Directorate were combined to form the Federalnaya Sluzhba Bezopasnosti (FSB), the Federal Security Service.

On December 18, the TsSR was dissolved, and the Sluzhba Vneshney Razvedki Rossii (SVR), or Russian Foreign Intelligence Service, was established. The former TsSR's activities were folded into the SVR. The SVR is the equivalent of the American CIA, Great Britain's M16, and Israel's MOSSAD.

Unlike its KGB predecessor, the First Chief Directorate, the SVR is an independent agency. As such, it reports directly to the Russian president.

Kryptos

Located in the northeast corner of the new CIA headquarters building courtyard at the GEORGE BUSH CENTER FOR INTELLIGENCE is a sculpture entitled *Kryptos.*

The sculpture, by Washington, D.C.–based artist James Sanborn, incorporates a number of themes, from Native Americana to North American geology to the art of information gathering and the science of cryptology. The piece consists of a large S-shaped sheet of copper emerging from a red granite slab. A "special message" of some 2,000 encoded letters has been cut into the sheet, suggesting a paper printout from a computer.

Kryptos was dedicated on November 3, 1990.

KUBARK

KUBARK is the CIA cryptonym for the Agency's headquarters in LANGLEY, VIRGINIA.

See also MOTHER "K."

L

Langer, William Leonard (1896–1977)

A scholar and prolific writer, William Leonard Langer held senior positions in both the CIA and the OFFICE OF STRATEGIC SERVICES (OSS), the World War II predecessor organization to the CIA.

Born in Boston, Massachusetts, on March 16, 1896, to German immigrants Charles Rudolph Langer and Johanna Rockenbach, young Langer lost his father when he was only three years old. Langer attended Harvard, graduating with an A.B. degree in 1915. For the next two years, he taught German at Worcester Academy, also in Massachusetts. While at Worcester he studied international relations at nearby Clark University.

Langer's scholarly pursuits were temporarily placed on hold when the United States entered World War I. In December 1917, he enlisted in the U.S. Army and was deployed to France, where he served in a chemical warfare unit. When the war ended he wrote a history of his unit. He then returned to Harvard as a graduate student in history.

During the winter of 1921–22, Langer did research for his Ph.D. thesis in Vienna, in Austria's Imperial Archives. He simultaneously studied Russian. In 1923, he received a Ph.D. He taught modern European history at Clark for the next four years. He then returned to Harvard, where he served as an assistant professor (1927–31) and an associate professor (1931–36). In 1936, he was named the

Archibald Cary Coolidge Professor of History, a chair he would hold until 1964.

When America entered World War II in December 1941, Langer became a member of the board of analysts in the OFFICE OF THE COORDINATOR OF INFORMATION (COI), the precursor to the OSS. When the latter was established in the summer of 1942, he became its deputy chief and then chief of its Research and Analysis Branch. For his service with the OSS, he was awarded the Medal of Merit.

When the war ended in 1945, Langer was appointed director of the Office of Intelligence Research at the U.S DEPARTMENT OF STATE. In 1946, he was named special assistant to the secretary of state, then returned to Harvard.

In the wake of the North Korean invasion of South Korea in 1950, DIRECTOR OF CENTRAL INTELLIGENCE (DCI) WALTER BEDELL SMITH persuaded Langer to leave Harvard temporarily to establish a unit that would sharpen the CIA's FINISHED INTELLIGENCE skills. As a result, Langer created the OFFICE OF NATIONAL ESTIMATES (ONE). ONE consisted of two elements: an intelligence estimates staff, responsible for drafting NATIONAL INTELLIGENCE ESTIMATES; and the BOARD OF NATIONAL ESTIMATES (BNE), tasked with reviewing the NIEs.

Langer served as assistant director for national estimates at the CIA until 1952. During that same period, he was a member of the National War College's advisory board and a trustee for the Carnegie Endowment for International Peace.

From 1960 to 1961, Langer sat on the PRESIDENT'S FOREIGN INTELLIGENCE ADVISORY BOARD (PFIAB). From 1964 to 1977, he served as professor emeritus at Harvard. He was the director of the Russian Research Center (1954–59) and the Center for Middle East Studies (1954–56).

Throughout his academic career, Langer lectured at the University of Chicago, Columbia University, Yale University, and the Fletcher School of Law and Diplomacy. Upon leaving academia, he served as president of the Harvard Pierian Foundation (1969–73). He was also an editorial adviser to the Houghton Mifflin Company, Harper & Row, and the American Heritage Publishing Company.

Langer published numerous works, including *With "E" of the First Gas* (1919, later published as *Gas and Flame in World War I*), *The Franco-Russian Alliance, 1890–1894* (1929), *European Alliances and Alignments, 1871–1890* (1931), *The Diplomacy of Imperialism, 1890–1902* (1935), *Our Vichy Gamble* (1947), *The Challenge to Isolation, 1937–1940* (1952), *The Undeclared War, 1940–1941* (1953), *Conyers Read, 1881–1959: Scholar, Teacher, Public Servant* (1963), *Political and Social Upheaval, 1832–1852* (1969, later published as *The Revolutions of 1848*), *Explorations in Crisis: Papers on International History* (1969), *The New Illustrated Encyclopedia of World History* (1975), and *Up from the Ranks: The Autobiography of William L. Langer* (1975, later published as *In and Out of the Ivory Tower: The Autobiography of William L. Langer*).

Langer won numerous academic awards including the Bancroft Prize from Columbia University, the Golden Plate Award from American Academy of Achievement, and several honorary doctoral degrees.

Langer died in 1977. He was 81.

Langley, Virginia (CIA headquarters)

Langley, Virginia, where CIA headquarters, also known as the GEORGE BUSH CENTER FOR INTELLIGENCE, is located, is in fact a neighborhood of McLean, Virginia. Agency insiders often refer to CIA headquarters simply as "Langley."

The name "Langley" originated before the town of McLean was founded, in 1910. In 1719, Virginia planter Thomas Lee purchased a tract of land from the sixth Lord Fairfax (for whom Fairfax County, in which McLean is located, was named). Lee named the tract "Langley," after his ancestral home in England. Lee never actually lived on the land, but it soon became home to many European settlers. A few were wealthy settlers to whom the Crown had granted land, and they established large plantations in the area.

As expected, the history of the Langley area is as colorful as that of any of the Potomac-area regions of Northern Virginia. During the War of 1812, British military forces laid siege to Washington, forcing President James Madison and his wife Dolley to flee to the safety of family and friends in Langley. During the American Civil War, Langley became a Union army stronghold in Virginia. It was home to two forts, Camp Griffin and Camp Pierpont, which protected nearby Washington, D.C.

The year 1903, with the establishment of the Great Falls & Old Dominion Railroad, was a defining one for Langley. John McLean, president of the Washington Gas and Light Company and future editor of the *Washington Post,* and Senator Stephen B. Elkins of West Virginia collaborated on construction of a railroad that would bring vacationing Washingtonians to nearby Great Falls and provide people who worked in Washington the choice of living outside of the city. In 1906, the railroad began operating, and the population of Langley and nearby Lewinsville quickly grew. In 1910, the post offices of these towns closed, and a new post office, McLean, was opened. In 1959, the U.S. government broke ground for the CIA headquarters building. Construction was completed in 1961, adding another chapter to McLean's long history.

Despite the name change in 1910, "Langley" is still used to describe the area, and very often to refer to CIA headquarters.

Lansdale, Edward Geary (1908–1987)

A career Air Force officer, Edward Geary Lansdale served in both the CIA and the OFFICE OF STRATEGIC SERVICES (OSS), the World War II predecessor organization to the CIA. He also served as the U.S. DEFENSE DEPARTMENT's senior officer for OPERATION MONGOOSE, a project aimed at toppling the regime of Cuban leader FIDEL CASTRO during the early 1960s.

Lansdale was born in Detroit on February 6, 1908, to Henry "Harry" Lansdale—an automotive industry executive who developed the NAPA auto parts company into a billion-dollar-a-year business—and Sarah Frances Philips. Because of his father's business, young Lansdale moved often. But the family finally settled in Los Angeles when Lansdale was 14 years old. He attended Los Angeles High School, where he joined the Junior Reserve Officers Training Corps, rising to the top cadet post. In 1926, he graduated from high school. The following year, he enrolled in the University of California at Los Angeles (UCLA), where he majored in English.

Active in a number of campus activities, including the college humor magazine, (the *Claw*) and ROTC, Lansdale surprised his family when in 1931 he left UCLA without a degree. He relocated to New York, hoping to both find work as a newspaperman and perhaps attend the Columbia University School of Journalism. Unable to find newspaper work, he accepted a position as a railroad clerk.

In 1935, he returned to California and accepted an advertising job offered by his brother Phil.

Lansdale's advertising career seemed to be taking off when the Japanese attacked Pearl Harbor in 1941. Applying for active military service, he was initially rejected because of an enlarged thyroid discovered during a physical examination. Undaunted, he applied for a health waiver, and in early 1943 he was approved for limited service as an officer in the San Francisco office of the U.S. Army's Military Intelligence Service (MIS).

Not long after, Lansdale applied to and was accepted by the OSS. On December 22, 1943, he was promoted to captain. He spent the remainder of the war in New York City, working for the MIS and the OSS. In August 1945, he was reassigned to Headquarters U.S. Armed Forces Western Pacific, in the Philippines. There he served as chief of the Intelligence Division's analysis branch, responsible for managing many of the particulars of the Japanese surrender of the Ryukyu island chain.

On June 19, 1947, Lansdale was reassigned to the Army's G-2 (intelligence) branch, assisting the government of the Philippines in its efforts against the communist Huk (Hukbalahap) guerrilla forces, which were trying to topple the legitimate government. Lansdale was soon appointed public information officer (PIO) in the Philippines and promoted to lieutenant colonel. As PIO, he worked directly with top leaders and military officers in the Philippine government. He also worked closely with journalists and local business leaders, often assuming responsibilities far above his rank.

On September 26, Lansdale transferred from the Army to the newly established U.S. Air Force (created by the NATIONAL SECURITY ACT OF 1947 from the wartime U.S. Army Air Forces), in the rank of major. In late 1948, he returned to the United States for training in Air Force intelligence at Lowry Air Force Base, in Denver, Colorado. He was then appointed an instructor at Craig Air Force Base, near Selma, Alabama.

On November 13, 1949, Lansdale was detached from the Air Force to work with the CIA as a member of the Far East Division of the OFFICE OF POLICY COORDINATION (OPC), then the Agency's covert action arm.

In September 1950, Lansdale was posted to the Philippines under COVER of the Joint U.S. Military Advisory Group. From 1951 through 1954, he was CHIEF OF STATION (COS) of the CIA's OPC station in Manila. In that capacity, he worked directly with Philippine defense minister Ramon Magsaysay, employing a mix of propaganda, counterinsurgency techniques, and community development programs (winning the hearts and minds) that ultimately helped the Philippines crush the Huk rebellion. Lansdale's efforts became a model for future counterinsurgency operations by the United States. (Unfortunately, the model would produce far less success in Vietnam, where the agency was constantly competing with the U.S. DEPARTMENTS OF STATE and DEFENSE over the best strategy for the war.)

In 1953, Lansdale was ordered to Vietnam, where he was to assess the French situation. In June 1954 he was made chief of the Saigon Military Mission, a group under the CIA but separate from the CIA station.

In the late 1950s Lansdale was transferred to Washington, D.C. There, he assisted retired general Graves B. Erskine in the Defense Department's Office of Special Operations. Lansdale also became the chief Department of Defense representative at U.S. Intelligence Board meetings. In April 1960, he was promoted to brigadier general.

On November 30, 1961, Lansdale became the U.S. Defense Department's senior leader for Operation MONGOOSE, a post–BAY OF PIGS project aimed at toppling the communist regime in Cuba through a myriad of actions including propaganda operations, sabotage, and ASSASSINATION PLOTS against Castro. Lansdale's CIA counterpart was WILLIAM KING HARVEY. However, MONGOOSE was abandoned after the CUBAN MISSILE CRISIS of October 1962. The following year, Lansdale retired from the Air Force at the rank of major general. From 1965 through 1968, he served in Vietnam as a civilian assistant to the U.S. ambassador.

On February 23, 1987, Lansdale died of heart failure at his home in McLean, Virginia. He was 79.

LANYARD

LANYARD was the code name for a satellite intelligence project aimed at gaining higher-resolution imagery than its predecessor program, ARGON. Utilizing the existing framework of CORONA, LANYARD flew one successful mission in 1963.

See also SATELLITE INTELLIGENCE/SURVEILLANCE OPERATIONS.

Lee, Andrew Daulton (1952–)

Andrew Daulton Lee (aka the "Snowman," so named because of his involvement in cocaine trafficking) was convicted of espionage in 1977. Lee, together with accomplice CHRISTOPHER JOHN BOYCE, sold top-secret CIA satellite documents to the KGB in Mexico City. He was sentenced to life in prison.

See also FALCON AND SNOWMAN.

"legal"

A legal is a CIA officer who is operating in a hostile country but is protected by diplomatic immunity. In most cases, a legal is officially (usually as a COVER) connected to the American embassy in that country. A legal is supposed to have immunity from arrest. A legal is sometimes referred to as an INSIDE MAN.

See also ILLEGAL.

"legend"

A legend is a complete COVER story developed for an operative in the field.

legislative oversight of intelligence

The U.S. Congress has been responsible for legislative oversight of the CIA since the establishment of the Agency in 1947. However, until the executive and congressional committees of the mid-1970s were created, oversight responsibilities existed only within the armed services committees of the House and Senate.

Prior to the famous ROCKEFELLER COMMISSION and the CHURCH and PIKE COMMITTEES, the DIRECTOR OF CENTRAL INTELLIGENCE and his representatives interacted directly with the respective chairmen of the armed services committees. Formal hearings and testimony regarding American intelligence activities were rare or nonexistent.

Following allegations of misdeeds on the part of the CIA and the FEDERAL BUREAU OF INVESTIGATION (FBI) in 1975, President Gerald Ford established an investigative body that would investigate those agencies and hold hearings. It was known as the Rockefeller Commission. The Senate and House, both feeling that the presidential panel was a whitewash, created their own investigative bodies, respectively, the Church and Pike Committees. The committees found that there had indeed been unauthorized activities conducted by U.S. intelligence bodies and that future permanent legislative oversight was needed.

On May 19, 1976, the SENATE SELECT COMMITTEE ON INTELLIGENCE (SSCI) was established. Just under two months later, on July 14, the House of Representatives followed suit by creating the HOUSE PERMANENT SELECT COMMITTEE ON INTELLIGENCE (HPSCI). The SSCI and HPSCI, together with the armed services and the foreign relations and foreign affairs committees, were tasked with overseeing the activities of the U.S. intelligence community and authorizing the programs of the individual intelligence agencies.

In 1980, the INTELLIGENCE OVERSIGHT ACT was passed, establishing the current structure by making the SSCI and the HPSCI the only two oversight committees for the CIA. However, the two appropriations committees, given their constitutional role of appropriating funds for all federal activities, also maintain limited oversight responsibilities. The CIA also maintains an Office of Congressional Affairs, which deals directly with oversight issues.

The SSCI and the HPSCI receive all CIA FINISHED INTELLIGENCE products. Additionally, CIA officials present over 1,000 briefings each year to members of Congress as well as various congressional committees and staffs.

See also EXECUTIVE OVERSIGHT OF INTELLIGENCE.

Library, CIA

Boasting some 125,000 books and 1,700 different periodicals, the CIA Library is an expansive repository of information. Located at CIA headquarters in LANGLEY, VIRGINIA, the library maintains three primary collections—reference, circulating, and historical intelligence.

The reference collection includes basic research tools such as encyclopedias, dictionaries, commercial directories, atlases, diplomatic lists, and telephone books from around the world, as well as computers, CD ROMs, and commercial database services. The circulating collection consists of monographs, newspapers, consumer-interest and trade magazines, and professional journals. The historical intelligence collection is an open-source repository in itself, dedicated to the collection, retention, and exploitation of material dealing with global intelligence.

The CIA Library also maintains reciprocal interlibrary-loan programs with other domestic libraries, giving the Agency's employees access to virtually any current or out-of-print book or publication. All three collections are regularly updated, with a focus on current intelligence objectives and priorities. Unfortunately, like the CIA EXHIBIT CENTER, the CIA Library is not open to the general public.

light cover

In CIA parlance, light COVER describes the diplomatic credentials used by CIA officers overseas. For instance, an officer protected by light cover may claim that he or she works as a member of the U.S. embassy staff.

Lindsey, Franklin Anthony (1916–)

In American intelligence circles, Franklin Anthony Lindsey was considered to be an expert in guerrilla and paramilitary operations.

Lindsey was born in Kenton, Ohio, on March 12, 1916. In 1938, he graduated from Stanford University; for the next year, he was employed by the U.S. Steel Corporation.

In 1940, Lindsey joined the U.S. Army and was transferred to the OFFICE OF STRATEGIC SERVICES (OSS), the World War II precursor organization to the CIA. He spent much of his time during the war in the field, participating in operations behind Nazi lines in southern Austria. He also served as the head of an OSS Balkan unit detached to Marshal Josip Broz Tito and his Yugoslav partisans. In 1945, he was made chief of the American military mission to Yugoslavia. When the war ended, he was discharged at the rank of lieutenant colonel and awarded the Legion of Merit.

Lindsey returned to the United States, where he enrolled in Harvard University as a graduate student. He also became executive assistant to Bernard Baruch, the U.S. representative to the United Nations Atomic Energy Commission.

In 1947, he became a consultant to the U.S. House of Representatives Committee on Foreign Aid, which conducted a feasibility study on the proposed Marshall Plan—the plan to rebuild wartorn Europe. The following year, he relocated to Paris, where he worked with the Economic Cooperation Administration.

In 1949, Lindsey was recruited into the CIA. There he was assigned to the OFFICE OF POLICY COORDINATION (OPC), the Agency's early covert-action arm. He soon became the chief of OPC's Eastern European Division. He led the division in a program of training Eastern European agents in spycraft operations. The agents were then infiltrated into their native Eastern bloc nations, where they conducted all manner of espionage work for the CIA. He also served as the CIA representative on a joint British/American Special Policy Committee that coordinated paramilitary/clandestine action operations, codenamed VALUABLE, against the Albanian communists beginning in 1949. However, the ALBANIAN OPERATIONS were compromised on several fronts, forcing the CIA to withdraw from the project in 1953. Lindsey resigned from the CIA that same year.

Lynch, Grayston L. (1923–   )

Credited as the man who fired the first shot in the ill-fated invasion of Cuba at the BAY OF PIGS, Grayston L. Lynch was the CIA's on-site commander during the actual landing operation.

Lynch, born in Texas, was considered to be a soldier's soldier. On June 6, 1944, he landed with American forces at Normandy. He fought in the Battle of the Bulge. He later saw action at Heartbreak Ridge in Korea. During America's involvement in SOUTHEAST ASIA, he reportedly served with the Special Forces in Laos. He left the Army in 1960 at the rank of captain and joined the CIA.

During Operation ZAPATA, the ill-fated invasion of FIDEL CASTRO's Cuba at the Bay of Pigs in April 1961, Lynch commanded the landing operation. He fired the first shot of the operation when a Cuban jeep patrol spotted his landing party hitting the beach. He also reportedly shot down two Cuban warplanes from the deck of his command ship, the *Blagar*.

Following the Bay of Pigs disaster, Lynch directed over 2,100 Miami-based secret missions against Cuba as part of OPERATION MONGOOSE, a post–Bay of Pigs project aimed at toppling the communist regime in Cuba. Lynch directly participated in 113 of those missions.

In 1998, Lynch published *Decision for Disaster: Betrayal at the Bay of Pigs,* an invasion memoir written 20 years earlier, in which he claimed that the administration of President John Kennedy had been largely to blame for the invasion force's failure at the Bay of Pigs. Operation ZAPATA, according to Lynch, "may have been the politically proper way to fight a war, according to the rules laid down by the 'armchair generals' of Camelot. But we called it murder."

See also ROBERTSON, RIP.

M

MacLeish, Archibald (1892–1982)

Soldier, Pulitzer prize–winning poet, and librarian of Congress, Archibald MacLeish (aka Archibald Fleming) served his country in myriad ways. But during World War II, his most important work was with the U.S. War Department's Office of Facts and Figures and the OFFICE OF STRATEGIC SERVICES (OSS), the wartime precursor organization to the CIA.

MacLeish was born on May 7, 1892, in Glencoe, Illinois, to Andrew MacLeish, a successful dry-goods merchant, and Martha Hillard, a college professor. As a boy, MacLeish lived on a 17-acre Lake Michigan estate. But his somewhat rebellious nature compelled his mother to send him to Hotchkiss, a private school noted for strict discipline. As a young man, he attended Yale University, where he majored in English, became chair of the *Yale Literary Monthly,* and excelled in sports. He graduated from Yale in 1915.

When America entered World War I in 1917, MacLeish joined the U.S. Army, initially volunteering as an ambulance driver, later serving in the field artillery and rising to the rank of captain (his brother Ken, a fighter pilot, was killed in action). Following the war, he enrolled at the Harvard Law School, graduating at the head of his class in 1919. He then taught law for a semester in Harvard's government department but rejected an offer to teach at the Law School. Instead he worked briefly as an editor for the *New Republic* magazine.

In September 1920, MacLeish joined the law firm of Choate, Hall, and Stewart in Boston. He proved to be a fine lawyer. But in February 1923, on the day of his promotion to partner in a Boston law firm, he gave up the practice of law and relocated to Paris with his wife and children. There, he devoted his time to his family and to writing poetry.

In Paris MacLeish befriended such members of the famous 1920s expatriate literary community as Kay Boyle, Ezra Pound, E. E. Cummings, John Dos Passos, F. Scott Fitzgerald, James Joyce, and Ernest Hemingway (with whom he developed a close relationship). As a poet, MacLeish published a number of collections, including *The Happy Marriage* (1924), *The Pot of Earth* (1925), *Streets on the Moon* (1926), and *The Hamlet of A. MacLeish* (1928).

MacLeish returned to the United States in the late 1920s in order to research the history of the Spanish conquest of Mexico, eventually publishing *Conquistador* (1932). The book won him a Pulitzer Prize. From 1920 to 1939, he served as a member of *Fortune* magazine's editorial board. During that period, he wrote two radio dramas meant to foster a greater sense of American patriotism and warn Americans against the danger of fascism, which was spreading across Europe.

In 1939, President Franklin Roosevelt appointed MacLeish librarian of Congress. He served in that capacity for the next five years. MacLeish was a thorough administrator. He reorganized the library's offices and established a series of poetry readings. He simultaneously served as both the director of the Department of War's Office of Facts and Figures and the assistant director of the Office of War Information.

During America's involvement in World War II, MacLeish worked directly with WILLIAM J. "WILD BILL" DONOVAN, the head of the OSS, presenting him with plans to analyze the strengths and weaknesses of Axis military and intelligence forces.

In 1944, MacLeish was appointed assistant secretary of state for cultural affairs. When the war ended in 1945, he became the first American member of UNESCO—the United Nations Educational, Scientific, and Cultural Organization—chairing the first UNESCO conference in Paris.

In 1949, MacLeish was named Harvard's Boylston Professor of Rhetoric and Oratory. He served in that capacity until 1962. During that same period, MacLeish published *Collected Poems* (1952), which earned him a second Pulitzer, as well as the National Book Award and the Bollingen Prize. His *J.B.* (1958), a poetic drama based on the Old Testament book of Job, became a Broadway hit and earned him a third Pulitzer.

From 1963 to 1967 he held the post of Simpson Lecturer at Amherst College. In 1965, he won an Academy Award for his screenplay of *The Eleanor Roosevelt Story.*

Among his many other works are *The Wild Wicked Old Man* (1968), *The Human Season* (1972), *Collected Poems, 1917–1982* (1985), *Riders on the Earth* (1978), and *Scratch* (1971), a play based on Stephen Vincent Benét's *The Devil and Daniel Webster.*

MacLeish died in April 1982. He was a few weeks shy of 90.

mail-intercept operations

One of the most controversial CIA projects to be exposed during the 1975 CHURCH COMMITTEE hearings (the Select Committee to Study Governmental Operations with respect to Intelligence Activities) was the Agency's mail-intercept program, which existed from 1952 to 1973.

In a program code-named HT-LINGUAL (unofficially, the CI PROJECT), CIA officers based in the United States intercepted some 215,000 letters mailed to and from the Soviet Union and China. The sealed envelopes were surreptitiously opened by the officers (utilizing a method known as the FLAPS AND SEALS technique), read, and photographed at a special CIA mail facility in New York's La Guardia Airport, screened for microdots and secret writing,

and their mailing and return addresses recorded, before being reentered into the postal system.

The project, initiated by the Agency's controversial COUNTERINTELLIGENCE chief JAMES JESUS ANGLETON, began as a plan for simply recording the information on the exteriors of certain suspect envelopes. In 1955, CIA operations chief and future DIRECTOR OF CENTRAL INTELLIGENCE (DCI) RICHARD MCGARRAH HELMS expanded the project to include the systematic opening of mail in a "secure" room at La Guardia.

A subproject of HT-LINGUAL was KMSOURDOUGH, the cryptonym for an Agency mail-intercept operation based in San Francisco, California, from September 1969 to October 1971. The operation, unknown to U.S. postal officials, targeted mail from an unspecified Asian nation, later presumed to have been the People's Republic of China.

Known unofficially by the nickname WEST POINTER, KMSOURDOUGH was a project wherein CIA operatives surreptitiously picked up envelopes at a U.S. post office, stuffed them in their pockets, and delivered them to the CIA's TECHNICAL SERVICES DIVISION (TSD) for evaluation. Concluding that it was producing few counterintelligence leads, the Agency shut down the HT-LINGUAL project in 1973. HT-LINGUAL was disclosed during the Church Committee hearings in 1975, but the "Asian nation" targeted in KMSOURDOUGH was not.

Marine Corps intelligence, U.S.

Marine Corps intelligence is an arm of the U.S. Marine Corps responsible for collecting, controlling, exploiting, and defending information pertaining to Marine land, sea, and air operations, while denying any potential adversary the ability to do the same.

Like its Army, Navy, and Air Force counterparts, Marine Corps intelligence is overseen by the DEFENSE INTELLIGENCE AGENCY (DIA). Marine Corps intelligence also reports to the president, through the NATIONAL SECURITY ADVISOR (NSA). Additionally, the service's activities are overseen—and coordinated with the efforts of the other members of the U.S. INTELLIGENCE COMMUNITY— by the CIA's DIRECTOR OF CENTRAL INTELLIGENCE (DCI).

See also AIR FORCE INTELLIGENCE; ARMY INTELLIGENCE; NAVAL INTELLIGENCE.

MASINT (measurement and signature intelligence)

A CIA acronym for *measurement and signature intelligence,* MASINT is simply intelligence collected by means of identifying the "signature" features of electromagnetic emissions. For example; radar signals, acoustic or sound

John Alex McCone shaking hands with President John F. Kennedy after being sworn in as director of central intelligence   (JOHN F. KENNEDY LIBRARY)

sources, nuclear test detonations, and lasers are all potential sources of MASINT.

See also ALL-SOURCE INTELLIGENCE; INTELLIGENCE CYCLE; INTELLIGENCE DISCIPLINES, FIVE PRIMARY.

McCone, John Alex (1902–1991)

John Alex McCone is best known as the DIRECTOR OF CENTRAL INTELLIGENCE (DCI) who served as a member of President John Kennedy's secret Executive Committee, or EXCOMM, during the CUBAN MISSILE CRISIS of 1962.

McCone was born in San Francisco, California, to Alexander J. McCone and Margaret Enright on January 4, 1902. In 1922, McCone graduated from the University of California. He initially began work in the steel business, going on to start up several steel and construction-related companies. In 1937, he became one of the cofounders of Bechtel-McCone, which was destined to become one of the

world's largest construction companies. Another McCone company, the California Shipbuilding Corporation, built ships for the U.S. government during World War II. But his success was so great that McCone's detractors accused him of being "a war profiteer," an allegation that led to a federal investigation in 1946 wherein it was charged that McCone and his associates had made $44 million on an investment of $100,000.

McCone soon left the private sector and entered government service. He briefly served on a presidential panel and then became an assistant to Secretary of Defense James V. Forrestal (the first defense secretary, in 1948). In that capacity, McCone outlined the U.S. DEFENSE DEPARTMENT's first budgets and assisted in the establishment of the CIA. President Harry Truman appointed McCone undersecretary of the Air Force in 1950. He then briefly left government service.

Considered to be one of the staunchest anticommunists of his day, McCone garnered national attention when in 1956, as a trustee of the California Institute of Technology (CIT), he publicly castigated CIT professors who backed an American-Soviet nuclear test-ban treaty. He argued that the faculty members had been duped by communist propaganda. He returned to the government in 1958, when President Dwight Eisenhower named him chairman of the Atomic Energy Commission (AEC).

McCone was appointed DCI by President Kennedy, assuming the post on November 29, 1961. When Kennedy announced in September 1961 that McCone was his choice to succeed ousted DCI ALLEN WELSH DULLES, many Washington insiders, liberals in particular, were taken aback. Though Dulles, who had overseen the disastrous invasion of Cuba at the BAY OF PIGS, was considered a somewhat dangerous director, McCone seemed even more hawkish. But the McCone choice was pure political strategy. Kennedy needed support from conservatives, who were prone to attack his foreign policy decisions; he had to fire Dulles after the Bay of Pigs; and McCone, who was charged with cleaning house at the Agency, could be directly controlled from the Oval Office. Additionally, McCone was not nearly as interested in covert operations as Dulles had been. McCone's forte was intelligence analysis.

In September 1962, a NATIONAL INTELLIGENCE ESTIMATE was issued predicting that the Soviet Union would not install offensive missiles in Cuba. McCone disagreed with the estimate, arguing that recently installed Soviet surface-to-air missiles were there to defend planned ballistic missile sites against air attacks. His conclusion was correct.

In mid-October, the CIA produced detailed aerial photographs of Soviet missile installations being constructed on Cuba. The missiles, once operational, would have been able to destroy much of the continental United States within minutes after being launched. McCone, who was vacationing on the French Riviera, returned to Washington to supervise CIA activities in what would become known as the Cuban missile crisis.

McCone resigned as DCI on April 28, 1965, and reentered private business. He became a member of the board of International Telephone and Telegraph (ITT) and was directly involved in that company's proposal to fund partially a CIA operation aimed at preventing Dr. Salvador Allende Gossens, a Marxist candidate for the Chilean presidency, from coming to power in 1970. ITT officials, as well as officials of several other American-owned companies with operations in CHILE, feared that Allende would nationalize their businesses if elected. ITT's proposal was rejected, and Allende won. But in 1973, he was killed and his government overthrown in a military coup led by Chilean army general Augusto Pinochet. The Pinochet forces were not supported by the CIA. However,

the CIA was aware of a coup plot, and there were "intelligence collection relationships" between the Agency and many of its planners.

McCone, who continued to serve as a consultant to the CIA, died in Pebble Beach, California, on February 14, 1991. He was 89.

McCord, James Walter, Jr. (ca. 1918/24–   )

James Walter McCord, Jr., was one of the five burglars arrested for breaking into the WATERGATE complex in the summer of 1972. He was also a CIA operative, with an elusive background.

McCord was born on July 26 (between 1918 and 1924) in Waurika, Oklahoma. On December 7, 1941, the United States entered World War II. The following year, McCord joined the FEDERAL BUREAU OF INVESTIGATION (FBI), serving in "radio intelligence." In 1943, he left the FBI and entered the U.S. Army Air Corps.

When World War II ended in 1945, McCord enrolled in the University of Texas, from which he later graduated. In 1948, he returned to the FBI, and in 1951 he joined the CIA.

McCord initially served in the Agency's Office of Security. He was purportedly involved in OPERATION ZAPATA, the ill-fated invasion of Cuba at the BAY OF PIGS in 1961. He served in Europe during the early 1960s and eventually became the CIA's physical security division chief. In 1970, he left the Agency and soon thereafter opened McCord Associates, Inc., a private security firm based in Rockville, Maryland.

But McCord's life took a dark turn when he was recruited by E. HOWARD HUNT and BERNARD BARKER, both former CIA operatives, for work with the Republican National Committee's "Committee to Re-elect the President" or CREEP. With CREEP, McCord became one of the infamous White House "PLUMBERS," a group of freelance operatives hired to "plug leaks" within the administration of President Richard Nixon.

On the night of June 17, 1972, McCord and four other plumbers—Eugenio Martinez, Virgilio Gonzalez, Frank Sturgis, and Barker—broke into the Washington, D.C., Watergate complex with the objective of obtaining information from the Democratic Party's national headquarters office there. The five men were discovered and arrested. The burglary proved to be one of the greatest political malefactions in American history. The scandal, which involved the highest levels of government in a number of illegal activities, forced Nixon to resign from the presidency in 1974, in order to avoid impeachment. It also resulted in CIA activities being exposed to the light of public scrutiny to a degree that the Agency had never before experienced.

McCord was convicted and sentenced to a term of imprisonment in 1973. He was released in 1975.

Memorial Garden, CIA

Designed as a "tranquil and reflective retreat" for CIA headquarters employees, the beautiful CIA Memorial Garden is situated on a gently sloping hillside between the original headquarters building and the Agency's auditorium at CIA headquarters in LANGLEY, VIRGINIA.

The garden features a blend of natural and landscaped plants surrounded by rock outcrops and a large pond. A brass plaque set in fieldstone adjacent to the pond is inscribed with the words: "In Remembrance of Those Whose Unheralded Efforts Served a Grateful Nation."

The CIA Memorial Garden was designed in 1995 by Sheila Brady of Oehme, Van Sweden & Associates, a landscape architectural firm. The garden was dedicated in 1996.

See also BOOK OF HONOR; *KRYPTOS*; MEMORIAL WALL, OFFICE OF STRATEGIC SERVICES.

Memorial Wall, CIA

The CIA Memorial Wall is a silent tribute to the nearly 80 men and women of the CIA who were killed during their Agency service. Located in the lobby of the original CIA headquarters building in LANGLEY, VIRGINIA, the wall bears 79 bronze stars, each representing a deceased Agency officer. Below the stars on a marble shelf, the glass-encased BOOK OF HONOR is displayed. The book features a corresponding gold star for each of the wall's stars, as well as inscribed names for over half of the honored dead (only the names of those CIA officers whose Agency-related deaths have been declassified are listed in the Book of Honor).

An inscription on the Memorial Wall above the stars reads: "In Honor of Those Members of the Central Intelligence Agency Who Gave Their Lives in the Service of Their Country." The inscription, the stars, and the Book of Honor are flanked by the flags of the United States and the CIA.

In a ceremony commemorating the 78th star on June 8, 2001, DEPUTY DIRECTOR OF CENTRAL INTELLIGENCE (DDCI) John E. McLaughlin made the following comments: "Those who seek the essence of our Agency—its ethic, its spirit, its drive—need only come to this wall. For each day, in this building and throughout the world, the men and women of the CIA strive to keep faith with those whose extraordinary commitment we honor here." A 79th star was added to memorialize the life of CIA operations officer JOHNNY MICHAEL "MIKE" SPANN, the first American killed in action during the war against TERRORISM. Each year, a Memorial Day ceremony is held at the Memorial Wall to honor Agency employees killed in the line of duty.

The CIA Memorial Wall was commissioned by the CIA Fine Arts Commission in May 1973 and unveiled in July 1974. It was designed and sculpted by artist Harold Vogel.

See also *KRYPTOS*; MEMORIAL GARDEN, CIA; MEMORIAL WALL, OFFICE OF STRATEGIC SERVICES.

Memorial Wall, Office of Strategic Services

Dedicated in 1992 on the 50th anniversary of the founding of the OFFICE OF STRATEGIC SERVICES (OSS), the OSS Memorial honors operatives killed in action while serving as members of the OSS (the CIA's predecessor organization) during World War II.

Located opposite the CIA MEMORIAL WALL in the lobby of the original CIA headquarters building in LANGLEY, VIRGINIA, the OSS Memorial Wall consists of a single star and above it an inscription that reads: "In Honor of Those Members of the Office of Strategic Services Who Gave Their Lives in the Service of Their Country." To the right of the star and inscription stands a statue of OSS director WILLIAM J. "WILD BILL" DONOVAN; it was dedicated in 1988. Below the star and to the left is an OSS Memorial book, listing the names of OSS members killed during the war. The memorial is flanked by the flags of the United States and the CIA.

See also BOOK OF HONOR; *KRYPTOS*; MEMORIAL GARDEN, CIA.

Meyer, Cord (1920–2001)

Known as a "titan" and "one of the great minds of covert action," CIA officer Cord Meyer was considered to be a master in the manipulation of the foreign press during the COLD WAR. But Meyer's was a tragic life.

Born in Washington, D.C., on November 10, 1920 (the 145th birthday of the U.S. Marine Corps), young Meyer was one of four brothers (two sets of twins), all of whom were destined to become Marine Corps officers. Raised in New England and Europe, Meyer graduated from St. Paul's School in Concord, New Hampshire, in 1939, and enrolled in Yale University, from which he graduated in 1942 with bachelor's degrees in English and philosophy.

With World War II in full swing, Meyer joined the U.S. Marine Corps Reserve. He was commissioned a second lieutenant in 1943 and shipped out to the South Pacific. As a weapons platoon commander, he saw close combat against the Japanese on Guam.

During a grenade attack in 1944, Meyer suffered a severe head wound that cost him his left eye (tragically, his twin brother Quentin would be killed during the invasion of Okinawa). For his service, Meyer was awarded a Purple Heart, a Bronze Star, and a Presidential Unit Citation. He was discharged at the rank of captain.

In 1946, Meyer won an O. Henry Prize, Best First-Published Story, for his short story *Waves of Darkness*, a fictional account of the fighting on Guam that appeared in the *Atlantic Monthly*. A portion of that piece reads: "The only certain fruit of this insanity will be the rotting bodies upon which the sun will impartially shine tomorrow. Let us throw down these guns that we hate." Meyer later won an MGM Atlantic Prize for the same story.

Having written several pieces about the war, Meyer began working on a series of articles proposing a permanent world government organization and, in at least one instance, criticizing the newly formed United Nations (UN). In 1947, he was a key figure in the establishment of the United World Federalists (UWF), an organization whose primary aim was to transform the UN into a "true world government" with absolute power over its member nations. Such a world government, he believed, was essential if the world was to avoid a nuclear holocaust. That same year, he published *Peace or Anarchy,* a book detailing the views of the UWF. He also became active in the creation of the American Veterans Committee, an organization dedicated to the idea that veterans in postwar America should receive no special treatment.

Meyer soon became disillusioned with the world federalist movement, believing that the communists would never respect or adhere to the requirements of the UWF. In 1949, he left the UWF for Harvard University, where he began researching the origins of the cold war. But with the test detonation of an atomic bomb by the Soviet Union that same year, the Berlin blockade of the previous year, and the communist invasion of South Korea, his dreams of permanent arms control and an end to war began to dissipate.

In 1951, after receiving a Ph.D. from Harvard, Meyer was recruited into the CIA's OFFICE OF POLICY COORDINATION (OPC) by ALLEN WELSH DULLES, chief of the Agency's CLANDESTINE SERVICE (and destined to become DIRECTOR OF CENTRAL INTELLIGENCE). With OPC, Meyer worked in the newly established International Organizations Division (IOD), which provided clandestine support to noncommunist organizations worldwide. The IOD also managed RADIO FREE EUROPE (RFE) and Radio Liberty (RL), the CIA's propaganda-disseminating radio stations in Europe.

Two years after joining the CIA, Meyer was temporarily relieved of duties after he was accused by the FEDERAL BUREAU OF INVESTIGATION (FBI) of being a communist sympathizer. An Agency hearing eventually acquitted him of all charges. Former UN ambassador Jeane J. Kirkpatrick would later say, "He [Meyer] was young and idealistic and very much involved in the one-world movement. But, he was a consistent anti-communist."

In 1954, Meyer became chief of the IOD. He became chief of the CIA's Clandestine Service Covert Action Staff when the IOD merged with it in 1962. In July 1967, he was named assistant deputy director for plans (operations).

During this period Meyer's personal life was mired in two tragedies and a controversy that reached the highest levels of government. Shortly after World War II, Meyer had married Mary Pinchot, an artist. In 1959, their nine-year-old son Michael was killed in an automobile accident. The couple divorced soon thereafter. In 1964, Mary was found shot to death in a remote area along the old Chesapeake & Ohio Canal towpath near Washington, D.C.

A few days after her death, Mary's sister, Tony Pinchot, and Pinchot's new husband, Benjamin C. Bradlee (the future *Washington Post* editor who became famous for directing the WATERGATE investigation) allegedly found CIA COUNTERINTELLIGENCE chief JAMES JESUS ANGLETON attempting to break into Mary's house. Angleton claimed he was trying to recover her diary. In his memoirs, *A Good Life,* Bradlee contends that the diary was discovered later that day by himself and Pinchot. According to Bradlee, the diary revealed an adulterous relationship between Mary and President John Kennedy. "After reading only a few phrases it was clear that the lover had been the President of the United States, though his name was never mentioned," wrote Bradlee. Mary Meyer's murder was never solved.

In 1967, Meyer's work with the Agency came to light when *Ramparts* magazine (a liberal political publication) revealed that the CIA, under Meyer's direction, had provided financial support to the National Student Association as part of an anticommunist campaign. The revelation initiated politically based criticism of the CIA from both the left and the right.

In 1972, Meyer again felt the heat of public scrutiny when it was revealed that he had asked a former world federalist colleague, who was then working in the publishing industry, to allow the Agency to review galley proofs of a book that dealt with the CIA's alleged connection to drug trafficking in SOUTHEAST ASIA.

In 1973, Meyer was made CHIEF OF STATION (COS) in London, a post he held until 1976. It was during his time in London that congressional hearings into CIA misdeeds were held in Washington. His COS responsibilities included allaying British fears that the American inquiries might endanger their own sources.

Upon his return from London, Meyer served briefly as special assistant to DEPUTY DIRECTOR OF CENTRAL INTELLIGENCE (DDCI) E. HENRY KNOCHE. Meyer retired from the CIA in 1977.

During the 1980s and 1990s, Meyer was a lecturer at Georgetown University's School of Foreign Service. He was also a columnist for the *Washington Times.* In addition to *Peace or Anarchy,* he wrote and published *Facing Reality* (1980).

Meyer, who spent his last years in a long-term-care facility, died of complications at 80 from lymphoma on March 13, 2001. A three-time recipient of the Distinguished Intelligence Medal, Meyer was buried in Arlington National Cemetery.

See also CHURCH COMMITTEE; PIKE COMMITTEE.

MI5

MI5 (Military Intelligence, Department 5), the British COUNTERINTELLIGENCE Agency, is the United Kingdom's counterpart organization of the counterintelligence branches in both the CIA and the FEDERAL BUREAU OF INVESTIGATION (FBI).

MI6

MI6 (Military Intelligence, Department 6), or British Secret Service, is the United Kingdom's counterpart organization of the CIA.

MICE

In CIA and U.S. INTELLIGENCE COMMUNITY parlance, MICE is an acronym for money, ideology, compromise, and ego—the four keys that can be used to turn someone into a traitor or a DOUBLE AGENT.

Money (M) and ideology (I) are usually considered the primary motivating factors for traitors. However, compromise (C) is also a strong motivator. Compromise is broken down into three subcategories: heterosexual, homosexual, and nonsexual (being compromised by an activity that one does not want disclosed but does not involve sexual activity).

Ego (E) has often served as a motivator when the individuals in question are either disgruntled or feel that to "turn" proves that they are "smarter" than their peers, and that if they do they cannot be discovered.

Midday Intelligence Report (MID)

The *Midday Intelligence Report* (MID) is an update of the *NATIONAL INTELLIGENCE DAILY* (NID), a compilation of significant current-intelligence matters pertaining to national policy. The *MID*, prepared only by the CIA, is delivered to key policy makers each afternoon.

Mighty Wurlitzer

"Mighty Wurlitzer" was a term coined by FRANK GARDINER WISNER, onetime head of the CIA's OFFICE OF POLICY COORDINATION, to describe the Agency's vast intelligence-gathering and propaganda network during the early years of the COLD WAR, the competition between the United States and the Soviet Union following World War II. According to writer Daniel Brandt, "Wisner created the first 'information superhighway.' But this was the age of vacuum tubes, not computers, so he called it his 'Mighty Wurlitzer.'"

mind-control drug testing

In the early 1950s, the CIA's TECHNICAL SERVICES DIVISION (TSD) began a series of mind-control drug testing projects aimed at discovering or developing a substance that would enable Agency scientists to control or disable the human mind.

The initial project, code-named MKULTRA, was the result of reports that American prisoners of war in Korea were being brainwashed by their communist captors. In April 1953, DIRECTOR OF CENTRAL INTELLIGENCE (DCI) ALLEN WELSH DULLES authorized the TSD to begin MKULTRA. Documentation produced years later revealed that MKULTRA was a vast series of mind-control drug experimentation subprojects. The drugs under development included substances that would:

- "Promote illogical thinking and impulsiveness to the point where the recipient would be discredited in public."
- "Increase the efficiency of mentation and perception."
- "Prevent or counteract the intoxicating effect of alcohol."
- "Promote the intoxicating effect of alcohol."
- "Produce the signs and symptoms of recognized diseases in a reversible way so that they may be used for malingering, etc."
- "Render the indication of hypnosis easier or otherwise enhance its usefulness."
- "Enhance the ability of individuals to withstand privation, torture and coercion during interrogation and so-called 'brainwashing.'"
- "Produce amnesia for events preceding and during their use."
- "Produc[e] shock and confusion over extended periods of time and capable of surreptitious use."
- "Produce physical disablement such as paralysis of the legs, acute anemia, etc."
- "Produce 'pure' euphoria with no subsequent letdown."
- "Alter personality structure in such a way that the tendency of the recipient to become dependent upon another person is enhanced."
- "Cause mental confusion of such a type that the individual under its influence will find it difficult to maintain a fabrication under questioning."
- "Lower the ambition and general working efficiency of men when administered in undetectable amounts."
- "Promote weakness or distortion of the eyesight or hearing faculties, preferably without permanent effects."

MKULTRA lasted from 1953 to 1964. MKSEARCH, which succeeded MKULTRA, began in 1966 and continued until 1972. The Agency's mind-control drug testing came to light during the executive and congressional hearings of the mid-1970s.

See also AMAZON NATURAL DRUG COMPANY; CHURCH COMMISSION; GOTTLIEB, DR. SIDNEY; KING, J. C.; OLSON, FRANK; PIKE COMMISSION; ROCKEFELLER COMMISSION.

MKNAOMI

MKNAOMI was the code name for a project initiated by the CIA's TECHNICAL SERVICES DIVISION (TSD) and aimed at developing poisons for use by the CIA and its clients. (The letters MK represented the TSD. NAOMI represented the project itself.)

MKSEARCH

MKSEARCH was the code name for the continuation of Project MKULTRA, the CIA's drug experimentation/behavioral-modification program that lasted from 1953 to 1964.

Federal funding for MKSEARCH began in 1966 and continued until 1972. MKSEARCH was a parent project under which a number of drug experimentation subprojects were funded by the federal government, with little or no knowledge outside of the Agency's TECHNICAL SERVICES DIVISION (TSD). (The letters MK represented the TSD; SEARCH represented the project itself.)

See also AMAZON NATURAL DRUG COMPANY; CHURCH COMMISSION; GOTTLIEB, DR. SIDNEY; KING, J. C.; MIND-CONTROL DRUG TESTING; MKULTRA; OLSON, FRANK; PIKE COMMISSION; ROCKEFELLER COMMISSION.

MKULTRA

MKULTRA was the code name for a secret CIA project conducted from 1953 to 1964 that involved MIND-CONTROL DRUG TESTING and behavioral modification.

MKULTRA was a parent project under which a number of drug experimentation subprojects were funded by the federal government, with little or no knowledge outside of the Agency's Technical Services Division (TSD). (The letters MK represented the TSD; ULTRA represented the project itself.)

See also AMAZON NATURAL DRUG COMPANY; CHURCH COMMISSION; GOTTLIEB, DR. SIDNEY; KING, J. C.; MKSEARCH; OLSON, FRANK; PIKE COMMISSION; ROCKEFELLER COMMISSION.

MOCKINGBIRD, Operation

Operation MOCKINGBIRD was a CIA project launched in the late 1940s aimed at recruiting American journalists and media companies for Agency propaganda work. The effort was overseen by FRANK GARDINER WISNER, one of the Agency's early covert-action experts; ALLEN WELSH DULLES, a future DIRECTOR OF CENTRAL INTELLIGENCE (DCI); and RICHARD M. HELMS, another future DCI. Numerous accounts of the operation suggest that a fourth key player was Philip Graham, the publisher of the *Washington Post*.

Over time, the Agency's media assets allegedly included the American Broadcasting Company (ABC), the National Broadcasting Company (NBC), the Columbia Broadcasting System (CBS), *Time, Newsweek,* the Associated Press (AP), United Press International (UPI), Reuters, the *New York Times,* Hearst Newspapers, Scripps-Howard News, and the Copley News Service. At the height of MOCKINGBIRD, approximately 25 news organizations and 400 journalists were alleged to have been involved either directly or indirectly at some level with the CIA.

mole

A mole is a member of an intelligence service who reports the activities of that organization to an opposing or hostile intelligence organization. The term "mole" began to be widely used in CIA and other U.S. intelligence community circles during the 1970s.

The origin of the word is unclear. Some have attributed it to famed British spy novelist John Le Carré. However, Sir Francis Bacon made mention of "moles" in his 1622 history of King Henry VII: "Hee was careful and liberal to obtaine good Intelligence from all parts abroad. . . . He had such moles perpetually working and casting to undermine him." A mole is also known as a "penetration agent." Moles are often confused with DOUBLE AGENTs, operatives who serve two opposing intelligence organizations. In the early 1960s, JAMES JESUS ANGLETON, the CIA's then chief of COUNTERINTELLIGENCE, became convinced that the Agency had been penetrated by numerous moles after it was revealed that his friend and former British intelligence officer HAROLD ADRIAN RUSSELL "KIM" PHILBY had supplied the Soviets with Western secrets for nearly 30 years. Philby defected to the Soviet Union in 1963. Angleton's exaggerated fears of a mole-infested CIA led to his being abruptly retired in 1974.

MONGOOSE, Operation

Operation MONGOOSE was a long-term, but unsuccessful, CIA project aimed at toppling the communist regime in Cuba through a range of actions including propaganda operations, sabotage, and ASSASSINATION PLOTS against Cuban leader FIDEL CASTRO.

Initiated on November 30, 1961, by U.S. president John Kennedy, MONGOOSE was directed by EDWARD GEARY LANSDALE, a U.S. Air Force officer and former CIA COUNTERINSURGENCY specialist; WILLIAM KING HARVEY, head of the operation's sabotage/paramilitary arm, known as TASK FORCE W; and Attorney General Robert Kennedy. Mongoose was abandoned after the CUBAN MISSILE CRISIS of October 1962.

Moore, Edwin G., II (1921–)

Edwin G. Moore II was a retired CIA employee who was found guilty of conducting espionage activities for the Soviet Union in the late 1970s.

On December 21, 1976, in a bungled attempt to sell Agency secrets to the Soviets, Moore tossed a package containing classified CIA documents over the fence of a Washington, D.C., apartment complex where Russian officials working for the Soviet embassy were residing. The Russians, who feared the package might be a bomb, immediately contacted the FEDERAL BUREAU OF INVESTIGATION (FBI). When FBI agents opened the box, they found not only the CIA documents but a note from Moore addressed to the Soviets demanding $3,000 for the documents and an additional $197,000 for promised further material.

The following day, Moore was arrested after the FBI arranged a false DROP that he believed was his payment from the Soviets. A search of Moore's Bethesda, Maryland, home revealed 10 large crates of classified CIA documents that he had hoped to sell.

A former Agency mapmaker and logistician with 22 years of service, Moore had retired from the CIA in 1973. Though financial gain was considered to be a strong motivation for his treason, he was also disgruntled because he believed that he had not received promotions that he deserved while with the Agency.

Moore, who insisted throughout his trial that he was a "pawn of the Agency," pled not guilty by reason of insanity. Still, he was convicted of conducting espionage activities against the United States and sentenced to 15 years in prison. The Court also ordered that he undergo psychiatric treatment. Moore was granted parole in 1979.

Mossad Le Aliyah Beth (MOSSAD)

The Mossad Le Aliyah Beth, or MOSSAD, the Israeli intelligence service, is Israel's counterpart to the CIA. Israel is a staunch American ally. As the MOSSAD is considered one of the world's foremost intelligence-gathering and covert-action entities, the CIA considers it a key source of both Middle Eastern and global intelligence for the United States.

Mother "K"

Mother "K" is an affectionate term used by CIA employees to describe CIA headquarters in LANGLEY, VIRGINIA. The term was derived from KUBARK, the Agency's cryptonym for CIA headquarters.

movies, television, and popular culture, CIA in

The mystique surrounding the CIA—as well as its World War II predecessor organization, the OFFICE OF STRATEGIC SERVICES (OSS)—has for decades spawned countless books (fiction and nonfiction), magazine articles, movies, and television programs that have portrayed the Agency in both a good and bad light.

In everything from JAMES BOND books and films, where the British Secret Service's top agent, 007, often works with CIA counterparts; to author Tom Clancy's military-techno thrillers; to television's *The X-files;* to film director Oliver Stone's conspiracy plots—the CIA has been viewed with both guarded admiration and skepticism by audiences who have never been able to understand fully its responsibilities or the scope of its power.

Indiana University history professor Jonathan Nashel wrote that during the COLD WAR's zenith, "the CIA attained an almost mythical public power. This is remarkable, especially when one considers that the organization and its forerunner, the Office of Strategic Studies, were initially viewed with an instinctive distrust—a distrust of the mandate to spy based on principles of American liberty and self-reliance." He added, "In this sense, the CIA has become both a safety valve and a repository for the dark side of America's foreign policy history." For many Americans, however, the growing historical distance of the Vietnam War as well as increased congressional oversight of the U.S. INTELLIGENCE COMMUNITY has created an evolving perception of the CIA, which is today one more of fascination than distrust.

Prior to the SEPTEMBER 11, 2001, TERRORIST ATTACKS ON THE UNITED STATES, two new CIA-based television dramas were slated that were predicted to appeal to America's fascination with foreign intelligence and the men and women involved in espionage work. The programs, CBS's *The Agency* (the first program allowed to film segments in CIA headquarters) and ABC's *Alias* have since begun airing; the proverbial jury of American opinion is still out on their success. Still, the programs reflect something of a post–cold war about-face in the way the American public views its CIA. This can be attributed to an evolving perception that though the CIA is still secret, it is somehow more accessible. Some of the mystique that has fueled the Agency's portrayal in pop culture has been stripped away by the fact that Agency officials have become more public, and not in the sense of being under scrutiny.

In a role considered "out of the box" for a DIRECTOR OF CENTRAL INTELLIGENCE (DCI), GEORGE JOHN TENET was sent to mediate a peace accord between the Israelis and the Palestinians. Though Tenet brought about only temporary peace, he was viewed as a compassionate DCI, not one simply directing those who move in the shadows. In the past, when CIA officers were killed in the line of duty, the American public was unaware of it. Family members were often provided COVER stories about an officer's demise. But when CIA officer JOHNNY "MIKE" SPANN became the first American serviceman killed during America's WAR AGAINST TERRORISTS, the general public was allowed to mourn his loss.

America is beginning to view the CIA as an organization where ordinary Americans do extraordinary things.

The alternative press, however, still points to the CIA as the source of all manner of conspiratorial misdeeds—ASSASSINATION PLOTS, MIND-CONTROL DRUG TESTING, and manipulation of the self-determination of other nations. Both the alternative and the mainstream press point to turncoats like ALDRICH HAZEN AMES and ROBERT PHILIP HANSSEN as proof that the U.S. Intelligence Community is not adequately policing itself. Thus, to many Americans, the CIA is still, as the late senator Frank Church once stated, "a rogue elephant on a rampage." But its face in popular culture is clearly evolving in a favorable direction.

See also FLEMING, IAN LANCASTER.

mugbook

A "mugbook" is a photographic file containing pictures and biographical sketches of hostile spies operating within the region of responsibility for a given CIA station. Agency officers operating in the region must familiarize themselves with the mugbook for that station. Mugbooks are maintained by stations worldwide.

Murphy Commission

The Murphy Commission (officially the Commission on the Organization of the Government for the Conduct of Foreign Policy) was a panel created in 1975 and chaired by former deputy secretary of state Robert D. Murphy. The commission was to consider and make recommendations regarding the formulation and implementation of national security processes. It focused a great deal on intelligence matters that directly effected the CIA. Though the commission suggested the need to correct "occasional failures to observe those standards of conduct that should distinguish the behavior of agencies of the U.S. Government," it also stressed the importance of intelligence to national-security policy making and was generally supportive of the U.S. INTELLIGENCE COMMUNITY.

Like other intelligence fact-finding bodies, the Murphy Commission noted that there was a fundamental problem in that the DIRECTOR OF CENTRAL INTELLIGENCE (DCI) has "line authority" over the CIA but "only limited influence" over other member agencies of the Intelligence Community. The commission, however, did not suggest a fundamental change in the existing organizational structure, holding that it was "neither possible nor desirable to give the DCI line authority over that very large fraction of the intelligence community that lies outside the CIA."

What the commission did recommend was that the DCI's office be placed in close proximity to the Oval Office, and that the DCI have regular direct contact with the president. Murphy envisioned a DCI delegating authority for day-to-day CIA management to a deputy, thus allowing the DCI to focus more attention on Intelligence Community tasks. The commission also recommended that the title of DCI be changed to DIRECTOR OF FOREIGN INTELLIGENCE (DFI).

The Murphy Commission provided for a means of oversight, including a strengthening of the PRESIDENT'S FOREIGN INTELLIGENCE ADVISORY BOARD, or PFIAB (a 16-member panel appointed from among trustworthy and distinguished persons outside of government), and a more extensive review of covert operations, by a high-level interagency panel. Murphy suggested that though Congress should be notified of covert actions by the Intelligence Community, the president should not sign off on such notifications, since it might be damaging to associate "the head of State so formally with such activities." It was further recommended that Intelligence Community requirements and capabilities be established at the NATIONAL SECURITY COUNCIL (NSC) level. The commission also recommended that the process of establishing such requirements and capabilities be institutionalized in a five-year plan.

A consolidated budget for foreign intelligence should, according to Murphy, be prepared and approved by an interagency entity, as well as the Office of Management and Budget, before being submitted to Congress.

Though the commission acknowledged ECONOMIC ESPIONAGE, it did not see a need for members of the Intelligence Community to expand efforts in this area. Instead, the commission recommended that the analysis arms of the U.S. DEPARTMENTS OF STATE, Treasury, Commerce, and Agriculture, and the Council of Economic Advisers, be strengthened.

Finally, the Murphy Commission noted the replacement of the BOARD OF NATIONAL ESTIMATES (BNE) by the national intelligence officers (NIOs) who were to draw upon analysts from the Intelligence Community to draft NATIONAL INTELLIGENCE ESTIMATES (NIEs). This practice was criticized because it created more work for the ANALYSTS and because NIEs had been largely ignored by senior State Department officials, who in recent years had made their own intelligence assessments based on their own sources of information gleaned from competing agencies. The commission instead recommended that a small staff of analysts be assigned to work with the NIOs in drafting the NIEs. Those analysts were to ensure that differences of opinion were clearly presented for the consumers of FINISHED INTELLIGENCE.

National Estimates, Board of (BNE)

The Board of National Estimates (BNE) was a panel created during the tenure of DIRECTOR OF CENTRAL INTELLIGENCE (DCI) WALTER BEDELL SMITH that reviewed the NATIONAL INTELLIGENCE ESTIMATES (NIEs) drafted by the Agency's OFFICE OF NATIONAL ESTIMATES (ONE). The BNE then worked directly with other members of the U.S. intelligence community and negotiated the final form of the NIEs.

The BNE was abolished in 1973 by DCI WILLIAM E. COLBY and replaced with the NATIONAL INTELLIGENCE COUNCIL (NIC).

National Estimates, Office of (ONE)

In the wake of the North Korean invasion of the South in 1950, DIRECTOR OF CENTRAL INTELLIGENCE (DCI) WALTER BEDELL SMITH persuaded Harvard professor WILLIAM LEONARD LANGER to forgo his scholarly pursuits temporarily in order to establish a unit that would sharpen the CIA's FINISHED INTELLIGENCE. Langer accordingly created the Office of National Estimates (ONE). ONE consisted of two elements: an intelligence estimates staff, responsible for drafting NATIONAL INTELLIGENCE ESTIMATES; and the BOARD OF NATIONAL ESTIMATES (BNE), which reviewed the NIEs.

In 1973, the BNE was replaced, by DCI WILLIAM E. COLBY, with the NATIONAL INTELLIGENCE COUNCIL.

National Imagery and Mapping Agency (NIMA)

A key component of the U.S. INTELLIGENCE COMMUNITY, the National Imagery and Mapping Agency is a U.S. DEPARTMENT OF DEFENSE (DoD) agency responsible for providing timely, accurate, and highly detailed images (photographs or other representations of natural or man-made features, objects, or activities on the earth), intelligence gleaned from images, and geospatial information in support of American military operations and national civilian consumers of intelligence.

NIMA was established on October 1, 1996, through the consolidation of the Defense Mapping Agency (DMA), the Central Imagery Office (CIO), the Defense Dissemination Program Office (DDPO), and the National Photographic Interpretation Center (NPIC), as well as certain imagery-related elements of the DEFENSE INTELLIGENCE AGENCY (DIA), the NATIONAL RECONNAISSANCE OFFICE (NRO), the Defense Airborne Reconnaissance Office (DARO), and the CIA. Through its management of the U.S. Imagery and Geospatial Information System (USIGS), NIMA provides American intelligence consumers with critical data necessary to achieve and maintain "dominant awareness" of the mission areas in which they operate.

Headquartered in Bethesda, Maryland, NIMA operates facilities in Northern Virginia, Washington, D.C., and St. Louis, Missouri. The agency also has liaison officers and technical and support personnel stationed around the world. As a member of the U.S. INTELLIGENCE COMMUNITY, NIMA is under the coordinating supervision of the DIRECTOR OF CENTRAL INTELLIGENCE (DCI).

In November 2001, the SCOWCROFT PROPOSAL—a comprehensive recommendation to bring the NRO, the NATIONAL SECURITY AGENCY (NSA), and NIMA under the direct control of the DCI—was released. The proposal, issued by retired lieutenant general Brent Scowcroft (a former National Security Advisor), was made to President George W. Bush roughly two months after the SEPTEMBER 11, 2001, TERRORIST ATTACKS ON THE UNITED STATES. It argued that by bringing the three DoD agencies under the CIA, rivalries would be reduced and programs would be consolidated, thus increasing the coordination of intelligence efforts.

National Intelligence Authority (NIA)

The National Intelligence Authority (NIA) was a short-lived post–World War II entity that served as a senior authority to the CENTRAL INTELLIGENCE GROUP (CIG), the immediate predecessor organization to the CIA. As such, the NIA is considered to be the immediate predecessor organization to the NATIONAL SECURITY COUNCIL (NSC).

Established in 1946 by President Harry Truman, the NIA comprised a White House representative and the individual secretaries of state, war, and Navy. The NATIONAL SECURITY ACT OF (SEPTEMBER) 1947 dissolved the NIA and the CIG and created the NSC and CIA.

National Intelligence Council (NIC)

The National Intelligence Council (NIC) is a group of senior experts and analysts drawn from the ranks of the U.S. INTELLIGENCE COMMUNITY, as well as elsewhere in the public and from the private sectors. They are appointed by and report to the DIRECTOR OF CENTRAL INTELLIGENCE (DCI).

Best known as the organization that produces NATIONAL INTELLIGENCE ESTIMATES, or NIEs (a strategic estimate of the capabilities, vulnerabilities, and possible courses of action of hostile foreign nations and other "threatening" foreign entities), the NIC focuses on the substantive problems of selected geographic regions of the world and such functional areas as economics and weapons proliferation. Aside from serving as a strategic intelligence think tank, the NIC supports the DCI in his role as head of the U.S. Intelligence Community by providing him with accurate FINISHED INTELLIGENCE. The

NIC was established in 1973, by DCI WILLIAM E. COLBY. The NIC replaced the BOARD OF NATIONAL ESTIMATES.

National Intelligence Daily (NID)

The *National Intelligence Daily* (*NID*) is a compilation of significant current intelligence matters pertaining to national policy. It is delivered by the CIA to institutional members of the U.S. INTELLIGENCE COMMUNITY and major American military commands on a daily basis. The *NID* is prepared by the Agency's DIRECTORATE OF INTELLIGENCE in concert with the DEFENSE INTELLIGENCE AGENCY (DIA), the STATE DEPARTMENT's Office of Intelligence and Research (INR), and the NATIONAL SECURITY AGENCY (NSA).

national intelligence estimate (NIE)

A national intelligence estimate (NIE) is a strategic estimate of the capabilities, vulnerabilities, and possible courses of action of hostile foreign nations and other "threatening" foreign entities (terrorist organizations, rogue military units, etc.).

Coordinated by the CIA, NIEs represent the collective view of the U.S. INTELLIGENCE COMMUNITY and are thus considered the highest form of FINISHED INTELLIGENCE. Once prepared (usually by the ANALYSTs from the various agencies who sit on the NATIONAL FOREIGN INTELLIGENCE BOARD), NIEs are signed by the DIRECTOR OF CENTRAL INTELLIGENCE (DCI) and forwarded to the NATIONAL SECURITY COUNCIL (NSC). The DCI's signature is not a formality; the DCI has historically had the last word on NIEs. "The first, and by all odds most important, legal and constitutional aspect of the National Intelligence Estimate is that it was and is the director's estimate, and its findings are his," writes SHERMAN KENT, considered to be the most influential person in the development of NIEs. "Although many experts from perhaps all intelligence components of the community participated in the production of the papers in the NIE series, and although the intelligence chiefs themselves formally passed on the final text, they could not bend its findings to suit their own judgments contrary to the will of the DCI."

See also SPECIAL NATIONAL INTELLIGENCE ESTIMATE.

National Intelligence Survey (NIS)

The *National Intelligence Survey* (*NIS*) was an encyclopedic compendium of basic, global intelligence information produced by the CIA and issued to Congress for nearly two decades. Born of the 1954 HOOVER COMMISSION—an executive-branch organization chaired by former president Herbert Hoover and tasked with determining ways to reduce the size and increase the efficiency of the post-war federal bureaucracy—the *NIS* was first issued to members of Congress in 1955. According to the commission report, "the *National Intelligence Survey* is an invaluable publication which provides the essential elements of basic intelligence on all areas of the world. There will always be a continuing requirement for keeping the Survey up-to-date."

In order to keep the survey current, the CIA began issuing the WORLD FACTBOOK as an annual addendum. The *World Factbook* was first published in a classified edition in 1962. The first unclassified version of the *World Factbook* was released in 1971. In 1973, the *NIS* program was terminated. The *World Factbook* was first made available to the general public through the U.S. Government Printing Office in 1975. It is currently one of the most widely used informational and reference texts in the English-speaking world.

National Reconnaissance Office (NRO)

The National Reconnaissance Office (NRO) is the component of the U.S. INTELLIGENCE COMMUNITY responsible for America's spaceborne reconnaissance. This mission is accomplished through the NRO's research on and development, acquisition, and operation of America's intelligence satellites. The NRO gathers intelligence to support critical national security operations, monitoring arms-control agreements and conventional military operations and exercises, and warning U.S. military forces in the event of a nuclear attack on the United States or any of its allies. The NRO also monitors natural disasters such as floods, storms, and other environmental factors.

Established in 1961, the NRO is an agency of the U.S. DEPARTMENT OF DEFENSE (DoD) and is funded through the National Reconnaissance Program (NRP) of the National Foreign Intelligence Program. For years, the official existence of the NRO was a secret. But on September 18, 1992, the NRO's existence was declassified.

The NRO is staffed by personnel from CIA, the armed forces, and DoD civilians. The director of the NRO is appointed by the president and confirmed by the Congress as the assistant secretary of the Air Force for space. The DIRECTOR OF CENTRAL INTELLIGENCE has the responsibility, exercised in concert with the secretary of defense, for operating the NRO. The DCI, who also establishes the priorities and requirements for the collection of the NRO's satellite information, oversees the office as the coordinating head of the U.S. INTELLIGENCE COMMUNITY.

In November 2001, the SCOWCROFT PROPOSAL—a comprehensive recommendation to bring the NRO, the NATIONAL SECURITY AGENCY (NSA), and NATIONAL IMAGERY AND MAPPING AGENCY (NIMA) under the direct control of the DCI—was released. The proposal, issued by retired lieutenant general Brent Scowcroft (a former NATIONAL SECURITY ADVISOR), was made to President George W. Bush roughly two months after the SEPTEMBER 11, 2001, TERRORIST ATTACKS ON THE UNITED STATES. It argued that by bringing the three DoD agencies under the CIA, rivalries would be reduced and programs would be consolidated, thus increasing the coordination of intelligence efforts.

National Security Act of 1947

The National Security Act of 1947 reorganized the post–World War II national defense/intelligence structure of the United States and created both the NATIONAL SECURITY COUNCIL (NSC) and the CIA.

The act, passed on July 26, 1947, and effective on September 18, created the U.S. DEFENSE DEPARTMENT (which unified the former Departments of War and the Navy, and created the Air Force); the NSC, which consisted of the president, vice president, and secretaries of defense and state; and the CENTRAL INTELLIGENCE AGENCY (CIA). The National Security Act of 1947 is considered to be the most sweeping reorganization of the American defense structure since the establishment of the Department of the Navy in 1798.

National Security Advisor

The National Security Advisor is the U.S. president's principal adviser on all matters related to American national security. As such, he or she is one of the chief consumers of CIA-produced FINISHED INTELLIGENCE.

National Security Agency (NSA)

The National Security Agency (NSA) is the member of the U.S. INTELLIGENCE COMMUNITY primarily responsible for exploiting foreign electromagnetic signals and protecting and developing electronic information critical to U.S. national security. Known as the "codemaker and codebreaker" of the federal government, the NSA is the self-described "largest employer of mathematicians in the United States and perhaps the world."

Located in Fort Meade, Maryland, the NSA was established in 1952 as an agency of the U.S. DEPARTMENT OF DEFENSE (DoD). It is successor of the U.S. Army's Signal Intelligence Service, which is best known within the Intelligence Community as the entity that cracked the famous VENONA codes, intercepted Soviet intelligence messages cabled between 1940 and 1948. Though the NSA is an independent DoD agency with a culture of secrecy paralleling that of the CIA, as a member of the Intelligence Community it is ultimately overseen by the DIRECTOR OF CENTRAL INTELLIGENCE (DCI).

In November 2001, the SCOWCROFT PROPOSAL—a comprehensive recommendation to bring the NSA, the NATIONAL RECONNAISSANCE OFFICE (NRO), and NATIONAL IMAGERY AND MAPPING AGENCY (NIMA) under the direct control of the DCI—was released. The proposal, issued by retired lieutenant general Brent Scowcroft (a former NATIONAL SECURITY ADVISOR), was made to President George W. Bush roughly two months after the SEPTEMBER 11, 2001, TERRORIST ATTACKS ON THE UNITED STATES. It argued that by bringing the three DoD agencies under the CIA, rivalries would be reduced and programs would be consolidated, thus increasing the coordination of intelligence efforts.

See also SIGINT.

National Security Council (NSC)

The National Security Council (NSC) is the highest-ranking executive council. It is responsible for advising the president of the United States on matters related to the integration of domestic, foreign, and military policies that affect national security.

Established by the NATIONAL SECURITY ACT OF 1947, the NSC comprises four statutory members including the president, the vice president, the secretary of state, and the secretary of defense. The DIRECTOR OF CENTRAL INTELLIGENCE (DCI) and the chairman of the JOINT CHIEFS OF STAFF (JCS) are statutory advisers to the NSC. The NSC's chief staff officer serves as assistant to the president for national security affairs. With the exception of the president, the NSC is the only entity senior to the CIA in matters of foreign intelligence.

naval intelligence, U.S.

Naval intelligence is an arm of the U.S. Navy responsible for collecting, controlling, exploiting, and defending information pertaining to Navy sea and air operations while denying any potential adversary the ability to do the same.

Like its Army, Air Force, and Marine Corps counterparts, the Naval Intelligence Service is overseen by the DEFENSE INTELLIGENCE AGENCY (DIA). The Naval Intelligence Service also reports to the president, through the NATIONAL SECURITY ADVISOR. Additionally, the service's activities are overseen—and coordinated with the efforts of the other members of the American INTELLIGENCE COMMUNITY—by the CIA's DIRECTOR OF CENTRAL INTELLIGENCE (DCI).

See also AIR FORCE INTELLIGENCE; ARMY INTELLIGENCE; MARINE CORPS INTELLIGENCE.

Nedzi Committee

The Nedzi Committee was the first House Select Intelligence Committee created after the establishment in January 1975 of the U.S. Senate's CHURCH COMMITTEE (officially, the Select Committee to Study Governmental Operations with Respect to Intelligence Activities). Established on February 19, 1975, the Nedzi Committee was chaired by Congressman Lucien N. Nedzi (D-Michigan). Like the Church Committee, the Nedzi Committee was directed to investigate allegations of illegal activities on the part of the FEDERAL BUREAU OF INVESTIGATION (FBI) and the CIA. However, five months after it was established, the Nedzi Committee was replaced by the U.S. House's PIKE COMMITTEE.

Nicholson, Harold James (1950–)

Harold James Nicholson, a branch chief for the CIA, is the highest-ranking Agency officer ever convicted of espionage.

Nicholson was born in Woodburn, Oregon on November 17, 1950. On October 20, 1980, Nicholson began working for the CIA. He held numerous posts in his Agency career. He began as an officer specializing in intelligence operations against several foreign intelligence services. His work primarily targeted the KGB, or KOMITET GOSUDARSTVENNOY BEZOPASNOSTI (the Soviet Committee for State Security). From 1982 to 1985, he was posted to the Philippines, where he had direct contact with targeted Soviet officials. He was subsequently reassigned to Bangkok, Thailand (1985–87) and Tokyo (1987–89).

In 1990, Nicholson was named CHIEF OF STATION (COS) in Bucharest, Romania. Two years later, he was named deputy COS in Kuala Lumpur, Malaysia. There, he met with Russian intelligence officers and purportedly began selling American secrets to them.

Nicholson returned to the United States on July 5, 1994, and began working as an intelligence tradecraft instructor at the CIA's Special Training Center (STC) in Virginia. He served in that capacity until July 1996.

On the surface, Nicholson's career seemed to be on a stellar track. However, things began to unravel when he underwent a week-long series of routine polygraph examinations beginning on October 16, 1995. During one of the examinations, an Agency polygrapher recorded as "inconclusive" Nicholson's response to the question: "Are you concealing contact with any foreign nationals?"

On December 4, Nicholson was directed to submit to another polygraph exam, which he attempted to manipulate by taking deep breaths. A subsequent review of his records indicated that Nicholson had been traveling overseas twice each year since his return from Malaysia and that there had been a number of unexplainable deposits to his banking accounts.

In July 1996, Nicholson was posted to CIA Headquarters in LANGLEY, VIRGINIA, where he served as a Branch Chief in the Directorate of Operation's Counterterrorism Center. For the next several months, Nicholson was placed under surveillance by the FEDERAL BUREAU OF

INVESTIGATION (FBI). Among the particulars revealed were that he had held an unauthorized meeting with intelligence officers from the SVR, or SLUZHBA VNESHNEY RAZVEDKI ROSSII (the Russian Federation's foreign intelligence service). The FBI intercepted postcards mailed to his handlers, recovered classified information from his laptop computer, and observed him photographing classified materials. A search of his office also revealed several classified documents related to Russia and unrelated to his Agency duties.

Nicholson was arrested on November 16. On March 3, 1997, he pled guilty to charges of espionage. In June, he was sentenced to 23 years in prison.

nonofficial cover

In CIA parlance, a "nonofficial cover" operative, or NOC, is a spy or a human-source intelligence asset.

In the wake of the SEPTEMBER 11, 2001, TERRORIST ATTACKS ON THE UNITED STATES, an article appeared in the British newspaper *The Guardian* that said, "In the resurgent Islamist movements of the Middle East, Pakistan and Afghanistan, it seems the CIA has no NOCs at all."

NUCINT (nuclear intelligence)

An acronym for "nuclear intelligence," NUCINT is simply intelligence gathered by means of the collection and analysis of radiation and other effects of radioactive sources. For instance, a test detonation of a nuclear weapon would create a radiation signature that might be detected and analyzed by the experts in the U.S. INTELLIGENCE COMMUNITY.

"Oh So Secret"

"Oh so secret" was a nickname given to the OFFICE OF STRATEGIC SERVICES (OSS), the World War II precursor organization to the CIA. The OSS was so christened because of its nature as a covert action/intelligence organization. Because of the high percentage of prominent "Eastern Establishment" personnel in its ranks, the OSS was also referred to as "OH SO SOCIAL" and "OH SUCH SNOBS."

"Oh So Social"

"Oh so social" was the best-known nickname given to the OFFICE OF STRATEGIC SERVICES (OSS), the World War II precursor organization to the CIA. The OSS was so christened because a high percentage of the organization's members were members of the elite "Eastern Establishment," men and women who before the war had been educated in Ivy League schools and had been prominent business leaders, politicians, lawyers, and society figures. A similar but lesser-known nickname for the Office was "OH SUCH SNOBS." Because of its nature as a covert action/intelligence organization, the OSS was also referred to as "OH SO SECRET."

"Oh Such Snobs"

"Oh such snobs" was a nickname given to the OFFICE OF STRATEGIC SERVICES (OSS), the World War II precursor organization to the CIA. The OSS was so christened because a high percentage of the organization's members were members of the elite "Eastern Establishment," men and women who, before the war, had been educated in Ivy League schools and were prominent business leaders, politicians, lawyers, and society figures. A similar, better-known, nickname for the Office was "OH SO SOCIAL." Because of its nature as a covert action/intelligence organization, the OSS was also referred to as "OH SO SECRET."

Olson, Dr. Frank R. (?–1953)

Dr. Frank R. Olson was a civilian employee of the U.S. Army who committed suicide after unwittingly ingesting hallucinogenic drugs administered during a CIA drug experiment.

Not knowing that he was being used as a guinea pig, Olson consumed approximately 70 micrograms of LSD when he drank a glass of Cointreau on November 19, 1953. The drug had been placed in the bottle from which he was served. Shortly after consuming the Cointreau, Olson began exhibiting symptoms of extreme paranoia and schizophrenia.

Dr. Robert Lashbrook, an employee of the Agency's TECHNICAL SERVICES DIVISION (TSD) who mixed the LSD into the Cointreau, accompanied Olson to psychiatrist Harold Abramson's office in New York City. Abramson, who allegedly been indirectly funded by the Agency, was considered an expert in the field of hallucinogenic drug research. But Olson's condition worsened over the next several days.

On November 28, 1953, Olson fell to his death from a 10th-story window in New York's Statler Hotel.

See also AMAZON NATURAL DRUG COMPANY; CHURCH COMMISSION; GOTTLIEB, DR. SIDNEY; KING, J. C.; MIND-CONTROL DRUG TESTING; MKSEARCH; MKULTRA; PIKE COMMISSION; ROCKEFELLER COMMISSION.

one-time pad

In cryptographic parlance, a one-time pad consists of small sheets of paper or silk inscribed with CIPHERs used to decode or encode messages.

operational group (OG)

Operational groups were self-contained paramilitary units of the OFFICE OF STRATEGIC SERVICES (OSS), the World War II predecessor organization to the CIA. They were unlike the OSS's three-man JEDBURGH teams, OGs were larger units, trained and organized like British commando teams. Members of OGs wore uniforms and in many cases carried standard military-issue weapons and equipment. In some military circles, OGs are considered the forerunner of U.S. Army Special Forces.

Operations Advisory Group (OAG)

The Operations Advisory Group (OAG) is a senior inter-departmental organization that oversees CIA high-risk covert operations. The OAG traces its lineage to the early OPERATIONS COORDINATING BOARD (OPB). The OPB was later renamed the SPECIAL GROUP, as well as the 5412 GROUP. During the administration of President John Kennedy, the Special (5412) Group was known as the 303 COMMITTEE—after a room number in the executive office complex in Washington, D.C. During the administration of President Richard Nixon, the 303 Committee became known as the 40 COMMITTEE. After the CHURCH COMMIT-TEE hearings of 1975 and the subsequent establishment of the INTELLIGENCE OVERSIGHT BOARD (IOB), the 40 Committee was renamed the OPERATIONS ADVISORY GROUP.

The Operations Advisory Group includes representatives from the U.S. DEPARTMENT OF STATE, the U.S. DEPARTMENT OF DEFENSE, the JOINT CHIEFS OF STAFF (JCS), the Oval Office, and the CIA.

Operations Coordinating Board (OCB)

The Operations Coordinating Board or OCB was the first in a series of senior interdepartmental organizations tasked with overseeing the CIA's high-risk covert operations.

On September 3, 1953, President Dwight Eisenhower issued EXECUTIVE ORDER (EO) 10483, which created the OCB (EO 10483 also eliminated the Psychological Strategy Board). The OCB comprised eight members, including the undersecretary of state (chairman), the deputy secretary of defense, the director of the Foreign Operations Administration, a representative of the president (to be designated), the undersecretary or corresponding official of any executive agency that has been assigned responsibility for the implementation of national security policies, the special assistant to the president for national security affairs, the director of the U.S. Information Agency, and the DIRECTOR OF CENTRAL INTELLIGENCE (DCI). Other members, invited from time to time, were representatives from the U.S. DEPARTMENT OF STATE, the U.S. DEPARTMENT OF DEFENSE, the JOINT CHIEFS OF STAFF (JCS), the Oval Office, and the CIA.

On February 19, 1961, President John Kennedy issued a directive abolishing the OCB. All OCB functions were rolled into the SPECIAL GROUP.

See also 5412 COMMITTEE; 40 COMMITTEE; OPERA-TIONS ADVISORY GROUP; 303 COMMITTEE.

Operations Course

The Operations Course, or "Ops Course," is an intensive, 18-week, closed-door training program that prospective CIA case officers must complete before being posted.

See also CAREER TRAINEES; FARM, THE; ISOLATION; PEARY, CAMP; and SWAMPY, CAMP.

Operations, Directorate of

See DIRECTORATES, CIA.

Ortiz, Peter Julien (1913–1988)

Colonel Peter Julien Ortiz was one of the most decorated Marine Corps officers of World War II. He was also one of the most storied operatives in the OFFICE OF STRATEGIC SERVICES (OSS), the wartime predecessor organization to the CIA.

Born in New York on August 5, 1913, to a French-Spanish father and an American mother, Ortiz spent much of his boyhood in France. As a young man, he was a student at the University of Grenoble, in the French Alps.

In 1932, at the age of 19, Ortiz joined the French Foreign Legion. He soon saw action in Africa and was decorated for heroism; he was wounded in 1933. Ortiz rose through the ranks from private to acting lieutenant; he was offered a permanent commission if he agreed to a reenlistment of five years. He rejected the offer and returned to the United States. Settling in California, where his mother lived, Ortiz working briefly as a Hollywood film technical adviser on military matters.

When World War II erupted in Europe, Ortiz returned to the legion. He reenlisted in October 1939 and received a battlefield commission in May 1940. In June, he was wounded during a raid on one of his unit's gasoline dumps that had been captured by the Germans. Ortiz, riding a motorcycle, led the attack; during the withdrawal he was shot in the hip, the bullet hitting his spine before existing his body. Temporarily paralyzed, he was easily captured. He spent the next 15 months as a prisoner of war in Germany, Austria, and Poland. Despite his wound, he attempted to escape on numerous occasions, finally succeeding in October 1941. In December, he returned to the United States.

On June 22, 1942, Ortiz enlisted in the U.S. Marine Corps and attended "boot camp" at Parris Island, South Carolina. The Marines, recognizing and placing great value on his previous training and experience—as well as the fact that he could speak English, French, German, Spanish, and Arabic—awarded Ortiz a commission on August 1. Following two months as an assistant training officer and after a brief stint at the Corps's wartime parachute training school at Camp Lejeune, North Carolina (he had previously completed the legionnaire parachute course), Ortiz was directed to Tangier, Morocco, where he was posted as an assistant naval attaché. However, the posting was a COVER for his true activities.

Ortiz was tasked with organizing and leading a unit of Arab tribesmen in scouting operations along the German lines in Tunisia. Not long after Ortiz began his work, the commandant of the Marine Corps received a dispatch from Major General WILLIAM J. "WILD BILL" DONOVAN, director of the OSS. A portion of the dispatch reads: "While on reconnaissance on the Tunisian front, Captain Peter Ortiz, U.S.M.C.R., was severely wounded in the right hand while engaged in a personal encounter with a German patrol. He dispersed the patrol with grenades. Captain Ortiz is making good recovery in hospital at Algiers. The Purple Heart was awarded to him."

In April 1943, Ortiz was temporarily reassigned to Washington, D.C., and in May he was detached to the OSS. In July, he was sent to England, where he underwent further training in special operations. Soon after, he was dropped by parachute into France to aid units of the French underground and assist in the rescue of downed Allied pilots. Though his peers wore civilian clothes in order to blend with the populace, Ortiz often wore his Marine uniform. The French who cheered his defiance, but the Germans were alerted by rumors of an American commando in Marine green.

Of all the tales surrounding Ortiz's exploits, none is more colorful than the wildly daring "café toast." One night while drinking incognito with several German officers at a bar in Lyons, Ortiz became agitated when one of the officers, unaware that Ortiz was an American OSS operative, cursed President Franklin Roosevelt. The officer then cursed the United States of America, and then the U.S. Marine Corps. Why or if he actually cursed the Marine Corps was a puzzle, since the Germans had probably never met a U.S. Marine on the battlefield. Nevertheless, it was a blanket condemnation of everything Ortiz held dear.

Ortiz, politely excusing himself from the table, returned to his apartment, and changed into the dress uniform of a Marine captain, complete with airborne wings and combat decorations. He then draped a cape over his shoulders to conceal his uniform and returned to the bar. There he was raucously greeted by his drinking partners.

Ortiz ordered a round of drinks. When the beverages were served, he tossed back the cape, revealing his uniform and a .45 automatic pistol. The Germans were speechless. "A toast!" Ortiz shouted. "To the President of the United States." He leveled his pistol at the officers as they emptied their glasses. He called for another round of drinks and proposed a toast to the U.S. Marine Corps. Again the Germans drained their glasses. A smiling Ortiz then eased backward out of the bar and vanished into the night. Another version has Ortiz shooting it out with the Germans, even killing a few, before disappearing into the back alleys of Lyon.

In May 1944, days before the famous D-day landing at Normandy, Ortiz and other members of his team were withdrawn and sent to England for regrouping and further assignment. On August 1, he returned to France at the head of an OPERATIONAL GROUP, or OG (armed and uniformed OSS teams for direct action against the Nazis).

When the war ended, Ortiz worked as an actor in, and as the subject of, films by the famed Hollywood director JOHN FORD, also a former member of the OSS. Two Ford-directed movies depicted the exploits of Ortiz—*13 Rue Madeleine* (1946), starring James Cagney, and *Operation Secret* (1952), starring Cornel Wilde. Additionally, Ortiz played bit parts in *Twelve O'Clock High* (1949), *Rio Grande* (1950), *When Willie Comes Marching Home* (1950), *Spy Hunt* (1950), *Sirocco* (1951), *What Price Glory* (1952), *Retreat, Hell!* (1952), *Commando Cody: Sky Marshal of the Universe* (1953), *Rocky Jones, Space Ranger* (1954), *Jubilee Trail* (1954), *King Richard and the Crusaders* (1954), *Son of Sinbad* (1955), *A Lawless Street* (1955), *Blast Off* (1956), *7th Cavalry* (1956), *The Wings of Eagles* (1957), and *The Halliday Brand* (1957).

Ortiz died on May 16, 1988, in Prescott, Arizona, and was subsequently buried in Arlington National Cemetery. He was 75.

OSINT (open-source intelligence)

An acronym for open-source intelligence, OSINT is simply intelligence gathered from a variety of such sources as the mass media, commercial (nonproprietary) information and imagery, official government reports, and expert reports.

See also ALL-SOURCE INTELLIGENCE; INTELLIGENCE CYCLE; and INTELLIGENCE DISCIPLINES, FIVE PRIMARY.

OSS

See STRATEGIC SERVICES, OFFICE OF.

outside man

In CIA parlance, an "outside man" is a CASE OFFICER who operates on foreign soil as a private citizen with no overt connection to the American government. Unlike an INSIDE MAN, who officially works out of an American embassy or consulate, an outside man has no official U.S. government cover and consequently no diplomatic immunity. An outside man is sometimes referred to as an ILLEGAL.

OXCART

Oxcart was the code name for the CIA's A-12 development project. The A-12 was a single-seat predecessor to the twin-seat SR-71 BLACKBIRD, a high-altitude strategic reconnaissance aircraft utilized by both the CIA and the U.S. Air Force.

See also U-2 DRAGON LADY AIRCRAFT.

P

Parallel Organizations

See FOREIGN INTELLIGENCE SERVICES.

PBSUCCESS, Operation

PBSUCCESS was the code name for the CIA's operations against the regime of Guatemalan president Jacobo Arbenz Guzmán that led to the 1954 coup d'état in that country.

See also GUATEMALA, COUP D'ÉTAT IN.

Pearson, Norman Holmes (1909–1975)

Norman Holmes Pearson directed the COUNTERINTELLI-GENCE operations of the OFFICE OF STRATEGIC SERVICES (OSS), the World War II predecessor organization to the CIA.

Pearson was born in Gardner, Massachusetts, on April 13, 1909, to Chester Page Pearson and Fanny Holmes Kittredge. A writer, editor, and collector of rare books, Pearson graduated from Yale University, first earning a bachelor's degree in 1932, then a Ph.D. in 1941. He also earned degrees from Oxford (an A.B. in 1932 and an M.A. in 1941) and attended the University of Berlin.

When World War II erupted, Pearson was teaching English literature at Yale. In 1942, he joined the OSS as a liaison officer with the British Secret Intelligence Service (SIS)

counterintelligence branch. He also directed the OSS's own counterintelligence branch, X-2, supervising the accumulation of some 1 million files on enemy agents and hostile organizations. He believed strongly in his work and felt that a similar effort should continue after the war.

Pearson earned a number of American and foreign decorations for his wartime service including, the Medal of Freedom (United States); Médaille de la Reconnaissance and Chevalier de la Légion d'Honneur (France); Knight of St. Olaf, First Class (Norway); and Knight of Dannebrog, First Class (Denmark).

After the war, Pearson returned to the Yale faculty where he soon earned a reputation as one of that institution's most distinguished scholars. Pearson won two Guggenheim fellowships—the first from 1948 to 1949, the second from 1956 to 1957.

Pearson died in 1975.

Peary, Camp

Camp Peary is the CIA's top-secret training facility, or "boot camp," for fledgling spies. Located near Williamsburg, Virginia, Camp Peary is a 10,000-acre site where the CIA's CAREER TRAINEES learn Agency tradecraft before being directed either to the field or to further specialized training. Camp Peary is also known to Agency insiders as ISOLATION, THE FARM, and CAMP SWAMPY.

Peers, William Raymond (1914–1984)

William Raymond Peers was the second and final commanding officer of DETACHMENT 101, the first paramilitary unit operated by the OFFICE OF STRATEGIC SERVICES (OSS), the World War II predecessor organization to the CIA. He later worked as a detached Army officer with the CIA. Peers was best known for overseeing the Vietnamera investigation of the My Lai massacre in the late 1960s.

Peers was born in Stuart, Iowa, on June 14, 1914, to Harry D. Peers and Milfred Stigers. As a boy, Peers was a stellar athlete. He wrestled and played rugby and football. He attended the University of California at Los Angeles, graduating in 1937. The following year, he joined the U.S. Army.

When World War II erupted, Peers was dispatched to the China-Burma-India Theater, where in 1943 he assumed command of the OSS's Detachment 101. The detachment, established in 1942 under the command of MAJOR CARL FREDERICH EIFLER, conducted sabotage and resistance operations behind Japanese lines in Burma.

After the war, Peers worked with the CIA, the Office of the Secretary of Defense, and the Department of the Army from 1949 until 1965. He served as special assistance to the JOINT CHIEFS OF STAFF (JCS) in Washington, D.C., from 1965 until 1966. In 1967, during the Vietnam War, he served as commander of the Fourth Infantry Division (1967) and the First Field Force (1968).

On November 26, 1969, General William C. Westmoreland, chief of staff of the Army, directed Peers to head the investigation into the atrocities committed by American soldiers—Vietnamese civilians had been shot, many of them execution-style—at the village of My Lai on March 16, 1968. Peers tackled his assignment tirelessly for four months, often working six or seven days per week. He listened to the attestations of nearly 400 witnesses, compiling some 20,000 pages of testimony. In December, he and his staff flew to Vietnam, where he visited the actual site of the massacre. Peers had initially disbelieved many of the allegations against the American soldiers, but he learned better. His findings (officially, *The Peers Report on the My Lai Massacre*) were published in March 1970. The four-volume report criticized a number of high-ranking Army officers for their participation in an initial cover-up. It also pointed to a number of commissioned and noncommissioned officers as directly responsible for the massacre, chief among them Lieutenant William Calley.

Following Vietnam, Peers served with the Eighth U.S. Army in Korea (1971–73). Peers retired from the Army in 1973, having attained the rank of lieutenant general. He received numerous decorations for his military service, including the Distinguished Service Medal with three oak-leaf clusters, the Silver Star, the Legion of Merit, the Distinguished Flying Cross, the Bronze Star with oak-leaf cluster, the Air Medal with oak-leaf cluster, the Joint Service Commendation Medal, the Army Commendation Medal, and a Presidential Unit Citation. Among his civilian awards were an honorary doctorate from Myongju University in Seoul, Korea, and the Eisenhower Distinguished Membership Award from People to People International.

Peers wrote and published two books, *Behind the Burma Road* (1963) and *The My Lai Inquiry* (1979). He also contributed to a variety of military journals on topics relating to guerrilla warfare and counterinsurgency operations.

Peers died of a heart attack on April 6, 1984, in San Francisco, California. He was 69.

Pelton, Ronald William (1942–)

Ronald William Pelton was a bottom-tier staffer at the NATIONAL SECURITY AGENCY (NSA) who, in order to avoid personal bankruptcy, began selling secrets to the Soviets. Those secrets included the highly sensitive CIA/NSA/U.S. Navy project IVY BELLS. He was caught after being revealed by a Soviet intelligence officer who defected to the United States.

Pelton, who for 14 years served as a communications specialist with the NSA, resigned in 1980. Faced with serious financial difficulties, he almost immediately began making contact with Soviet officials. He first reportedly visited the Soviet embassy in Washington, agreeing to sell classified information to the KGB. He then made several trips to Vienna, where he met and was debriefed by Soviet operatives.

The Soviets knew that Pelton had access to a great deal of sensitive information, but they offered him little in terms of monetary reward. He accepted anyway. From 1980 to 1983, he received an estimated $35,000 from the Soviets for information about American intelligence-gathering projects including IVY BELLS. An offshoot of the CIA's PROJECT JENNIFER, IVY BELLS was a joint NSA–U.S. Navy operation, overseen by the CIA, wherein Soviet dispatches were intercepted from a Soviet communications cable on the bottom of the Sea of Okhotsk.

A few years later, Vitaly Sergeyevich Yurchenko, a former KGB security officer at the Soviet embassy in Washington, defected to the United States and began to provide information to the CIA. Yurchenko's information uncovered the treasonous activities of former CIA officer EDWARD LEE HOWARD. He also disclosed the activities of a "walk-in" from the NSA who had telephoned the Soviet embassy and said, "I have some information to discuss with you, and to give to you." Yurchenko referred to the walk-in as "Mister Long."

The CIA passed the information on to the FEDERAL BUREAU OF INVESTIGATION (FBI). The bureau researched its archived recordings of wire-tapped calls to the Soviet embassy and found the tape. The recording was then played to a handful of NSA employees, who recognized Pelton's voice. A voice analysis later confirmed it.

On November 25, 1985, the FBI arrested Pelton in Annapolis, Maryland, where he was working as a sailboat salesman. DIRECTOR OF CENTRAL INTELLIGENCE (DCI) WILLIAM JOSEPH CASEY wanted Pelton tried without revealing any of the particulars of the IVY BELLS project. Casey believed that the Soviets could have missed something that might be brought to light in a trial.

On June 5, 1986, Pelton was found guilty on two counts of espionage, one count of conspiracy, and one count of disclosing classified communications intelligence. He was subsequently sentenced to three consecutive life terms plus 10 years.

Pentagon Papers

A secret U.S. government study of American involvement in Southeast Asia that was made available to the *New York Times* by a former Pentagon employee in 1971 become known as the *Pentagon Papers*.

A 47-volume report commissioned by Secretary of Defense Robert S. McNamara in June 1967, the *Pentagon Papers* was written by a team of 34 researchers, all of whom had been granted access to classified information. The report, some 3,000 pages of classified analysis and another 4,000 pages of appended documents, was completed in early 1969. It covered the period from the close of World War II to May 1968 and made mention of CIA operations and estimates. The study revealed a considerable degree of miscalculation and public deception in the prosecution of the Vietnam War by U.S. policy makers.

In 1971, DANIEL ELLSBERG, one of the authors, released the *Pentagon Papers* to the media. On June 13, the *New York Times* began publishing a series of articles based on the study. The story was then picked up by a number of other newspapers, including the *Washington Post* and the *Boston Globe*. The U.S. government obtained an injunction that temporarily prevented the publication of further stories. But the U.S. Supreme Court ruled in favor of the media, and the stories continued to be published.

Ellsberg, who contended that he was willing to risk a prison sentence to end the war, was indicted on several counts, including converting government property to personal use (via a copy machine), possessing government documents, conspiracy, theft, and espionage. His first trial was declared a mistrial in 1972 after Ellsberg's attorneys successfully argued that the papers were in the public domain and therefore did not constitute a threat to national security. The following year, just as Ellsberg was preparing for a second trial, the judge dismissed all charges when it was revealed by the WATERGATE prosecutors that the Nixon White House had directed former CIA dirty-tricks master EVERETTE HOWARD HUNT to burglarize the offices of Dr. Lewis J. Fielding—Ellsberg's psychoanalyst—in an attempt to uncover personal information that might damage Ellsberg's reputation. It would later be discovered that the CIA had supplied Hunt with a wig, a camera, a speech-altering device, and false identification papers for the operation.

Citing government misconduct, the judge declared that Ellsberg and the American public had been "victims of a conspiracy to deprive us of our civil liberties." Ellsberg regarded the judge's ruling as "the defrocking of the Wizard of Oz."

The *Pentagon Papers* have since been released in book form and made available to the general public.

Persian Gulf War, CIA operations in the

Though many of its activities remain classified, the CIA was actively involved at all levels of planning and operations during the 1990–91 Persian Gulf War.

In July 1990, Iraqi president Saddam Hussein began massing offensive military forces near the Kuwaiti border. As the buildup increased, the CIA warned American policy makers that Iraq would indeed attack Kuwait. The week prior to Iraq's invasion, the CIA accurately assessed that an Iraqi attack was "highly likely" within a few days if Kuwait failed to accept Baghdad's demands. Agency officials also noted that the Iraqi force was large enough to move through Kuwait and deep into Saudi Arabian territory.

On August 1, the day prior to the invasion, the CIA stated, "Baghdad almost certainly believes it is justified in taking military action to reclaim its 'stolen' territory and oil rights. It is also possible . . . that Saddam has already decided to take military action against Kuwait."

When the invasion was launched, the Agency organized round-the-clock task forces in the DIRECTORATES of Operations and Intelligence. The Directorate of Operations increased the strength of its overseas stations in order to handle the anticipated increases in intelligence collection and related requirements. The Directorate of Intelligence increased the number of ALL-SOURCE and IMAGERY INTELLIGENCE (IMINT) ANALYSTs. Soon after the U.S. Central Command (CENTCOM) established its headquarters in Saudi Arabia, the CIA deployed Joint Intelligence Liaison Element (JILE) teams to CENTCOM headquarters. JILE teams provided vital intelligence information to deployed American military forces.

From the Iraqi invasion of Kuwait in August 1990 through the American deployment phase (Operation Desert Shield) and subsequent attack (Operation Desert Storm) on the Iraqi army, until the cease-fire in late February 1991, CIA officers and analysts constantly gathered and assessed raw information and turned it into vital FINISHED INTELLIGENCE for the American military. As such, the Agency was able to produce "thousands of intelligence cables, reports, and briefings on Iraq," all the while protecting its own assets.

Referring to the stellar intelligence produced, General Colin Powell, then chairman of the JOINT CHIEFS OF STAFF, said, "No combat commander has ever had as full and complete a view of his adversary as did our field commander. Intelligence support to Operations Desert Shield and Desert Storm was a success story."

GEORGE HERBERT WALKER BUSH was the American president who oversaw Operations Desert Storm and Desert Shield. Bush was a former DIRECTOR OF CENTRAL INTELLIGENCE (DCI).

Ph.D. intelligence

Ph.D. intelligence was a derogatory term used by the late director of the FEDERAL BUREAU OF INVESTIGATION (FBI), J. EDGAR HOOVER, to refer to the CIA. Hoover, who considered the Agency his chief rival, often mocked the number of Ivy League scholars serving in the CIA.

See also COWBOYS VS. SCHOLARS.

Philby, Harold Adrian Russell (Kim)
(1912–1988)

Harold Adrian Russell "Kim" Philby was a British Secret Service officer who, some historians have contended, was in line for the top spot at MI6, the United Kingdom's counterpart organization to the CIA, when instead he became one of the most notorious DOUBLE AGENTs of the 20th century. The *London Times* would dub him "the most remarkable spy in the history of espionage." The CIA would consider him anathema to its own espionage network.

Born in Ambala, India, on January 1, 1912, to the son of a high-ranking British civil service officer, Philby was nicknamed "Kim" after the fictional boy spy hero created by novelist Rudyard Kipling. While studying at Cambridge University in the early 1930s, Philby became a communist, as did a number of his colleagues, including Donald Maclean, Guy Burgess, Anthony Blunt, and John Cairncross. Years later the five men would betray many of the West's most sensitive secrets, eventually becoming known as the CAMBRIDGE FIVE.

During the Spanish Civil War, Philby worked as a combat correspondent for the *London Times*. When World War II erupted in 1939, he was posted to France. There, in 1940, he took part in the evacuation of Amiens, just before the capitulation of the French government to the Germans. That same year, Philby began working for the British Secret Intelligence Service (SIS), also known as MI6. By 1944, he was in charge of all British intelligence operations against the Soviet Union—a perfect position for a Soviet double agent.

In 1949, Philby was transferred to Washington, D.C., where he served as liaison between MI6 and the member agencies of the U.S. Intelligence Community—chief among them the CIA and the FEDERAL BUREAU OF INVESTIGATION (FBI), the CIA's domestic counterpart. This gave him access to some of the West's most vital secrets, which he forwarded to his handlers in Moscow.

Arguably, Philby's greatest betrayal was disclosing Western attempts to infiltrate, and in some cases conduct, paramilitary operations in the Eastern bloc countries. In the early 1950s, he compromised a series of joint CIA/British Secret Service covert-action projects conducted in Albania from 1949 to 1953. The operations were aimed at overthrowing the totalitarian government of Prime Minister Enver Hoxha.

Code-named VALUABLE, the ALBANIAN OPERATIONS were the first such attempt by the CIA. FRANK GARDINER WISNER, then head of the CIA's OFFICE OF POLICY COORDINATION (OPC), described them as a "clinical experiment to see whether larger rollback operations would be feasible elsewhere." Unfortunately for the Agency, the operations were a dismal failure—because, no doubt, of Philby's betrayal.

In 1951, however, things began to unravel, albeit temporarily, for Philby when his Cambridge colleagues Burgess and Maclean (who were working for the British Foreign Office in Washington, D.C.) were suspected of

Harold Adrian Russell "Kim" Philby (HULTON ARCHIVE)

espionage against the West. Just before being arrested and interrogated, both men escaped to the Soviet Union.

Philby himself was accused of warning them after FBI director J. EDGAR HOOVER told the *New York Daily News* that his intelligence sources pointed to Philby as the "third man." Hoover blamed MI6 for not being on top of the matter, contending that British intelligence was protecting Philby because he was a well-heeled member of its "old-boy network." British officials did investigate the allegations against Philby, but the evidence was deemed circumstantial and not sufficient to indict and prosecute him for treason.

Philby continued working as a field operative for the SIS, and in 1956 he was posted to Beirut, Lebanon. In addition to his intelligence work, he worked as a journalist, penning pieces for the *Economist* and the *London Observer*. During his time in Beirut he again began passing secret information to Moscow. But the difficulties associated with a double life began to take its toll on the MI6 operative. Slipping into a state of chronic depression, he often drank himself into stupors, and he became somewhat sloppy in his work.

In January 1963, Nicholas Elliot, a former SIS station chief in Lebanon, accused Philby of spying for the Soviets. Philby denied the allegations but realized that his betrayals were catching up with him. On January 23, 1963, he escaped to Russia on the Soviet freighter *Dolmatova*.

In Moscow, Philby was paid a comfortable salary by the Soviet government and promoted to the rank of general in the KOMITET GOSUDARSTVENNOY BEZOPASNOSTI, or KGB (the Committee for State Security). Philby began an extensive debriefing process wherein he provided the Soviets detailed information about Western intelligence agencies, operations, spies, and counterspies.

The defection and subsequent revelations stunned the leaders of the CIA, chief among them JAMES JESUS ANGLETON, the Agency's head of COUNTERINTELLIGENCE. Angleton had lunched with Philby every week for months. He had considered Philby a close friend.

In 1968, Philby published his memoirs, *My Silent War: The Soviet Master Spy's Own Story*. The book, written under his nickname "Kim," attempted to defend his actions against the West.

Philby died on May 11, 1988, in Moscow, where he was buried in a military cemetery. He was 76.

Phillips, David Atlee (1922–1988)

A 25-year veteran of covert operations, David Atlee Phillips is best known as a public defender of the CIA during some of the Agency's darkest years.

Born in Fort Worth, Texas, on October 31, 1922, Phillips was a tall, handsome boy with natural leadership abilities. He attended William and Mary College from 1940 to 1941, and then Texas Christian University from 1941 to 1942. He started out as a professional actor, but his stage career was temporarily sidelined by World War II.

In 1943, Phillips enlisted in the U.S. Army Air Corps, rising to the rank of sergeant and serving as a member of a bomber crew. During a mission over German-occupied territory in Europe, his plane was shot down, and he was captured. He spent a year in a prisoner of war camp but eventually escaped and linked up with American ground forces marching toward Germany. When the war ended in 1945, he was awarded a Purple Heart and an Air Medal.

Phillips again worked as an actor. He also worked as a radio announcer and a playwright. He then moved to Chile, where he continued to write. In 1948, Phillips attended the University of Chile. The following year, he launched a commercial printing service and became the publisher and editor of the *South Pacific Mail*, an English-language newspaper.

Phillips entered the CIA in 1950 as a "contract employee." He initially worked as a part-time agent for the CLANDESTINE SERVICE but soon moved up to a full-time position as a CASE OFFICER.

Phillips left Chile in 1954 and began working as an assistant for EVERETTE HOWARD HUNT, an Agency operations officer who was destined to become one of the infamous White House "PLUMBERS." With Hunt, he engaged in psychological warfare operations against the regime of Jacobo Arbenz Guzmán before and during the CIA's 1954 COUP D'ÉTAT IN GUATEMALA.

Phillip's responsibility was to foment BLACK PROPAGANDA via the radio. Through the "Voice of Liberation," an Agency-owned radio FRONT, he broadcast material intended to strike fear in the ranks of communists and sympathizers of Arbenz Guzmán while at the same time rallying people who might aid the CIA-supported rebels. The broadcasts worked.

On June 18, 1954, a CIA-sponsored army of some 150 Guatemalan expatriates, Hondurans, Nicaraguans, and American mercenaries led by rebel colonel Carlos Castillo Armas crossed the Honduran border into Guatemala and began marching on Guatemala City. Though trained and equipped by the CIA, Armas's meager force would have been no match for the 6,000-man Guatemalan army and air force. But its size was greatly exaggerated by Phillips's Voice of Liberation announcements, which were believed by Guatemalan government troops. This in turn panicked many of Arbenz Guzmán's military commanders, and on June 25 the regime collapsed.

After Guatemala, Phillips was reassigned to CIA headquarters and was appointed as a staff specialist in psychological warfare. From 1956 through 1958, he served as an operations officer in "deep COVER," first in Cuba, then in Lebanon. In late 1958, he resigned briefly from the CIA.

He operated a public relations firm for American businesses in Cuba and continued as a part-time contractor of the Agency.

When FIDEL CASTRO came to power in 1959, Phillips's business began to falter. He returned to the CIA as a full-time staff officer in March 1960 and was assigned to the project to topple the Castro regime in Cuba. Phillips, chief propaganda officer for the project, and other Agency planners believed that the Cuban problem could be addressed in much the same way that operations had been conducted in Guatemala. But it was not to be.

In April 1961, after months of Phillips-organized radio broadcasts, over 1,500 exiled Cuban freedom fighters began hitting the beaches along Cuba's southwestern coastline in a CIA-sponsored operation known as OPERATION ZAPATA, or the BAY OF PIGS INVASION. Doomed from the start, the invasion was crushed by Castro in three days. Though it was both a strategic and moral victory for the Cuban president, the outcome of the invasion had less to do with Castro's combat talents than with the CIA's inability to assess the willingness of the Cuban people to rise up against Castro and President John Kennedy's failure to provide promised air and naval gunfire support for the émigrés on the ground.

After Cuba, Phillips was reassigned to the CIA station in Mexico City, Mexico. There he served as a senior covert-action officer. In 1965, he was appointed CHIEF OF STATION (COS) in Santo Domingo in the Dominican Republic. He served in that capacity until 1967.

In 1968, Phillips returned to Agency headquarters, where he was named chief of the Cuban Operations Group (COG) of the Western Hemisphere Division. He oversaw the collection of intelligence on Cuban military operations around the world and managed the Agency's intelligence-gathering operations within Cuba. In 1970, he was made COS in Brazil. In 1972, he was reassigned to the COS post in Venezuela. In 1973, he returned to headquarters as chief of the Agency's Western Hemisphere Division.

Phillips retired from the CIA in 1975, the controversial YEAR OF INTELLIGENCE, when the Agency underwent both public and congressional scrutiny. The Senate CHURCH and House of Representatives PIKE COMMITTEEs leveled all manner of accusations against the CIA and the FEDERAL BUREAU OF INVESTIGATION (FBI), and morale at the Agency was at an all-time low. In response, Phillips began speaking out against the numerous charges of illegal activities being directed at the Agency. He also founded the ASSOCIATION OF FORMER INTELLIGENCE OFFICERS (AFIO), an organization that he felt would serve as a "public defender" of the Agency.

In 1977, Phillips wrote what has since been referred to as a "breezy, anecdotal account of his career," *The Night Watch: 25 Years of Peculiar Service.* He would also write several other works, including a "how to" book for young men and women seeking careers in the field of intelligence.

After struggling with cancer, Phillips, 65, died at his home in Bethesda, Maryland, on July 7, 1988. He was buried in Arlington National Cemetery.

PHOENIX, Operation

Operation PHOENIX was a controversial special project in the Vietnam War wherein Vietcong leaders were identified by U.S. intelligence officers to be targeted by U.S. forces. The project was directed by future DIRECTOR OF CENTRAL INTELLIGENCE (DCI) WILLIAM EGAN COLBY.

PHOTINT (photographic intelligence)

An acronym for photographic intelligence, PHOTINT is simply intelligence gathered by means of collecting and analyzing photographs. In recent years, the term PHOTINT has been replaced with IMINT, or IMAGERY INTELLIGENCE.

See also ALL-SOURCE INTELLIGENCE; INTELLIGENCE CYCLE.

Pike Committee

In the wake of the WATERGATE SCANDAL, allegations about CIA plots—some true, some false—began emerging in congressional circles and in the court of public opinion. Executive and congressional fact-finding panels were formed to investigate alleged abuses of power by both the CIA and its domestic counterpart, the FEDERAL BUREAU OF INVESTIGATION (FBI).

The Pike Committee was the second House Select Intelligence Committee formed to investigate the CIA and the FBI. Established in mid-1975, during the YEAR OF INTELLIGENCE, the Pike Committee replaced the first House Select Intelligence Committee, also known as the NEDZI COMMITTEE. The Pike Committee was chaired by Congressman Otis Grey Pike (D-New York), an outspoken former Marine Corps combat pilot who initially butted heads with the CIA over what should be disclosed in public.

CIA staffers who worked closely with both the CHURCH COMMITTEE (officially, the U.S. Senate's Select Committee to Study Governmental Operations with Respect to Intelligence Activities) and the Pike Committee investigative staffs were unable to develop the same sense of cooperation as with the Church Committee.

To say that there was bad blood between the Agency and Pike's staffers would be an understatement. The committee's staffers were "absolutely convinced that they were dealing with the devil incarnate," recalled CIA officer Richard Lehman. "They [the members of the Pike Committee] were loaded for bear." Donald Gregg, a CIA officer and Vietnam veteran, agreed. "The months I spent with the Pike Committee made my tour in Vietnam seem like a picnic," he said. "I would vastly prefer to fight the Viet Cong than deal with a polemical investigation by a Congressional committee, which is what the Pike Committee [investigation] was."

Nonetheless, the Pike Committee's report argued, unlike the Senate Church Committee, that the CIA was not out of control. The Pike Committee never published an "official" final report, because an early draft was leaked to the *Village Voice,* an alternative newspaper in New York, before a final security review was completed. This was considered an embarrassment to the House of Representatives.

Pike himself concluded, "I wound up the hearings with a higher regard for the CIA than when I started. We did find evidence, upon evidence, upon evidence where the CIA said: 'No, don't do it.' The State Department or the White House said, 'We're going to do it.' The CIA was much more professional and had a far deeper reading on the down-the-road implications of some immediately popular act than the executive branch or administration officials. One thing I really disagreed with [Senator Frank] Church on was his characterization of the CIA as a 'rogue elephant.' The CIA never did anything the White House didn't want. Sometimes they didn't want to do what they did."

Both the Church and Pike Committees were formed as a result of an inconclusive investigation of unauthorized CIA activities by the ROCKEFELLER COMMISSION in January 1975. The latter had been established by President Ford and chaired by Vice President Nelson Rockefeller. Congress felt that the commission's findings had been "whitewashed."

Pit, the

In CIA parlance, "the Pit" has two uses. The first describes a basement area of the Agency's headquarters building where classified documents were once destroyed. According to Henry S. A. Becket's *Dictionary of Espionage,* ashes from the pit were dumped into the Potomac River through the 1970s. When environmentalists complained, it was transported to a landfill in West Virginia.

A second use describes the isolated, windowless area in CIA headquarters where crisis operations are often conducted.

Plans Directorate

See DIRECTORATES, CIA.

Plumbers

The "Plumbers" were a secret and illegal White House unit tasked with stopping news leaks and keeping track of President Richard Nixon's political opponents.

The Plumbers are best known as the operatives responsible for two of Washington's most famous burglaries. The first was the September 1971 break-in at the office of Dr. Lewis J. Fielding, the psychoanalyst of DANIEL ELLSBERG, author of THE *PENTAGON PAPERS.* In that operation, the Plumbers were looking for information that might damage Ellsberg's reputation. The team leader during the Fielding burglary was EVERETTE HOWARD HUNT, a former CIA officer. Hunt was purportedly supplied by the CIA with a wig, a camera, a speech-altering device, and false identification papers for the operation.

The second famous Plumbers operation was the 1972 break-in at the Democratic National Headquarters office in the WATERGATE complex in Washington, D.C. The Watergate burglary, also led by Hunt, with George Gordon Liddy, a former special agent and supervisor with the FEDERAL BUREAU OF INVESTIGATION (FBI), evolved into one of the greatest political malefactions in U.S. history. The Watergate scandal involved the highest levels of government in a number of illegal activities designed to help Nixon win reelection during the 1972 presidential campaign. It forced Nixon to resign from the presidency in 1974 in order to avoid impeachment proceedings. It also resulted in the exposure of CIA activities to public scrutiny to a degree which the Agency had never before experienced.

The events began to unfold on the night of June 17, when five plumbers—Eugenio Martinez, Virgilio Gonzalez, Frank Sturgis, BERNARD BARKER, and JAMES WALTER MCCORD, JR.—broke into the Watergate complex with the objective of obtaining information from the Democratic Party's national headquarters office. Barker had once been recruited by the Agency while he was a Cuban policeman. McCord was a former CIA officer. The five men were arrested after being discovered in the building by a roving security officer.

Policy Coordination, Office of (OPC)

The Office of Policy Coordination (OPC) was a quasi-independent branch of the CIA, responsible for covert action.

Established in 1948 under the direction of FRANK GARDINER WISNER, the OPC quickly became able to conduct effective and secret propaganda, sabotage, subversion, and all manner of resistance operations against hostile nations. Few outside Wisner's circle would know what those operations entailed. Future DIRECTOR OF CENTRAL INTELLIGENCE (DCI) WILLIAM E. COLBY would later write that Wisner had created "the atmosphere of an order of Knights Templars, to save freedom from Communist darkness."

In January 1951, DCI WALTER BEDELL SMITH sought to bring the OPC under stricter control. Smith brought the

Agency's two clandestine arms—the OFFICE OF SPECIAL OPERATIONS (or OSO, the secret intelligence arm) and the OPC—under the newly created post of DEPUTY DIRECTOR for plans (DDP), thus creating the CIA's CLANDESTINE SERVICE (CS). Future DCI ALLEN WELSH DULLES was named the CS's first DEPUTY DIRECTOR for plans (DDP). Dulles was to supervise the functions of both the OPC and OSO (Wisner would succeed Dulles as DDP in August 1951). But it took until August 1952 to merge the two offices effectively into one cohesive entity—the DIRECTORATE of plans (the future Directorate of Operations).

Pollard, Jonathon Jay (1954–)

Jonathon Pollard was an American ANALYST in NAVAL INTELLIGENCE who, during the 1980s, illegally provided Israel classified information that resulted in the deaths of a number of CIA operatives in the Eastern bloc during the COLD WAR. He became the first American found guilty of spying for an American ally.

Pollard was born in Galveston, Texas, on August 7, 1954. He was the youngest child of Morris Pollard, a noted microbiologist, and Molly Pollard, a homemaker. Soon thereafter, Pollard's father accepted a faculty position at the University of Notre Dame, and the family moved to South Bend, Indiana. Despite the fact that Notre Dame was a Roman Catholic institution and the Pollard's were Jewish, the family was welcomed with open arms.

As a boy, young Pollard quickly developed a deep respect for the newly founded nation of Israel; his parents often telling him stories of courageous Israeli warriors and the struggle for a Jewish state. Pollard vowed that he would one day aid Israel.

Pollard graduated from high school with honors and was accepted at California's Stanford University. There, he initially enrolled in the university's pre-medical program but switched to political science. As a student, Pollard began to spin incredible stories about himself. He told friends he held dual Israeli/United States citizenship, that he was an officer in the Israeli army, and that he was a member of the MOSSAD LE ALIYAH BETH, or MOSSAD (the Israeli parallel organization to the CIA). At one point, he produced a revolver, saying that he needed it for protection and that he had once killed an Arab while guarding an Israeli kibbutz. Ironically, he never joined any of the campus Jewish organizations.

Pollard graduated from Stanford with a B.A. in 1976. He briefly attended law school at Notre Dame, then won admission to the Fletcher School of Law and Diplomacy at Boston's Tufts University. He studied at Tufts for two years but did not graduate.

In 1977, while still in law school, Pollard attempted to join the CIA but was rejected after a polygraph test indicated that he may have used illegal drugs. Two years later, he was hired by U.S. naval intelligence as a civilian intelligence research specialist. In that capacity, he worked at the Field Operational Intelligence Office in Suitland, Maryland. The navy did not know of the CIA's findings regarding their new employee. He would work in naval intelligence for a total of seven years.

Over time, Pollard became disturbed by what he believed was the U.S. INTELLIGENCE COMMUNITY's unwillingness to share all Middle East–related intelligence with Israel. He, in fact, believed that Soviet military hardware was falling into Arab hands unnoticed by the Israelis, who were relying upon American intelligence for such information.

In November 1985, Pollard was arrested for passing top-secret materials to Israel: The materials included various documents related to Iraq, Syria, and Libya. It was also discovered that Pollard had provided Israeli intelligence authorities with classified information pertaining to American military intelligence and diplomatic codes, the names of nearly 100 U.S. agents operating in the Middle East, U.S. INTELLIGENCE COMMUNITY deciphering techniques and targets, foreign communications intercepts; and combat contingency plans for the Middle East. Much of the information eventually found its way into Soviet hands, resulting in the arrests and executions of numerous agents working for the CIA and operating in Eastern bloc countries.

In March 1987, Pollard was sentenced to life in prison. Since his conviction and sentencing, Pollard supporters, including the government of Israel, have lobbied for his release, arguing that his sentence for passing information to an ally was "grossly disproportionate." The CIA contends that Pollard is a threat to U.S. national security and should remain in prison.

Pope, Allen Lawrence (1927–2000)

Allen Lawrence Pope, a pilot with CIVIL AIR TRANSPORT (CAT), one of the CIA's better-known proprietary airlines, was shot down by Indonesian troops in 1958 and nearly executed.

A graduate of the University of Florida, Pope served in the U.S. Air Force, flying combat missions during the Korean War. Following the war, he worked briefly for a private airline in Texas. He signed on with CAT, which was operating in the Far East, and flew a number of airdrop missions in support of the besieged French troops who were fighting the Vietminh at Dien Bien Phu.

During the 1958 INDONESIAN rebellion, Pope flew missions in support of the CIA-backed rebels. On May 18, while flying a bombing mission against Indonesian loyalists, he accidentally attacked a church during services, killing most of the congregation. He was subsequently shot down and captured. Following a brief trial, he was sentenced to death. Fortunately, the U.S. government successfully appealed for his release, and he returned to the United States in July 1962.

Pope then began flying for Miami-based Southern Air Transport, another CIA-owned airline.

Powers, Francis Gary (1929–1977)

Francis Gary Powers was the U-2 pilot who, flying for the CIA in 1960, was shot down by a Soviet surface-to-air missile over Soviet territory.

Powers was born in Burdine, Kentucky, on August 17, 1929, to Oliver Powers, a coal miner, and Ida Ford. Family tradition has it that young Powers was persuaded by his father to seek a career other than coal mining. When he was 14 years old, Powers made his first flight and then dreamed of nothing but being a pilot. He graduated from Tennessee's Milligan College in 1950 and enlisted in the U.S. Air Force.

In 1952, Powers earned an officer's commission and pilot's wings through the Aviation Cadet Program. He was then assigned to the Strategic Air Command (SAC). With SAC, he obtained a top-secret clearance and soon captured the interest of the CIA.

In 1955, Powers and several other aviators were recruited by the Agency to begin flight training in the U-2 high-altitude reconnaissance aircraft. Nicknamed the "Dragon Lady," the U-2 had been designed by the Lockheed Aircraft Corporation for the Air Force. The latter

Francis Gary Powers (LIBRARY OF CONGRESS)

had rejected the design as unsuited to the service's needs. The CIA viewed it as an effective aerial platform for monitoring the Soviets' developing intercontinental ballistic missile (ICBM) and long-range bomber capability during the early days of the COLD WAR. In order to fly for the CIA, Powers had to resign his Air Force commission. He also assumed the COVER of Francis G. Palmer, a Lockheed pilot.

On May 1, 1960, Powers was flying a U-2 on a mission to reconnoiter the reported construction of a Soviet ICBM base at Plesetsk when his aircraft developed engine trouble. He was forced to reduce his altitude and was subsequently shot down over Sverdlovsk. He was able to escape from the doomed aircraft but was apprehended by Soviet authorities on the ground.

Powers was tried on charges of espionage and imprisoned. But in early 1962 he became a bargaining chip in one of the most dramatic spy-swapping episodes of the cold war. On the morning of February 10, Powers was exchanged for COLONEL RUDOLF IVONOVICH ABEL, a Soviet spy who in 1957 had been arrested in New York and convicted of espionage activities against the United States.

Powers and Abel were brought by their captors to opposite ends of the Glienecker Bridge, which spanned a lake separating West Berlin from the East German city of Potsdam. Negotiators discussed the swap in the center of the bridge, where a white painted line marked the geographical division of East and West. The two spies stared at each other from opposite sides and then crossed the bridge into their respective versions of freedom.

Back in the United States, Powers worked briefly for the CIA, then as a test pilot for the Lockheed aircraft company.

Powers was working as a radio station's traffic-reporting helicopter pilot when, on August 1, 1977, while flying over Encino, California, his helicopter ran out of fuel and crashed. Powers and a cameraman who had been covering brushfires near Santa Barbara were killed. For years, rumors circulated that Powers's death had been part of a conspiracy. After all, the conspiracy theorists argued, how could such an experienced aviator make such a simple, fatal mistake?

Powers, who was only days from celebrating his 48th birthday, was buried in Arlington National Cemetery.

President's Board of Consultants on Foreign Intelligence Activities (PBCFIA)

Established by Dwight Eisenhower in 1956, the President's Board of Consultants on Foreign Intelligence Activities (PBCFIA) is the predecessor executive-level board of the PRESIDENT'S FOREIGN INTELLIGENCE ADVISORY BOARD (PFIAB).

President's Daily Brief (PDB)

The *President's Daily Brief* (PDB) was a published compilation of significant intelligence matters issued to the president on a daily basis by the CIA. The *PDB*, also known as the *President's Daily Intelligence Publication,* or the *Daily Summary,* was replaced by the CURRENT INTELLIGENCE BULLETIN (CIB) on February 21, 1951.

President's Foreign Intelligence Advisory Board (PFIAB)

The President's Foreign Intelligence Advisory Board, or PFIAB, is a 16-member citizen panel appointed from among trustworthy and distinguished persons outside of government. Chosen on the basis of achievement, experience, and integrity, the board members serve without compensation and are maintained within the executive office of the President.

The PFIAB continually reviews the performance of all government agencies engaged in the collection, evaluation, or production of intelligence or in the execution of intelligence policy. It also assesses the adequacy of management, personnel, and organization within the U.S. INTELLIGENCE COMMUNITY, advising the president on all matters concerning the objectives, conduct, and coordination of the community's activities. Additionally, the board makes recommendations for actions to improve and enhance the performance of the intelligence efforts of the United States.

Established by President John Kennedy on May 4, 1961, the PFIAB is the successor of the PRESIDENT'S BOARD OF CONSULTANTS ON FOREIGN INTELLIGENCE ACTIVITIES (PBCFIA), which was created by President Dwight Eisenhower in 1956. The PFIAB has served every American president, with the exception of President Jimmy Carter, since the Kennedy administration.

President's Intelligence Oversight Board (IOB)

In 1976, President Gerald Ford established the President's Intelligence Oversight Board (IOB) as a White House entity with oversight responsibilities for the legality and propriety of intelligence activities. The primary task of the IOB is to prepare reports for the president detailing any intelligence activities that the board believes may be unlawful or contrary to an EXECUTIVE ORDER or presidential directive. The board also has the authority to refer such reports to the attorney general's office.

In 1997, the IOB was made a standing committee of the PRESIDENT'S FOREIGN INTELLIGENCE ADVISORY BOARD (PFIAB), a panel established to review the performance of all government agencies engaged in the collection, evaluation, or production of intelligence, or in the execution of intelligence policy.

P Source

"P Source" was the code name for the CIA's Ivy League connection during the early days of the Agency. During the 1950s, the CIA recruited heavily from Ivy League schools, such as Harvard, Princeton, and Yale. The P stood for "professor."

R

Raborn, William Francis, Jr. (1905–1990)

Vice Admiral William Francis Raborn, Jr., was chief of the U.S. Navy's Special Projects Office, which produced the first Polaris ballistic-missile submarine. He was also a DIRECTOR OF CENTRAL INTELLIGENCE (DCI).

Raborn was born the son of William Francis Raborn, a farmer, and Cornelia Victoria Moore on June 8, 1905, in Decatur, Texas. As a boy, Raborn attended public schools in Oklahoma. As a young man, he attended the U.S. Naval Academy in Annapolis, Maryland, graduating in 1928.

In the Navy, Raborn initially served as a gunnery officer on three ships—one battleship and two destroyers. In 1934, he earned the wings of a naval aviator. He then served on aircraft carriers and cruisers.

Following the U.S. entry into World War II in 1941, Raborn was assigned to direct the Free Gunnery School at Kaneohe, Hawaii. In 1943, he was transferred to the Office of the Deputy Chief of Operations for Air, where he headed aviation gunnery training until 1942. He was then made executive officer of the USS Hancock, an aircraft carrier in the Pacific theater. The Hancock was in several campaigns, including Iwo Jima and Okinawa, and Raborn was awarded a Silver Star for his actions when the ship was hit during a kamikaze attack. After the war, he was promoted to captain and assigned to the staff of the commander of a carrier task force.

From 1949 until 1950, Raborn served as operations officer for the Commander, Fleet Air, West Coast. From 1952 through 1954, he served as the assistant director of guided missiles in the Office of the Chief of Naval Operations. In 1955, he was selected to head the Navy's Polaris missile program. For the remainder of his naval career, he was instrumental in the development of ballistic missile submarines and their weapons and navigation systems.

Raborn was appointed by President Lyndon Johnson to serve as DCI. He served in that capacity from April 1965 until June 1966. But, with no prior experience in matters of intelligence or foreign affairs, he proved a rather ineffective DCI. In fact, conversations circulating among Agency professionals of Raborn's alleged gaffes and blunders soon began appearing in the press, and the admiral was forced to resign after only 14 months in office.

Following his brief term with the CIA, Raborn entered the private sector. He initially served as vice president of California-based Aerojet General. He then founded the W. F. Raborn Co., Inc., serving as its president from 1970 until 1986.

Raborn was the recipient of the Distinguished Service Medal, the Robert J. Collier Trophy of the National Aeronautics Association, and the National Security Medal, among others.

Raborn died at 85 of cardiac arrest at his home in McLean, Virginia, on March 7, 1990. He was buried on the grounds of the U.S. Naval Academy.

See also RICHARD MCGARRAH HELMS.

RADINT (radar intelligence)

RADINT is an acronym for radar intelligence. This form of intelligence is gathered by intercepting and analyzing the signals emitted by radar.

See also ALL-SOURCE INTELLIGENCE; INTELLIGENCE CYCLE.

Radio Free Europe (RFE)

Established in 1950, Radio Free Europe (RFE) is a broadcasting organization with a stated mission of "promoting democratic values and institutions." Its original purpose was to broadcast news to Eastern bloc countries during the COLD WAR.

During the first two decades of its existence, funding for RFE was channeled through the CIA. Since 1971, however, funding has been granted directly by Congress, most of it disbursed as grants from the Broadcasting Board of Governors of the U.S. Information Agency. In 1975, RFE merged with RADIO LIBERTY (RL), which, founded in 1951, was responsible for similar broadcasting within the Soviet Union.

In 1991 the Soviet Union collapsed, and the RFE/RL budget was reduced. Broadcasting ceased in some areas but was begun in others. RFE/RL currently operates throughout Europe, Russia, the Caucasus, Central Asia, and the Middle East. The broadcasts include news and political commentary, sports, and music.

Radio Liberty (RL)

See RADIO FREE EUROPE.

raven

In CIA parlance, a "raven" is a male agent who works as a prostitute in order to gather intelligence from someone who possesses knowledge of a hostile nation's secrets. The raven's mission is to engage in sexual activity with the targeted person and gather the intelligence through pillow talk or blackmail.

The sexual activity usually takes place in a prearranged room or residence equipped with hidden cameras and recording devices. Such a place is known as a "raven's nest."

See also SWALLOW.

Robertson, William (Rip) (–1973)

Texas-born William "Rip" Robertson was one of two non-Cuban senior ground officers commanding the CIA-supported assault force (the second officer was GRAYSTON LYNCH) during the 1961 invasion of Cuba at the BAY OF PIGS. Robertson was a tall, raw-boned former Vanderbilt football player and Marine Corps frogman whose skin was so sun-wizened that the Cuban exiles under his command nicknamed him "the alligator."

Poster advertising Radio Free Europe   (LIBRARY OF CONGRESS)

Robertson joined the CIA soon after the Agency was established in 1947 and participated in the COUP D'ÉTAT OF GUATEMALA in 1954.

Together with Lynch, Robertson directed the landing operation during the ill-fated invasion of Cuba at the Bay of Pigs in April 1961. He commanded the force from the deck of his command ship, the *Barbara J,* and was one of the first men ashore.

In 1973, Robertson died of malaria in Laos.

Rockefeller Commission

The Rockefeller Commission (the U.S. President's Commission on CIA Activities within the United States) was a presidentially appointed panel tasked with investigating illegal domestic activities on the part of the CIA. The alleged misdeeds also included ASSASSINATION PLOTS against foreign political leaders.

Seeds for the investigation were planted when on May 9, 1973, an Agency list, known as the FAMILY JEWELS, of over 300 "questionable" CIA activities was compiled under the orders of DIRECTOR OF CENTRAL INTELLIGENCE (DCI) JAMES R. SCHLESINGER—a virtual outsider when it came to the CIA's clandestine affairs. Schlesinger had decided that he needed to know what he—and his DEPUTY DIRECTOR of Operations (DDO), WILLIAM EGAN COLBY—might not be aware of. But the Family Jewels weren't the only problem facing the Agency.

In December 1974, Seymour Hersh, a reporter for the *New York Times,* published a scathing exposé of the CIA, alleging that the Agency had illegally spied on antiwar activists during the Vietnam War. The article argued that the spying constituted domestic activities that violated the CIA's charter.

President Gerald Ford was not completely unaware of the CIA's illegal activities, but he was genuinely disturbed by the allegations of Agency-sponsored ASSASSINATION PLOTS. Ford wanted a full report, but with discretion. That, combined with calls by prominent Democrats for an investigation, compelled Ford to create an investigative body chaired by Vice President Nelson Aldrich Rockefeller, in an attempt to head off a Senate investigation. However, the commission—established in 1975 during what would become known as the "YEAR OF INTELLIGENCE"—did not prevent Congress from creating its own investigative bodies. Both the Senate and the House felt that the commission's findings were "whitewashed." Thus, the Senate would establish the CHURCH COMMITTEE (officially, the Select Committee to Study Governmental Operations with Respect to Intelligence Activities) chaired by Senator Frank Church. The House would establish the PIKE COMMITTEE (officially, the House Select Intelligence Committee) chaired by Congressman Otis Pike.

rogue elephant

"Rogue elephant" was a characterization by SENATOR FRANK CHURCH (D-Idaho) of the CIA. Church used the term in 1975 during the CHURCH COMMITTEE hearings (officially, the Select Committee to Study Governmental Operations with Respect to Intelligence Activities) into alleged misdeeds on the part of the CIA and its domestic counterpart, the FEDERAL BUREAU OF INVESTIGATION. Church, believing that the Agency was out of control and with virtually no oversight, declared that the CIA was a "rogue elephant . . . on a rampage."

roll-out

In CIA parlance, to "roll out" is to remove surreptitiously a letter from an envelope by tightly rolling the letter inside of the envelope, using a special set of pincers, and then extracting it from the unsealed gap at a top corner of the envelope. The letter can then be read or photographed. It is then replaced by simply reversing the technique. This method can be done with all manner of long, thin instruments, including a split chopstick or a pair of knitting needles.

See also FLAPS AND SEALS; HT-LINGUAL.

Roosevelt, Kermit, Jr. (Kim) (1916–2000)

A grandson of President Theodore Roosevelt, Kermit "Kim" Roosevelt was the CIA officer who directed Operation AJAX, the Agency's 1953 COUP D'ÉTAT IN IRAN.

Roosevelt was born in Buenos Aires, Argentina, on February 16, 1916, to Kermit Roosevelt, Sr.—a soldier, writer, and professional adventurer—and Belle Willard. As a boy, young Roosevelt attended Groton, an elite college preparatory school near Boston, Massachusetts. He graduated from Harvard University in 1938. He then taught history at Harvard until 1939, and at the California Institute of Technology (CIT) until 1941.

During World War II, Roosevelt served in both the OFFICE OF THE COORDINATOR OF INFORMATION (COI) and the OFFICE OF STRATEGIC SERVICES (OSS), predecessor organizations to the CIA. Following the war, Roosevelt wrote an official history of the OSS and another book entitled *Arabs, Oil, and History.*

Roosevelt joined the CIA soon after its establishment in 1947. He initially served as political operations assistant to the chief of the Agency's CLANDESTINE SERVICE. He was eventually named the CIA's chief of the plans (operations) DIRECTORATE's Near East and Africa Division.

In 1953, Roosevelt, operating from a SAFE HOUSE in the Iranian capital of Tehran, organized and directed the CIA-sponsored coup d'état in IRAN, which overthrew the de facto regime of Dr. Mohammad Mossadegh and subsequently restored the shah of Iran, Mohammad Reza Pahlavi, to his throne.

The Iranian operation made Roosevelt an instant hero. Eisenhower ordered him to Washington for a personal debriefing. The shah presented Roosevelt at a private dinner with a gold cigarette case and the toast: "I owe my throne to God, my people, my army, and you." Winston Churchill, who invited Roosevelt to his London bedside where he was recovering from a stroke, exclaimed, "Young man, if I had been but a few years younger, I would have loved nothing better than to have served under your command in this great venture."

Roosevelt retired from the CIA in 1957 and became vice president of public relations for Gulf Oil. He later became a partner in a Washington, D.C.–based public relations firm.

Roosevelt died in Cockeysville, Maryland, on June 8, 2000. He was 84.

S

safe house

A safe house is an inconspicuous "house" or dwelling where spies and other covert operatives may hide or take refuge, or from which they may safely conduct clandestine activities without fear of discovery. For instance, the base of operations from which CIA officer Kermit Roosevelt directed the Agency-sponsored COUP D'ÉTAT IN IRAN in 1953 was a safe house in the Iranian capital, Tehran.

San Romain, Jose Perez (Pepe)

Jose Perez "Pepe" San Romain was the senior émigré commander of a CIA-trained force of Cuban expatriates destined to invade Cuba in the ill-fated BAY OF PIGS operation in 1961.

A former Cuban military officer loyal to the regime of Fulgencio Batista y Zaldívar, San Romain was imprisoned after organizing a revolt against his own army. When FIDEL CASTRO came to power in the late 1950's, San Romain was released.

The CIA looked upon San Romain as perfect to lead the attack called for by OPERATION ZAPATA, the invasion of Cuba at the Bay of Pigs. He was familiar with command. He had been educated at Cuba's military academy. He had trained at U.S. Army installations—Fort Benning, Georgia, and Fort Belvoir, Virginia. He had expressed willingness to serve in the Cuban invasion force as either an officer or ordinary soldier. He had no qualms about taking orders from American officers—a fact that would be an asset during the invasion and during the postinvasion establishment of a new Cuban government.

During the ill-fated invasion, San Romain commanded BRIGADE 2506, also known as "La Brigada Asalto," the anti-Castro landing force. San Romain is best remembered for his final frantic radio transmission to the Americans before he and a number of his soldiers fled the battlefield. "I have nothing left to fight with," he shouted as communist tanks moved against his position. "Am taking to the woods. I can't wait for you." He reportedly added, "How can you people [Americans] do this to us, our people, our country?"

satellite intelligence/surveillance operations

The CIA has often relied on information gleaned from satellite intelligence/surveillance operations in order to gather intelligence about nations or entities hostile to the United States or its allies. Coordinating such efforts with other members of the U.S. INTELLIGENCE COMMUNITY as well as the armed forces, the Agency has pioneered many operations that have produced America's current satellite intelligence/surveillance capabilities.

Among the Agency's earliest such projects were the CORONA, LANYARD, and ARGON satellite operations, which, together with the efforts of the U.S. Air Force and the NATIONAL RECONNAISSANCE OFFICE (NRO), collected hundred of thousands of images of the earth's surface from 1960 through 1972. On February 22, 1995, President Bill Clinton ordered the declassification of over 860,000 images collected during the CORONA, LANYARD, and ARGON operations. Today, the NRO (a DEPARTMENT OF DEFENSE entity established in the early 1960s) is primarily responsible for America's satellite intelligence/surveillance operations. The office is staffed by personnel from CIA, the armed forces, and DoD civilians. The director of the NRO is appointed by the president and confirmed by the Congress as the assistant secretary of the Air Force for space.

The DIRECTOR OF CENTRAL INTELLIGENCE (DCI) has the responsibility, which is exercised in concert with the secretary of defense, of operating the NRO. The DCI, who also establishes collection priorities and requirements, oversees the office as the coordinating head of the Intelligence Community.

In November 2001, the SCOWCROFT PROPOSAL—a comprehensive recommendation to bring the NRO, the NATIONAL SECURITY AGENCY (NSA), and the NATIONAL IMAGERY AND MAPPING AGENCY (NIMA) under the direct control of the DCI—was released. The proposal, issued by retired lieutenant general Brent Scowcroft (a former NATIONAL SECURITY ADVISOR), was made to President George W. Bush roughly two months after the SEPTEMBER 11, 2001, TERRORIST ATTACKS ON THE UNITED STATES. It argues that by bringing the three DoD agencies under the CIA, rivalries could be reduced and programs could be consolidated, thus increasing the coordination of intelligence efforts, particularly in the realm of satellite intelligence/surveillance operations.

Schlesinger, Arthur Meier, Jr. (1917–)

Arthur Meier Schlesinger, Jr., is a two-time Pulitzer Prize–winning author and historian. He is also a former intelligence ANALYST for the OFFICE OF STRATEGIC SERVICES (OSS), the World War II predecessor organization to the CIA.

Born in Columbus, Ohio, on October 15, 1917, to Arthur Meier Schlesinger, Sr., and Elizabeth Bancroft, young Schlesinger was destined for a life of power and privilege. He attended Harvard University, majoring in history and literature. He graduated summa cum laude from Harvard in 1938. A member of the Society of Fellows at Harvard, he also became a fellow at Cambridge University.

In 1939, Schlesinger published his first historical biography, *Orestes A. Brownson: A Pilgrim's Progress* (originally his senior honors thesis at Harvard), followed by *The Age of Jackson*, an evaluation of President Andrew Jackson's administration. The latter became a best-seller (Schlesinger received the Pulitzer Prize for that work in 1946).

In December 1941, the United States entered World War II, and in 1942 Schlesinger joined the Office of War Information. That same year, he transferred to the newly established OSS and the office's Research and Analysis branch, serving in Washington, London, and Paris.

After the war, Schlesinger returned to freelance writing and other academic pursuits. He served as an associate professor at Harvard University (1946–54), a professor of history at Harvard (1954–62), a special assistant to President John F. Kennedy (1961–63), and a special assistant to President Lyndon Johnson (1963–64).

In 1965, Schlesinger wrote *A Thousand Days: John F. Kennedy in the White House,* for which he was awarded a second Pulitzer Prize. The following year, he became the Albert Schweitzer Professor in the Humanities at the University of New York in New York City, serving in that capacity until 1995.

Schlesinger is the author of countless magazine and newspapers articles. His other books include *The Vital Center* (1949), *The General and the President* (1951), *The Age of Roosevelt,* volume 1, *The Crisis of the Old Order 1919–1933* (1957), *The Age of Roosevelt,* volume 2, *The Coming of the New Deal* (1958), *The Age of Roosevelt,* volume 3, *The Politics of Upheaval* (1960), *Kennedy or Nixon: Does It Make Any Difference?* (1960), *The Politics of Hope* (1963), *Paths of American Thought* (1963), *The National Experience* (1963), *The Bitter Heritage: Vietnam and American Democracy 1941–1966* (1967), *The Crisis of Confidence: Ideas, Power and Violence in America* (1969), *History of American Presidential Elections* (1971), *History of U.S. Political Parties* (1972), *The Imperial Presidency* (1973), *The Dynamics of World Power* (1973), *Congress Investigates* (1975), *Robert Kennedy and His Times* (1978), *The Almanac of American History* (1983), *The Cycles of American History* (1986), *The Disuniting of America* (1991), *Running for President: The Candidates and Their Images* (1994), *History of American Life* (1996), *A Life in the 20th Century* (2000), and *Innocent Beginnings* (2000).

Aside from his two Pulitzers and numerous other awards, Schlesinger is the recipient of the National Institute and American Academy of Arts and Letters Gold Medal in History and Biography, the Ohio Governor's Award for History, the Eugene V. Debs Award in Education, and the Fregene Prize for literature (Italy). He is a Guggenheim fellow, an American Academy of Arts and Letters grantee, a Decorated Commander of the Order of Orange-Nassau (the Netherlands), and a recipient of the Ordem del Libertador (Venezuela). Additionally, Schlesinger has won countless honorary doctoral degrees.

See also BRUCE-LOVETT REPORT.

Schlesinger, James Rodney (1929–)

James Rodney Schlesinger was the shortest-reigning DIRECTOR OF CENTRAL INTELLIGENCE (DCI). He once reportedly said, "This [the CIA] is a gentleman's club, and I am no gentleman."

Schlesinger was born in New York City on February 15, 1929, to Julius Schlesinger and Rhea Rogen, a middle-class Jewish couple who soon found themselves struggling through the Great Depression. Nevertheless, young Schlesinger was well provided for. He was educated at Harvard University, earning a B.A. in 1950, an M.A. in 1952, and a Ph.D. in 1956. He taught economics at the University of Virginia from 1955 to 1963. In 1960, he published *The Political Economy of National Security*.

In 1963, Schlesinger accepted a position with the RAND Corporation, an academic think tank specializing in research and analysis projects for decision makers in both the corporate world and the federal government. There he worked until 1969, in the later years as director of strategic studies. In 1969, he joined the administration of President Richard Nixon as assistant director of the Bureau of the Budget. In this capacity, he devoted most of his time to matters of national defense as they related to the federal budget.

In December 1970, Nixon directed Schlesinger, by now the deputy director of the U.S. Office of Management and Budget, to examine how the organizational structure of the intelligence community should be changed to bring about greater efficiency and effectiveness, short of legislation. The result was the SCHLESINGER REPORT (officially, A Review of the Intelligence Community), a 47-page review of the intelligence community, complete with recommendations for a basic reform of management, including the establishment of a DIRECTOR OF NATIONAL INTELLIGENCE, a proposal that was not accepted.

In 1971, Nixon named Schlesinger chairman of the Atomic Energy Commission (AEC). Schlesinger brought about extensive organizational changes in an effort to improve the commission's regulatory performance.

On February 2, 1973, Nixon appointed Schlesinger DCI, a post he would hold only until July 2. Schlesinger was not a popular DCI. Not long after assuming the post, he began systematically to fire or retire nearly 1,400 CIA employees. Officially, his actions were the result of downsizing after the Vietnam War. But Agency insiders felt that he was hauling out what he perceived to be deadwood left over from the earliest days of the Agency. Schlesinger's firings would be overshadowed only by the HALLOWEEN MASSACRE, a mass firing nearly five years later. Soon, rumors began surfacing suggesting that CIA facilities and perhaps Agency operatives had been used in some of the illegal activities surrounding the WATERGATE SCANDAL. That, combined with the CIA's alleged 1971 involvement in the burglary of the office of Dr. Lewis Fielding (the psychiatrist of DANIEL ELLSBURG, author of *THE PENTAGON PAPERS*) outraged Schlesinger, who refused to be further blindsided by Agency misdeeds.

Schlesinger, an outsider when it came to the CIA's clandestine affairs, decided to find out what else he might not be aware of. On May 9, he and DEPUTY DIRECTOR OF OPERATIONS (DDO) WILLIAM COLBY directed current and former CIA employees to report (to the DCI) any illegal CIA activities of which they were aware. A portion of the directive reads: "All the senior operating officials of this Agency are to report to me [Schlesinger] immediately on any activities now going on, or that have gone on in the past, which might be construed to be outside of the legislative charter of this Agency." Thus, the FAMILY JEWELS were assembled—a 693-page compendium of some 300 possible CIA transgressions including domestic spying, MAIL INTERCEPTIONS, MIND-CONTROL DRUG TESTING, and foreign ASSASSINATION PLOTS.

On May 10, one day after the Family Jewels directive and just over three months after assuming the directorship of the CIA, Nixon nominated Schlesinger to the post of secretary of defense. Following his congressional confirmation, Schlesinger became the 12th secretary. He served in that capacity from July 2, 1973, until November 19, 1975. The following year, he was named a visiting scholar at the Johns Hopkins School for Advanced International Studies.

When newly elected Jimmy Carter moved into the White House in January 1977, he appointed Schlesinger his special adviser on energy matters and subsequently named him the head of the newly established DEPARTMENT OF ENERGY. Schlesinger became the first secretary of energy on October 1977, a position he would hold until his retirement in July 1979.

Schlesinger left public life, but he continued writing and lecturing. He was also employed as a senior adviser to Lehman Brothers, Kuhn Loeb, Inc. of New York City, and as a senior adviser at Georgetown University's Center for Strategic and International Studies in Washington, D.C.

During the presidential campaign of 1996, Schlesinger, along with former secretaries of defense Caspar Weinberger and Donald Rumsfeld, nuclear scientist Edward Teller, and former DCI JAMES WOOLSEY, argued in favor of a nationwide system of satellites, radars, and missile interceptors by the year 2003. Independent polls, however, showed that the public had little interest in it, and the issue was shelved.

As a member of a 1997 Council on Foreign Relations policy-impact panel addressing the future of the CIA, Schlesinger made the following comments: "How best to equip the Agency to deal with the problems of the 21st century? One of the things that ought to be done is to avoid the kind of constant attack under which the Agency has suffered in recent years. If the leaders of the Agency are continuously called to the Hill or to press conferences to defend the legitimate operations of the Agency, it will vitiate the basic purpose of having a secret intelligence agency."

Schlesinger report

In December 1970, President Richard Nixon directed future DIRECTOR OF CENTRAL INTELLIGENCE (DCI) JAMES RODNEY SCHLESINGER (then the deputy director of the U.S. Office of Management and Budget) to examine how the organizational structure of the U.S. intelligence community should be changed to bring about greater efficiency and effectiveness, short of legislation. The result was the Schlesinger report (officially, A Review of the Intelligence Community), a 47-page review of the community, complete with recommendations for a basic reform of management, including the establishment of a DIRECTOR OF NATIONAL INTELLIGENCE (a proposal that was not accepted).

The report suggested that though there had been a marked increase in the size and expense of the intelligence community over the years, there had also been an "apparent inability to achieve a commensurate improvement in the scope and overall quality of intelligence products." Schlesinger noted that in many cases the intelligence community had "unproductively" duplicated intelligence collection efforts and that there had been a failure at the planning level to coordinate the allocation of resources. He also cited the failure of policy makers to specify their needs to the producers of FINISHED INTELLIGENCE.

The report pointed to what Schlesinger saw as a lack of substantive, centralized leadership within the intelligence community, an inability to "consider the relationship between cost and output from a national perspective." Schlesinger argued that this had resulted in a fragmented intelligence effort.

The report suggested that a DNI position be created, thus freeing up the DCI to concentrate on reducing intelligence costs, increasing intelligence production, and improving the quality of analysis. The creation of a DNI would again be proposed by DCI STANSFIELD TURNER in 1985, in the BOREN-MCCURDY INITIATIVE of 1992, by U.S. Senator Dianne Feinstein (D-California) in June 2002, and in December 2002 by a congressional panel tasked with investigating possible intelligence shortcomings leading to the SEPTEMBER 11, 2001, TERRORIST ATTACKS ON THE UNITED STATES.

The report also advocated the establishment of a Coordinator of National Intelligence (CNI), who would act as the executive-level overseer of the intelligence community. The CNI, Schlesinger believed, would provide more direct presidential representation in all intelligence issues.

The Schlesinger report was completed in March 1971.

School of the Americas (SOA)

The U.S. Army School of the Americas (SOA), a U.S.-based military training center for Latin American military forces, has come under tremendous criticism, as many of its graduates have allegedly engaged in human rights abuses in and around their own countries. Reportedly, those abuses were documented in SOA training manuals, which in many cases had been based on early, classified CIA operations manuals. The SOA has often, though incorrectly, been said to be operated by the Agency.

Located at the Army's infantry installation at Fort Benning, Georgia, the SOA has trained approximately 60,000 Latin American soldiers (both officer and enlisted) from 22 countries in the art of conventional infantry combat, counterinsurgency and special warfare, counternarcotics operations, and military intelligence. The initial U.S. government consensus was that efficient armies trained and supported by the United States would provide a substantive defense against Soviet incursions against North America's southern flank during the COLD WAR. But many of the SOA's graduates returned home and allegedly engaged in all manner of human rights abuses—including torture, assassination, and mass executions—against combatants and noncombatants. Some, in fact, became "assets," or agents, of the CIA.

The SOA was established in 1946 as the U.S. Army Caribbean Training Center in Panama. Its purpose was to assist in creating a sense of professionalism within the Latin American and Carribean military forces. The center was renamed the School of the Americas in 1963. In 1984, under the terms of the 1977 Panama Canal treaties, the school was transferred from Panama to Fort Benning.

In recent years, legislation has been introduced aimed at closing the SOA. The first such bill, introduced in the U.S. House of Representatives on February 5, 1997, stated that "the United States Army School of the Americas graduates include some of the worst human rights abusers in our hemisphere."

Graduates of the SOA include El Salvador's death-squad leader Roberto D'Abuisson; Panamanian dictator and convicted drug dealer Manuel Noriega; Haitian coup leader Raoul Cedras; 19 Salvadoran soldiers linked to the 1989 murder of six Jesuit priests, the priests' housekeeper, and the housekeeper's daughter; Colonel Julio Roberto Alpirez, a Guatemalan military officer linked in the deaths of an American innkeeper; Hector Gramajo, a former Guatemalan defense minister found liable in a U.S. court for the abduction, rape, and torture of Sister Dianna Ortiz, an American citizen; Argentinian dictator Leopoldo Galtieri, leader of the "dirty little war" and responsible for the deaths of 30 civilians; two of the three killers of Archbishop Oscar Romero of El Salvador; 10 of the 12 officers responsible for the murder of 900 civilians in the El Salvadoran village of El Mozotem; and three of the five officers involved in the 1980 rape and murder of four American churchwomen living in El Salvador.

The initial bill to close the SOA was defeated, as was a second bill in 1998. But in 1999, Congress voted 230–197 to cut approximately 10 percent of the SOA's funds.

On January 17, 2001, the SOA was redesignated the WESTERN HEMISPHERE INSTITUTE FOR SECURITY COOPERATION, or WHISC (DEPARTMENT OF DEFENSE officials often refer to it as "WHINSEC"). The name change was part of an ongoing Defense Department effort to repair the SOA's image.

Science and Technology, Directorate of
See DIRECTORATES, CIA.

Scowcroft proposal
The Scowcroft proposal was a comprehensive recommendation to bring three major U.S. DEFENSE DEPARTMENT (DoD) intelligence agencies under the direct control of the DIRECTOR OF CENTRAL INTELLIGENCE (DCI). The proposal, based on the findings of a panel headed by retired lieutenant general Brent Scowcroft (the chairman of the PRESIDENT'S FOREIGN INTELLIGENCE ADVISORY BOARD and a former NATIONAL SECURITY ADVISOR), was made to President George W. Bush in November 2001.

Under the proposal, the agencies to be transferred included the NATIONAL RECONNAISSANCE OFFICE (NRO), which develops intelligence satellite systems; the NATIONAL SECURITY AGENCY (NSA), which is in charge of electronic intercepts; and the NATIONAL IMAGERY AND MAPPING AGENCY (NIMA), which handles imagery intelligence systems and mapping.

Bush created the Scowcroft panel in May 2001, directing DCI GEORGE J. TENET to conduct a comprehensive review of the existing intelligence system. The panel was ordered to produce plans for a revamping of the system in order to meet the challenges of new technologies and new threats to the United States.

In the wake of the SEPTEMBER 11, 2001, TERRORIST ATTACKS ON THE UNITED STATES, the panel took on added significance.

If the proposal is accepted, it will constitute one of the largest ever overhauls of the U.S. INTELLIGENCE COMMUNITY.

Scranage, Sharon M. (1955–   )
Sharon M. Scranage was a CIA employee who, together with her boyfriend MICHAEL SOUSSOUDIS, turned over classified information to intelligence officials of the government of Ghana. She was caught after a routine polygraph test aroused the suspicions of Agency officers.

In 1985, Scranage, a 30-year-old operations-support assistant at the CIA's station in Ghana, was persuaded by her lover, Soussoudis, a Ghanaian intelligence operative, to provide him with classified U.S. information, including secret cables. She copied the material in shorthand at her office, then later recopied it in longhand. Scranage also disclosed the identities of CIA officers, agents, and informants operating in the region, resulting in the arrest and imprisonment of at least eight CIA assets. In his book *Inside the CIA*, Ronald Kessler writes, "She [Scranage] handed Soussoudis virtually everything there was to know about the CIA's activities in Ghana." Additionally, much of what Scranage turned over to Soussoudis was reportedly forwarded by Kojo Tsikata, chief of Ghanaian intelligence, to Cuba, Libya, East Germany, and the Soviet Union.

The case began to surface in 1983 when Scranage invited an officer from the Agency's Office of Security to her home for dinner. At some point during the evening, the officer passed through Scranage's bedroom on the way to the bathroom and noticed a photograph, taped to her vanity mirror, of Soussoudis in Scranage's bed. The officer later warned her against becoming romantically involved with locals, particularly people connected with the Ghanaian government (Soussoudis was a first cousin of Ghanaian prime minister Jerry Rawlings). Not long after the dinner, the CIA's CHIEF OF STATION directed Scranage to end her relationship with Soussoudis. Scranage said she would, but the affair continued.

In the summer of 1985, Scranage was reassigned to the United States. She was then ordered to submit to a routine polygraph test for reposting. The test revealed deception, but Scranage denied any wrongdoing. Eventually she admitted to providing Soussoudis with classified information because he had threatened to end their relationship. Scranage agreed to cooperate with the FEDERAL BUREAU OF INVESTIGATION (FBI) in order to arrest Soussoudis.

Indicted on 18 counts of providing classified information to a foreign country, Scranage subsequently pled guilty to one count under the espionage code and two counts of violating the recently passed INTELLIGENCE IDENTITIES PROTECTION ACT OF 1982. The remaining charges were dropped.

On November 26, 1985, Scranage was sentenced to a five-year prison term. The sentence was later reduced to two years. Soussoudis received a 20-year sentence but was exchanged for several imprisoned Ghanaian agents who had worked for the CIA.

seal of office, CIA
The strikingly beautiful CIA seal of office, also known as the CIA emblem, was approved by presidential mandate in 1950.

Provided for in the CENTRAL INTELLIGENCE AGENCY ACT OF 1949, the seal was designed with three primary symbols in mind. Like most federal emblems, the CIA seal features the head of an American eagle, the national bird and a symbol of strength and vigilance. The seal also

Seal of the Central Intelligence Agency   (CENTRAL INTELLIGENCE AGENCY)

features the radiating points of a scarlet compass rose, which represents the intelligence data collected from around the world as converging at a central point. It is described in official heraldic terms as follows:

> Shield: Argent, a compass rose of sixteen points gules.
> Crest: On a wreath argent and gules an American bald eagle's head erased proper.
> Below the shield on a gold color scroll the inscription 'United States of America' in red letters and encircling the shield and crest at the top the inscription 'Central Intelligence Agency' in white letters.
> All on a circular blue background with a narrow gold edge.

President Harry Truman formally approved and set forth the establishment of the CIA seal with EXECUTIVE ORDER 10111, on February 17, 1950.

Federal law prohibits use of the CIA seal, or "any colorable imitation" of the seal, in any manner intended to convey the impression that such use is "approved, endorsed, or authorized" by the CIA.

secret intelligence (SI)

Secret intelligence (SI) is a term used to describe intelligence gathered by covert means. In most cases, this involves intelligence gathered by HUMINT or human intelligence sources (spies and other covert operatives).

The Encyclopedia of American Intelligence and Espionage states that SI is "generally synonymous with espionage."

secret writing (SW)

Secret writing (SW) is a CIA tradecraft term that describes the art of using special inks or special carbon papers (impregnated with chemicals) to write messages clandestinely. The utilization of special inks is known as the "wet system." The utilization of special carbon papers is known as the "dry system."

In secret writing, the messages are not visible to the human eye unless the recipient uses special chemicals to reveal them. A hostile operative intercepting the paper or document inscribed with the hidden message would be unable to see it. With no knowledge of a hidden message, he or she would have no reason to treat the paper with a special chemical.

Senate Select Committee on Intelligence (SSCI)

The Senate Select Committee on Intelligence (SSCI) is one of two congressional bodies tasked with overseeing, and sometimes investigating, the actions of the U.S. INTELLIGENCE COMMUNITY.

Established on May 19, 1976, the SSCI was created as a result of the congressional hearings held in the mid-1970s that investigated alleged misdeeds on the part of the CIA and the FEDERAL BUREAU OF INVESTIGATION (FBI). The SSCI's counterpart in the House of Representatives is the HOUSE PERMANENT SELECT COMMITTEE ON INTELLIGENCE (HPSCI).

See also CHURCH COMMITTEE; PIKE COMMITTEE; ROCKEFELLER COMMISSION.

September 11, 2001, terrorist attacks on the United States

On September 11, 2001, the U.S. INTELLIGENCE COMMUNITY—and to a much greater extent, the nation and the world—was shocked by the worst terrorist attack on American soil in history. It was an unexpected attack that was initially viewed as a failure on the part of the CIA.

At 8:45 A.M., American Airlines Flight 11—a Boeing 767 originating from Boston, Massachusetts, enroute to Los Angeles, California—crashed into the north tower of the World Trade Center in lower Manhattan, New York City. Initial reports indicated that the aircraft might have been a small charter plane that had accidentally veered off course and crashed into one of the two 110-story structures.

Intelligence Community officials immediately began to fear that the plane had been hijacked and deliberately flown into the building. Eighteen minutes later, those fears were confirmed when a second aircraft, United

Airlines Flight 175, also from Boston enroute to Los Angeles, slammed into the south tower of the World Trade Center.

Within minutes, the Federal Aviation Administration (FAA) shut down all New York City area airports. The Port Authority of New York and New Jersey closed all bridges and tunnels in the New York area.

At 9:30 A.M., President George W. Bush, speaking at a school in Sarasota, Florida, announced that the nation had suffered an "apparent terrorist attack."

Air traffic nationwide was halted at 9:40.

Three minutes later, American Airlines Flight 77—a Boeing 757 originating from Washington's Dulles International Airport enroute to Los Angeles—reversed course and crashed into the Pentagon, headquarters of the U.S. DEPARTMENT OF DEFENSE, in Northern Virginia.

The White House was immediately evacuated, Bush left Florida, and the first of the twin World Trade Center towers collapsed, killing thousands.

A fourth plane, United Airlines Flight 93—originating from Newark, New Jersey, enroute to San Francisco, California—crashed in a remote area southeast of Pittsburgh, Pennsylvania. Flight 93's target was never confirmed, a group of passengers had apparently stormed the cockpit and attempted to regain control of the aircraft. The plane had plummeted nose first into the Pennsylvania countryside, killing all aboard.

All federal office buildings were evacuated in Washington. The United Nations building in New York was also evacuated.

The total count for dead and missing fluctuated, eventually settling on more than 3,000 people killed within an hour and a half.

The military forces of the United States, both at home and abroad, were immediately placed on a high state of alert, and Bush began courting allies—chief among them, the United Kingdom—as he developed a coalition for action against the perpetrators of the attacks.

The CIA and the FEDERAL BUREAU OF INVESTIGATION (FBI), working in concert with other American and foreign intelligence agencies, concluded that all four planes had been hijacked by followers of 44-year-old Islamic militant leader OSAMA BIN LADEN. From one of his numerous secret lairs in Afghanistan, bin Laden announced that neither he nor his followers had anything to do with the attacks. But the evidence was overwhelming and was confirmed not just by the U.S. government but by the heads of state and the intelligence agencies of a number of nations allied to the United States.

A multimillionaire Saudi Arabian national, bin Laden was singled out as the principal source of direction and funding for al-Qaeda (Arabic for "the base"), a worldwide network of terrorist cells whose primary aim was the destruction of Israel and the West, and whose primary

tactic had been suicide bombings against civilian and military targets around the globe.

Bin Laden was born in Saudi Arabia to a Yemeni family in 1957. He left Saudi Arabia in 1979 to fight against the Soviet invasion of Afghanistan. The Afghan rebels opposing the Soviets were financially supported by the United States. It was during that period that bin Laden himself allegedly received security operations training from the CIA (both the Agency and bin Laden, however, have denied any such relationship). In Afghanistan, bin Laden founded the Maktab al Khidimat (MAK), an organization that recruited freedom fighters from around the world and aided in the importation of weapons and equipment for the Afghan resistance. After the Soviet pullout in 1989, bin Laden's faction turned its focus on opposing the United States and its allies in the Middle East. Like many Arabs, bin Laden hated Israel and wanted the total collapse of that nation. He also hated Israel's allies, chief among them the United States, and he believed that Western culture in general was corrupting Islam.

At some point, bin Laden returned to Saudi Arabia to work in his family's construction business. However, in 1994, he was expelled because of his antigovernment activities in that country. He relocated to the African country of Sudan. Two years later, U.S. government pressure led the Sudanese government to expel bin Laden. He then returned to Afghanistan. According to American intelligence sources, bin Laden was involved in numerous attacks on Western targets prior to the attacks of September 11—the 1992 bombing of a Yemeni hotel (where American servicemen were lodging), killing two Australians; the 1993 World Trade Center bombing, which killed six people and wounded more than 1,000; a 1995 car-bomb detonation in Riyadh, Saudi Arabia; a 1993 attack on American troops in Somalia in which 18 American soldiers were killed; a 1995 truck-bomb detonation in Dhahran, Saudi Arabia, in which 19 American soldiers were killed; the 1995 assassination attempt on Egyptian president Hosni Mubarak; the 1998 embassy bombings in Kenya and Tanzania, which killed 224 people and wounded nearly 5,000; and the 2000 attack on the guided-missile destroyer USS *Cole* in the port of Yemen, killing 17 American sailors and wounding 40 others.

In August 2001, the CIA received information from a number of sources suggesting that bin Laden was "increasingly determined" to strike on American soil. Unfortunately, that intelligence was not specific enough to prevent the attacks of September 11. Additionally, it was determined by early 2002 that both the CIA and the FEDERAL BUREAU OF INVESTIGATION (FBI—the Agency's domestic counterpart organization) had failed to share related information that might have produced more precise FINISHED INTELLIGENCE. The CIA, the FBI, and the NATIONAL SECURITY

Smoke pours from the twin towers of the World Trade Center after they were hit by two hijacked airliners in a terrorist attack on September 11, 2001, in New York City   (ROBERT GIROUX/GETTY IMAGES)

AGENCY (NSA—the U.S. INTELLIGENCE COMMUNITY member primarily responsible for electronic intelligence) were also blamed for failing to develop a single, cooperative counterterrorism plan and a single definition of terrorism. At the time of the attacks, bin Laden and his chief lieutenants were harbored by Afghanistan's ruling Taliban party, a militant Islamic sect sympathetic to al-Qaeda. The Taliban was engaged in a civil war with the Northern Alliance, a marginally equipped group of Afghan freedom fighters opposed to the Taliban's iron-fisted rule.

As American and British warships steamed to the region and special forces commandos reportedly began scouting operations in and around Afghanistan, bin Laden issued the following statement: "We hope that these brothers [the suicide hijackers] will be the first martyrs in the battle of Islam in this era against the new Jewish and Christian crusader campaign that is led by the Chief Crusader Bush under the banner of the cross."

On September 12, 2001, the day after the terrorist attacks, DIRECTOR OF CENTRAL INTELLIGENCE (DCI)

GEORGE J. TENET made the following comments in a briefing before the employees of the CIA.

Yesterday, the entire American people—joined by men and women around the globe—recoiled in horror at the barbaric acts against our country. In my hometown of New York, at the Pentagon, and in the skies over Pennsylvania, the bloody hand of evil struck again and again, stealing thousands of innocent lives.

As the devastating toll of terror comes into focus, we are sure to find among those who were lost friends, colleagues, and others we hold dear.

Our thoughts and prayers are with all the victims, with those searching and caring for them, and with those who mourn them. I urge all of you to take the time to think of brothers and sisters that we, as Americans, have lost and to pray for those who survive them.

The images of fire and destruction are forever etched in our minds. And in our hearts, amid the numbing shock, there has been profound grief and renewed resolve.

As President Bush said last night, the search for the sponsors of these unspeakable acts has already begun. Our Agency is among the leaders of that search.

The fight against those who use the weapon of terror to menace and murder is necessarily hard. The shield of fanaticism—wielded by those ready to forfeit their lives to achieve their twisted dreams—is not easily pierced. But it has been pierced before, and it will be pierced again.

Though we did not stop the latest, terrible assaults, you—the men and women of CIA and our Intelligence Community—have done much to combat terrorism in the past. Hundreds, if not thousands, of American lives have been saved by the brave men and women of our Counterterrorism Center, our Directorate of Operations, our analysts, our scientists, our support officers—all who work relentlessly every day against this difficult target. I know that together, we will do even more in the future.

The response yesterday from our counterterrorism center, the Ops Center, Global Support, our entire Security Staff, and many, many others was absolutely magnificent. Today, I am—as I always have been—very, very proud of all the men and women in this organization.

The important thing for us now is to do our job. To run to ground a vicious foe—one without heart or pity. A foe who has killed Americans, but who hopes in vain to kill the ideals and values that define all of us as Americans. The terrorists behind these atrocities—and those who give them shelter and support—must never know rest, ease, or comfort. The last word must not be theirs. For the future must belong to the champions of freedom, not its enemies. That is our aim—today, tomorrow, always. This is a time for us to come together: To bring all our talents to bear in a steely determination to do what we are called to do—protect our fellow citizens.

It is our turn again to step up to a challenge, and to meet it as we meet all challenges: With commitment and courage.

Put some spirit in your step, square your shoulders, focus your eyes . . . . [W]e have a job to do.

Many years ago, Winston Churchill—a giant of democracy—recalled his reaction on hearing the news of another surprise attack on America, this one at Pearl Harbor: There were, he wrote, "many, not only in enemy countries [who] might discount the force of the United States. Some said they were soft, others that they would never be united. They would fool around at a distance. They would never come to grips. They would never stand blood-letting." But, Churchill concluded, "I had studied the American Civil War, fought out to the last desperate inch. American blood flowed in my veins. I thought of a remark which Edward Grey had made to me more than thirty years before—that the United States is like a gigantic boiler. Once the fire is lighted under it, there is no limit to the power it can generate."

Indeed there is not.

In comments to CIA employees on September 26, President George Bush said:

> We are on a mission to make sure that freedom is enduring. We're on a mission to say to the rest of the world, come with us—come with us, stand by our side to defeat the evil-doers who would like to rid the world of freedom as we know it. There is no better institute to be working with than the Central Intelligence Agency, which serves as our ears and our eyes all around the world.
>
> This is a war that is unlike any other war that our nation is used to. It's a war of a series of battles that sometimes we'll see the fruits of our labors, and sometimes we won't. It's a war that's going to require cooperation with our friends. It is a war that requires the best of intelligence. You see, the enemy is sometimes hard to find; they like to hide. They think they can hide, but we know better.
>
> This is a war that not only says to those who believe they can disrupt American lives or, for that matter, any society that believes in freedom, lives. It's also a war that declares a new declaration, that says if you harbor a terrorist you're just as guilty as the terrorist; if you provide safe haven to a terrorist, you're just as guilty as the terrorist; if you fund a terrorist, you're just as guilty as a terrorist.

In the wake of the attacks, blame was heaped on numerous federal agencies—not the least of them the CIA—for failing to predict and counter the actions of bin Laden and al-Qaeda. "There was no intelligence," said Representative Curt Weldon (R-Pennsylvania), a senior member of the House Armed Services Committee. "This was a massive operation and it's a failure that was caused by a lack of resources. Our government failed the American people." Bush disagreed, stating, "in order to make sure that we're able to conduct a winning victory, we've got to have the best intelligence we can possibly have. And my report to the American people is that we've got the best intelligence we can possibly have thanks to the men and women of the CIA."

In an October 6 interview for CNN—entitled "Target Terrorism: The Investigation Continues; Intelligence Community Retraces Its Steps; How Can Attacks Be Prevented?"—CIA spokesperson Bill Harlow stated, "As you know, the war on terrorism didn't begin on September 11 at the CIA. We've been working on that for a long time. Our Counterterrorism Center, in fact, was set up in the mid-1980s. In the last four years, the size of it has doubled, and in the last four weeks, it's doubled again.

"We have ANALYSTS, operators, people detailed to us from the FBI, from the FAA, from the Department of Defense, all working together on this target. Not just the Counterterrorism Center but throughout the agency, all of our assets are devoted to this very important target."

According to Harlow, HUMINT (human intelligence) is the core of what the CIA does on a day-to-day basis. But that the Agency, just like other U.S. government agencies, was reduced in size during the early 1990s. "More than 20 percent," he said. That fact has been addressed since 1997 under the directorship of Tenet.

"Our clandestine training facility this year graduated five times as many students as graduated from that facility in 1996," said Harlow. "We're working on dealing with the question of language capabilities. . . . three times as many people with capabilities in Arabic. Our last graduating class from the clandestine facility had 22 different languages represented among the students there." Unfortunately, said Harlow, "It's not the kind of thing which you can fix in a day or a week or a month." He added, "It is a war against terrorism, and in wars, sadly, some battles will be lost. Obviously, the events of September 11 were a very serious blow, but I can assure you that all of us are focused on the mission of taking care of the terrorist target and working overseas. It is a very difficult target, much more difficult than the conventional wars that we've been used to, and one that requires a great deal of resources and assets."

The CIA, which was on the ground in the region almost immediately after the attacks of September 11, began coordinating the efforts of the Northern Alliance with the special military forces of the United States and the United Kingdom.

In the days following September 11, President Bush granted the CIA what was considered in some circles the broadest covert operations powers in the history of the Agency.

According to a report in the *Washington Post,* "President Bush last month signed an intelligence order directing the CIA to undertake its most sweeping and lethal covert action since the founding of the agency in 1947, explicitly calling for the destruction of Osama bin Laden and his worldwide al-Qaeda network, according to senior government officials.

"The president also added more than $1 billion to the agency's war on terrorism, most of it for the new covert action. The operation will include what officials said is 'unprecedented' coordination between the CIA and commando and other military units."

On October 7, 2001, the United States and its allies launched a massive retaliatory air and naval strike against the forces of the ruling Taliban in Afghanistan and bin Laden's al-Qaeda terrorist network in that same country.

See also TERRORISM, CIA'S INVOLVEMENT IN THE WAR AGAINST.

Shackley, Theodore George, Jr. (Ted)
(1927–2002)

Nicknamed the "Blonde Ghost," Theodore George "Ted" Shackley, Jr., is best known as the Agency operative who directed the CIA's JMWAVE station in Miami during the early 1960s.

Shackley was born in Massachusetts on July 16, 1927. He served in the U.S. Army from 1945 to 1947, and in 1951 he graduated from the University of Maryland. He returned to the Army during the Korean War, serving from 1951 to 1953 and attaining the rank of first lieutenant. Shackley then joined the CIA, accepting a position with the CIA CLANDESTINE SERVICE.

After the failed invasion of Cuba at the BAY OF PIGS in 1961, Shackley became chief of the Agency's Miami station, code-named JMWAVE. Utilizing the COVER of ZENITH TECHNICAL ENTERPRISES, JMWAVE was the headquarters from which OPERATION MONGOOSE, a series of suboperations against Cuban leader Fidel Castro, was planned and directed during the 1960s.

Located in a refurbished former U.S. Navy blimp facility on the University of Miami's south campus, Zenith Technical Enterprises offices posted hours of operation and gave the appearance of a nondescript government electronics research and development contractor conducting classified work for the U.S. DEPARTMENT OF DEFENSE and other federal agencies. Behind the corporate cover, however, the Agency was planning and initiating all manner of BLACK operations against Castro's regime, including the infiltration into Cuba of intelligence-collection teams, supply of weapons and equipment to support the Cuban underground, support to commando raids, and other operations aimed at destroying Cuba's agricultural and industrial infrastructure. When MONGOOSE ceased after the CUBAN MISSILE CRISIS in 1962, JMWAVE operations ended, and Shackley was reassigned.

In 1965, Shackley was posted to the CIA station in West Berlin. The following year, he was transferred to Laos, where he served as CHIEF OF STATION (COS) until 1968, when he was named COS in Saigon, Vietnam. In that capacity, he was involved in the controversial special project code-named OPERATION PHOENIX. The project involved identifying and targeting Vietcong leaders during the Vietnam War. He later served briefly in Chile.

Shackley became chief of the CIA Clandestine Service's Western Hemisphere Division in 1972, and he served in that capacity until the middle of 1973. He then held posts in the East Asia Division and as deputy to the CS chief. His final assignment was with the Agency's Policy and Coordination Staff.

Shackley retired from the Agency in 1979 and then served on the transition team for the incoming administration of President Ronald Reagan. Two years later, his book *The Third Option: An American View of Counterinsurgency Operations* (1981) was published.

Shackley was allegedly involved in the 1985–87 IRAN-CONTRA SCANDAL. He later served as a lecturer on topics related to unconventional warfare. Among awards he received was the Distinguished Intelligence Medal, which he won three times.

Sheinwold, Alfred (1912–1997)

Alfred Sheinwold was best known as a bridge-playing expert and newspaper columnist. He also served with the OFFICE OF STRATEGIC SERVICES (OSS), the World War II predecessor organization to the CIA.

Sheinwold was born the son of Nathan Sheinwold and Mary Sugarman in London, England, on January 26, 1912. The family came to the United States and settled in Brooklyn in 1921. Sheinwold became a naturalized citizen in 1940. While studying economics at the City College of New York (now known as the City College of the City University of New York), he began playing bridge and soon developed such a knack for the game that he became known as the "King of Bridge." He won a number of prestigious bridge tournaments, including the North American Open Team Championship, the North American Men's Championship, and the North American Mixed Pair Championship. He also coached several teams competing at the international level, including the 1985 North American team that won the bridge world championship. He graduated from the City College of New York, earning a B.S.S. (bachelor of science in surveying) in 1933.

When America entered World War II in 1941, Sheinwold joined the U.S. Army. He was transferred to the OSS, where he became chief of the cryptographic security section of the OSS Message Center. In that capacity, from 1942 to 1945, he was responsible for deciphering garbled messages from the various OSS stations worldwide. He was also tasked with ensuring the security of messages, as well as training the Office's cryptographers.

After the war, Sheinwold's passion for bridge led him to write a syndicated newspaper column, *Sheinwold on Bridge*, which appeared in over 200 newspapers for nearly 40 years. He was also a regular contributor to bridge magazines, and he wrote 13 books related to bridge and other card and board games. One of those books, *Five Weeks to Winning Bridge* (1959), became a best-seller. In 1996, he was inducted into the Bridge Hall of Fame in Philadelphia, Pennsylvania.

Following a stroke, Sheinwold died in Sherman Oaks, California, on March 8, 1997. He was 85.

siblings

Siblings is a CIA term used to refer to officers employed by the sometimes rival DEFENSE INTELLIGENCE AGENCY (DIA). The unofficial rivalry between the two agencies began when the DIA was established in 1961. From the beginning, some CIA officials felt that the DIA was encroaching on Agency territory. It was believed that the DIA was too involved with CIA-controlled spy satellite operations. The rivalry also stemmed from fiscal concerns, wherein both agencies found themselves competing for budget dollars. However, by virtue of the coordinating and oversight authority of the DIRECTOR OF CENTRAL INTELLIGENCE (DCI), the CIA is senior to the DIA within the U.S. INTELLIGENCE COMMUNITY.

sick think

"Sick think" is synonymous with CLANDESTINE MENTALITY.

See also CONSPIRATORIAL NEUROSIS; DREAM-WORLD SPOOKOLOGY.

SIGINT (signals intelligence)

An acronym for signals intelligence, SIGINT is simply intelligence gathered by means of intercepting and analyzing electromagnetic signals. SIGINT is an amalgamation of COMINT and ELINT.

See also ALL-SOURCE INTELLIGENCE; INTELLIGENCE CYCLE; INTELLIGENCE DISCIPLINES, FIVE PRIMARY.

signal site

A signal site is a prearranged fixed location, usually in a public place, where a CIA field officer or an agent can place a predetermined mark to alert a contact person of operational activity. For example, a foreign agent working for the CIA might place a piece of tape on a certain telephone pole in order to signal his or her HANDLER that he has completed an intelligence-gathering assignment and will place coded intelligence documents at a previously determined DROP.

Skull & Bones Society

The Skull & Bones Society is a controversial secret fraternity of select Yale University students. It is said to be "one of the nation's most exclusive and powerful secret societies." Former members, also known as "bonesmen," of the Skull & Bones have served as U.S. presidents, senators, secretaries of state, national security advisors, attorneys general, Supreme Court justices, university presidents, and chief executive officers of *Fortune 500* companies. Many of the early members of the CIA were "bonesmen," including JAMES JESUS ANGLETON, RICHARD MERVIN BISSELL, WILLIAM PUTNAM BUNDY, WILLIAM SLOAN COFFIN, JR., WILLIAM F. BUCKLEY, JR., and President GEORGE H. W. BUSH.

sleeper

In CIA parlance, a "sleeper" is an operative or agent who waits until a predetermined time or a given signal before going into action, then either gathering intelligence or conducting a special or covert operation. The sleeper is sometimes directed to wait for years before going operational.

In the wake of the SEPTEMBER 11, 2001, TERRORIST ATTACKS ON THE UNITED STATES, the agencies of the U.S. INTELLIGENCE COMMUNITY determined, and issued public warnings that, sleepers under the direction of terrorist leader OSAMA BIN LADEN might be located throughout the United States.

Sluzhba Vneshney Razvedki Rossii (SVR)

The Sluzhba Vneshney Razvedki Rossii (Russian Foreign Intelligence Service, or SVR), is Russia's current foreign intelligence service. The SVR is the direct descendent of the First Chief Directorate of the KGB (KOMITET GOSUDARSTVENNOY BEZOPASNOSTI), the infamous Soviet espionage arm.

On October 24, 1991, Soviet president Mikhail Gorbachev abolished the KGB, and with it the First Chief Directorate. Most of the KGB's functions and assets were transferred to several separate organizations. Foreign intelligence, being one of the most critical arms of Soviet defense, was the first element of the KGB to establish a separate identity. Thus, the intelligence-gathering and analysis activities of the First Chief Directorate were immediately reestablished as the Tsentralnaya Sluzhbza Razvedkyin or TsSR (Central Intelligence Service).

On December 18, the CSR was dissolved, the SVR was established, and the CSR's activities were folded into the SVR. Newly elected president Boris Yeltsin appointed Yevgeni Primakov—the former first deputy chairman of the KGB and chief of the First Chief Directorate—as head of the SVR.

Unlike the First Chief Directorate, the SVR is an independent agency and reports directly to the president. The SVR is the Russian Federation's counterpart organization to the American CIA, Great Britain's MI6, and Israel's MOSSAD.

SMERSH

SMERSH was the acronym for the feared SMERT SHPIONAM (literally "death to spies") ASSASSINATION units of the KOMITET GOSUDARSTVENNOY BEZOPASNOSTI, or KGB.

SMERT SHPIONAM

SMERT SHPIONAM, or SMERSH (literally, "death to spies"), was the name of the feared ASSASSINATION units of the KOMITET GOSUDARSTVENNOY BEZOPASNOSTI, or KGB.

Established from the counterintelligence units of the NKVD by Soviet premier Joseph Stalin in 1943, SMERSH was overseen by Stalin but officially directed by the Soviet general staff during World War II. As the Soviet armies advanced against the enemy, SMERSH battalions followed, rooting out dissidents from among the ranks of the Red Army and executing Soviet soldiers deemed cowardly.

According to *On the Front Lines of the Cold War: Documents on the Intelligence War in Berlin, 1946 to 1961,* a publication released by the History Staff of the CIA's *Center for the Study of Intelligence,* SMERSH was "theoretically" responsible for counterintelligence operations. In fact, it was "Stalin's tool for eliminating subversion and collaboration in territories recaptured from the Nazis. After the war, it was primarily engaged in interrogating and executing returning Soviet prisoners of war."

In 1946, control of SMERSH was returned to Soviet intelligence, eventually falling under the umbrella of the First Chief Directorate of the KGB, the CIA's parallel organization in the former Soviet Union. (The CIA has never maintained a SMERSH counterpart entity.) SMERSH was supposedly abolished when the Soviet Union collapsed in 1991.

IAN FLEMING, author of the well-known JAMES BOND novels, first introduced SMERSH to Western readers through his books.

Smith, Walter Bedell (1895–1961)

Best known as General Dwight Eisenhower's wartime chief of staff, General Walter Bedell Smith was also one of the earliest DIRECTORS OF CENTRAL INTELLIGENCE.

Smith was born in Indianapolis, Indiana, on October 5, 1895, the son of William Long Smith and Ida Frances Bedell, both buyers for a dry-goods company. When he was 15 years old, Smith decided to enter military service. He enlisted in the Indiana National Guard. In 1913, he entered active service, and in 1916 he deployed with the U.S. Army's Mexican border expedition. He briefly attended Butler University in Indianapolis, then worked as a mechanic.

When the United States entered World War I in 1917, Smith was ordered back into active service. He completed officer training at Fort Benjamin Harrison, Indiana, in November, was commissioned a second lieutenant, and was assigned to the 39th Infantry Regiment, Fourth Division. In April 1918, his division left for France. He fought at Chateau-Thierry and in the third Battle of the Marne. He was wounded and returned to the United States.

Smith advanced in rank slowly between the world wars. He was promoted to captain in late 1929 and a decade later became a major. He held a variety of staff posts during the 1920s and 1930s. He also served as an instructor and attended a number of professional schools, including the

General Walter Bedell Smith   (NATIONAL ARCHIVES)

Infantry School at Fort Benning, Georgia; the Command and General Staff School at Fort Leavenworth, Kansas; and the Army War College in Washington, D.C. With war imminent in late 1939, he was ordered to Washington to assist in the rapid building of a new American army.

In February 1942, Smith was named secretary of the JOINT CHIEFS OF STAFF (JCS) and U.S. secretary of the Combined Chiefs of Staff (with the British military service chiefs). In September he was named chief of staff for the European Theater of Operations and chief of staff to General Dwight Eisenhower. Smith served with Eisenhower until the latter's departure from Europe after the war. Smith also negotiated the surrenders of Italy and Germany, personally accepting their surrenders for the Allies.

Promotions were rapid in the late prewar and early war years. Smith became a lieutenant colonel in April 1941, a colonel in August, a brigadier general in February 1942, a major general in December, and a lieutenant general in January 1943.

After the war, Smith was appointed ambassador to the Soviet Union, a post he would hold from 1946 until 1949. In March 1949, he assumed command of the U.S. First Army in New York.

The following year the Korean War erupted, surprising the U.S. government, which blamed the CIA for a lack of substantive warning. As a result, Smith was appointed DIRECTOR OF CENTRAL INTELLIGENCE (DCI) by President Harry Truman, serving in that capacity from October 7, 1950, to February 9, 1953. Smith was considered a tough, effective DCI. As one of his first acts, he sought to bring both the OFFICE OF POLICY COORDINATION (or OPC, the CIA's covert-action arm) and the OFFICE OF SPECIAL OPERATIONS (OSO, the CIA's SECRET INTELLIGENCE arm) under DCI control. In January 1951, he brought the two offices under the newly created post of deputy director for plans (DDP), thus creating the CIA's CLANDESTINE SERVICE (CS). He then named future DCI ALLEN WELSH DULLES the CS's first deputy director for plans (DDP). Smith received his fourth star in 1951.

When Eisenhower became president in 1953, Smith was moved from the DCI's position to that of undersecretary of state. During that period, the CIA was directly involved in the successful COUP D'ÉTAT IN GUATEMALA, an Agency-sponsored operation launched after the socialist regime of President Jacobo Arbenz Guzmán attempted to nationalize American-owned companies operating in that country. Smith had a major financial interest in one such company, UNITED FRUIT.

In May 1954, Smith served as the American representative to the Geneva Far Eastern Conference, arranged to discuss Korean reunification and a settlement of the war in Indochina (Vietnam). He resigned from the State Department in October and entered the private sector. He then held executive-level positions with the American Machine and Foundry Company, RCA, and Corning Glass.

On August 6, 1961, Smith died of a heart attack in Washington, D.C., and was buried in Arlington National Cemetery. He was 65.

soft targets

"Soft target" is a CIA term used to describe a hostile nation, a potentially hostile nation, or a nation friendly to enemies of the West that covert operatives find easy to penetrate and obtain information from. For example, during World War II, Spain and Portugal were considered to be soft targets.

See also HARD TARGET.

Souers, Rear Admiral Sidney William
(1882–1973)

Rear Admiral Sidney William Souers was the first official DIRECTOR OF CENTRAL INTELLIGENCE (DCI), not including WILLIAM J. "WILD BILL" DONOVAN, who was the director of the OFFICE OF STRATEGIC SERVICES (OSS), the World War II precursor organization to the CIA. As such, Souers presided over the CENTRAL INTELLIGENCE GROUP (CIG), the immediate predecessor to the CIA.

Souers was born on March 30, 1882, in Dayton, Ohio. He briefly attended Purdue University but graduated from Miami (Ohio) University in 1914. He worked for a year as a reporter for the *New Orleans Item,* then took a position with Lousiana's Mortgage Security Company. Five years after joining the company, he was named its president. For the next few years, he served in several senior executive positions and on the boards of a number of national corporations.

Souers was named commissioner of the Port of New Orleans in 1928. The following year, he was commissioned a lieutenant commander in the U.S. Naval Reserve. Retaining his commission, he moved to St. Louis, Missouri, and in 1932 was named senior intelligence officer for the region. In 1940, he was called to active service and named senior intelligence officer for the Ninth Naval District, Great Lakes, Illinois.

On December 7, 1941, the Japanese attacked Pearl Harbor, drawing America into World War II. A few months later, in 1942, Souers was appointed intelligence officer for the Sixth Naval District, based in Charleston, South Carolina. That same year, he was named chief of intelligence for the Caribbean Sea Frontier, San Juan, Puerto Rico.

Souers was a key figure in the development of submarine warfare countermeasures, which led to his promotion to rear admiral in 1943. He then assumed the post of assistant director for the Office of NAVAL INTELLIGENCE in Washington, D.C. He was appointed deputy chief of naval intelligence in 1944. The war ended in August 1945.

On January 23, 1946, Souers was appointed director of the newly created CIG by President Harry Truman. At a private luncheon the following day, Truman presented Souers a black cloak, black hat, and a wooden dagger. The president then read a humorous directive that outlined some of the responsibilities of the chief of "Centralized Snooping."

Though reluctant to accept the directorship, and serving for less than five months, Souers was instrumental in ensuring that the CIG survived beyond his tenure and fulfilled its role as the coordinating agency for all American intelligence activities. Souers's leadership skill was reflected in his ability to assemble a staff of experienced, primarily military intelligence officers from the U.S. DEPARTMENTS OF STATE, War, and the Navy. He also managed to gain responsibility for the STRATEGIC SERVICES UNIT, the OSS's remaining foreign intelligence assets, which had been placed under the Department of War when the OSS was disbanded after the war. Under Souers, the CIG also collated the massive amount of

daily cables and dispatches from the War, Navy, and State Departments, producing for the White House a comprehensive intelligence summary known as the *Daily Summary.*

Souers was replaced as DCI by Air Force general HOYT VANDENBERG on June 10. Briefly returning to private life, Souers was recalled to public service when in May 1947 he was asked to establish an intelligence branch for the U.S. Atomic Energy Commission (AEC). Months later, he was named executive secretary of the NATIONAL SECURITY COUNCIL. He served in that capacity until 1950.

Souers died on January 14, 1973. He was 80.

Soussoudis, Michael (unknown)

Michael Soussoudis was a Ghanaian national who persuaded his American lover, CIA secretary Sharon M. Scranage, to provide him with classified Agency information, which he then turned over to senior Ghanaian intelligence officers.

Soussoudis—a 39-year-old first cousin of the Ghanaian prime minister (Jerry Rawlings), a Ghanaian intelligence operative, and a traveling business consultant with homes in both Ghana and the United States—had developed a romantic relationship with Scranage. But in 1985, Soussoudis threatened to break up with her unless she provide him with classified U.S. information from the CIA's Ghana station, where she worked. Scranage complied, turning over secret cables that she copied in shorthand at the office, then recopied in longhand for Soussoudis. Scranage also disclosed the identities of CIA officers, agents, and informants operating in the region, resulting in the arrest and imprisonment of at least eight CIA agents. In his book *Inside the CIA,* Ronald Kessler writes, "She [Scranage] handed Soussoudis virtually everything there was to know about the CIA's activities in Ghana."

As Soussoudis received the information, he passed it on to Kojo Tsikata, chief of the Ghanaian intelligence service. The latter then reportedly forwarded it to Cuba, Libya, East Germany, and the Soviet Union.

The case began to surface in 1983 while Soussoudis was out of the country on business. Scranage invited an officer from the Agency's Office of Security to her home for dinner. At some point during the evening, the officer passed through her bedroom on the way to the bathroom and noticed taped to her vanity mirror a photograph of Soussoudis in Scranage's bed. The officer later warned her against becoming romantically involved with locals, particularly people connected with the Ghanaian government.

Not long after the dinner, the CIA's CHIEF OF STATION directed Scranage to end her relationship with Soussoudis. Scranage said she would, but the affair continued when Soussoudis returned.

In the summer of 1985, Scranage was reassigned to the United States, where she was ordered to submit to a routine polygraph test for reposting. The test revealed deception, and Scranage eventually admitted to providing Soussoudis with classified information. She then agreed to cooperate with the FEDERAL BUREAU OF INVESTIGATION (FBI) in order to arrest Soussoudis.

In July, Soussoudis was picked up by the FBI at a Holiday Inn in Springfield, Virginia. He was charged with eight counts of espionage. He pleaded nolo contendere, a virtual admission of guilt, and was sentenced to 20 years in prison. His sentence was suspended on the condition that he leave the United States. He was quickly exchanged for several imprisoned Ghanaian agents who had worked for the CIA. Scranage received a five-year prison sentence, reduced to two.

In the ensuing years, Soussoudis became heavily involved in Ghanaian politics.

Southeast Asia, operations in

CIA involvement in Southeast Asia lasted for nearly two decades, from the mid-1950s through 1973. Though the U.S. government and many of its entities were blamed for America's ultimate failure in Southeast Asia, the Agency performed credibly, often conducting operations outside of its sphere of responsibility.

In the mid-1950s, CIA operatives began training police forces and paramilitary units for the government of South Vietnam. Simultaneously, the Agency began organizing, recruiting, training, and equipping a number of Meo tribesmen in Laos for conventional and unconventional warfare

President Truman awarding the Distinguished Service Medal to Admiral Sidney Souers   (PAUL BEGLEY, NAVAL PHOTO CENTER)

against the communists. This force of Meo tribesmen would, by 1962, be known as L'ARMÉE CLANDESTINE (the Secret Army). The army, which grew to some 30,000 Laotian fighters and 17,000 mercenaries from Thailand, fought communist Pathet Lao and North Vietnamese soldiers who were attempting to overthrow the government of Laos. This conflict was known as the "Secret War in Laos."

Large-scale involvement on the part of the CIA in both Laos and Vietnam began in 1962. By 1965, the Agency was conducting a myriad of intelligence-gathering operations, as well as all manner of covert-action projects aimed at combating the communists in North Vietnam and guerrillas operating in South Vietnam. Many of the operations involved the deployment of CIA officers who worked directly with U.S. and allied ground forces in the field and CIA pilots who flew transport and intelligence-gathering missions. In the *Encyclopedia of American Intelligence and Espionage*, G. J. A. O'Toole quotes former CIA officer Harry Rositzke as saying, "The CIA became an all-purpose instrument of action like the OFFICE OF STRATEGIC SERVICES during the war with Germany and Japan."

Though covert action was a primary responsibility of the CIA during the conflict in Southeast Asia, the Agency also provided U.S. government consumers of intelligence, chief among them the armed forces, with substantive FINISHED INTELLIGENCE. CIA-gathered and analyzed intelligence provided American military leaders with an accurate pictures of the enemy's actual strength. This intelligence, however, conflicted with enemy-strength figures estimated by the U.S. Army. For instance, in 1967, the Army estimated that some 270,000 enemy soldiers were operating in the field. CIA estimates were twice that number.

In January 1968, Vietcong and North Vietnamese forces launched coordinated attacks on virtually all of South Vietnam's major cities and provincial capitals, as well as U.S. military installations and fire bases throughout the country. The attacks, known as the Tet offensive, forced the Army to revise its enemy-strength figures. The CIA continued providing substantive finished intelligence, but the Agency became increasingly "pessimistic" about the eventual outcome of the war.

When the Paris Peace Accords of 1973 ended America's involvement in Vietnam, the number of CIA operatives was dramatically reduced. In neighboring Laos, l'Armée Clandestine was also disbanded.

In his book *CIA and the Vietnam Policymakers: Three Episodes 1962–1968*, CIA historian Harold P. Ford made the following conclusions as to the Agency's efforts during the war:

> From the early 1950's onward, CIA's assessments in the main proved more accurate than those of any other US Government entity, and CIA's analytic record on Vietnam compares favorably with its endeavors in the counterinsurgency field. CIA officers fairly consistently insisted their

analyses showed that military force alone would not win the war; that our South Vietnamese creation, the GVN, was not proving adequate to the political-military task; that we should not underestimate the enemy's covert presence throughout South Vietnamese society; that we should not underestimate the enemy's staying power; that US bombing efforts were not appreciably slowing the enemy's progress in the South; that the enemy would try to match US escalation rather than meaningfully negotiate; and that ill-founded official claims of great progress distorted reality to the detriment of policy objectives. CIA's record of candor is all the more remarkable because CIA officers often had to brave pressures from senior political and military officers to "get on the team" and to support the war effort with more optimistic findings and estimates.

See also AIR AMERICA; PHOENIX OPERATION.

Spann, Johnny Michael (Mike) (1969–2001)

Johnny Michael "Mike" Spann was the first American killed in overseas combat during the war against terrorism. He died while serving as a CIA officer. Spann, a 32-year-old employee in the CIA's SPECIAL ACTIVITIES DIVISION (the paramilitary arm of the DIRECTORATE of Operations) was serving as an interrogator in Afghanistan at the time of his death.

A native of Winfield, Alabama, Spann played football at Winfield City High School, where he developed a local reputation for being "tough as nails." He attended Auburn University, earning a bachelor's degree in criminal justice. He then served eight years as an officer in the U.S. Marine Corps, rising to the rank of captain. He joined the CIA in June 1999.

In the weeks following the SEPTEMBER 11, 2001, TERRORIST ATTACKS ON THE UNITED STATES, Spann received orders to Afghanistan. He told his family, "I'm going to do something about this," referring to the attacks on American soil. He was dispatched to northern Afghanistan, where he worked closely with U.S. Special Forces who were actively seeking terrorist leader OSAMA BIN LADEN. The Special Forces were coordinating operations with the Northern Alliance—Afghanistan's rebel opposition to the military forces of Afghanistan's ruling Taliban. The latter were providing safe haven for bin Laden.

On November 25, Spann was interrogating captured Taliban soldiers in the fortress of Kala Jangi, near Mazar-e-Sharif, when the prisoners, who had smuggled weapons into the compound, revolted. In the ensuing battle to regain control of the fortress, he was killed. Though the Agency did not release the details of his death, some reports indicated that Spann was greatly outnumbered in close quarters and died in a hand-to-hand struggle.

Of Spann, DIRECTOR OF CENTRAL INTELLIGENCE (DCI) GEORGE JOHN TENET said, "He was no stranger to challenge or daring. He came to us from the United States Marine

Johnny Michael "Mike" Spann (AP WORLD WIDE)

Corps, whose traditions he loved and whose values of courage and commitment he carried with him to the end."

Spann's death was marked by the addition of the 79th star to the MEMORIAL WALL at the GEORGE BUSH CENTER FOR INTELLIGENCE, CIA headquarters in LANGLEY, VIRGINIA. Of the 78 other employees who have died on duty, 35 remain anonymous for reasons of national security. The last two CIA officers to die on duty, in 1998, remain unidentified.

See also TERRORISM, CIA'S INVOLVEMENT IN THE WAR AGAINST.

Special Activities Division (SAD)

The Special Activities Division (SAD) is the paramilitary or special operations arm of the CIA's DIRECTORATE of Operations.

Special Group

The Special Group was a senior interdepartmental organization tasked with overseeing the CIA's high-risk covert operations during the 1950s and early 1960s. Also known

as the 5412 GROUP, the Special Group traced its lineage to the early OPERATIONS COORDINATING BOARD (OCB). The OCB was later renamed the 5412 Group, or simply the Special Group. During the administration of President John Kennedy, the Special Group was known as the 303 COMMITTEE—after a room number in the executive office complex in Washington, D.C. The group was later known respectively as the 40 COMMITTEE and then the OPERATIONS ADVISORY GROUP.

Members of the Special Group included representatives from the U.S. DEPARTMENT OF STATE, the U.S. DEPARTMENT OF DEFENSE, the JOINT CHIEFS OF STAFF (JCS), the Oval Office, and the CIA.

Special Group Augmented (SGA)

Established in November 1961, the Special Group Augmented (SGA) was an executive-level interagency group established by the CIA for the sole purpose of overseeing and carrying out the dictates of OPERATION MONGOOSE, the CIA project aimed at ousting FIDEL CASTRO's regime in Cuba.

One of the SGA's initial duties was to place COUNTERINTELLIGENCE expert WILLIAM KING HARVEY in charge of TASK FORCE W, the CIA operational group responsible for sabotage and paramilitary operations conducted by anti-Castro guerrilla units against Cuba. The SGA was abandoned, along with MONGOOSE, after the CUBAN MISSILE CRISIS of October 1962.

Special National Intelligence Estimate (SNIE)

Special National Intelligence Estimate (SNIE) is a strategic assessment of the capabilities, vulnerabilities, and possible courses of action of a hostile foreign nation or other threatening foreign entities (terrorist organizations, rogue military units, etc.). It is issued during an emergency situation or during any event related to national security in which time is of the essence. SNIEs are also referred to as "rush estimates."

See also NATIONAL INTELLIGENCE ESTIMATES.

Special Operations Executive (SOE)

Established in July 1940, the Special Operations Executive (SOE) was a British "special operations" organization ordered by Prime Minister Winston Churchill to "coordinate all action, by way of subversion and sabotage, against the enemy overseas."

Serving as both a model for and the parallel organization to the U.S. OFFICE OF STRATEGIC SERVICES, or OSS (the World War II predecessor to the CIA), the SOE trained commandos for covert operations against the Axis powers during the war. "In mansions that stretched from the Highlands to the New Forest agents were taught how to kill with their bare hands; how to disguise themselves; how to derail a train; and even how to get out of a pair of handcuffs with a piece of thin wire and a diary pencil," wrote Nigel Morris in an article for the BBC. "If an agent survived these tests and a grueling parachute course they were ready to go."

At peak strength, the SOE comprised some 13,200 operatives, 3,200 of which were women. Organizationally, the SOE fell under the umbrella of the British Chiefs of Staff and was subject to Foreign Office veto when operations were conducted in neutral countries.

The war in Europe ended in the spring of 1945. The war in the Pacific ended in the fall. The SOE was disbanded in January 1946.

Special Operations, Office of (OSO)

The Office of Special Operations or OSO was the first secret intelligence-gathering arm of the CIA.

See also CLANDESTINE SERVICE AND POLICY COORDINATION, OFFICE OF.

Special Policy Committee (SPC)

The Special Policy Committee (SPC) was a panel of representatives from the U.S. DEPARTMENT OF STATE, the CIA, the British Foreign Office, and the British Secret Service (MI6). The committee coordinated paramilitary and clandestine action efforts during the ALBANIAN OPERATIONS of 1949–53. Code-named VALUABLE, the Albanian operations were a series of joint CIA/MI6 suboperations aimed at overthrowing the communist government of Albanian prime minister Enver Hoxha.

The SPC was composed of four member representatives. The State Department representative was ROBERT PRATHER JOYCE, an expert on the Balkans and a former member of the OFFICE OF STRATEGIC SERVICES (OSS), the World War II predecessor organization to the CIA. The CIA representative was FRANKLIN ANTHONY LINDSEY, also a former OSS operative; he had fought alongside Josip Broz Tito's partisans during World War II and was currently serving as chief of the East European Division of the OFFICE OF POLICY COORDINATION's (OPC), the CIA's early covert-action arm. The British Foreign Office representative was George Jellico, a wartime veteran of the elite Special Air Service (SAS). The MI6 representative was HAROLD ADRIAN RUSSELL "KIM" PHILBY, one of the infamous CAMBRIDGE SPIES who had been working for the Soviets and who would ultimately betray the Albanian operation to the communists.

Special Procedures Group (SPG)

The Special Procedures Group was the first covert-action arm of the CIA. Established in 1947 by DIRECTOR OF CENTRAL INTELLIGENCE (DCI) ROSCOE HENRY HILLENKOETTER, the SPG was intended to influence the Italian elections in 1948.

The SPG was eventually named the Office of Special Projects (OSP), which was in turn the predecessor office to the Agency's OFFICE OF POLICY COORDINATION (OPC), the quasi-independent branch of the CIA, established under the direction of FRANK GARDINER WISNER in 1948, responsible for covert action.

See also ITALIAN OPERATIONS.

Special Projects, Office of (OSP)

The Office of Special Projects or OSP was the direct predecessor to the OFFICE OF POLICY COORDINATION (OPC), the covert-action arm of the CIA. Established in June 1948, the OSP descended from the SPECIAL PROCEDURES GROUP, the Agency's first covert-action arm.

spikes, dead drop

Dead DROP spikes are hollow spikes that can hold items delivered by spies or assets to a prearranged location or dead drop. The spikes, which vary in size, are waterproof, have a screw-top or fixed-latch lids, and can be pounded into the ground like a tent stake and thus concealed.

SR-71 (A-12) Blackbird aircraft

Arguably the most recognizable of the high-altitude reconnaissance aircraft ever operated by the CIA was the Lockheed-Martin A-12 (single seat) and the SR-71 (twin seat) Blackbird. But unlike its older sister, the U-2 Dragon Lady, much of the Blackbird's history remains shrouded in mystery.

Developed in the 1950s and 1960s by aircraft designer Clarence "Kelly" Johnson at Lockheed's famous "Skunk Works" in Burbank, California, the Blackbird began as two aircraft, the A-12 and the YF-12 (known in its earliest developmental stages as the A-11). With the exception of crew capacity, the A-12—a single-seat, high-altitude strategic reconnaissance aircraft—was nearly identical to its future twin-seat brother, the SR-71. The YF-12 was also similar in design but was developed as a high-altitude strategic interceptor capable of attacking and destroying high-speed Soviet bombers with air-to-air missiles. The YF-12 never became operational.

At the time of the Blackbird's development, the U-2 Dragon Lady was operational and could outperform any other high-altitude aircraft in the world. But it had become increasingly vulnerable to Soviet surface-to-air missiles.

In 1960, a U-2 flown by CIA pilot FRANCIS GARY POWERS was shot down by a Soviet SA-2 missile over Soviet airspace. At that point, the CIA realized that high-altitude, marginally maneuverable aircraft like the Dragon Lady and the Blackbird were better suited to the reconnaissance role than to the air combat role.

Several A-12s that had been configured for both reconnaissance and attack missions were soon delivered to the CIA. Aside from onboard cameras, the A-12 was fitted with a centerline pod capable of carrying either a one-megaton nuclear bomb or an air-launched drone fitted with an array of sophisticated photographic and infrared sensing equipment. The aircraft were flown by the U.S. Air Force Strategic Air Command and by former Air Force-turned-CIA pilots until the introduction of the SR-71 in 1964.

The purpose behind the SR-71 was simple, according to Johnson: "It makes no sense to just take this one or two steps ahead, because we'd be buying only a couple of years before the Russians would be able to nail us again. No, I want us to come up with an airplane that can rule the skies for a decade or more."

Development of the SR-71 began in February 1963, four months after the CUBAN MISSILE CRISIS. The aircraft's maiden flight took place on December 22, 1964. Soon Air Force SR-71s were operational. A-12s, however continued in service for another four years.

The highlight of the A-12's history was Operation BLACKSHIELD. In May 1967, CIA pilots began flying A-12s out of Kadena Air Base on the Japanese island of Okinawa. From that time until June 1968, A-12s flew numerous sorties over Vietnam and North Korea. The A-12s were then replaced by SR-71s, flown by Air Force pilots. But photographic intelligence (PHOTINT) gleaned from the SR-71 missions continued to be forwarded to the Agency.

Then as now, the Blackbird was the fastest, highest-climbing reconnaissance aircraft in the U.S. arsenal. It has

The SR-71 Blackbird aircraft   (NATIONAL ARCHIVES)

a top speed of Mach 3.5 (over three times the speed of sound, or 2,500 miles per hour). It can fly higher than 100,000 feet. It has a range of over 2,500 miles on one tank of gas; it is intercontinental if refueled in flight. It can survey over 100,000 square miles of the earth's surface in one hour. Physically, the aircraft is unlike anything developed before or since. It is a twin-engined platform, constructed of titanium that at extremely high flight temperatures elongates up to six inches. It is 107.4 feet (32.74 meters) long, and 18.5 feet (5.64 meters) in height, with a wingspan of 55.6 feet (16.95 meters).

The collapse of the Soviet Union, the subsequent U.S. military downsizing, and the escalating costs of the SR-71 (intelligence gleaned during SR-71 missions was utilized by the CIA, the U.S. Navy, and the Air Force, but funding for the aircraft was drawn from SAC's coffers) forced the Blackbird into retirement on January 26, 1990. But when Iraqi forces invaded Kuwait in August, the aircraft was brought back into service. The SR-71 was again retired in 1998. A few SR-71s are still in use by the National Aeronautics and Space Administration (NASA) for high-speed research.

The SR-71 was originally named the RS-71. Lockheed renamed it when President Lyndon Johnson accidentally reversed the letters during his announcement of the aircraft's existence in 1964.

Staatssicherheitsdienst (STASI)

The Staatssicherheitsdienst, or STASI, was the East German Secret Police, also known as the Ministry for State Security. During the COLD WAR, the STASI maintained a vast database on East German citizens built through a network of spies and informants loyal to the communists. The STASI was one of the CIA's most notorious counterparts during the height of the cold war.

State, U.S. Department of

The U.S. Department of State is a cabinet-level organization and one of three non–Defense Department components of the U.S. INTELLIGENCE COMMUNITY. As the senior U.S. foreign affairs agency, the department is responsible for a variety of diplomatic foreign assistance missions, which include advancing the president's foreign policy and facilitating other American objectives and interests throughout the world. The State Department is both a collector of raw intelligence data and a primary consumer of FINISHED INTELLIGENCE produced by the CIA.

The department maintains a Bureau of Intelligence and Research (INR), responsible for gathering all-source intelligence, analyzing that intelligence, as well as global events for department planners and policy makers, and working with other members of the Intelligence Community to ensure that American intelligence activities adequately support foreign policy and national security goals. The

INR also serves as a departmental review entity for counterintelligence and law enforcement activities. The bureau also analyzes geographical data as it relates to international boundary issues.

As a member of the Intelligence Community, the State Department and its INR fall under the coordinating jurisdiction of the DIRECTOR OF CENTRAL INTELLIGENCE (DCI).

stay-behind nets

Stay-behind nets were post–World War II spy networks set up by the United States and allied governments to collect intelligence and create guerrilla resistance forces in the event of a Soviet invasion of the West or a communist takeover of any Western nation.

Though the stay-behind operation was officially established in 1952, such nets had been in existence since the end of the war. Military forces and intelligence entities vacating certain areas in Europe following temporary occupation directed many of their officers and assets to stay behind for the purposes of espionage or sabotage if needed.

Considered the brainchild of future DIRECTOR OF CENTRAL INTELLIGENCE (DCI) ALLEN WELSH DULLES, the nets were the responsibility of future DCI WILLIAM EGAN COLBY. Attached to the Scandinavian branch of the OFFICE OF POLICY COORDINATION's Western European Division, Colby was tasked with establishing and overseeing the nets in the primary areas of U.S. responsibility—Sweden, Finland, and areas of Europe not overseen by the British. The United Kingdom was responsible for establishing stay-behind nets in France, Belgium, Holland, Portugal, and Norway.

Stay-behind nets are not new to the espionage world. During the American Revolution, the Continental Army established such nets in areas from which it was forced to withdraw.

See also COLD WAR.

Steinberg, Saul (1914–1999)

For more than 50 years the artwork of celebrated cartoonist Saul Steinberg graced the covers and pages of the *New Yorker* magazine, elevating comic illustration to the level of fine art. His talent also enabled him to serve the Allied war effort as a propaganda artist with the OFFICE OF STRATEGIC SERVICES (OSS), the World War II predecessor organization to the CIA.

Born near Bucharest, Romania, on June 15, 1914, to Maurice Steinberg, a commercial printer and box manufacturer, and Rosa Jacobson Steinberg, a confectioner, young Steinberg was recognized as a natural artist with a keen aesthetic eye. Steinberg family tradition has it that he found his mother's cakes too beautiful to eat. He studied sociology and psychology at the University of Bucharest, then moved to Milan, Italy, where he received a doctoral degree in architecture from the Reggio Politecnico in 1940.

In Italy, Steinberg began his career as an artist. He also founded a magazine, *Bertoldo*, with famed Italian novelist Giovanni Guareschi, and it was in the magazine that he began publishing his drawings. He would later say that the only reason he didn't become a writer was that he had not been born into "a good language."

In 1941, with World War II in full swing, Steinberg fled Fascist Italy for the United States, using a counterfeit passport that he had stamped himself. The passport enabled him to escape to Portugal and ultimately Ellis Island, in New York City. However, the U.S. quota for Romanians had been filled, and he was deported to the Dominican Republic. From there, he began selling cartoons to the *New Yorker*, in hopes that the publication would support his return and entry into the United States. His first drawing appeared on October 25, 1941, in the *New Yorker*. The piece was a humorous rendition of a "reverse centaur"—a horse's head and man's rear end. In 1942, Steinberg was allowed to enter the United States, and he settled in New York.

For Steinberg, 1943 was a red-letter year. He became a U.S. citizen; his first American show was held, at the Wakefield Gallery in Manhattan; he married painter Hedda Lindenberg Sterne; he was commissioned an ensign in the U.S. Navy; and he was assigned the task of teaching Chinese guerrillas the art of blowing up bridges in the China-Burma-India Theater. Soon thereafter, he was recruited into the OSS by the Office's director, WILLIAM J. "WILD BILL" DONOVAN, and assigned to North Africa and Italy. There, he was directed to draw a series of anti-Axis cartoons aimed at the opposition community inside Germany.

Steinberg created macabre, though somewhat melodramatic, images of German leader Adolf Hitler with skulls in the background, and of Italian leader Benito Mussolini with a distorted face. These images, among other drawings, were dropped behind enemy lines and published in *Das Neue Deutschland,* an underground newspaper established by the OSS. Back in the States, the *New Yorker* was publishing his anti-Axis drawings as well as his reports via images from around the world. Many of his drawings depicted military life on the front; they were published in a single volume entitled *All in Line* (1945).

In 1945, Steinberg was released from the OSS, and in 1946 he was honorably discharged from the Navy. That same year, his work was included in *Fourteen Americans,* a highly touted show at New York's Museum of Modern Art. The show was his first major recognition as an artist.

Steinberg's art career took off in the early postwar years. But his place in the art world was always a question in his mind. "I don't quite belong to the art, cartoon or magazine world," Steinberg once said. "So the art world doesn't quite know where to place me."

At the close of his life, Steinberg had completed just under 650 drawings, including 85 covers for the *New Yorker*. The latter included his famous panoramic view of the Western world as seen from Manhattan's Ninth Avenue looking due west. He once said that had royalties been paid, "I could have retired on this painting."

In addition to *All in Line*, books of his work included *The Art of Living* (1949), *The Passport* (1954), *The Labyrinth* (1960), *The New World* (1965), *The Inspector* (1973), and *The Discovery of America* (1993).

"Saul Steinberg was the greatest artist to be associated with this magazine [the *New Yorker*], and the most original man of his time," wrote art critic Adam Gopnik.

Steinberg died in New York on May 12, 1999. He was one month shy of his 85th birthday.

Steinem, Gloria (1934–)

A leader in the late-20th-century women's rights movement and founding partner of *Ms.* magazine, Gloria Steinem was also for a brief time collaterally employed by the CIA.

Steinem was born in Toledo, Ohio, on March 25, 1934, to Leo Steinem, a traveling antiquities dealer, and Ruth Nuneviller, a former suffragist and newspaper columnist who suffered from incapacitating depression. Steinem's parents divorced in 1944. Her father moved to California, her older sister went off to college, and young Steinem was left to take care of her mother. Steinem became a voracious reader, with dual dreams of going to college and dancing in New York's Radio City Music Hall as a Rockette. She enrolled in Smith College (Northampton, Massachusetts) in 1952. She graduated Phi Beta Kappa in 1956 with a bachelor's degree in government and a Chester Bowles Asian Fellowship to study in India for two years.

En route to India, Steinem made a stopover in England that changed her life. Having just broken off her marriage engagement with her college sweetheart, she realized that she was pregnant with his baby. Not wanting to jeopardize her career, she decided on an abortion and located a British doctor who was willing to perform the operation (at that time, abortions were illegal in the United States and in nearly all cases in the United Kingdom). Without telling anyone, she had the abortion and continued on to India.

From 1958 to 1962, Steinem worked for Independent Research Service, a nonprofit educational foundation that recruited American students to travel to international youth festivals to discuss democracy with their communist counterparts. The foundation was later revealed to be funded by the CIA. Steinem, considered to be politically left of center, became the foundation's director. She expressed no qualms about the foundation's, thus her own, affiliation with the Agency. "Far from being shocked by this involvement, I was happy to find some liberals in government in those days, who were far-sighted and cared enough to get Americans of all political views to the festival," Steinem said in a 1967 interview for the *New*

York Times. She contended that most Americans who attended the various international festivals when she was working for the foundation were in fact communist sympathizers. She added, "I was never asked to report on other Americans or assess foreign nationals I had met."

Steinem left the foundation in 1962 and soon began a stellar career as a journalist. Her first byline garnered a modicum of recognition when that same year *Esquire* magazine published her "Moral Disarmament of Betty Coed," a piece that dealt with the growing sexual revolution in America. In 1963, she wrote for *Show* magazine a stunning exposé of Hugh Hefner's Manhattan Playboy Club entitled "I Was a Playboy Bunny." She then began writing regularly for a variety of top-tier magazines, including *Vogue* and *McCalls*.

By 1968, Steinem was writing a weekly column for *New York* magazine (a publication she cofounded), which reflected her interests and commitment to the women's liberation movement. But she wanted a magazine that would bring women's issues to the forefront of mainstream America. As a result, in January 1972, the first issue of *Ms.* magazine debuted. "We called it the spring issue," Steinem recalled years later. "We were really afraid that if it didn't sell it would embarrass the women's movement. So we called it spring so that it could lie there on the newsstands for a long time." Her caution was unfounded; the initial 300,000 copy run of *Ms.* sold out in just over a week. It also generated some 26,000 subscription orders and more than 20,000 reader letters. Today, *Ms.* magazine stands as the premier feminist publication in the United States and the world.

Aside from her published articles and essays, Steinem has authored numerous books, including *The Thousand Indias* (1957), *The Beach Book* (1963), *Wonder Woman* (1972), *Outrageous Acts and Everyday Rebellions* (1983), *Marilyn: Norma Jeanne* (1986), *Revolution from Within: A Book of Self-Esteem* (1992), and *Moving beyond Words* (1994). Her awards include the Penney-Missouri Journalism award, the Ohio Governor's Award for Journalism, the Bill of Rights Award from the Southern California branch of the American Civil Liberties Union, *McCalls* magazine's Woman of the Year, the Woodrow Wilson International Center for Scholars Fellowship, and an induction into the National Women's Hall of Fame.

Despite the fact that she once shunned the institutions of marriage and motherhood, Steinem, 66, married David Bale in September 2000.

Stephenson, Sir William Samuel (Intrepid)
(1896–1989)

Sir William Samuel Stephenson, code-named INTREPID, was a Canadian-born intelligence officer who directed British intelligence operations in the Western Hemisphere during World War II. He is credited with coordinating the exchange of intelligence between Great Britain and the United States. His influence also helped shape American intelligence and special operations capabilities, particularly through his work with the OFFICE OF STRATEGIC SERVICES (OSS), the wartime predecessor organization to the CIA.

Stephenson was born at Point Douglas, near Winnipeg, Manitoba, on January 11, 1896. When World War I erupted, he enlisted in the Royal Canadian Engineers, rising to the rank of sergeant and eventually earning a field commission. In 1916, he was wounded in a gas attack; he recovered after a short period of convalescence. He returned to active duty on August 16, 1917, this time as an aviator in the Royal Flying Corps. For the remainder of the war he served as a flight commander with 73 Squadron, credited with shooting down 27 enemy aircraft (12 of which were confirmed).

Aside from earning the title "ace" (pilots with five or more aerial kills), Stephenson won the Military cross, the Distinguished Flying Cross (DFC), and the French croix de guerre. His citation for the DFC reads: "This officer has shown conspicuous gallantry and skill in attacking enemy troops and transports from low altitudes, causing heavy casualties. His reports, also, have contained valuable and accurate information. He has further proved himself a keen antagonist in the air having, during recent operations, accounted for six enemy aeroplanes." On July 28, 1918, Stephenson, flying a Sopwith Camel, was shot down and captured by the Germans.

After the war, Stephenson manufactured and raced airplanes, and he became a financial speculator. He was also credited with inventing the wire-photo transmitter, a forerunner of the modern facsimile (fax) machine. At the University of Manitoba in the early 1920s, he developed a radio method of transmitting photographs without the use of telephone or telegraph wires. He took this method to Great Britain in order to market it for newspaper use. In 1924, a radio-transmitted photograph—the first ever—appeared in the *London Daily Mail.*

Over time, Stephenson developed global business interests as well as a number of solid contacts within the British intelligence community. During the 1930s, his businesses required that he travel extensively throughout Europe. This enabled him to observe German preparations for war firsthand. He reported his findings to the British government.

World War II erupted in 1939. With the Nazi conquest of France the following year, the United Kingdom saw a need to reinforce Anglo-American relations. Britain turned to Stephenson. In April 1940, he was appointed a Secret Intelligence Service, or SIS (MI6), station chief in New York. In that capacity, he was primarily tasked with countering threats against British war supplies by Nazis and Nazi-sympathizing saboteurs. In 1941, Stephenson's New York operation was given the name British Security Coordination (BSC), and Stephenson himself was given the code name INTREPID. With the BSC, he oversaw the sorting and dissemination of all signals intelligence (SIGINT) intercepts to Canadian, British, and U.S. intelligence authorities. He also assisted in the coordination and implementation of Allied intelligence efforts. As such, he became well connected not only with MI6 officials but with the American and British heads of state, the British Home and Foreign Offices, the British War cabinet (including members of the Joint Intelligence Committee), Britain's domestic security service (M15), and the SPECIAL OPERATIONS EXECUTIVE (SOE), Britain's senior covert-action arm.

Among the tasks undertaken by BSC was the capturing or killing of enemy spies in North America. These operations included assassinations by both snipers and trained automobile drivers who neutralized their targets by way of hit-and-run automobile accidents. These operations would later inspire a number of postwar spy novel writers, among them IAN LANCASTER FLEMING, future author of the JAMES BOND series.

Fleming, a Royal Navy intelligence officer who briefly trained under Stephenson, would later write of his instructor, "He is the man who became the scourge of the enemy throughout the Americas."

Soon, MI6 assigned Stephenson the task of recruiting and training special operations agents for SOE's sabotage and subversion operations in Europe and Latin America. Stephenson then established Special Training School 103, or "Camp X," a 260-acre BSC-administered special operations training center near Whitby, Ontario. At Camp X, American and a few British special operations trainees were instructed in the arts of special warfare. Many of the Americans were members of the newly established U.S. intelligence/covert-operations agency, the OFFICE OF STRATEGIC SERVICES (OSS).

Borne of Major General WILLIAM J. "WILD BILL" DONOVAN'S OFFICE OF THE COORDINATOR OF INFORMATION (COI), the OSS was the precursor organization to the CIA. Stephenson worked closely with Donovan in the establishment of the OSS.

In addition to BSC's SIGINT work, the OSS, and Camp X, Stephenson was responsible for forwarding top-secret dispatches across the Atlantic and managing a string of MI6 stations throughout Central and South America.

Not one to skirt action in which he was so involved, Stephenson flew over France in the tail gunner's seat of an Allied bomber during the June 6, 1944, invasion of Normandy.

Six months after Normandy, both Stephenson and Donovan drafted letters to President Franklin Roosevelt appealing for some form of American central intelligence authority and asking that the strong wartime intelligence coordination between the Americans and the BSC be continued in the long term. It was not to be. Roosevelt died on April 12, 1945, and was succeeded by Vice President Harry Truman. The OSS was dissolved by Truman in October, and Stephenson's BSC was ordered out of the United States.

In recommending Stephenson for a knighthood at war's end in 1945, Prime Minister Sir Winston Churchill wrote, "This one is dear to my heart." In addition to being knighted, Stephenson was awarded the Order of Canada and the William J. Donovan Award. He became the first non-American to win the Presidential Medal of Merit, America's highest civilian award.

Stephenson remained in intelligence after the war. In the early years of the COLD WAR, Stephenson played an important role in Canada's handling of the defection to that country of a Russian cipher clerk, Igor Gouzenko. In 1985, he was named "Intelligence Branch Patron." This title was bestowed upon him after serving as the first Intelligence Branch colonel commandant from 1982 to 1985.

Stephenson died in Bermuda on January 31, 1989. He was 93.

On May 2, 2000, CIA executive director David W. Carey accepted a replica statuette of Stephenson presented to the CIA by the Intrepid Society of Winnipeg, Manitoba, Canada. Accepting the award, Carey stated, "INTREPID may not have technically been the father of CIA, but he's certainly in our lineage." The statuette has been placed in the main entryway of CIA's new headquarters building at the GEORGE BUSH CENTER FOR INTELLIGENCE.

Stockwell, John Robert (1937–)

John Robert Stockwell was a senior CIA operations officer who in the late 1970s published *In Search of Enemies*, which the Agency charged violated a secrecy agreement.

Stockwell was born to William Foster Stockwell and Wilora Baker in Angleton, Texas, on August 27, 1937. In 1955, Stockwell joined the U.S. Marine Corps Reserve, serving until his retirement at the rank of major in 1977. In 1959, he earned a B.A. degree from the University of Texas. From 1959 until 1962, he served on active duty in the Marine Corps. He left the Corps to accept a position as foreman with the McCallum Landclearing Company in Alice, Texas. He then became a market research analyst for the Denver, Colorado–based Gates Rubber Company.

Stockwell joined the CIA in 1964. He served as chief of base in Lubumbashi, Katanga (from 1967 until 1969); CHIEF OF STATION (COS) in Bujumbura, Burundi (from 1969 until 1971); and provincial officer in charge in Tay Ninh, South Vietnam (from 1972 until 1973).

From 1975 through 1976, Stockwell served as chief of the CIA's Angola Task Force. In that capacity, he headed a series of covert paramilitary operations in support of UNITA (União Nacional para a Independência Total de Angola, or National Union for the Total Independence of Angola) and FNLA (Frente Nacional de Liberte de Angola, or National Front for the Liberation of Angola), two pro-Western guerrilla organizations, against the pro-Soviet MPLA (Movimento Popular para a Libertação de Angola, or Popular Movement for the Liberation of Angola). But the operations ended in failure, for which he blamed many of his fellow officers, charging them with "incompetence, irrationality, and amorality."

Stockwell then left the Agency to write and publish *In Search of Enemies* (1978). The book was not approved by the CIA, and in 1980 the Agency sued Stockwell, alleging that he had wittingly violating his pre-hiring secrecy agreement. The Agency sought all profits from the book. But in June 1980, an agreement was reached wherein Stockwell would pay the U.S. government only any future profits.

A contributor to a variety of professional journals, Stockwell is also the author of *Red Sunset* (1982) and *The Praetorian Guard* (1991). He has also written a number of screenplays, including *The Company Man, Special Access,* and *Almost Heaven.*

Strategic Services, Office of (OSS)

Established as an intelligence/counterintelligence/covert-action entity during World War II, the Office of Strategic Services (OSS) was the largest and most storied of the predecessor organizations to the CIA.

When the Japanese attacked Pearl Harbor in late 1941, the only centrally controlled U.S. intelligence entity was WILLIAM J. "WILD BILL" DONOVAN's marginally staffed OFFICE OF THE COORDINATOR OF INFORMATION (COI), which had been established only four months prior. Previous intelligence and COUNTERINTELLIGENCE efforts had fallen under the respective domains of the Departments of the Navy and War and the FEDERAL BUREAU OF INVESTIGATION (FBI). But their efforts suffered from poor coordination, duplication, and sometimes rabid organizational rivalry.

On June 13, 1942, President Franklin Roosevelt redesignated the COI as the Office of Strategic Services. Under Donovan's leadership, it quickly morphed into one of history's most famous central intelligence organizations. The OSS was responsible for espionage and sabotage in the countries that had been overrun and occupied by the Germans, Italians, and Japanese. Donovan recruited his OSS officers from among the nation's toughest, most experienced soldiers and resourceful civilian leaders in the private and public sectors. Because a high percentage of those recruited were well-heeled members of the "Eastern Establishment," the OSS earned the nicknames "OH SO SOCIAL" and "OH SUCH SNOBS." The organization's covert nature resulted in a third nickname—"OH SO SECRET." Still, most of those recruited were seconded from the American armed forces. U.S. Army (including Army Air Corps) personnel constituted approximately two-thirds of OSS strength; civilians accounted for another quarter. The remainder were drawn from the ranks of the U.S. Navy, Marine Corps, and Coast Guard.

OSS candidates had to undergo grueling combat training that tested their mental, physical, and emotional limits. Trainees were encouraged to be creative and inventive in their thinking, and trained operatives were allowed a great deal of freedom in accomplishing their missions.

At peak strength in 1944, over 13,000 Americans (8,500 men and 4,500 women) worked for the OSS, performing a myriad of tasks and working in concert with resistance forces and the intelligence/ special-operations units of Allied nations. Roughly, 7,500 OSS employees (including 900 women) served in overseas posts.

The OSS had seven branches:

1. Research & Analysis
2. Morale Operations
3. Labor Division
4. Special Operations
5. SECRET INTELLIGENCE
6. COUNTERINTELLIGENCE (also known as X-2)
7. DETACHMENT 101 (the Office's paramilitary unit).

Over a four-year period, the office cost the taxpayers $135 million (nearly $1.1 billion in current dollars).

Donovan was a tireless and inspirational leader, but he was considered in many circles to be a mediocre administrator. Soon, tales of OSS waste and inefficiency began circulating. As the war drew to a close, Donovan fought for the establishment of a peacetime intelligence service based on the OSS model. But the combination of his detractors, the death of Roosevelt, the growing American fear of a "super" intelligence agency, and the lack of support from the incoming president, Harry Truman, signaled the death knell of the OSS or any OSS-based organization.

In a final address to his operatives, Donovan said, "We have come to the end of an unusual experiment. This experiment was to determine whether a group of Americans constituting a cross section of racial origins, of abilities, temperaments and talents could meet and risk an encounter with the long-established and well-trained enemy organizations. . . . You can go with the assurance that you have made a beginning in showing the people of America that only by decisions of national policy based upon accurate information can we have the chance of a peace that will endure."

When the war ended, Truman saw no further need of a large national intelligence agency. Consequently, the OSS was disbanded in October 1945. Its services were transferred to other government entities. The office's operational arm, redesignated the STRATEGIC SERVICES UNIT (SSU), moved to the War Department. OSS research and analysis units were brought under an INTERIM RESEARCH AND INTELLIGENCE SERVICE and transferred to the STATE DEPARTMENT.

The perception of a growing Soviet threat to U.S. national security, however, resulted in the establishment of a CENTRAL INTELLIGENCE GROUP (CIG) in January 1946. The CIG was created from the remains of the OSS. The following year, the NATIONAL SECURITY ACT OF 1947 was passed; it reorganized America's Defenses and established a CENTRAL INTELLIGENCE AGENCY (CIA) under a NATIONAL SECURITY COUNCIL (NSC).

The OSS served as the training ground for many of the leaders and personnel who formed the new CIA. Among those leaders were four future DIRECTORS OF CENTRAL INTELLIGENCE (DCI): ALLEN WELSH DULLES, RICHARD MCGARRAH HELMS, WILLIAM E. COLBY, and WILLIAM J. CASEY.

Donovan, who never held a post in the CIA, is considered to be the father of American central intelligence and the unofficial first DCI.

See also GREAT GESTAPO FEAR.

Strategic Services Unit (SSU)

Strategic Services Unit was the name given to the operational arm of the OFFICE OF STRATEGIC SERVICES (OSS), the World War II precursor to the CIA, when President Harry Truman disbanded the OSS in October 1945. SSU activities were transferred to the War Department, while OSS research and analysis units were brought under an INTERIM RESEARCH AND INTELLIGENCE SERVICE and transferred to the STATE DEPARTMENT.

When the CENTRAL INTELLIGENCE GROUP (CIG)—the immediate predecessor organization to the CIA—was established in January 1946, the NATIONAL INTELLIGENCE AUTHORITY (NIA) began dismantling the SSU. Some of the SSU's components were assigned to the new CIG. Others remained within the War Department.

The SSU as an entity was officially abolished on October 19, 1946.

stringer

A stringer is a freelance or part-time agent who works for an intelligence agency like the CIA, usually for specific projects and for set rewards. Stringers are not Agency employees, nor are they permanently on call.

Most stringers are specialists in particular fields (e.g., burglaries, document photographing, deliveries, decoys) and are recruited for specific missions. In nearly all cases, stringers are motivated by money. Of all the kinds of intelligence operatives, they are considered the least reliable.

Studeman, Admiral William Oliver (1940–   )

A former director of both NAVAL INTELLIGENCE and the NATIONAL SECURITY AGENCY (NSA), Admiral William Oliver Studeman served two U.S. presidents and three DIRECTORS OF CENTRAL INTELLIGENCE (DCI) as the DEPUTY DIRECTOR OF CENTRAL INTELLIGENCE (DDCI). He also served as acting DCI, twice.

Studeman was born on January 16, 1940, in Brownsville, Texas, to Oliver Jennings Studeman and Gail McDavitt. Studeman earned a bachelor's degree from the University of the South at Sewanee, Tennessee, in 1962. The following year, he was commissioned an ensign in the U.S. Navy. From 1966 through 1967, he studied at the Defense Intelligence School. He earned a master's in international affairs from George Washington University in 1973. That same year, he attended the Naval War College. From 1974 until 1975, he served as an analyst at the NAVAL INTELLIGENCE Support Center in Washington, D.C. He was then posted as an executive assistant at the Office of Naval Intelligence, also in Washington.

In 1976, Studeman was transferred to Norfolk, Virginia, where he served on the staff of Commander in Chief, Atlantic Fleet. He was assistant chief of staff to the commander of the Sixth Fleet in Gaeta, Italy, from 1978 through 1980. He returned to the Naval War College in 1981. From 1981 through 1988, he held a variety of senior staff posts and commands in the Washington area, all directly related to forward planning and intelligence, including a term as director of naval intelligence. He was awarded an honorary doctorate in strategic intelligence from the Defense Intelligence College in 1987. In 1988, he was appointed director of the NSA, a primary member of the U.S. intelligence community.

In January 1992, Studeman was appointed DDCI by President GEORGE HERBERT WALKER BUSH. He was confirmed by the Senate in April, resigning from the NSA that same month. He briefly served as acting DCI during the period (January 21 to February 5, 1993) between the terms of DCIs ROBERT MICHAEL GATES and R. JAMES WOOLSEY. On January 10, 1995, Studeman was appointed interim DCI by President Bill Clinton. He served in that capacity until May 9.

On April 6, 1995, Studeman made the following comments to the U.S. House of Representatives Judiciary Committee regarding the increasing danger to Americans by international terrorists:

> International terrorism remains one of the deadliest and most persistent global threats to U.S. security. The motives, perpetrators, and methods of terrorist groups are evolving in ways that complicate analysis, collection, and counteraction and require the ability to shift resources flexibly and quickly. The rise of the new breed of terrorist who is interested in inflicting mass death and

destruction does not bode well for the future security of American interests. These groups can strike at any time, anywhere, spurred by seemingly unrelated events for which they judge the United States to be blameworthy. They have a widening global reach and a high degree of technical proficiency with more sophisticated weapons and tactics.

Studeman retired from the Agency in July 1995. In 1996, he joined TRW, an aerospace defense contractor, becoming vice president and deputy group manager for intelligence and information superiority.

Studeman's awards include the Legion of Merit with two gold stars, the Distinguished Service Medal (for both naval and intelligence service), and the President's National Security Medal.

SVR
See SLUZHBA VNESHNEY RAZVEDKI ROSSII.

swallow
In CIA parlance, a "swallow" is a female agent who works as a prostitute in order to gather intelligence from someone who possesses knowledge of a hostile nation's secrets. The swallow's mission is to engage in sexual activity with the targeted person and gather the intelligence either through pillow talk or blackmail.

In order to be able to blackmail the targeted person into disclosing secrets, the sexual activity usually takes place in a prearranged room or residence equipped with hidden cameras and recording devices. Such a place is known as a "swallow's nest."

See also RAVEN.

Swampy, Camp
CAMP PEARY, Virginia, the CIA's top-secret "boot camp" for fledgling spies, is often referred to by Agency insiders as "Camp Swampy," THE FARM, or ISOLATION.

See also CAREER TRAINEES.

T

tank

"Tank" is a CIA term used to describe the soundproof, sound-secure rooms found in many CIA stations worldwide. Tanks are often set up with reinforced walls and voice-scrambling devices so that conversations within the room are impervious to the internal and remote eavesdropping technologies employed by hostile intelligence organizations.

In his book *Spectrum,* novelist David Wise describes a London-based tank as resembling "a streamlined railroad car on stilts, . . . actually a room within a room. It rested on steel legs above the floor. A speaker had been mounted on the outside, and when the tank was in use, a noise-making tape emitted a loud steady sound of whirring machinery. Tanks are bug-proof—but also windowless; they tend to get stuffy."

Taylor Commission

The Taylor Commission was an executive-level body commissioned by President John Kennedy on April 22, 1961, to ascertain the reasons for the failure of OPERATION ZAPATA, the ill-fated BAY OF PIGS INVASION, that same month. Comprising former army chief of staff General Maxwell Taylor (the commission's chairman), Attorney General Robert Kennedy, former chief of naval operations Admiral Arleigh Burke, and DIRECTOR OF CENTRAL INTELLIGENCE

(DCI) ALLEN WELSH DULLES, the group compiled a 53-page classified report that was submitted to Kennedy on June 13, 1961. Declassified in 1977, the report critiqued the operation's conception, development, and implementation phases. Blame was leveled in all quarters.

The report pointed out that the CIA, under White House direction, had organized and trained Cuban exiles to overthrow the Cuban government of FIDEL CASTRO. ZAPATA, originally intended by the administration of President Dwight Eisenhower as a guerrilla operation, was supposed to operate within the parameters of a NATIONAL SECURITY COUNCIL (NSC) directive that, among other things, called for "plausible U.S. deniability." When Kennedy came to power, however, ZAPATA evolved into a large-scale amphibious invasion involving refitted bombers, supply ships, and landing craft. The report stated that "the magnitude of ZAPATA could not be prepared and conducted in such a way that all U.S. support of it and connection with it could be plausibly disclaimed." Much blame was heaped on ZAPATA's planners at the Agency's DIRECTORATE of Plans (Operations) for not keeping the president fully abreast of the expanding nature of the operation. But the report also criticized the U.S. STATE DEPARTMENT, the JOINT CHIEFS OF STAFF, and the Kennedy administration for ultimately acquiescing and approving ZAPATA. This had been done, according to the report, with an inadequate grasp of all the military particulars by the latter three entities. The commission contended that the operation was ill conceived, with little chance of success. The report also suggested that the decision to cancel American air support over the landing zones was a factor in ZAPATA's failure.

In conclusion, the report stated: "The Executive Branch of government was not organizationally prepared to cope with this kind of paramilitary operation. There was no single authority short of the President capable of coordinating the actions of CIA, State, Defense and USIA [U.S. Information Agency]. Top level direction was given through ad hoc meetings of senior officials without consideration of operational plans in writing and with no arrangement for recording conclusions reached."

The report recommended courses of action in the realm of "planning, coordination, effectiveness, and responsibility" for future COLD WAR operations. The report also recommended the establishment of a Strategic Resources Group (SRG) composed of subsecretarial representatives from the CIA, as well as the Departments of State and Defense. The SRG would have direct access to the president and would serve a planning/coordinating entity for future paramilitary operations, taking account of the opinions of the JCS.

Interestingly, the Taylor Commission reaffirmed the U.S. commitment to ousting Castro. Its findings greatly influenced Kennedy's desire to manage better the overall intelligence-gathering/covert-action process. While the Taylor Commission conducted its examination, CIA inspector general LYMAN B. KIRKPATRICK, JR., under the direction of Dulles, conducted his own investigation into the Agency's shortcomings during the Bay of Pigs. The result was the KIRKPATRICK REPORT. Though it remains classified, insiders believe that much of the Kirkpatrick Report was highly critical of Dulles, who was himself relieved as DCI by Kennedy.

TECHINT (technical intelligence)

An acronym for technical intelligence, TECHINT is simply intelligence collected through technological means, as opposed to HUMINT (human intelligence) or human-source intelligence that is collected by means of officers, agents, or informers.

See also ALL-SOURCE INTELLIGENCE and INTELLIGENCE CYCLE.

Technical Services, Office of (OTS)

The Office of Technical Services—formerly known as the TECHNICAL SERVICES STAFF (TSS) or the TECHNICAL SERVICES DIVISION (TSD)—is a laboratory (design and experimentation) branch of the CIA's DIRECTORATE of Science and Technology.

Technical Services Division (TSD)

See TECHNICAL SERVICES, OFFICE OF.

Technical Services Staff (TSS)

See TECHNICAL SERVICES, OFFICE OF.

TELINT (telemetry intelligence)

An acronym for telemetry intelligence, TELINT is intelligence derived from the interception, processing, and analysis of the telemetry data gathered from foreign missiles, aircraft, and space vehicles. TELINT is a special category of SIGINT, or signals intelligence.

See also ALL-SOURCE INTELLIGENCE; INTELLIGENCE CYCLE.

Tenet, George John (1953–   )

George John Tenet was the DIRECTOR OF CENTRAL INTELLIGENCE (DCI) who presided over the CIA through the turn of the century and into the dark early years of America's War against Terrorism.

Born one of twin boys to Greek immigrants John and Evangelia Tenet in Flushing, New York on January 5, 1953, young Tenet attended public school in Queens and religious classes at St. Nicholas Greek Orthodox Church. At St. Nicholas, he and his brother served as altar boys. As a teenager, Tenet, nicknamed "the mouthpiece," attended Cardozo High School and held an after-school job as a restaurant busboy. As a young man, he attended Georgetown University's School of Foreign Service in Washington, D.C. He spent his summers at home in New York, where he waited tables at a bar in Queens. In 1976, he earned a bachelor's degree from Georgetown. He then went on to Columbia University's School of International Affairs, where he earned a master's degree in 1978.

After Columbia, Tenet returned to Washington and began working for the American Hellenic Institute, a Greek-American lobbying organization. In 1982, he joined the staff of Senator John Heinz (R-Pennsylvania). He served with Heinz for over three years, both as a legislative assistant (working on national security and national energy issues) and as a legislative director.

In the summer of 1985, Tenet was named to the post of designee to the vice chairman of the SENATE SELECT COMMITTEE ON INTELLIGENCE. The vice chairman was Senator Patrick Leahy (D-Vermont). The following year, Tenet was promoted to staff director for the committee. In that capacity, he managed the activities of some 40 staffers. He was also tasked with coordinating all of the oversight and legislative activities of the committee. Those activities included strengthening covert-operation reporting requirements, establishing a CIA inspector general, and introducing legislation that would reorganize the U.S. INTELLIGENCE COMMUNITY. He also directed the committee's oversight efforts regarding arms control negotiations between the United States and the Soviet Union.

In 1992, Tenet was appointed to President-elect Bill Clinton's national security transition team. When Clinton moved into the White House, he named Tenet special assistant to the president and senior director of intelligence programs for the NATIONAL SECURITY COUNCIL (NSC). In that capacity, Tenet served as the chief intelligence adviser to NATIONAL SECURITY ADVISOR Anthony Lake. He also coordinated presidential decision directives in a myriad of areas related to intelligence, COUNTERINTELLIGENCE, and covert action.

In July 1995, Tenet was named DEPUTY DIRECTOR OF CENTRAL INTELLIGENCE (DDCI) under DCI JOHN DEUTSCH. When Deutsch announced his resignation in December 1996, he recommended Tenet for the post of interim DCI. Lake was nominated for the post of DCI but withdrew his name from consideration.

George John Tenet   (ASSOCIATED PRESS)

Clinton then himself nominated Tenet for the post, stating that he "played a pivotal role in leading the intelligence community in meeting the demands of the post–cold war world." Tenet was appointed DCI on July 11, 1997. He proved to be a versatile director.

In a move considered out of the box for a DCI, Tenet was tasked with mediating a peace accord between the Israelis and the Palestinians. Both parties agreed to a fragile truce designed to end months of fighting. But the cautious optimism began to wane as bloodshed continued, eventually began to increase, and ultimately reemerged as a veritable civil war.

Tenet's directorship placed him in the position of being able to glean some unnerving insight into the future. "What are the threats that keep me awake at night?" Tenet asked rhetorically during a lecture at Georgetown University on October 18, 1999. "International terrorism, both on its own and in conjunction with narcotics traffickers, international criminals and those seeking weapons of mass destruction. You need go no further than OSAMA BIN LADEN."

On September 11, 2001, Tenet's fears were realized when the United States was attacked by four civilian airliners commandeered by suicide pilots directly linked to bin Laden and his al-Qaeda terrorist network. Two of the planes slammed into the towers of New York City's World Trade Center. One plane was flown into the Pentagon, the Northern Virginia–based headquarters of the U.S. DEPARTMENT OF DEFENSE. The fourth plane crashed into the Pennsylvania countryside after passengers attempted to regain control of the aircraft from the hijackers. With over 3,000 people killed, it was the worst terrorist attack on American soil in history. In the wake of the attacks, Tenet made the following comments before a group of CIA employees:

> The terrorists behind these atrocities—and those who give them shelter and support—must never know rest, ease, or comfort. The last word must not be theirs.
>
> For the future must belong to the champions of freedom, not its enemies. That is our aim—today, tomorrow, always.
>
> This is a time for us to come together. To bring all our talents to bear in a steely determination to do what we are called to do—protect our fellow citizens.
>
> It is our turn again to step up to a challenge, and to meet it as we meet all challenges: With commitment and courage.
>
> Put some spirit in your step, square your shoulders, focus your eyes. . . . We have a job to do.

In the weeks following the attacks, rumors began surfacing which suggested that Tenet would be fired. The attacks had been too horrific; someone within the executive ranks of the U.S. INTELLIGENCE COMMUNITY would have to be held accountable. As of September 2002, he still serves as DCI and has the full public support of the president and the Intelligence Community.

terrorism, CIA's involvement in the war against

In the wake of the SEPTEMBER 11, 2001, TERRORIST ATTACKS ON THE UNITED STATES, the United States and its allies launched a massive retaliatory air and naval strike against the forces of the Taliban in Afghanistan and against the bases of al-Qaeda—the terrorist network of Saudi-born terrorism mastermind OSAMA BIN LADEN.

The strikes, which began on October 7, had been preceded by American and British special operating forces that scouted the region for intelligence on al-Qaeda's bases. The CIA, which was on the ground in the region almost immediately after the attacks of September 11, began coordinating the efforts of the Northern Alliance—Afghanistan's rebel opposition to the Taliban—with the military forces of the United States and the United Kingdom.

At the time of the initial allied attack, the Northern Alliance launched a ground offensive against the Taliban. Agency operatives reportedly provided weapons, money, and intelligence, as well as interrogating prisoners captured during the fighting.

In October, U.S. Army Rangers and Delta Force commandos began conducting offensive ground operations against the Taliban. That same month, the *Washington Post* revealed that in the days following September 11, President George W. Bush had granted the CIA the broadest covert-operations powers in the history of the Agency. According to the report, "President Bush last month signed an intelligence order directing the CIA to undertake its most sweeping and lethal covert action since the founding of the agency in 1947, explicitly calling for the destruction of Osama bin Laden and his worldwide Al Qaeda network, according to senior government officials.

"The president also added more than $1 billion to the agency's war on terrorism, most of it for the new covert action. The operation will include what officials said is 'unprecedented' coordination between the CIA and commando and other military units."

Despite previously issued executive bans on assassinations, the CIA was reportedly granted authority from Bush that would have enabled the Agency to kill targeted individuals connected to al-Qaeda. The authority was the first such expansion of the Agency's covert-action powers since the congressional inquiries (the CHURCH and PIKE COMMITTEES) into CIA misdeeds restrained the Agency in the mid-1970s.

According to a follow-up article in the *Washington Post,* "The Bush administration has concluded that executive orders banning assassination do not prevent the president from lawfully singling out a terrorist for death by covert action. The CIA is reluctant to accept a broad grant of authority to hunt and kill U.S. enemies at its discretion, knowledgeable sources said. But the agency is willing and believes itself able to take the lives of terrorists designated by the president."

In October a small number of cases of the deadly anthrax disease began to appear throughout a variety of locations within the United States, particularly along the eastern seaboard. By year's end, some 18 cases would be confirmed; 11 of those cases would be of the dangerous inhalation form of anthrax, seven would be the less serious skin form. Five people would ultimately die of the disease. On October 25, a trace amount of deadly bio-terror anthrax spores was found in the Agency's mail room at CIA headquarters in LANGLEY, VIRGINIA. The mail room was closed, and some CIA employees were treated with antibiotics. Some members of the U.S. INTELLIGENCE COMMUNITY suggested that the anthrax attack might well have been the work of a domestic terrorist. Others believed it might have been the work of bin Laden and al-Qaeda, but there was no substantive evidence to suggest it.

The day following the discovery of anthrax in the Langley mail room, Bush signed into law the Anti-Terrorism Act (also known as the USA Patriot Act of 2001, or Public Law 107-56). The act is a sweeping set of guidelines granting unfettered power to all agencies involved in combating terrorism.

Exactly one month later, JOHNNY MICHAEL "MIKE" SPANN, a CIA operations officer in Afghanistan, was killed during a prison uprising launched by captured Taliban fighters who had smuggled weapons into their holding compound near Mazar-e-Sharif. Spann, a 32-year-old former U.S. Marine who had joined the Agency in June 1999, became the first American combat fatality in Afghanistan.

On November 26, American Marines began landing in southern Afghanistan, "ramping up" ground operations in the region. Three days later, soldiers from the U.S. Army's 10th Mountain Division began moving into Afghanistan from the north. In the months that followed, the United States and its allies broadened the scope of offensive military operations beyond the borders of Afghanistan. As in most previous conflicts since 1947, the CIA was on the ground before uniformed American forces.

terrorist

In CIA parlance, a terrorist is one who engages in premeditated, politically motivated violence against noncombatant targets with the intention of inflicting casualties and striking fear in an audience, and thus influencing that audience. Terrorists are often clandestine agents or participants in subnational or international groups.

The suicide pilots who commandeered the civilian airliners and crashed them into the Pentagon in Northern Virginia and the World Trade Center in New York City were terrorists. They belonged to the international terrorist group al-Qaeda, which is directed by terrorist leader OSAMA BIN LADEN.

See also QUESTIONS AND ANSWERS.

third-country operations

"Third-country operations" is a CIA term used to describe intelligence-gathering operations based in a neutral or "third party" country in which there is no particular government intelligence interest for the Agency. For example, during the COLD WAR, both the CIA and the KOMITET GOSUDARSTVENNOY BEZOPASNOSTI conducted Latin American intelligence-gathering operations from the third country of Mexico. The latter was considered a haven for political exiles and revolutionaries; thus, it was rich in information for both the United States and the Soviet Union.

303 Committee

The 303 Committee was a senior-level interdepartmental organization that oversaw CIA high-risk covert operations during the 1960s. As such it was one of many predecessors of the OPERATIONS ADVISORY GROUP.

Named after a room number in the executive office complex in Washington, D.C., the 303 Committee comprised representatives from the U.S. DEPARTMENT OF STATE, the U.S. DEPARTMENT OF DEFENSE, the JOINT CHIEFS OF STAFF, the Oval Office, and the CIA.

The 303 Committee traces its lineage to the early OPERATIONS COORDINATING BOARD (OPB). The OPB was later renamed the SPECIAL GROUP and was also known as the 5412 GROUP. During the administration of President John Kennedy, the Special (5412) Group became known as the 303 Committee. During the administration of President Richard Nixon, the 303 Committee was renamed the 40 COMMITTEE.

Tibet, operations in

From 1953 through the mid-1960s, tens of thousands of CIA-trained Tibetan guerrillas conducted operations against communist Chinese forces that had invaded Tibet in 1951.

The Chinese had controlled Tibet as a sovereign state since 1907, but the communists' aim was to assert absolute control over the Buddhist kingdom. As a result, the CIA began training and equipping Tibetan refugees, who it then returned to Tibet to attempt to oust the Chinese and contain communism in the region. They were resupplied by airdrops. A number of the Tibetans were flown to the United States and secretly trained at a remote CIA facility known as Camp Hale in Colorado's Rocky Mountains.

The Chinese, however, achieved absolute control in 1965. The Agency continued modest operations in the region for a brief time after the Chinese takeover.

Tofte, Hans V. (1912–1987)

Hans V. Tofte was an effective wartime operations officer serving in both the OFFICE OF STRATEGIC SERVICES (or OSS, the World War II precursor to the CIA) and the CIA. But his career was tarnished by an embarrassing violation of Agency security regulations.

Tofte was born in 1912 in Copenhagen. When he was 19, he joined East Asiatic, a Danish shipping company. The company sent him to Peking (Beijing), where he was to learn to speak Chinese. Two years later, he was transferred to Kirin, Manchuria. There he spent most of the next eight years of his East Asiatic career, making frequent jaunts through northern China and Korea.

When World War II erupted in 1939, Tofte returned to Denmark, where he served a brief stint in the anti-Nazi Danish underground. Soon he traveled to New York City, where he was recruited by SIR WILLIAM STEPHENSON of the British Secret Intelligence Service (SIS).

Tofte was commissioned in the SIS, with the rank of major in the Indian army. He was sent to Singapore, where he established an effective supply operation for the Chinese forces fighting the Japanese. His operations included organizing guerrilla units.

When Singapore fell in 1942, he returned to America. Tofte enlisted in the U.S. Army and was quickly reassigned to the OSS. Stationed first in Cairo, he was transferred to a parachute training unit in Palestine.

In October 1943, Tofte directed a seaborne transport and resupply operation that transported weapons and equipment to Yugoslav and Albanian partisans by small and medium-sized boats, which were able to break through the Nazi blockade in the Adriatic Sea.

By the summer of 1944, Tofte had been reassigned to the London headquarters of the Secret Intelligence Branch of the OSS. He was soon posted to Dijon, France, where he coordinated the efforts of Allied intelligence officers inside Germany. When the war ended, he was discharged as a major; he entered private business.

When the Korean War erupted in 1950, Tofte was recruited into the CIA, accepting a position in the OFFICE OF POLICY COORDINATION (OPC), the Agency's covert-action arm. He was instrumental in establishing several CIA operations bases in Japan. He established escape-and-evasion plans for U.S. pilots and air crew-men downed behind enemy lines. He organized guerrilla operations in North Korea. Tofte also directed OPERATION TROPIC, a series of suboperations conducted by "third force" guerrilla units on the Chinese mainland. After Korea, Tofte was reassigned to the Western Hemisphere Division and later the Domestic Operations Division.

On July 1966, Tofte and his wife, who were building a new home, placed an ad in the *Washington Post* offering a basement apartment for rent for $150 per month. Kenneth R. Slocum, a fledgling CIA employee, responded and was shown the apartment by Tofte's 86-year-old mother-in-law. As Slocum toured the apartment, he opened a closet door to find a number of CIA documents stamped "secret." The following day, Slocum returned to the apartment with a CIA security officer and asked Tofte's mother-in-law if he might be permitted a second walk-through. The security officer confiscated the documents.

Tofte was immediately suspended from work pending further investigation. He filed a lawsuit against the Agency and DIRECTOR OF CENTRAL INTELLIGENCE (DCI) RICHARD M. HELMS, charging them with the theft of some $30,000 worth of jewelry belonging to his wife.

The affair soon became something of a public embarrassment to the Agency. On September 15, Tofte was fired.

Tofte died on August 24, 1987. He was 75.

tree shaker

In the CIA jargon of the 1950s, a "tree shaker" was an AGENT PROVOCATEUR.

TROPIC, Operation

Operation TROPIC was the code name for a series of air operations (1951–55) flown over North Korea, China, and the Soviet Union by pilots with CIVIL AIR TRANSPORT (CAT), one of the CIA's air proprietary companies.

The flights, which transported over national borders guerrilla teams and foreign agents working for the CIA's OFFICE OF POLICY COORDINATION (or OPC, the Agency's early covert-action arm), were successful in terms of inserting and extracting the operatives. The pilots, all volunteers who made little more than 10 dollars an hour, were well trained and exhibited tremendous courage. However, the operatives themselves (foreign nationals known as "third force" teams—anticommunists not allied with the Nationalist Chinese on Taiwan) were poorly trained and marginally motivated. They accomplished very little on the ground.

One of the most dramatic moments during Operation TROPIC occurred on November 29, 1952. That evening,

a CAT aircraft transporting two OPC officers—RICHARD GEORGE FECTEAU and JOHN THOMAS "JACK" DOWNEY—was shot down by communist forces. The pilot and copilot were killed in the crash. Fecteau and Downey were taken prisoner. Initially, the U.S. government denied that Fecteau and Downey were CIA officers. The official story was that the two men were civilian employees of the U.S. Army on a "routine flight" from Seoul, South Korea, to Japan.

Fecteau, who was sentenced to 20 years in prison, was released in December 1971 after serving 19 years. Downey, who was sentenced to life, was released in March 1973 after President Richard Nixon admitted publicly that both men were CIA officers.

Truscott, Lucian King, Jr. (1895–1965)

Lucian King Truscott, Jr. (or Lucian King Truscott II), is best known for his combat generalship during World War II. He also served in the CIA during the Agency's early years.

Truscott was born into a military family on January 9, 1895, in Chatfield, Texas. He was raised in both Texas and Oklahoma. As a young man, he briefly taught school in Oklahoma.

When America entered World War I, Truscott enlisted in the U.S. Army and was quickly selected for officer candidate school. In 1917, he was commissioned a second lieutenant of cavalry. Between wars, he served in a variety of cavalry assignments, including an instructor's post at the Army's Cavalry School and at the Command and General Staff School.

When World War II erupted, Truscott joined Lord Louis Mountbatten's combined staff, where he was instrumental in the development of the U.S. Army's Ranger units, based on the model of the British commandos. Commanding his Rangers, Truscott saw combat at Dieppe, France, and in North Africa. He rose quickly through the ranks. His major commands included the Third Infantry Division (March 1943), VI Corps in Sicily and Italy (February 1944), the 15th Army in Italy and southern France (October 1944), the Fifth Army in Italy (December 1944), and the Third Army in Germany (October 1945). At the close of hostilities, he commanded the American occupation forces in Bavaria and served in a number of advisory capacities.

Truscott earned numerous awards and decorations, including the Distinguished Service Cross, the Distinguished Service Medal, the Legion of Merit, and the Purple Heart, and the French Croix de Guerre. In 1947, Truscott retired from military service.

In 1951, Truscott was recruited by the CIA and appointed CHIEF OF STATION of the Agency's CLANDESTINE

SERVICE in West Germany. Three years later, President Dwight Eisenhower tasked Truscott with resolving a number of "jurisdictional disputes" between the Agency and the intelligence organizations of the armed forces. In *The Encyclopedia of American Intelligence and Espionage,* G. J. A. O'Toole states that Truscott also served as "Eisenhower's unofficial watchdog of the CIA, reporting on planned covert action."

Years later, William Corson, a former intelligence officer in the U.S. Marine Corps, testified before the U.S. Senate that Truscott, upon discovering that the CIA had plotted without authorization to assassinate Communist Chinese leader Chou En-Lai during the mid-1950s, confronted DIRECTOR OF CENTRAL INTELLIGENCE (DCI) ALLEN WELSH DULLES with his findings. Dulles terminated the operation.

Truscott died in Alexandria, Virginia, on September 12, 1965, and was buried in Arlington National Cemetery. He was 70.

Turner, Stansfield (1923–)

Admiral Stansfield Turner was one of the Agency's most outspoken, and occasionally unpopular, DIRECTORS OF CENTRAL INTELLIGENCE (DCI).

Turner was born to Oliver Stansfield Turner and Wilhelmina Josephine Wagner in Highland Park, Illinois, on

Stansfield Turner (LIBRARY OF CONGRESS)

December 1, 1923. Turner attended Massachusett's Amherst College from 1941 to 1943, but he graduated from the U.S. Naval Academy, in Annapolis, Maryland, in 1946, officially a member of the class of 1947. As a newly commissioned ensign, he attended Oxford University on a Rhodes Scholarship. He earned a master's degree from Oxford in 1950.

Turner spent a total of 31 years in the Navy, holding numerous commands in peace and war, including a minesweeper, a destroyer, a guided-missile cruiser, and a carrier task group. He was also president of the Naval War College, commander of the U.S. Second Fleet, and commander in chief of North Atlantic Treaty Organization (NATO) forces in southern Europe.

Turner's former Annapolis classmate, President Jimmy Carter, appointed him to the post of DCI in 1977. Turner served from March 9 of that year to January 20, 1981. It was a tenure mixed with substantive successes and a few decisions that would earn him a degree of disfavor in the eyes of some Agency insiders.

On October 31, 1977, Turner issued some 820 pink slips to CIA employees, in an action that became known as the HALLOWEEN MASSACRE. He conducted the mass firing as a method of "cleaning house" after the 1975–76 congressional investigations of Agency misdeeds. It forced 147 career officers into early retirement, sacked an additional 17, and eliminated nearly all of the OSS veterans and CIA charter officers. It also eliminated much of the CIA's HUMINT capacity and severely damaged Agency morale. Opponents of the mass firing, like THEODORE SHACKLEY, a former deputy director of the Agency's CLANDESTINE SERVICE, argued that the reduction in force could have been accomplished through "peer review and attrition"; he considered the firings "insensitive" and wholly demoralizing.

The Halloween Massacre was the second such wave of firings at the CIA in less than five years. In early 1973, DCI JAMES SCHLESINGER, an unpopular appointee of President Richard Nixon, had fired or retired nearly 1,400 CIA employees. Officially, Schlesinger's actions were the result of downsizing after the Vietnam War. But Agency insiders felt that Schlesinger was hauling out what he perceived to be deadwood left over from the earliest days of the Agency. Schlesinger's firings where conducted over a period of four months and did not disproportionately target senior career officers.

As DCI, Turner instituted a number of reforms; not the least of which was institution of the NATIONAL INTELLIGENCE COUNCIL (NIC), a group of senior experts and analysts drawn from the ranks of the intelligence community, as well as experts from the public and private sectors. In Turner's mind, the NIC effectively replaced the BOARD OF NATIONAL ESTIMATES, which had been dissolved during the tenure of DCI WILLIAM E. COLBY. In January 1981,

President Ronald Reagan appointed WILLIAM J. CASEY as Turner's replacement.

Turner retired from the Agency, but he continued to involve himself in the business of national intelligence, and he was somewhat critical of his successors. His first book, *Secrecy and Democracy: The CIA in Transition,* published in 1985, suggested that the CIA under Reagan seemed to be based on the OFFICE OF STRATEGIC SERVICES (OSS) model, where Casey had begun his intelligence career during World War II. According to Turner, "almost any covert action to help win the war was considered acceptable, and the more the better. Translating that attitude to the peacetime conditions of the 1980's was a serious mistake." That same year, Turner outlined his views for intelligence reform in a proposal to Congress recommending a reduction in the emphasis on covert action. Turner also proposed a charter for the intelligence community. But the proposal's most important recommendation involved the future of the office of DCI. According to Turner, "the two jobs, head of the CIA and head of the Intelligence Community, conflict. One person cannot do justice to both and fulfill the DCI's responsibilities to the President, the Congress, and the public as well."

Turner's proposal recommended a separation of the two primary DCI responsibilities, by creating a head of the CIA, reporting to a DIRECTOR OF NATIONAL INTELLIGENCE (first proposed in the SCHLESINGER REPORT of 1971).

Since 1981, Turner has lectured widely on strategic nuclear policy and has become a professor and senior research scholar at the University of Maryland's Center for International and Security Studies.

Aside from *Secrecy and Democracy,* Turner has written three other books: *Terrorism and Democracy* (1991), *Caging the Nuclear Genie: An American Challenge for Global Security* (1997), and *Caging the Genies: A Workable Plan for Nuclear, Chemical and Biological Weapons* (1998).

Turner has become a staunch advocate of a post–COLD WAR strategy that involves what he calls "strategic escrow." Simply put, strategic escrow would be a mutual pact between the United States and Russia whereby both nations would unilaterally remove the nuclear warheads from approximately 1,000 intercontinental ballistic missiles. Those warheads would then be stored at least 300 miles from their potential launching sites. Neutral observers would monitor both nations. Both nuclear arsenals, according to Turner, could be reduced to less than 1,000 weapons each in less than five years. "The fact that 30,000 nuclear warheads are around in Russia and the United States and that our government has no plan for reducing that number below 20,000 in the next decade should be unacceptable to us as citizens," Turner wrote in

a 1999 article for the *Washington Post.* "No military officer could imagine a war that required 30,000 of these warheads. And it is not only costly to maintain them, it is dangerous. It tells the world how important we believe these weapons to be, even though without them we are still the strongest military power in the world."

In the wake of the SEPTEMBER 11, 2001, TERRORIST ATTACKS ON THE UNITED STATES, media criticism of Turner resurfaced. A number of newspapers across the country blamed the former DCI for what they believed was his eradication of the Agency's human-intelligence-gathering element during his tenure as director. "If I did all these terrible things they're suggesting, why didn't the six directors in the 24 years that has since transpired, give people an opportunity to correct what I did?" Turner asked during an October 2001 interview on Fox News's *O'Reilly Factor.* "I'm proud of the way I ran the CIA. For these people to say that September 11 is due to something I did over 24 years ago is ludicrous."

In the wake of the terrorist attacks, Turner proposed legislation whereby foreign nationals living in the United States but associated with known terrorists would be immediately deported to their countries of origin. The deportation order would be issued by the attorney general on the recommendation of either the DCI or the director of the FEDERAL BUREAU OF INVESTIGATION (FBI). "I base this concept on the idea that any foreign person coming to this country is privileged," said Turner. "That person does not have a right to come to this country. And that we're foolish when the situation is as serious as it is today to let terrorists stay in this country and plot their terrorist activities, as they did for the September 11 event. Instead, we should, on the recommendation of the director of the FBI or the CIA, let the Attorney General pass judgment as to whether there is sufficient evidence to give real meaning to the idea that these people are supporting terrorist activities, and then the Attorney General should have the authority, if he so rules, just to deport them, send them off to another country, to their own country."

Turner is the recipient of numerous military and intelligence decorations, including the Distinguished Intelligence Medal, the Distinguished Service Medal, the Legion of Merit, and the Bronze Star.

Turner proposal

The Turner proposal was an intelligence reform plan issued by former DIRECTOR OF CENTRAL INTELLIGENCE (DCI) STANSFIELD TURNER to Congress in 1985.

The proposal, which outlined Turner's views for restructuring the U.S. intelligence community, recommended a formal charter for the community, as well as a reduction in its emphasis on covert action. But the proposal's most important recommendation involved the future of the office of DCI. According to Turner, "the two jobs, head of the CIA and head of the Intelligence Community, conflict. One person cannot do justice to both and fulfill the DCI's responsibilities to the President, the Congress, and the public as well."

The Turner proposal recommended a separation of the two primary DCI responsibilities, by creating a head of the CIA, reporting to a DIRECTOR OF NATIONAL INTELLIGENCE, or DNI. The idea was not accepted. It had been first suggested in the SCHLESINGER REPORT of 1971, and it would again be proposed in the BOREN-MCCURDY INITIATIVE of 1992, by U.S. Senator Dianne Feinstein (D-California) in June 2002, and in December 2002 by a congressional panel tasked with investigating possible intelligence shortcomings leading to the SEPTEMBER 11, 2001, TERRORIST ATTACKS ON THE UNITED STATES.

U

Ulmer, Alfred Conrad, Jr. (1916–2000)

Alfred Conrad Ulmer, Jr., was one of the few continuously serving intelligence field officers who worked for three of the CIA's predecessor organizations before serving with the Agency.

Ulmer was born on August 26, 1916, in Jacksonville, Florida, to Alfred Conrad Ulmer and Ruth Clementine Porter. Ulmer worked as a newspaper reporter for the *Jacksonville (Florida) Journal* from 1935 until 1937. He also attended Princeton University, in New Jersey, earning an A.B. degree in 1939. Following Princeton, he served on the public relations staff of Benton & Bowles, one of the world's largest advertising firms.

When America entered World War II in 1941, Ulmer joined the U.S. Naval Reserve, serving in NAVAL INTELLIGENCE and eventually rising to the rank of lieutenant commander. In that capacity, he was detached to the OFFICE OF STRATEGIC SERVICES (OSS), the World War II precursor organization to the CIA. With the OSS, he served in Egypt as a part of a joint American-British unit comprising OSS operatives and members of Britain's SPECIAL OPERATIONS EXECUTIVE (SOE). He later served as chief of the Germany-Austria section of the Office's SECRET INTELLIGENCE Branch in Italy.

When the war ended in 1945, Ulmer was posted to Austria. There he remained, working through the evolutionary period during which the OSS was disbanded, the remains of the OSS's Secret Intelligence Branch were rolled into the new STRATEGIC SERVICES UNIT (SSU), the SSU was rolled into the new CENTRAL INTELLIGENCE GROUP (CIG), and the CIG was reestablished as the CIA.

With the CIA, Ulmer served as CHIEF OF STATION in a variety of foreign posts, including Spain (from 1948 until 1950), Greece (from 1953 until 1955), France (from 1958 until 1962), and the United Kingdom (from 1962 until 1975).

A widely held belief within Agency circles was that Ulmer was being groomed to succeed FRANK GARDINER WISNER as chief of the CIA's CLANDESTINE SERVICE. But Ulmer's direct leadership of the Agency's involvement in the failed INDONESIAN REBELLION of 1958 removed him from the running. Ulmer retired from the CIA in 1962 and pursued a number of private business ventures.

Ulmer earned numerous awards for his military and civilian service, including the Bronze Star (American), the Intelligence Medal of Merit (American), and the Order of the Phoenix (Greek).

In 1992, Ulmer suffered a severe stroke. He died on June 22, 2000. He was 83.

United Fruit

The United Fruit Company was an American-owned, Guatemalan-based banana-growing and shipping business that became a major bone of contention between the U.S. and Guatemalan governments during the early 1950s. It also led to a CIA-backed COUP D'ÉTAT IN GUATEMALA.

In the spring of 1951, Socialist Democrat Jacobo Arbenz Guzmán, a former revolutionary who had the support of both the Guatemalan army and the local communist party, was elected president of Guatemala on a popular platform of land reform. When he assumed office, 70 percent of Guatemala's arable lands were owned by less than 2.5 percent of the planter class, most of whom were not even in the country. Almost immediately, Arbenz Guzmán began to institute a number of social and economic reforms, including a strengthening of the unions and a redistribution of land to some 100,000 peasants, whose incomes averaged less than eight dollars per month.

Unfortunately for American business interests in Guatemala, Arbenz Guzmán's reforms included the expropriation in 1953 of private property including over 400,000 acres of banana plantation lands owned by United Fruit, the largest landowner in the country. Arbenz Guzmán also demanded that United Fruit and other such companies pay more taxes.

Arbenz Guzmán initially offered to purchase United Fruit—its expansive banana orchards, railroads, and telephone lines—for a paltry $600,000 in long-term nonnegotiable bonds. The offer was essentially what the company had declared was its taxable land value. United Fruit then made an unsuccessful counteroffer of $16 million.

U.S. president Dwight Eisenhower, who had inherited the developing Guatemalan problem from Harry Truman, described Arbenz Guzmán's offer as "woefully inadequate," adding that the government confiscation of United Fruit land was a "discriminatory and unfair seizure."

United Fruit had close ties to the CIA. GENERAL WALTER BEDELL SMITH, a former United Fruit executive who was later named to the company's board of directors, was a former DIRECTOR OF CENTRAL INTELLIGENCE (DCI). Several congressmen with national security interests had invested in the company. The Dulles brothers, Secretary of State John Foster Dulles and DCI ALLEN WELSH DULLES, had provided legal services for United Fruit through their association with the New York–based law firm of Sullivan & Cromwell.

In 1954, the CIA supported a successful coup d'état in Guatemala, an operation that would ultimately serve as a model for the ill-fated invasion of Cuba at the BAY OF PIGS. Arbenz Guzmán was forced to flee the country; and land reform policies were rescinded, including those that had been instituted against United Fruit.

U-2 (Dragon Lady)

The U-2 spy plane, also known as the "Dragon Lady," is probably best known as the type of high-altitude reconnaissance aircraft that CIA pilot FRANCIS GARY POWERS was flying when he was shot down over the Soviet Union by a surface-to-air SA-2 missile in 1960.

Developed by aircraft designer Clarence L. "Kelly" Johnson at the now-famous Lockheed Martin "Skunk Works" in Burbank, California, the U-2 was initially rejected by the U.S. Air Force. But the CIA chose it as an air reconnaissance platform that could monitor the Soviets' developing intercontinental ballistic missile (ICBM) and long-range bomber capabilities during the early days of the COLD WAR.

In 1954, DIRECTOR OF CENTRAL INTELLIGENCE (DCI) ALLEN WELSH DULLES directed his special assistant RICHARD MERVIN BISSELL, JR., to oversee the development of a high-flying aircraft, fitted with special cameras, that could overfly communist territory unopposed. On December 9, the CIA contracted with Lockheed, and development of the U-2 began. The following year, the first test flight was made. By May 1956, four U-2s and six pilots were based in Turkey. The following month, U-2s began flying missions for the CIA over the Soviet Union. The first flight covered the cities of Moscow and Leningrad (now St. Petersburg). For the next four years, the aircraft, flying at altitudes of over 70,000 feet, photographed Soviet ICBM testing sites, air bases, and manufacturing centers. The aircraft's capabilities were remarkable. At that time, no Soviet surface-to-air missile could reach the altitudes at which the U-2s flew. In a single flight, U-2 cameras could snap up to 4,000 high-definition photographs of an area over 2,100 miles long and 30 miles wide.

By the spring of 1960, however, the Soviets had vastly improved the range and accuracy of their surface-to-air missiles. On May 1, 1960, a U-2 flown by Francis Gary Powers was on a mission to reconnoiter the reported construction of an ICBM base at Plesetsk when it developed engine trouble. Powers was forced to reduce his altitude and was shot down over the Soviet city of Sverdlovsk. Powers was captured and later exchanged for COLONEL RUDOLF IVONOVICH ABEL, a Soviet spy imprisoned in the United States.

On October 14, 1962, the U-2 again made history when it photographed the installation of Soviet-built intermediate range ballistic missiles in Cuba, thus setting off the CUBAN MISSILE CRISIS. During the crisis, on October 27, another U-2 was shot down; its pilot, Major Rudolph Anderson, was killed. From 1964 to 1966, the U-2 made overflights of China.

Physically, the U-2 is unlike anything developed before or since. It is a one-engined, single-seat platform. It is 63 feet (19.2 meters) long and 16 feet (4.8 meters) in height, and it has a wingspan of 103 feet (30.9 meters). The aircraft has a range of over 7,000 miles

U-2 "Dragon Lady"   (NATIONAL ARCHIVES)

(6,090 nautical miles); a ceiling, or maximum altitude, of over 70,000 feet (21,212 meters); and a classified speed well over 475 miles per hour (Mach 0.58).

The U-2's unconventional design gives it gliderlike flying characteristics but makes the aircraft extremely challenging to land. Additionally, the U-2's high-altitude mission requires the pilot to wear a full pressure suit, which makes it difficult to manipulate the aircraft controls.

Modified versions of the aircraft are in use today, and they are projected to continue flying well into the 21st century. The U-2 is currently operational as a U.S. Air Force reconnaissance aircraft.

U-2 incident

On the morning of May 1, 1960, villagers near the Soviet city of Sverdlovsk were startled by the shriek of a crippled jet aircraft flying at treetop level. Rushing out of their homes, they heard a terrific crash and explosion, and saw a distant, curling plume of smoke. Above them descended a parachutist. The villagers ran toward the parachutist, assuming that he was Russian.

When the parachutist landed, the villagers noticed that he was unlike any aviator they had ever seen before. The parachutist was a burly man wearing an odd-looking steel-gray flight suit, brown boots, a white helmet, a pistol, and a sheath knife. When asked if he was injured, the parachutist replied in a language they had never heard before. The language was English, and the parachutist was FRANCIS GARY POWERS, a CIA reconnaissance pilot, and he had just been shot down by a Soviet surface-to-air SA-2 missile.

Powers, who was flying a U-2 spy plane over Soviet airspace, had been on a mission to reconnoiter the reported construction of an intercontinental ballistic missile base at Plesetsk, in northwestern Russia. His aircraft had developed engine trouble. Forced to reduce his altitude, he had been attacked and shot down. He was subsequently apprehended by Soviet authorities and turned over to the KGB.

Having been assured by the CIA that no evidence of the U-2's reconnaissance purposes would ever be revealed, U.S. president Dwight Eisenhower publicly denied that Powers was on a spy mission. Soviet premier Nikita Khrushchev soon publicly released evidence, in the form of pieces of Power's aircraft and equipment.

Powers was tried in Soviet court, charged with espionage, and sentenced to 10 years in prison. In February 1962, however, he was exchanged in a dramatic COLD WAR spy swap for Soviet intelligence operative COLONEL RUDOLF IVONOVICH ABEL. The latter had been arrested earlier by the Americans when it was discovered that he had established an elaborate spy network in New York during the 1950s.

During Powers's trial, Roman Rudenko, the chief prosecutor, lashed out at the American U-2 program, referring to it as "a graphic example of criminal collusion between a big American capitalist company, an espionage center, and the US military."

Years later, DIRECTOR OF CENTRAL INTELLIGENCE (DCI) GEORGE JOHN TENET would say that Rudenko's statement was "pretty close" to the truth. However, Tenet added, "the U-2 revolutionaries got it right. They were brilliant. They were willing to think big and think different and take risks. They drew ideas, information, and strength from a variety of disciplines and from each other. And they formed public-private partnerships that would last."

V

Vandenberg, Hoyt Sanford (1899–1954)

Lt. Gen. Hoyt Sanford Vandenberg was the second official DIRECTOR OF CENTRAL INTELLIGENCE (DCI) and one of the key early leaders who helped establish the Agency as a preeminent intelligence organization.

Vandenberg was born to William Collins Vandenberg, a bookbinder and street-car company president, and Pearl Kane, on January 24, 1899, in Milwaukee, Wisconsin. Vandenberg grew up in Lowell, Massachusetts.

When the United States entered World War I, Vandenberg joined the U.S. Army as an officer candidate and began training in Plattsburgh, New York. However, the war ended before his training was completed. He then sought and won an appointment to the U.S. Military Academy at West Point, New York. He graduated on June 12, 1923, and was commissioned a second lieutenant, with orders to the Air Service Flying School at Brooks Field, Texas. There he earned his pilot wings in February 1924. He went on to graduate from the Army's Advanced Flying School at Kelly Field, Texas, in September.

Vandenberg was initially assigned to the Third Attack Group, also at Kelly Field, where he eventually assumed command of the 90th Attack Squadron. In 1927, he became an instructor pilot at the Army Air Corps Primary Flight School at March Field, California. In May 1929, he transferred to Schofield Barracks, Hawaii. There he joined the Sixth Pursuit Squadron, assuming command of the unit

within six months. He returned to Texas in 1931 as an instructor pilot at Randolph Field. By 1933, he was a flight commander and deputy stage—primary training—commander. The following year, he entered the Air Corps Tactical School at Maxwell Field, Alabama. In June 1936, he graduated from the Command and General Staff School at Fort Leavenworth, Kansas. He briefly returned to Maxwell Field as a flight instructor, and then entered the Army War College in September. In 1939, he was assigned to the Plans Division in the Office of the Chief of Air Corps.

In the aftermath of the Japanese attack on Pearl Harbor in 1941, Vandenberg served as both operations officer and training officer of the Air Staff. Throughout World War II, he held organizational and operational posts. He traveled throughout the world and flew a number of missions over hostile territory. He also held a variety of deputy commands and commands. By war's end, he was serving as assistant chief of the Air Staff at U.S. Army Air Forces headquarters.

In 1946, Vandenberg, was named assistant chief of staff for ARMY INTELLIGENCE. That same year, he was appointed by President Harry Truman to serve as director of the CENTRAL INTELLIGENCE GROUP (CIG), the immediate predecessor organization to CIA. Vandenberg served from June 10, 1946, to May 1, 1947.

An an Air Force officer with a great deal of wartime command experience, Vandenberg realized the importance of coordinated intelligence gathering and effective analysis. That in turn influenced his approach to the group's development. During his first months as DCI, Vandenberg lobbied for an increased CIG budget and an expansion in the number of personnel. He also oversaw the group's jurisdictional victories—over the FEDERAL BUREAU OF INVESTIGATION (FBI), the CIG's domestic counterpart, for foreign COUNTERINTELLIGENCE and foreign intelligence gathering. He also established the beginnings of a special-operations capability within CIG. In principle, he created a new intelligence organization with virtually all of the powers (excepting covert action) of the OFFICE OF STRATEGIC SERVICES (OSS), the World War II predecessor organization to the CIA.

When he was succeeded as DCI by REAR ADMIRAL ROSCOE HILLENKOETTER, Vandenberg continued campaigning for a permanent "central intelligence agency," testifying before Congress on matters related to the proposed reorganization of the national intelligence structure. On September 18, 1947, the NATIONAL SECURITY ACT became effective. The act, which created the U.S. DEPARTMENT OF DEFENSE (bringing Army, Navy, and newly established Air Force Departments under one civilian defense chief) and the NATIONAL SECURITY COUNCIL (the president, vice president, and secretaries of defense and state), also established the CIA.

In 1947, Vandenberg was named vice chief of staff of the Air Force and promoted to full (four-star) general. The following year, he was named chief of staff. He served in that capacity for more than five years. He retired from the Air Force in June 1953.

He died of complications from cancer on April 2, 1954. He was 55.

VENONA project

The VENONA project was an effort conducted by the U.S. Army's Signal Intelligence Service, the predecessor organization to the NATIONAL SECURITY AGENCY (or NSA, now a member of the U.S. INTELLIGENCE COMMUNITY) in which Soviet intelligence cables from 1940 through 1948 were collected and decrypted into legible text. Those messages, exchanged by the KGB (KOMITET GOSUDARSTVENNOY BEZOPASNOSTI, the Soviet intelligence/counterintelligence agency) and the GRU (GLAVNOYE RAZVEDYVATELNOYE UPRAVLENIYE, the Soviet military intelligence corps) with their agents operating in the Western Hemisphere, provided extraordinary insight into Soviet attempts to infiltrate the highest levels of the U.S. government.

On February 1, 1943, the Signal Intelligence Service began decoding the messages that had been sent over commercial telegraph lines. Between 1947 and 1952, most of the intercepted cables that were susceptible to decoding had been translated and analyzed. The effort to crack the message codes continued until 1980. During that period, the FEDERAL BUREAU OF INVESTIGATION (FBI) was able to use VENONA intelligence to identify a number of Soviet assets operating in the West. The CIA also used decrypted VENONA cables to identify KGB agents beginning in 1953.

On July 11, 1995, a ceremony was held at the GEORGE BUSH CENTER FOR INTELLIGENCE in LANGLEY, VIRGINIA, wherein DIRECTOR OF CENTRAL INTELLIGENCE (DCI) JOHN M. DEUTCH announced the release of 49 translated VENONA documents. The documents were related to Soviet espionage activities directed at the U.S. government's early atomic weapons programs. Since then, thousands of VENONA messages have been declassified and made available to the public. "The Intelligence Community does not own national security secrets," said Deutch during the release announcement. "They are a trust that we hold for the American people. We must guard these secrets as long as the information is relevant to the protection of our freedom and then it is our obligation to make them available to the public. The information that we are now declassifying helps the American people understand the contribution that intelligence and law enforcement make to protecting this nation."

Vietnam, operations in

See SOUTHEAST ASIA, OPERATIONS IN.

W, Task Force

Task Force W was the CIA operational group responsible for sabotage and paramilitary operations conducted by anti-Castro guerrilla units against Cuba during OPERATION MONGOOSE, the CIA's all-encompassing covert-action effort aimed at eliminating Cuban leader FIDEL CASTRO during the early 1960s.

During the CUBAN MISSILE CRISIS of 1962, WILLIAM KING HARVEY, the director of Task Force W, sent more than one intelligence team into Cuba without the knowledge of either President John Kennedy's EXECUTIVE COMMITTEE or of DIRECTOR OF CENTRAL INTELLIGENCE (DCI) JOHN MCCONE. One of the teams was captured by the Cubans (October 25). Another team destroyed a Cuban industrial complex (November 8), which increased tension during the final days of the crisis. Harvey's actions elicited strong criticism of the Agency from Attorney General Robert Kennedy, who wanted to terminate Task Force W. It continued to operate until 1963, when it became known as the Special Affairs Staff.

Walker, John Anthony, Jr. (1937–)

John Anthony Walker, Jr., known unofficially in U.S. Navy circles as "JOHNNY WALKER RED," was the ringleader of the notorious WALKER FAMILY SPY RING.

Walker was born in Scranton, Pennsylvania, in 1937 and, like many other turncoats, was raised in a dysfunctional family. His father was a physically abusive alcoholic. In fact, the elder Walker beat his wife so severely that young Walker began plotting to kill his father when he was only 10 years old. As a boy, Walker exhibited dual-personality traits. He had few friends, save for two, which he always kept apart. With one friend, he was always courteous, trustworthy, and respectful of other people and their property. With the other friend, he was something of a juvenile delinquent—shooting out automobile headlights, rolling old tires in front of passing cars, setting fires, throwing rocks through school windows, and stealing money from various places, including church donation boxes. He attended a Catholic school, where he was considered a marginal student and poor athlete whose avoidance of extracurricular activities led him even to refuse to have his picture made for the yearbook.

When he was 17, Walker was arrested for attempted burglary. When police began interrogating him, he admitted to committing six other burglaries. He was subsequently sentenced to a period of probation. His older brother, Arthur, a naval officer, persuaded the judge to lift the probation so that Walker could enlist in the Navy. The judge agreed, as he believed Walker might benefit from Navy discipline. Walker then took and passed the high school equivalency test as well as a two-year-college-level equivalency test.

In 1956, once in the Navy, he immersed himself in the world of radio operations, electronics, signals, and CRYPTOGRAPHY. He was regarded as "bright, energetic, and enthusiastic" and was promoted quickly.

Married and with three children, everything seemed to be going well, at least on the surface. Each time Walker was promoted, he put the increase in his pay into a savings account. But saving money became an obsession for both Walker and his wife, Barbara. They refused to tip waitresses in restaurants. They bought powdered milk instead of fresh milk for their children. Walker wore his shoes until they could no longer be resoled. When deployed, he avoided "liberty call" in foreign ports. In 1965, however, he withdrew his savings and used them, together with money from a loan, to purchase a house near Charleston, South Carolina, and turn it into a bar. But the bar failed to produce a profit. Soon his finances and his marriage were on the rocks.

The failures were apparently more than he could bear. In late 1967, a desperate Walker stole his first document from the Navy. He then approached the Soviets and offered his services for the purposes of espionage. Strolling up to the Soviet embassy in Washington, D.C., he boldly asked to see "someone in security." He had taken with him a month's code-key settings for a ciphering machine used where he worked at the Navy's command center for Atlantic Fleet submarine forces in Norfolk, Virginia.

Promising future deliveries, Walker demanded $1,000 per week and a cash advance. He was then introduced to officials from the KGB, who agreed to his terms. They also provided Walker with a tiny Minox camera so that he could surreptitiously photograph top-secret materials.

With Walker providing key cards used for enciphering messages as well as technical manuals on the encryption devices themselves, the Soviets were able to learn the routes of American submarines and gain advance knowledge of American bombing operations against North Vietnam.

For 17 years, Walker's actions would compromise countless classified messages sent and received by members of the U.S. intelligence community, including the CIA. "He [Walker] himself knew very little," former DIRECTOR OF CENTRAL INTELLIGENCE (DCI) ROBERT MICHAEL GATES would later say. "But what he did was hand the Russians the keys to our communications."

Once the KGB had established him as an agent, it ordered him not to meet with any of its officials in the United States. Instead, he was directed to travel overseas—once to Hong Kong, usually to Austria—where he received training, money for his services, and further instructions. "We received from him the most valuable

information on the military strategic and tactical plans of the U.S.A. against the U.S.S.R., including the combat employment of atomic submarines equipped with the nuclear missiles," Alexander Sokolov, the former Washington fixed-post intelligence networks officer of the KGB's First Chief Directorate, later recalled. "He provided us with the figures which allowed us for many years to read secret information of the U.S. Defense Department, the State Department, the Agency for National Security and other important state structures. Walker has been considered to be the most valuable source of such information for Soviet intelligence."

Walker used his newfound wealth to purchase all manner of luxury items. He bought a boat, an airplane, and a new house, which he allowed his wife to furnish and decorate as she pleased, regardless of cost. He threw

John Anthony Walker, Jr., left, is escorted by a U.S. federal marshal (ASSOCIATED PRESS)

parties for his fellow sailors, sometimes inviting prostitutes and other women with whom he was having affairs. He drank often and used marijuana. But it never seemed to impair his work.

When asked where his money came from, Walker said he made it from his bar and other investments, like a short-lived car-stereo operation with his brother, Arthur, and a Virginia Beach–based detective agency. As a COVER for his treasonous activities, he portrayed himself as a staunch anticommunist. He even went so far as to join ultra-right-wing political organizations like the JOHN BIRCH Society, and even the Ku Klux Klan.

Facing imminent retirement from the Navy, Walker recruited as a second spy one of his mates, Jerry Alfred Whitworth, a Navy communications specialist. Walker retired from the Navy in 1976. Whitworth worked with Walker from 1975 to 1982, providing highly classified material related to naval communications.

In 1980, Walker lured his older brother, Arthur, into the scheme. At Walker's suggestion, Arthur took a job with the VSE Corporation, a Chesapeake, Virginia–based defense contractor, for the sole purpose of gaining access to classified material. Over the next two years, Arthur provided his younger brother with numerous surreptitiously photographed documents, all classified, that dealt with the construction and design of American naval vessels. Most of the money Arthur received he returned to Walker to repay a debt.

In 1983, Walker recruited his son Michael, who at that time was on active duty aboard the aircraft carrier USS *Nimitz*. Michael then began providing classified Navy documents to his father for sale to the Soviets.

In 1985 Walker and his wife, Barbara, separated. Barbara, who would later claim she had had no knowledge of her son's involvement, went to the FEDERAL BUREAU OF INVESTIGATION (FBI) to inform on her husband. On May 20, Walker was arrested at a Maryland motel after making a roadside drop to be picked up by KGB operatives. Within days, his son was arrested aboard ship, and the Walker family spy ring began to collapse.

On October 28, both Walker and his son pled guilty to six charges of espionage under a plea bargain wherein Walker agreed to testify against Whitworth and provide complete information on what the Soviets had received, in exchange for a lesser sentence for his son. On November 6, 1986, Walker received two life sentences plus 10 years to be served concurrently.

Years, later in an interview for the History Channel, RICHARD L. HAVER, a former interrogator and executive director of the CIA's COMMUNITY MANAGEMENT STAFF, said, "Walker was a catastrophe. It was a disaster. John Walker may be the single most damaging traitor in recent American history."

Walker will be eligible for parole in 2015.

Walker family spy ring

The Walker family spy ring was a group of four American conspirators, all of whom served in the U.S. Navy, who committed espionage for the Soviet Union over a period of nearly two decades. Their actions inflicted substantive damage on the U.S. intelligence community, including the CIA. The ringleader was JOHN ANTHONY WALKER, JR., a U.S. Navy chief warrant officer considered by Soviet intelligence officials to be their most important spy in America during the 1970s.

Walker's coconspirators were Michael Lance Walker, John's son and a U.S. Navy petty officer; Arthur James Walker, John's brother and a retired U.S. Navy lieutenant commander; and Senior Chief Radioman Jerry Alfred Whitworth, John's friend and a U.S. Navy communications specialist.

John Walker's treasonous activities began after making some financial investments that turned sour. To make up for his losses, he approached the Soviets in October 1967 and offered his services for the purposes of espionage.

Strolling up to the Soviet embassy in Washington, D.C., Walker boldly asked to see "someone in security." He had taken with him a month's code-key settings for a ciphering machine used where he worked at the Navy's command center for Atlantic Fleet submarine forces in Norfolk, Virginia. Promising future deliveries, he demanded $1,000 per week and a cash advance. He was then introduced to officials from the KGB, who agreed to his terms. They also provided Walker with a tiny Minox camera so that he could surreptitiously photograph top-secret materials.

With Walker providing key cards used for enciphering messages as well as technical manuals on the encryption devices themselves, the Soviets were able to learn routes of American submarines and gain advance knowledge of American bombing operations against North Vietnam. For 17 years, Walker's actions would compromise countless classified messages sent and received by members of the U.S. intelligence community, including the CIA. "He [John Walker] opened up windows way beyond just Navy access for extended periods of time," said RICHARD L. HAVER, a former interrogator and executive director of the CIA's COMMUNITY MANAGEMENT STAFF, in an interview for CNN. "And when someone compromises your secure communications, they have compromised your entire system."

A few years after his initial contact with the Soviets, and facing imminent retirement from the Navy, Walker recruited Jerry Whitworth. The latter worked in the spy ring from 1975 to 1982, providing John Walker with highly classified material related to naval communications. For his services, Whitworth received approximately $332,000.

Arthur Walker was lured into the scheme in 1980 when, at his brother's suggestion, he took a job with the VSE Corporation, a Chesapeake, Virginia–based defense contractor, for the sole purpose of gaining access to classified material. Over the next two years, Arthur provided John with numerous surreptitiously photographed documents, all classified, that dealt with the construction and design of American naval vessels. Arthur received about $12,000 for his services, much of which he returned to John to repay a debt.

In 1983, John recruited his son Michael, who at that time was on active duty, serving aboard the aircraft carrier USS *Nimitz*. The younger Walker then began providing classified Navy documents to his father for sale to the Soviets.

The spy ring began to collapse when in late 1984 John Walker and his wife, Barbara, separated. Barbara, who would later claim she had had no knowledge of her son's involvement, went to the FEDERAL BUREAU OF INVESTIGATION (FBI) on November 23 to inform on her husband. Some sources allege that Barbara had been aware of her son's involvement but went to the FBI fearing that her daughter, Laura, who was being encouraged by Walker to enlist in the U.S. Army, was also about to be lured into the spy ring. Whitworth, realizing that the FBI was closing in, reportedly attempted to arrange a meeting with the bureau in order to bargain for immunity from prosecution.

On May 20, 1985, John was arrested at a Rockville, Maryland, motel after making a roadside drop. On May 28, his son, Michael, was arrested on board the *Nimitz* off Haifa, Israel. A search of Michael's berthing space revealed 15 pounds of stolen classified material hidden near his bunk. The following day Arthur was arrested. On June 3, the FBI arrested Whitworth. All four men were charged with conducting espionage activities for the Soviet Union.

On August 9, 1985, Arthur Walker was found guilty of seven counts of espionage. He was sentenced to three life terms and fined $250,000. On October 28, both John and Michael Walker pled guilty to six charges of espionage under a plea bargain wherein John agreed to testify against Whitworth and provide complete information on what the Soviets had received, in exchange for a lesser sentence for his son.

On November 6, 1986, John received two life sentences plus 10 years, to be served concurrently. Michael was sentenced to 25 years in prison. On August 28, Jerry Whitworth was convicted on 12 counts of espionage and one count of tax evasion. He was subsequently sentenced to 365 years in prison and a fine of $410,000.

Whitworth's actions were considered the most damaging, as he had reportedly provided the Soviets with key lists that would have enabled them to decipher American naval communications as well as uncover classified information about the design of sensitive cryptographic equipment.

On February 16, 2000, Michael Walker—having served the mandatory 15 years of his 25-year sentence—was released from a halfway house in Boston. Both John and Arthur Walker will be eligible for parole in 2015.

walk-in

In CIA parlance, a walk-in is a DEFECTOR who literally "walks in" to an embassy, consulate, or other such installation and declares his or her intentions, perhaps to request political asylum or to offer his or her services as an agent for the intelligence services of that nation.

Wall of Honor

See MEMORIAL WALL, CIA.

Watergate scandal

The Watergate scandal, which lasted from 1972 to 1974, was the greatest political malefaction in U.S. history. The scandal involved the highest levels of government in a number of illegal activities designed to help President Richard Nixon win reelection during the 1972 presidential campaign. Its discovery forced Nixon to resign from the presidency in 1974 in order to avoid impeachment proceedings. It also resulted in CIA activities being exposed to a degree of public scrutiny that the Agency had never before experienced.

The events began to unfold on the night of June 17, 1972, when five men—Eugenio Martinez, Virgilio Gonzalez, Frank Sturgis, BERNARD BARKER, and JAMES WALTER MCCORD, JR.—broke into the Washington, D.C., Watergate complex with the objective of obtaining information from the Democratic Party's national headquarters office. Barker had once been recruited by the Agency when he was a Cuban policeman. McCord was a former CIA officer.

The five men, known as the White House "PLUMBERS," were arrested after being discovered in the building by a roving security officer. Not long after their arrests, it was discovered that the men had been operating under the direction of EVERETTE HOWARD HUNT, a former CIA operative, and George Gordon Liddy, a former special agent and supervisor with the FEDERAL BUREAU OF INVESTIGATION (FBI).

When the FBI deepened its investigation into the matter, Nixon attempted to divert its attention from the White House by deepening the CIA's implication. RICHARD M. HELMS, then DIRECTOR OF CENTRAL INTELLIGENCE (DCI), resisted. That was viewed as disloyalty by the president, and on February 2, 1973, Nixon relieved Helms as director, replacing him with JAMES R. SCHLESINGER.

Though no substantive evidence linking the CIA to the Watergate scandal has ever been produced, rumors continue to circulate suggesting that the Agency was implicated at some level, beyond the involvement of former operatives.

weapons and assassination devices

CIA field operatives, though usually not considered combatants, must be trained and equipped to handle all manner of conventional weapons and personal weapons. The reasoning is simple: though the CIA operatives' primary mission is to collect intelligence, if they are discovered, the only possible chance of escape might be the immediate and skillful employment of deadly force with a weapon.

Field operatives are often equipped with easily concealed close-combat weapons, for *defensive* purposes. Such weapons might include small knives, blades, and daggers (some similar to ice picks); brass knuckles; small pistols with silencers; single-shot devices mounted in ballpoint-pen cases, hollowed-out cigars, pipes, and cigarettes; empty flashlights; belt buckles; and lipstick tubes.

During intelligence-gathering operations and covert actions, field operatives must sometimes use a variety of *offensive* weapons, including silenced pistols and silenced submachine guns, crossbows, and garrotes. The latter, a long strand of serrated wire with brass or wooden handles, is most commonly used to eliminate enemy guards; one approaches the victim from behind, loops the wire over his head (around the neck), and then tightens the loop until the victim is dead.

During the early 1960s, several unconventional, and unsuccessful, weapons were either used or considered by the CIA in ASSASSINATION PLOTS against Cuban leader FIDEL CASTRO. Among those weapons were poison pills, a box of botulism-laced cigars, a ballpoint pen–concealed hypodermic needle that contained botulism, and exploding seashells.

During that same period, the Agency planned to assassinate Congolese leader Patrice Emery Lumumba. The plan was for a CIA-hired executioner to inject poison into Lumumba's food or toothpaste. The operation was never conducted; Lumumba was eventually killed by his own political rivals.

Assassination devices utilized by the CIA's counterpart agencies since World War II have included walking canes concealing poison-gas-propellent mechanisms or poison needles, cigarette packs and wallets with poison gas propellents, poison-dart-firing pistols, and small tubes and tobacco pipes designed with single-bullet-firing mechanisms.

Whether used for offensive or defensive purposes, current CIA weapons are constantly being upgraded; also, new developments are being added to the Agency's arsenal. The weapons are becoming increasingly sophisticated as new technologies are brought to bear. But field requirements demand that the most important characteristics of a CIA operative's personal weapons never change—effectiveness and concealability.

See also CONGO, OPERATIONS IN THE.

Webster, William Hedgcock (1924–   )

William Hedgcock Webster was the only DIRECTOR OF CENTRAL INTELLIGENCE (DCI) who also held the post of director of the FEDERAL BUREAU OF INVESTIGATION (FBI).

Webster was born on March 6, 1924, in St. Louis, Missouri, to Thomas M. Webster and Katherine Hedgcock. Commissioned in the U.S. Naval Reserve, Webster served during World War II and in the postwar occupation period (1943 to 1946), as well as briefly during the Korean conflict (1951 to 1952). In 1947, he graduated from Massachusett's Amherst College. Two years later, he finished Washington University Law School. After graduation, he moved to St. Louis, Missouri, where he practiced law for 22 years, including a stint as U.S. attorney for Missouri's Eastern District from 1960 to 1961. In 1971, he was appointed a judge in the Eastern District. In 1973, he was named to the U.S. Court of Appeals, Eighth Circuit. He served in that capacity until 1978, when he was appointed director of the FBI by President Jimmy Carter.

Webster assumed the post of FBI director at a time when the bureau was reeling from disclosures of FBI misdeeds by the CHURCH and PIKE COMMITTEES. Webster, however, was able to return much of the prestige lost by the FBI, and he increased the Bureau's effectiveness in the areas of organized crime and foreign espionage.

President Ronald Reagan appointed Webster director of the CIA in 1987; he served in that capacity from May 26 of that year to August 31, 1991. According to documents published by the CIA's History Staff, Webster worked tirelessly as DCI to emphasize the Agency's accountability in the public eye. Whereas DCI WILLIAM J. CASEY had managed the CIA independently, Webster recognized the Agency's subordination to national policy. He tightened the reigns on the CIA's internal review process and defined standards by which clandestine activities would be judged for practicality, competency, and consistency with U.S. foreign policy and American values. Thus, as in his work as FBI director, Webster was able to recover much of the Agency's lost prestige.

When Webster retired from the CIA, he returned to the practice of law, becoming a senior partner in the Washington, D.C.–based firm of Milbank, Tweed, Hadley

William Webster, meeting with President Ronald Reagan   (RONALD REAGAN LIBRARY)

& McCloy. Webster has since served as a public lecturer, television analyst, and an unofficial adviser to members of the U.S. INTELLIGENCE COMMUNITY.

Following the February 2001 arrest of FBI COUNTER-INTELLIGENCE officer ROBERT PHILIP HANSSEN on charges of conducting espionage activities against the United States, Webster was appointed to head a special commission that investigated security shortcomings and concluded that there had been "a pervasive inattention to security" inside the FBI.

In late October 2002, in the wake of dozens of scandals involving sizable corporations nationwide, Webster was appointed head of special accounting oversight board for the Securities and Exchange Commission (SEC). Soon it was disclosed that SEC chairman Harvey Pitt had failed

to inform fellow commissioners that Webster had overseen the audit committee of a company under investigation for fraud. The flap forced Pitt to resign from the SEC, and on November 12, Webster resigned from the board. "I now believe my continued presence on the board will only generate more distractions which will not be helpful to the important mission of the board," Webster stated in his letter of resignation. "Those who know me will appreciate that I do not abandon duty lightly."

Among Webster's awards are numerous honorary doctorates from a variety of colleges and universities. He is also the recipient of the Distinguished Alumnus Award from Washington University, the Stein Award from Fordham University, the Law Award from the University of Virginia, the National Service Medal from the Freedom

Foundation, the Theodore Roosevelt Award, the Presidential Medal of Freedom, the National Security Medal, the Silver Buffalo Award from the Boy Scouts of America, and the Distinguished Service Award from the American Legion, and others. He has also earned recognition as Father of the Year for 1986, and Man of the Year by the *St. Louis Globe Democrat*.

Welch, Richard Skeffington (1929–1975)

Richard Skeffington Welch was the CIA's Athens CHIEF OF STATION (COS) who in 1975 was gunned down by terrorists after his name and address had been published in a spy cult magazine. His death was blamed on PHILIP AGEE, a former Agency employee who reportedly had ties to the magazine.

Welch was born on December 14, 1929, in Hartford, Connecticut. He later attended Classical High School in Providence, Rhode Island. In 1951, he graduated from Harvard University and soon thereafter joined the CIA.

Assigned to the Agency's CLANDESTINE SERVICE, Welch initially served at CIA headquarters in LANGLEY, VIRGINIA. He was then posted to CIA stations in Athens and on the Mediterranean island of Cyprus. He then held posts in Guatemala (1966), Guyana (1967), and a second assignment at Langley. In 1972, he was made chief of station in Peru.

Welch returned to Athens in June 1975, this time as station chief. But his tour was short-lived. In late 1975, the English-language *Athens News* published his name, title, home telephone number, and home address, along with the particulars of other Agency operatives in the region. Similar information had been previously published about him in the Washington, D.C.–based *Counterspy* magazine (the predecessor to the *Covert Action Information Bulletin,* now the *Covert Action Quarterly*), a publication for which Agency turncoat Philip Agee wrote editorials.

On December 23, Welch was shot and killed on his doorstep by masked gunmen as he returned from a Christmas party with his wife. A group calling itself the "Revolutionary Organization of November 17" (the date referred to an uprising two years earlier) later claimed credit for the assassination. The CIA blamed Agee for Welch's death, but the former spy denied any responsibility.

The edition of *Counterspy* that published Welch's contact information also published the following statement by Agee to potential enemies of the CIA: "The peoples victimized by the CIA and the economic exploitation that CIA enforces can bring pressure on their so-often compromised governments to expel the CIA people. And, in the absence of such expulsion, which will not be uncommon, the people themselves will have to decide what they must do to rid themselves of CIA."

At the time of his death, Welch was 46.

Western Hemisphere Institute for Security Cooperation (WHISC)

The Western Hemisphere Institute for Security Cooperation is the current name of the infamous SCHOOL OF THE AMERICAS. WHISC is located at Fort Benning, Georgia, a U.S. Army infantry base.

WEST POINTER

WEST POINTER was the unofficial nickname for Operation KMSOURDOUGH, a CIA mail-intercept operation based in San Francisco, California, from September 1969 to October 1971.

See also FLAPS AND SEALS; HT-LINGUAL.

wet work

"Wet work" describes the act of assassination. The term originated within the Soviet intelligence community but is today used by officers of, and agents employed by, the CIA.

white propaganda

In CIA parlance, white propaganda refers to manipulated information in broadcast or published statements that makes no attempt to conceal its origin. White propaganda differs from BLACK PROPAGANDA in that the source of the latter is not revealed.

See also GRAY PROPAGANDA.

Wisner, Frank Gardiner (1909–1965)

Frank Gardiner Wisner was one of the CIA's early covert-action zealots.

Born in 1909 in Laurel, Mississippi, to Frank George Wisner, a no-nonsense timber magnate, and Mary Gardiner, a tender-hearted schoolteacher, young Wisner developed a straightforward perception of right and wrong. As a boy, he was an excellent athlete, excelling in track and field, and a fair student whose marginal performance in the classroom was balanced by enthusiasm and quick-wittedness. His father, who supported higher education for blacks, was not well liked by local Ku Klux Klansmen. Wisner witnessed occasional cross burnings on his family's property, which reinforced his principled concepts.

In 1931, Wisner graduated from the University of Virginia and in 1934 earned his juris doctor degree from its law school, finishing third in his class. In 1936, his recognized athletic prowess from his college days was enough to earn him an invitation to the Olympic trials. For the next several years he practiced law in New York City at the Wall Street firm of Carter, Ledyard, & Milburn.

When America entered World War II in 1941, Wisner joined the U.S. Naval Reserve and was assigned to NAVAL INTELLIGENCE. Less than two years later, he was recruited into the OFFICE OF STRATEGIC SERVICES (or OSS, the wartime predecessor organization to the CIA) by his friend WILLIAM J. "WILD BILL" DONOVAN, its head.

Wisner was sent to Turkey, and was soon appointed station director in Istanbul. There, he established a complex espionage network covering much of southeastern Europe. He was able to provide vital information to the U.S. Army Air Forces regarding the Ploesti oil fields in Romania, which in August 1944 were bombed.

In September, Wisner was reassigned to Bucharest, where he took over OSS operations in Romania. When the Soviets entered Bucharest in March 1945, Wisner's men shifted their focus from the Germans to the Russians; they were able to penetrate and gather intelligence from Soviet military headquarters as well as from the offices of the Romanian Communist Party. When the Germans surrendered in May, Wisner was sent to Wiesbaden, Germany.

In October 1945, President Harry Truman disbanded the OSS, and in 1946 Wisner returned to his legal practice. But after wartime espionage work, civilian life seemed dull and purposeless. Additionally, Wisner had developed a deep hatred of communism and was impelled to combat it in any way possible.

Not long after returning to the States, Wisner joined the U.S. Council on Foreign Relations. In 1947, he joined the U.S. DEPARTMENT OF STATE, becoming deputy assistant secretary of state for occupied countries. In that capacity, he was responsible for managing the problems associated with the stream of refugees entering Western Europe from the East. He was also tasked with gathering intelligence from the war-ravaged areas of Europe.

The following year, Wisner transferred from the State Department to the newly established CIA. There he was made chief of the OFFICE OF POLICY COORDINATION (OPC), the Agency's early covert-action arm. In the OPC, Wisner was able to create an entity within the Agency that could effectively and secretly conduct propaganda, sabotage, subversion, and all manner of resistance operations against hostile nations. Few would know, outside of Wisner's circle, what those operations entailed.

Future DIRECTOR OF CENTRAL INTELLIGENCE (DCI) WILLIAM E. COLBY would later write that Wisner had created "the atmosphere of an order of Knights Templars, to save freedom from Communist darkness." Evan Thomas, author of *The Very Best Men,* would echo that view. "To work for Frank Wisner was romantic and dashing," Thomas wrote. "Over time the amateurs would become cynics, and intelligence would become a cult. But in 1948 it was still a crusade."

During the Soviet BLOCKADE OF BERLIN in 1948, several suggestions were made as to how the communists might be countered. One of the more provocative ideas was proposed by Wisner. The OPC chief, along with several top-ranking U.S. Army officers, believed that Berlin could be taken by force. After all, the Soviets had yet to develop the atomic bomb. The idea was to send in a self-contained task force complete with engineers, artillery, armor, and a small force of infantry. The task force would launch from one of the Western-occupied zones and fight its way toward the capital city. The proposal was shelved in favor of something less confrontational—the Berlin Airlift, a series of some 300,000 air transport flights into West Berlin, delivering an average of 5,000 tons of life necessities every day for nearly a year.

In 1951, the OPC and the OFFICE OF SPECIAL OPERATIONS (OSO), the Agency's SECRET INTELLIGENCE arm, were brought under the newly created CIA CLANDESTINE SERVICE. The following year, the OPC and the OSO merged to form the new DIRECTORATE of Plans (the predecessor of the current Directorate of Operations), and Wisner was named DEPUTY DIRECTOR for plans (DDP). Under his leadership, the Plans Directorate achieved a number of successes, including the COUPS D'ÉTAT IN IRAN and GUATEMALA as well as the U-2 spyplane program.

Unfortunately, by the end of 1956, the stress of intelligence work had begun to take its toll on the DDP. Twice hospitalized for mental and physical exhaustion, Wisner was reassigned to a less stressful post as CHIEF OF STATION (COS) in London. He resigned from the CIA in 1961.

In 1965, Wisner committed suicide at his home in Galena, Maryland. He was 56.

See also MIGHTY WURLITZER.

witting

In CIA circles, the term *witting*—which simply means "aware"—describes someone who is aware of the underlying role of a COVER organization or of an individual operating with a cover. For instance, during the Vietnam War, an employee of AIR AMERICA who knew that the airline was a cover for CIA operations in Southeast Asia would be considered "witting."

Woolsey, R. James (1941–   )

R. James Woolsey was a DIRECTOR OF CENTRAL INTELLIGENCE (DCI) who resigned from the CIA after assuming much of the blame for the Agency's mishandling of the ALDRICH AMES spy case.

Woolsey was born on September 21, 1941, in Tulsa, Oklahoma, to Robert James Woolsey and Clyda Kirby. Graduating from Stanford University in 1963, Woolsey was named a Rhodes Scholar in 1965. In 1968, he received his law degree from Yale University. Following Yale, he served a brief tour as a U.S. Army officer (from 1968 until 1970), earning the rank of captain. In that capacity, he served both as a program ANALYST in the Office of the Secretary of Defense and as an adviser to the U.S. delegation to the Strategic Arms Limitation Talks (SALT I) in Helsinki, Finland, and Vienna, Austria. He also worked as a program analyst for the NATIONAL SECURITY COUNCIL (NSC).

From 1970 through 1973, Woolsey served as general counsel for the U.S. Senate Armed Services Committee. He then joined Shea & Gardner, a Washington, D.C.–based law firm, in which he would continue to practice law, except when in public service. He served as undersecretary of the Navy from 1977 to 1979, and from 1989 to 1991 he was ambassador and U.S. representative to the negotiations on the Conventional Armed Forces in Europe Treaty.

On February 5, 1993, President Bill Clinton, a fellow Rhodes Scholar, appointed Woolsey director of the CIA. He served in that capacity until January 10, 1995. During his confirmation hearing, Woolsey stated that though the Soviet Union was now a "slain dragon," the post–COLD WAR world was "a jungle filled with a bewildering variety of poisonous snakes, and in many ways the dragon was easier to keep track of."

On February 21, 1994, CIA COUNTERINTELLIGENCE officer Aldrich Hazen "Ricky" Ames was arrested by the FEDERAL BUREAU OF INVESTIGATION (FBI) for selling secrets to the Soviets related to operatives working behind the IRON CURTAIN for the Americans and the British. The ensuing trial revealed that Ames had disclosed the names of every Western officer and Russian agent operating in the Soviet Union; many of the Russian agents had since been arrested by the Soviets and executed for spying. It

was a catastrophic revelation, and Woolsey was made a scapegoat.

Woolsey's subsequent resignation, however, was prompted by what some believe was the mishandling of the Ames case. The DCI was roundly criticized by lawmakers and intelligence experts for refusing to punish seriously anyone in the CIA for allowing Ames's treachery to go undetected. Simultaneously, allegations that females employed by the Agency were being treated as second-class citizens began to surface, as did allegations that the CIA had provided monetary support to the oppressive military regime in Guatemala.

Woolsey—who, some journalists have contended, did not want the DCI's posts in the first place (he had wanted to be secretary of defense)—was replaced by JOHN M. DEUTCH, who was himself to come under fire for incompetence. Woolsey returned to the firm of Shea & Gardner in 1995, but he continued to speak out on intelligence-related issues. "When you're collecting intelligence, you have to traffic with severely unpleasant people," said Woolsey during a 1998 PBS panel discussion. "You can't just collect intelligence from nice people. And you're going to be buying information or encouraging information be given to you by some fairly rugged customers."

In the wake of the SEPTEMBER 11, 2001, TERRORIST ATTACKS ON THE UNITED STATES, Woolsey became something of an "unofficial point man" in the American allegations that Iraqi dictator Saddam Hussein was directly linked to the attacks. The U.S. DEPARTMENT OF DEFENSE dispatched Woolsey to the United Kingdom, to investigate any possible connection between Hussein and the attacks on America. Woolsey has since lectured extensively on the subject and has appeared on a number of television news programs as an analyst.

X-2

Considered an "elite within an elite," X-2 was the counterespionage branch of the OFFICE OF STRATEGIC SERVICES (OSS), the World War II predecessor organization to the CIA.

Established by OSS director WILLIAM J. "WILD BILL" DONOVAN in early 1943, X-2 was the OSS liaison unit to British intelligence for ULTRA—the British communications intelligence system that broke Axis CODEs and CIPHERs during the war. Prior to X-2, the British security forces, utilizing intelligence gleaned from ULTRA intercepts, had captured nearly every German intelligence operative in the United Kingdom. Deals were cut with many of those operatives, who became DOUBLE AGENTs, sending bogus reports to Berlin. The British sought American help in this effort but insisted that the Americans imitate British security practices so as to protect the secrecy of ULTRA. Out of this arrangement X-2 was born.

Under the direction of former Justice Department law clerk James Russell "Jimmy" Murphy, X-2 became a unique, somewhat independent, branch within the OSS. X-2 operatives controlled the passkeys to many Allied intelligence puzzles, and they could veto operations proposed by other operational branches of the OSS without explanation. Consequently, many of the most talented OSS operatives were assigned to X-2.

Y

Year of Intelligence (1975)

In CIA circles, the year 1975 was considered to be the "Year of Intelligence," the year in which a series of Agency scandals became public. It was also a year in which a number of inquiries were launched into alleged CIA misdeeds, probes that would forever limit the Agency's ability to conduct secret operations without congressional oversight. Four panels were convened in 1975 in order to conduct investigations and investigative hearings into alleged illegal activities on the part of the U.S. intelligence community, in particular the FEDERAL BUREAU OF INVESTIGATION (FBI) and the CIA.

The seeds were planted in December 1974, when Seymour HERSH, a reporter for the *New York Times,* published a scathing exposé of the CIA, alleging that the Agency had illegally spied on antiwar activists during the Vietnam War. The article pointed out that the spying had violated the CIA's charter. When Democrats called for an investigation, President Gerald Ford created a "blue ribbon" investigative body, chaired by Vice President Nelson Rockefeller, in an attempt to head off a congressional investigation.

The body, established in early 1975, was known as the ROCKEFELLER COMMISSION (officially, the U.S. President's Commission on CIA Activities within the United States). It was to investigate alleged illegal domestic activities on the part of the CIA. The alleged misdeeds included ASSASSINATION PLOTS against foreign leaders and possible involvement in the assassination of President John Kennedy. But the Rockefeller Commission did not prevent the Senate and the House from creating their own investigative bodies.

The Senate entity was known as the CHURCH COMMITTEE (the Select Committee to Study Governmental Operations with Respect to Intelligence Activities); established in January, it was chaired by Senator Frank Church (D-Idaho). The Church Committee investigated alleged illegal CIA activities worldwide, including possible Agency-sponsored assassination plots against foreign leaders, foreign coups d'état, unauthorized spying on American citizens, and lack of governmental oversight.

The NEDZI COMMITTEE, the first House Select Intelligence Committee, was established in February. This body was replaced five months later with the PIKE COMMITTEE (the second House Select Intelligence Committee), a fact-finding panel established by the U.S. House of Representatives and chaired by Congressman Otis Pike (D–New York).

Year of the Spy (1985)

In CIA circles, the year 1985 was considered to be the "Year of the Spy," in which a series of espionage scandals rocked the foundations of the U.S. intelligence community. Those scandals included the spy cases of RONALD PELTON, JONATHON J. POLLARD, EDWARD LEE HOWARD, and the WALKER FAMILY SPY RING.

In all these cases, substantive intelligence community secrets (including sensitive CIA information) had been disclosed to foreign intelligence agencies.

Z

Z, Unit

Unit Z was a special COUNTERINTELLIGENCE unit, composed of American and British operatives, which was attached to the U.S. OFFICE OF STRATEGIC SERVICES (OSS), the World War II predecessor organization to the CIA.

ZAPATA, Operation

Operation ZAPATA was the code name for the BAY OF PIGS INVASION, the CIA-backed invasion of Cuba in 1961. The name was taken from the Zapata Peninsula and the Zapata swamps, which were just beyond the beachhead at the Bay of Pigs.

Zenith Technical Enterprises

Zenith Technical Enterprises was the Florida-based COVER company for the CIA's research and planning operations at JMWAVE, the code name for the Miami station from which operations against Cuban leader FIDEL CASTRO were launched during the 1960s.

Located in a refurbished U.S. Navy blimp facility on the University of Miami's south campus, Zenith Technical Enterprises maintained offices with posted hours of operation and the appearance of a nondescript government electronics research and development contractor conducting classified work for the U.S. DEPARTMENT OF DEFENSE and other federal agencies. A civilian guard who checked identification cards was posted at the front gate. This aroused no suspicion, as any such government research installation would post guards.

Behind the corporate cover, however, the Agency was planning and initiating all manner of BLACK OPERATIONs against Castro's regime, including the infiltration into Cuba of intelligence-collection teams, supplying weapons and equipment to support the Cuban underground, and supporting commando raids and other operations aimed at destroying Cuba's agricultural and industrial infrastructure.

Excepting the CIA's LANGLEY, VIRGINIA, headquarters, Zenith Technical Enterprises was the Agency's largest installation. With an annual budget of over $50 million, the company maintained some 300 permanent American employees, who controlled approximately 6,000 Cuban émigré agents.

ACRONYMS, ABBREVIATIONS, AND CODE NAMES

ACIS	Arms Control Intelligence Staff	Blackbird	A-12 and SR-71 reconnaissance aircraft
AEC	Atomic Energy Commission		
AFSA	Armed Forces Security Agency	BLACKSHIELD	code name for A-12 aircraft reconnaissance missions off Okinawa
A-11	Blackbird aircraft (prototype of YF-12)		
		BND	Bundesnachrichtendienst (West Germany's foreign intelligence service)
AIOC	Anglo-Iranian Oil Company		
AJAX	code name for the Iranian Coup d'état in 1953		
		Cambridge Five	group of British double agents— Harold Adrian Russell "Kim" Philby, Donald Maclean, Guy Burgess, Anthony Blunt, and John Cairncross
ALERT	code name for ongoing U.S. civil defense exercise from 1954 to 1962		
A-2	U.S. Air Force intelligence		
ARGON	code name for a satellite-intelligence mapping project which lasted from 1962 to 1964	CAT	Civil Air Transport
		CENTCOM	U.S. Central Command
		CHAOS	code name for a program of domestic spying on American citizens that lasted from 1959 to 1975
A-12	CIA version of Blackbird reconnaissance aircraft (predecessor to the SR-71)		
		Church Committee	The 1975 Select Committee to Study Governmental Operations with Respect to Intelligence Activities
AZORIAN	code name for the preparatory phase of Project JENNIFER		
BCCI	Bank of Credit and Commerce International	CI	counterintelligence
		CIA	Central Intelligence Agency
BfV	Bundesamt für Verfassungsschutz (German Federal Office for the Protection of the Constitution	CIB	*Current Intelligence Bulletin*
		CIC	U.S. Army's Counterintelligence Corps
		CIG	Central Intelligence Group
BI	Bureau of Investigation (the predecessor organization to the FBI)	CIO	Central Imagery Office

CNI — coordinator of national intelligence
COB — chief of base
COG — Cuban Operations Group
COI — coordinator of information
COINTELPRO — acronym for the counterintelligence program of the Federal Bureau of Investigation from 1956 to 1971
COMINT — communications intelligence
CORONA — code name for the CIA's first satellite reconnaissance program begun in 1958
COO — chief of outpost
COS — chief of station
DA — Directorate of Administration
DARO — Defense Airborne Reconnaissance Office
DCI — director of central intelligence
DCID — DCI's directive
DESERT SHIELD — code name for the coalition deployment phase of the Persian Gulf War
DESERT STORM — code name for the coalition combat-operations phase of the Persian Gulf War
DDA — deputy director of administration
DDCI — deputy director of central intelligence
DDI — deputy director of intelligence
DDNI — deputy director of national intelligence
DDO — deputy director of operations (descendent of DDP)
DDP — deputy director of plans (predecessor to DDO)
DDPO — Defense Dissemination Program Office
DDS&T — deputy director of science and technology
DFI — director of foreign intelligence
DGI — director general of intelligence
DI — directorate of intelligence
DIA — Defense Intelligence Agency
DMA — Defense Mapping Agency
DNI — director of national intelligence (proposed position)
DO — Directorate of Operations
DOD — Domestic Operations Division
Dragon Lady — U-2 reconnaissance aircraft
DS&T — Directorate of Science and Technology
ELINT — electronic intelligence
ENDURING FREEDOM — code name for the series of military action/intelligence-gathering operations against terrorist leader Osama bin Laden that began in 2001.

EO — executive order
EXCOM — executive committee of the CIA
EXCOMM — President John Kennedy's executive committee during the Cuban missile crisis of 1962
FBI — Federal Bureau of Investigation
FBIS — U.S. Foreign Broadcast Information Service
FNLA — Frente Nacional de Liberte de Angola (National Front for the Liberation of Angola)
FUBELT — code name for operations conducted during the early 1970s aimed at undermining the Chilean government
GID — General Intelligence Division
GOLD — code name for the Berlin Tunnel
GRU — Glavnoye Razvedyvatelnoye Upravleniye (Soviet Military Intelligence)
G-2 — U.S. Army intelligence
Hezbollah — Arabic for "Party of God"
HTLINGUAL — code name for a CIA mail intercept operation that lasted from 1952 to 1973
HUMINT — human intelligence
Huston Plan — a Nixon White House plan proposing an increase in domestic intelligence gathering
ICBM — intercontinental ballistic missile
IMINT — imagery intelligence
INFINITE JUSTICE — initial code name for Operation ENDURING FREEDOM
INR — U.S. State Department's Office of Intelligence and Research
INTREPID — code name for William Stephenson
IOB — U.S. Intelligence Oversight Board (a subcommittee of the PFIAB)
IOD — International Organizations Division
IRR — *Intelligence Information Report*
ISR — intelligence, surveillance, and reconnaissance
IVY BELLS — code name for an operation wherein Soviet dispatches transmitted over a Soviet communications cable lying on the bottom of the Sea of Okhotsk were monitored
JCS — Joint Chiefs of Staff
JEDBURGH — code name for three-man Allied paramilitary teams during World War II
JENNIFER — code name for a mission aimed at recovering a portion of a sunken Soviet submarine in 1974

Jib	a man-sized dummy
Jihad	Arabic for "holy struggle" or "holy war"
JILE	Joint Intelligence Liaison Element
JMWAVE	code name for the Miami station from which operations were launched against Cuban leader Fidel Castro during the 1960s
JROTC	Junior Reserve Officer Training Corps
KGB	Komitet Gosudarstvennoy Bezopasnosti (Soviet Committee for State Security)
KMSOURDOUGH	code name for a CIA mail-intercept operation from 1969 to 1971
KUBARK	code name for CIA headquarters in Langley, Virginia
LANYARD	code name for satellite intelligence program undertaken in 1963
MASINT	measurement and signature intelligence
MI	military intelligence
MICE	money, ideology, compromise, and ego
MID	*Midday Intelligence Report*
MI5	Military Intelligence, Department 5 (British Counterintelligence Service)
MI6	Military Intelligence, Department 6 (British Secret Service or Secret Intelligence Service)
MKNAOMI	code name for a project aimed at developing poisons for use by the CIA
MKSEARCH	code name for a drug experimentation/behavioral modification project conducted from 1966 to 1972
MKULTRA	code name for a drug experimentation/behavioral modification project conducted from 1953 to 1964
MOCKINGBIRD	code name for an operation aimed at recruiting American journalists for CIA work
MONGOOSE	code name for a series of operations aimed at eliminating Fidel Castro
MOSSAD	Mossad Le Aliyah Beth (Israeli Intelligence Service)
MPLA	Movimento Popular para a Libertação de Angola
NATO	North Atlantic Treaty Organization
Nedzi Committee	the first House Select Intelligence Committee established in 1975
NIA	National Intelligence Authority
NIC	National Intelligence Council
NID	*National Intelligence Daily*; Great Britain's Naval Intelligence Division

NIE	national intelligence estimate
NIMA	National Imagery and Mapping Agency
NKVD	Narodny Kommissariat Vnutrennykh Del (Soviet People's Commissariat for Internal Affairs)
NPIC	National Photographic Interpretation Center
NRO	National Reconnaissance Office
NSA	National Security Agency
NSC	National Security Council
NUCINT	nuclear intelligence
NWC	Naval War College
OAG	Operations Advisory Group
OCB	Operations Coordinating Board
OCS	Officer Candidate School
OEO	Office of Economic Opportunity
OG	Operational Group of the Office of Strategic Services
OHS	Office of Homeland Security
OIC	officer in charge
OMB	Office of Management and Budget
ONE	Office of National Estimates
ONI	Office of Naval Intelligence
OPC	Office of Policy Coordination
OPTINT	optical intelligence
OSINT	open-source intelligence
OSO	Office of Special Operations
OSP	Office of Special Projects
OSS	Office of Strategic Services
OTP	one-time pad
OTS	Office of Technical Services
OXCART	code name for the A-12 aircraft development project
PBCFIA	President's Board of Consultants on Foreign Intelligence Activities
PBSUCCESS	code name for the Guatemalan operations that led to the 1954 coup d'état in that country.
PDB	President's Daily Brief
Pentagon Papers	the U.S. Defense Department's secret history of the Vietnam War
PFIAB	U.S. President's Foreign Intelligence Advisory Board
PHOENIX	code name for special project targeting enemy leaders during the Vietnam War
PHOTINT	photographic intelligence
Pike Committee	the second House Select Intelligence Committee, established in 1975
Plumbers	secret White House team tasked with stopping news leaks and keeping track of President Richard Nixon's political opponents

P Source	code name for the CIA's Ivy League connections during the 1950s
RADINT	radar intelligence
RFE	Radio Free Europe
RL	Radio Liberty
Rockefeller Commission	President's Commission on CIA Activities within the United States
ROTC	Reserve Officer Training Corps
SAD	Special Activities Division
SAM	surface-to-air missile
SAS	British Special Air Service
Schlesinger Report	a 1971 Review of the intelligence community
Scowcroft Proposal	proposal to transfer three defense intelligence agencies to the CIA in 2001
SEALs	U.S. Navy commandos trained for special operations in the combined environments of SEa, Air, and Land
SGA	Special Group Augmented
SI	secret intelligence
SIE	special intelligence estimate
SIGINT	signals intelligence
SIS	Secret Intelligence Service (British Secret Service or MI6)
SLBM	submarine-launched ballistic missile
SNIE	special national intelligence estimate
SOA	School of the Americas
SOE	British Special Operations Executive
SMERSH	the acronym for KGB's feared SMERT SHPIONAM (literally, Death to Spies) ASSASSINATION units.
SPC	Special Policy Committee
SPG	Special Procedures Group
SRG	Strategic Resources Group
SR-71	Air Force version of Blackbird reconnaissance aircraft
SSU	Strategic Services Unit
STC	Special Training Center
SVR	Sluzhba Vneshney Razvedki Rossii (Russian Federation's foreign intelligence service)
TECHINT	technical intelligence
TELINT	telemetry intelligence
TROPIC	code name for a series of air operations flown over North Korea, China, and the Soviet Union by CAT pilots during the 1950s.
TSD	Technical Services Division
TSS	Technical Services Staff
2506	code name for the brigade of Cuban exiles at the Bay of Pigs
ULTRA	code name for a British code-breaking system against the Germans during World War II
UNITA	União Nacional para a Independência Total de Angola
USA	United States of America; U.S. Army
USAF	U.S. Air Force
USIGS	U.S. Imagery and Geospatial Information System
USMC	U.S. Marine Corps
USN	U.S. Navy
U-2	Dragon Lady reconnaissance aircraft
VALUABLE	code name for the Albanian operations from 1949 to 1953
VENONA	code name for project wherein Soviets messages from 1940 to 1948 were intercepted and decrypted
W	code name for task force employed during Operation MONGOOSE
WEST POINTER	the nickname for KMSOURDOUGH
WHISC	Western Hemisphere Institute for Security Cooperation (formerly School of the Americas)
X-2	counterintelligence unit of the Office of Strategic Services
YF-12	strategic attack version of Blackbird aircraft
ZAPATA	code name for the Bay of Pigs invasion in 1961

Central Intelligence Agency Command Organization Chart

Director (DCI)*
Deputy Director (DDCI)*

Executive Director (EXDIR)
Deputy Executive Director (D/EXDIR)

- Office of Inspector General*
- Office of General Counsel*
- Office of Congressional Affairs
- Office of Public Affairs
- Office of Protocol
- Diversity Plans & Programs

Deputy Director of Intelligence for Community Management*
Assistant Director of Intelligence for Administration*

- ADCI/Collection*
- EXDIR/Intelligence Community Affairs
- ADCI/Analysis & Production*

Associate Director of Central Intelligence for Military Support
- Office of Military Affairs

SA/DCI/Foreign Intelligence Relations

National Intelligence Council

Center for the Study of Intelligence
Office of Equal Employment Opportunity
Ombudsman/Alternative Dispute Resolution

Executive Secretary
- DCI Analytic Support Team
- DCI Action Center
- Operations Center

SCIENCE & TECHNOLOGY
- Chief Scientist
- Open Source Collection
- In-Q-Tel Interface Center
- Office of Advanced Technologies & Programs
- Office of Development & Engineering
- Office of Technical Collection
- Office of Technical Service
- Business strategies & Resources Center
- Program Analysis & Systems Engineering Staff

OPERATIONS
- Regional & Transnational Issues Division
- Counterintelligence Center
- Counterterrorist Center
- National HUMINT Requirements Tasking Center
- Resources, Plans & Policy Staff

INTELLIGENCE
- Office of Asian Pacific & Latin American Analysis
- Office of Near Eastern, South Asian & African Analysis
- Office of Russian & European Analysis
- Office of Transnational Issues
- Collection Requirements & Evaluation Staff
- DCI Crime & Narcotics Center
- DCI Weapons Intelligence, Nonproliferation & Arms Control Center
- Office of Policy Support

Chief Financial Officer
- Corporate Staff
  - Business Systems
  - Plans & Analysis
  - Procurement Executive
    - Budget
    - Finance

Chief Information Officer
- Corporate Staff
  - Information Services Infrastructure
    - Architecture & Systems Engineering
    - Enterprise Program Management Office
  - Information Management Services
  - Application Services

Global Support
- Mission Integration Staff
  - Deployed Support
  - Facilities Support
    - Logistics Support
    - Imaging & Publishing Support
  - Transportation Support

Human Resources
- HR Improvement Team
- HR Strategy & Planning
  - Medical Services Office
    - Recruitment Office
    - Training & Development Office
  - Pay & Benefits Office

Security
- NRO Security
- Center for Security Evaluation
  - Protective Programs Group
    - Personnel Security Group
    - Plans & Resources Group
    - Industrial & Area Security Programs
  - Security Services Group
  - Information Security Group

Legend
- CIA
- Intelligence community
- * Statutory position nominated by the president, confirmed by the Senate

Central Intelligence Agency

CENTRAL INTELLIGENCE AGENCY: QUESTIONS AND ANSWERS

As America's preeminent intelligence organization, the CIA is often asked to shed light on many of its most guarded secrets. Of course, the nature of the Agency's mission requires that the vast majority of its secrets not be disclosed to the public.

However, the Agency does provide public, declassified answers to all general questions. Following are the 14 most frequently asked questions of the CIA and adaptations of the Agency's official, published answers, including four questions and answers pertaining to terrorism.

Question 1: What does the CENTRAL INTELLIGENCE AGENCY (CIA) do?

The Central Intelligence Agency's primary mission is to collect, evaluate, and disseminate foreign intelligence to assist the president and senior U.S. government policy makers in making decisions relating to the national security. The Central Intelligence Agency does not make policy; it is an independent source of foreign intelligence information for those who do. The Central Intelligence Agency may also engage in covert action at the president's direction, in accordance with applicable law.

Question 2: Who works for the Central Intelligence Agency?

The CIA carefully selects well-qualified people in nearly all fields of study. Scientists, engineers, economists, lin-

guists, mathematicians, secretaries, accountants, and computer specialists are but a few of the professionals continually in demand. Much of the Agency's work, like that done in academic institutions, requires research, careful evaluation, as well as writing of reports that end up on the desks of this nation's policy makers. Applicants are expected to have a college degree with a minimum GPA of 3.0 and must be willing to relocate to the Washington, D.C., area. Selection for Agency employment is highly competitive. Employees must successfully complete polygraph and medical examinations and background investigations before entering on duty. The Agency endorses equal employment opportunity for all employees.

Question 3: How many people work for the Central Intelligence Agency, and what is its budget?

Neither the number of employees nor the size of the Agency's budget can, at present, be publicly disclosed. A common misconception is that the Agency has an unlimited budget, which is far from true. While classified, the budget and size of the CIA are known in detail and scrutinized by the Office of Management and Budget and by the Senate Select Committee on Intelligence, the House Permanent Select Committee on Intelligence, and the Defense Subcommittees of the Appropriations Committees in both houses of Congress. The resources allocated to the CIA are subject to the same rigorous examination and approval process that applies to all other government organizations.

In 1997, the aggregate figure for all U.S. government intelligence and intelligence-related activities—of which the CIA is but one part—was made public for the first time. The aggregate intelligence budget was $26.6 billion in fiscal year 1997 and $26.7 billion for fiscal year 1998. The intelligence budget for fiscal year 1999 has not been publicly released.

Question 4: Does the Central Intelligence Agency give public tours of its headquarters buildings?

No. Logistical problems and security considerations prevent such tours. The CIA provides an extremely limited number of visits annually for approved academic and civic groups. A brief tour is available on the CIA website.

Question 5: Does the Central Intelligence Agency release publications to the public?

Yes. The CIA releases millions of pages of documents each year. Much of this is material of historical significance or personal interest that has been declassified under Executive Order 12958 (a presidential order outlining a uniform system for handling national security information) or the Freedom of Information Act (FOIA) and Privacy Act (statutes that give U.S. citizens access to U.S. government information, or U.S. government information about themselves, respectively). The Agency handles thousands of cases each year and maintains the CIA's Electronic Document Release Center at www.foia.ucia.gov to release this information to the public and to provide guidance for requesting information. Some released information of significant public interest or historical value is also available at the National Archives and Records Administration. Specific copies of any previously declassified records are available directly from the CIA FOIA office.

The Agency frequently releases items of more general public interest on its website. The site includes general information about the CIA, unclassified current publications, speeches and congressional testimony, press releases and statements, employment information, and basic references, including the *CIA World Factbook*. Many documents, including the *CIA World Factbook*, reports on foreign economic or political matters, maps, and directories of foreign officials are also available in hard copy; these are listed in "CIA Maps and Publications Released to the Public," which is also available from the Office of Public Affairs. Publications on this list may be purchased from the Government Printing Office, the National Technical Information Service, and the Library of Congress. Most CIA publications are classified, however, and are not publicly available.

Question 6: Does the CIA spy on Americans? Does it keep a file on individuals?

By law, the CIA is specifically prohibited from collecting foreign intelligence concerning the domestic activities of U.S. citizens. Its mission is to collect information related to foreign intelligence and foreign counterintelligence. By direction of the president in Executive Order 12333 of 1981 and in accordance with procedures issued by the director of central intelligence and approved by the attorney general, the CIA is restricted in the collection of intelligence information directed against U.S. citizens. Collection is allowed only for an authorized intelligence purpose—for example, if there is a reason to believe that an individual is involved in espionage or international terrorist activities. The CIA's procedures require senior approval for any such collection; depending on the collection technique employed, the sanction of the attorney general and director of central intelligence may be required. These restrictions on the CIA have been in effect since the 1970s.

Question 7: Who decides when the CIA should participate in covert actions, and why?

Only the president can direct the CIA to undertake a covert action. Such actions usually are recommended by the National Security Council (NSC). Covert actions are considered when the NSC judges that U.S. foreign policy objectives may not be fully realized by normal diplomatic means but military action is deemed too extreme an option. Therefore, the Agency may be directed to conduct special activity abroad in support of foreign policy, where the role of the U.S. government is neither apparent nor publicly acknowledged. Once so tasked, the director of central intelligence must notify the intelligence oversight committees of the Congress.

Question 8: The CIA has been accused of conducting assassinations and engaging in drug trafficking. What are the facts?

The CIA does neither. Executive Order 12333 of 1981 explicitly prohibits the Central Intelligence Agency from engaging, either directly or indirectly, in assassinations. Internal safeguards and the congressional oversight process assure compliance. Regarding recent allegations of CIA involvement in drug trafficking, the CIA inspector general found no evidence to substantiate the charges that the CIA or its employees had conspired with or assisted contra-related organizations or individuals in drug trafficking to raise funds for the contras or for any other purpose. In fact, the CIA plays a crucial role in combating drug trafficking by providing intelligence information to the Drug Enforcement Administration, the Federal Bureau of Investigation, and the State Department.

Question 9: Who oversees the CIA? Does it act on its own initiative?

Both the Congress and the executive branch oversee the Central Intelligence Agency's activities. In addition, the CIA is responsible to the American people through their elected representatives, and, like other government agencies, it acts in accordance with U.S. laws and executive orders. In the executive branch, the National Security Council—including the president, the vice president, the secretary of state, and the secretary of defense—provides guidance and direction for national foreign intelligence and counterintelligence activities. In Congress, the Senate Select Committee on Intelligence and the House Permanent Select Committee on Intelligence, as well as other committees, closely monitor the Agency's reporting and programs. The CIA is not a policy-making organization; it advises policy makers on matters of foreign intelligence. It conducts covert actions only at the direction of the president.

Question 10: Where is the Central Intelligence Agency's headquarters? Is it in Langley or McLean, Virginia?

Technically, CIA headquarters is in both. "Langley" is the name of the McLean neighborhood in which CIA headquarters, also known as the George Bush Center for Intelligence, is located.

The town of McLean was founded in 1910. Before that time, the area where CIA headquarters is located was known as Langley. In 1719, Virginia planter Thomas Lee purchased a tract of land from the sixth Lord Fairfax (for whom Fairfax County, the county in which McLean is located, was named). Lee named the tract "Langley," after his ancestral home in England. Though Lee never actually lived on the land, the Langley area soon became home to many European settlers. A few were wealthy settlers to whom England had granted land, and they established large plantations in the area.

During the War of 1812, President James Madison and his wife Dolley fled the British siege of Washington to the safety of family and friends in Langley.

During the American Civil War, Langley was a Union stronghold, in the Southern state of Virginia. Two forts—Camp Griffin and Camp Pierpont—housed Union soldiers who were stationed there to protect nearby Washington, D.C.

With the building of the Great Falls & Old Dominion Railroad, 1903 became a defining year for Langley. John McLean, president of Washington Gas and Light Company and future editor of the *Washington Post,* and Senator Stephen B. Elkins of West Virginia collaborated on construction of a railroad that would bring vacationing Washingtonians to nearby Great Falls and provide people who worked in Washington the choice of living outside of the city.

In 1906, the railroad began operating, and the population of Langley and nearby Lewinsville quickly grew. In 1910, the post offices of these towns closed, and a new post office, McLean, was opened.

In 1959, the U.S. government broke ground for the CIA headquarters building. Construction was completed in 1961, adding another chapter to McLean's long history. Despite the name change in 1910, the name "Langley" is still used to describe the area.

Question 11: What is the Central Intelligence Agency's role in combating international terrorism?

The Central Intelligence Agency supports the overall U.S. government effort to combat international terrorism by collecting, analyzing, and disseminating intelligence on foreign terrorist groups and individuals. The CIA also works with friendly foreign governments and shares pertinent information with them.

Question 12: Has the CIA ever provided funding, training, or other support to Osama bin Laden?

No. Numerous, recent comments in the media have reiterated a widely circulated but incorrect notion that the CIA once had a relationship with Osama bin Laden. But the CIA has never employed, paid, or maintained any relationship whatsoever with Osama bin Laden.

Question 13: Are there restrictions on the CIA's recruitment of criminals and other unsavory characters?

The guidelines at issue simply require field officers to obtain prior CIA headquarters approval before establishing a relationship with an individual who has committed serious crimes, human rights abuses, or other repugnant acts.

The CIA has never turned down a field request to recruit an asset in a terrorist organization. Furthermore, the CIA does not avoid contact with individuals—regardless of their past—who may have information about terrorist activities.

There seems to be a misunderstanding regarding whether or not the CIA has been prevented from dealing with "unsavory" characters who might be able to provide information on terrorism and other threats to U.S. national security. A number of commentators have stated that the CIA is banned by regulations from doing so and now gathers intelligence only from individuals of high personal integrity—individuals who do not have access to the type of information our country needs. This perception is wrong.

Internal CIA regulations governing the recruitment of such individuals were issued in 1995 in response to congressional calls for wider notification when the Agency has a relationship with an "unsavory" individual. This was generated by a concern that the CIA was dealing in the early 1990s with people in Central America who were involved in human rights abuses.

It is understandable that the American people are now examining ways to provide the U.S. Intelligence Community with greater authority to deal with the terrorist threat, and it is possible that modifications of the Agency's current guidelines will result from this examination. But make no mistake, the CIA has been working relentlessly against the terrorist target, and the Agency is not constrained from recruiting individuals with unsavory backgrounds.

The greatest challenge is to penetrate the terrorist networks themselves. This effort requires an extensive analytic effort to understand shadowy terrorist organizations, train CIA officers in their language, deploy them within the culture, and support them in the dangerous and enormously difficult mission of penetrating these groups. These challenges are the focus of the CIA's efforts.

Question 14: How is terrorism defined?

The Intelligence Community is guided by the definition of terrorism contained in Title 22 of the U.S. Code, Section 2656(d). The term "terrorism" is defined there as premeditated, politically motivated violence perpetrated against noncombatant targets by subnational groups or clandestine agents, usually intended to influence an audience.

The term "international terrorism" means terrorism involving the territory or the citizens of more than one country.

The term "terrorist group" refers to any group that practices, or has significant subgroups that practice, international terrorism.

DIRECTORS OF THE CENTRAL INTELLIGENCE AGENCY

Since 1946, 18 presidential appointees have held the post of director of central intelligence (DCI). This does *not* include, MAJOR GENERAL WILLIAM J. DONOVAN, director of the Office of Strategic Services (OSS), who is considered to be the *first* head of U.S. central intelligence.

1. REAR ADMIRAL SIDNEY WILLIAM SOUERS, appointed by President Harry Truman, served as DCI from January 23, 1946, to June 10, 1946.
2. LIEUTENANT GENERAL HOYT SANFORD VANDENBERG, appointed by President Harry Truman, served as DCI from June 10, 1946, to May 1, 1947.
3. REAR ADMIRAL ROSCOE HENRY HILLENKOETTER, appointed by President Harry Truman, served as DCI from May 1, 1947, to October 7, 1950.
4. GENERAL WALTER BEDELL SMITH, appointed by President Harry Truman, served as DCI from October 7, 1950, to February 9, 1953.
5. The Honorable ALLEN WELSH DULLES, appointed by President Dwight Eisenhower, served as DCI from February 26, 1953, to November 29, 1961.
6. The Honorable JOHN ALEK McCONE, appointed by President John F. Kennedy, served as DCI from November 29, 1961, to April 28, 1965.

7. VICE ADMIRAL WILLIAM FRANCIS RABORN, JR., appointed by President Lyndon Johnson, served as DCI from April 28, 1965, to June 30, 1966.
8. The Honorable RICHARD McGARRAH HELMS, appointed by President Lyndon Johnson, served as DCI from June 30, 1966, to February 2, 1973.
9. The Honorable JAMES RODNEY SCHLESINGER, appointed by President Richard Nixon, served as DCI from February 2, 1973, to July 2, 1973.
10. The Honorable WILLIAM EGAN COLBY, appointed by President Richard Nixon, served as DCI from September 4, 1973, to January 30, 1976.
11. The Honorable GEORGE HERBERT WALKER BUSH, appointed by President Gerald Ford, served as DCI from January 30, 1976, to January 20, 1977.
12. ADMIRAL STANSFIELD TURNER, appointed by President Jimmy Carter, served as DCI from March 9, 1977, to January 20, 1981.
13. The Honorable WILLIAM JOSEPH CASEY, appointed by President Ronald Reagan, served as DCI from January 28, 1981, to January 29, 1987.
14. The Honorable WILLIAM HEDGCOCK WEBSTER, appointed by President Ronald Reagan, served as DCI from May 26, 1987, to August 31, 1991.
15. The Honorable ROBERT MICHAEL GATES, appointed by President George H. W. Bush, served

as DCI from November 6, 1991, to January 20, 1993 (Gates had also served as acting DCI from December 18, 1986, to May 26, 1987).

16. The Honorable R. JAMES WOOLSEY, appointed by President Bill Clinton, served as DCI from February 5, 1993, to January 10, 1995.

17. The Honorable JOHN M. DEUTCH, appointed by President Bill Clinton, served as DCI from May 10, 1995, to December 15, 1996.

18. The Honorable GEORGE JOHN TENET, appointed by President Bill Clinton, has served as DCI from July 11, 1997 to present.

DEPUTY DIRECTORS OF THE
CENTRAL INTELLIGENCE AGENCY

1. KINGMAN DOUGLASS, appointed by DCI SIDNEY W. SOUERS, served as DDCI from March 2, 1946, to July 11, 1946 (Douglass's position was considered to be in an acting capacity).

2. BRIGADIER GENERAL EDWIN K. WRIGHT, appointed by DCI HOYT S. VANDENBERG, served as DDCI from January 20, 1947, to March 9, 1949.

3. The Honorable WILLIAM H. JACKSON, appointed by DCI ROSCOE H. HILLENKOETTER, served as DDCI from October 7, 1950, to August 3, 1951.

4. The Honorable ALLEN W. DULLES, appointed by DCI WALTER BEDELL SMITH, served as DDCI from August 23, 1951, to February 26, 1953.

5. GENERAL CHARLES PEARRE CABELL, appointed by President Dwight Eisenhower, served as DDCI from April 23, 1953, to January 31, 1962.

6. LIEUTENANT GENERAL MARSHALL S. CARTER, appointed by President John Kennedy, served as DDCI from April 3, 1962, to April 28, 1965.

7. The Honorable RICHARD MCGARRAH HELMS, appointed by President Lyndon Johnson, served as DDCI from April 28, 1965, to June 30, 1966.

8. VICE ADMIRAL RUFUS L. TAYLOR, appointed by President Lyndon Johnson, served as DDCI from October 13, 1966, to February 1, 1969.

9. LIEUTENANT GENERAL ROBERT E. CUSHMAN, JR., appointed by President Richard Nixon, served as DDCI from May 7, 1969, to December 31, 1971.

10. LIEUTENANT GENERAL VERNON A. WALTERS, appointed by President Richard Nixon, served as DDCI from May 2, 1972, to July 7, 1976 (Walters also served as acting DCI, from July 2, 1973, to September 4, 1973).

11. The Honorable E. HENRY KNOCHE, appointed by President Gerald Ford, served as DDCI from July 7, 1976, to August 1, 1977 (Knoche also served as acting DCI, from January 20, 1977, to March 9, 1977).

12. The Honorable JOHN F. BLAKE, appointed by President Jimmy Carter, served as DDCI from August 1, 1977, to February 10, 1978 (Blake also served as acting DDCI, from August 1, 1977, to February 10, 1978).

13. The Honorable FRANK C. CARLUCCI, appointed by President Jimmy Carter, served as DDCI from February 10, 1978, to February 5, 1981.

14. ADMIRAL BOBBY R. INMAN, appointed by President Ronald Reagan, served as DDCI from February 12, 1981, to June 10, 1982.

15. The Honorable JOHN N. MCMAHON, appointed by President Ronald Reagan, served as DDCI from June 10, 1982, to March 29, 1986.

16. The Honorable ROBERT M. GATES, appointed by President Ronald Reagan, served as DDCI from

April 18, 1986, to March 20, 1989 (Gates also served as acting DCI, from December 18, 1986, to May 26, 1987).

17. The Honorable RICHARD J. KERR, appointed by President George Bush, served as DDCI from March 20, 1989, to March 2, 1992 (Kerr also served as acting DCI, from September 1, 1991, to November 6, 1991).

18. ADMIRAL WILLIAM O. STUDEMAN, appointed by President George Bush, served as DDCI from April 9, 1992, to July 3, 1995 (Studeman also served as acting DCI, from January 21, 1993, to February 5, 1993, and from January 11, 1995, to May 9, 1995).

19. The Honorable GEORGE J. TENET, appointed by President Bill Clinton, served as DDCI from July 3, 1995, to July 11, 1997 (Tenet also served as acting DCI, from December 16, 1996, to July 11, 1997).

20. GENERAL JOHN A. GORDON, appointed by President Bill Clinton, served as DDCI from October 31, 1997, to July 1, 2000.

21. JOHN E. MCLAUGHLIN, appointed by President Bill Clinton, has served as DDCI from October 19, 2000, to the present.

BIBLIOGRAPHY

Acocella, Nick. *Moe Berg: Catcher and Spy.* ESPN Internet Ventures, 2000. Available on-line. URL: espn.go. com/classic/biography/s/berg_moe.html

Adams, James. *Sellout: Aldrich Ames and the Corruption of the CIA.* New York: Viking Penguin, 1995.

Aguilar, Luis. *Operation Zapata.* Frederick, Md.: University Publications of America, 1981.

Albin, Kira. *Julia Child: A Butcher, a Baker, a Mover & Shaker.* El Cerrito, Calif.: Grand Times, 1997. Available on-line. URL: grandtimes.com/mags/child.html

Almanac of Famous People. Farmington Hills, Mich.: Gale Group, 2001.

Ambrose, Stephen E. *Ike's Spies: Eisenhower and the Espionage Establishment.* Jackson: University Press of Mississippi, 1999.

"America's New War." CNN.com, 2001.

Andrew, Christopher. *For the President's Eyes Only: Secret Intelligence and the American Presidency from Washington to Bush.* New York: HarperCollins, 1995.

Andrew, Christopher, and Vasili Mitrokhin. *The Sword and the Shield: The Mitrokhin Archive and the Secret History of the KGB.* New York: Basic Books, 1999.

Archer, Jules. *SuperSpies: The Secret Side of Government.* New York: Delacorte Press, 1977.

Archibald MacLeish. New York: Poetry Exhibits, Academy of American Poets, 2000. Available on-line. URL: poets.org

"Architect of Policy: William Putnam Bundy." *New York Times,* May 29, 1964.

Arkin, William M. *National Security Research on the Internet.* Paul H. Nitze School of Advanced International Studies, Johns Hopkins University. Washington, D.C.: Center for Strategic Education, 2000. Available on-line. URL: sais-jhu.edu/cse/products/

Arthur Joseph Goldberg 1908–1990. Farmington Hills, Mich.: Contemporary Authors Online, Gale Group, 2000. Available on-line. URL: galegroup.com

Atkinson, Rick. *Crusade: The Untold Story of the Persian Gulf War.* New York: Houghton Mifflin, 1993.

Auster, Bruce B., and Edward Pound. "You Can Take This Job and Shove It: Retired Admiral Bobby Ray Inman Rejects Nomination to Secretary of Defense Position." *U.S. News & World Report,* January 31, 1994.

Aydintasbas, Asla. *The Midnight Ride of James Woolsey.* San Francisco: Salon.com, December 20, 2001.

Babcock, Charles R. "Spy Agency Infighting Hurt U.S., Turner Says: Ex-CIA Director Critical of Rise in Covert Actions." *Washington Post,* May 13, 1985.

"Bagley, Mary Louise Harrington." *Arlington National Cemetery Website,* April 4, 2000. Available on-line. URL: arlingtoncemetery.com

Barber, David. *Archibald MacLeish's Life and Career.* Urbana-Champaign: University of Illinois Department of English, Modern American Poetry, 2001. Available on-line. URL: english.uiuc.edu/maps/poets/m_r/macleish/life.htm

Bardsley, Marilyn. *J. Edgar Hoover.* The Crime Library. Dark Horse Multimedia, 1998. Available on-line. URL: crimelibrary.com/hoover/bardsley.htm

Barry, John. "CIA's Man at the Bay of Pigs." *Miami Herald,* July 16, 1998.

Becket, Henry S. A. *The Dictionary of Espionage: Spookspeak into English.* Briarcliff Manor, N.Y.: Stein and Day, 1986.

Bedard, Paul, John T. Sellers, and Richard J. Newman. "Bad Guys Wanted: John Deutch, the Former CIA Director, Is Accused of Being the Worst Director Ever." *U.S. News & World Report,* March 13, 2000.

Berger, D. H. *The Use of Covert Paramilitary Activity as a Policy Tool: An Analysis of Operations Conducted by the United States Central Intelligence Agency, 1949–1951,* Unpublished paper. Quantico, Va.: Marine Corps Command and Staff College, (n.d.). Available on-line. URL: fas.org/irp/eprint/berger.htm

"Berlin Blockade: The American Experience." Public Broadcasting Service, 2000. Available on-line. URL: pbs.org/wgbh/amex/bomb/peopleevents/pandeAMEX49.html

"Berlin Blockade." *The History Channel,* A&E Television Network, 2001.

Berry, Jr., F. Clifton. *Inside the CIA: The Architecture, Art & Atmosphere of America's Premier Intelligence Agency.* Montgomery, Ala.: Community Communications, 1997.

Best, Richard A., Jr., and Herbert Andrew Boerstling. *Proposals for Intelligence Reorganization 1949–1996: The Intelligence Community in the 21st Century.* Washington, D.C.: Permanent Select Committee on Intelligence, House of Representatives, 104th Congress, February 28, 1996. Available on-line. URL: access.gpo.gov/congress.house/intel/ic21/ic21018.html

"Big Ego, Big Money Cited as Alleged Spy's Motivation." CNN.com, February 21, 2001.

"A Biography of Osama bin Laden." PBS Frontline, 2001. Available on-line. URL: pbs.org

Bissell, Richard M., Jr. *Reflections of a Cold Warrior: From Yalta to the Bay of Pigs.* New Haven, Conn.: Yale University Press, 1996.

Blair, Tony. *Text of the Prime Minister's Speech to Parliament Regarding Osama bin Laden and Al Qaeda.* London: 10 Downing Street, October 4, 2001.

Blake, Peter. "Cartoon Critic: Saul Steinberg's Drawings Were Often Witty Criticisms of Contemporary Architecture." *Architecture,* September 1999.

Blau, Stacey E. "Poised to Become CIA Head. *The Tech,* May 5, 1995.

Blum, William. *Killing Hope: U.S. Military and CIA Interventions since World War II.* Monroe, Me.: Common Courage Press, 1995.

Borger, Julian. "How the CIA Lost Its Edge." *The Guardian,* October 16, 2001.

Boxer, Sarah. "Saul Steinberg, Epic Doodler, Dies at 84." *New York Times,* May 13, 1999.

Bradlee, Benjamin C. *Ben Bradlee: A Good Life—Newspapering and Other Adventures.* New York: Simon and Schuster, 1995.

Brandt, Daniel. *Journalism and the CIA: The Mighty Wurlitzer.* San Antonio, Tex.: NameBase NewsLine, no. 17, April–June 1997. Available on-line. URL: pir.org/news17.html

Brenner, Philip. *The National Security Archive: Turning History on Its Head.* Washington, D.C.: George Washington University Gelman Library, 1995–2001.

Buckley, William F., Jr. Letter to W. Thomas Smith, Jr. March 12, 2001.

Buranelli, Vincent, and Nan Buranelli. *Spy/Counterspy: An Encyclopedia of Espionage.* New York: McGraw-Hill, 1982.

Burns, Robert. "CIA Honors 2 Spies Who Survived Imprisonment in China for 20 Years." Associated Press, July 3, 1998.

Casey, Dennis. "Limping Lady Begins Spy Career in the Early 1940s." *U.S. Air Force Air Intelligence Agency,* April 26, 2000. Available on-line. URL: 64-baker-street.org

Caza, Shawn. *History: Cheka to KGB.* NKVD & KGB Web Page. January 1998. Available on-line. URL: sovietarmy.com

"The Central Intelligence Agency." *Defense Security Service Website,* 2001. Available on-line. URL: dss.mil/

Chang, Laurence, and Peter Kornbluh. *The Cuban Missile Crisis, 1962.* New York: New Press, 1998.

Chardy, Alfonso. "Homeland Office to Coordinate Security." *Miami Herald,* September 29, 2001.

CIA Biographic Register on Che Guevara. Langley, Va.: Office of Central Reference, CIA, August 1964.

CIA History Staff. "Fifteen DCIs' First 100 Days." *Studies in Intelligence* 38, no. 5, 1995. Available on-line. URL:cia.gov/csi/studies/95unclass/100days.html

"CIA Subsidized Festival Trips: Hundreds of Students Were Sent to World Gatherings." *New York Times,* February 21, 1967.

CIA Support to the U.S. Military during the Persian Gulf War. Langley, Va.: DCI Persian Gulf War Illnesses Task Force, June 16, 1997.

Cockburn, Alexander, and Jeffrey St. Clair. *Whiteout: The CIA, Drugs, and the Press.* London and New York: Verso, 1998.

Cohen, Adam. "The CIA's Year-Round Camp for Spies." *Time,* December 2, 1996.

"Cold War: CNN Perspectives." CNN, 2001.

Cold War: Postwar Estrangement. Washington, D.C.: Soviet Archives Exhibit, Library of Congress, 2001.

Available on-line. URL: loc.gov/exhibits/archives/colp.html

Committee for State Security. Washington, D.C.: Federation of American Scientists Intelligence Resource Program, November 26, 1977. Available on-line. URL: fas.org

Contemporary Authors Online. Farmington Hills, Mich.: Marquis Who's Who, Gale Group, 2001. Available on-line: URL: galegroup.com

Conway, J. North. *American Literacy: Fifty Books That Define Our Culture and Ourselves.* New York: William Morrow, 1993.

Copeland, Larry. "CIA Identifies War Casualty in Prison Riot. *USA Today,* November 29, 2001.

"Cuba, Memorandum for the Record." *Foreign Relations of the United States.* Vol. 10, *Cuba.* Washington, D.C.: U.S. Department of State, January 28, 1961.

Cullather, Nicholas. *Operation PBSUCCESS, the United States and Guatemala, 1952–1954.* Washington, D.C.: History Staff, Center for the Study of Intelligence, Central Intelligence Agency, 1994. Available on-line. URL: cia.gov/csi/bulletin/csi7.htm

Davis, Kenneth C. *Don't Know Much about History.* New York: Crown, 1990.

———. *Don't Know Much about Geography.* New York: William Morrow, 1992.

Deacon, Richard. *Spyclopedia: The Comprehensive Handbook of Espionage.* New York: William Morrow, 1988.

Defense Almanac. Washington, D.C.: Armed Forces Information Service, September 19, 2000.

Degregorio, William A. *The Complete Book of U.S. Presidents.* New York: Barricade Books, 1993.

De La Rue, Keith. *The Name's Fleming, Ian Fleming.* Pascoe Vale, Australia: Keith De La Rue's Island in the Big Pond, 1998. Available on-line. URL: users.bigpond.com/-Kdelarue/

Delgado, James P. "Back to the Bay of Pigs." U.S. Naval Institute *Proceedings,* April 2001.

Deriabin, Peter, and Tennent H. Bagley. *The KGB: Masters of the Soviet Union.* New York: Hippocrene, 1990.

Dettmer, Jamie, and Kenneth R. Timmerman. "Carlucci Sets the Record Straight concerning His Involvement in the Congo." *Insight on the News,* August 20, 2001.

Detzer, David. *The Brink: Cuban Missile Crisis 1962.* New York: Thomas Y. Crowell, 1979.

DIA WebSite. Defense Intelligence Analysis Center, September 2000. Available on-line. URL: dia.mil/

Dictionary of Hispanic Biography. Farmington Hills, Mich.: Marquis Who's Who, Gale Group, 1996. Available on-line. URL: galegroup.com

Did You Know? Background on Archibald MacLeish. Great Neck, N.Y.: Poem Finder, Roth Publishing, 1999. Available on-line. URL: poemfinder.com

DiEgidio, Tom. *Salon People: Leo Castelli.* San Francisco: Salon.com, September 11, 1999.

DoD Dictionary of Military Terms. Fort Belvoir, Va.: Defense Technical Information Center, January 2001.

Dornan, James E., Jr. *The U.S. War Machine.* New York: Crown, 1978.

Douglas, Martin. "William P. Bundy, 83, Dies: Advised Three Presidents on American Policy in Vietnam." *New York Times,* October 7, 2000.

Earley, Pete. *Confessions of a Spy: The Real Story of Aldrich Ames.* New York: G. P. Putnam's Sons, 1977.

Edward L. Howard Case. Global Spy, 2000. Globalscan International, Crescent Springs, Kentucky. Available on-line. URL: spynews.net/2000Edition.html

Ellis, Rafaela. *The Central Intelligence Agency.* Broomall, Pa.: Chelsea House, 1988.

Elliston, Jon. *MKULTRA.* Parascope, 1966. Available on-line. URL: parascope.com/ds/mkultrao.htm

Emery, Fred. *Watergate: The Corruption of American Politics and the Fall of Richard Nixon.* New York: Touchstone, 1995.

Encyclopedia Britannica. Chicago: 2000.

Encyclopedia of World Biography. Farmington Hills, Mich.: Marquis Who's Who, Gale Group, 1998. Available on-line. URL: galegroup.com

Ensor, David. "CIA Spy Hunter Talks to CNN about Notorious Turncoats." CNN, May 29, 2000. Available on-line. URL: cnn.com

Farago, Ladislas. *The Game of the Foxes: The Untold Story of German Espionage in the United States and Great Britain during World War II.* New York: David McKay, 1971.

Farnsworth, Elizabeth, interview with Burton Hersh. *Online NewsHour with Jim Lehrer.* Arlington, Va.: MacNeil-Lehrer Productions and PBS, April 30, 1996. Available on-line. URL: pbs.org/newshour/bb/remember/colby_4-30.html

———, interview with Senator Richard Shelby, Senator Robert Kerrey, former director of central intelligence R. James Woolsey, and former CIA analyst Melvin Goodman. *Online NewsHour with Jim Lehrer.* Arlington, Va.: MacNeil-Lehrer Productions and PBS, October 26, 1998. Available on-line. URL: pbs.org/newshour/bb/middle_east/july-dec98/cia_10-26.html

Fegley, Randall Arlin. *Encarta Online Encyclopedia.* "Mobutu Sese Seko." Redmond, Wash.: Microsoft, 2001. Available on-line. URL: africana.com

Fenton, Ben. "He Cannot Be Brains behind the Attacks." News.Telegraph.Co.UK, Telegraph Group Limited, October 3, 2001.

Fernandez-Zayas, Marcelo. *A Man Called Macho.* Organo Oficial de la Sociedad Economica de Amigos del Pais, May 11, 2000. Available on-line. URL: amigospais-guaracabuya.org/oagmf023.html

The Final Report of the Assassination Records of the Review Board (as Mandated by the John F. Kennedy Assassination Records Collection Act of 1992). Kennedy Assassination

Records Review Board, September 1998. Available on-line. URL: indiana.edu/~oah/kennedy/

Ford, Harold P. "A Tribute to Sherman Kent." *Studies in Intelligence,* fall 1980. Available on-line. URL: cia.gov/csi/books/shermankent/1tribute.html

———. *CIA and the Vietnam Policymakers: Three Episodes 1962–1968.* Washington, D.C.: Central Intelligence Agency, Center for the Study of Intelligence, 1997. Available on-line. URL: cia.gov/csi/books/vietnam/

Foreign Relations of the United States, 1945–1950: Emergence of the Intelligence Establishment. Washington, D.C.: U.S. Department of State, January 20, 2001.

Foreman, Jonathon. "Special Forces: No Magic Bullet." *New York Post,* October 15, 2001.

"Former CIA Director Honors 129 Local Eagles." *Yankee Clipper Clipboard,* February 10, 2001. Available on-line. URL: yccbsa.org/eagles/gatherings/gates2001.htm

Forster, Arnold, and David Kirschenbaum. *CIA Aims at Pollard for Scapegoating.* Toronto: Justice for Jonathon Pollard, November 25, 1994. Available on-line. URL: jonathonpollard.org

"A Fragile Ceasefire—Negotiated by George J. Tenet between Israel and Palestine." *Maclean's,* June 25, 2001.

"Frank C. Carlucci to Succeed William P. Clark as Chairman of US-ROC (Taiwan) Business Council." *PR Newswire,* August 16, 1999.

Franklin, Jane. *Cuba and the United States: A Chronological History.* Chicago: Ocean Press, 1997.

Fray, William C., and Lisa A. Spar. *Yalta (Crimea) Conference.* New Haven, Conn.: Avalon Project at Yale University Law School, April 4, 2001. Available on-line. URL: yale.edu

Frazier, Howard. *Uncloaking the CIA.* New York: Macmillan, 1978.

Funk & Wagnalls. *The Presidents.* Indianapolis, Ind.: Curtis, 1989.

"The Future of the CIA." Policy Impact Panel transcript. Washington, D.C.: Council on Foreign Relations, February 18, 1997.

Gellman, Barton. "CIA Weighs 'Targeted Killing' Missions: Administration Believes Restraints Do Not Bar Singling Out Individual Terrorists." *Washington Post,* October 28, 2001.

Germanotta, Tony. "A Local Spy Peddles a World of Secrets: John A. Walker Jr., a Norfolk Sailor and Private Investigator, Recruited Family Members into His Espionage Ring." *Virginian-Pilot,* November 28, 1999.

"Gestapo." *Museum of Tolerance Online.* Simon Wiesenthal Center, 1999. Available on-line. URL: wiesenthal.com

Gettleman, Marvin E., Jane Franklin, Marilyn B. Young, and H. Bruce Franklin. *Vietnam and America.* New York: Grove Press, 1995.

Geyer, Georgie Anne. *Guerrilla Prince: The Untold Story of Fidel Castro.* Boston: Little, Brown, 1991.

"Gilmore, Gates Headline Charter Day." *William and Mary News,* January 15, 1998.

Gloria Steinem. Santa Rosa, Calif.: National Women's History Project, 1997–2000. Available on-line. URL: nwhp.org

"Gloria Steinem." Greenville, S.C.: *Glass Ceiling Website,* 1999–2000. Available on-line. URL: theglassceiling.com

Greaves, William. *Ralph Bunche: An American Odyssey.* New York: William Greaves Productions and PBS, 2001. Available on-line. URL: williamgreaves.com

Grigg, William Norman. "John Birch: A Patriotic Exemplar." *New American,* December 13, 1993. Available on-line. URL: thenewamerican.com

Gup, Ted. *The Book of Honor.* New York: Random House, 2000.

———. "Star Agents." *Washington Post Magazine,* September 7, 1997.

———. "The Two Mikes. *Cornell,* November/December 2000.

Gullo, Karen. "Justice, CIA Revamping for Security." Washington, D.C.: Associated Press, November 9, 2001.

H.R. 611 to Close the United States Army School of the Americas. Washington, D.C.: U.S. House of Representatives, February 5, 1997.

Haines, Gerald K. "Looking for a Rogue Elephant: The Pike Committee Investigations and the CIA." *Studies in Intelligence,* 1998–1999. Available on-line. URL: cia.gov/csi/studies/winter98-99/art07.html

Hansen, Ralph, and Deborah J. Roberts. *The Frank Church Papers: A Summary Guide.* Boise, Idaho: Albertsons Library Special Collections, Boise State University, 1988.

Henwood, Doug. "Spooks in Blue." *Grand Street,* spring 1988. Available on-line. URL: cia-on-campus.org/yale.edu/henwood.html

Hersh, Burton. *The Old Boys: The American Elite and the Origins of the CIA.* New York: Charles Scribner's Sons, 1992.

Hersh, Seymour. "Huge CIA Operation Reported in U.S. against Anti-War Forces, Other Dissidents in Nixon Years." *New York Times,* December 22, 1974.

Herzog, Jeff. "Woolsey Discusses CIA, US Security." *Yale Daily News,* October 14, 1998.

Hillenbrand, Barry. "America's Unseen Hand." *Time,* August 23–30, 1999.

"A Historical Perspective on CSIS." *Canadian Security Intelligence Service homepage,* 2001. Available on-line. URL: csis-scrs.gc.ca/eng/menu/welcome_e.html

Historical Review Program: JFK Assassination Records Project Completed. Langley, Va.: CIA, Center for the Study of Intelligence, spring 1999. Available on-line. URL: archives.gov/research_room/JFK/

"The History of Espionage." NBCi.com, 2000.

"A History of Foreign Assistance." *U.S. Agency for International Development Website*, 2001. Available on-line. URL: usaid.gov

Hodgson, Lynn Philip. *Inside Camp X.* Ontario, Canada: Blake Books, 1999.

Honn, Aaron. "God and Man at Yale: 45 Years Later." *Yale Daily News*, February 15, 1996.

Hougan, Jim. *Secret Agenda: Watergate, Deep Throat, and the CIA.* New York: Random House, 1984.

Hyland, Jason P., and David B. Shear. *Remembering the Cold War.* Chapel Hill: Triangle Institute for Strategic Studies, University of North Carolina, 1991.

Ingraham, Jane. "For God and Country." *New American*, September 4, 1995.

Jeffreys-Jones, Rhodri. *CIA & American Democracy.* New Haven, Conn.: Yale University Press, 1989.

Johnson, Haynes. *The Bay of Pigs: The Leaders' Story of Brigade 2506.* New York: W. W. Norton, 1964.

Johnson, Loch K. *Secret Agencies: U.S. Intelligence in a Hostile World.* New Haven, Conn.: Yale University Press, 1996.

———. *A Season of Inquiry: The Senate Intelligence Investigation.* Lexington: University Press of Kentucky, 1985.

Johnson, Sterling Rock. "Detachment 101 Harried Japanese in Burma and Provided Close Support for Regular Allied Forces." *World War II*, 2001. Available on-line. URL: burmastar.org.uk/detach101.htm

Kalugin, Oleg Danilovich. *The First Chief Directorate: My 32 Years in Intelligence and Espionage against the West.* New York: St. Martin's Press, 1994.

Kehoe, Robert R. "1944: An Allied Team with the French Resistance." *Studies in Intelligence*, winter 1998–99. Available on-line. URL: cia.gov/csi/studies/winter98-99/art03.html

Kerry, John, and Hank Brown. *The BCCI Affair: A Report to the Committee on Foreign Relations, United States Senate.* Washington, D.C.: 102nd Congress, 2nd Session, Senate Print 102-140, December 1992. Available on-line. URL: fas.org/irp/congress/1992_rpt/bcci/

Kessler, Ronald. *Inside the CIA: Revealing the Secrets of the World's Most Powerful Spy Agency.* New York: Simon and Schuster, 1992.

Kiger, Jack J. *Discovery Channel Online: Inside the CIA.* Bethesda, Md.: Discovery Communications, 2000. Available on-line. URL: discovery.com

Kilzer, Louis C. *Churchill's Deception: The Dark Secret That Destroyed Nazi Germany.* New York: Simon and Schuster, 1994.

Knightley, Phillip. *The Second Oldest Profession: Spies and Spying in the Twentieth Century.* New York: W. W. Norton, 1986.

Koeller, David W., and Kat Magnuson. *The Cuban Missile Crisis 1962.* Chicago: North Park University. History Department. The Web Chronology Department, May 8, 1999. Available on-line. URL: campus.northpark.edu/history/WebChron/World/CubanMissile.html

Kornbluh, Peter. *Bay of Pigs Declassified: The Secret CIA Report on the Invasion of Cuba.* New York: New Press, 1998.

Kunhardt, Philip B., Jr., Philip B. Kunhardt III, and Peter W. Kunhardt. *The American President.* New York: Kunhardt Productions, 2000. Available on-line. URL: americanpresident.org

Lamb, Brian. *Booknotes: America's Finest Authors on Reading, Writing, and the Power of Ideas.* New York: Random House, 1997.

———. *Booknotes: Life Stories—Notable Biographers on the People Who Shaped America.* New York: Three Rivers Press, 1999.

Laqueur, Walter. *A World of Secrets: The Uses and Limits of Intelligence.* New York: Basic Books, 1985.

Lehrman, Karen. "What Julia Started." *U.S. News & World Report*, September 22, 1997.

Lemann, Nicholas. "Escape Artist: The Carlucci Technique." *New Republic*, August 1, 1988.

Lert, Frederic. *Wings of the CIA.* Paris: Histoire and Collections, 1998.

Lever, Bob, and Jean-Michel Stoullig. "Attacks Represent Colossal Failure for US Intelligence." Agence France Press, September 12, 2001.

Liddy, G. Gordon. *Will: The Autobiography of G. Gordon Liddy.* New York: St. Martin's Press, 1980.

"Lockheed U-2D Dragon Lady." *Museum of Aviation Flight and Technology Center Website*, 2001. Available on-line. URL: museum.flight-history.com

Loeb, Vernon. "Tenet, Krongard Alter CIA Power Structure." *Washington Post*, May 1, 2001.

———. "Deutch Apologizes for Mishandling Secrets on Home Computers." *Washington Post*, February 23, 2000.

Loeb, Vernon, and John F. Harris. "Deutch's CIA Clearance Suspended." *Washington Post*, August 21, 1999.

Loftis, John, and Mark Aarons. *The Secret War against the Jews.* New York: St. Martin's Griffin, 1994.

Lonergan, Michael. *Affidavit in Support of Complaint, Arrest Warrant and Search Warrants: United States v. Harold J. Nicholson.* Alexandria, Va.: U.S. District Court, Eastern District of Virginia, November 15, 1996. Available on-line. URL: cicentre.com

Lumpkin, John J. "CIA Doubles Counterterrorism Staff." Associated Press, October 8, 2001.

———. "CIA Operative Dies in Prison Riot." Associated Press, November 28, 2001.

Mackey, Sandra. *The Iranians: Persia, Islam, and the Soul of a Nation.* New York: Dutton, 1996.

"Major Investigations: Aldrich Hazen Ames." FBI.gov, 2001.

Marquis Who Was Who. Farmington Hills, Mich.: Marquis Who's Who, Gale Group, 2001. Available on-line. URL: galegroup.com

Marquis Who's Who in America. Farmington Hills, Mich.: Marquis Who's Who, Gale Group, 2001. Available on-line. URL: galegroup.com

Marquis Who's Who in American Education. Farmington Hills, Mich.: Marquis Who's Who, Gale Group, 2001. Available on-line. URL: galegroup.com

Marquis Who's Who in American Law. Farmington Hills, Mich.: Marquis Who's Who, Gale Group, 2001. Available on-line. URL: galegroup.com

Marquis Who's Who in American Politics. Farmington Hills, Mich.: Marquis Who's Who, Gale Group, 2001. Available on-line. URL: galegroup.com

Marquis Who's Who in American Women. Farmington Hills, Mich.: Marquis Who's Who, Gale Group, 2001. Available on-line. URL: galegroup.com

Marquis Who's Who in the East. Farmington Hills, Mich.: Marquis Who's Who, Gale Group, 2001. Available on-line. URL: galegroup.com

Marquis Who's Who in Entertainment. Farmington Hills, Mich.: Marquis Who's Who, Gale Group, 2001. Available on-line. URL: galegroup.com

Marquis Who's Who in Government. Farmington Hills, Mich.: Marquis Who's Who, Gale Group, 2001. Available on-line. URL: galegroup.com

Marquis Who's Who in Science and Engineering. Farmington Hills, Mich.: Marquis Who's Who, Gale Group, 2001. Available on-line. URL: galegroup.com

Marquis Who's Who in the South and Southwest. Farmington Hills, Mich.: Marquis Who's Who, Gale Group, 2001. Available on-line. URL: galegroup.com

Marquis Who's Who in the World. Farmington Hills, Mich.: Marquis Who's Who, Gale Group, 2001. Available on-line. URL: galegroup.com

Matloff, Maurice. *American Military History: Army Historical Series.* Washington, D.C.: Office of the Chief of Military History, U.S. Army, 1969.

McCormick, Donald. *The Master Book of Spies.* London: Hodder Causton, 1973.

McDonald, J. Kenneth. *CIA Early Years 1947–50.* Washington, D.C.: Central Intelligence Agency, Center for the Study of Intelligence, March 17, 1994.

McLaughlin, Martin. "The Crisis in Washington: What History Tells Us." *World Socialist Web Site,* April 4, 1998. Available on-line. URL: wsws.org

McNamara, Robert S. *In Retrospect.* New York: Random House, 1995.

Melton, H. Keith. *The Ultimate Spy Book.* New York: DK, 1996.

"Memorials: Alfred Conrad Ulmer, Jr. '39." *Princeton Alumni Weekly,* September 13, 2000.

Mendez, Antonio J. *The Master of Disguise: My Secret Life in the CIA.* New York: William Morrow, 1999.

Merriam Webster's Dictionary of American Writers. Springfield, Mass.: Merriam Webster, 2001.

Mills, Anthony E. "Jedburgh Teams WWII." *Jedburgh Research WebPage,* 2000. Available on-line. URL: jedburgh.demon.co.uk/

Minnery, John. *The CIA Catalog of Clandestine Weapons, Tools, and Gadgets.* Fort Lee, N.J.: Barricade Books, 1990.

Mirsky, Jonathon. "Mission Impossible: An Account of the CIA's Secret Operations in Tibet." *New York Times,* July 18, 1999.

Montgomery of Alamein, Field Marshall Viscount. *A History of Warfare.* Cleveland: World, 1968.

Moore, Don. *The Clandestine Granddaddy of Central America.* Fulton, Mo.: Monitoring Times Magazine, 1989.

Moore, Nigel. "Mission Impossible: The Special Operations Executive 1940–46." *British Broadcasting Corporation Online,* 2001. Available on-line. URL: bbc.co.uk

Moskin, J. Robert. *The U.S. Marine Corps Story.* New York: McGraw-Hill, 1982.

Murphy, David E., Sergei A. Kondrashev, and George Bailey. *Battleground Berlin: CIA vs KGB in the Cold War.* New Haven, Conn.: Yale University Press, 1997.

Murray, William. *A Short Biography of Captain Nathan Hale.* Seattle, Wash.: TimePage, 2000. Available on-line. URL: seanet.com

Nagorski, Andrew. "Rolling Back the Iron Curtain: 'Containment' Was the Official Postwar Policy. but Two New Books Show That Washington Was Far More Ambitious." *Newsweek* (international edition), May 8, 2000.

Nashel, Jonathon. *CIA and American Popular Culture.* South Bend: Indiana University South Bend, Office of Academic Affairs, February 16, 2001. Available on-line. URL: iusb.edu/~acadaff/deansem/ deansem00.html#Abstract4

Noonan, Peggy. *When Character Was King: A Story of Ronald Reagan.* New York: Viking Penguin, 2001.

"Obituary: Alfred Sheinwold." *Los Angeles Times,* March 9, 1997.

"Obituary: 'Intrepid'—Sir William Stephenson." *Time,* February 13, 1989.

Ogilvie, John. *Ogilvie's English Dictionary.* London: Blackie and Son, 1903.

Oleg Kalugin: Professor. Alexandria, Va.: Centre for Counterintelligence and Security Studies, 2000. Available on-line. URL: cicentre.com

"Operation Alert: The American Experience." Public Broadcasting Service, 2000. Available on-line. URL: pbs.org

O'Reilly, Bill. "Interview with Admiral Stansfield Turner." *The O'Reilly Factor,* Fox News, October 3, 2001.

Orlov, Colonel Alexander. "A Hot Front in the Cold War: The U-2 Program: A Russian Officer Remembers." *Studies in Intelligence,* winter 1998–1999. Available on-line. URL: cia.gov/csi/studies/winter98-99/art02 .html

Ostrovsky, Victor. *The Other Side of Deception: A Rogue Agent Exposes the MOSSAD's Secret Agenda.* New York: HarperCollins, 1995.

O'Toole, G. J. A. *Honorable Treachery: A History of U.S. Intelligence, Espionage, and Covert Action from the American Revolution to the CIA.* New York: Atlantic Monthly Press, 1991.

———. *The Encyclopedia of American Intelligence and Espionage: From the Revolutionary War to the Present.* New York: Facts On File, 1988.

Palmer, Raymond. *The Making of a Spy.* United Kingdom: Aldus Books, 1977.

Parrish, Thomas. *The Simon and Schuster Encyclopedia of World War II.* New York: Simon and Schuster, 1978.

Patterson, Michael Robert. "Arlington National Cemetery Biographies." *Arlington National Cemetery WebSite,* 2000. Available on-line. URL: arlingtoncemetery.com

Payne, Ronald, and Christopher Dobson. *Who's Who in Espionage.* New York: St. Martin's Press, 1984.

———. Counterattack: *The West's Battle against the Terrorists.* New York: Facts On File, 1982.

Pease, Lisa. "David Atlee Phillips, Clay Shaw, and Freeport Sulphur." *Probe,* March–April 1996.

Peraino, Kevin, and Mark Hosenball. "A Dreamer with No Fear: Mike Spann, the First Combat Casualty in Afghanistan, Had Come a Long Way from Winfield, Alabama." *Newsweek International,* December 10, 2001.

Peterzell, Jay. *Reagan's Secret Wars,* CNSS Report no. 108. Washington, D.C.: Center for National Security Studies, 1984.

Pincus, Walter. "Intelligence Shakeup Would Boost CIA: Panel Urges Transfer of NSA, Satellites, Imagery from Pentagon." *Washington Post,* November 8, 2001.

"The Playboy Interview: Philip Agee." *Playboy,* August 1975.

Pluta, Stefan A. *Affidavit in Support of Criminal Complaint, Arrest Warrant and Search Warrants: United States of America v. Robert Philip Hanssen (aka B, Ramon Garcia, Jim Baker, and G. Robertson).* Alexandria, Va.: U.S. District Court for the Eastern District of Virginia, February 16, 2001. Available on-line. URL: fas.org/irp/ops/ci/hanssen_affidavit.html

"The Poison Designed to Produce an African Disease." *New African,* November 2000.

Powers, Thomas. *Inside the Department of Dirty Tricks.* Boston: Atlantic Monthly Press, August 1979.

Prados, John. *President's Secret Wars: CIA and Pentagon Covert Operations since World War II.* New York: William Morrow, 1986.

———. "Woolsey and the CIA." *Bulletin of the Atomic Scientists,* July–August 1993. Available on-line. URL: thebulletin.org

Prothero, Stephen. "Skulls in the Closet." Salon.com, January 21, 2000.

Quirk, Robert E. *Fidel Castro.* New York: W. W. Norton, 1995.

Reagan, Ronald. *Remarks on Signing the Intelligence Identities Protection Act of 1982.* Langley, Va., June 23, 1982.

"Recent Major Espionage Cases in the United States." Associated Press, February 20, 2001.

Reeves, Jay. *First American Killed in Afghanistan.* Associated Press, November 28, 2001.

"Reference Newsmakers: Fidel Alejandro Castro Ruz. ABC News Internet Ventures, 2001. Available on-line. URL: abcnews.go.com

Remnick, David. "Time 100: Vladimir Ilyich Lenin." *Time,* April 13, 1998.

Richelson, Jeffrey T. *A Century of Spies: Intelligence in the Twentieth Century.* New York: Oxford University Press, 1995.

Richelson, Jeffrey T., and Michael L. Evans. *The National Security Agency Declassified.* Washington, D.C.: National Security Archive Electronic Briefing Book no. 24, January 13, 2000. Available on-line. URL: gwu.edu

Risen, James. "Once Again, Ex-Agent Philip Agee Eludes CIA's Grasp." *Los Angeles Times,* October 14, 1997.

———. "Secrets of History: The CIA in Iran." *New York Times Magazine,* April 15, 2000.

Robbins, Ron Cynewulf. "Great Contemporaries: Sir William Stephenson, 'Intrepid': This One Is Dear to My Heart." *Winston Churchill Home Page,* second quarter 1990. Available on-line. URL: winstonchurchill.org

Romerstein, Herbert, and Eric Breindel. *The Venona Secrets: Exposing Soviet Espionage and America's Traitors.* Washington, D.C.: Regnery, 2000.

Rose, Alexander. "Congo in Crisis." *National Post,* August 21, 2000.

The Scribner Encyclopedia of American Lives. Farmington Hills, Mich.: Marquis Who's Who, Gale Group, 2001. Available on-line. URL: galegroup.com

"Secretaries of Defense: James R. Schlesinger." *Defense Special Reports Online,* Armed Forces Information Service, 2001. Available on-line. URL: defenselink.mil/afis

Shane, Scott. "CIA Officer Died in Jail Revolt: Agency Identifies Interrogator Killed at Afghan Fortress; Second American Escaped; Paramilitary Effort Signals Changing Role in Terrorism Fight." *Baltimore Sun,* November 29, 2001.

Sheppard, R. Z. "Now Batting for the OSS: A Biography Traces the Life of Moe Berg, Major Leaguer and Spy." *Time,* August 15, 1994.

Shirer, William L. *The Rise and Fall of the Third Reich: A History of Nazi Germany.* New York: Simon and Schuster, 1960.

"Sir William Stephenson, CC, MC, DFC." Ottawa: Canadian Forces Intelligence Branch Association, 2001. Available on-line. URL: intbranch.org/steven.htm

"A Sloppy Spymaster." *Bulletin of the Atomic Scientists,* November 2000.

Small, Melvin. "Grounds for Impeachment: Nixon, Watergate, and the White House Horrors." *USA Today,* November 1, 1998.

Smith, Charles. "The Information Vacuum Cleaner: National Security Agency Casts Wide Net of Global Surveillance." *WorldNet Daily,* April 9, 2000.

Smith, Russell Jack. *The Unknown CIA: My Three Decades with the Agency.* McLean, Va.: Pergamon-Brassey's International, 1989.

Sokolov, Alexander. "John Walker Spy Files: How John Walker Was Recruited." *Global Spy,* 1999. Available on-line. URL: spynews.net

Solomon, John. "CIA Cited Growing Risk of Attack." Associated Press, October 4, 2001.

Sontag, Sherry, and Christopher Drew. *Blind Man's Bluff: The Untold Story of American Submarine Espionage.* New York: HarperCollins, 1998.

Soviet Union: A Country Study. Washington, D.C.: Library of Congress Federal Research Division, May 1989.

Spannuaus, Edward. "The Mysterious Origins of J. Edgar Hoover." *American Almanac,* August 2000.

Sterling, Claire. *The Terror Network.* New York: Holt, Rinehart, and Winston, 1981.

Studeman, Admiral William O. *Remarks Made at the Signing of the Executive Order Declassifying Early Satellite Imagery: Early Satellites in US Intelligence.* Langley, Va.: Central Intelligence Agency, February 24, 1995. Available on-line. URL: cartome.org/ciacorona95.htm

Suvorov, Viktor. *Spetsnaz: The Inside Story of the Soviet Special Forces.* New York: W. W. Norton, 1988.

Tarpley, Webster G., and Anton Chaitkin. "George Bush: The Unauthorized Biography." Washington, D.C.: *Executive Intelligence Review,* 1992.

Tenet, George J. *Open Letter from the Director of Central Intelligence.* Langley, Va.: CIA, December 13, 2000. Available on-line. URL: cia.gov/public_affairs/press_release/index.html

———. *Statement by the Director of Central Intelligence.* Langley, Va.: CIA, April 3, 1998. Available on-line. URL: gov/cia/public_affairs/press_release/index.html

———. "An Intelligence Success Story: The U-2 Program—The DCI's Perspective." *Studies in Intelligence,* winter 1998–1999.

"Text of Osama bin Laden's Statement in the Aftermath of Allied Strikes in Afghanistan." Associated Press, October 7, 2001.

"They Also Served." *History Net,* Cowles History Group, 1998.

"This Week in Black History." *Jet,* August 21, 2000.

Thomas, Evan. *The Very Best Men: Four Who Dared: The Early Years of the CIA.* New York: Simon and Schuster, 1995.

Thompson, Mark, and Elaine Shannon. "The Trouble Within: CIA Chief Woolsey Battles Accusations That He's Failing to Bring His Agency in from the Cold War Era." *Time,* August 1, 1994.

Thomson, David. "How False Was My Valley." *New Republic,* January 31, 2000.

Troy, Thomas F. *Donovan and the CIA: A History of the Establishment of the Central Intelligence Agency.* Frederick, Md.: University Publications of America, 1984.

Turner, Stansfield. "A Way Out of Nuclear Stalemate." *Washington Post,* November 1, 1999.

"Under Suspicion: The Case against Robert Hanssen." CNN.com, 2001.

Uninspiring Quotations. Okotoks, Alta., Canada: Canadian Centre for Teaching Peace, 1998. Available on-line. URL: peace.ca/

Verne, Lyon. "Domestic Surveillance: The History of Operation CHAOS." *Covert Action Information Bulletin,* summer 1990.

Volkman, Ernest. *Espionage: The Greatest Spy Operations of the 20th Century.* New York: John Wiley and Sons, 1995.

———. *Warriors of the Night: Spies, Soldiers, and American Intelligence.* New York: William Morrow, 1985.

Walcott, John. "Taking the Bull by the Horns." *U.S. News & World Report,* March 1, 1993.

"Walker Was 'Intrinsically Evil.'" *Employees Guide to Security Responsibilities.* Washington, D.C.: Security Research Center of the Defense Security Service, U.S. Department of Defense, 2001. Available on-line. URL: defenselink.mil/

Walsh, Lawrence E. *Final Report of the Independent Counsel for Iran/Contra Matters.* Vol. I, *Investigations and Prosecutions.* Washington, D.C.: U.S. Court of Appeals for the District of Columbia Circuit, August 4, 1993.

Warner, Michael. "Salvage and Liquidation: The Creation of the Central Intelligence Group." *Studies in Intelligence,* 1995. Available on-line. URL: cia.gov/csi/studies/96unclass/salvage.htm

"Watergate." *World Book Encyclopedia.* Chicago: World Book, 1999.

"Watergate 25." *Washington Post,* June 1997.

Weinkopf, Chris. "Salon People: William F. Buckley, Jr." *Salon,* September 3, 1999.

Westmoreland, William C. *A Soldier Reports.* Garden City, N.Y.: Doubleday, 1976.

What Is the School of the Americas? Washington, D.C.: School of the Americas Watch, 2001. Available online. URL: soaw.org

"Who Is Osama bin Laden?" BBCNews, September 18, 2001. Available on-line. URL: news.bbc.co.uk/

William L. Langer: Historian of Diplomacy 1896–1977. Cambridge, Mass.: Notable American Unitarians, 2001. Available on-line. URL: harvardsquarelibrary.org/ unitarians/index.html

"William Stephenson." *Aerodrome,* October 19, 2001. Available on-line. URL: theaerodrome.com/aces/ canada/stephenson2.html

Wilson, Barbara A. "Women Who Were Spies." *Military Women Veterans,* 2000. Available on-line. URL: userpages.aug.com/captbarb/

Wise, David. *The Spy Who Got Away: The Inside Story of Edward Lee Howard, the CIA Agent Who Betrayed His Country's Secrets and Escaped to Moscow.* New York: Random House, 1988.

Woodward, Bob. *Veil: The Secret Wars of the CIA, 1981–1987.* New York: Simon and Schuster, 1987.

———. "CIA Told to Do 'Whatever Necessary' to Kill Bin Laden—Agency and Military Collaborating at 'Unprecedented' Level; Cheney Says War against Terror 'May Never End.'" *Washington Post,* October 21, 2001.

Woodward, Bob, and Thomas E. Ricks. "U.S. Was Foiled Multiple Times in Efforts to Capture bin Laden or Have Him Killed—CIA Trained Pakistanis to Nab Terrorist but Military Coup Put an End to 1999 Plot." *Washington Post,* October 3, 2001.

Wyden, Peter. *Bay of Pigs: The Untold Story.* New York: Simon and Schuster, 1979.

Yost, Graham. *The CIA.* New York: Facts On File, 1989.

———. *The KGB: The Russian Secret Police from the Days of the Czars to the Present.* New York: Facts On File, 1989.

Zabecki, David T. "The 'Man Who Never Was' Pulled Off One of the Greatest Deceptions in Military History— after His Death." *World War II,* November 1995.

Ziff, John. *Espionage & Treason.* Philadelphia: Chelsea House, 2000.

INDEX

Note: Page numbers in **boldface** indicate major treatment of a subject. Page numbers in *italics* refer to illustrations and photographs.